in CHAINS

ONE WEEK LOAN

(1987)

Also by Robert Gildea

EDUCATION IN PROVINCIAL FRANCE

BARRICADES AND BORDERS: EUROPE 1800–1914

FRANCE 1870–1914

THE PAST IN FRENCH HISTORY

FRANCE SINCE 1945

MARIANNE
in CHAINS

In Search of the
German Occupation
1940–1945

ROBERT GILDEA

PAN BOOKS

First published 2002 by Macmillian

This edition published 2003 by Pan Books
an imprint of Pan Macmillan Ltd
Pan Macmillan, 20 New Wharf Road, London N1 9RR
Basingstoke and Oxford
Associated companies throughout the world
www.panmacmillan.com

ISBN 0 330 48865 1

3 5 7 9 8 6 4 2

A CIP catalogue record for this book is available from
the British Library.

Typeset by SetSystems Ltd, SaffronWalden, Essex
Printed and bound in Great Britain by
Mackays of Chatham plc, Chatham, Kent

All Pan Macmillan titles can be ordered through our website,
www.panmacmillan.com
or by phone through Bookpost, 01624 677237

To the memory of

RICHARD COBB
(1917–1996)

Contents

List of Illustrations

LIST OF ILLUSTRATIONS

Acknowledgements

First of all I would like to thank my family – Lucy-Jean, Rachel, Georgia and William – who agreed to be uprooted and live in France for a year in 1996–7, to make research on this book possible. The birth of our youngest, Adam, during the stay in France meant that we all returned home the richer. Many friends made our French stay enjoyable: in particular I would like to mention Pierre-André and Monique Vincent, who were always ready to welcome and look after us in Angers.

I am grateful to the British Academy, the Leverhulme Trust, the Modern History faculty, Oxford, and Merton College, Oxford, for their generous support in funding this project.

I am indebted to my research assistant, Isabelle Goldsztejn, who laboured in the Paris archives while I explored the provinces, and with whom I had a valuable exchange of ideas. The local correspondents of the Institut d'Histoire du Temps Présent – Julien Papp in Tours, Franck Liaigre in Nantes and Marc Bergère in Angers – gave me excellent guidance in the early stages of my research. Among the numerous archivists who helped me, not least in my dealings with the French administration, I would like to thank Jacques Mourier, Élisabeth Verry and Vivienne Miguet, Departmental Archivists respectively of Indre-et-Loire, Maine-et-Loire and Loire-Atlantique. I would also like to thank Abbé Gérard Lefeuvre, the Diocesan Archivist of Nantes, for his wisdom and unstinting generosity.

Among local historians who advised me and supplied me with documentation I must thank above all Michel Lemesle in Angers and Louis Oury in Nantes. Others who offered me assistance and advice, and to whom I owe so much, include Émile Aron, Marcel Girard, André Bellegarde and Marie-Paule Fresneau in and around Tours,

ACKNOWLEDGEMENTS

Claude Bougreau in Chinon, Michel Ancelin in Saumur, Paul Grenouilleau, Violette Lemasson, Marinette Rameau, Aymar de Sauvebeuf and Jean-Paul Vincent in Angers, M. Gilabet at Doué, Pierre Hervé at Saffré, Isabelle de Paysac in Versailles and Jérôme Scorin in Nancy.

A number of colleagues and friends read and commented with great insight on various drafts of the book, and gave much encouragement. I would like to register my thanks to Philippe Burrin, Ruth Harris, Sudhir Hazareesingh and Karma Nabulsi. Felicity Bryan, my agent, prevailed on me to write in a more accessible style and supplied constant enthusiasm and encouragement. At Macmillan Tanya Stobbs saw the possibilities of the project and Georgina Morley at Macmillan improved the manuscript and sustained me with good humour. Lastly I would like to thank my research student Jessica Irons for her dedication and high standards in compiling the bibliography and checking the proofs.

MAPS

Occupied France, 1940-45

Loire-Inférieure

MAYENNE

SARTHE (river)

MAINE-ET-LOIRE

Loire

Thouet

DEUX-SÈVRES

ILLE-ET-VILAINE

Mayenne

Rougé
Châteaubriant
St-Julien-de-Vouvantes
Moisdon-la-Rivière
Derval
Nozay
St-Mars-la-Jaille
Varades
Ancenis
Riaillé
Erdre
Nort-sur-Erdre
Ligné
Le Loroux Bottereau
Vallet
Clisson

VENDÉE

LOIRE-INFÉRIEURE

MORBIHAN

St-Nicolas-de-Redon
Vilaine
Isac
Nantes (canal)
Brest (canal)
Canal
Guémené-Penfao
Blain
Ponchâteau
St Gildas-des-Bois
Savenay
Montoir-de-Bretagne
Herbignac
Guérande
St-Nazaire
Le Croisic
Paimbœuf
St Père en Retz
Pornic
Le Pellerin
Bourgneuf-en-Retz
Machecoul
Légé
St-Philbert-de-Grandlieu

NANTES
Rezé
Vertou
Aigrefeuille-sur-Maine
Orvault
St-Herblain
La Chapelle-sur-Erdre
St-Étienne-de-Montluc
Carquefou

Loire

Noirmoutier

Pocket of St-Nazaire
August 1944–May 1945

20 kilometres

Maine-et-Loire

Indre-et-Loire

Introduction

The rules of the Academy of Tours forbid the audience from asking the speaker questions but not, it appears, from causing a riot. In 1997 I was invited to present a paper to this society of local notables and antiquaries by its president, a Jewish doctor, professor, writer and former member of the Resistance. Having undertaken a certain amount of oral history in the region, I entitled my talk 'What the French of the Loire valley think in 1997 of the German Occupation'. The gist of the presentation was that under the four years of Occupation more complex relationships than those of brutal oppression had developed between Germans and French and that far from always going hungry the French had managed to keep themselves fed and even enjoy themselves. The president, who had recently suffered a bereavement, was unable to attend and the secretary, chairing the meeting in his place, had difficulty keeping order. At one point a man got to his feet and shouted, 'What about the 230 people who were shot in Tours during the Occupation?' At another moment, when I cited a country-dweller who said that her family had never wanted for food under the Occupation, there was a wave of murmuring and shaking of white heads in the room. Although two teachers whom I knew approached me after the talk to endorse what I had said, I was left with the feeling that I had defaced the tablets of stone on which the official history of the Occupation and Resistance had been written.

The officers of the Academy, now rejoined by the president, wined and dined me in some style and the secretary invited me to submit my paper for publication in the proceedings of the Academy. Having read it, however, he returned it to me saying that, 'While each of the examples rings true, your audience, myself included, failed to find in

1

it the precise reflection of our collective memory of the German Occupation.' The Occupation, during which he had taught at the Lycée of Orléans, he said, was characterized by four things: cold, hunger, the absence of freedom and above all fear. 'At any moment', he explained, 'you could be arrested for a subversive remark, a contravention of the curfew, a violation of German legislation, a little transaction on the black market, or for listening to the BBC.'[1] He criticized me for giving too much space to the 'small minority of petty Angevin and Vendean nobles' from further down the Loire who clearly sympathized with the Vichy regime, and then invited me to return to Tours to interview a Freemason who represented the more progressive opinions of Touraine.

The following summer I duly returned to Tours to record the interview, fully prepared to revise many of my previous opinions. What I heard, however, was the exact opposite of what I had expected. While the interviewee's father had indeed been a Freemason, he himself had steered well clear of an organization that was anathema to the Vichy regime and would have jeopardized his career. As a middle-ranking official in the prefecture of Tours, he had also kept well clear of the Resistance. Since he was in charge of the distribution of industrial products locally he was obliged to negotiate with the Germans and initially, he said, tried to resist their demands. But the Germans told him bluntly, 'If that is how you feel, Monsieur, you will be in Germany tomorrow morning.' At the trial of the secretary-general of the prefecture of Bordeaux, Maurice Papon, earlier that year, he added, it had been suggested that it was possible for French officials to resist the Gestapo. 'That is simply not true,' he asserted. To reinforce his point he told the story of two fellow officials and a friend who had annoyed the Germans or become involved in resistance and whose imprudence or stupidity had been rewarded by arrest, deportation or death. As for the Jews, he said, actually shedding a tear, 'The Gestapo were arresting everybody. And to think that it happened in our country. We helped them to escape when we could, but we couldn't always.'[2]

The president and the secretary of the Academy of Tours, and the latter's wife, were invited to the lunch that followed the interview at the official's house, in Tours. Each took a radically different view of the Occupation. The secretary, who had returned my paper to me with a clear signal that it would not be published in the proceedings of the Academy, returned to his theme of the extreme severity of the Occupation. As an example he cited a French school inspector who told him not to set his pupils Latin texts from Tacitus, lest the Germans deemed that it encouraged resistance. His wife Camille sweetly contradicted him, suggesting that the Occupation posed no difficulties for those who went about their ordinary business. The prefecture official, in jovial mood, now boasted of what he called 'the first act defying the enemy'. He recalled that, returning from the army after the defeat in 1940 to his home village, where on an isolated road a pine-log barrier signalled the demarcation line between the zone occupied by the Germans and the Free Zone, he amused the locals by painting the tail of the grocer's dog red, white and blue and sending it under the barrier into the Occupied Zone. Meanwhile, on his arrival at the lunch, the president had quietly slipped me a cutting from a local paper from the time of the Papon trial entitled 'Was there a Papon in Touraine?' This argued that the prefectoral corps in Touraine, which included our host, had been 'good servants of Vichy'.[3] At lunch the resister questioned the patriotism of most French people under the Occupation, citing French officers in his POW camp in 1940 who with German officers had toasted the death of 'the whore' (*la gueuse*), as the Republic was known to its enemies. After we left the house where the lunch had been held, he referred to queues of French people eager to see the anti-Semitic Nazi propaganda film, *The Jew Süss*, stretching right around the block. He himself had forfeited both his professorship at the hospital and his medical practice as a result of Vichy's anti-Semitic legislation, had been threatened with arrest after a German soldier was shot in Tours in 1942, and had fled for his life to the Free Zone, where he joined the Resistance.

The most striking thing about these incidents is that in ordinary homes more than fifty years after the event the German Occupation is still a subject of heated debate, and a debate that is far from being resolved. This is explained in part by the shame and guilt felt by French people about the Occupation. Shame: a country that prided itself on its greatness was brought to its knees after a six-week war and was occupied, bullied and plundered by the hereditary enemy. Guilt: the country that defined itself from the French Revolution as being the cradle of liberty should hand over power to an authoritarian regime that was a puppet of the Third Reich, try to suppress all dissent, and hand over to the Germans Jews who had sought asylum in France as well as Jews who were fully French citizens, for deportation to Auschwitz. The explanation of the debate, however, also lies in the fact that the French have never faced up to their wartime past in any sustained and systematic way.[4] Unlike in South Africa, no Truth and Reconciliation Commission was ever set up to allow the French openly to express their anger and remorse. After the first wave of purges for collaboration which were rapidly wound up in the interests of national unity several decades passed before the recent spate of trials for crimes against humanity – of the Gestapo chief in Lyon, Klaus Barbie (1987), of the Milice leader Paul Touvier (1994) and of the secretary-general of the prefecture of the Gironde, Maurice Papon (1997–8) – and arguably the waters of perception are now even muddier than before. Obstacles in the way of establishing an agreed version of the truth are not only intellectual. Much is at stake ideologically and politically in the interpretation of the Occupation period, and rival views are propagated and defended by interest groups who are constantly vigilant lest their orthodoxy be challenged and they refuse to give an inch in the struggle to impose their views as orthodoxy.

The conversation at Tours suggested that there were three competing interpretations of what conditions were like in France under the German Occupation. The first was that resistance was the highest form of honourable conduct. For want of something grander, small gestures of resistance, such as sending a dog with a tricolour tail into the Occupied Zone, were magnified to assert the patriotic credentials of the 'good Frenchman', but it is interesting that the president of the Academy, who had resisted most, said least about it. The second view, on which the president concentrated, was that the Occupation was characterized less by the oppression of the Germans than by the cowardice and treachery of the French. Many, far from resisting, welcomed the demise of the Republic to further their ambitions and were happy to persecute Freemasons, communists and Jews, whom Vichy blamed for France's decline and defeat. This was the story of the 'bad French' about whom subsequent generations felt such shame and guilt. The third view, that of the official in private and of the secretary in conversation, was that in what amounted to a Nazi dictatorship or SS state it was almost impossible to resist. The best option was to keep one's head down and concentrate on more important things like finding enough food to eat and fuel to keep warm. There was, to complicate matters, even a fourth view, expressed almost inaudibly by the secretary's wife and plainly contradicting what her husband had said. This was that in some respects the German Occupation had been benign, that the Germans had not been vicious towards those who minded their own business and that some sort of accommodation between French and Germans had been possible. However, like the contributions of the Dormouse at the Mad Hatter's Tea Party, these opinions were dismissed as irrelevant and shelved without discussion.

This local conversation would be of little consequence if it did not echo debates which have long gone on at a national level in France. Despite the argument that Nazi tyranny was so pervasive that all resistance was impossible, it was important for the French to recover a sense of honour and dignity by asserting that after their armies had been defeated they began actively to resist the German Occupation, as civilians, as best they could. Those who emerged from hiding, returned from German camps and came to power after the Liberation were in a position to write the history of the 'good French' who had resisted and claimed through their virtuous actions the authority to rule France. The account of the Resistance that they elaborated effectively became a religion, with a number of articles of faith. The first was that it began on 18 June 1940 when General de Gaulle, speaking on the BBC, called upon the French not to give up the struggle. In this way he became the repository of French legitimacy, coming into his inheritance on 25 August 1944 when he marched down the Champs-Élysées in liberated Paris. The second was that it was a pure and heroic movement, with a long roll-call of martyrs who died in the struggle to drive out the occupying forces. The third was that, however diverse the origins and opinions of the participants, the Resistance expressed a common commitment to such eternal French values as the Rights of Man and a One and Indivisible France. The fourth was that, though active resisters were a small minority, the Resistance was approved and supported by the vast mass of the French people, who emerged from the Occupation with their pride intact, since only a handful of traitors had collaborated with the enemy. The fifth article of the credo was that the Resistance, which continued the struggle where the French army had left off, had an indisputable military significance and alongside the Allies contributed significantly to the liberation of France.[5]

The dominance of this story of the 'good French', however, was countered by the story of the 'bad French' who had not resisted but collaborated actively with the German occupiers. In his study of Vichy France published in 1972 the American historian Robert Paxton argued that at least until 1943 most French people had supported the Vichy regime which had declared for a policy of 'collaboration' with Germany. He also calculated that those who resisted the Germans had numbered no more than 2 per cent of the adult population, increased to a maximum of 10 per cent if those willing to read clandestine material put out by the Resistance are included.[6] This interpretation was supported by Marcel Ophuls' 1970 film, *Le Chagrin et la pitié*, subtitled 'Chronicle of a French Town under the Occupation'. This showed the French to be far from heroic but self-seeking, cowardly, deceitful and self-deceiving. So much did it challenge the official view of the 'good French' that it was not shown on French television for ten years.[7] More recently still, Resistance heroes who had enjoyed a virtual cult of personality, such as Jean Moulin, who was tortured to death by Klaus Barbie in 1943, or Raymond and Lucie Aubrac, who worked with Moulin and survived, have had their reputations challenged. It has been suggested, for instance, that Moulin, de Gaulle's emissary to unite the squabbling Resistance movements in France, was in fact a Soviet agent, while Raymond Aubrac, who fell into Gestapo hands in 1943 and was then released, had been turned into an agent of Klaus Barbie and betrayed Moulin.[8]

In recent years the story of the 'bad French' has begun to bite because of the debate about the involvement of Vichy France in the Holocaust. This was documented by Robert Paxton and Michael Marrus in 1981 and by Serge Klarsfeld in 1983.[9] On 16 July 1992 Jewish organizations ensured maximum profile for the commemoration of the fiftieth anniversary of the round-up of 12,000 Jews by the French police under René Bousquet working hand in glove with the SS. President Mitterrand attended the ceremony but refused to accept any responsibility on the grounds that the crime had been committed not by the Republic, which had been abolished in 1940, but by the Vichy state. The following year René Bousquet, who was a friend of Mitterrand and thought to be protected from justice by him, was shot dead by a lone gunman who called at his flat. At the round-up commemoration in 1995 the new president of the Republic, Jacques Chirac, called the deportation a 'collective offence' for which the French must take responsibility.[10] This admission marked a breakthrough in the French coming to terms with their past instead of heaping all blame for it on to a regime that had long gone and had been declared 'null and void' by General de Gaulle, although not everyone agreed that the French should be so repentant. The Gaullist politician Philippe Séguin, whose father had died fighting for the Resistance, denounced the 'climate of permanent collective expiation and self-flagellation of which a certain number of French people are becoming sick and tired'.[11] Some historians, too, pointed out that the current debate had become so 'Judaeo-centric' that the German Occupation and Vichy had been reduced to a detail of the Holocaust.[12]

The story of the 'good French' was increasingly tarnished but it was far too uncomfortable for French national identity simply to replace it with a story of the 'bad French'. One way out was to make a distinction between the Vichy regime, which was admittedly bad, and the French people, who were basically good. Vichy may have deported Jews, it was said, but many more were saved than perished because ordinary French people fed, hid or otherwise helped them in their distress. Former President Giscard d'Estaing, whose family had weathered the Occupation in the Auvergne, argued at the time of the Papon trial that the French people may have welcomed the new head of state, Marshal Pétain, in 1940 but soon parted company with his government. Moreover, he asserted, 'Between 90 and 95 per cent of French people did not even speak to a German during the five years of the Occupation. I am telling the French youth of today so that they do not have cause to be ashamed of their grandparents.'[13] The theme of a major international conference organized by Jean-Pierre Azéma and François Bédarida in Paris in 1990 was *Vichy and the French*, suggesting that the two were now considered distinct entities.[14] From the tension between the 'good French' and the 'bad French' emerged the 'poor French', who were portrayed, like the Jews, as victims and martyrs who had suffered intolerably under the Occupation from cold, hunger and fear. Dominique Veillon's work on the survival of the French under occupation argues that 'for the majority of the population, daily life was reduced to the obsession with food and cold. In the towns the average French person spent a good deal of their time looking for something to put in the pot.'[15] The term *les années noires* – the dark years – first popularized in the title of a diary published in 1947 – was resurrected in the 1990s by leading historians Azéma, Bédarida and Rousso, and also adopted by Julian Jackson to characterize his 2001 survey of Vichy France.[16]

Is it possible to find out, one may well ask, what *really* happened in France under the German Occupation? Are the true answers not there, buried in the archives? As an admirer of Richard Cobb, who after the war revealed to British and French historians alike the richness of French departmental archives, in his case for the period of the French Revolution, I was convinced that the secrets of life under the Occupation in *la France profonde* lay in the departmental, municipal and Church archives of provincial France. The archives of the wartime period were closed for several decades after the Liberation but a law of 3 January 1979 liberalized access by laying down a thirty-year rule. Exceptions were made for files 'containing information likely to harm private individuals or concerning state security or national defence', which were closed for sixty years, and judicial documents, including purge trials, which were closed for 100 years. Special dispensation might be granted to the bona fide historian, file by file, subject to the consent of the branch of the administration, police or judiciary which had deposited the files in the archives. Cautious officials, however, concerned less about state security than the good standing of the administration, may be reluctant to grant access to any documentation which might show that administration – of Vichy or otherwise – in a bad light. Over half the files consulted for this study were formally closed and special dispensation kindly granted. But some areas were more reluctant than others: in one department the archivist had to negotiate on my behalf with the prefecture for several months before access was permitted to a single classified file relating to the Occupation's short-, medium- and long-term legacies. French archives were supplemented by the archives of German military administration, some of whose files were captured at Tours, some of which are kept in Paris, but most of which are preserved in the Bundesarchiv-Militärarchiv at Freiburg-im-Breisgau. There was, interestingly, no problem of access to the German archives in Freiburg, perhaps because the German state ceased to exist for some years after the war and its workings were exposed by the Allies. Typically, however, access to a short run of photocopies from the Freiburg archives relating to the assassination of the military governor of Nantes in 1941, and deposited in Nantes by a local historian, has been assumed by the mayor of Nantes as if they originated from the municipal administration.

Even once access is granted there is no guarantee that the files have not been weeded to remove compromising documents. In 1946, for instance, the prefect of Maine-et-Loire sent round to his services a circular headed 'Destruction of documents concerning racial distinctions between French people', in which he explained that under the law of 9 August 1944 which re-established republican legality, 'all traces of the exceptional legislation passed under the Occupation must be eradicated and all documents relating to Jewish identity must be destroyed'. The telltale copy of this circular discovered in the archives of the *arrondissement* of Cholet was annotated in pencil at the subprefecture: 'Do we have any here? If so, destroy them. Notify police superintendent, captain of gendarmerie, mayors.' The police commissaire of Cholet duly reported a week later that 'the police commissariat of Cholet no longer has any files or indexes concerning Israelites who were resident in this district'.[17]

Censorship can be exercised informally as well as formally by those who have a vested interest in a certain interpretation of the Occupation. One local historian of the Occupation period told me that he had received a number of threatening telephone calls during his publishing career and showed me one document only on condition that I would not publish it. It was a letter written in 1982 by the widow of General Feldt, who had headed the German military administration in Angers in the latter part of the Occupation, recalling that her husband had been welcome in the château of one of the leading notables of the city, and that because of the shortage of petrol suffered by French people he regularly gave a lift to the man's mother on his way to the city centre. The practitioner of this perfect example of 'cohabitation' could not be revealed without risk of a lawsuit because the habitual narrative of events would immediately present it as a form of collaboration.

One of the shortcomings of administrative records, rich though they are, is that things are seen through the filter of the official mind. Of course it is possible to gain some impression of private lives and private opinions from reports written by the police or gendarmerie, from the interviews undertaken by investigating magistrates, or simply from letters of complaint or denunciation sent in to the administration. More eloquent were the diaries and written recollections I managed to trace, the jewel among which was the unpublished wartime diary of the bishop of Nantes, which the diocesan archivist was initially unwilling to let me see because the events were still too close. Organizations specializing in collecting data from the Occupation period, such as the Comité d'Histoire de la Deuxième Guerre Mondiale, have also amassed an archive of recollections collected in the years after the war,[18] but these are relatively patchy and may not answer the questions in which the modern historian is interested. For these reasons about fifty interviews were undertaken in the period 1996–9 with survivors of the period and in a few cases their close relations.

There is a school of thought that dismisses oral history as unreliable evidence, as the ranting of old men and women.[19] My own experience, however, shows that with the passage of time those who witnessed the Occupation are willing to talk about it candidly as never before. In order to find interviewees I had myself interviewed by a local paper under the heading, 'Angevins, tell me about your life under the Occupation'.[20] The day the article appeared, having fun with my 'tweed jacket, understatements and deceitfully candid look behind the glasses', the phone never stopped ringing. Contacts established in this way quickly led to others and lines were traced to neighbouring departments. Only one individual I approached flatly refused to speak to me. Initially, I went to interviews equipped with a list of questions, but I soon discovered that it was pointless to try to corroborate the details of events external to people's lives and which occurred over fifty years ago. It became clear that the best approach was to allow the interviewee freedom to 'tell the story' of his or her experience and then to probe more at specific points. There is no doubt that many who experienced the Occupation are still marked by events that transformed their lives: the death of a friend in an aerial attack, the arrest and subsequent execution of a loved one, or even a bungled operation for appendicitis and what seemed like an eternal diet of beans.[21] These events are etched in the memory and often provide the subjects around which interviewees will construct a narrative.

Naturally, an individual's story of his or her experiences under the

Occupation is not wholly personal but is shaped by the collective memories and accounts that have dominated discussion of the Occupation over the intervening years. Interviewees often adopt a particular discourse, seeking to align their own lives with the model of the Resistance, like the official who sent the tricolour dog into the Occupied Zone or the former printer who told me that when the Germans arrived in his town in 1940 and threw cigarettes to the crowd he solemnly crushed with his foot the one that fell close to him and then spat on it.[22] Others, by contrast, expound a 'Pétainist' version of events which is effectively taboo in public discourse but often voiced very forcefully in private by individuals who clearly believe that their view has not been given credence. They will argue for example that most French people supported Marshal Pétain as the only alternative to the direct rule of a Gauleiter, that the Resistance was composed of 'bandits', 'terrorists' or communist subversives whose folly provoked German reprisals against innocent civilians, and that the Resistance had no significant role in the liberation of France, which was achieved by Allied armies.

There are occasionally moments in an interview, however, when an account that has been carefully constructed hits an obstacle and something that has been hidden then breaks the surface. If the dominant line is that the Vichy regime collaborated with the Germans but ordinary French people bore no responsibility for this, an individual such as our printer might construct a story to show that he never had any dealings with Germans, until he lets slip that Germans did talk to him in his office and that sometimes he drank with them. Sometimes interviewees rehearse a familiar script while the taperecorder is playing and say what they really mean after it has stopped. Thus the mayor of a village which had narrowly escaped German reprisals in 1944 as a result of Resistance activity in the area confided as I was about to leave, 'In any case, I am against the Resistance.' This moment has been called a 'rupture in the narrative' or 'boundary crossing', when the 'hidden transcript' beneath the rehearsed narrative suddenly begins to play.[23] This allows the interviewer to glimpse the possibility of an alternative reading of events, such as the more or less amicable 'cohabitation' of French and Germans periodically, and sharply contrasting attitudes to the Resistance.

The interviewer has to listen sympathetically and build a bond of trust with the interviewee in order that the latter can feel safe delivering an account that may well be sensitive or difficult to relate. It may be that the British historian, who is not readily identified with a particular camp, is able to elicit more confidences. The danger arises, however, that the interviewer may become persuaded, even seduced, by a point of view that is deeply felt but by its nature one-sided.[24] Survivors of a massacre in Touraine at the hands of the Germans in 1944, provoked by a Resistance attack on a German convoy, were reluctant to criticize the Resistance when I met them in 1997, but demonstrated by their tears in the graveyard what they really felt. Returning home, I too burst into tears. I had clearly been won over to a viewpoint that was critical of the recklessness of much Resistance activity, but also needed to distance myself and recover objectivity. The next issue was how to write about the experience. Could the account of the survivors be integrated into the overall story as anything other than 'opinion', 'voice' or 'memory'? Should it be weighed differently from the official documentation, which was just as likely to have been produced from a particular angle and in order to persuade superiors?

With few exceptions, the interviews undertaken were with ordinary French people who could offer an account of what the German Occupation was like for those who experienced it in the small towns and villages of France. Enough has been written about the major politicians and statesmen, the leading resisters and collaborators.[25] My own work concentrates on workers and peasants, manufacturers and landowners, women and children, Catholics and Jews, notables and officials up to the rank of prefect, closely integrated into the fabric of provincial life. The fine work of Philippe Burrin has explored how French and Germans found ways of 'accommodating' each other in Occupied France, but moves in the exalted sphere of high politics, big business and leading intellectuals rather than in that of ordinary people.[26] Pierre Laborie has investigated the attitudes of ordinary people as 'public opinion', using the data thrown up by Vichy's secret mail-opening service. It takes the pulse of changing popular opinion to Vichy, but treats the French people as a bloc and opinion as something that can be traced on a graph.[27] My own approach is to locate ordinary people in the communities to which they belonged. This might be a neighbourhood, village, town or *pays*, an area with a distinct geographical or historical identity, usually a small town and its hinterland.[28] What matters about the community is less the given area than the unwritten rules that govern its members and do not apply to outsiders.[29] The perspective of the local community makes it possible to reassess the complex relations between French and Germans, between Vichy and the French and among the French themselves, not according to some higher code of 'good' and 'bad' actions that was handed down at the Liberation but according to what the community thought was good or bad for it under the Occupation.

This study therefore begins by taking the lid off one small town in *la France profonde*, with fewer than 6,000 souls: the picturesque and historic Chinon. Behind the beautiful façade a world of faction and intrigue, rivalry and treachery, highlighted by the unusual circumstances of the Occupation, is explored. The lens then widens to take in the Loire valley as a whole as a typical region of Occupied France, in so far as any region may be deemed typical in the rapidly changing French landscape. Although the Loire and its tributaries provide a unity, what emerges is that even in this limited area the Occupation was experienced very differently: from large seaports with a substantial German presence to isolated hamlets where Germans were rarely seen; from cathedral towns which endorsed the reactionary philosophy of the Vichy regime to villages where stones were thrown at religious processions; and from communist strongholds in railway suburbs to the fiefs of nobles still perfumed by the *ancien régime*. What it offers is a cross-section of communities in which the challenges of the Occupation can be explored: displacement and absence, work and play, physical and spiritual needs, and concentric circles of conflicting loyalties.

The lightning German offensive of May–June 1940 defeated the French armies, toppled the government and cut the country in two. The northern two-thirds of the country was placed under German military rule, and the so-called Free Zone in the south was governed by a new regime based in the Massif Central spa town of Vichy.[30] Under the armistice concluded between the French and German governments, the occupation of northern France was provisional until the end of the war and Vichy remained formally sovereign in the Occupied Zone as well as in the south. In practice, however, the French administration in the Occupied Zone continued to administer, but virtually out of contact with Vichy. The French civil administration

13

was therefore obliged to do business daily with the German military administration, and soon each mirrored the other at the local, departmental and regional levels. The Germans were happy to let the French administration continue to administer under a system of indirect rule, so long as it delivered public order and a flow of resources for the needs of the Wehrmacht. They drew a distinction between the western provinces of German-occupied Europe, where effective local government ensured the delivery of order and resources, and the eastern provinces, such as Poland and the Balkans, where the indigenous government commanded less loyalty, and the German military found itself from the start fighting a guerrilla war with local populations. For its part the French administration, isolated from Vichy, found that the confidence of the Germans could even increase its authority over its charges. Moreover, the brutal relationship of occupier and occupied was tempered by the sharing of a common set of military, cultural and even religious values which made it easier to reach agreement. The German Occupation was in many ways less dictatorship and more negotiation between two (admittedly unequal) bureaucracies to contain discontent and defuse crises before they erupted into open violence.

The presence of the Germans affected ordinary people and communities as well as the military. Their arrival in 1940 was preceded by rumours of atrocities they had committed en route, which might entail rape, violence or robbery. Many of these, however, were recycled from the Great War and this time the Germans were keen to make a good impression in order to facilitate Franco-German cooperation.[31] Units marched through French towns and villages, occupied public buildings and hotels, and were sometimes billeted on private family homes for weeks or months. French people were taken on by the Germans as cleaners, cooks and laundrywomen, relationships of service that frequently led to sex. Vehicles, horses and foodstuffs were requisitioned, but many businesses were offered contracts to supply the German military, and informal opportunities to trade with Germans on the black market multiplied. The influential image of the French as passive victims of the Occupation has to be set against ample opportunities for profit and pleasure that many were only too ready to take. Some of course simply pursued self-interest; but just as administrations tried to define what was legal in terms of private relations between French and Germans, so French communities fixed the bounds of what was morally acceptable and what was not. How morality was defined collectively by the French under the Occupation, as opposed to how it was defined after the Liberation, is an important theme that will be explored in this book.

Relations between the French in the Occupied Zone and the Vichy government are also explored from the viewpoint of the community. Having dissolved parliament and the *conseils généraux* – the French equivalent of county councils – Vichy was in theory more authoritarian than any regime since the First Empire of Napoleon I. It was also seen to be reactionary, taking revenge on the politicians of the Third Republic who were held responsible for France's decline and the defeat of 1940, and abolishing the Republic. Marianne, symbol of the Republic, was henceforth in chains. And yet, isolated in the Free Zone, Vichy was unable to provide much support for the French administration in the Occupied Zone, which therefore became very dependent for the cultivation of consent on local notables. These were the most prominent figures in the towns and villages because of their wealth, profession or family connections, and served as mayors and local councillors – the lowest layer of local administration that could not be dissolved.[32] Some mayors and councillors were purged, on the grounds that they were not reliable rather than for the ideological reason that they belonged to the dominant parties of the Third Republic, the radicals and the socialists. What mattered for Vichy was 'rallying' to the new regime, and plenty of radicals and socialists had voted full powers to Marshal Pétain on 10 July 1940 when parliament convened for the last time in the casino of Vichy. Pierre Laval, who intensified the collaboration between Vichy and the Third Reich when he became head of government in 1942, realized that the politicians of the Third Republic were also local notables with great influence in their constituencies and acknowledged the need to embed the administration more firmly in the locality. He thus restored the *conseils généraux* in all but name. Local notables essentially mediated between Vichy, the Germans and the local community, delivering order and resources for the first two, but protecting the autonomy and interests of the latter. They had performed such a function since 1940, when many mayors opened the doors of their towns and cities to the advancing Germans for fear that resistance would provoke bombardment and massacre. Such feats of local if not national patriotism wonderfully increased their authority for the course of the Occupation. Whether, as the pressure grew, they were successful in defending the interests of all members of the city equally, is open to question. In the long run, arguably, peasants and workers obtained a better service than Jews.

Another buffer between the French population and the German authorities was the Catholic Church. The Catholic hierarchy was undeniably loyal to Marshal Pétain, and was doubtless more assiduous in its concern for absent prisoners of war and conscripted workers than persecuted Jews. As an institution, however, it limited the influence of Nazism, and it also played a key role providing hope for those struck by pain and grief. In the chaotic world of Occupied France it interceded with saints and the Virgin Mary for the protection and salvation of believers, perceived for many a year as a more hopeful source of deliverance than the Allied invasion that never seemed to come.

French people did of course suffer terrible hardships under the Occupation, but they were more than traumatized souls queuing for the next loaf of bread or dodging the bombs. As a result of defeat and Occupation French society was in a state of shock: normal patterns of life were disrupted, moral certitudes were undermined, raw nerves were exposed. And yet, far from being atomized and cowed, the French formed new relationships, built new networks and discovered new forms of solidarity in order to deal with the challenges and crises inflicted by the Occupation. What is most striking about the French under the Occupation is not how heroic or villainous they were but how imaginative, creative and resourceful they were in pursuit of a better life.

Solidarity did not, in the course of things, mean solidarity with anybody. One of the most marked consequences of the Occupation was the narrowing of horizons. Frightened by the unfamiliarity and unpredictability of the new order, people fell back on their families, their churches, their trades, their villages, towns and *pays*. Communities also divided against themselves. Old tensions erupted under stress, and some individuals whose loyalties to Vichy or the Germans were suspect risked becoming the object of denunciation and persecution. The witch-hunt was a corollary of communities falling back upon themselves. The denunciation of suspects, which was deemed highly unpatriotic after the Liberation, was welcomed under the Occupation as a patriotic gesture.[33]

16

The moral universe of Occupied France was notoriously murky. What was right and what was wrong, what patriotic and what unpatriotic, may have been crystal clear in 1944, but not before. Much of the confusion may be explained by conflicts of loyalty within a succession of concentric circles. Just as individuals were retreating to the village, town or *pays*, so, ironically, the Vichy regime demanded greater sacrifices for the benefit of a France that had almost ceased to exist. Should a farmer, for instance, hand over his harvest to the Vichy agency to supply urban markets at fixed prices, or should he keep some back to feed his family, his regular clients whom he would supply at a fair price, or Parisians or Germans from whom he could make a killing? Was hoarding unpatriotic or was it patriotic to refuse to supply the Vichy agency on the grounds that it might pass on the stocks to the Germans?

Matters were complicated by the fact that there was not one *patrie*: there were two or three. The French might be loyal to Vichy as the established or legitimate government. They might however feel loyal to de Gaulle and the Free French in London, later to become the provisional government of the Republic in Algiers, on the grounds that they considered Pétain to be a usurper and a traitor. They might even have a first loyalty to Moscow, on the grounds that after 1941 the Soviet Union was alone in resisting Hitler militarily and alone preserved the hope of the delivery of Europe. If the object of patriotism was contested, so was the manner in which it might be expressed. It could be done by 'moral force', peacefully, by laying a wreath at a statue of Joan of Arc or coming out on to the streets at a time appointed by the BBC. Rebuilding a patriotic community symbolically was enough for many, but for others it did nothing to loosen the grip of the occupier or stir up insurrection. This minority believed in 'physical force' patriotism, including the assassination of members of the Army of Occupation. Such actions might be considered the height of patriotism by the Communist Party, but were decried by the local community in which the assassination took place, some of whose members were executed as a collective punishment because the culprit himself could not be found. Here loyalty and even sacrifice to the ideal of a fighting France was diametrically opposed to loyalty to the interests of a town or city which simply wanted to see out the Occupation with as little grief as possible.

The outbreak of war between Germany and the Soviet Union in

June 1941 fundamentally changed the balance of forces and the tempo of the Occupation in France. Not only did it cause communists in France to open a 'home front' against the Germans in the hope of provoking a domestic uprising; it also caused the Germans to step up the war against the enemy within – notably communists and Jews – and massively to increase their resources and labour for what was now a total war. From this moment the negotiated period of the Occupation may be said to have ended. As armed resistance increased, the Germans no longer trusted the French authorities to deliver the public order and resources they required. Collaboration as a system of indirect rule, involving cooperation between French and German authorities, gave way to collaboration as the imposition of terms on the French administration and police, and a shift of influence from the German military to the German secret police. Hostage-taking ended, but was replaced by a systematic terror against communists, the deportation of foreign and many French Jews, and the conscription of French labour for the armaments factories of the Reich.

German repression and the labour draft provoked more resistance, but each new Resistance organization was liable to be denounced, discovered, and its members executed or deported. Just as significant was the alienation of local communities whose reserves and manpower were now under attack. French officials and local authorities were squeezed between the increasingly greedy and brutal German authorities and the increasingly angry and frightened local populations. They were placed in an impossible predicament: forced to affect loyalty to Vichy and the Germans if they were to keep their jobs, but risking rejection by local populations if they failed in their duty of protection. Increasingly they resorted to dissembling and the double game, a less and less reliable link in the chain of command.

At the same time incessant Allied bombing raids on German installations in France paralysed the German war economy. Even before the Allied landings of June 1944 the German military machine had virtually ground to a halt. The fear of a Resistance dominated by the communists was a powerful incentive to prevent revolution as the Germans left, secure the continuity of the French state and ensure that the Liberation was less a power struggle between Gaullists and Vichy than an orderly transfer of power between Vichy officials and the officials-in-waiting of the new Republic. The doctrine of republican legitimacy required that all those who had voted full powers to Marshal Pétain or been appointed by him should be removed. Loyalty to one's town or *pays* was no longer sufficient in 1944, and some indication had to be given of sincere commitment to the Resistance and the General over the water. Against this, however, the need for efficacy and continuity in government meant that, especially at local level, notables were carried over and wielded their influence much as before. In this area as in others the Liberation was a moment of dashed hopes and unfulfilled dreams.

At this point we return from our search for the Occupation in the archives to memories of Occupation that were being constructed even as the Liberation took place. As soon as he returned to Paris, General de Gaulle brought down the tablets of the Resistance for the admiration of the crowd. Over the next few decades, locally as well as nationally, the story of the heroic Resistance of the French people was rehearsed and commemorated. The 'bad French' were marginalized and 'poor French' were recast as extras supporting the 'good French'. Discordant voices wishing to tell other stories were drowned out. And yet those other voices continued to make themselves heard, in their own small theatres rather than on the national stage, in public with their own shrines and monuments, or else in private among like-minded disciples and anyone who might care to listen. The final part of this book attempts to give space to this multiplicity of accounts, not only out of a sense of historical fairness, but because these stories, as much as the records of the archives, offer new clues and new insights to the historian in search of Occupied France.

1. CHINON

'Chinon is so full of quaintness', wrote an English lady sketching in Touraine in the 1920s, 'that the trouble is to find the bits which most repay one's time.' Examining the medieval houses as potential subjects for her pen, Margaret Aulton observed that 'queer turrets hang from odd corners, jutting gables shade tiny windows; cornices and brackets, weather-worn and scarred, carved weirdly in ancient oak into figures, animals and grotesque heads, stretch above the windows of little shops'.[1] At about the same time a local writer, René Boylesve, taking Chinon as the setting for a story of provincial bourgeois life, *La Jeune Fille bien élevée*, noted that 'its most recent buildings date from the time of Louis XIV; most are from the fifteenth and sixteenth centuries. Some are half-timbered, ornamented with naive sculptures, others are built from the soft stone of the region, with turrets capped by knobbly cones, pierced by smiling mullioned windows. . . . If you look up to examine the detail of a skylight or gable,' he continued, 'you will be surprised and delighted to see steep rocks way above the object attracting your gaze, sprouting clumps of elm or young oaks here and there, on the summit of which lie the magnificent ruins of the three châteaux where Joan of Arc once passed.'[2]

Squeezed between the tranquil Vienne, a tributary of the Loire, and a sharply rising cliff, the town was indeed dominated by the ruins of the three keeps which had been the Plantagenet Henry II's favourite residence in France and where he had died in 1189. Ten years later his son, Richard the Lionheart, died in Chinon having been wounded while laying siege to a nearby castle. Their tombs, along with that of Eleanor of Aquitaine, Henry's wife and Richard's mother, lie a dozen miles away in the abbey of Fontevrault. Subsequently the château of Chinon was the stage for an even more significant event, recalled by George Bernard Shaw in scene ii of his 1924 play *Saint Joan*. There, in the throne room, in 1429, Joan of Arc met the indecisive French king, Charles VII, and declared that she would raise the siege of Orléans and have him crowned at Reims. The people of Chinon themselves never forgot this moment of destiny, and erected a dramatic equestrian statue in Joan's memory when her cult enjoyed a revival at the end of the nineteenth century. In 1929, when the 500th anniversary of her epic journey was commemorated, a crowd of 50,000 turned out to attend the celebrations at Chinon presided over by the highest dignitaries of army and Church.[3]

There was more to Chinon, however, than medieval quaintness and overgrown grandeur. The celebrations in honour of Joan of Arc had been organized by the town's Commercial and Industrial Union rather than by the republican authorities, who looked askance at the junketings of their right-wing rivals. After they took control of the constituency and town in 1877–8, in the wave of elections which saw the back of the royalist and Catholic notables who had controlled French politics for so long, the republicans launched a national subscription to commission a statue of the Renaissance humanist writer, François Rabelais. Dressed in his doctor's gown for which he had discarded his monk's habit, open book in one hand, pen in the other, he gazed towards the town hall as if to endorse its new occupants, an ironic smile playing on his lips. In the eyes of the republicans he was a precursor of Voltaire, who had directed his barbs against the intolerance and superstition of the feudal regime and the Catholic Church and pointed the way to the democratic and secular order that they were about to inaugurate. Unveiling the statue in 1882, the local republican deputy who had headed the subscription campaign addressed the bronze man in an anticlerical rhetoric worthy of his subject. 'How you whipped the hypocritical, clawing, sanctimonious, vestimented enemies of the people,' he declared, 'all those hideous, snotty-nosed, catarrhal and worm-eaten clerics.'[4]

The Rabelais of the republicans, for all their spite, was a high-minded patron of the desperately serious political battle they were waging. Another side of Rabelais was lost on their Victorian minds but appealed to nineteenth-century Romantics and twentieth-century modernists.[5] This was the Rabelais of *Gargantua* and *Pantagruel*, ordained the 'priest of laughter' by Victor Hugo, who drew on the exuberance of popular culture and seemed to write from the belly. The world of this Rabelais is neither witty nor refined; it is a topsy-turvy one of satire and subversion, oaths and obscenities, eating and drinking on a vast scale, urinating and defecating. At one point the young Gargantua regales his father Grandgousier with his experiments designed to find the perfect bum-wipe. He has tried a lady's veil, a hood, a neckerchief, some silk ear-pieces, a page's bonnet and a cat which unfortunately scratched his perineum. He tries herbs and vegetables, sheets and curtains, hay and straw, wool and paper, a hen and a pigeon, but finally concludes, citing the Oxford theologian Duns Scotus as an authority, that the perfect article for the task is a plump and downy goose, its head held between the legs.[6] This is not to argue that Chinonais were obscene Rabelaisians but that Rabelais was a familiar point of reference for many of them, and this reading resonated on more than one occasion under the Occupation.

The contradictions of the town – its beauty, quaintness and traditions, its intense civic pride, and the risk of subversion and obscenity – were laid bare by the German Occupation. Until then tensions and animosities within the population of under 6,000 were effectively controlled by the social and political hegemony of the provincial bourgeoisie, which had kept at bay challenges from nobles, clergy and the working classes. The Occupation, however, undermined the conventions on which provincial society was built, throwing up new antagonisms and dangerously raising the stakes for the conflicts that were played out.

On Wednesday, 19 June 1940, as German forces approached Chinon, frantic negotiations took place between the mayor and the French military commander in the vicinity. The military commander was under instructions to defend the bridges over the Loire and the Vienne to ensure an orderly retreat for the French army, but the mayor was fearful that any defence of the town would provoke artillery bombardment and Stuka attacks. Thirty miles away the city of Tours was bombed for three days and engulfed in flames. Eventually the French commander saw reason and as the population hid in their cellars in the early hours of 21 June Mayor Henri Mattraits stood alone on the *quai* as the German troops entered the town without incident. He later explained to the municipal council that Chinon – 'open to everyone . . . proud to be able to show its natural beauty and artistic riches to tourists the world over' – had been fortunate not to suffer the same fate as Tours. One of the assistant mayors then thanked the mayor 'on behalf of the decent and hard-working population of Chinon' for remaining at his post, day and night, inspiring confidence in the citizens by his sangfroid, and duly announced that he had 'deserved well of the town'.[7]

The German military and Feldgendarmerie requisitioned hotels to serve as their headquarters and the local population settled down to life under the Occupation. No sign of any discontent was manifested until the autumn, and then French and German authorities collaborated to defuse it. On 11 November 1940, anniversary of the victory over Germany in 1918, students parading on the Champs-Élysées in Paris in defiance of a German ban were arrested by German police and the Paris universities were closed until further notice. The main effect was that Paris students returned to their home towns and continued to demonstrate there. In Chinon, fly-posters appeared on the walls announcing ironically, 'French people! Listen to this appeal to the population: male and female workers are required to narrow the English Channel.' The local military commander at Chinon, the Kreiskommandant, summoned his French opposite number, the young subprefect Paul Cay, and warned that if such posters or graffiti appeared again, severe punishment would be meted out to the townsfolk. Far from clamping down without reflection, the German authorities were prepared to talk to French officials and – in 1940 at least – to give the French a chance to mend their ways. The subprefect in turn summoned the mayor of Chinon, Dr Henri Mattraits, and the principal of the college, Auguste Correch. These two had been educated together and served together in the trenches of Flanders. They were patriots but they could see no sense in gratuitous provocation, particularly as they were held personally responsible by the German authorities for keeping order in the town. The principal agreed to lecture his pupils and the mayor to have words with the families of students to ensure that youthful high spirits did not run out of control again.[8]

There were some ways of expressing patriotic feeling that were not regarded as undue provocation by the Germans. The most obvious was the annual celebration of Joan of Arc Day in Chinon. To be sure, they banned the traditional procession through the streets to the château, for marches were regarded as militaristic and unacceptable. Every May, however, there were three days of prayer

24

followed by a Sunday Mass at which a leading churchman from Tours or Angers gave a panegyric on the saint. The usual message was that Joan had been sent from God to save the Church and had been burned alive by the English. In Chinon the sermon of 1941 was devoted to the piety, faith and sacrifice of Joan, while in 1943 Canon Panaget from Angers, a hero of two wars, spoke of Joan's journey from serving the family home to serving the fatherland. The Church's control of the cult kept radical–socialist Mayor Mattraits away in 1941 but he duly attended in 1943, along with Subprefect Cay, Principal Correch, the captain of the gendarmerie and leading magistrates. The commemoration of Joan of Arc in fact brought civic and ecclesiastic authorities together in a town usually split between clericals and anticlericals, and though the references to Joan's patriotism always cited her struggle against the English, she served in an unspoken way as a symbol of national independence and invincibility that was as much anti-German as anti-English.[9]

Even closer to the town's sense of pride and identity was the statue of Rabelais. This came under threat during the Occupation because, being cast in bronze, it attracted the attention of the government agency responsible for recycling metals in short supply. Statues of Joan of Arc were protected as too important to be melted down, but the statue of Rabelais, whose message did not sit well with the conservative, moralistic tones of Vichy's National Revolution, was at risk. The statue was duly earmarked for removal early in 1942 and Chinon was forced to present Rabelais in a new light in order to hold on to him. The municipal council petitioned Marshal Pétain on behalf of 'the father of the French language . . . born in this region that he loved so much and which inspired most of his works'. The local antiquarian society, the Amis du Vieux Chinon, also published a protest, asserting that 'for the Chinonais, Rabelais is not just a famous writer but a legendary figure, the genius of the region, the very incarnation of their little fatherland'. The blatant appeal to Vichy's desire to root populations in their localities, so that they could imbibe the lessons of their ancestors and the earth which gave birth to them and to which they returned, paid off: the Minister for Industrial Production decided that Rabelais could stay on his pedestal.[10]

Such a victory was a tribute to the influence of the local press, run by local politicians who in Touraine belonged to the Radical–

Socialist Party, the ruling party of the Third Republic. Chinon under the Occupation in fact had two weekly newspapers, *Le Républicain de Chinon*, owned by the former radical–socialist deputy and pig-farmer Léon Courson, and *Le Chinonais*, managed by Albert Gue-non, each with a circulation of 2,500. When the German authorities ordered the closure of *Le Républicain de Chinon* in 1942, the Vichy prefect suggested that they might like to close *Le Chinonais* too, as both kept republican sentiment alive and periodically criticized the Vichy regime.[11] In fact both newspapers survived until the Liberation, when paradoxically they were closed down to give a free run to *La Nouvelle République*, the new regional paper based at Tours that underpinned the Liberation authorities. Local identity and a local voice were thus paradoxically better expressed under the Occupation and Vichy than afterwards.

Similarly, it would be wrong to imagine that under the Occupation French society was atomized and crushed and that people did little but cower in their homes. Associative life was sometimes diverted into new channels, but it went on with much the same energy as before. In the autumn of 1940 Chinon was honeycombed by clubs and societies which testify to the sociability of the inhabitants. The total membership of the various societies was 3,000 men, 300 women and 170 children. There were the old boys' associations of the college, the lay municipal school and the private Christian Brothers' School, the lay and Catholic youth clubs, the scouts, a workers' education association, the Saint-Jean Choir and a Concert Society, two hunting clubs called 'La Chasse' and 'La Protection Chinonaise', two general sporting clubs called 'L'Avant-garde chinonaise' and 'La Rabelaisienne', two *boules* societies, a horse-racing association, a tennis club, a cycling club, a fishing club, the Friends of the Central Plateau which indulged in 'healthy pursuits' for men, the Amis du Vieux Chinon specializing in local history, the municipal colony holidays organization, self-help groups for the victims of industrial accidents, the Firemen's Friendly Society, the Friends of the Hospital, a landlords' association and a consumer cooperative for buying shoes.[12]

Not all these societies continued uninterrupted through the Occu-pation: some changed their spots while others responded to new challenges such as the needs of the 1.5 million French prisoners of war in German camps. Hunting was dealt a blow when, for security reasons, the German authorities ordered all guns to be handed in at town halls and threatened severe penalties if any weapons were discovered. Only German officers and their French cronies hunted with firearms, while the ordinary peasant, who had secured the right to hunt in the French Revolution, had to fall back on clandestine hunting at night or catching rabbits with ferrets and nets, as during the *ancien régime*. Organizations in uniform, such as the scouts, were regarded by the German authorities as a paramilitary threat to the Army of Occupation and closed down. But the Chinon scouts deftly renamed themselves the Open-air Chinon Youth and were duly authorized by the Feldkommandantur at Tours. The Vichy regime was keen on sport as a way to train a youth heathy in body and mind, and Chinon took advantage of subsidies made available to build a municipal sports ground and swimming pool.[13] New kinds of transport called for new kinds of races, such as the bicycle-and-25-kilo-trailer race held in May 1941 to make a competitive sport of monotonous trips with trailers into the country in search of food. The race finished at the municipal stadium, where Dr Mattraits blew the whistle to start the final of the departmental football knock-out sponsored by the Angers-based *Petit Courrier*, which the Chinon team won 4–0.[14] The Touraine Boat Club held rowing regattas on a local lake, while horse racing became a special attraction, one spectacular high point being a meeting organized in July 1943 to raise funds for the POWs. Prizes were offered by the local demobilized soldiers, veterans, repatriated prisoners, the prisoner support committee, the municipality, the Commercial and Industrial Union and the Peasant Corporation. The seriousness of the fund-raising did not detract from the splendour of the occasion, with press reporting that 'the race-goers milled about in their thousands at the weigh-in and in the paddock. Elegant outfits brightened up the stands, giving the appearance of a multi-coloured garden.'[15]

All of this does not disguise the fact that there was much hardship under the Occupation, and a widening gulf between those who were making large profits and those who were struggling. Despite government attempts to fix prices and ration goods, the competition for supplies from urban consumers and the Germans created a black market in which prices were driven relentlessly upward. In the summer of 1942 holiday-makers descended on the region from Paris, buying up stocks of potatoes and beans at inflated prices from a delighted peasantry, with the result that those living on fixed incomes like pensioners, small *rentiers*, workers and white-collar employees had little left.[16] By the following summer the gap between those having difficulty feeding and clothing their families and those making 'scandalous fortunes' in a manner 'dangerous for social order' had become a matter of concern to the authorities.[17] Chinon was rocked by a scandal involving the trafficking of local wines by a dentist from Lille, Charles Graeve, who had set up in Chinon after the outbreak of war. After a bad year in 1939 the Chinon wines of 1941 and 1942 were excellent, commanding a ready market. Buying wine for 60–80 francs a litre, Graeve was selling it in the Paris region for 450–500 francs. Involved with him were his twenty-three-year-old son, Étienne, who was about to be appointed an official of the Peasant Corporation set up by Vichy to run agriculture, and his thirty-year-old daughter, Élisabeth, who was employed by the Vichy Youth Administration. The subprefect tried to warn the local press off publishing the story, because the Graeve family were well connected within the Vichy administration, but investigations revealed 'a vast black market organization with ramifications throughout France'. It did not do for those with responsible posts in the Vichy régime to preach the rhetoric of 'Travail, Famille et Patrie' (Work, Family and Fatherland), to the extent of appearing in their official functions at Mothers' Day celebrations, while publicly flaunting the millions of francs they had made on the black market. Eventually Étienne was interned administratively by the prefect and Élisabeth forced to resign, but the affair demonstrated extraordinary depths of corruption and hypocrisy at the heart of the Vichy system.[18]

Black marketeers sprang up in Occupied France like mushrooms after rain. So also did denouncers, who took the opportunity to appeal to the German military administration when they felt persecuted by the French authorities. Denunciation, from one perspective, was a patriotic act, bringing to the attention of the authorities illegalities, disloyalties and threats to the state which might otherwise remain hidden. But it also represented a betrayal of the secrets of the community which were perhaps best kept from the prying of the French state, let alone of the German authorities. Its magic was that it gave extraordinary powers to the weaker members of the community, in particular women, but its poison divided communities against themselves in the most bitter way. Chinon itself was almost torn apart by a series of denunciations at the centre of which was a personage who could not have been more different from the *Jeune Fille bien élevée* of Boylesve's novel. That young woman, who is never even given a name, is a model of perfect self-sacrifice, educated to be the perfect wife. She marries the man chosen for her by her convention-bound family, rather than the man she loves, denying herself the last chance of an exit by fainting during the marriage ceremony for fear of spoiling her veil. By contrast, Madeleine Longuépée, the scourge of Chinon during the Occupation, was the antithesis of the provincial lady: a former dressmaker from a less fashionable provincial town, middle-aged, childless and divorced, she was kept by Adalbert Chevalier, the owner of the Café des Terrasses, and was passionately jealous of the husband of Chevalier's daughter by a previous marriage, a successful doctor of North African Jewish origin. A woman so ill at ease in Chinon discovered, however, that the German Occupation provided her with ample opportunity for revenge against society and she did not hesitate to exploit this possibility.

Madame Longuépée inaugurated her role as wicked stepmother in the late summer of 1940 by denouncing the Jewish doctor, Mehmed Kapandji. Kapandji was working as a surgeon for the Red Cross in Châtellerault hospital when he was summoned by two German officers. They said that he had been denounced both as a Jew and for practising medicine illegally by the woman living with his father-in-law. These were the early days of the Occupation, however, before anti-Semitic policies began to bite. Instead of arresting him, the Germans warned Kapandji, 'Don't trust that woman, she could bring you all sorts of misfortune.' Frustrated at first, Mme Longueépée became only more determined to impress the Germans and spread terror around her.

The Germans, as conquerors, took the view that defeated Frenchmen had forfeited the right to Frenchwomen, who now belonged to them. After a hard day giving orders, the Kreiskommandant of Chinon and his men repaired to the Café des Terrasses, where Chevalier had put up a photograph of Hitler and a notice welcoming 'our German friends'. For their delight Chevalier was happy to lay on young girls such as Simone Peltier, who was just fifteen when the Germans invaded, had failed to find a job after leaving school, and was still living with her parents when she fell under the spell of Mme

Longuépée. Simone had sex with Germans both in the bar and on a sofa in a cellar opposite. After a row with Chevalier, she went to the French gendarmerie to complain, and the French authorities launched an inquiry into 'the incitation of minors to debauchery'. By the time the French police arrived, however, Chevalier had placed hen cages in the cellar and claimed to be raising chickens. Simone retracted her story, no doubt under pressure from Chevalier and Longuépée, but the French pursued their inquiry through the examining magistrate, Leopold Florens, and the Procureur de la République (leading magistrate) at Chinon, M. Ponset.

The French inquiry did not get far down the road. Ponset and Florens were summoned to the Feldkommandantur at Tours in November 1940, told that they had been defeated, and ordered to hand over all files concerning immoral acts. Ponset affected to rule Chinon like a robed noble of the eighteenth century, declaring 'I have the Kreiskommandant [of Chinon] entirely in my hands, I can do with him exactly as I want, I will continue to enforce French laws and ignore German ones and no one will notice.' These words were relayed by Chevalier to the Germans, who promptly arrested Ponset. Ponset, for his part, was convinced that Chevalier was only doing as instructed by his mistress, Mme Longuépée, 'the inspirer of his deeds', who had gone to pull strings with the German authorities in Paris to ensure that Ponset was brought low.

The Kreiskommandant of Chinon made clear that he had a quite different notion of where power lay. He told Florens, who was also questioned, that 'We are the victors! You have been beaten! The women, even the children of your country, are no longer yours! Our soldiers have the right to have fun, and if you do anything to slight the honour of the German army you will be arrested, like M. Ponset. Chevalier and others are there to keep an eye on you.' But Chevalier was no more than putty in the hands of Mme Longuépée. A year later he confessed to Florens that 'all the evil comes from that woman Longuépée. The woman is a tyrant. She subjugates me. Listen, *Monsieur le juge*, it was she who had M. Ponset arrested. She went to Paris to fix it.' Florens told the magistrate preparing Mme Longuépée's trial after the Liberation that he had never interviewed the woman, 'but she had the reputation of a shrew at Chinon, extremely dangerous for the Resistance because of the contacts with the

German milieux. Not because of her charm but because of her diabolical intelligence and spirit of evil.'[19]

Mme Longuépée's malice was not exhausted by the arrest of Procureur Ponset, who was in fact released by the Germans after three weeks on condition that he move to a post in unoccupied France. Around the same time she was in Mme Gauthier's grocery shop in Chinon when M. Bagarie the postman came in. When Mme Gauthier asked for news of his son, Bagarie said that the boy was delighted to be in the Free Zone, away from the 'Boche'. Mme Longuépée intervened to say that the Germans were going to win the war, whereupon Bagarie replied that those who served them deserved to be shot one day. Bagarie was far from being a resister: he was a former gendarme who sent his children to Church school and sold large numbers of photographs of Marshal Pétain to raise money for the charitable Secours National. But Mme Longuépée was determined to lure him into her trap. She returned to the attack, defending Marshal Pétain's policy of collaboration with Germany, upon which Bagarie was alleged to have taken a photograph of the Marshal and, making an appropriate gesture, announced that it was fit only for toilet paper. In another context this rerun of Gargantua's experiment would have provoked the laughter it deserved, but it was promptly reported by Mme Longuépée and Gauthier to the Feldkommandantur of Tours. Bagarie was hauled before a German military court and sentenced to ten months in prison for insulting both the German army and Marshal Pétain.

When the Post Office investigated the case they found that there was more to it than a vendetta between Mme Longuépée and Bagarie. Bagarie was a schoolfriend of Ponset, and Mme Longuépée, having got rid of Ponset, wanted to do the same to his friends and allies. She was able to take Mme Gauthier the grocer along with her because she was able to blackmail her. She knew that Mme Gauthier had had an affair with a French officer at Saumur while her husband had been away at the front in 1940 and had given birth to a stillborn child. Mme Gauthier, for her part, was keen to have Bagarie out of the way because her husband, who had a temporary job with the Post Office, coveted Bagarie's permanent one. The Germans were quite happy to release Bagarie so long as Gauthier was given his job. But this violation of administrative proprieties was unacceptable to

31

the French postal services. As far as they were concerned, Bagarie was a good employee whose southern temperament had got the better of him, while Gauthier was a bad one. More importantly, to let two women of 'deplorable morals' dictate who was to be employed in the Post Office was out of the question.[20]

After a third incident in the space of five months arose, the French authorities endeavoured to recover control of the situation. Mme Josseaux, wife of the bank manager of the Chinon branch of the Crédit Lyonnais, went into a grocer's shop in Chinon (we are not told if it was Mme Gauthier's) and met the Kreiskommandantur's cook, who was buying fruit for her German employers. 'You can give them the fruit-stones,' observed Mme Josseaux wryly, 'that is good enough for them.' Mme Josseaux was duly denounced and arrested, but at this point the subprefect, Paul Cay, had had enough. He warned his opposite number the Kreiskommandant of the 'deplorable effect that these arrests – based for the most part on the accounts of people of the most dubious conduct and morality – may have on the population'. He told the prefect more explicitly that the arrests were made after denunciations by people accredited with the Kreiskommandantur. 'Whether it is Mme Longuépée of Porte du Château, Mme Gauthier of rue Jean-Jacques Rousseau, Mlle Crosnier of place Jeanne d'Arc, Mme Pichon and her daughter of rue Marceau, Mme Albertini and her daughter of rue Voltaire, Mlle Meunier of rue Marceau, Mlle Simone Peltier of les Closeaux, Mme Mireille Beury of les Grésillons, both in Chinon commune, Mme Galle at Beaumont, Mme Delory of the rue du Mûrier, their bearing betrays without doubt the mission that they are accomplishing.'[21] This litany conveys a fear that behind the public façade of male office-holding the town was effectively being run by a mafia of women who exercised an insidious influence at the Kreiskommandantur. The French authorities tried to persuade the Germans, in the interests of orderly and hierarchical administration, not to listen to women who had come into contact with them through menial employment or sex. They hoped that the Germans' own concern with order and hierarchy would induce them to see eye to eye and terminate the reign of these females.

After her break with Chevalier and Longuépée, Simone Peltier went to live with a member of the collaborationist Milice called Crosnier in a nearby hamlet, where she terrorized the local inhabitants by threatening to have anyone who crossed her arrested by the Germans. At the Liberation Crosnier was found in a wood with his hands tied behind his back and two bullets in his head, in what turned out to be a settling of scores within the Milice.[22] Chevalier, Longuépée and Peltier were arrested, interned and sent for trial. Two peasants and a grocer testified against Simone Peltier as an immoral person addicted to the easy life and easy money, and she was sentenced to three years' imprisonment for denunciation. At their own trials Chevalier and Longuépée accused Peltier of lying about the scenes of debauchery with Germans alleged to have gone on at the café. Longuépée admitted that she had reported Bagarie for wiping his bottom with a photo of Marshal Pétain but she denied that she had denounced people to the Germans and argued that on the contrary she had used her contacts with the Germans to save young men from being sent on forced labour service to the Reich. Meanwhile, Chevalier claimed that he had hidden three Jewish doctors who had been entrusted to him by his son-in-law Kapandji in a flat that he owned in Paris. The Cour de Justice was not convinced: Longuépée was sentenced to five years in prison, and Chevalier to ten.[23]

All sorts of arguments were found after the Liberation by those standing accused to demonstrate that far from collaborating with the Germans they had engaged in acts of resistance. To have sheltered Jews was a powerful defence, not least because under the Occupation Jews were at risk even before racial deportations began in the summer of 1942. On the night of 5 February 1942 a German sentry on duty at a German petrol station near the railway tracks in Tours was jostled and shot in the stomach by a civilian, and died a few days later. By way of reprisals the German authorities immediately arrested fifty hostages drawn from those sectors which were seen to be hampering the German war effort: communists and Jews. Among those arrested were two Jews who had come to Chinon from Metz in Lorraine at the outbreak of war in 1939: Marc Cahen, aged fifty-two, and his son, Jean, nineteen, a pharmacy student at Tours. Subprefect Cay went to the Kreiskommandantur to investigate, only to find that the order to arrest had come from the Feldkommandantur at Tours. At Tours Prefect Tracou, a former naval officer, managed to persuade the Feldkommandant, Colonel Kloss, to release those who could not possibly have committed the crime: eleven Jews, two communists who were sick, and two schoolteachers. Tracou and

Kloss then acted in concert, trying to persuade the higher military authorities not to execute the hostages, on the grounds that the killer must have been a terrorist from outside town. The hostages remained in custody, however, many Jews were later deported (whether these included Marc and Jean Cahen is not known), and on 21 February the Germans executed six 'fanatical communists' who had been sentenced by Vichy's exceptional courts, the Sections Spéciales, and were in prison at Fontevrault.[24]

Acts of resistance proved extremely dangerous, as much because of denunciation or silliness as a result of the effectiveness of the French police or Gestapo. Just north of Chinon, in the broad valley between the Loire and the Indre, Albert Malécot, secretary of the *mairie* of the village of Huismes, found a meadow that looked ideal for parachute drops or for small planes to land, which in March 1943 was code-named the 'Gide terrain'. He also recruited a small number of men from the surrounding villages of Huismes, Bréhémont and Rivarennes to service any drops or landings. Unfortunately the cover was somehow blown, and on 19 January 1944 the Gestapo raided Malécot's home and shot him dead. On 4 March the Gestapo struck again, arresting five men from Huismes, two from Bréhémont and two from Rivarennes. One managed to flee, one was never discovered, but all those arrested were deported to Germany and only one returned.[25]

Although there were patriots willing to risk their lives to help liberate France, local French officials and notables generally tried as far as possible to minimize direct confrontation by trying to cushion the burdens of the Occupation, negotiate their way out of local crises, and maintain a continuity of administration for as long as possible. In Chinon itself there were three key players. First, there was the subprefect, the prefect's representative in the town by virtue of the fact that it was the head of an *arrondissement*, which generally coincided with an electoral constituency. Paul Cay remained subprefect for almost the entire Occupation, until April 1944 when he fell out with the new prefect. The German authorities had no reason to complain about him, noting that he worked well with them, although, since they were based in Tours, they in fact saw little of him.[26] He served the Vichy regime honourably, but he was alert to the changing balance of forces and climate of opinion. After the Anglo-American landing in North Africa in November 1942 he reported to the prefect that the normally calm and indifferent population was beginning to express pro-Allied and Gaullist sentiments with some force. He confessed that 'our role is very delicate', but while advising his superior that 'we must enforce a more rigid discipline than ever', he was himself making secret contacts with the Resistance and taking silent steps towards the regime-in-waiting.[27]

The other two main players in the town were elected notables, one the mayor, the other Chinon's representative on the *conseil général*, the department's elected assembly which fulfilled an advisory role alongside the prefect in Tours. Both were doctors of medicine and both were members of the Radical–Socialist Party, which subscribed to the principles of the French Revolution but was firmly committed to private property and social order. There, however, the resemblance ceased.

Henri Mattraits (1882–1948) was a solid, respectable local figure, son of Benoît Mattraits, Chinon's mayor in the Belle Époque (1898–1912). He was elected to the *conseil général* in 1929, succeeding Camille Chautemps, one of the bosses of the Radical–Socialist Party locally as well as nationally. Mattraits became mayor of Chinon in 1934 and was confirmed in office by the Vichy regime in 1941 on the grounds that he had stood at his post when the Germans arrived in 1940 and that since then, although the radical–socialists were anathema to Vichy, he was considered to have 'rallied' to the new regime. In fact the abolition of the *conseils généraux* by Vichy created an opening for Mattraits. He became a member of the small, seven-man administrative commission which replaced the *conseil général* in 1941, and in 1942 became a member of the *conseil départemental*, a revived *conseil général* in every way except that it was appointed, not elected.

The other doctor, Pierre Labussière (1905–44), was entirely different. Younger, and not a local but from the small town of Loches, he was unmarried and had a reputation for frank speaking, usually facilitated by alcohol, which he consumed in abundance. His dress was invariably unkempt, which scandalized the burghers of Chinon but endeared him to the rural populations who formed the backbone of his clientele and electors. Compared by his colleague Émile Aron to Grandgousier, he was a Rabelaisian figure in his closeness to folk ways, his appetite for the bottle, his oaths and obscenities, and general violation of the conventions of bourgeois taste.[28] He stood against Mattraits in the election to the *conseil général* in 1937, plying his voters with drink and attacking Mattraits as a hypocrite, a liar and crypto-clerical, and duly defeated him, a humiliation for which Mattraits never forgave him. As member of the *conseil général* for the canton, Labussière would normally have been appointed to Vichy's *conseil départemental* in 1942, but a confidential report warned that his loyalty to Pétain was doubtful, that he 'passed for an Anglophile', and that though he wielded influence among his rural clientele 'his demagogy and his slovenliness gave him an unsavoury popularity'.[29] Accordingly he was passed over.

What festered as a little local rivalry in Chinon reached a critical and even fatal point as a result of the politics of the German Occupation. One of the impositions that the French government had to agree to in 1943 was the Service du Travail Obligatoire (STO) or forced labour service in Germany for young men of military service age. In February 1944 Pierre Labussière was performing a routine medical examination for sixty young men conscripted for STO in Chinon, in the presence of five medical students, a Red Cross nurse, three gendarmes, a delegate of the STO administration and a man from the prefecture. At one point he knocked a photograph of Marshal Pétain on to the floor. He was then alleged to have spat on it and torn it up, exclaiming 'Bastard', 'Old fart' and 'Judas'. When the nurse, Mlle Rivière, voiced a protest, he riposted, going one better than postman Bagarie in Rabelaisian creativity, 'And you can put it between your legs, where it belongs!'

Most of the people present, knowing the excesses of Pierre Labussière, took the outburst in good part. Paul Cay, the subprefect, tried to smooth things over, informing the prefect that Labussière had not thrown the picture on to the floor but had knocked it down accidentally while reaching for a towel. He said that the doctor, whose eccentricities verged on mental instability, regretted his actions, and he pointed out that the issue had been blown up out of all proportion because of the political dimension, in particular the old rivalry with Mayor Mattraits. Others, however, were not prepared to let things go. Mlle Rivière made clear to the subprefect her sense of outrage. The new prefect at Tours, Fernand Musso, was an out-and-out collaborationist, keen to erase the memory that he had worked before the war with the Jewish interior minister Georges Mandel, and he was under strong pressure from collaborationist movements to deal firmly with the Resistance. He was extremely suspicious of Cay, who he sensed was in league with the Resistance, and indeed made a trip to Chinon in March 1944 to denounce the Maquis as a 'Bolshevik danger' and to stress that 'order must be maintained by whatever means necessary'. He was intimidated by the Germans, in particular by the Gestapo, who saw Labussière as a critic of Franco-German collaboration, liable to sabotage the recruitment of STO labour to Germany, and wanted him punished.

The Labussière affair permitted several birds to be killed with one stone. On 20 March 1944 Musso ordered the internment of Labussière and informed his superior, the regional prefect at Angers, that the German authorities in Tours were demanding that Labussière be handed over to them on his release. The regional prefect, Charles Donati, fixed the internment period at one month but told Musso that under the terms of the agreements between the French police and the SS only communists could be handed over to the German police after their sentence was completed. Paul Cay tried to persuade Musso to keep Labussière in French custody longer and therefore safe from the Gestapo. But Cay was summarily dismissed by Musso, whose patience was at an end, and ordered to a new subprefecture in the Massif Central. Instead of leaving he went underground and joined the Resistance locally. Meanwhile Labussière was released on 22 April, promptly arrested by the Gestapo on 25 April, and deported to Germany. He died on 6 June 1944 at Neuengamme.[30]

At the Liberation the rules of the game immediately changed. Patriotism meant to have resisted the Germans or persuaded others that one had done so, and to be free of compromising relationships with the Vichy regime, which was now deemed null and void. Paul Cay emerged from his brief period of hiding to be appointed secretary-general of the prefecture, the right-hand man of the new Liberation prefect. By contrast Prefect Musso was arrested, brought to trial in Angers, where he was felt to be safer from the vengeance of the population of Tours, and duly sent to prison.[31]

The position of Henri Mattraits was more complicated. The new republican regime decided that there was nothing wrong in holding office under Vichy, provided that it was an office to which one had been elected under the Republic. Mattraits had been elected mayor in 1934, which conferred legitimacy, but he had accepted office on Vichy's *conseil départemental* without having being the elected *conseiller général* for the canton of Chinon. He had lost that seat to Pierre Labussière in 1937, but in 1943 Vichy passed over Labussière as unfit for office and gave Mattraits the chance of sweet revenge. Mattraits was disqualified from sitting on the *conseil général* when it was revived after the Liberation, and also ran the risk of being disqualified as mayor.

From the beginning of the Liberation Mattraits campaigned to hold on to the town hall. In an eloquent defence of his conduct he told the council that he had protected Chinon during four years 'under the German jackboot'. He had suffered threats from German officers demanding supplies and accommodation and had been offered the blandishments of invitations to film shows and banquets, which he had systematically refused. Forgetting that the campaign to save the statue of Rabelais had been waged against Vichy, he claimed that 'one of our most glorious victories was to prevent our most cherished statue from being turned into German bullets'. The policy of non-cooperation he had pursued, Mattraits concluded, was 'another form of resistance that lasted for four years'.[32] This, however, did not prevent the new prefect from dissolving the municipal council of Chinon and appointing a 'provisional municipal delegation' of local Resistance leaders. With splendid irony its ceremonial inauguration was presided over on behalf of the prefect by Paul Cay, who announced how delighted he was to be back in Chinon.[33] The name of Mattraits was not so much as mentioned.

Free and fair municipal elections were scheduled for April and May 1945, and in the interim the battle-lines were drawn between the Resistance leaders and the local community. Auguste Correch, the college principal and assistant mayor to Mattraits in the latter part of the Occupation, declared for the former mayor, saying that Mattraits 'had never been the servant of the Vichy government and, faithful to the republican tradition, he never looked for any personal profit. He did his duty entirely.'[34] Mattraits took the head of one list under the system of proportional representation adopted, while the rival group, composed of members of the provisional delegation, headed their list with Pierre Labussière, who as a deportee had the crown of a resister but, unknown to the electorate, was already dead.

In the first ballot Mattraits was elected top of the poll by a local population which honoured him as their father figure and protector during the Occupation and had no time for those who had leapt aboard the Resistance bandwagon at the last moment; ten were elected from Mattraits' list, only Labussière from the other. After the second ballot the Mattraits list had secured seventeen of the twenty-three seats on the council and on 18 May Mattraits was duly elected mayor. The verdict of the popular vote nevertheless clashed with the rules of republican legitimacy and, despite an appeal from the council majority to de Gaulle, Mattraits was once again officially deposed. In the end the Resistance faction of the council did not benefit either. Auguste Correch was elected mayor and immediately paid homage to the devotion of Dr Mattraits, who had served Chinon 'with courage, probity, dignity and disinterestedness during a difficult and danger-ous period'.[35] Three years later Mattraits died and was buried with great pomp after a funeral attended by representatives of the munic-ipal council, the medical body, the hospitals, the court, the teachers and schoolchildren, the public employees, the gendarmerie and the population of Chinon and surrounding villages. Giving the oration, Correch reiterated Mattraits' role as the saviour of his people and the plebiscite which had returned him to office in 1945. Unfortu-nately, he said, Mattraits had received an 'odious and outrageous reward' in the form of dismissal and, despite the lobbying of power-ful friends, they had 'come up against a Marmorean decision made by they did not know who, and they did not know where'. Even the local leaders of the Resistance now paid homage to Mattraits at a funeral which demonstrated eloquently that the concerns and aspira-tions of the local community and the concerns and aspirations of the Resistance were far from being the same.[36]

What general questions about France under the German occupation can be teased from the experience of one small town? The first lesson is that the German occupation disrupted social and economic rela-tions in a multitude of ways, driving local people either to form new networks of solidarity or to break ranks and seek private advantage. Food shortages meant that consumers took their bicycles and trailers out to farmers they knew in order to stock up. Christian Beugnet of Chinon recalls cycling 10 or 15 kilometres to see M. Peraud, a miller, who he says was 'in our sector' and 'an honest chap, who tried to satisfy everyone except when the economic inspectors were about. Then he said, "Not today."' This implied a clientage between townsmen and farmers who knew and trusted each other, evading the sparsely provided official market for their mutual benefit. Under the Occupation, adds Beugnet's wife Léonie, 'People knew each other better.'[37] This 'grey market' in which goods were sold locally at a fair price was quite different from the long-distance black market engaged in by the Graeve family, selling to Parisians and Germans, in which huge profits could be made. The Germans, of course, did not pay for everything: tribute, produce, raw materials, transport and labour services were generally requisitioned without compensation. But much they did pay for in secret deals, and their appetite for the finer things of life was insatiable. The fact that the Graeve children were part of the Vichy administration demonstrated also that the desire for gain could eat away at the interior of a regime that had made a point of attributing the defeat of 1940 to selfishness and decadence and preaching the gospel of morality and self-sacrifice.

The tension between those who became involved in the German webs of power, profit and pleasure and those who fought to maintain the integrity of the local community and keep matters under the control of local notables was well illustrated by the Chevalier–Longuépée affair. While the magistrates were keen to ensure the supremacy of French law and sort out the petty disputes of the community locally, others were prepared to exploit for financial gain the Germans' sense that they had a right to the women of the defeated nation and to appeal to their German protectors over the heads of the local magistrates in order to get their way. For the least considered members of society such as women, who were denied the vote under the Third Republic and were expected, if bourgeois, to remain in the domestic sphere, the Occupation offered exciting possibilities of wielding power over those who conventionally despised them. Those who were shunned by conventional family-based small-town communities by dint of being separated, divorced, living in sin or by prostitution, who were drawn into relationships with Germans through domestic service, serving in bars or providing information, and were insulted as 'Boche', were now able to cast a spell by invoking the demonic force of the Germans and have their enemies imprisoned or spirited away to foreign parts.[38]

The second lesson, however, is that despite such aberrations local French authorities were generally astute in mediating between the pressures imposed by the Germans and the fears and frustrations of the local populations for whom they were responsible. In Chinon the commemoration of Joan of Arc Day and the defence of the statue of Rabelais increased the prestige of the local authorities in the eyes of their citizens. The irresponsible daubing of anti-German graffiti could not be tolerated, however, and the same authorities were obliged to demonstrate to the Germans that they had the matter under control. The Germans were happy with a system of 'indirect rule', whereby French local government was allowed a certain autonomy so long as it could deliver public order. The Chevalier–Longuépée affair showed the risk of allowing private individuals direct access to the Germans who then dictated terms to the French authorities. The latter eventually managed to convince the Germans that to allow the likes of Mme Longuépée to terrorize a small town by repeated denunciations was in the interests of neither of them, and indirect rule was restored. Even the killing of the German sentry in Tours, the repercussions of which reached as far as Chinon, did not prevent negotiations between the prefect and the Feldkommandant at Tours to defuse the situation and to divert German reprisals on to hard-core communist militants. The Labussière affair finished tragically because the new prefect Musso went down the road of close collaboration with the Gestapo and a hard line against the Resistance, rather than playing a more cunning game that might have kept local incidents hidden from German prying and saved the doctor.

The final lesson is how the meaning of patriotism evolved between 1940 and 1945. Henri Mattraits, lionized in 1940 for saving his town from destruction and standing firm on the *quai* as the Germans marched in, was thrust aside in 1945 for having accepted office under Vichy against the rules of republican legitimacy invented by the government-in-waiting. To have been a good shepherd, a father to one's people, when the French state had to all intents and purposes ceased to exist, was now not enough. It was necessary to have resisted the Germans or at least to have refused unelected office in the Vichy regime, and only a surfeit of the former was enough to purge the latter. Pierre Labussière, who had fallen foul of Vichy by his indiscreet abuse of Marshal Pétain and of the Germans for allegedly undermining STO, was acclaimed as a Resistance hero but was also a martyr to the cause. The most effective navigation of the fickle tides of patriotism was that of Paul Cay. Though a Vichy official, he was sensitive to the changing balance of power between the Allies and the shifting opinions of French citizens and was careful not to lock himself into a lost cause. He played an expert double game, giving his superiors to believe that he was committed to the regime while secretly building bridges to the Resistance. Rumbled by his superiors a few months before the Liberation, he abandoned Vichy just in time to secure credibility with the shadow republican government that was forming and to ensure his promotion at the Liberation as the new prefect's right-hand man at Tours. Contrary to the myth elaborated by de Gaulle, there was for the overwhelming majority of French people no unbroken thread between the General's appeal to continue the struggle in June 1940 and his march down the Champs-Élysées in liberated Paris in August 1944. Most French people followed Pétain for most of the Occupation, then de Gaulle. To abandon one for the other too soon was dangerous, to do it too late imprudent. In Vichy France choices guided by heroism were rarely as conducive to survival as those based on an ability to see one step ahead in a very murky world.

2. ENCOUNTER

On 18 June 1940, as the recently formed government of Marshal Pétain sued for an armistice, General de Gaulle, broadcasting on the BBC, famously told the French people that although the battle of France was lost, the war – a world war – was not over.

> Crushed by superior mechanical force today, we can conquer in the future by virtue of a superior mechanical force. There lies the destiny of the world ... Whatever happens, the flame of French resistance must not be extinguished and will not be extinguished.[1]

That Tuesday, a fine day, the French were unlikely to be tuning into the BBC or even to pay much heed to de Gaulle's message if they happened to hear it. The German army had swept all before it in a lightning campaign since 5 June. The government abandoned Paris on 10 June and declared it an 'open city' which would not be defended against the oncoming Germans, who entered it on the 14th. The roads were clogged by a jumble of retreating soldiers and civilians fleeing for fear of atrocities the Germans might commit, as they had on the previous invasions in 1870 and 1914. The prefect of Loire-Inférieure reported a 'veritable wave of refugees' driven before the German armies, confident that if they could cross the Loire they would somehow be safe.[2] By the middle of June there were over 250,000 refugees in his department, Belgians followed by inhabitants of the Nord/Pas-de-Calais, the Ardennes and Alsace-Lorraine. Marinette Rameau, a young bourgeoise of Angers, whom we shall meet again in the next chapter, noted in her diary on 17 June that 'the spectacle on the roads is lamentable: routed soldiers in twos and threes, refugees pulling the most heterogenous vehicles with difficulty ... Exhausted, they are walking like automatons towards a single vague goal: the south.' Her parents gave a short lift to a woman, wearing all her jewels, travelling with her son; they were bound for Bordeaux and hoped in the midst of all the chaos that the boy would still be able to take his *baccalauréat*.[3] As the Germans inexorably approached, families in threatened towns had to decide whether to stay or go. While the Rameaus quickly returned home, another bourgeois family of Angers, hearing bombs falling on the local aerodrome, decided to leave the city for the island of Noirmoutier off Nantes where they had a secondary home and were convinced they would be safe. By the end of the month, however, 4,000 Germans had occupied the island, taking over the summer chalets and swimming in the sea every morning.[4]

As the German forces drove south, the French high command tried one last throw of the dice: to hold up the enemy on the Loire by blowing up the bridges across the river, and defending the towns along it, allowing the retreating army as much time as possible to keep ahead of the invaders. The decision to defend the Loire and its towns struck panic into the hearts of local citizens, municipal authorities and refugees. A wedge was driven between the military commanders and civilians who understood that any defence of their town would expose it to aerial and artillery bombardment and a potential massacre in the streets. Since the rumours of atrocities committed by German soldiers were turning out to be groundless (and it later transpired that they were under strict instructions to act with discipline and courtesy) civilians became much more fearful of the consequences of resisting than of surrender.

In the annals of the French military one operation stood out as worthy of its glorious past. Saumur, less than 20 miles west of Chinon, overlooked by a chocolate-box castle as perfect as that of Chinon was in ruins, was the home of the French Cavalry School, from which many of the military élite graduated. For three days, from 19 to 21 June 1940, the cadets of the school undertook a heroic defence of the Loire over a wide front in order to protect the retreat of the French army. When further resistance became impossible a small unit gathered to bear away the standard of the school, lest it fall into German hands. Almost immediately the cadets of Saumur acquired a mythical status which will be examined later.[5]

In June 1940, however, in Saumur as elsewhere, soldiers and civilians were at each other's throats over the question of resistance or surrender. The mayor of Saumur, a vigorous radical–socialist called Robert Amy, whose son was in fact killed in action that month, was desperate to prevent his town being turned into a battlefield. According to the government, towns of over 20,000 inhabitants were to be declared 'open cities' and would not be defended, but Saumur was not big enough to fall into that category. Meanwhile, the commander of the Cavalry School, Colonel Michon, was adamant that his orders were to defend Saumur and the Loire and that he counted on the mayor's patriotism to support his efforts. The general commanding the sector, whom Amy reached by telephone, refused to change his orders and equally refused to order the evacuation of the town. On 19 June the Germans began to shell Saumur and the population hid in either cellars or limestone caves in the cliffs, or fled. On the 20th the Germans entered the town, seized the elderly Procureur de la République, Louis Ancelin, as a hostage, and took him by sidecar to military headquarters at Chinon. There the German general threatened reprisals against Saumur for the killing by French fire of a German sent to parley under a white flag, thereby violating the laws of war. Ancelin replied that he knew nothing of the incident and was not a soldier but a magistrate, although he had been four times wounded in the Great War as an officer and held the Legion of Honour. At this the German general saluted him, saying, 'We respect the combatants of the last war, who defeated us, but we despise the little rabbits of this one.' Ancelin was released and driven back by Major Wahrenburg, a portly Prussian who was to take command at Saumur and, as a magistrate in civilian life, looked forward to sorting out with Ancelin differences between French and German law thrown up by the Occupation.[6]

For mayors and magistrates the overriding concern in June 1940 was not resistance but avoiding military confrontation that could inflict terrible damage on the civilian population. Mayors summoned emergency meetings of town councillors and other notables, including bishops who had not been welcome in town halls for the seventy-year duration of the anticlerical Third Republic, in order to construct a lobby for cease-fire. Frantic telephone conversations took place between mayors and the government, now evacuated to Bordeaux, about whether their town was to be treated as an 'open city', between mayors and military commanders asking them to leave rather than defend the town, and ultimately directly between mayors and German military commanders about its surrender. They were not operating in a vacuum but under pressure from the local population and passing refugees who were so averse to combat that they were prepared to disarm French soldiers who were too keen to have a go at the Boche.

Tours had been capital of France for two days, on 12–13 June 1940, after the French government, as in 1870, abandoned Paris in the face of the approaching Germans. While the ministers set up base in the château of Cangé, a few miles to the east on the outskirts of Amboise forest, Churchill and his staff arrived with a Hurricane squadron for a meeting of the Supreme Allied War Council at the prefecture of Tours. The airfield had already been cratered by German bombs, no one came to meet them, and a café owner who claimed he was closed had his arm twisted to provide lunch for the British prime minister. At the prefecture Churchill found Interior Minister Mandel, Clemenceau's former secretary, shouting orders down two telephones at once and inspiring hope 'like a ray of sunshine'. Unfortunately, though, Mandel was not a member of the Supreme War Council, convened at 3.30 p.m. with eight Britons and two Frenchmen, the dithering premier Paul Reynaud and the silken secretary of the French war cabinet, Paul Baudouin. Reynaud asked, on behalf of his government, what Britain's attitude would be if the French, notwithstanding the Franco-British agreement of 28 March not to conclude a separate peace with Germany, did so if the worst came to the worst. Churchill replied that the British government could not agree to release the French from their obligations, but said that they would not descend to reproaches or recriminations if they did sue for an armistice.[7] It was no doubt a mistake that Churchill was not invited to address the French ministers at Cangé, to stiffen their resolve, for their meeting at 5 p.m. was dominated by the 'defeatists' under Marshal Pétain, who now made a formal proposition that government seek an armistice with Germany, as 'the necessary condition of the survival of eternal France'.[8] As the ministers headed off for Bordeaux, the population of Tours unwittingly made clear that their sympathies lay more with Pétain than Churchill: the fighting must stop. The Germans resumed their bombardment of the aerodrome and the city and arrived on the banks of the Loire on 18 June.

That day, as de Gaulle in London appealed to the French to

continue the fight, a delegation of the inhabitants of a neighbourhood to the east of the railway tracks at Tours marched to the Hôtel de Ville and told the mayor that if the city were defended they would not hesitate to throw themselves in front of the cannon of the French artillery-men.[9] The mayor, Ferdinand Morin, himself of working-class origin, a practical socialist rather than an ideologue and from the pacifist wing of the party, convened a meeting with the prefect and archbishop of Tours, Mgr Gaillard, and made desperate calls to Bordeaux to have the city confirmed as open. But he was confronted by a military commander who claimed to have orders to hold up the Germans on the Loire for forty-eight hours. At 11 p.m. on 18 June the bridges over the Loire to the north of the city centre were blown up and a motley collection of troops, many of them North African, took up positions in such places as the municipal library. The following morning they opened up on the Germans from the library with machine-guns and the Germans riposted by shelling the city. The wind whipped up a fire which burned for three days, killing about 100 people, destroying many ancient buildings and leaving 9,000 homeless.[10] The librarian reported that pages of burning books were carried as far as Azay-le-Rideau and Chinon.[11] On 20 June the Germans demanded the surrender of the city, and in an extraordinary scene of biblical symbolism, the mayor, prefect and (according to some accounts) the archbishop set off in the mayor's own fishing boat across the Loire to where the Germans awaited them.[12] Hoping against hope that the military had done their duty and that the civilians would remain disciplined, Morin promised on his honour and his life that there would be no resistance if a truce were granted, and the Germans entered Tours at dawn the following day.

Whereas after the return of de Gaulle in 1944 some act of resistance was required for honour, in 1940 as the French state collapsed loyalties shrank very sharply from the *patrie* to one's own town or village. The duty of a mayor in these circumstances was to show personal bravery by staying at his post but as father of his community not to expose his charges to unnecessary dangers. In July, while Morin was away in Vichy voting full powers to Marshal Pétain to restore the French state, the municipal council of Tours unanimously endorsed a motion that by going to meet the Germans and offering his honour and life as a guarantee he had 'deserved well of the city' by averting its 'total ruin'.[13] To underline the point, Morin was presented the following year with an embossed presentation volume the size of a pavement slab, signed by literally thousands of Tourangeaux, 'workers and intellectuals, shopkeepers and civil servants, whatever their divergences of opinion of diversity of condition in the past', according to the assistant mayor, who wished to thank Morin for saving the city and sparing hundreds of innocent lives.[14]

To the west, at Angers, the same battle between soldiers and civilians was fought out. The Germans began to bomb the railway station and, although it had been announced on the radio that towns of over 20,000 inhabitants would be declared open cities, on 18 June French soldiers began to set up machine guns on the banks of the Maine in front of the medieval château. The inhabitants of the neighbourhood implored them not to fire on the Germans, for fear of the consequences.[15] The local military commander was insistent that Angers should be defended, but the mayor, Victor Bernier, a tight-lipped and sharp-featured pharmacist, called an emergency council meeting which resolved that Angers was not in a position to stand a siege and did not want to see bridges blown up or women, children or the elderly evacuated.[16] The deadlock was broken the following day by a phone call from a French-speaking Captain Stein of the approaching German forces who claimed to be with a division and threatened to reduce Angers to ashes with heavy artillery and Stukas if the slightest resistance was shown. The French commander was persuaded not to defend the bridges over the Maine which led to the city centre, although he did not exclude a defence of the Loire, to the south of the city. Mayor Bernier travelled by car with the prefect and a French officer to meet the Germans some miles north of the city and, like Morin, offered himself as a guarantee that there would be no resistance.[17] On 20 June the local press carried an announcement that 'all resistance and all armed opposition is formally prohibited and will be severely punished by the French authorities. The prefect and mayor appeal for calm, coolness and discipline on the part of the population.'[18] As one Angers merchant wrote to a colleague who had left the city with his family, 'Our good city gave itself up like a flower.'[19] No discredit was done to the mayor, however. On the contrary, Victor Bernier was warmly thanked by the municipal council for 'sparing the inhabitants a certain and useless massacre', and duly remained in office until the last year of the Occupation.[20]

At Nantes, the largest city in the region, the process of occupation went more smoothly in the short term, but the mayor did not distinguish himself either by a bravura performance as the Germans approached the city or by tactful and disciplined conduct subsequently. The idea of a 'Breton redoubt' or a bridgehead in Brittany permitting the British to support a last stand of the French army, which Churchill had tried to sell to Reynaud in the early part of June, quickly evaporated.[21] There was no issue about Nantes being declared an open city, no frantic telephone calls or dangerous missions by car or boat. The Germans simply streamed in on lorries and motorcycles, while the Nantais crowded the pavements to gawp at them. 'Civilians surrounded the soldiers and tried to question them, showing no animosity, while the Germans took photos of them,' a schoolmaster wrote disapprovingly in his diary. 'Similarly, as the the troops crossed the place Royale, the German soldiers waved at the children, inviting them to wave back, while other soldiers filmed the scene for propaganda purposes.'[22] The curé of Sainte-Croix noted that the Nantais were hanging out of their windows to look at the Germans, while in the evening the German soldiers invaded the shops and markets, 'mass-buying jewellery, silk stockings and binoculars, etc.'.[23] There seemed to be an atmosphere of festivity rather than of mourning.

Nantes, however, was a busy sea-port with a large population of seamen, dockers, factory workers and prostitutes and a tradition of left-wing politics, a simmering urban pot in a calm rural hinterland over which nobility and clergy still exercised influence almost unchallenged. Brothels were temporarily closed, but German soldiers shot the doors down and queued up four or five to a bedroom in seedy hotels to which the prostitutes had repaired. On the second night of the Occupation a German sentry, jostled by a passing black man, riddled him with bullets and tossed him into the Loire.[24] The Feldkommandant or German military governor in Nantes was concerned by the indiscipline of his own troops but even more by the threat of resistance from the local population. Resuming a practice that had operated in occupied parts of France in 1870 and 1914–18, he required the municipality to draw up a list of hostages, preferably of notables with influence, of whom twenty a day would be kept at a hotel to guarantee the good order of the population. The municipality convened the town's main authorities and organizations and a list of 300 potential hostages was drawn up.[25] The bishop, Mgr Villepelet, offered himself for the first watch in the Hôtel Vendée and provided a list of thirty clergy. After a week the hostages were simply required to stay the night and the curé of Sainte-Croix noted that he had dined soberly with an architect, museum conservator and industrialist next to Germans who were loudly quaffing champagne.[26] Early in July the Feldkommandant ruled that, given the 'loyal and peaceful attitude of the population up to now', hostages had no longer to sleep at the hotel but simply remain in town.[27] The system was still operating a year later when the president of the Commercial Court, designated a hostage for the third or fourth time, complained that it should be democratized and all electors included.[28] Democratized it was a month later, with terrible results.

At the end of the day it was the mayor rather than a rota of hostages who answered for the good behaviour of the population. From the late summer of 1940 things in Nantes started to get worse, not better, and it soon transpired that the mayor was not part of a solution but part of the problem. For mayors to survive politically it was necessary for them to tread a difficult path between being a father of their citizens, protecting them against German aggression, and maintaining cordial relations with the German military authorities, insulating them from popular violence. Auguste Pageot, an emotional and somewhat tactless socialist, failed on both counts, and did not last in office beyond the first Christmas of the Occupation. One of the most common acts of resistance was to cut the communications cables laid by the German military for the effective functioning of their machine. Unable to find the culprits, the Germans responded by imposing massive fines on the local community, a collective punishment that was strictly forbidden under the Hague Convention of 1907, but to which they resorted anyway. After one telephone cable was cut at Nantes on 8 August 1940 the Feldkommandantur imposed a collective fine of 2 million francs, followed by a second fine of 5 million francs when a second cable was cut on 8 September. Mayor Pageot claimed that he was unable to demand a further sacrifice from his townsfolk, and was already in trouble because of another incident. During the night of 30–1 August the war memorial in honour of the dead of 1870, which depicted a nude hero of antiquity slaying a dragon, was overturned by chains attached to a lorry. The Germans wanted the municipality to remove the prone statue, which was attracting crowds and becoming a threat to public order, and telephoned the town hall three times to have something done. Mayor Pageot, however, wanted to make patriotic capital out of the incident, and proposed to lead the municipal council in a body to lay a wreath on the ruin. He stormed into the Feldkommandantur where the Feldkommandant and the prefect had just agreed that the statue must be removed and that French and German police should conduct parallel investigations into who was responsible: one theory was that the culprits were fairground people. Pageot interrupted them to protest at what he called a premeditated provocation by the Germans which 'wounded our most worthy patriotic sentiments to the depths of our hearts', and said that he was ordering the work to remove the statue to cease, so that the people of Nantes could meditate more deeply on the brutality of the Occupation. The following day the municipal council met to consider Pageot's motion to lay a wreath as a body, but was split; accordingly, the mayor went alone before lunch to lay a wreath with a tricolour ribbon inscribed from the 'town of Nantes'.[29]

As a result of this incident and others, the exasperated Feldkommandant realized that he could no longer work with Pageot, who was arrested on 10 October and thrown into prison. When the municipal council voted their solidarity with their mayor, the Feldkommandant thought of having them arrested too, but decided against it. He himself was treading a narrow path between insisting on the cooperation of the French authorities and averting any measure that would needlessly provoke the Nantais. He hesitated between court-martialling the mayor and releasing him on condition that he resigned, but this Pageot refused to do until just before Christmas. He was duly released from prison and exiled to the Free Zone to prevent him stirring up more trouble in Nantes.[30] The striking thing about the episode as a whole is that the prefecture at Nantes supported the Feldkommandant against a mayor who was less patriotic than irascible and rude, and that the Nantais did not rise up – as the Feldkommandant feared they might – to protest against the dismissal of their mayor. Franco-German accommodation was an art that had to be learned in the interest of all parties, and most parties managed it extremely well.

The settlement of this issue involved German authorities not only in Nantes but also in Angers and Paris and set in motion the institutional framework of the military administration which the Germans imposed on Occupied France. This resembled a colonial administration with the difference that it was exercised over a highly civilized western European country. At the pinnacle was the Militär-befehlshaber in Frankreich (MBF) or military commander in France, based in Paris at the Hôtel Majestic, avenue Kléber. The two generals who occupied this post were cousins who sprang from the Prussian military aristocracy, Otto von Stülpnagel until the spring of 1942, then Carl-Heinrich von Stülpnagel.[31] Born respectively in 1878 and 1886, they were representatives of German military might from the Imperial age and far from being Hitlerian. Otto, as we shall see, disagreed with his superiors over the ruthless strategy of reprisals implemented by the Army High Command in 1941, while Carl-Heinrich struggled against the tightening grip of the secret police and was executed as a traitor after the bomb plot of 20 July 1944 against Hitler. Under the military command for the whole of France were the four regional military administrations: District B, based in Angers, was the so-called South-western Region. The first regional commander, General Karl-Ulrich Neumann-Neurode, born in Silesia in 1876, was a shadowy figure of whom little is known except that he loved animals.[32] In July 1942 he was replaced by General Kurt Feldt, a West Prussian of the 24th Panzer Division, who was ten years younger. Subordinate to the regional commander were the Feldkommandants, one to each department, whose opposite numbers were the French prefects. In April 1941 the Vichy government gave some of their prefects new responsibility as regional prefects, supervising a group of departments and hoping to operate with more clout vis-à-vis the German military. The crucial interface of Feldkommandant and prefect, however, was scarcely changed. At the base of the German military administration were the Kreiskommandants, one to each *arrondissement*, whose opposite numbers were the French sub-prefects. This was the link that operated, for example, in the small town of Chinon.[33]

The organization chart of corresponding authorities of course says very little about the reality of relations between French and German officials, which were more than simply a brutal relationship between occupiers and occupied. Negotiations had to be entered into, and negotiations were facilitated by good personal relations and a common cultural framework of military honour, European civilization

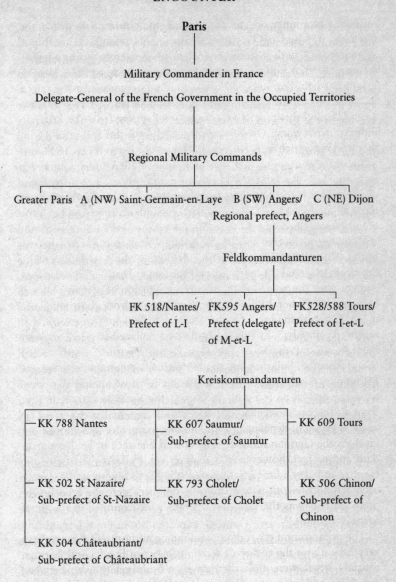

Paris

Military Commander in France

Delegate-General of the French Government in the Occupied Territories

Regional Military Commands

Greater Paris   A (NW) Saint-Germain-en-Laye   B (SW) Angers/   C (NE) Dijon
Regional prefect, Angers

Feldkommandanturen

FK 518/Nantes/   FK595 Angers/   FK528/588 Tours/
Prefect of L-I   Prefect (delegate)   Prefect of I-et-L
of M-et-L

Kreiskommandanturen

— KK 788 Nantes   KK 607 Saumur/   ⊢ KK 609 Tours
Sub-prefect of Saumur

— KK 502 St Nazaire/   KK 793 Cholet/   KK 506 Chinon/
Sub-prefect of St-Nazaire   Sub-prefect of Cholet   └ Sub-prefect of
Chinon

└ KK 504 Châteaubriant/
Sub-prefect of Châteaubriant

and Christian religion. The defusing of the Pageot affair in Nantes, for example, was made possible by the good working relationship of the Feldkommandant, the prefect's interpreter and the ruling notables of Nantes. The Feldkommandant, Lieutenant-Colonel Hotz, was no stranger to Nantes when he arrived as military governor in 1940. Born in 1877 at Wertheim-am-Main, he had learned French while serving in the garrison of Metz, which from 1871 to 1918 was part of Imperial Germany. Attached to the Bavarian general staff during the First World War, he then went into industry and was in Nantes from 1930 to 1933 as manager of Brandt of Düsseldorf, which was diverting the waters of a tributary of the Loire into an underground canal system through the city centre with funds from the Dawes Plan. Highly musical, Hotz bought the latest popular songs from Les Trois Rossignols and played the piano in the salons of the bourgeoisie and nobility of Nantes.[34] After he returned to Nantes in 1940 he was invited to play the trumpet at the château of the Marquise Yolaine de Sesmaisons outside Nantes. Her husband, Olivier de Sesmaisons, belonged to a military nobility which could trace its ancestry back to the time of Saint Louis and as a large landowner was an influential local politician.[35] According to their sons, whom I interviewed in 1998, the French and German military castes were drawn together by 'a sense of honour, courtesy and the chivalric spirit', which transcended national boundaries.[36] Unlikely though this may seem at the time of the Third Reich, it should be remembered that these German officers of the military administration were usually in their sixties, trained in the Second Reich and veterans of the 1914–18 war, during which they had learned to respect their opposite numbers in the French military.

National boundaries were also transcended by a sense of belonging to a common European civilization. Hotz's link with the prefecture was Edmond Duméril, a German master at the Lycée Clemenceau who was seconded as interpreter at the prefecture to liaise with the occupying authorities. Duméril expected to meet a large brutal Prussian at the Feldkommandantur but instead found 'an old man, dry, short, dressed in an artillery officer's uniform', with a 'broad smile and kindly expression'. He discovered that they had studied, ten years apart, under the same professors at the University of Tübingen. The ages of these individuals were as important culturally as militarily. Duméril regarded Hotz, aged sixty-three, as a representative of the old, civilized Germany, quite different from the young Nazi Schuster who was his immediate subordinate in the military administration. While Schuster listened to Hitler's every word on the radio, Hotz hid a history book under his papers and in conversation applauded Duméril's citation of Goethe's words on the death of Schiller.[37]

A third factor that brought French and German elites together was organized religion. Most Germans admittedly were Protestants, and Mgr Villepelet, bishop of Nantes, used the excuse that his cathedral was Catholic to deny the German authorities the right to use it.[38] Relations with Hotz's successor, Baron von und zu Bodman, were much better, because he was a Bavarian Catholic. 'He is so distinguished and well educated,' mused the bishop when they met in December 1941, 'one can sense that he is of noble race.' They spoke of the baron's origins in Munich, and the bishop asked him if he knew Cardinal Falhauber. 'Not only do I know him,' replied the baron, raising the stakes, 'but I also know the Pope, who I often saw at Munich when he was nuncio. I even went to his coronation.' Moving on to royalty, he spoke of Queen Elizabeth of the Belgians, widow of King Albert, who was a Bavarian princess, of the young King Leopold who had recently remarried, and of the royal children.[39] Mgr Villepelet, a doctor's son but a prince of the Church, felt much more at ease with this ambassador of the German Reich than he ever had with French republican officials elected or appointed under the Popular Front.

In the Angers region the key relationship was between the French prefect (later regional prefect), Jean Roussillon, and the Feldkommandant, Colonel Kloss. Kloss was clear that the French administration must bend to German will and expressed pleasure at the intention of the prefect and his subordinates 'to work loyally with the Germans'. He was clear also that German authority and the German military must be accorded respect. But he realized, too, that if the French were to consent in any way to German rule it would be necessary to maintain at least the illusion that they were still being run by French administrators who enjoyed some independence. For his part Roussillon needed to extract as many concessions as possible from the German authorities to make the Occupation tolerable for the French. On the other hand, given the lack of communication with the French government at Vichy in the non-occupied part of

France, Roussillon came to learn that the support of the German military regime actually gave him an authority and effectiveness vis-à-vis the French population that he could not otherwise have contemplated. The relationship between Feldkommandant and prefect was therefore much more complex than a simple one of command and obey, reproducing as it did the system of 'indirect rule' between colonizers and indigenous elites as developed in the British Empire by Frederick Lugard, former governor-general of Nigeria.[40]

A good working partnership was built up between Roussillon and Kloss, the former reporting that relations were 'more than courteous: they are almost trusting and based on a reciprocal loyalty. They could quite easily become cordial.' Thanks to this 'spirit of comprehension with Kloss,' he clarified, 'the measures ordered by the Military High Command [in Paris] are applied with moderation and flexibility in Maine-et-Loire'.[41] Unfortunately, the build-up of confidence on a local level was all too often interrupted by the redirection of officials in accordance with the wider needs of the military or civil bureaucracies. In April 1941 Colonel Kloss moved from Angers to Tours, from where he was to run both Indre-et-Loire and Maine-et-Loire as a single large Feldkommandantur. Roussillon regretted the departure of Kloss who, he said, had kept the German military on a tight leash and prevented them from abusing the French population. Now, he said, 'We are confronted by subaltern officers who do not care to shoulder too much responsibility and do not have the same authority or influence over the troops.' He took solace from Kloss's promise to visit Angers once a week, a promise that, given his busy schedule, he was not able to keep. Roussillon's opposite number from this point was less the regional commander General Neumann-Neurode, whom he nevertheless found 'considerate' and 'courteous' when they did meet, than General Dr Medicus, chief of the administrative section of District B. After a couple of months Roussillon was heaping the same praises on Medicus that he had accorded to Kloss, saying that his influence had grown rapidly in the District, that his 'pro-French sympathies, which he demonstrated at every possible opportunity', had made the confident relationship that he had enjoyed with Kloss still stronger and had even served to reinforce the authority of the French administration. After Medicus returned to Angers following a brief posting to Greece in the summer of 1941 Roussillon was even more extravagant with his superlatives, praising the German's 'perfect propriety and and remarkable understanding of the French mentality'.[42]

Meanwhile, the French authorities in Tours were in their turn discovering the advantages of having Colonel Kloss at the Feldkommandantur. His predecessor, Captain Marloh, had been particularly harsh and unyielding, and no tears were shed when he and his team were sent off to Belorussia. Jean Chaigneau, the prefect of Indre-et-Loire, said that he was 'delighted by the ease and courtesy of my relationship with the German authorities, which are due in large measure to the understanding of Colonel Kloss'.[43] The German authorities were similarly impressed by Chaigneau, not least because he had a distinguished career in the 1914–18 War. 'He works well and conscientiously with the German administration,' noted one confidential report. 'His reputation as a clever and energetic administrative civil servant goes before him.' A comparison with the number two in the prefecture of Tours, Secretary-General René Feld, confirms that the German ideal of a good French official was one who was brisk, straight-dealing and even courageous with it. Feld, the Germans observed, always worked hard to meet German demands fully but was 'soft of character'.[44] His shifty conduct may have been explained by the need to conceal his Romanian-Jewish origins by over-zealousness in the German cause. The French saw only the over-zealousness and in some circles in Tours his reputation was crisply summed up by his nickname: Feld-kommandant.[45]

Relations between French and German officials were established not only within a system of personal contacts and common cultural assumptions but also within a legal framework defined by both the armistice convention and international law. When the Germans arrived in Nantes, notices immediately went out to the civil authorities instructing them to 'use all their energy to ensure that no individual undertakes any act of hostility against the German army or the German military command'. Once French armies had laid down their arms it was understood that all resistance would cease; and yet the Germans were worried in the early days that the Occupation would encounter massive popular opposition. The Kommandantur of Nantes told the town hall that 'any passive resistance, act of violence, sabotage or work stoppage must be prevented with the utmost rigour, and the guilty parties arrested and punished'. He went on to list the crimes that were subject to martial law:

'1. Assistance given to non-German soldiers in occupied territory; 2. Transmission of information to the detriment of the German army and Reich; 3. Assistance to French POWs; 4. Offences against the German army and its commanders'. He added a further list of punishable offences: street gatherings, distribution of leaflets, public meetings and demonstrations, and any other activity hostile to Germany.[46]

This may have seemed like law by *Diktat* but in fact the Germans were operating within the terms of international law governing occupation administrations drafted by the great powers at The Hague in 1907 and added to by France and Germany in the Armistice Convention of 1940. The Armistice was not a peace treaty and made provisions for a situation that was by definition temporary, before any peace treaty was signed. Military occupation, moreover, did not abolish French sovereignty, which extended formally into Occupied France, but balanced it against the security needs of the occupying forces. The French government was free to make laws but always within the requirements of German military security. In pursuit of that security the German authorities could make their own laws and if necessary overrule French laws that conflicted with them. The French people were guaranteed protection of their lives, property and religion so long as they admitted defeat, obeyed the occupying authorities and offered no resistance. Resistance by non-combatants was not the same as war by soldiers: it was regarded as violating the laws of war and was punished under martial law. Under military occupation resources might be requisitioned for the needs of the Army of Occupation, but only in so far as the country could bear the burden and on issue of receipts which would later be honoured. One basic principle laid down was that communities could not be considered collectively responsible for acts committed by individuals. Collective punishments, such as hostage-taking or collective fines, were thus prohibited.[47]

Despite the legal attempt to reconcile French sovereignty and German security, in practice they tended to conflict. When French rights came up against German military security, which was to give way? There was no international tribunal to which appeal could be made. Communications between French authorities in the Occupied Zone and Vichy were deliberately frustrated by the Germans and had to be carried on indirectly through the Delegate-General of the

French Government in the Occupied Territories (DGGFTO), who from January 1941 was Fernand de Brinon, together with a delegate of the interior minister, the rather faceless Jean-Pierre Ingrand of the Conseil d'État, all resident in Paris. Ingrand effectively had the powers of a 'minister *in partibus*', while the Delegate-General had the status of ambassador and in effect was serving in a foreign country under German rule.[48] It did not help that de Brinon was himself highly devious and manipulative, intent on ingratiating himself with the Germans as a counterweight to Vichy rather than defending French interests, a path that led to his being shot as a collaborator after the war. In the event the French administration in the Occupied Zone was very much isolated from Vichy and left to fend for itself. The extent of French sovereignty depended on daily negotiations between French and German authorities in the regions and departments. As well as the declarations of cordiality and trust we have witnessed there were veritable wars of nerves, feinting and fencing, threats and blandishments, bluff and counter-bluff, claims to more power or resources than were actually to hand.

One issue over which French and German authorities struggled for the upper hand was the appointment and dismissal of mayors. Vichy legislation on local government was applicable in all parts of France, and at the end of 1941 the German authorities renounced the right to have a say in the appointment of mayors as a result of talks in the Franco-German commission overseeing the terms of the Armistice.[49] In practice, the German authorities were happy to respect the local administration in place, so long as it effectively carried out the task of maintaining order, that is, of insulating the Army of Occupation from any popular discontent. Towns like Nantes and Saint-Nazaire, large ports with a tradition of labour militancy, were regarded as particularly sensitive. The warm relationship between Feldkommandant Hotz and the prefecture of Loire-Inférieure did not prevent Hotz, as we have seen, from arresting the clumsily patriotic socialist mayor, Pageot, forcing him to resign, and exiling him to the Free Zone. Hotz's successor at Nantes, Baron von und zu Bodman, may have been emollience itself in his dealings with the bishop of Nantes, but when it came to Ferdinand Blancho, the socialist mayor of Saint-Nazaire who resigned in opposition to Vichy but remained the hero and possible demagogic leader of the dockers, he brooked no compromise. During heated debates in February 1942

Regional Prefect Roussillon argued that Blancho was under police surveillance and that tougher action would only provoke the dockers. Bodman insisted that it was precisely his influence over the dockers that made his departure necessary, and Blancho was duly put on a train for Paris, whence he travelled south and joined the Resistance.[50]

The rules of the Occupation thus evolved according to case law rather than legal principle. This was the situation as much in the judicial system as in the administration. In order to protect the security of the military, the Germans established a network of military courts to administer martial law. Any action deemed to threaten German military security was brought before the military court, although other cases were left to the French system of civil and criminal courts. The German military courts were tough, but not arbitrary, and worked according to set procedures. The accused was entitled to defence provided by a French barrister, although the pleading had to be in German. In Nantes, the defence was generally provided by Maître Guineaudeau, with Duméril on hand to translate. 'Until the death of Hotz,' Guineaudeau reported after the war, 'we obtained a good deal from the staff of the German justice system. I would say that they had a sort of professional conscience to which we could appeal. The judges did not think in the same way as the police. Often we were able to save heads.'[51]

One of the tasks of the French defence was to convince the German judges that opposition to the Occupation was often ritual or comic rather than a threat to security. The twenty-three-year-old son of a magistrate who amused himself and German soldiers by drawing caricatures of them in the Grand Café on the place de la Bourse at Nantes, for example, found himself in deep water when he drew a caricature of the Führer which they found insulting. He was sentenced to two months in prison by the military court until French lawyers persuaded the Germans to have a greater sense of humour and he was released. Similarly, a country priest who let the children in his Sunday-school group laugh at a scarecrow wearing a German helmet was threatened with three months in prison until the French defence convinced the court that 'to laugh while passing by but without stopping was not an offence'. More tricky was the case of Arthur Martineau, a sixty-five-year-old cement merchant of Sainte-Marie-de-la-Mer who had an obsessive desire to cut German telephone wires. On the first occasion his death penalty was lifted after the French medical witness convinced the court that he had suffered brain damage as a result of a cerebral haemorrhage. Unfortunately, after his release he repeated the offence and was promptly shot.[52]

The German system of military justice was neither as severe as might be imagined, at least in the early years of the Occupation, nor as pervasive. When the German military administration of District B tried to take cognizance of the case of two traders illegally selling above the fixed price and Prefect Roussillon resisted, he was supported by de Brinon in Paris who argued that under the Hague Convention occupying powers were authorized to act to ensure public order, but while price hikes might in theory affect public order, there was no reason for them not to be dealt with by the French courts. Sometimes the German military courts themselves did not wish to become involved in exclusively French matters.[53] When one man in Touraine tried to bring a defamation suit against two brothers who had called him a 'bandit' and a 'Boche', the German military court promptly returned the dossiers to the French court, saying that it was 'a quarrel between two French people'.[54] This is not to say that any case that went before the French courts was dealt with leniently and with due process. The Vichy government invented its own system of exceptional courts, the so-called Sections Spéciales, in order to deal with the communist threat. Immortalized by the Costa-Gavras 1975 film, they were found not just in Paris but wherever a regional Appeal Court could mutate into one of them. They effectively spared the Germans the business of repression they would otherwise have had to undertake themselves, and made a speciality of arbitrariness. The Section Spéciale of Angers sat for the first time in September 1941 and was particularly fond of handing out heavy sentences to anyone who so much as sang the *Internationale*. One young man received three years for singing it in a café, while a tax official received five years for teaching it to a band of peasants in a farm courtyard and conducting them.[55]

Negotiating the Occupation involved not only individuals but communities. Any critical moment, such as the death of a French or German person in confused circumstances, might suddenly bring a community where life was otherwise uneventful into a matrix which involved the Occupation forces, the Feldgendarmerie and French police, mayors and their councils, the subprefect and Kreiskommandant, the prefect and Feldkommandant, and possibly higher authorities too. Everything here was at stake, from finding the guilty party to calming local troops and the local community and preserving the reputation and honour of the French and German authorities. Three deaths in two communities within the space of a couple of months may be used to investigate French and German nerves at their rawest and negotiating skills at their highest premium.

After the heroic fighting by the military cadets of Saumur in June 1940 the Cavalry School was turned into a temporary POW camp, before evacuation to camps in Germany was organized. On Christmas Eve 1940 three French soldiers escaped from the camp and took refuge in a labourer's cottage. They were tracked down by German soldiers and one of the Frenchmen was shot as he hid under a bed. The funeral was attended by the subprefect, Robert Milliat, who was writing a book on the epic achievement of the cadets of Saumur, by notables of the town, by veterans' associations and also, in a spirit of reconciliation, by an escort of German soldiers and two German officers representing the camp commander.[56] Good relations in the town seemed to weather this incident, but two months later they were threatened when a roofer named Frank Le Cosquer was killed by a German patrol doing its rounds in Saumur. The version of the Feldgendarmerie was that Le Cosquer, arrested for being without papers, proceeded to kick and punch his captors and was shot while trying to escape. Milliat told the Kreiskommandant, Major von Wahrenburg, that such trigger-happiness was regrettable and that it would be better if German soldiers only used their weapons when their lives were in danger. He underlined his point by attending the funeral, at which 1,500 citizens turned out, in full uniform and at the head of the municipal council. Wahrenburg felt that this demonstration had been instigated by the prefect, and Kloss wrote angrily to Roussillon to protest at this challenge to the Wehrmacht's honour. Roussillon replied that Le Cosquer had been an 'honest worker who gave no trouble' and that he had acted both to 'appease the painful emotions that had gripped the community' and to 'restore a climate indispensable to a good understanding between the Army of Occupation and the civilian population'. Kloss refused to give way, saying that if the prefect had been apprised of the full facts he would not have turned the funeral into a demonstration.[57]

The stubbornness of both parties left the tension in Saumur

unresolved. Relations were not helped by another killing, a day before, in the usually quiet town of Cholet. Though an industrial centre, Cholet was an outpost of the Vendée and firmly under the control of paternalistic employers and the Catholic Church. There was great confusion and bewilderment, therefore, when a German soldier, Corporal Müller, was shot late at night by a civilian with a revolver who then escaped into the darkness. Suspecting an act of resistance, Colonel Kloss immediately had the mayor arrested, decreed a curfew after 8 p.m., closed all cafés and restaurants, and imposed a fine of 1 million francs on the townspeople. This time the funeral was staged as a German military occasion, with a band playing and a volley of rifles, to impress the local people with the honour attributed to an ordinary German soldier. The mayor, Alphonse Darmaillacq, a textile factory owner, later wrote that he was forced to follow the cortège. Kloss, however, who came to Cholet, said that 1,000 townsfolk attended, the men bareheaded 'in the French custom', that the mayor, subprefect and police commissioner expressed their sympathy personally to him, and that the mayor offered a substantial reward to anyone helping with the arrest of the culprit.

All was not clear in Cholet, however, and doubts about the identity of the murderer accumulated. The Kreiskommandant of Cholet, Major von Trotha, persuaded Kloss to reopen the case. No serious crime had been committed in Cholet for seventeen years and relations between the Choletais and Germans had been good. The murderer was said to have spoken in German before he pulled the trigger. Müller had become separated from his mates between the Café-restaurant Tamisier and the Café Coeffard, a house of ill repute, because he went to meet a stranger at the Hôtel de France and was shot as he crossed the main square. It emerged that German soldiers often went out in civilian clothes at night, particularly when they were visiting brothels, so the evidence increasingly pointed to the fact that Müller was shot by a German soldier in civvies. It was not just a question of righting a wrong but of mollifying French public opinion. The German war effort was demanding more and more industrial labour and French workers had to be attracted on to projects such as building the Atlantic warships in Brittany. To alienate a usually quiet industrial town like Cholet by levying a massive fine to punish a crime that might not even have been committed by a Frenchman was simply counter-productive. On 28 April 1941 Kloss therefore made the unprecedented gesture of refunding the million-franc fine to the citizens of Cholet.[58]

The German authorities came to realize that the efficient functioning of the Occupation involved a trade-off between maintaining order by sticks and maintaining goodwill by carrots. In the case of Saumur Kloss refused to cede, on the grounds that a common worker dealt with harshly was the price paid for good order and any apology would impugn the honour of the army, whatever resentment was felt by the community. In the case of Cholet the honour of the army had already been secured by a magnificent funeral, and the collective fine imposed on a community that was probably not responsible did not make good order more secure. On the contrary, true Vendeans that they were, the Choletais were taking refuge in a sullen opposition that could eventually undermine the German war effort. Harsh yet rational, the German military authorities understood that the tacit consent of the French people was indispensable to the success of the Occupation.

3. COHABITATION

In one of the great classics of the Occupation, Vercors' *Le Silence de la mer*, finished in October 1941 and published by an underground press in Paris early in 1942, a German officer, Werner von Ebrennac, is billeted on a French family comprising the narrator and a young woman, his niece. Every evening, after his work at the local Kommandantur, the officer tries to make conversation, saying how much he has always loved France, how much French literature complements German music, how they should unite as wife and husband and how, as in *Beauty and the Beast*, the love of beautiful France will liberate the German from his beastly imprisonment and reveal the handsome prince within. The niece, to whom these words are subliminally directed, never raises her eyes from her sewing and never speaks, the narrator continues to smoke his pipe, and the officer, confronted by an unyielding silence, never sits down and soon withdraws with the words, '*Je vous souhaite une bonne nuit*'. The story hinges on his visit to Paris, where his friends are preparing the 'wonderful union of our two peoples'. He returns, having met soldiers who had experienced the horrors of the Russian front, who have a totally different perspective on the Franco-German relationship. He confides to the narrator and his niece that the soldiers laughed at his naïveté, given the world-wide struggle for power, pointing out that the real plan was not to seduce France but to destroy it, body and soul, and ensure that she could never rise again. 'Adieu,' he declares and is gone the next morning when silence descends on the narrator and his niece also.[1]

Fifty-five years after the publication of Vercors' book, I visited Marinette Rameau in her oak-beamed family home in the Angevin countryside close to the Loire. Born in 1909, she might have been the same age during the war as the niece in *Le Silence de la mer*. She is a tall, elegant and still beautiful woman, who not only kept a diary of her wartime experiences but is happy to talk about them freely. She never married and it is as if some of the most significant emotional moments of her life occurred under the Occupation. This, for Marinette Rameau, meant a succession of German officers billeted on the family's town house in Angers on the promenade facing the château across the Maine. The most memorable of them was Captain Wilhelm Koester, who arrived on 21 July 1940. Whereas Werner von Ebrennac, asked by the narrator of *Le Silence de la mer*, whether, given his name, he was not descended from a French Protestant driven out by Louis XIV, regretted that he was not, Wilhelm Koester declared, 'I love to speak French . . . I admire your culture; my wife is of southern origin, her ancestors from Vignolles [Charente] came to Germany after the Revocation of the Edict of Nantes, but we are now Catholics.' Marinette's mother proposed to serve the officer in the study, but he insisted, 'Madame, you do not understand. I wish to eat at your table. Choose: do you prefer to have a civilized officer, or four soldiers who will be much less so?' Far from freezing Koester out, the Rameau family acceded to his request. Marinette, whose eyes were for handsome men rather than for sewing, was delighted. She discovered that Koester, aged forty-seven, was a sculptor and director of the Fine Art School at Trier. 'I have to admit,' she wrote, 'he is very distinguished and perfectly educated.' His orderly, Willi Gehendges, turned out to have been his pupil at Trier. Marinette noted that he spoke little French but 'plays the violin like a virtuoso, and by heart: Beethoven, Schubert, Mozart, Strauss, Neapolitan romances and modern tunes'.[2] Her only regret was that the captain and his orderly stayed for less than a month, and when I interviewed her in 1996 she told me the whole story again, rhapsodizing about the virtues of 'le capitaine.'![3]

Marinette Rameau's appreciation of the cultivation of the German military was reinforced in May 1944, when 'a French Apollo' turned up at the house with an accommodation slip issued by the Kommandantur. Her mother tried to turn him away, saying that her rooms were reserved for Germans, but the Apollo was a leader of the French counter-insurgent Milice and would not take no for an answer. A month later, returning from the family retreat on the Loire, Marinette found vomit in the garden, cigarette ends trodden into the stair carpet, wine-glass stains on the pedestal table, bullet holes in the bedroom walls and two more Milice soldiers still in bed. She complained to the Milice headquarters and then reprimanded the uninvited lodgers. 'I have to tell you, Messieurs,' she scolded, 'that we have had Germans throughout the war in the rooms that you occupy. They were always clean and polite and would never have done what I have just seen in the garden, or left the doors wide open. It is painful to me to observe that this is the behaviour of French people. You ought to be ashamed of yourselves.'[4]

These stories of German officers billeted on French homes could scarcely be more different. The difference lies not in the portrayal of the officers, who are equally refined and civilized, but in the reaction of their French hosts. The first was greeted by a persistent and glacial silence, the second, if Marinette Rameau was as loquacious then as she is now, was probably carried away on a torrent of words. One explanation may simply be that not all families responded in the same way to their guests, but it must be remembered that *Le Silence de la mer* is a political parable, a lesson in patriotic behaviour for the Occupied French written as the initial goodwill between French and Germans began to turn sour. It is a warning not to trust to appearances, to beware of the mailed fist in the glove. Marinette Rameau's story may be the romantic daydreams of a thirty-one-year-old spinster, but it is significant that her judgement was confirmed as the war continued, as a result of the bad behaviour not of the Germans but of the French. Moreover, despite the official postwar orthodoxy that contact with Germans was reprehensible, fifty years on she is still captivated by the memory of Captain Koester. This is not to say that Vercors' account is fiction and Rameau's reality, but that relations between French and Germans under the Occupation cannot be reduced to German oppression confronted by French patriotism. Despite the obvious inequality of power between the parties, interactions between the two were multifaceted, subtle and complex. From Marinette Rameau's account we can understand that the Germany of Goethe and Beethoven was never quite eclipsed for many French people by the Germany of Hitler, that the clash of Latin and Teuton was disturbed by Germans fluent in French and by Germans descended from French stock, and finally that the German officer, cultivated and honourable as well as virile, exercised a magnetic attraction, particularly over French women.

The experience of Marinette Rameau of a succession of Germans billeted on the family home was not necessarily typical. The German Occupation did not mean that the country was constantly teeming with troops looking for accommodation. True, in the autumn of 1940 the German military authorities required the French administration to undertake a sort of Domesday Book of every village, to ascertain how many officers, NCOs, troops and horses could be accommodated in each commune, first under ordinary billeting (one bed per soldier) and second under heavy billeting, with the troops sleeping on straw. For the village of Ligueil near the demarcation line in Touraine, for example, with a population of 2,028, ordinary billeting would mean 35 officers, 71 NCOs, 905 troops and 247 horses, while heavy billeting meant the same number of officers and NCOs but 2,258 troops and 428 horses.[5] In the event fears of Occupation on this scale were not realized. Unless they were part of the military administration in larger centres, German troops were generally on the move and never stayed long in one particular place. Most small towns and villages were troubled for a few days or weeks at the beginning of the Occupation, and for a few days or weeks at the end, and sometimes a little in between, but rarely more. A historical survey undertaken on a commune-to-commune basis in Maine-et-Loire (Anjou) in 1948 makes possible a fine calibration of the German presence. In the Mauges the village of Andrezé was occupied between 21 and 23 June 1940 and 8 August and 8 November 1942, when the troops moved into the Free Zone; no damage was reported. The nearby village of Le Fuilet was occupied between 21 and 29 June and 14 and 25 July 1940. The mayor reported that the German forces occupied the town hall, broke chairs, made holes in the wall and removed flags and his scarf of office; when they returned in 1944, headlong in retreat, they stole twenty bicycles. An analysis of over 200 reports received reveals that only 10 per cent of communes in Anjou said that they were occupied throughout the war, 15 per cent were never occupied at all, and in between 26 per cent were occupied once, 29 per cent twice and 20 per cent more than twice.[6]

Clearly the impact of the German Occupation was very uneven. Cities, ports, suburbs close to airfields, administrative and communication centres saw more Germans than out-of-the-way villages. Germans were reluctant to stay outside the *bourg* or village nucleus in isolated farmsteads because of a sense of insecurity. Rural dwellings were not attractive because only one room was generally heated, serving as both kitchen and living room for the family. The mining village of Nyoiseau in rural north Anjou was inspected three times as possible accommodation for German troops and each time rejected as unsatisfactory. On the last occasion, early in 1944, the secretary of the town hall told the German officer that 'this is a mining area and if your soldiers start drinking with them, it could turn nasty'.[7] Given the choice, German officers expressed a preference for elegant châteaux and seaside villas. Well-connected politicians, industrialists and generals were often able to pull strings to avoid their properties being taken over. General Huntziger, who had lost the battle of Sedan in June 1940 and now represented France at the commission to oversee the Armistice at Wiesbaden, was able to keep his villa at the fashionable resort of La Baule out of German hands.[8] But the ancient Duc de Blacas, mayor of the pious and picturesque town of Beaupréau in the Mauges, who had no such connections, had to suffer three invasions of his château by German officers between June and September 1940. Not only did he receive no notice, he complained, and had to provide beds, sheets, washbasins, tables, chairs, a typewriter and a radio, but the Germans used up 15 tons of his pure Welsh anthracite which would be impossible to replace for the winter, given the British blockade.[9] Maybe the cold finished him off, for he died the following year.

In the towns, the Germans requisitioned public buildings such as barracks, convents, schools and halls, and also took over the hotels. Busy seagoing and trading cities like Nantes had giant hotels with up to 200 rooms, but the hotels in less commercial, more military and administrative centres like Angers were much more modest, with between thirty and fifty rooms on average. This caused problems when Angers was chosen by the Germans as the capital of its military administration for the whole of south-west France. In the summer of 1940 there were 8,000 German soldiers forces in the city, out of a total of 10,000 in the department. Although there were four barracks which could house over 5,000 men, and convents and schools could accommodate another 1,000 – at least until term began in September – and châteaux for the general staff were plentiful in the noble-ridden countryside, many officers and men still had to be billeted *chez l'habitant*, as the French had it, in private accommodation.[10] This meant not only large town houses like that of the Rameau family but much more basic housing too, of both middle- and working-class families.

Like any lodgers, there were good and bad among the Germans living with private families. The Rameau family's first two lodgers had ugly duelling scars and drank Pommery champagne by the case into the early hours. Marinette's mother, who had the room beneath them, was greatly relieved when they left after four days.[11] Colonel de Sauvebeuf, who ran the charitable Secours National in Angers, had four German soldiers billeted on his house near the château in August 1940. On the sixth night they brought home some 'women of loose morals' and made so much noise that he had to ask them to be quiet. It should not be imagined, however, that the French had to suffer in silence. Regularly they complained to the Feldkommandantur and were often obliged. Sauvebeuf asked the Feldkommandantur to inform the soldiers that he kept a 'respectable house' and that they should behave with more decorum.[12] Odette Goxe, whose middle-class family lived frugally in the predominantly working-class faubourg Saint-Michel, received a mixed bag of lodgers. The first officer, she recalls, looked like a pimp and spied in cafés, creating a bad impression in the neighbourhood. She went to the Feldkommandantur to complain, and they removed him. The second officer came back drunk and burst into the children's bedroom by mistake. As she left for the Kommandantur, the terrified officer asked her not to say that he had had women back, or he would be sent to the Russian front. The third officer, she subsequently learned, was the director of the military prison at Angers, who had a ferocious reputation. At home, however, he was open and friendly, and asked Mme Goxe's permission to take her children to the funfair, where he spoiled them. On their return the youngest child was triumphant: 'You see,' he proudly proclaimed, 'he didn't kill me!'[13]

It may be that to seek redress successfully from the occupying authorities was unusual, but it should be underlined that the Germans, while keeping the French on a tight leash, were keen initially not to alienate them unnecessarily. This coexistence was facilitated by the attitude of Germans posted to France. Many came as sexual and gastronomic tourists as much as soldiers. The *douceur* of France and of parts of France like the Loire valley in particular, was something to cherish. After the Russian front was opened up, the alternative of service in France seemed like a dream, and even in comparison with Germany, as the war progressed, France was seen as a land of plenty. '*Leben wie Gott in Frankreich*' was a phrase much used by German soldiers to sum up the ease of life in France.[14] Lieutenant Helmut Voss, before the war a municipal employee and former member of the Social Democratic Party, now in charge of one of the Angers barracks, told of a soldier who had shot himself rather than go to Russia, and of the joy of troops who learned that they were being posted back to France, especially after the cold winter of 1941–2. Helmut Radssat came to Angers from the Sudetenland early in 1944, and remained for five years, first on active service, then as a POW. 'France was the country for which many German soldiers were nostalgic,' he recalled, 'particularly those who had fought on the Russian front.' They had a special affection for the canteen of the Verneau barracks in Angers. 'The precious aroma of wine and brandy was quite new to me. In Germany such luxuries were becoming more and more scarce. It was in those barracks that I learned to know and appreciate good wines. We could also buy toiletries, lingerie for women, and so on. Things that we had not been able to obtain in Germany for a long time, particularly of that quality.'[15]

Although the formal relationship between Germans and French was that of occupier and occupied, there were other ways of defining the relationship which broke up this sharp contrast. Since the Armistice Germans and French were no longer at war, but the war continued around them and in one sense made them both its victims. This was particularly the case after the Russian campaign began to take its toll. In addition, moreover, not all Germans in Occupied France were soldiers. Some were civilians, for example builders and building workers employed by the Todt Organization on defence work. One of the projects on the outskirts of Angers was the conversion of the Château de Pignerolles into a bunker-bound command centre for naval activity in the Atlantic. The lodger in the Rameau household in the autumn of 1942 was a Rhinelander, Josef Liesenhof, a civilian whose Cologne building firm was working on the château. Marinette Rameau noted in her diary that he was not chauvinistic and asked her repeatedly, '*Warum der Krieg*? I have nothing against you so why should we be enemies?' And she replied, '*Ja, warum*? I ask myself the same question.'[16] Two German workers involved in the same project lodged for five or six months in the Leterme household, of which the father was a quantity surveyor, using the bedroom of a daughter who had just married and moved out. Michel Leterme, then aged twelve, remembers that they were ordinary, decent men who drank coffee in the kitchen and shared their cigarettes. In their rudimentary French their constant refrain was '*La guerre, grosse malheur*'.[17]

Michel Leterme's father was a veteran of the 1914–18 War who, like many graduates of the trenches, kept his helmet hanging up at home as a badge of that confraternity. The confraternity, interestingly, existed not only between French or Allied veterans but also between French and German soldiers who, though they were supposed to be hereditary enemies according to the propaganda, had endured the same unspeakable experiences in the trenches. Jacques Hervé, whose family lived in Tours and went to Germany under the Service du Travail Obligatoire (STO) in 1943, recalls that a café owner next door escaped deportation to Germany after the intervention of a German soldier who had been held a prisoner in Tours in 1918, and was eager to do a favour for a fellow veteran of the Great War.[18] Bonds formed by military honour which were stronger than national animosity went back a long way. Léon Mousseau, a country doctor at Saint-Mathurin on the Loire, sent his wife and children for safety to his mother-in-law's house in the Vendée. When a German officer was billeted there an old aunt took him to see the portraits and war decorations of ancestors going back to the First Empire. The officer clicked his heels and said, 'Madame, I pay homage to our unfortunate adversaries!'[19]

It is true that German respect for French military honour was severely dented in 1940. The French soldiers of 1940 had not shown the same valour as their fathers of 1914 and duly forfeited the esteem the German military showed for their equals. In the *Blitzkrieg* of June 1940 the Germans were astounded by the absence of French resistance. 'Where is the enemy?' wrote a member of the Swabian division approaching the Loire. 'On the right a couple of men disappeared into the bushes. But of the enemy nothing is to be seen. Where are the *poilus*?'[20] We have already seen how the German general who accepted the surrender of Saumur told the procureur, Louis Ancelin, that the Germans respected the combatants of the last war, who defeated them, but despised the little rabbits of 1940, who ran away.[21] Helmut Voss observed that just as French men failed to do their duty so French women now showed their mettle. For him, French women were holding the country together, making their houses spotless in the morning, but then doing themselves up in the afternoon to take a walk with their children and their husbands, who themselves seemed to do little else than hang about on street corners and prop up the bar in cafés. The women, he said, were defined by 'intelligence, elegance of appearance and speech. After the shock of the defeat they showed strength of will and energy, and were able to cope much more quickly than the men.'[22]

For the German military this was not just a question of an appreciation of French manners. They took the view that by failing to defend their homeland, French men had also forfeited the right to their womenfolk.[23] It was not that the conquerors assumed the right to rape the women of the defeated nation, but the power to seduce was one of the fruits of victory. Frenchwomen, for their part, were equally fascinated by the *Übermenschen* who had taken control of their country. A million and a half Frenchmen were in German POW camps, leaving their women alone to fend for themselves. German soldiers, on the other hand, were surrounded by the aura of victory, had the benefit of an artificially strong currency which enabled them to offer Frenchwomen nylons, jewellery and drinks, and, according to one woman from Touraine, 'They were the best-looking men I have ever seen.'[24]

The Occupation opened up many possibilities for relations between French women and German men but this did not mean that there were no rules. The German authorities forbade marriage between German soldiers and the women of defeated nations, and Slavs working in Germany who had sex with German women might be punished by death. Germans were also obsessed by the threat to their troops of venereal disease and demanded that the French authorities keep prostitution under control. On the other hand they regarded any interference by those authorities in relations between German soldiers and French women as a slight to their honour. The French had their own rules about what was proper and what not in relations between French women and German soldiers. To have sex was a challenge to the French family, community and country, but the rules that applied at the Liberation when 'horizontal collaboration' was punished by head-shaving and possibly prosecution for intelligence with the enemy were not necessarily the same under the Occupation, when single women were coming up against Germans in their employment and social situations. The 1940 catechism of the socialist Jean Texcier, *Conseils à l'occupé*, which recommended that the French should be 'correct' with the Germans but not friendly, said nevertheless that French men should not refuse Germans a light, nor interfere with a French girl negotiating business with a German soldier, who would get 'only what he paid for'.[25]

Some relationships between German soldiers and French women were entirely bound by the codes of courtly love. Helmut Voss, for example, fell in love with the French secretary of the German captain who was in charge of the city of Angers. She was 'a delightful young woman with sparkling blue eyes, always beautifully dressed' who, when he found an excuse to go to her office each Saturday, greeted him with the words, 'Here comes Mr Faithful'. Once he came across her at the theatre where she had gone with her girlfriend, and was smitten by her 'perfect manners, charm, friendliness and yet distance', for obviously she did not want the relationship to develop. Other relationships were less discreet and transgressed the boundaries of what it was licit to do with Germans and what illicit. Marinette Rameau tells of a German officer called Hubert who used to visit the dentist's wife in a white convertible, bringing her all sorts of delicacies such as game. The dentist's surgery was on the second floor of a block in Angers in which her father had the office of his veterinary supply business. One day, coming out of the office where she was typing, Marinette bumped into the dentist's wife, 'wearing white satin pyjamas and red shoes', in the arms of the German. Later, she said, the dentist's wife had a child who was 'very blond' and was generally assumed to be Hubert's.[26] Berthe Vaillant, wife of an official at the prefecture of the Creuse, came to Ligueil near the demarcation line with her daughter Denise in 1940 to look after her ninety-year-old mother. A few months later the German customs service established an office at Ligueil and Denise, aged thirty-five, met a customs officer called Müller, who began to come round to the house, singing in German as Berthe played the piano. Then the recitals became parties and the parties feasts; German officers started to come from as far as Tours and Châtellerault and the postmistress and other local women joined in the celebrations, dancing with the officers. Clearly they enjoyed spending time with well-bred officers who drove up in large cars. Sometimes the officers stayed the night: as Berthe said, 'I never refused the Germans a room.' Caught by the Forces Françaises de l'Intérieur (FFIs) at the Liberation, Denise admitted having sex with Germans and said she had fled the town for fear of having her head shaved. Making merry with Germans was not well regarded in a small community and getting too close was likely to attract accusations of treachery. The postman and doctor were among those who claimed that the dancing women were all Gestapo informers and the house an 'information bureau' for the Germans. Berthe and Denise Vaillant went before the Cour de Justice at Tours in December 1944. The charge of denunciation was not proven, but Denise was sentenced to five years in prison for 'relations with the enemy'. What was regarded as a challenge to the integrity of the community under the Occupation was seen as much more serious by the courts at the Liberation, although rumour and gossip alone were not enough to convict.[27]

Receiving Germans at home was frowned upon more than meeting them in bars, cafés and restaurants. Relations developed easily between waitresses, barmaids, landladies and Germans who were often regular customers, tended to drink a good deàl and tipped generously. Marie-Louise Coiscault, who served in her parents' bar, L'Artichaut, in the river-crossing town of Chalonnes-sur-Loire, was nineteen when the Germans arrived in 1940. Among the daily customers she became friendly with Corporal Müller, from the Saarland. There is a photograph of her, her friend Jeanne and Müller in a meadow close to the town, arms linked and smiling at the camera. After Müller left Chalonnes Marie-Louise sent him food parcels, and supplied his German comrades who remained with eggs, meat and potatoes in return for soap and pâté. She wished to marry Müller after the war and wrote to his family. Instead she was taken to court where she protested that she had not had relations with other German soldiers, although naturally she had been obliged to serve them and talk to them when they came into the café. In spite of this she was deprived of her civic rights for five years and required to live outside Chalonnes for a year.[28]

Sometimes during the Occupation itself members of the community complained that relations between French women and German soldiers were going too far. In March 1941 a group of French women were seen waving goodbye to a contingent of German soldiers leaving the railway station of the seaside town of Le Croisic. The following day a notice went up on the wall of the auction house listing the women who had 'come to bid fond farewells to the occupying troops'. They included the nineteen-year-old daughter of the owner of the Au Bon Vin Nantais café, the landlady of the Café de Paris and her barmaid, also nineteen. The local subprefect who investigated the incident was more concerned with the act of denunciation than with the leave-taking, and suspicion fell on a former railway employee of Le Croisic station who was thought to bear a personal grudge. The inquiry was inconclusive, but suggests that in 1941 informing was regarded as a greater threat to the fabric of the community than waving goodbye to Germans.[29]

Frenchmen naturally contested the German view that their victorious soldiers had first claim on their women. There were particular hot spots like the port districts of Nantes and Saint-Nazaire which teemed with German soldiers and sailors, and hot times like Saturday nights when drink flowed freely. One fight in Nantes in September 1941, for example, led to the wounding of two German soldiers and the arrest of two Frenchmen, with both the French and German police involved. For the French police commissioner this was not a question of the rights and wrongs of sleeping with Germans but a matter of public order. It was also like any other busy night around the little cafés of the quai de la Fosse, where musicians played, and the square in front of the Bourse, where a funfair was often set up. 'There,' he said, 'all the young people, males and females, and soldiers too, get together every night and particularly on Saturdays, Sundays and holidays. Incidents often happen in these places because of the mingling of males and females and above all because of the abuse of alcohol.'[30]

Between flirting, picking up girls, buying rounds and paying money for casual sex the demarcation lines were extremely fuzzy. Both the French and the German authorities attempted to isolate prostitution from other relationships and regulate it under well-established procedures for reasons of public health and public order. But to control a range of sexual activity through regulations designed for a well-defined category of prostitutes who were registered, kept in brothels and subjected to medical inspection was extremely difficult. Scarcely three weeks after the arrival of the Germans in Angers the Kommandantur instructed the local police chief to clamp down on what he called 'covert prostitution' going on in hotels, cafés, bars and even private houses where there were many 'debauched women'. Inverting the conventional balance of menace between occupiers and occupied, he insisted that 'These women who practise covert prostitution represent a very great danger for German soldiers . . . they are a veritable plague.' Suspects, he said, should be arrested, medically inspected, sent to the dispensary if they were found to be infected and properly registered if they admitted to being prostitutes; establishments which allowed such women to ply their trade should be closed down. A sweep by the French police in Angers discovered 37 women in brothels, 25 registered prostitutes working privately, and 41 covert prostitutes, of whom 12 were found to be contagious. Separate brothels were established for Frenchmen and German soldiers, with an élite brothel for German officers. Notices were pinned up in all brothels and in the homes of girls working privately to the effect that girls were not allowed to attract clients from windows or on the street and had to take at least one bath a week, and that German soldiers should use condoms and be issued with cards with the name and address of their contact, who could be traced if they developed VD. The clampdown did little to minimize the problem, however: the number of prostitutes discovered in Angers rose in the weeks before Christmas 1940 to 60 in brothels and 60 registered individuals, with 10 covert workers, and the number of covert workers suddenly rose again to 30 in February 1941.[31]

One problem with the regulation of prostitution was that the Germans' message was ambivalent. They demanded action by the French police to guard against the scourge of VD, but as a point of honour they were reluctant to allow interference in the amorous pursuits of German soldiers. In 1943, for example, an incident flared up in Cholet when Mlle Denise Lacomme was officially registered as a prostitute by the French police. This provoked her suitor, Karl Speyer, who oversaw the shoe industry in the west of France for the purposes of the German war economy, to burst into the police station to announce that her registration was 'an offence to the German army', and that he was going to 'shoot all her lovers, have all the officers who contributed to her registration imprisoned as Gaullists and put a bullet in the police inspector too'. The Gestapo Chief in Angers, Ernst, told Regional Prefect Roussillon to dismiss the inspector in question for 'anti-German activities'. The inspector was summoned to the Feldkommandantur at Angers and told that Mlle Lacomme would not undergo a medical inspection. He expressed surprise, since he had orders from the Feldkommandantur to clamp down on clandestine prostitutes like Mlle Lacomme, an out-of-work hairdresser who plied her trade from the terrace of the Hôtel Blanchard, opposite the railway station. He had no idea why Speyer was so angry, given that he was 'only one number on a long list'. For the French authorities it was intolerable that such a woman should make their police look ridiculous. The regional prefect stood firm and refused to dismiss the inspector. For his part, Ernst realized that the German authorities also stood to look ridiculous by hitching their honour to a such a dubious woman, and withdrew the dismissal order.[32]

As the Occupation wore on it became more and more difficult to deal with prostitution and the public order issues associated with it. German troops returning from service on the Russian front looked to have a good time in France and did not take no for an answer. In the sleepy town of Ancenis, on the banks of the Loire, soldiers who had done twenty-two months on the Eastern Front had a particular fondness for the Au Bon Muscadet café, where they were 'attracted more by the charms of Mme Dubillot [the landlady] than by the drinks'. Finding the café closed one evening, they started firing off their pistols. A fortnight later, finding the Stella brothel in the town closed, they fired off more shots, wounding a fisherman in his boat. The distraught mayor tried to convince the Kreiskommandant and prefect to set up mixed patrols of French and German gendarmes to keep a watch on such brothels, but even the Kreiskommandant had little authority over troops who rarely stayed long in the area. Meanwhile, a local doctor who tended the wounded fisherman was concerned that the presence of the Germans was driving up prostitution at an alarming rate: 'minors, wives of POWs, mothers of small children are causing a veritable scandal which is having a disastrous effect on the morality of our young people'.[33]

If the line between casual relationships and prostitution was difficult to draw, so also was that between employment and casual sex. The German Occupation created a multitude of employment possibilities for women as cleaners, laundrywomen, bar staff and waitresses in the Soldatenheime or officers' casinos, and menial work often developed into sexual relationships. In seaside resorts such as La Baule, Pornichet and Le Croisic, where many of the military and naval forces working at Saint-Nazaire were housed in holiday villas, local girls taken on formally as maids in the villas were happy to provide a more generous service.[34] Slightly above the ruck, Simone Deflandre, a gay divorcee in her early thirties who had been a nurse and masseuse, ran the Bar de la Plage and in addition supervised the maids who worked in the villas at La Baule, went out with Captain Piel, a dental surgeon in civilian life who not only wined and dined her in restaurants but also looked after her teeth.[35]

Cohabitation between French and Germans was as much about money as about sex. Obviously the Germans were in a position to plunder, exploit and fleece the French for the benefit of their war economy. But just as personal encounters between French and Germans were not only about rape but about patterns and codes of love and sex, so also economic relations were constructed according to certain norms and were not always to the disadvantage of the French. Requisition was not the same as theft: a note was issued to the provider in respect of goods requisitioned which was redeemable in theory at least from the French or German authorities. Nor did the Germans only take: leading sectors of the French economy boomed under the Occupation because of German orders, while Germans were always ready to pay handsomely for scarce items or luxuries on the black market.

Inevitably things were not always as ordered as this. Less than three months after the Armistice the curé of Le Loroux near the demarcation line sent an anguished letter to Marshal Pétain saying that since 24 June the commune had been occupied by 210 Germans and eighty horses. The German soldiers had taken over the schoolhouse, billeted themselves on the inhabitants and in some cases driven them out, removed furniture from houses, taken hay and straw for their horses and wood and groceries for themselves, and done military exercises in the beetfields. 'Do the terms of the Armistice', he asked, 'permit German forces to respect nothing, to take what families require for their own needs without the permission of the French authorities, to steal whatever they want without any requisition order for the disgusting pleasure of reducing people to the greatest misery?' An agricultural official from Tours went to the village to see, and reported back that there were now only eighty soldiers and that Germans taking wood and coal was nothing unusual although perhaps they might now gather hay and straw from other communes as well. He said that nothing had in fact been taken without a requisition receipt being issued, that 'relations between the population and the troops were correct' and that for his part the mayor had not complained.[36]

Similar abuses went on in Nantes, where the Germans ruled that all goods that had entered the port since 3 September 1939 were legitimate war booty and confiscated stocks of tea, coffee, sugar, chocolate, rice and vegetable oil. Ordinary troops were more interested in consumer goods and, waving blank requisition slips or indeed no slips at all, piled into the city's department stores where, according to the prefect, they took 'radios, fridges, champagne, flowers, expensive antique or modern furniture, carpets, curtains, luxurious dinner services, watches, chandeliers, bicycles, cars and even pleasure boats'.[37] He complained to Feldkommandant Hotz, who was prepared to rein in his subordinates if they went too far. When a Luftwaffe officer took the car of the head of the women's teacher training college in Nantes on the grounds that 'she did not like Germans', issuing a requisition note and then taking it back because it compromised him, then dragging her to the Feldkommandantur and keeping her waiting for two hours, Hotz 'became crimson, as if he were going to fly into a violent temper'. He declared that to take a car without issuing a requisition note was theft and that no innocent person should be held in the Kommandantur without his orders.[38]

The French, who prided themselves on their Gallic cunning, found many ways to get around the threat of requisition. Periodically, farmers were required to take their horses to town so that the Germans could make a selection. Odile Talon, a farmer's daughter from outside Angers who regularly went out with Germans and had influence with them, was able to get some peasants who came to her exempted.[39] Alternatively, tricking the Germans served peasant self-interest and was later presented as patriotism. René Bretault, from the Angevin village of La Pommeraye, recalls that he took a twenty-five-year-old nag before the German commission and was told, '*Raus!*'[40] Sometimes the trade in horses went in favour of the locals. When the Germans arrived in Loire-Inférieure they noted that the horses were in short supply because in the previous year the *French* army had requisitioned 8,800 horses, 50 per cent more than they themselves would have done. Since they had an interest in getting in the crops, not least to ensure fodder, they actually lent their own military horses to French farmers for the duration of the harvest.[41]

The Germans in general regarded France as a rich country but a backward and unproductive one, whose resources needed to be developed rationally if exploitation on a long-term basis was to be a success. Helmuth Voss, in Angers, compared France to 'a beautiful older woman'. 'The houses, fields and gardens', he said, 'are somewhat neglected, the whole seems unplanned and disconnected, the technology is thirty years out of date and makes us smile, the looks are seductive only from a certain distance'.[42] Shortly after he arrived in Angers Feldkommandant Kloss called a meeting of the prefect, his economic advisers, a number of mayors and leading producers, and impressed on them the need to increase productivity: in particular, he made clear, the yield of the wheat harvest must be increased the following year by 25 per cent. He emphasized that this cooperation was in deliberate contrast to the way the French had treated the Rhineland when they occupied it in 1923, and duly reported that 'the French authorities and economic leaders are quite ready to work according to the directives of the military administration and to take and follow through the necessary measures'.[43]

One obsession of the German authorities was the amount of agricultural land that lay fallow or abandoned. The French argued that productivity was limited by the number of farmers held by the Germans as POWs, but the Germans would not accept this explanation.[44] On one occasion they demanded the dismissal of the Director of Agricultural Services of Indre-et-Loire, whom they saw as the cat's paw of 'the Jew Aaron' [sic], former president of the Chamber of Agriculture of Indre-et-Loire, for sabotaging their drive to increase the wheat harvest.[45] Another obsession was the plague of Colorado beetles that infested the potato crops. Each June they issued instructions that peasants should spray their crops, and that children should be taken out of school three days a week to collect and destroy the pests. In July 1941 the Feldkommandantur of Loire-Inférieure complained that the potato fields were still infested and demanded another campaign in August, but this provoked the riposte of rural mayors that the children were on holiday, the teachers gone, and the farmers did not want children in their fields anyway.[46] A final obsession of the Germans was the infestation of slaughter-houses, tanneries, butcher's shops, dairies and even restaurants with rats. The chief veterinary officer in Tours, Dr Herbig, told the prefect that the vermin were destroying food and fodder, propagating disease and undermining buildings, and ordered a campaign of destruction by traps and poison in the summer of 1941. Unhappy with the result, he ordered a second campaign in the autumn.[47] The Germans remained frustrated by the incompetence of the French and suspected that their foot-dragging was deliberate.[48]

The German authorities were concerned primarily with the economic contribution the French could make, but were also seduced by their artistic treasures. Of course the financial value of the treasures was important, but there is evidence that the Germans could be better conservationists than the French. In the autumn of 1940, for example, Professor Dr Count Metternich, the head of the army's artistic conservation, visited Touraine with a delegation of about twenty German museum directors and conservationists to inspect its historic buildings.[49] He made sure that the treasures of Versailles, which had been moved for protection to the depository of Brissac outside Angers, received adequate supplies of scarce coal to ensure heating to the correct temperature.[50] A list of châteaux was drawn up which for artistic reasons were not to be occupied by the German forces, including those of Chenonceaux, Villandry, Ussé, Azay-le-Rideau, Langeais, Brissac and Saumur.[51] After a visit to the château of Saumur the subprefect complained to the mayor, much to the amusement of the Kreiskommandant, that the windows were broken, the collection was scattered and the caretaker refused to show them round because he said it was his rest day.[52] Even when military needs took precedence over art, as in the case of nineteenth-century bronze statues which could be melted down, the German authorities were prepared to listen to arguments for why certain statues of peculiar historic significance should be preserved. We have already seen how the statue of Rabelais at Chinon was saved, as were the Joans of Arc of Chinon and Nantes and the René d'Anjou of Angers. However, the statues of the nineteenth-century sculptor David d'Angers in Angers and the statue of Balzac in Tours, among others, were considered to be more useful as German bullets than as monuments to French artistic pride.[53]

The contribution that France could make to the German war

effort was of course central, and here it is clear that it was German production orders that lifted the French economy out of the recession into which it had been plunged after the defeat of 1940. War industries no longer had any purpose, the British imposed a blockade that caused severe shortages of coal and thus of electricity, and workers were laid off – first women, then men. In Loire-Inférieure the Germans calculated in August 1940 that a third of the workforce of 85,000 were unemployed.[54] The Vichy government encouraged local chambers of commerce to reduce unemployment by schemes to clear bomb damage, build local roads or improve the water supply, but it was paying a vast amount to Germany as reparation and tribute under the Armistice and had no funds available for Keynesian economics. Orders from the Wehrmacht, the Luftwaffe and above all from the Kriegsmarine to sustain the war effort were the obvious alternative for French firms to stay in business.

The experience of the small town of Cholet, as traditional economically as it was politically, with textiles and shoe manufacture the staple industries, may serve as an example. In the spring of 1941 the municipal council was reduced to finding work for 150 unemployed men by enlarging the cemetery.[55] Then some high-tech industries such as Radio-Électrique and the armaments firm Société Alsacienne were relocated to Cholet from Paris or German-annexed Alsace, and were soon receiving German orders for ships' radios and pistols respectively. So wide was the market for supplying the armed forces that even the traditional textile industries in Cholet were inundated with orders for blackout material, carpeting, bedlinen and even handkerchiefs. Traditional firms in nearby towns also flourished. Bessonneau of Angers employed 3,000 workers making ropes, sail-cloth and tarpaulin, and later diversified into nine-man tents and camouflage netting, whilst Châteaubriant and Fougères now produced snowshoes and army leathers for the Russian front.

The demand for finished goods soon began to outstrip the availability of labour and materials and the Germans adopted a policy of concentration, closing down some smaller and less efficient firms in order to allow the larger units to develop. In February 1942 the Feldkommandantur of Tours presented the prefect with a list of eleven firms, including a porcelain factory, a typewriter factory and the Mame printworks, that would have to close.[56] However, Touraine was also the location of a number of advanced precision

industries that expanded by virtue of military orders, such as the
Société Générale d'Optiques of Tours, or Barbier-Bernard and
Turenne of Amboise which made field-glasses, periscopes and glass
for headlights and searchlights, and the Compagnie des Cables which
made the cables crucial for military communication in Occupied
Europe.

The biggest contractors in the region were the shipyards, railway
works and aircraft factories of the Nantes/Saint-Nazaire area. At
Nantes were the Chantiers de la Loire, the Chantiers de Bretagne and
the Chantiers Dubigeon, at Saint-Nazaire the massive Chantiers et
Ateliers Penhoët and Chantiers de la Loire, both with over 3,000
workers. All these received orders from November 1940 to build
destroyers, tugs, torpedo boats, speedboats, U-boats, air-traffic-
control boats, tankers, transport ships, whalers and trawlers. Associated engineering works received orders for turbines and motors,
steelworks for sheet metal.[57] Meanwhile, at Nantes, the Compagnie
Générale de Construction de Locomotives (Batignolles-Chatillon)
was devoting 90 per cent of its output to the Reichsbahn early in
1941, whilst the Société Nationale de Construction Aéronautique du
Sud-Ouest (SNCASO) at Nantes-Bouguenais agreed an order in April
1941 to build Heinkel 111 aircraft worth 4 million man-hours over
two years.[58] From May 1942 there was a surge of orders not only
from Heinkel of Rostock but from Junkers of Magdeburg, Focke
Wulf of Bremen and BMW aircraft motors of Munich.[59] To see that
these orders were efficiently met the Germans set up a separate war-
economy administration, the Rüstungsinspektion, which patterned
itself on the hierarchy of the military administration. In 1942 the
Rüstungsinspektion B (SW Frankreich), with responsibility for production in Maine-et-Loire, Indre-et-Loire, Sarthe, Mayenne and Ille-
et-Vilaine (but not Loire-Inférieure), was moved from Tours to Le
Mans and placed under Korvettenkapitan Fock, who was directly
answerable to Paris. One of its goals was to increase the number of
Rüstungsbetriebe or Rü-Betriebe producing almost totally for the
German military and Vorzugsbetriebe or V-Betriebe working partly
for them. By September 1942 there were forty-nine Rü-Betriebe in
the Le Mans region but a year earlier there had been thirty in Loire-
Inférieure alone, demonstrating its exceptional importance for the
German machine.[60] The workers in these factories generally enjoyed
advantageous conditions, such as fuller rations than the average

and protection from the Germans' periodic campaigns to recruit labour.

The German military machine required not only the delivery of military hardware but also enormous building projects such as the Atlantic Wall to fend off potential invasion, and the construction of U-boat bases at Lorient and Saint-Nazaire from which the campaign against Allied Atlantic convoys could be launched. These projects were promoted by the Todt Organization and involved huge contracts with construction companies like the Entreprise des Travaux Publics Dodin at Nantes, which themselves often subcontracted to consortia such as the Nantes group of twenty-seven firms set up in July 1943. After the war Henri Dodin and the director of the consortium argued that initially he had refused contracts but the Germans threatened to requisition his workforce and plant.[61] Accept them they did, however, using labour conscripted by the Todt Organization which was often employed under atrocious conditions. One man sent to build the submarine base at Saint-Nazaire said that everything was geared to obtaining the quickest possible results: they worked from 7 a.m. to 7 p.m. alongside Spaniards, Portuguese, Italians, Czechs, Poles, Russians and Arabs, and continued through air-raid warnings (for which no shelters were provided anyway). The food was plentiful but lousy, they slept on 5-cm-thin mattresses, and the hygiene was non-existent. 'The workers are like civilian prisoners,' he said, whose release date was not known.[62] Meanwhile, the Entreprises Dodin made a profit of between 50 and 80 million francs working on German defences.[63]

There has been much debate about how free employers were to work for the Reich or not and whether 'economic collaboration' may be considered in the same way as other forms of collaboration. What employers said after the war about having their arms twisted is difficult to gauge. In 1943, according to the Rüstungskommando of Le Mans, the owner of a foundry at Sainte-Jamme-sur-Sarthe initially refused an order to make 50,000 15.5-cm shells, but mainly because he thought his factory would promptly be bombed by the Allies; he was soon induced to change his mind.[64] The term 'survival collaboration' has been invented by historians to define working for the Germans on pain of seeing their plant and/or labour requisitioned, but these same historians argue that German orders were 'the driving force of the French economy' under the Occupation, accounting for up to 70 per cent and even 90 per cent of firms' orders.[65] The temptations, moreover, were not confined to shipyards, engineering plants and building enterprises. The German war machine created a vast market, not only for military hardware and buildings but for food, drink, scrap metal and luxuries. It imposed price restrictions and legislated against hoarding, but goods were in such short supply and demand so intense that even the Germans were unable to prevent the flourishing of a black market and were in fact instrumental in developing it. The French, meanwhile, were only too delighted to procure wanted goods and sell them to the Germans at exorbitant prices.[66]

Those who profited included not only hardened speculators but otherwise menial individuals with an eye for a good deal. Among the first, Roger Flamant was well known in the La Baule area. Before the war he had had a large textile dye-works at Anor in the Nord, which he sold and went to Morocco to make another fortune. During the war he became a property developer in the resorts of La Baule and Le Pouliguen, buying up large villas and turning them into flats ready to do holiday business after the war. He was well connected with the German authorities, who sold him materials from buildings they had demolished and even lent him lorries to transport them.[67] At the other end of the spectrum was Raymond Couturier, a mechanic and foreman at the SNCASO works at Château-Bougon, who also ran a café called L'Envol. After the Germans arrived he gave up his job at the aircraft factory to concentrate on his café, and then made a fortune hiring out horses and carts for the German air-base at Château-Bougon and supplying the Germans with black market goods into the bargain.[68]

Some speculators had their fingers in a number of pies. M. Maud, for example, had a clandestine abattoir at Montreuil-Bellay in Anjou and delivered meat to the Germans billeted at the Cavalry School of Saumur. He also had a secret distillery which sold liquor to the Germans at 500 francs per litre and exported the rest by rail to Nancy. With his profits he obtained supplies of sugar, copper and bronze which he sold to the Germans, and also did a trade in new and second-hand bicycles, hunting rifles which had been left at the Cavalry School and small arms which had been abandoned by British soldiers in 1940.[69] Other speculators were more specialized and more organized. Georges Besson, a commercial traveller, was the head of a trafficking ring which bought up wine from Touraine winegrowers at between 8 and 15 francs a bottle and then sold it to German clients in Paris for 55 francs. Equipped with passes issued by corrupt Germans, they were able to send lorry-loads to the capital without being stopped by French or German authorities, and the five ringleaders were said to have made 1.5 million francs in three months.[70]

Occupied France was full of rags-to-riches stories along the lines of Dutourd's *Au Bon Beurre*. In the little village of Coueron, outside Nantes, Joseph Aubineau was a labourer in 1940. After the arrival of the Germans he worked for them as a carpenter, then bought a cart, then a lorry and became a road haulier. He was said to have been involved in an 'intense black market trade with the Germans, supplying them with wine, pork, poultry, eggs, etc. ... he was reputed to be the biggest trafficker in the region'.[71] In many ways it was impossible to cohabit with the Germans and not make money out of them. Those who got into trouble at the Liberation were seen to have gone too far, in particular to have preferred German clients to local customers, or to have combined profit with sex. Mme Laurence Morandeau, who kept a café in the same village of Coueron, was accused of saying that she preferred one German customer to twenty French ones, and of indulging with her daughter Suzanne in 'veritable orgies' with them while her husband took pictures of them with a camera stolen from work. She denied the orgies as 'pure invention' and stated baldly, 'I did like all traders, I served Germans in my café because I had to, but I never collaborated with them.'[72] One is inclined to believe her and the thousands like her who simply did business with the Germans because they were good customers, with money to spend. Some, like the Morandeau family, finished up in court, but most got away with it and went on to make money out of the next wave of foreigners. As one peasant joked, 'During the Occupation I worked for the Germans and now I am going to work for the Americans.'[73]

The sullen rejection of the Germans represented by Vercors in *Le Silence de la mer* has to be set against a more nuanced analysis of cohabitation between French and Germans which held good at least for the first two years of the Occupation. The image, evoked by Philippe Burrin of the 'blind town' refusing to make eye contact with the Germans, was more patriotic ideal than reality.[74] Beyond the power relations of the French and German authorities there were manifold private relations between French and Germans which tended to revolve around money and sex. These relations were not arbitrary but governed by certain rules negotiated between French and Germans and among the French themselves. To receive Germans at home, for example, unless they were billeted, was felt to be different from being seen with them in a public place under the public gaze. To accept German production orders openly was not the same thing as trafficking with Germans on the black market. Very often the measure of what was acceptable was its impact on the community: production orders might keep the local economy afloat and people in work, whereas trafficking deprived the locality of scarce resources. The impact of the Germans was not wholly negative: naturally they wished to exploit France's resources to the full but this might entail developing traditional practices and eliminating vermin and pests. It has also been calculated that the Germans did their bit to tackle France's demographic deficit by fathering between 50,000 and 70,000 children.[75] Perspectives also changed with time, so that practices tolerated by communities weakened by evacuation and the absence of POWs in 1940 were judged harshly in 1944 when communities were seeking to rebuild themselves after the Liberation. Sexual misdemeanours were punished more harshly than economic collaboration, partly because they might be linked to intelligence of the enemy and the denunciation of compatriots, partly because the threat to family, community and male honour was felt to be much greater. The perspective of 1944 should not, however, prevent us from remembering that in many respects Occupied France was another country where they did things differently.

4. SEPARATION

At the end of June 1940 Odette Goxe returned to Angers from the island of Noirmoutier, off the Brittany coast, where she had fled with her mother, Ninette Bordereau, and her young children, in an attempt to find her father, who had been taken prisoner by the Germans. French forces, which had collapsed and fled west and south before the German advance, had been rounded up in their tens of thousands and herded into makeshift prisoner-of-war camps. Odette discovered that her father was with his whole regiment in a camp of 30,000 men near Le Mans, but when she arrived the Germans had suspended all visits because of women rioting outside the camp. Back in Angers on 2 July she witnessed another column of prisoners being marched through the town on their way to the Le Mans camp. There was a 'surge of solidarity that could not have been predicted at that time of food restrictions', recalls Odette Goxe. 'From all the windows and doorways people brought the captured soldiers everything they had: sugar, bread, wine. The order was given for the column to stop so that this unprecedented gesture could be completed in safety.' Odette returned to Noirmoutier 'completely shattered by all these emotions and in real need of rest'. Meanwhile her mother, though in no doubt about the 'calvary' her husband was having to endure, took solace from the firm belief that he would be home soon.[1]

This story sheds light on the predicament of both refugees and POWs in the turbulent summer of 1940. The Bordereau/Goxe family were luckier than many refugees, in that they had not travelled far and their return to Angers was relatively unimpeded. Others were less fortunate. Early in July the Germans decided that because of military operations all refugees would have to stay south of the Loire and Cher rivers, so those who had fled before the advancing German armies were now unable to return home.[2] The Germans were keen that the refugees should not remain idle but help bring in the harvest where possible.[3] Later in the month they divided up the Occupied Zone into five sub-zones, with different rules applying to each. Those who had fled from the Paris region or from between the Seine and the Loire were allowed to return; those who had come from between the Seine and the Somme could only return if they were farmers or employed in the public services; while those who had come from north of the Somme, essentially the departments of the Nord, Pas-de-Calais, Aisne and Somme, were not allowed to return at all. Belgians and Dutch were obliged to go home, and pressure was put on those who had left Alsace and Lorraine, now annexed by Germany, to go back. The German authorities ordered a census of all Alsatians and Lorrainers, allegedly for statistical purposes, but rumours began to spread that those who did not go back would have their property confiscated. Elizabeth Walter, who had come to Nantes from Strasbourg in September 1939 and was now employed at the prefecture, wrote to her employers on behalf of a number of her compatriots who wanted to stay in Nantes, asking for clarification.[4] The last official repatriation train for Alsatians and Lorrainers had in fact left Nantes at the end of October, one of the many which furrowed the country in the late summer and autumn of 1940, taking refugees back to their place of origin, free of charge if they could not pay. Numbers in the Loire valley declined from 250,000 in Loire-Inférieure in June to only 18,000 in October, and in Maine-et-Loire, during the same period, from 100,000 to under 10,000.[5]

While the refugees were going home, the POWs were behind barbed wire in camps, remaining for a number of months in France, often in the most atrocious conditions. Some buildings that the Germans took over, such as the Cavalry School of Saumur, provided reasonable accommodation, but Brittany became a veritable gulag of encampments in the open fields: 20,000 at Savenay, 30,000 at Châteaubriant. Until barbed-wire fences were in place the German sentries kept their human flocks together simply by promising that they would soon be liberated.[6] The water was suspect, there was little food, no sanitation, no shelter, and in the pouring rain the ground turned to mud underfoot. The local hygiene inspector was worried about an outbreak of typhus or dysentery, exacerbated, he feared, by the presence of African prisoners.[7] The bishop of Nantes, who visited the camps early in July, was more concerned about the prisoners' souls and ensured that soldier-priests who had been captured were provided with portable altars.[8] The Marquise de Sesmaisons, whose own husband was a prisoner of war and who worked for the Red Cross, harassed the German authorities to obtain permission for prisoners to work outside the camps or even be released. She was 'Providence itself', said one local mayor, 'counting neither time, nor effort, nor expense'.[9] Veterans of the 1914–18 War at Nantes, headed by Léon Jost, a businessman with the Legion of Honour whose leg had been shot off in the Great War, together with two lawyers, Alexandre Fourny and Fernand Ridel, set up a committee to provide food supplies to the camps. Under the cover of this charity the committee organized escapes to the Free Zone for over 2,000 POWs. For their pains seven of the committee and its female secretary were arrested in January 1941 and sentenced by a German military court to prison terms.[10]

These stories reveal a great deal about the experience of French prisoners of war, their families and local communities. The shadow of the 1.5 million POWs hung like a pall over Occupied France. In the three departments under review here there were 45,000 POWs at the end of 1942, 10 per cent of the active population.[11] With as many soldiers prisoner as there were soldiers killed in the 1914–18 War, most families in France were without a husband, father, brother or son. These separations caused both material hardship and mental anxiety, for no one knew when the loved one would return and fervent hopes were repeatedly disappointed.[12] For all the anti-feminist rhetoric of the Vichy regime, which preferred women to stay at home and bring up children,[13] women were increasingly called upon to take on new responsibilities and new roles – they were 'liberated' in fact if not in law. The response of French communities to the POW tragedy was powerful and imaginative. The 'surge of solidarity' evoked by Odette Goxe continued throughout the Occupation in the form of committees to raise funds and send parcels to loved ones hundreds of miles away in German Stalags and Oflags. The fate of the prisoners was a major concern of the government, which managed to get some of them brought home, and also of the Church, which promoted national days of prayer as well as aid. And yet the picture was not all rosy. The whole issue of POWs revealed schisms as well as solidarities in French society: power struggles between and within organizations involved in supporting the prisoners; tensions between local communities or businesses wishing to care for *their* prisoners and representatives of central organizations wanting them to take a wider view; political conflicts between those involved in what was supposed to be charity; and even corruption and crime festering under the cover of doing good.

In the early months of the Occupation French women unable to trace their husbands laid siege to the authorities. Mme Bonin, a mother of three from a working-class suburb of Angers, told the prefect that she had had no news of her husband four months after the defeat. 'I am very anxious about what has happened to him and why he has not come home,' she said. 'Life is very hard and I only have my military benefit to live on.'[14] When POWs were found and logged, prefects were lobbied from all sides – municipalities, government departments, magistrates, politicians, bishops and private firms – requesting that they intercede with the German authorities for the release of members of their staff as a matter of priority and special urgency. The archbishop of Tours wrote both to the Feldkommandant to urge the release of priests and schoolmasters in holy orders who had borne arms, and to the Red Cross on behalf of priests who had been military chaplains or stretcher-bearers and thus should not be held under the Geneva Convention.[15]

The German authorities were not minded to be generous. They entertained requests only in respect of certain categories, such as farmers, workers in vital industries and civil servants who were totally indispensable. Feldkommandant Marloh of Tours decided in August 1940 to consider no more than five or ten applications a week, while Feldkommandant Kloss of Angers ruled in September that requests would have to be drawn up in French and German and sent not to him but to the Prisoner-of-War Information Bureau in Paris.[16] For the Germans the French POW population represented an immense resource of hostages, the promise of whose return home could be used to exert pressure on the French to behave well. Later in the war it was used as a bargaining counter, to exchange (on very unequal terms) for French labour needed in Germany to turn the wheels of the Reich's economy. But, as we have seen, the Germans also had an interest in the functioning of the French economy, required to sustain the Army of Occupation and the German war machine itself. So, for example, they were prepared to allow French POWs to leave their camps in the summer of 1940 to help bring in the harvest. The fact that nearly a third of French POWs were of agricultural backgrounds, rising to 60 per cent in the case of Angevin POWs, made this policy economically sensible.

Letting POWs work in the fields was of course a security risk, whether they were under German or French guard. In Touraine, which was bifurcated by the demarcation line, the first escape was registered in mid-August 1940. In September there were few, but in October there was a rash of escapes, as POWs pretended to go for walks on Sunday or claimed they were going to bathe in the Vienne. Sometimes they escaped not just in ones or twos but in groups of six or eight from the same farm, and in March 1941 fifteen North African prisoners escaped from their rural accommodation by piercing the wall at the back of a cupboard.[17] Escapes also took place from legitimate POW camps. Three prisoners escaped from the Cavalry School of Saumur on Christmas Eve 1940; they took refuge in a labourer's cottage in Saumur and one was shot dead while hiding under a bed.[18] After such incidents the German authorities decided that the time had come to move French POWs en masse to Germany. The first contingent of 1,000 from Saumur left on 6 January, followed by 1,200 ten days later. After that the escape stories were mainly those of French African troops whom the Germans were not keen to import. In February thirty-four escaped and Kreiskommandant Colonel Baron von Gall threatened to impose a collective fine on the town. Subprefect Robert Milliat called a meeting of the police, gendarmerie and Catholic and Protestant Church leaders to put pressure on individuals, notably in the Red Cross, who were suspected of helping escapes.[19] It seems that the meeting was something of a charade. In March over 100 African soldiers escaped from the Cavalry School and Feldkommandant Kloss duly imposed a fine of 500,000 francs on Saumur, which was advanced from municipal funds and recouped by an extraordinary tax on the townsfolk. When another batch of Africans escaped in April, an irate von Gall summoned Milliat and threatened another fine of 500,000 francs. Milliat replied judiciously that he would do his best to find them but 'my honour as a Frenchman would forbid me from handing them over if they were discovered'.[20] This patriotic commitment by a local official towards Africans who, though black, were soldiers in the French army, contrasts eloquently with the treatment meted out to Jews, many of whom were French, a year or so later.

From time to time small batches of prisoners returned to France, either for good or for a period of leave. First there were the sick, then fathers of large families such as the Marquis de Sesmaisons, with his eight children, who returned on 27 December 1940. In the spring of 1941 a number of farmers returned, then in the summer veterans of the 1914–18 War, for whom the Germans had a particular respect, such as Colonel Canon Panaget. The trickle of homecomings encouraged speculation about more returns that was often wildly exaggerated. Contradictory rumours spread in the Mauges in the spring of 1941 to the effect that mayors were going to be able to select one POW in their commune who could come home, or alternatively that peasants with more than 20 hectares would be released.[21] Such were the rumours of an imminent 'massive' release of prisoners that Feldkommandant Kloss and Prefect Roussillon had to act in concert to scotch them for fear that painful disappointment would fuel social unrest.[22] It took more than a press communiqué to silence rumour, however, and in July 1941, just after the German invasion of Russia, it was being whispered that *all* French prisoners would be home before the end of the year, to make room for the torrent of Russian POWs.[23]

For the vast majority of POWs the trip to Germany was the beginning of a term which ended only in the spring or summer of 1945. To overcome the pain of separated families, communities and churches invented a multitude of different ways to stay in touch, and these efforts were often reciprocated by the soldiers in the camps. Indeed, it would be fair to say that fund-raising and support activities on behalf of the POWs were among the greatest stimulants of sociability under the Occupation, drawing divided families out of their isolation, rallying the wider community around households in difficulty, and mobilizing the faithful to look after their spiritual needs.

Support for the POWs was generated locally, but it was also vigorously promoted by the government. For the Vichy regime encouraging concern for the prisoners was a way of stressing the message that France had been punished for past errors of self-indulgence, was in a period of mourning, and must seek regeneration through altruism and solidarity. A committee to support the POWs was set up in virtually every commune in France, and communes that were slow to respond were rapped sharply over the knuckles. To reply, as did the mayor of a small commune near Saumur, that the locals were too selfish and difficult and that at the age of seventy-two he no longer had the energy to dragoon them into action, was not good enough.[24]

In fact, the enthusiasm with which most communities set about raising funds in order to send food parcels to the POWs was remarkable. At a time when all public gatherings had to be authorized by the German authorities for security reasons, and the French authorities showed a marked disapproval of merry-making, POW events provided an excellent excuse for combining duty and pleasure. Fund-raising became the rationale for *boules* competitions, for football matches between neighbouring communes, for concerts and amateur dramatics which played fast and loose with the Germans' keenness to spot any political content in plays. Tombolas and lotteries were particularly popular, although a cut was taken of all funds raised by the Secours National, the national charity which legally enjoyed a charity monopoly. The annual *kermesse* or patronal festival, usually held in the summer or early autumn, was geared up to helping the POWs. One commune near Saumur in September 1942, for example, boasted a bar, pâtisserie stall, fairground attractions such as the greasy pole and quoits, weight-throwing and jumping competitions, a theatrical show and children's games.[25] A year later another Angevin commune organized a fund-raising event at which it was demonstrated that the parcels they had sent, if piled on top of each other, would be two and a half times as high as the Eiffel Tower and that the string used would reach round the commune nine times.[26]

The Secours National, which ran successive campaigns for a variety of good causes, devoted a week in November 1941 to mobilize the country's youth to collect funds for the POWs. It was promoted not only as a money-spinner but as a way to promote solidarity between young people who had not yet reached military age and those who had served their country and paid a price. 'Solidarity shares' worth 50 centimes each were sold in schools by the pupils, in workshops and businesses by apprentices and trainees, and on the streets by both of them.[27] In Angers, boys and girls aged between twelve and twenty put on different variety events, interspersed by a film and a live broadcast by Marshal Pétain, which were attended by the regional prefect.[28] Another event held in Angers a year later, organized by the Popular Education Secretariat and patronized by the glitterati of Catholic and conservative notables, raised funds specifically to send books to the POWs. It was promoted as 'the only way for them to escape from moral isolation', and made much of the fact that with paper in short supply books were now comparatively rare and expensive.[29]

In all these fund-raising and networking activities a key role was played by the Catholic Church. Its most obvious contribution was to organize national days of prayer for the POWs and to devote collections taken in church specifically to them. This offered an opportunity for Church and state, which had not enjoyed good relations under the Third Republic, to draw together, and for men, who had traditionally left the business of worship mainly to women, to return to the fold. On one of the prayer days, 29 November 1942, Mgr Villepelet, bishop of Nantes, noted: 'At 3 p.m. I led a procession of prisoners' wives, mothers, daughters and sisters to Notre-Dame de Miséricorde, and at 5 p.m. in the cathedral there was a wonderful turnout of men, with the prefect and mayor in the front row. Great crowds in both churches, with sermons given by the Abbé Lordonné and Father Marboeuf, both freed prisoners'.[30] Collections that day went to the Chaplaincy for Prisoners of War in Paris, which sent portable altars, altar linen, vestments, Bibles, service books, communion wine and wafers to the Catholic priests who had themselves been taken prisoner and were authorized to serve as chaplains in the camps.[31] Locally a system of spiritual adoption was developed, whereby each diocese took a particular interest in camps where soldiers from that area were particularly concentrated: Stalag IA for the diocese of Angers, Stalag IXB for that of Nantes, and Stalag IVC for that of Tours. At Stalag IA the chaplain organized a day of prayers to coincide with one held in Angers, and one of the prisoners who was subsequently liberated reported 'how comforting it was for all of us to know that at the same moment we were united in fervent prayer for our dear France'.[32]

This points to another of the links forged between France and Germany, the intense correspondence exchanged between bishops and the clergy of their diocese imprisoned in the camps. Some of the clergy, such as the Angevin curé René Sallé, tried to remain in good spirits. 'Abbé Vergnaud, curate of Vern, and Abbé Gohier, seminarist from Challan, as well as the Salesian Abbé Hardy are here with me,' he wrote to the bishop of Angers, Mgr Costes, 'and there are a few Angevins, good types, good Christians, with whom we have prayer meetings from time to time.' More pessimistic was Michel Guéry, who had been working on a large German farm. 'It is so hard. For two years I didn't meet either a priest or a seminarist.' Now he was part of a work team attached to the camp hospital and was able to help with religious services there. 'In spite of that,' he confessed, 'my thoughts rarely leave my dear diocese, I dream of my parish, of the young people above all . . . It is hard to be deprived of all that at an age when one should be throwing oneself into it. May our suffering be offered up for the future harvest.'[33] The relationship between young cleric in exile and bishop was summed up by one priest from the diocese of Nantes in a camp in the Tyrol who, after relating how POW fathers pinned pictures sent by their children to their bunk beds with tears in their eyes, reflected, 'Are you not, after all, the father of the great sacerdotal family of the diocese and are not the priest-prisoners, exiled for nearly four years, a little more your children because they are more unfortunate?'[34]

In all this correspondence about fathers and children what is missing is the wife and mother. Yet the imprisonment of husbands and fathers in German camps affected no one more than French women, who were left with the burden of raising children and keeping the family fed, clothed and housed without the benefit of the traditional breadwinner. For the Vichy regime, moving close to the Catholic Church for this purpose, the duty of women was to return to the home to have children and to educate them as pious and virtuous mothers. Men had failed to defend the nation but to regenerate it was the task of women. Mothers, proclaimed the archbishop of Tours for Mother's Day 1941, were 'a factor of first importance in the work of moral and social restoration that we all want to see for our country' and sermons must exalt 'the maternal virtues: the spirit of faith, the spirit of sacrifice, sleepless vigilance and constant self-abnegation'.[35] 'France will be what mothers have made it,' echoed the mayor of the small town of Baugé on Mother's Day 1942. Mothers had 'simply obeyed this double imperative of Genesis: "Be ye fruitful, and multiply" and "In sorrow thou shalt bring forth children". Always smiling and resigned, they have agreed to be this mission and the holocaust of this redemption.' Reluctantly, he conceded that the wife would have to substitute for the husband, if the latter were mobilized, taken prisoner or died for the *patrie*, but at the same time 'remaining the mother, the good mother, the *maman*'.[36]

The law of 11 October 1940 excluded married women from employment in the public sector, except where the husband's income was insufficient for the household.[37] Mme Talbot, who had been appointed a philosophy teacher at Cholet girls school in 1939–40, was told in 1941 that the post was no longer available. She would have to make way for a young woman under thirty who would pursue a career in teaching and besides, some male teachers being moved from the Lycée of Brest because of the danger of air attacks now needed jobs at Cholet.[38] Married women were given incentives to stay at home, such as the priority card that allowed women with small children the right to get to the front of the food queue or a special ration card if they were pregnant or breast-feeding. They were encouraged to have big families by the award of medals each Mother's Day – bronze for five children, silver for eight, gold for ten – legitimate of course. The fifteenth child had the honour of having Marshal Pétain himself as a godfather. When, for example, the Huteau family of Nantes, described by the local priest as honest working class, had their fifteenth child, they received a silver thimble, a large cheque and a photograph of the Marshal. The delighted father replied that the photograph would be 'framed and given a place of honour in our little home, so that my [*sic*] children will grow up under his gaze'.[39] How the mother responded we do not know.

This laudable ideal of the wife and mother did not correspond to the reality of life under the Occupation. Life was hard for all women, not least for the wives of POWs. In the first place, how were women whose husbands were in POW camps supposed to have legitimate children? The allowance they received from the authorities was meagre, the whole fund-raising business seemed to be a fraud. In June 1942, on the second anniversary of the Armistice, with the soldiers still behind barbed wire, a chain of handwritten letters was passed from hand to hand in Nantes, calling on the wives of POWs to protest. Fine speeches had been made, they said, but nothing had been done. In particular, huge amounts of money had been collected for the prisoners and given to the Red Cross to ensure a free parcel for each prisoner, but the cost of the goods was then charged to the families. A demonstration took place outside the gates of the prefecture, and the prefect agreed to receive a delegation of women who demanded two parcels a month for their husbands, not one, and then complained that their allowances as wives of POWs were derisory. He dismissed the incident as inspired by communists but conceded in private that further demoralization of the families of prisoners might result in social unrest.[40]

Bread-rioting was a traditional activity for women who (even with husbands present) assumed responsibility for feeding the family.[41] Female labour was also traditional, at least among the working classes. Many women who would not necessarily seek work were driven on to the market under the Occupation. Some took jobs as seamstresses, laundrywomen or cleaners, if need be with the Germans. Others took over the family farm or business, sometimes employing a significant number of workers. Despite its scorn for women working, the Vichy regime eventually had to repeal the law against the employment of married women because of growing labour shortages, and came round to recognize that the contribution of the wives of farmers or artisans who were POWs was crucial to the survival of the enterprise. Pétain himself wanted to award medals to forty such women in each department on Labour Day 1943. Among those decorated at Angers were Georgette Brunet, who had left her own prewar job to run her husband's leather business, and Hélène Boisteau, who ran her husband's roofing business with eight workers. Unfortunately the authorities did not reckon with the pressures on working women: Mme Hubert of Allonnes, who had three children and ran her husband's butchery/charcuterie on her own, sent her apologies for not attending the ceremony on Sunday, 2 May, in Angers because the meat allocation arrived on the Saturday and there were no trains on Sundays.[42]

It was all very well for the Church and regime to preach the virtues of motherhood and family life, but the long absence of husbands in German POW camps put relationships under enormous strain. As the years passed some women inevitably looked for support, protection and love elsewhere. In small communities this did not pass unnoticed. The mayor of a winegrowing village near Saumur reported 'the behaviour or rather *misbehaviour* of two wives of prisoners in my commune, scandalizing the inhabitants and threatening the upright young men'. The prefect replied that under the law of 23 December 1942 to 'protect the dignity of the family home from which the husband is absent owing to the circumstances of war' a man might be fined for living with the wife of a POW, but only if the husband lodged a complaint. The mayor, furious, argued that the husbands were in a German camp and one who had been burned in an Allied air raid was nearly blind; he insinuated that the women were prostitutes and that the vice squad should be brought in. 'It is not with such examples that the young people of France will revive our poor country.' The wife of the injured POW later divorced, sold the farm and moved to Saumur where she ran a café.[43]

Sometimes husbands complained from POW camp and tried to begin divorce proceedings, but if Vichy was clear about one thing, it was that divorce should be made more difficult. The divorce law of 2 April 1942 prohibited divorce within three years of marriage and did not consider adultery sufficient grounds. So when POW Paul Urien told Prefect Dupard on hearing of his wife's behaviour, 'I have only disgust for that woman who is not worthy to bear my name . . . I never want to see her again,' Dupard replied that divorce was now difficult and slow, and there was no special provision for POWs.[44] In any case the husband was often just as much to blame for the breakdown of a marriage. Albert Loiseau, a POW from the working-class suburb of Saint-Pierre-des-Corps asked for a divorce and for his two children to be entrusted to his mother. A social worker told the prefect that his wife was 'without morality and shamelessly admitted that she was pregnant for the second time since her husband was taken prisoner', but that 'they got on very badly before the war. There were often rows when M. Loiseau came home drunk and beat his wife.' She saw no reason why Mme Loiseau should forfeit either the children, since she looked after them well, or the allowance due to her as the wife of a POW since she had nothing else to live on, and the prefect concurred with this judgement.[45]

In the final analysis the campaign of Vichy against immorality and its desire to protect the family were often at cross-purposes. This contradiction, however, allowed women in an impossible situation to begin a new life while retaining custody of the children or, in some cases, abandoning them. The wife of a POW could not be divorced simply because she was sleeping or cohabiting with someone else, and children were rarely taken away because there was nowhere else for them to go. Mme Vétault of Jumelles, whose husband was a POW in Saxony, eventually stopped writing to him and moved in with a butcher called Eugène Chaudronnier. She had already been prosecuted for an abortion and found not guilty, was now pregnant again by Chaudronnier and had put her four-year-old daughter by Vétault into an orphanage in Saumur. The French authorities took away her military allowance and decided to cut the family benefit she received for her daughter and give it and the daughter to Vétault's seventy-four-year-old father, but the grandfather wanted nothing to do with the idea. They also decided to prosecute Chaudronnier under the law of 23 December 1943 but there is no record of the outcome.[46] Mme Vétault, despite her perceived immorality, secured the family arrangement she wanted.

The position of POWs improved a little from the summer of 1942, when Prime Minister Pierre Laval negotiated with the Germans an exchange of French workers who would go to the Reich in return for POWs who would be reunited with their families in France.[47] This process, known as the *Relève*, was trumpeted by the Vichy government as a triumph of hard bargaining, but the small print revealed that only one POW would return for each *skilled* worker sent to Germany. The return of prisoners was thus only modest: only 100,0000 for France as a whole and 1,000 of the 14,400 POWs of Maine-et-Loire in the year after August 1942. In April 1943 prisoners who contracted to return to Germany as 'free workers' were allowed home briefly on leave, but this amounted to no more than 1,000 for France as a whole. Eight were given a reception by the mayor of Nantes but in the end three of them did not return to Germany: one was too sick and two went missing for family reasons.[48] In the summer of 1943, after the introduction of the Service du Travail Obligatoire (STO) made life extremely difficult for many families, Laval managed to negotiate the return of 2,000 POWs nationally as an exceptional measure. This provoked a hectic scramble to demonstrate need and revealed extraordinary circumstances such as that of the Piron family near Saumur. The parents, aged sixty-nine and fifty-nine, were farming 18 hectares with two daughters aged twenty-two and eighteen. A third daughter was married and of their eight sons three were POWs, one had been requisitioned for the Todt Organization and another for the STO, two were married with children and one was a boy aged twelve.[49] This was an extreme example of the disruption of family life by the German Occupation.

The return of POWs, however slow, added a new dimension to the solidarity required among French people. It was a case now not only of caring for POWs in German camps by sending parcels but also of caring for the returning POWs. A new organization was set up in the summer of 1942 to coordinate the different services that already existed and to cater for developing needs: the Maisons du Prisonnier. The general rule was one per department, at Tours, Angers and Nantes, but Saumur acquired one early in 1943 and then Cholet, claiming it had more POWs to cope with than Saumur, set one up. The Maisons dealt with questions of benefits, employment and even relationships. When a POW returned, the military allowance that had been paid to his wife was cancelled, but he became entitled to a range of concessions such as free public transport, free cinema entry and a free fishing permit. This implied that he would simply sit around relaxing, but clearly there were pressures to return to work as soon as possible. For those in agriculture or related trades – about 43 per cent of POWs in Loire-Inférieure, 52 per cent in Indre-et-Loire and 63 per cent in Maine-et-Loire – the demand was only too intense.[50] Nor did industrial workers find difficulty either recovering their old jobs or finding new ones, even without training, at a time when the Germans were stepping up labour recruitment for the Reich.[51] The biggest problems seem to have been experienced by the self-employed, such as M. Tijou of Saint-Pierre-des-Corps who complained that his painting and decorating business had been squeezed out by other businesses which had secured all the public works contracts, or the shoemaker M. Madelin who fell foul of the regulations governing the allocation of scarce raw materials, and received no leather or rubber because he had no registered clients.[52] Some ex-POWs made such a mess of things that they were soon on the road back to Germany. One man from Saint-Nazaire quarrelled so violently with his wife that he went back to Germany voluntarily, leaving his child and butcher's business to his mother-in-law. Another man, from Nantes, arrested for stealing sugar, and not having proof that he was a former POW, was put on a train against his will with a contingent of workers destined for the Reich only a few days before the city was liberated by the Americans.[53]

For all the energy that went into helping POWs and their families, the conflict and corruption endemic in Occupied France could not but infiltrate the very organizations which were supposed to demonstrate the solidarity of the French people in their hour of need. Some of the conflicts arose from political differences, others from tensions between local communities and more centralized authorities, or within local communities themselves. The collection of large quantities of money and goods in the midst of scarcity, moreover, was an invitation to some French people, who perhaps felt themselves worse off than the POWs, to cheat and pilfer. In some respects they were right. As the Atlantic ports were subjected to Allied aerial attack, culminating in the massive bombardment of Nantes on 16 September 1943, so the balance between the needy and those provided for subtly shifted, so that in a curious reversal of charity, at the end of the Occupation, POWs were sending the product of their collections to the bomb victims of their home towns.

Tensions within organizations set up to assist POWs were apparent from the summer of 1940. The committee set up in Loire-Inférieure by veterans headed by Léon Jost both to supply the makeshift prison camps in the department and to orchestrate escapes was not allowed to function without interference. Catholic and conservative institutions such as the Association Catholique des Chefs de Famille, which claimed 80,000 members in the department, muscled in under the leadership of the Marquis de La Ferronnays, president of the *conseil général*, and lobbied the prefect to become involved. As a result a departmental committee to assist POWs was set up, within which the veterans' escape committee continued to function covertly, but which became vulnerable to the prying of the Catholic conservatives. A row broke out between the veterans and the conservatives, as a result of which it was alleged that one of the conservatives, a certain M. Roger, denounced the veterans who, as we have seen, were arrested and court-martialled by the Germans. Sentenced to three years in prison in July 1941, a much worse fate awaited them following the assassination of the Feldkommandant of Nantes the following October.[54]

The departmental committee to assist the POWs in Loire-Inférieure came under further pressure the following winter because of differences in policy with the city of Nantes. The mayor of Nantes, Gaëtan Rondeau, took the view (as did the wives of the 5,500 POWs of Nantes) that the departmental committee handed out so few goods to prisoners' families that they had to fall back on their own rations to make up the parcels. As a result a separate Nantes committee was set up in February 1942 under a local barrister, Alexander Vincent, who was to become prefect of Loire-Inférieure at the Liberation. This undertook to provide a second, free parcel every month to the families of POWs, to supplement the one provided, at cost, by the departmental committee. It was to be financed by a grand tombola and to include cans of meat and vegetables supplied by local canning firms such as Cassegrain. The wives of POWs who demonstrated in June 1942 were pressing in the same direction as the Nantes committee and against the departmental committee, which as a result of the Nantes initiative reduced its allocation to Nantes.[55]

Local patriotism was always the order of the day when it came to collecting for POWs, and committees set up in each commune to support POWs had the prisoners of that commune particularly in mind. This clashed with the national overview of organizations like the Secours National, which wanted to spread the funds raised more widely. In the winter of 1940–1, for example, the Secours National ran a campaign to collect money for blankets, clothes and linen for POWS, relying on the generosity of communes, schools and businesses. When the money was forwarded, businesses and communes often requested that a proportion of it should be devoted to their particular prisoners, emphazising that the success of the collection was explained by the understanding of locals that they were giving to their own, but this was a request the Secours National was reluctant to meet.[56] In 1942 bureaucracy became even tighter, and local fund-raising events were required to give not only 50 per cent of their receipts to the Secours National but a further 20 per cent to a departmental commission which vetted all fund-raising events for POWs. This provoked clashes with promoters such as M. Vanneyre, president of the prisoners' committee of the Madeleine district of Angers. Told that he had not handed over enough money, he replied that donors had given directly to the Red Cross for parcels and for local families of POWs in difficulty. 'Why try to replace us?' he asked. If people knew that 70 per cent of their donations were being spirited off elsewhere they would stop giving, 'and who would have the right to blame them?'[57]

The struggle of local community against central authority was not the only fault-line to appear in the commitment to POWs. Even local communities which were supposed to have a common purpose and identity could be divided against themselves, and the prisoners' support committee simply became a forum in which local antagonisms were played out. Saint-Brévin-les-Pins was a commune at the mouth of the Loire opposite Saint-Nazaire, looking out over the Atlantic. About as far as one could get from the German border, it tended to attract a number of exotic outsiders who did not necessarily fit in with the locals. The prisoners' committee set up by Mayor Guillou in 1940 functioned without incident until the summer of 1942 when Auguste Hérault, a war-wounded shoemaker, Freemason and member of the League of Rights of Man, accused his political rival, Raoul Marchand, a shopkeeper and right-wing municipal councillor, of stealing chocolate from the parcels destined for POWs and selling it on the black market. The mayor called the committee to thrash out the matter, and after a row Hérault resigned. Guillou then filled up the committee with POWs who had been liberated, including Captain Amédée Modena, an Italian who had fought in the French Foreign Legion in 1914 and 1940 and had recently acquired French nationality. But Hérault did not give up the fight and allied with another outsider, retired captain Victor-Antoine Mas, who had come to Saint-Brévin as a refugee in 1940 and stayed. Mas revived the accusations of chocolate theft against Marchand in the press in September 1943, and Modena came to Marchand's aid. Hérault then laid into Modena, accusing him of being a Transalpine ruffian, a communist and a Jew, which ran the risk of drawing him to the attention of the Germans. After the Liberation Hérault tried to rally the new prefect to his version of events, while Modena argued that he had joined the Resistance and that Hérault and Mas were anti-Semites and collaborationists. A quarrel which started over chocolate bars for POWs thus exposed the fault-lines of a seaside village: Left against Right, natives against newcomers, self-styled resisters against supposed collaborators. The only compensation was that the slanging match was played out within the community rather than by means of denunciation to the Germans, which would have led to deportation and tragedy.[58]

Tensions between collaborationists and resisters in fact penetrated POW organizations at the highest level. Most subversive was the collaborationist Mouvement du Prisonnier, which recruited the wives and mothers of POWs by claiming to be able to bring about the liberation of their husbands or sons, and newly repatriated POWs by claiming that they had been responsible for their liberation. When the Maisons du Prisonnier were set up the Mouvement tried to ensure that its supporters were appointed to key positions. This led to a series of conflicts, exposures, resignations and dismissals which seriously undermined the Maisons and made them much less effective than they might have been. Jean Roussillon, regional prefect of Angers, was alerted to the danger early on and became extremely concerned by the Mouvement's plentiful resources, propaganda and contacts.[59] When the departmental delegate of the Mouvement, M. Oger, was appointed the director of the Maison du Prisonnier at Angers, Roussillon collected a dossier on his incompetence and tried to replace him by his own candidate, the hero of the pro-Vichy Catholics, Canon Panaget. Roussillon managed to have Oger's appointment cancelled in June 1943, but the Maison remained under the influence of M. Duchange, the secretary in charge of employing ex-POWs, who wore the uniform of the collaborationist Rassemblement Nationale Populaire (RNP) and was said to be in close touch with the Gestapo.[60] Meanwhile, Roussillon did not last the course himself, dismissed under German pressure in July 1943. In Touraine, similarly, the departmental delegate of the Mouvement, a schoolteacher named Philipon, acted as a veritable kingmaker in appointments to the Maison du Prisonnier. He unseated the first director, Landry, in August 1943, vetoed the proposed replacement, and finally sanctioned the appointment of a certain Georges Renault, a former notary's clerk and apartment manager.[61] By the end of 1943 it was fairly clear that the Maisons du Prisonnier of Angers and Tours were in the pocket of the Mouvement du Prisonnier.

The POW support movement was undermined from within not only by political conflict but also by corruption and crime. Fundraising events which sold foodstuffs in short supply became a front for black market operations, while the promotion of entertainment attracted 'impresarios' interested only in fleecing the organizers and their clientele. Laval tried to clamp down on such 'commercial enterprises' by setting up departmental commissions to approve all fund-raising events for POWs and by banning from them all buffets, lunches, dinners or public auctions of foodstuffs.[62] These measures did not, of course, manage to eliminate corruption, which went to the heart of the Maisons du Prisonnier themselves. M. Lardy, director of the Maison of Tours, surprised one of his aides, Colonel de Busnel, siphoning off for the benefit of the staff the 20 litres of milk that arrived every Sunday for the teas organized for the children of POWs.[63] In Angers one of the staff of the Maison, Bazely, used his contacts with freed prisoners who were winegrowers in the region to organize a vast black market operation in wine. He held court in the cafés around the Maison du Prisonnier, struck up friendships with German army lorry drivers to ensure transport, and resold the wines under the table to Angers retailers.[64] The final anti-social act at the expense of the POWs was theft of or from the parcels addressed to the prisoners in Germany. Here the best placed for crime were railway employees and warehousemen. If caught, they faced stiff sentences from the exceptional courts or Sections Spéciales set up by Vichy. Two railwaymen in Angers received terms of four and five years, and a ring of twelve individuals headed by a retired major who was in charge of the distribution centre for POWs in Angers, and including warehousemen, an accountant and even a woman driver for the Red Cross, were given sentences of between three and seven years.[65]

As the Occupation continued it seemed that the altruism of the French began to wear thin and that the tremendous solidarity that greeted the first initiatives in favour of the POWs gave way to self-seeking and corruption. At the same time, paradoxically, examples multiplied of POWs returning the compliment and organizing their own fund-raising networks to support loved ones at home who were becoming the collateral victims of Allied air attacks on the submarine bases, naval shipyards and and armaments factories of Lorient, Saint-Nazaire and Nantes. From 1941 the POWs of Stalag VIIIC set up departmental committees to strengthen ties between prisoners and their native *pays*. After the air attacks of April 1943 those from the five Breton departments including Loire-Inférieure formed a special regional group and raised 5,600 Reichsmarks or 11,200 francs for those left hurt or homeless in the Breton coastal towns. This was echoed by the 'Brittany' group of Stalag IIIA which sent 870 Reichsmarks for the Breton ports, specifying in particular Saint-Nazaire.[66] The bombing of Nantes on 16 September 1943 destroyed among other things its Maison du Prisonnier and killed fifteen of the staff or visitors. This tragedy provoked a wave of sympathy and support among POWs, who wrote to the mayor expressing the wish to adopt children who had been orphaned. Thus, for example, the POWs of Kommando 106 at Borna near Leipzig adopted Françoise, whose father had been a POW since 1940, whose mother had been killed on 16 September and whose grandmother, looking after her, was injured and left homeless.[67] The support of POWs was given in prayers as well as in money. Sergeant Louis Nouais, a priest-prisoner at Stammlager IVF, told the bishop of Nantes how shocked he was to hear of the death of Canon Boisellier, a stalwart of the diocese, on 16 September. 'The great suffering of the people of Nantes has been carried as far as IVF; I had to inform several comrades of the death of a wife or child, sometimes of several loved ones. Mass was celebrated on 3 October for the victims of the disaster.'[68] The wheel had come full circle, and whether inspired by Christian charity or a love of the *petite patrie*, those in exile who should have been helped were in their turn helping those at home who, for once, had greater need than they.

The case of POWs illustrates both the disruption of families and communities by defeat and occupation, and energetic attempts by those who had been separated to rebuild networks of solidarity. Communities rallied round to send food and messages to the POWs, and later on, when the war engulfed civilian populations in France, the POWs replied in kind with help to bomb victims. Churches were filled as many turned to pray for the release of their loved ones. Left in practice to fend for themselves, many women rose to the challenge of running farms or businesses as well as family. On the debit side stresses and strains inevitably undermined much of the work of solidarity. Some families broke up as women sought support and affection elsewhere. Fund-raising and charity sometimes provided opportunities for corruption and theft. Collective enterprises might be damaged by faction and politics. Tensions were evident between those who felt solidarity with POWs in their community and organizations seeking a broader national approach to the relief of suffering. As in so many respects, the Occupation drove people to narrow their horizons and give priority to family and community over national loyalties.

5. BREAD

In the first winter of the Occupation Georges Mazeaud, a glovemaker in the Saint-Lazare district of Paris, took up his pen and wrote 'with some shame' to a country cousin he scarcely knew but who for reasons of survival became a vital ally. 'We are hungry, my children, grandchildren, my wife and me. I never thought that at the age of 66 I could write that, but there it is. The food supply in Paris is absolutely inadequate, and many are undernourished.' Like most Parisians Mazeaud had roots in the provinces. He had left the village of Concourson-sur-Layon near Saumur as a baby in 1875 when his father sought a better life as a draughtsman in the capital, but now that cold and hunger gripped Paris the balance seemed to have shifted and all the advantages appeared to lie with the rustic relatives. Mazeaud's correspondent, Gaston Grenouilleau, was a forty-three-year-old winegrower and cooper at Concourson-sur-Layon, reputed for its soft Côteaux du Layon wines. Mazeaud asked whether he could send any surplus food he might have by registered mail, declaring it as a trade sample, up to the permitted weight of 3 kilos – 'bacon, cheese, butter, pasta, in fact anything you can eat'.[1]

Ten days later Mazeaud wrote again to say that he had just paid 80 francs for a skinny chicken: could Gaston please send poultry, beans, 'rillettes like Aunt Léontine's'. 'I said to my wife, as I wrote,' he added, 'that life is like a play: I was born at Concourson, I drank its milk, and now in my old age it is Concourson that will perhaps continue to keep me alive.' Now that the family connection was re-established and the shame diminished a little, Mazeaud asked whether Gaston could also send parcels to his son Roger, thirty-six, who had been demobilised in July and was a sales representative for a chemicals firm, his wife Suzanne and four-year-old daughter

Françoise; to his daughter Madeleine whose husband was a POW, and their twelve-year-old son Bernard; and to his eldest daughter Lucienne, whose husband was also a POW and was out of touch with her two teenage children in the Free Zone. A week later he wrote to thank Gaston for the first parcel that had arrived that day, saying 'The rillettes are wonderful and have the taste of Concourson.' On 30 January 1941 he acknowledged receipt of a joint of lamb, the first they had eaten for eight months, since May 1940.[2]

Mazeaud was a proud man and kept scrupulous accounts of what he owed Gaston. He also initiated a two-way traffic, taking orders for gloves and sending them to Concourson. Gaston was to take the money and use them to offset the debt. For while the countryside was awash with food, manufactured goods were generally hard to come by there. In April 1942, for example, Mazeaud sent twenty-nine pairs of gloves, worth between 18 and 30 francs each, having taken off the prices, telling Gaston that he could easily charge five francs more. His daughter Lucienne asked whether Gaston could send some bottles of white wine for her son's wedding and later sent a cheque for 200 francs to pay for the seventeen bottles delivered that had been 'le roi de la fête', enjoyed by twenty guests. Another of Georges's sons, Paul, who was in the clothing business, was supplied with food from the countryside by his own clients, but offered to send two smocks for the children, two shirts, a blouse for Gaston's wife Sidonie and a pair of work trousers worth 805 francs in return for some wine which was retailing for between 100 and 130 francs a bottle in Paris. Whether this was for personal consumption or a little private trade is uncertain.[3]

Meanwhile Mazeaud's requests for food continued – pork, mutton, beef, rabbit, duck, chicken, rillettes, sausages, butter – not swede, he joked, 'with which we are saturated'. The void seemed impossible to fill. 'Soon we will become vegetarians out of necessity,' he complained, 'and perhaps even have to do without bread. The women in particular spend half their time queueing for one thing or another.' Come the summer, however, he was requesting vegetables and regretting, 'I should have stayed at Concourson, instead of coming to Paris when I was 15 months old. Perhaps I would have some fields and some vines too. But I was young!' The following spring Mazeaud reflected, 'The most important thing in the world is to eat. We are almost reduced to the level of beasts.' In the spring of

1943 he told Gaston that they were becoming 'skeletons', his weight down to 54 kilos, and he spent some time in hospital with anthrax. There were often hiccups in the transport system – chickens going off in the summer heat, parcels sent by train getting stolen – and the Liberation did not suddenly bring plenty. On his seventieth birthday in February 1945 Mazeaud reflected wryly that 'The Allies helped us to victory but did not bring abundance nor even basic necessities.' He survived the war but his daughter Madeleine, though 'radiant' when her POW husband returned in 1945, had nevertheless been seriously weakened and died the following year. 'The war killed her little by little,' her father wrote.[4]

Georges Mazeaud never met Gaston Grenouilleau, either during the war or afterwards. But their correspondence, squeezed into a biscuit tin by Gaston's son Paul, suggests a great deal about survival during the Occupation. People went hungry, especially in large cities and above all in Paris. Those in the country, however, despite the pressure from the French and German authorities to hand over their produce, kept enough back for a parallel market supplying friends and relatives and in return acquiring the clothing and other manufactured goods they needed. Severe shortages and high prices set the French against each other in the struggle for survival, yet their inventiveness in getting by – the famous 'Système de Débrouillage' or 'Système D' – actually required them to establish new networks and to cooperate as never before. Survival was not only about queueing and scratching a meagre existence but developing family, neighbourhood and business contacts in order to make life possible.

Inventiveness and solidarity were at a premium because although the Vichy government put systems in place to deal with shortages and price rises these were neither effective nor popular. In each department it appointed a director-general of Supply (Ravitaillement), who was supposed to ensure that markets were supplied with agricultural produce, a Price Control Commission to make sure that price levels fixed by the administration to protect consumers were adhered to by businesses, and groups bringing together producers and traders in each product such as meat or milk to ensure that each trader obtained a fair supply of the goods available. Customers had to register with particular traders for the operation of rationing, which was introduced from September 1940. The population was divided into different categories for the purposes of food entitlement.

Thus children under six were entitled to 750ml of milk a day and children aged between six and twelve to 500ml. Adults between twenty-one and seventy were entitled to 350g of bread per day, at least at the beginning of the Occupation, 300g of meat and 50g of cheese a week, and 500g of sugar, 200g of butter, 200g of margarine and 50g of rice a month. Manual workers and farm workers were entitled to more food than white-collar workers, in respect of their exertions. These rations were actually higher than those fixed in Great Britain in January 1940, when an adult was entitled to only 4oz (113g) of butter and 12oz (340g) of sugar a month, but rations were always limited by what was available, and generally declined over the period of the war.[5]

Despite the energy spent on constructing and enforcing the official economy, the results were meagre. Many problems, to be fair, were beyond the control of the Vichy administrators. The British imposed a blockade on trade with France as they had during the Napoleonic wars, and British coal, on which much industry in the west of France depended, dried up. The Germans confiscated as war booty imported stocks of tea, coffee, sugar, rice, chocolate and Algerian wine they found in ports such as Nantes and Saint-Nazaire.[6] Integrating France into their war economy meant the systematic requisition of agricultural as well as industrial goods, and here the question of how far the Vichy administration acted as a 'shield' against the Germans became an issue. At times it seemed that the French Ravitaillement services acted less to protect French markets from German plundering than as vehicles of German greed. Colonel Constant Rouleau, Director-General of Supply for the five departments of the Angers region, was also responsible for supplying meat to the Germans in the twelve departments of Bezirk B and was accused after the war of doing nothing to temper German demands for oats, potatoes and any other produce. Rigid and authoritarian, he was said to have admired German discipline, put on his uniform to present his respects to German officers on New Year's Day, enthusiastically showed visitors a revolver and a hunting rifle they had given him, and went hunting with them on more than one occasion.[7]

In many ways the Angers region, known as the Garden of France, with its mixed agriculture of market gardens, cereals, vines and cattle-breeding, was less at risk from shortages than, for example, the Mediterranean coast with its wine monoculture and insufficient space given to wheat or livestock.[8] In the spring of 1941 the prefect of Maine-et-Loire reported that 'the food supply problem has become particularly serious in this department which until now had been in a privileged position because of its agricultural resources'. Fortunately, 'apart from a few incidents without importance in long queues in front of butchers' or other food shops, the population has endured this test with courage and dignity'.[9] Eighteen months later, in the winter of 1942–3, the assessment was more pessimistic:

> Housewives are complaining bitterly about the absence of butter, milk and cheese. They are saying that no oil has been available since November . . . Eggs have not been distributed in any rational way. Shopkeepers are complaining that they have not received the quantities corresponding to the number of clients registered with them, of which the *Ravitaillement* has been informed, so that they are completely unable to satisfy their customers. It is not rare to hear criticisms, even among shopkeepers, of the 'incompetence' of the services concerned.[10]

The large sea ports of Nantes and Saint-Nazaire, cut off from their overseas trade and less well served by the hinterland, were even worse off. In the winter of 1941–2 there were no vegetables on the market, and only an emergency convoy of 655 tonnes of potatoes sent to Nantes in February 1943 saved the situation. Just before Christmas 1943 a women's demonstration was planned to take place in front of the prefecture, to demand an increase in the bread ration, and only a last-minute deal prevented it from going ahead.[11]

The failure of the Vichy administration to keep markets adequately supplied was explained not only by objective shortages but by the fact that its policy of forcing producers to supply markets at fixed prices could be counterproductive. It gave rise to parallel circuits of supply and demand which offered goods at higher prices than the official rates and which therefore might be seen to exploit consumers, but were also more efficient in that the supply was generally kept up. In November 1940 a group of Angevin women sent a semi-literate letter to the prefect protesting at the unscrupulous profiteering of a number of traders. Stockings bought for 25 francs in Marseille were being sold in Angers for 125 francs. Cloth imported from Lyon was being sold at similar ridiculous prices: 'Madame Grégoire in the rue Corneille thinks Angevin women are stupid,' they continued, 'saying that even cuts of 300 francs a metre were going like hot cakes ... Meanwhile, blouse-sellers can't believe how much their bank accounts have grown since the war.'[12] Clearly, officials had to answer such complaints and be seen to do so, but there were dangers in being too heavy-handed. The stallholders of the Lafayette market in Angers complained the following summer that the police had come round ordering them to sell beans at less than the maximum price of 12 francs per kilo, because coarser beans had been mixed with the fine ones, and to sell sour cherries at 10 francs a kilo instead of 13 francs, a price for which only the Montmorency variety qualified. As a result, the stallholders packed up their wares and murmured that they would not be back the following Wednesday. The losers, said their spokesman, would be the inhabitants of the *quartier*, for producers could always remain on their farms and sell to wholesalers for prices that were every bit as good as, if not above, the maximum. He suggested that if the police were more diplomatic everyone's interests might be better served.[13]

Increasingly, producers and wholesalers boycotted the official market, preferring to sell to retailers or middlemen on the black market at prices way above the maximum. This had obvious benefits for them, but risked antagonizing those who were left out of the loop. At Tours, where vegetables also seemed to disappear from the market stalls, it was discovered that wholesale market gardeners were selling to greengrocers at way over the maximum price while providing them with fictitious legal invoices. The overpriced stocks were then kept at the back of the shop to be sold under the counter to customers willing to pay over the odds.[14] A hard-pressed woman from Amboise argued that

> there are two categories of consumers, the rich who eat and those who queue for an hour only to be told that there is nothing left. In the butchers' shops favoured customers place their orders and have them delivered to their houses; they are sure to eat. At the poultry merchant Leclerc the blind is hermetically closed but favoured customers are invited in at the side entrance where they are sold rabbit and other produce under the counter. It is shameful. Likewise in grocers' shops when you ask for some tins or chocolate to make a parcel to send to our dear prisoners in Germany you are told that there is nothing left. Not happy with starving the workers, these unscrupulous traders even refuse help for our prisoners.[15]

The market gardeners' syndicate of Cholet, finally, saw no reason to supply cauliflowers to the local market where produce was subject to price controls, if they could send them to Paris where they would fetch much higher prices paid by the restaurants, the rich and the Germans. 'It is unacceptable for some citizens to accumulate fortunes in a matter of months on the misery of others,' complained an employee of a Cholet firm when he found not a single cauliflower in the market that morning and reached for the language of the *sans-culotte*. 'These bad French people should be punished. Tough measures should be passed, including prison and the confiscation of their goods for organizers of famine.'[16]

The black market that developed in parallel to the official market may have been criticized as a Darwinian jungle of ruthless profiteering and exploitation, but it was more complicated than that. The black market was not a single market but a system of concentric circles. The wider and more impersonal the market, the more exploitative it was likely to be. The widest circle involved selling to distant clients in Paris or other large towns. The Graeve family of Chinon, whom we have already met, operated a large-scale racket buying Touraine wines for 60–80 francs per litre and selling it in the capital for up to 500 francs.[17] The police commissaire of Tours thought that most peasants in Touraine were happy to sell eggs to Parisians on holiday for 60–100 francs per dozen or butter for 100–150 francs per kilo. He pointed out that once peasants realized that their produce could command such prices they were reluctant to sell to local people for any less so that the inhabitants even of small towns found little in the marketplace.[18] Some Parisians already had ties with the countryside, either as regular holidaymakers before the war or, as at Chinon, because their government department or bank was evacuated to the provinces for a period in 1940 and they were able to exploit contacts made at that moment. Mathurin Legras, a member of a collaborationist group, wrote a ten-page diatribe to the prefect of Loire-Inférieure complaining of holidaymakers who toured the countryside with bicycles and double panniers, ceaselessly harassing the peasantry for produce, while 'in the hotels, around groaning tables, crowds of property-owners and bureaucrats of all sorts, stuffed themselves with pork rillettes, meat, game, butter and eggs . . . the only class that suffers from rationing is the proletariat'.[19]

The narrowest circle, like that of Georges Mazeaud and Gaston

Grenouilleau, was purely familial. Working people living in large cities suddenly discovered or rediscovered lost country cousins who, previously forgotten and even despised, now became of the greatest value. Sending food parcels from the country was often no more than gift-giving, or a bartering system swapping farm and manufactured produce. Money scarcely came into it except as a tally of debt and credit, although it might play a greater role if the exchange network extended beyond the family to other members of the community, or if Parisian relatives saw the opportunity for a little profit by selling family wine in an inflated market.

In between these two circles was an intermediate one which included friends, neighbours and clients. It was wider than the family circle but operated on the basis of personal, face-to-face contact. It was based on monetary exchange but set a fair price which offered a privileged supply to the customer and a decent return for the supplier. For this reason it has sometimes been called a 'grey market' rather than a black one. The ultimate sanction of this moral economy was denunciation of a too greedy supplier by an angry client to the French or German authorities. This served to limit the extent of the market, for suppliers were unwilling to do business with customers they did not know or trust.

The typical relationship of this kind evolved when the producer-stallholder no longer saw the benefit of selling on the official market but was willing to do deals with regular customers who came out to the farm. Michel Leterme, a boy at Angers during the Occupation, remembers cycling with his father 32 kilometres each way to Champigné to buy food from a farm. Of course there were farms closer in, but the farmer's wife at Champigné was known to them, as she used to have a stall in the market in Angers.[20] Given the small and diminishing bread ration, millers were particularly in demand. We have already met M. Peraud, the miller outside Chinon, visited by young Christian Beugnet who described him as being 'in our sector'.[21] At Chemillé, wrote a country doctor meanwhile, 'There was an uninterrupted procession of bicycles, of walkers, arriving with empty bags and returning delighted, loaded with flour.'[22]

Personal contact between suppliers and customers was one factor which kept prices fair; the other was the risk of denunciation, which in turn had an effect on the extent of the market. Andrée Trudeau, who worked in the ration-ticket office of Saumur, lived on her father's farm just above the château where wheat, wine and potatoes were grown. Trudeau had some wheat milled privately for his own consumption and found himself accosted by townspeople coming to his door keen to buy flour and potatoes. Andrée admits that such trade was illegal but denied that it was clandestine since 'everyone knew about it'. She points out that 'honest and conscientious as he was', her father did not overcharge them, arguing that he provided a fair and valued service. The great fear was being denounced, and on one occasion this happened to her father. Fortunately the fraud officers did not find his stocks of flour, but the lesson was clear: deal with those you know, not with outsiders.[23]

André Treulier, a winegrower at Le Thoureil, downstream along the Loire, talked to me in a cellar which was an Aladdin's cave of vintages going back before the war. As we sipped wine from the Occupation period he described an autarkic economy of the narrowest dimensions. 'There was not much to eat,' he says, and they had to 'piously conserve' what stocks they had in case of shortage. There was no black market, simply because they had 'nothing to sell'. Later he concedes that he did not want to sell to people he did not know, because they might be 'spies' and have him sent to jail as a 'public enemy'. He remembers hiding in the house while some unknown townspeople laid siege to his farm in order to buy, waiting for them 'to bugger off'. Prices, he says, rose fast, and they thought that they might make a lot of money, but unfortunately there was 'nothing to buy' so they simply saved. After the war he bought the vineyards he had been working, together with the manor house, from the two old ladies who owned it and turned himself into a seigneur of the Domaine de Norgevault. With his flat cap and blue overalls he looked like the peasant described by de Tocqueville in L'Ancien Régime, who appears poor in order to avoid paying too many taxes.[24]

Farmers and winegrowers generally did well under the Occupation. As a result, marriage between a bourgeois and a peasant was no longer beyond the realms of possibility, securing a food supply while not necessarily entailing social dérogation. Dr Mousseau of Saint-Mathurin described how the daughter of one of his patients, the widow of a magistrate, married a farmer who courted her by offering her chops and rillettes whenever he killed a pig, and the widow moved in for good measure.[25] The good fortune of shopkeepers has been admirably portrayed in Jean Dutourd's 1952 novel, *Au Bon Beurre*. A more provincial version of the Parisian dairy merchants might be the Cohu–Denis family of Trélazé, the *petit bourgeois* aristocrats of a working-class suburb of Angers. Like the farmers, shopkeepers who made a good living under the Occupation also seem to feel the need to deny that they engaged in the black market or made huge profits. They underline that they provided a good service, compensating for the failings of the official market, and demanded no more than a fair price. Lucienne Cohu, who with her husband had a charcuterie business in Trélazé, recalls that here was 'a big traffic in meat, but not within the trade. Masons and roofers began to kill animals and people bought from them, but the meat was cut up anyhow, it was sheer waste.' As supplies of pork from the authorities dried up, charcutiers had to fall back on beef. M. Cohu went out to farms in his gas-powered van in order to 'stock up secretly', purely to satisfy their customers. As for prices, 'We didn't take a lot of money. We were long established in the commune. We didn't want to exploit the German presence.' 'We never sold at more than the fixed price,' echo her daughter and son-in-law, Jacqueline and Louis Denis, who were bakers during the Occupation at Trélazé. Of course, some people sold at four or five times that price, but not the professionals. Later Jacqueline Denis takes out a collection of 'little notes' she received from customers at the time, one of them from an angry working-class woman. It reads:

> Do you want to drive people to steal? Don't complain if after all this the workers take everything they can from you. We want to stay honest but we are driven to do wrong. I told you that if I hadn't found myself pregnant against my will I would not lower myself again to ask for credit. I would rather put my children into care than continue to suffer for being honest.

'People had moments of wickedness,' explains Mme Cohu, 'if you had three children and no bread . . .'[26]

There is no doubt that the working classes did not do well out of the Occupation. The high point of their success had been in 1936, when the election of the Popular Front government had been greeted by a national wave of strikes which forced a raft of concessions including wage rises, a forty-hour week, paid holidays and collective bargaining.[27] The trade unions flexed their muscles, both in federations for each industry and in unions of all the industries of a town or department, meeting in the Bourse du Travail which would be subsidized by the local municipality. The Socialist and Communist Parties enjoyed unprecedented influence, the first in government, the second putting pressure on it from parliament, the unions and the street. The downturn had come after the Munich Agreement of 1938, when the government of Daladier turned to the right, ended the Popular Front, abolished the forty-hour week and defeated the striking unions, and then after the Nazi–Soviet Pact when the government dissolved the Communist Party.[28] This repression was only confirmed under the German Occupation and Vichy.

The burning issue for the working classes under the Occupation was the cost of living. The price of foodstuffs soared and wages simply failed to keep pace. It should not be imagined, however, that the workers were totally cowed under the Occupation. Strike action was limited and often only symbolic, but it was resorted to. The famous miners' strike in the Nord in May 1941 has attracted much attention but it was not the only example of industrial action in occupied France.[29] The industrial area of Nantes and Saint-Nazaire was also highly volatile. Moreover, although strikes were few, the fact that they occurred in plants harnessed to the German war machine raised the stakes sharply. Vichy and French employers were put under intense pressure by the Germans to settle disputes immediately, which weakened rather than strengthened their hand. And while Vichy was keen to deal ruthlessly with communists, it did not want to alienate the mass of the workers, whose hard work and political loyalty it wished to develop.

In March 1941 Marcel Blanchard, secretary of the CGT engineers' union of Saint-Nazaire since 1936, when he had been a driving force behind the strikes and factory occupations, urged a meeting of 600 shipyard and aviation workers in Saint-Nazaire to rejoin the union and pursue a campaign for wage rises. In response, on 2 May, the riveters of the Ateliers et Chantiers de la Loire at Saint-Nazaire led a go-slow and forced the management to make concessions. This was followed in August 1941 by a strike of dockers in Nantes, who refused to unload a shipment from Dakar until their wage demands had been met.[30] In October quarryers employed by the Entreprise de Travaux Publics de l'Ouest or Entreprises Dodin, which worked for the Todt Organization, went on strike and also turned out workers at a neighbouring quarry. The Todt Organization twisted the arm of the local Dodin manager to get the men to return to work at once, which they did after a day, but the subprefect of Saint-Nazaire discouraged punishment, given that in his opinion the strike was a response to the rising cost of living in the countryside, not to communist ideas.[31] By contrast, when the aviation workers of SNCASO at Nantes-Bouguenais went on strike in June 1942 the police took the view that they had been stirred up by a sixty-year-old militant called René Daniel, a shop steward who had been sacked from the Batignolles locomotive factory in 1938 for communist propaganda. They advised the prefect of Loire-Inférieure to intern him, although if possible without magnifying the incident, for fear of stirring up trouble in neighbouring factories where tempers were running high.[32]

How effective workers were in achieving their goals was conditioned by their industrial muscle as well as by the circumstances of the Occupation. At first sight their organization seemed rather fragile. Trade union membership had slumped since the strikes of 1938 and the clampdown on labour militancy which had followed. The advent of Vichy was seen by many in business and the administration as an opportunity to have done with organized labour for good. Many employers took this as a chance to cease all negotiation with trade unions, and some municipalities now decided to refuse unions access to the Bourse du Travail they subsidized.

In fact local officials and employers often acted prematurely, for it was the intention of neither the Germans nor Vichy to extinguish trade union activity. The German ordinance of 28 August 1940 which governed the formation of associations specifically allowed the meeting of organizations which had a purely economic or occupational function, so long as the local Kommandantur was informed in advance. Moreover, Vichy's Minister of Labour, the former trade unionist René Belin, spelled out to prefects that the law of 16 August 1940 which set up Comités d'Organisation (COs) to run each industry dissolved only *national* organizations of employers and workers, such as the CGT and CGPF, leaving intact departmental and local unions of unions, meeting in the Bourses du Travail. Prefect Roussillon was obliged to remind mayors that any bans on trade unions entering Bourses du Travail were mistaken and provocative, and that 'the minister has clarified that workers are to be treated on the same terms as employers, so that they do not feel in any way marginalized from the work of national regeneration being pursued by the head of state'.[33] Admittedly the Vichy government was not united, but the Labour Ministry and Marshal Pétain were explicit that regeneration meant social peace rather than industrial confrontation, and weaning the working class away from communism rather than eroding the benefits won by organized labour.

One area where labour and Vichy could agree was to raise very low wages. For the unions it was a question of defending workers against the escalating cost of living, while for the government it was to inoculate against communism and staunch the flow of labour to factories working for the Germans where the wages were up to twice as much. The law of 23 May 1941 permitted the authorities to increase 'abnormally low' wages but this required implementation at the local level. The animating force for labour in the Angers region was Raymond Déaud, leader of the tramway workers and secretary of the Maine-et-Loire union of unions. He presided over resolutions for a minimum wage from labour leaders at both a regional conference for the west of France in Rennes in July 1941 and a departmental conference in Angers the following November, which persuaded Prefect Roussillon to agree to a minimum wage of 1,000 francs per month or 5 francs 75 per hour for Nantes, though less for smaller towns in the region and women.[34]

The flexibility of the Vichy government on wages was at the end of the day a carrot to entice 'healthier' elements of the labour movement into accepting its Labour Charter, which was published on 4 October 1941.[35] The fight against communism would continue unabated, announced Interior Minister Pierre Pucheu, but officials were to try to end misunderstandings that had arisen between workers and employers and workers and the government, and 'avoid all propaganda that might depict the Marshal's government as reactionary and retrograde'.[36] The labour law, like most corporatist projects, was a massively ambitious redesigning of the architecture of industrial relations with the aim of eliminating both class war and rivalry between different trade union federations, notably the CGT and Catholic organizations. Its main provision was to establish a single trade union for each 'occupational family', merging employers, managers, white-collar workers, foremen and workers, locally, regionally and nationally. This would take some time to set up and in the meantime the collaboration of all these strata would be launched in each factory level in social committees which would deal not with running the business but with working conditions and welfare. The failure of Vichy in the long run to persuade workers of the benefits of the Labour Charter bears eloquent witness both to the weakness of a regime that was more authoritarian in theory than in practice, and to the vitality of the labour movement under the Occupation, a phenomenon that has hitherto been seriously underestimated.

The Labour Charter was a powerful challenge to organized labour. A minority of labour leaders saw it as a framework which they could either grasp in order to save the unions, or reject and risk annihilation. Foremost among the partisans of the Charter was Raymond Déaud, who from his base at the Bourse du Travail of Angers effectively served as the intermediary between René Belin and CGT leaders in the west of France.[37] For the 1941 conference of the Maine-et-Loire union of unions he brought in Marcel Roy, national secretary of the engineers' union, an anti-communist unionist close to Belin himself, to put the case for the Charter and 'a policy of involvement rather than one of abstention'. Déaud had a vision of a syndicalist state in which trade unionists would not only be free to build their labour empires but also participate in the political decision-making that had been the privilege of parliamentarians before 1940 and was now monopolized by bureaucrats. He challenged the 1943 conference of the Maine-et-Loire union of unions by asking, 'If tomorrow the trade union movement had the opportunity to send its representatives to the various assemblies responsible for running the country – and that without the trickery of political parties – would it not be well advised to seize it?'

Most trade unionists were suspicious of the Charter, however. They saw it as a trick by which all the gains they had made since 1936 could be rolled back. Catholic labour leaders feared that their separate organizations would be eliminated by the single union system. CGT leaders thought that it threatened the autonomy of trade unions that was consecrated by their own Charter of Amiens of 1906 and left no place for the local and departmental unions of unions based in the Bourses du Travail. The importance of local solidarity in the labour movement is underlined by the response of different industrial communities to the Charter. Saint-Nazaire, for example, responded in a quite different way to Nantes. This was mainly because of the stance of Marcel Blanchard, the former militant of 1936, and of his mentor, François Blancho, former socialist deputy and still mayor of Saint-Nazaire. Blancho attempted to negotiate a place for labour and working-class communities within the Vichy system at least until his resignation as mayor in May 1941 and even until he was required by Vichy, under pressure from the Germans, to move to the Free Zone in March 1942. Blanchard was singled out by more progressive elements in Vichy as a labour leader who had the confidence of the workers of Saint-Nazaire and, though a socialist, had helped to prevent those workers from falling prey to communism. The third member of the Saint-Nazaire team was Emmanuel Jouvance, secretary of the local union of unions and municipal councillor under Blancho, who was convinced that the labour movement was destined either to flourish within the framework of the Charter or die outside it. They paved the way for a high-profile visit to Saint-Nazaire by Regional Prefect Roussillon on 26 February 1942 at which representatives of employers, engineers, technicians and trade unions signed a solemn declaration in which they repudiated class struggle and committed themselves to 'the implementation of the Labour Charter at Saint-Nazaire in the spirit of union, loyalty and justice defined in the preamble to the law of 4 October 1941'.[38]

The labour movement of Nantes, by contrast, was hostile to the Charter. Communism was stronger there, thriving on the climate of fear and hatred caused by the execution of forty-eight hostages in Nantes and Saint-Nazaire on 22 November 1941.[39] Trade unionism was weak, with perhaps only 1,200 out of a possible 10,000 members, and the labour leaders saw opposition to the Charter as one way to build up support. Blanchard and Jouvance were unable to convince Auguste Péneau, secretary of the union of unions of Loire-Inférieure, that the Charter was the way forward. Péneau, nicknamed 'the fortress' by Jouvance, was sixty-four, a generation older than the Charter enthusiasts (Jouvance was fifty-three but Blanchard was forty, Roy thirty-nine and Déaud thirty-four) and wedded to the principles of the Charter of Amiens. Péneau scoffed,

> You make me laugh when you say that there will be no trade
> union activity when the Charter is implemented if we don't adopt

its machinery. I have already told you I would not give my little finger for it. Yesterday's trade unionism is sufficient unto itself. The workers must reject all collaboration with employers as required in the law. The role of shop stewards drawn from the union will be just as strong and sustained, indeed more so, when they operate independently as when they have to take account of the opinions of engineers, technicians, managers and even white-collar workers. I want to stay faithful to the trade unionism that has been our *raison d'être* and to which the workers are attached. In the future the workers will remember those who stuck to this system and did not seek for whatever reason to place trade unionism under government control. They will dump those who in any way forfeited their independence.[40]

For Jouvance, Péneau was a representative of Old Labour who was simply not alert to the requirements of the new order. In fact Péneau had a fine sense that the dogged attachment of the working classes to their old organizations and their deep suspicion of politics made the Charter's chances of success extremely small. Perhaps, far-sighted in his wisdom, he was also grooming himself for the end of the Occupation, when he would be elected president of the Liberation Committee of Loire-Inférieure, the local parliament of Resistance organizations.[41]

Whether in Nantes or Saint-Nazaire, despite the hard work of Blanchard and his team, the Charter remained a dead letter. The large shipyards and factories like SNCASO had still not set up social committees by the spring of 1944, and were reprimanded by Raymond Déaud in his capacity as emissary of the Social Committees Office.[42] One large plant where the social committee was given a fair trial was the main employer of the railway suburb of Saint-Pierre-des-Corps, the Compagnie Industrielle de Matériel de Transport (CIMT), which made rolling stock. The committee diluted shop stewards with representatives of fathers of large families, war veterans, young workers, female workers, categories which were suggested by the Vichy motto of Work, Family and Fatherland. When the social committee actually met in the spring of 1943, the shop stewards complained that their grievances had been rejected and that the director had told them that 'he would do what he liked and that if they didn't like that it would make no difference'.[43] As a result, when a new social committee was elected CGT unionists boycotted it and 80 per cent of the ballots were returned blank. The prefect of Indre-et-Loire concluded that 'the majority of workers in this important engineering works have made clear that they have no interest in the implementation of the Labour Charter'.[44]

The magnificent architecture of the single union scarcely ever got beyond the paper stage. Far from being 'single' the new unions never managed to overcome the traditional divisions of industry between different localities, Catholics and non-Catholics, employers and workers. Joseph Le Scellour, leader of the Catholic union of Trélazé, refused to join the 'single union' of miners on the grounds that it would be taken over by CGT if not communist elements dedicated to class struggle.[45] Under the Charter the single union was subdivided for each industry into four distinct unions of employers, engineers and managers, white-collar employees and foremen, and manual workers. At Nantes and Saint-Nazaire it was reported that attempts to set up these unions were undermined by the 'resistance' of white- and blue-collar unions.[46] Each union in the hierarchy had to draw up its own statutes which were officially endorsed and published in the *Journal officiel*. Since these publications were appearing right up to July 1944, it seems clear that few of them were functioning in any real way.[47] In the end even the administration seemed to lose interest in the Charter. Whereas early in 1942 Regional Prefect Roussillon had been on a tour of major industrial firms to urge support for the Charter, two years later the prefect of Loire-Inférieure, Gaudard, had more important things to do than attend the launch of the new unions. Invited to attend the inauguration of the single union of hairdressers on May Day 1944, he declined, and, although the hairdressers postponed the occasion until 22 May, he still sent his apologies.[48]

Securing the loyalty of the French peasantry was in theory a good deal easier for the Vichy government than winning that of the workers. The peasantry was regularly praised by Vichy as the backbone of economic life, defender of the patriarchal family and guardian of traditional values against the decadence and corruption of the cities.[49] Unemployed city youths were encouraged to return to the land both to relieve the shortage of labour suffered in the countryside because of the absence of POWS and to undergo moral regeneration. The underlying assumption was that in the work of national regeneration the peasantry, salt of the earth, led the way.

There was, however, a lesser-known Vichy discourse on the peasantry which expressed its exasperation with the peasants' reluctance to supply official markets with their produce and preference for either an autarkic economy providing for their own families and communities or lucrative black market activities. Regional Prefect Roussillon dug deep into the rhetoric of the French Revolution when he described them as *affameurs*, deliberately starving the industrial workers and small artisans of the towns, placing their private interest before the general interest. They were driven by a 'spirit of lucre', making 'undreamed of profits' and 'golden fortunes . . . Once the disinherited class,' he continued, 'the peasantry is now suffering the present hardships less than anyone else.'[50] Jean Chaigneau, prefect of Indre-et-Loire, went even further. He asserted that the peasantry were deliberately taking revenge on the urban population for the red peril of 1936 and the brief ascendancy of the urban workforce. Their 'engrained individualism' must now be replaced by 'the spirit of solidarity and mutual aid on a national scale'.[51]

The Vichy regime did not confine itself to criticizing the peasantry but developed a battery of officials and measures to bend them to the requirements of the national interest. Under Director-General of Supply Rouleau was a corps of Ravitaillement officials to ensure that delivery quotas were met, a hierarchy of economic control officials to enforce price controls and bring proceedings against those reaping illicit profits, and a gendarmerie which became increasingly involved in checking suspicious vehicles or raiding isolated farms in pursuit of black market activity in the countryside. One strategy adopted to fight the black market was to centralize the slaughter of livestock and the manufacture of dairy products in large abattoirs and commercial dairies, and to ban butter-making and slaughtering on farms. Another was to harness the support of the administration, the Church and the media for the 'battle of wheat', to ensure that stocks of grain were delivered to bridge the so-called *soudure* or gap between one harvest year and the next. In Loire-Inférieure, where the German presence was particularly dense and temptations to farmers correspondingly great, the subprefects of Saint-Nazaire and Châteaubriant toured the communes of their *arrondissements* in the spring of 1942 to urge the peasants to deliver their grain, and the new secretary of state for Ravitaillement, who had a reputation for tough talking, came in person to Nantes to exert further pressure.[52] Improved relations between Church and State under Vichy were used to persuade local bishops to exhort farmers via the diocesan weekly and the pulpit to hand over what remained of their grain stocks in the name of Christian charity.[53] Official communiqués appeared regularly in the press, farmers who had not met their quotas were named and shamed, and when articles critical of the government's punitive and incompetent supply policy appeared anonymously in the local press, the authors were tracked down and punished. In the case of *L'Écho de Paimboeuf*, the writer turned out to be a prominent defender of rural interests, Dutertre de la Coudre, a former deputy, mayor and *conseiller général* of Machecoul, but he was nevertheless reprimanded by the prefect of Loire-Inférieure and required to publish a recantation declaring his total loyalty to Marshal Pétain.[54]

Obviously the government had no alternative to adopting a tough stance against rural black market activities, but it is also clear that its policies did not cow the peasants and if anything made them more hostile, not to Marshal Pétain himself but to the administration in general and to the Ravitaillement in particular. After Prefect Chaigneau told the mayors of Indre-et-Loire that peasants must in future not kill pigs without informing the *mairie*, on pain of heavy punishment, he received a blast from someone who described himself as 'a true peasant':

> If the peasants are harassed this much one thing is clear, that in future they won't even bother to raise pigs. There is no law which can force someone to work if they don't want to so why should our wives squelch in manure if they are not allowed to send a lump of bacon to a son who is a POW or a married daughter who has left home and needs the extra to feed her family? If peasants were free to do as they wished things would be a lot better than they are at present, when we can't sell an egg or a rabbit without risking a prison sentence and the only freedom people have is to die of hunger. If the gendarmes start to raid farms to see what is going on, we haven't got guns any more but we have got forks. If you want peasants to do their duty then do yours first . . . back the peasants, don't bully them.[55]

The anger of the peasantry placed rural mayors in a difficult position. On the one hand they were supposed to be the agents of the government in the locality, no longer elected but appointed. On the other hand they were responsible to their local communities and that meant protecting the peasantry. The Marquis de Sesmaisons, mayor of La Chapelle-sur-Erdre outside Nantes and a leading figure in the agricultural organizations of Loire-Inférieure, told the prefect that he spoke for all the rural mayors in the department when he said that the rations and sanctions applied to farmers were ridiculous. In order to work the farmer should be allowed to 'eat as much as he wanted', not limited to a mere 350g of bread which was half of what he needed. In addition he should be allowed some autonomy in trading, the Ravitaillement and price controls should come down on 'flagrant and unjustified irregularities', but otherwise he advised to act with tact and discretion. Greater freedom, he suggested, would mean a more responsible and responsive attitude to the market on the part of peasants, not more autarky and black marketeering.[56]

The principal response of rural communities faced by repeated demands for meat, milk, eggs, potatoes, wheat and oats was a sulky non-cooperation. Mayors generally put themselves at the head of their discontented constituents and used the threat of resignation to devastating effect. Comte Henri de Champagny, a brilliant former soldier, the flamboyant mayor and *conseiller général* of Somloire in Anjou, who in the end was deported by the Germans, simply slashed the butter quota required from his commune from 375 to 50 kilos.[57] Jacques de la Grandière, mayor of Grez-Neuville and member of Vichy's Conseil National, said that the quota required of his commune was totally unjust. Why should they provide 75,000 eggs a year when a neighbouring commune of the same size was asked for only 9,000? 'That's it!' he told the director of Ravitaillement, 'I shall tell my constituents not to declare a single hen at the October census.' The Marquis du Puy, a keen hunter and mayor of Courléon, argued that the unfair size of his cattle quota compared with other communes made his position untenable and threatened resignation if it were not reduced.[58] Other less eloquent or well-connected mayors took refuge in stubborn silence. 'When he does not just refuse to execute orders,' the district Ravitaillement officer complained of one mayor, 'he indulges in a passive resistance by giving the impression that he knows nothing and can do nothing, a very easy way to slough off the duties of his office and refuse all responsibility.'[59]

The idea of 'passive resistance' to requisitions was greatly vaunted after the Liberation as a patriotic gesture. Since much Vichy requisitioning took place to meet German needs, farmers and farming communities were well placed to argue that autarky was patriotic. In Maine-et-Loire farmers refused to surrender their milk to the Maggi dairy company on the grounds that the butter made in the Maggi dairies was being used to grease the axles of German cars and lorries. Such silly rumours, the company told the prefect, was costing it 150 tons of butter a month, enough to feed 600,000 people.[60] There were in fact cases of the German authorities imposing collective fines on communes for non-fulfilment of quotas, and non-payment of these could equally be presented as patriotic. Gennes near Saumur was dealt a fine of 225,000 francs in 1943 for non-delivery of oats, which was shared out between twenty-eight farmers, but by March 1944 only eight farmers had paid a total of 20,000 francs and the mayor was trying to obtain credit from the state.[61] Patriotic the French peasants may have been, but in general they were acting on behalf of the *petite patrie*, that of their community or *pays*, rather than for the wider French *patrie*. It is significant that one of the areas most reluctant to deliver was the Mauges around Cholet. In 1793 the demand for conscripts for the revolutionary armies had triggered the Vendean revolt there, and 150 years later the same autarkic hostility was capable of driving the local peasantry to acts of violence against French officials in defence of their autonomy. The police noted that 'in the countryside, especially in the Cholet region, traditionally more refractory [than others], there was a marked particularist sentiment that war could provoke a will to resist government decisions'.[62] In the autumn of 1943 the authorities were complaining of 'a raising of shields' in the Mauges and a refusal to meet quotas of meat, milk and potatoes.[63] Early in 1944 there was a dramatic outbreak of violence in the Mauges commune of La Pommeraye, when two Ravitaillement officials who went to investigate a clandestine abattoir were accosted, accused of working for the Germans and threatened with reprisals after the war by an angry crowd of fifty people headed by the Catholic schoolteacher, a father of nine, and a winegrower who was the son of the mayor. As the officials left, the father was heard shouting at the crowd to puncture the tyres of their car. Intendant Ganot, head of Ravitaillement in Maine-et-Loire, asked the prefect for an exemplary punishment, both against the charcutier who ran the clandestine slaughter business and the leaders of the riot. 'The more difficulties Ravitaillement officials have to contend with,' he urged, 'the more authority they need to be given.'[64]

In fact, the more authoritarian the Vichy government became, the more rural communities resorted to isolationism and the black market. Fortunately Vichy had another instrument in play, the Peasant Corporation. Just as the Labour Charter was supposed to harness the working class to the higher goals of the national community, so the Peasant Corporation would restructure rural unions to bend farmers to the needs of the economy as a whole.[65] Corporative organization committees were set up at national, regional and departmental levels to organize one corporative agricultural union in each commune, each under the direction of a syndic, and then to marshal these unions into regional (in effect departmental) and national corporative unions, under their own regional and national syndics.

Unlike the Labour Charter, when the structures were implemented only to a limited extent, the hierarchy of the Peasant Corporation actually materialized quite successfully. The main question was whether it did the task set for it or not. At the annual meeting of 500 syndics from Indre-et-Loire at Tours in December 1943, which was due to elect a regional syndic, the national syndic, M. Pointier, with Regional Prefect Donati at his shoulder, told his audience that the Corporation must be 'the voluntary auxiliary of the Ravitaillement service'. 'It is up to us,' he continued, 'to make sure that quotas are delivered on time and not to leave this to the gendarmerie or the price-control bodies which have their own duties. The Corporation has one immediate interest: to ensure that an unbridgeable gulf does not open up between the urban and peasant populations.'[66]

The peasantry, however, had other ideas for the Corporation. In the first place farmers used it to seize control of agricultural unions, which had flourished since the end of the nineteenth century, from the large landowners. Henri de Champagny was a key figure in the Union Agricole de Maine-et-Loire and second in command of the regional corporative organization committee launched in September 1941 to develop the structures of the Corporation, but when the regional syndic of the Corporation came to be elected in Maine-et-Loire in 1942, he was defeated by Henri Dèze, an ordinary peasant who had won his activist spurs in the Parti Agraire of Henri Dorgères in the 1930s. His deputy, Eugène Forget, who was also close to Dorgères and had been a Parti Agraire candidate in Maine-et-Loire, reflected that 'this was the first time a peasant farming his own land had been elected to a position of departmental responsibility in an agricultural union. The least one can say about the Corporation in Maine-et-Loire was that it was decreed from on high but was the manifestation of free peasant opinion.'[67] Having taken over the Corporation, the peasantry made sure that it functioned less as an auxiliary of the Ravitaillement services than as a drag on its efforts. Henri Dèze lost no time in arguing for an end to the requisitioning of farmyard products such as eggs and poultry.[68] When Intendant Ganot stepped up fines for farmers who did not meet their quotas, Dèze conveyed to Regional Prefect Donati 'the anger rising amongst the rural population' in response to such measures.[69]

For all the threats, blandishments and restructuring of the Vichy government, the French peasantry was able to preserve much of its autarky and black market dealings. Punishments remained minimal, and of course only applied to the minority who were caught. In Maine-et-Loire a third of proceedings brought for price infringements were dropped, and only 15 per cent resulted in fines.[70] Fines for illegal slaughtering of livestock imposed on farmers, farm labourers and others (cattle-breeders, butchers, charcutiers, carpenters, and even a postman) in Loire-Inférieure ranged from 1,000 to 2,400 francs, which was very small beer.[71] There is plenty of evidence that fines such as those imposed by the Ravitaillement for non-delivery of quotas were not paid, 'covering with ridicule', said Prefect Tracou of Indre-et-Loire, 'both those who pay their fines and the administration'.[72] This was not only a question of inefficiency or incompetence on the part of the authorities. A balance had to be struck between the toughness urged by Intendant Ganot to ensure the authority of the public services and the discrimination and flexibility recommended by the Marquis de Sesmaisons to retain the cooperation of the peasantry. Commenting on a demonstration provoked by the arrest of three people accused of clandestine slaughtering for domestic consumption, not for the black market, the police chief of Tours argued against the 'excessive zeal' of some Ravitaillement officials which risked provoking serious incidents intended to 'put [the officials] in their place'.[73] The district chiefs of the Ravitaillement in Maine-et-Loire were advised by the prefect to 'reconcile the imperious needs of the Ravitaillement with the susceptibility of the mayors and their constituents'. They were to use persuasion, reminding peasants of the hunger suffered by townsfolk, and only then brandish the threat of judicial proceedings. In a word, they should be 'both forceful and subtle'.[74]

There was one other reason why the black market was never stamped out. The authorities, while mainly doing their duty to the best of their ability, were also caught up in the loop of corruption and crime. This seems to have been increasingly the case towards the end of the Occupation. When Frédéric Brémond, baker at Chalonnes-sur-Loire, was investigated by the local gendarmerie for black market acquisitions of wheat, one of the gendarmes pointed out that he was a valuable informer and it would be best if the authorities treated him leniently.[75] The Atlantic coast was even more like the Wild West. M. Hery, the district Ravitaillement chief of Guérande on the Breton coast, went native on the issue of clandestine slaughtering. He took the simple view that rations were not sufficient and that people should eat, not least those doing hard work for the Germans. He was said regularly to have given verbal permission to slaughter animals, assumed 'the air of a benefactor of the local population, and simply made up his own policy'.[76] Nearby at La Baule it was reported that a gendarme and two inspectors of the economic control service were frequently seen having free drinks at the bar of the Café Ramet, where they were on excellent terms with the landlord, and where the waitresses were involved in a substantial black market trade in cigarettes. Further inquiries suggested that economic service officials regularly ate with the tradespeople they were supposed to be inspecting at Nantes and Saint-Nazaire, and that the private gains available to those in authority far outweighed the benefits of doing things by the rules.[77]

At the end of the day the Vichy government was never as authoritarian as it pretended to be, both because it had to come to terms with vested interests, and because it was riddled by corruption. In addition, its attempts to control the economy in the national interest failed because it was unable to fulfil the task it set for itself to supply markets and because it was seen by too many sectors to be unjust. Parallel circuits of supply sprang up which the government attacked as selfish black marketeering. In fact, these circuits had distinct advantages: they balanced the supply of distant markets at a profit with the supply of local markets at a fair price, and they kept resources out of the hands of the Germans unless the Germans were prepared to offer black market prices. This defence of local and trade interests was reflected also in Vichy's attempts to set up corporative economic interests in the national interest. Although a few trade unionists saw the Labour Charter as the blueprint of a syndicalist state, most saw it as a threat to trade union organizations which survived under the Occupation and Vichy and which they were not prepared to jeopardize. By contrast the majority of the peasantry went along with the Peasant Corporation, but only because they managed to bend it to their own local and professional interests.

6. CIRCUSES

André Roussel is a dapper man, with swept-back grey hair and a clipped moustache, more suggestive of a barber than a rock star. Still living in Bléré, the small town near the demarcation line where he grew up, he reminisces about what young people like himself did under the Occupation. He left school at the age of fourteen in 1940 and worked in his father's grocer's shop six days a week. His contemporaries, he says, also started work young and wanted, come Sunday, 'to have a bit of a good time'. There were not many distractions. The Pagoda cinema, only open at weekends, was for family entertainment and children went with their parents. There were billiards at the Café du Chalet and ping-pong at the Café du Commerce, but the Café de la Ville was full of ageing card-players. The youth of the little town divided into age groups, each with its own meeting place, where they ate and played records at weekends. The older ones met at the old mill, the middle ones (of whom André was one) in a barn, the younger ones somewhere else. Sunday night was dance night for the older and middle ones, who each had their separate dances. André played the accordion for the middle ones, in a small band which had no name but whose drummer was called Quick. Generally they danced in a large cabin in the forest of Amboise, otherwise they found a barn belonging to one family or another. They were a tight-knit group, eight boys and eight girls, who all knew each other and had nothing to do with outsiders.

The most significant thing about the dances was that they were illegal. The Vichy government took the view that France was in mourning after her defeat and that so long as families were deprived of their loved ones in POW camps merry-making was to be banned. Dances took place in secret and news of an event was passed on by word of mouth, not unlike the contemporary rave, says André Roussel, though on a smaller scale. 'We were more afraid of the French gendarmes than of the German customs officers' who patrolled the demarcation line, he points out. The Germans were concerned only with security and 'couldn't care less, seeing that we weren't terrorists', whereas 'the gendarmes would have caught us, had they been able to'. They had lookouts posted on the road and 'when there was the slightest alert we turned everything off, just like in the Indo-China war [where he fought after 1945], we pretended not to know each other and we dispersed'. Defiance of the authorities, however, had nothing to do with the Resistance for André. He was, he says, completely apolitical. 'As a shopkeeper,' he explains, 'my father belonged to no party and neither did I. That is the best way. A shopkeeper must only ever listen to his customers' family news, and nothing else, if he wishes to keep his clientele.' Moreover, the world of the young people and of those he repeatedly calls 'the partisans' were completely divorced. Once just before the Liberation they decided to hold a dance in the street in the village of La Touche, but the 'partisans' (as he calls them) arrived in the area and started firing, so they scattered. 'I didn't know any partisans,' he asserts, 'I never went around with them, never associated with that lot.' He was, he repeats, 'only eighteen and the only thing that interested me was going out with girls and playing the accordion'.[1]

At the time, it is clear, the Vichy establishment was far more concerned about the morality of young people than about their politics. One veteran of two wars wrote to the prefect of Indre-et-Loire to complain of young people smoking on the streets of Tours. 'German officers have told me how surprised they are to see the practice tolerated, and I share their opinion entirely.' He also complained that schoolchildren of both sexes were cutting classes and going to the cinema on weekday afternoons, 'their books and papers under their arms'. The head of education in the department (who incidentally would become prefect at the Liberation) agreed that something had to be done about young people's idleness and the 'harmful refuge' they found in the back rows of cinemas.[2] Prefect Chaigneau responded by banning under-eighteens from cinemas on weekday afternoons, but clearly believed that more would have to be done to discipline their behaviour. 'The mentality of young people is still a cause for anxiety,' he reflected a few months later. 'They have a critical, sceptical and intolerant attitude that is fairly typical of that age together with a serious lack of moral sense and civic spirit. They let themselves go both physically and intellectually and are suspicious or scornful of the few among them who display energy and faith.'[3] Some of those few, who were involved in Catholic and lay youth movements, were told by the delegate of the Ministry of Youth in Touraine that the vices of young people included not only watching unsuitable films, but drinking too many aperitifs – in defiance of the prefect's ban of under-eighteens frequenting cafés without their parents – and reading pornographic magazines, which were still on sale in the kiosks of Tours despite a ban which the police seemed to have no interest in enforcing.[4]

One question that needs to be asked is what kind of associative life functioned under the Occupation. According to the account of André Roussel, there were few distractions and young people were obliged to fall back on entertaining themselves. To some extent he was correct. A youth club at Bléré run by former members of the Jeunesse Ouvrière Chrétienne (JOC), called the Artistic Cricket, was authorized by the French authorities in 1942, but another one, called Arts and Youth, was turned down the following year on the grounds that one such society existed already.[5] At Amboise, less than 10 kilometres away, in the autumn of 1940, there was L'Étoile, a popular education and sports society open to children over twelve, a ping-pong club at the Café du Château for boys over fourteen, and a cycling club based at the Café Belle Vue for boys over sixteen. Youth clubs or *patronages*, the main function of which was to keep young people off the streets, were attached to the schools, both the municipal lay *patronage* and the Association Saint-Denis for Church school pupils, both over 200 strong. For those interested in music there was the Amboise Municipal Band (36 men, 1 woman and 19 children) and the Amboise Philharmonic Society (18 men and 8 women). Mutual aid societies which flourished in the years before the Welfare State included the Amicable Association of Military Medal Holders, the Amboise 'Solidarity' based at the Café Desmazeau (men only) and the Amboise Amicable Association of State and Department Civil Servants, which was mixed. There were charitable organizations like the Association of Notre-Dame of Perpetual Grace, which numbered 110 women, and the Amboise Association for Free Assistance to the Poor Sick, run by fifteen men. Finally there was a gardening or allotment club, the Petit Jardinage Amboisien, the like of which became extremely popular under the Occupation as hobby converged with the benefits of an additional source of food.[6]

The pattern of associations, dedicated to sport, games, gardening, music, mutual aid and charity, was repeated with variations across all the towns of the region. In the railway suburb of Saint-Pierre-des-Corps, up the line from Amboise and Bléré, the biggest association was the mutual aid organization of the CIMT railway workshops, with 745 men and 28 women members. The CIMT also had a fishing club with 446 members, all male. There were a number of sporting clubs aimed at young people, from the Étoile Sportive Notre-Dame, for over-nines, and the Étoiles de la Médaille, for over-thirteens, to the Étoile Cycliste, based at the Café de l'Univers, with 120 members over fifteen. The Églantine football club, for youths over fifteen, seems to have acted as a cover for communist activity. One peculiarity of the town, which reflected the influx of immigrant labour into the railway workshops, was the presence of cultural associations for foreigners – the Masaryk Association for Czechs, about which the Feldkommandantur wanted to know more, and the Prosvita Ukrainian Association, which was closed down by the prefecture.

In Saumur, the only association for outsiders was the Cloucado del Soulel, founded in 1926 for French southerners, though the Protestant minority also had their own Benevolent Society run by Protestant society ladies. The literary pretensions of the town were indicated by its Society of Letters, Sciences and Arts, founded in 1910, aping that founded in Cholet in 1880, and the Society of Agriculture, Sciences and Arts of Angers which claimed to go back to 1685. There was more diversity among the sporting clubs than at Amboise, with a Saumuroise Athletic Union, started in 1903, for gymnastics, shooting and military training (now banned), a women's gymnastic club and a tennis club founded in the 1920s, and three cycling clubs, a rowing club, a rugby club, a road-walking club and an aeronautical club, all set up in the 1930s. Alongside these rather English-style and elitist clubs were more popular clubs devoted to 'boules, billiards and cards', with a particular enthusiasm for the Angevin version of boules de fort or crown bowls. One club where Saumur blazed a trail in 1929 was the Rallye Cor or hunting-horn society, for which the members dressed in hunting pink. It was copied by the elite of Cholet three years later, blending with its

Horse-racing Society presided over by industrialist and mayor Alphonse Darmaillacq and the Rural Hippomobile Society, formed to counteract the pernicious influence of the car. What otherwise characterized Cholet was the rash of associations set up to defend Catholic education, including the influential Catholic Association of Family Heads under the presidency of industrialist Bernard Pellau-mail, and the various veterans' associations differentiated by rank, class of recruitment or theatre of action. Though dominated by industrialists, Cholet was firmly committed to Catholic and military values in society.[7]

Such a survey, combined with what we know about trade-union activity and agricultural organizations, suggests that the French did not spend the Occupation cowering in their homes or too suspicious of their neighbours to cooperate socially. Civil society flourished, independently of any commitment to Resistance activity or otherwise. Of course, not all these associations were fully active in the autumn of 1940: many were undermined by the absence of their activists who were mobilized for the war and often then removed to POW camps. They also functioned under rules laid down by the French and German authorities, which were highly bureaucratic if not restrictive. But the Germans and the Vichy government did not have the same objectives, and the clash of those objectives often opened spaces in which associative life could blossom more than it might otherwise have done.

The obsession of the Germans was military security. No organiz-ation or movement that threatened the Wehrmacht could be allowed to stand. The German ordinance of 28 August 1940, which governed French associative life, prohibited the wearing of any uniforms or insignia as a way of eliminating paramilitary as well as military organizations. All processions were banned, and that included the traditional rag procession with floats of the *gadz'arts*, the students of the technical École d'Arts et Métiers at Angers.[8] Sporting organiza-tions were permitted so long as they were registered with Vichy's Commissariat for Physical Education and Sport, but sporting events charging entry required permission from the German authorities. Cultural organizations had to be registered, and in 1941 the Feld-kommandantur of Tours was concerned about an organization called the Future of the Proletariat which advertised a meeting at the Café de la Concorde in the local press. The panic did not die down until the police made clear that the society was 'essentially philanthropic and humanitarian' and did not discuss politics.[9] Theatrical and musical events also required permission from the German authorities, and the text of any play, song or libretto to be performed had to be submitted in advance for censorship to the Propagandastaffel. Public libraries were ordered to remove any anti-German works and report action taken to the military administration. For some reason the Bibliothèque Saint-Michel at Angers saw fit to take *Mein Kampf* off the shelves.[10] The curfew was used to ensure that no threat could be posed to the army under cover of darkness and restricted social life in cafés, restaurants, cinemas, and at dances and weddings. Where there were any security incidents the curfew was brought forward for a matter of days or weeks.

The concerns of the Vichy government were somewhat different. Security was not so important except in the case of the threat from communist activity which was aimed as much against the Vichy regime as against the Germans. Vichy was convinced, for example, that the Églantine football club of Saint-Pierre-des-Corps and the Nantes branch of Amis de la Nature to promote camping for workers were communist fronts.[11] The overriding policy of Vichy, however, was the moral regeneration of the French nation, by means of the National Revolution, to cure the ills which had led to defeat in 1940 and to pave the slow way to recovery. France had dropped out of the war. It was allowed an Armistice Army of 100,000 men, the same as the French had allowed the Germans after 1918, but after the Germans invaded the Free Zone in November 1942 even this was dissolved. Regeneration was thus to be not military but moral. Selfishness was to be replaced by dutifulness, decadence by discipline, individualism by community spirit, division by unity.

One of the main instruments of national regeneration for Vichy was the Légion Française des Combattants.[12] It was an alternative to a fascist party, considered far too revolutionary for the Vichy Old Guard, and brought together and replaced rival organizations of veterans in the name of new-found union. As a movement of veterans with banners, berets and uniforms, the Germans considered it a military threat and banned it in the Occupied Zone. In our three departments, the only place where it functioned was the unoccupied south-east sector of Indre-et-Loire centred on Loches. There it was founded by Dr Abribat, vice-president of the Touraine Poilus, and on 4 May 1941 the 1,300 legionnaires, drawn up on the place Verdun at Loches, in the presence of the mayor and his council, the 31st Infantry Regiment, the Compagnons de France, scouts, school-children and *patronages*, received their colours from General Auguste Laure, inspector-general of the Legion, and took the oath of loyalty to Marshal Pétain.[13] Although the German authorities banned the Legion in the Occupied Zone, they infuriated the Vichy regime by recognizing the four main veterans' movements that Vichy had dissolved in favour of the Legion, so long as they held no meetings, avoided politics and set up no military or sporting organizations.[14] At Saumur, the local branch of the National Union of Disabled, Discharged and Former Servicemen (UNMRAC) tried to exploit this loophole by coming 1,000 strong to lay wreaths at the war memorial on Armistice Day 1940. The row that ensued was not with the Germans but with the Vichy regime which argued that the veterans' organization was defunct under French legislation.[15] Interestingly enough, when nearly three years later Colonel Canon Panaget, the president of the Anjou section of the National Union of Combatants (UNC) and just back from a POW camp, wished to set up a Maison du Combatant in Angers along the lines of the Maison du Prisonnier, Regional Prefect Donati raised no objection because of the great prestige enjoyed by Panaget as a veteran of two wars and his ambition to link the men of 1939–40 with those of 1914–18.[16]

Two other militaristic organizations that the Germans refused to countenance in the Occupied Zone were the Chantiers de Jeunesse, which were camps for twenty-year-olds who would normally be doing military service, and the Compagnons de France, who were volunteers under twenty participating in land reclamation, forestry, harvesting and building sports fields.[17] The rather paltry equivalents promoted in Occupied France by the General Secretariat for Youth were Rural Youth Centres set up in a few requisitioned châteaux to put delinquent youths from Paris to work on agricultural projects in the hope that some might remain on the land. So sensitive was the German military administration that it ordered the closure of two of these camps, one of which was sited near the Breton coast, as security risks, before being persuaded that no possible threat existed.[18] But neither did the centres do much in the way of moralizing French delinquents or promoting the return to the land. Youths sent there thought only of how to escape. André Garnier, aged seventeen, was recaptured twice by the gendarmerie of Baugé after he got away from the centre of La Roussière and tried to return home to his mother in Angers. André Célarié was luckier, managing to escape from the same centre after a fortnight and make it to the Free Zone.[19] As for local farmers, they were predictably extremely reluctant to accept assistance from urban delinquents at the centres, which became a prey to other Vichy agencies keen to turn them into farm schools for the sons of peasant families who were already committed to the land.[20]

For the National Revolution to succeed, the motivation had to come spontaneously from existing organizations. Scouting was one of those paramilitary movements banned in the Occupied Zone, not least because the Germans suspected it of having English connections.[21] The fact that most scouts were under the wing of the Catholic Church and lay scouts numbered about a tenth of these did not seem to impress them. However, if scouts were good at one thing it was secrecy. They camouflaged their summer camps as *colonies de vacances*, hoisting the tricolour flag and lighting camp fires when Germans were at a safe distance. When the British and Americans began to bomb French ports and cities, they metamorphosed into Équipes Nationales which served as one of the emergency services, pulling victims from the rubble of buildings and administering first aid. In one sense too they had the last laugh. The 3rd Angers troop under Pierre-Yves Labbe founded a sea-scout group which had itself authorized as a sailing club. Then, in August 1944, as the Americans approached Angers, Labbe sent his lieutenant Louis Bordier over the small, ill-defended Pont des Pruniers to meet them and take the Germans in the rear.[22]

The largest and most influential instrument of national regeneration was without doubt the Secours National. Although not founded by Vichy – it was set up in 1915 and revived by the Republic on the outbreak of war in 1939 – it was given new powers under a law of 4 October 1940 to coordinate all agencies 'helping civilians afflicted by the war and its consequences'. Most important, it was given 'exclusive authority to make and permit public fund-raising', which gave it immense resources and the power effectively to dictate to all charitable organizations. The Secours National was a vast charity monopoly which launched waves of fund-raising such as its winter campaigns every November to collect food and clothing for evacuees, bomb victims, wives of POWs, the unemployed and low paid. 'Solidarity coupons' were on sale everywhere, in theatres, concert halls, cafés, restaurants, wine shops, schools and on the street. It was also a highly effective instrument of propaganda, less perhaps for the Vichy regime than for Marshal Pétain himself. The Secours National laboured under his 'high patronage', and sales of postcards of Pétain both raised money and stimulated the cult of personality. The target for sales in Indre-et-Loire in the winter of 1940–1 was 300,000, hardly less than the population of the department, and a year later the bishop of Angers claimed that each of his 100,000 church attenders had one.[23]

For the Secours National fund-raising and propaganda were important in themselves but always at the service of a wider aim, to restructure French society around the principle of solidarity. A reserve army captain, manager of a business at Niort but passing through Angers, was scandalized one cold February morning in 1941 to witness the 'selfishness' exhibited at the place Lafayette market. 'There was complete panic around the stall of a charcutier,' he told the prefect, 'with customers fearful that they would not be served.' To offset this kind of attitude he proposed a 'kindness week' that would weave together the bonds of social solidarity torn asunder by the struggle for survival. On the first day women and girls would take fruit and puddings to the sick in hospital, on the second men would take wine to gentlemen in old people's homes, on the third and fourth young people would have a collection for orphans and children would bring them sweets, and on the fifth and sixth days all Angevins would raise money for municipal charities.[24] Far from being treated as dotty, this suggestion was taken up by the prefect who called initially for a 'kindness week' in March, then simplified it to three days: a Day for Children, a Day for Families, and an Old People's Day. The main headache was not the appeal but obtaining lists of families who were hard up but not normally in receipt of charity. This involved close cooperation with the Catholic Church, which was far more knowledgeable about this sort of thing than the prefecture.

Fortunately the Secours National was not run by prefects but by departmental delegates assisted by action committees of representatives of the Church, charitable organizations, education, industry and agriculture. There were also Secours National delegates in each *arrondissement*, canton and even commune. The departmental dele-gate in Maine-et-Loire was Colonel François de Sauvebeuf, a Kipling-esque figure who had been educated by the Jesuits at Tours, trained at the Cavalry School of Saumur, and after he retired from the army in 1920 tried his hand variously at running a peat farm, a stud farm, and working for an oil company. His undistinguished professional career was amply compensated by his accumulation of the honours of notability in Anjou. By 1940, at the age of sixty, he was vice-president of the UNC under Colonel Panaget, secretary of one of the three Red Cross societies, that of the Military Wounded, and vice-president of the Society of Agriculture, Sciences and Arts of Angers. More controversially, he had joined the Croix de Feu of Colonel de la Rocque, a paramilitary organization of decorated soldiers of the Great War which was highly critical of the parliamentary Third Republic, and became president of the local Parti Social Français, the reactionary if not fascist party that replaced it after 1936. There is no doubt that de Sauvebeuf was a vigorous and effective head of the Secours National in Maine-et-Loire, but his political activity was to prove his Achilles heel as far as the German authorities were con-cerned.[25]

The activities of the Secours National were rich and diverse. It collected, sorted, mended and distributed large amounts of old clothes – over 80,000 articles of clothing in Maine-et-Loire in 1941. It took over the supervision of the Mutual Aid Kitchens of Angers, a network of nearly a dozen food *guichets* and cheap restaurants usually run by nuns, from the night shelter in the old Doutre quarter and the Brisepotière refectory for industrial workers from outside Angers who could not get home for lunch, to the Foyer de l'Ouvrière in the rue Pasteur which was intended as a safe haven for shopgirls, female office workers and women students. Some people could pay, while others had free or half-price vouchers. Many of the restaurants also served as school canteens, the poorer children having free lunches paid for by the municipality. Nearly 5,000 meals a day were served in November 1941 and the number was rising. In the winter of 1941–2 many more middle-class people, experiencing difficulties finding food themselves, turned to the kitchens.[26] For children, the Secours National supplied vitamin-enriched biscuits and sweets to schools, 41 tons of them in Maine-et-Loire alone in the winter of 1941–2. For working families, it developed allotments which were in extremely short supply, and distributed seeds and seedlings for vegetable growing. Last but not least it helped to organize summer camps and Christmas parties for children and Mother's Day celebrations to reward women who were doing their patriotic duty by raising large families. 'In a word,' concluded Colonel de Sauvebeuf, 'we want to found a school of generosity which will bring together as pupils all French people and happily replace the monstrous school of selfishness in which they have been educated for so many years.'[27]

The Secours National was a veritable engine of social solidarity, one of the most successful institutions of Vichy, although its hegemony did not go unchallenged. It had a reputation of being Catholic, bourgeois and right wing. Colonel de Sauvebeuf's first office had been in the house of the cathedral canon who had preceded him before his death in 1940, and stalwarts of the Angevin organization included such Catholic notables as Pierre Poisson, a commercial lawyer, his cousin Francis Poisson, vice-president of the Saumur Chamber of Commerce, and Joseph Le Sciellour, leader of the Catholic trade unions in Angers. Sauvebeuf tried to remedy this situation, seeking for example to add a representative from a 'left-wing union', but this never came off and the 'clerical complexion' of the organization was criticized even by Vichy government officials, from Interior Minister Darlan downwards, who feared an anticlerical backlash.[28] The affair of the contaminated biscuits in Maine-et-Loire illustrates ways in which opponents of Vichy reaction were able to exploit hostility towards the Secours National. Rumours began to spread that the vitimin-enriched biscuits distributed to schools by the Secours National were in fact contaminated by the tuberculosis bacillus, and parents began to stop their children accepting them. The rumours were whipped up by *Le Petit Courrier*, which was ostensibly the official organ of the prefecture, and Prefect Roussillon was forced to publish communiqués dismissing the rumours as totally unfounded.[29] The damage done to the authority of the Secours National was nevertheless considerable. Sauvebeuf himself was highly vulnerable as the local leader of the Parti Social Français, which became suspect to the Gestapo as anti-German. He was arrested in March 1943, deported to Germany, and died in Flossenberg in October 1944. After his disappearance the Secours National of Anjou never really recovered its direction.

One of the dilemmas faced by the Secours National was what

constituency it targeted. Its brief, to attend to the totality of the civilian population hit by the war, was impossible to fulfil. It did its fair share of good deeds for the traditional poor, but increasingly became obsessed by the new middle-class poor. One delegate in Touraine drew the attention of his superiors to 'the critical and profoundly sad situation of people living on small private incomes' from property or stock, which had lost value since the First War let alone the Second. He said that to offer help to these people was 'extremely delicate since they were accustomed to living comfortably and had never begged'. One case thrown up was a commercial traveller with nine children, who lost his job when the firm employing him collapsed in 1940 and became ill, but who as a house-owner was not entitled to benefit; the Secours National gave him 5,000 francs to cover his tax arrears.[30] In Angers concern was expressed that 'women white-collar workers of irreproachable morals and excellent appearance' had been driven out of the Foyer de l'Ouvrière restaurant by workers and tramps, and that a new respectable restaurant should be set up to serve them.[31] A preference was developed for helping the genteel poor back to independence and respectability rather than encouraging dependency among the traditional poor, who were rarely grateful anyway for what they were given. When Marie-Louise Poirier of Cholet complained of the 'swindle' by which she had been asked to pay 50 francs and contribute ten textile points from her ration book for what she called 'rags' from the Secours National, she was told that her attitude revealed 'a mean ingratitude and a marked hostility towards an organization of national solidarity', and that any further defamation would trigger judicial proceedings against her.[32] This patronizing attitude only confirmed to the underclass that they were not the first concern of the Secours National.

Although it could not possibly meet all its commitments, the Secours National antagonized other charitable organizations by rigidly defending its monopoly status. At meetings of the commission set up in Loire-Inférieure to approve all fund-raising events for POWs, the delegate of the Secours National antagonized the prisoners' organizations by voting against all requests to organize fund-raising events, on the grounds of the Secours National's formal monopoly of fund-raising. The fact that this authority might be delegated in practice to other charities was never considered.[33] This imperialistic attitude increasingly alienated other charitable and even public bodies which missed no opportunity to assert their own autonomy. For Christmas 1943 the Secours National of Touraine planned a single big party for all the children of evacuees, POWs and workers sent to Germany. But POWs' organizations, the employers of *La Dépêche du Centre* newspaper and the mayors of numerous communes insisted on having their own private parties and the principle of unity was shattered. Not surprisingly, Secours National fund-raising schemes to help those hit by Allied bombing and evacuated to less exposed regions met with concerted resistance. Not content to solicit charitable donations, it went over to a system of thinly disguised taxation. Traders in Touraine asked to contribute a fifth of the value of the patent tax they paid to the government coughed up only 6 per cent of what was demanded, many arguing that peasants, starting with the wealthiest winegrowers of Touraine, were now much richer than they were. These farmers were also asked for a sou (5 centimes) for each hectare, but despite letters to the rich winegrowers underlining 'the imperious duty of solidarity towards your co-citizens afflicted by the war', not one in twenty of them paid up.[34] Of course Touraine was a predominantly radical area on which the grip of Vichy was limited, but such opposition revealed significant fault-lines in the edifice of social solidarity.

Solidarity required from above was one thing; solidarity promoted spontaneously from below was another. The French needed no encouragement to get together for sport, culture or entertainment, where necessary in defiance of the rules imposed by Vichy and the German authorities. They were also able to exploit the contradictions between the Germans' priority of military security and Vichy's concern with moralization.

One of the great passions of French country life was hunting. A privilege confined to the nobility on horseback during the *ancien régime*, the practice had been democratized since the Revolution, and every Frenchman with a permit duly delivered by the *mairie* was entitled to stride out with his gun and shoot game. For security reasons the Germans could not tolerate this licence: orders were given that all firearms were to be handed in at the local *mairie* on pain of the severest penalties. Some guns were wrapped up in cloth or leather, hidden, buried or sunk to the bottom of ponds, but hiding a gun made an individual vulnerable to denunciation by a resentful neighbour or even a spouse, and was not undertaken lightly. In the autumn of 1941 the Germans realized that to turn town halls into arms dumps was also risky and required mayors to hand over their stocks to safe sites like the Caserne Blucher at Tours, where 11,000 weapons fetched up. While they were about it, they ordered any remaining firearms to be handed in, and the mayor of Bléré reported that he had received eight hunting rifles, five revolvers and fifty-two cartridges.[35] Earlier on the Germans showed no concern for weapons of merely historic interest such as muskets and blunderbusses, but in the spring of 1942 they demanded even these, together with swords, sabres and bayonets.[36] Such were their doubts that all weapons had been handed in that in August 1943 they declared an amnesty for any firearms still to be declared, and one mayor reported that he had taken to the Blucher barracks '1) a rifle without a butt; 2) an old pistol in poor repair and 3) an old musket'.[37]

Without their guns the French were unable to hunt and the privilege reverted to the German military, which was only too happy to indulge its taste for sport on its own terms. Touraine, with the forests of Amboise and Chinon, teeming with the wild boar and deer the French were not allowed to touch, was particularly attractive, and Dr Herbig in Tours served as the Germans' hunting officer. Herbig in fact liaised with the president of the Hunting Federation of Indre-et-Loire, the Baron de Champchevrier, and its secretary and treasurer, Louis Théret, an accomplished gamekeeper with indispensable knowledge of local game. The result was that the Germans issued licences to hunt to a few dozen individuals, such as the Baron de Champchevrier and the Comte de Blacas of Rigny-Ussé, effectively restoring the hunting privileges of the nobility abolished 150 years before. At the same time they allowed these landowners' gamekeepers to carry guns in order to combat poaching. Some hunts involved Germans and Frenchmen together, a form of collaboration that Frenchmen were reluctant to admit after the Occupation.[38] But in 1942 the mayor of Chênehutte-les-Tuffeaux complained that not enough Frenchmen with guns were permitted to go on a Franco-German boar hunt: only one had a gun whereas what was really needed was 'twenty-five or thirty good hunters', knowing the paths, and armed.[39] It should be added that the German military applied their own hierarchical rules to their own men, issuing permits to select officers and NCOs but never to ordinary soldiers.[40]

While this return to privilege was fine for French nobles and

German officers, it led to the same complaints as before 1789 from peasants about fields being overrun and crops spoiled by rampaging boar and plagues of rabbits. One concession won was that farmers were allowed to catch rabbits with ferrets, dogs or traps, but the Germans tended to take the view that French stories of plagues of wild animals were much exaggerated.[41] However, even the Germans could not put a stop to poaching, which for the French had become less a question of sport than of survival. When the carcass of a deer was found in the forest of La Ferrière in Anjou, the Germans threatened to impose a fine of a million francs on the village, until the subprefect of Segré persuaded them that the animal had been shot by ordinary German soldiers who had run off. Years after the Occupation it transpired that the deer had indeed been killed by Frenchmen, but from outside the commune.[42] Elsewhere hunting – or poaching as it was now called – went on more or less unimpeded. At La Pommeraye, where the Ravitaillement officials were to be accosted in 1944, there were 'nocturnal safaris' with the aid of guns hidden or provided by an obliging gendarme from Montjean. One night they returned at 4 a.m. with a bag of eighteen hares.[43]

While hunting was formally under strict control, fishing was less so, except for the close season for spawning between mid-April and mid-June. As with hunting, it became a necessity as well as a sport, as the number of workers in fishing clubs like that of the CIMT at Saint-Pierre-des-Corps demonstrates. The problem with fishing, however, was that there was a shortage of stock. In 1941, responding to pressure from the local fishing organization to allow fishing exceptionally on Sundays and public holidays during the close season to supplement meagre rations, Prefect Roussillon issued an order conceding this so long as the catch was used only for family consumption and not sold. But he was immediately overruled by the Ministry of Agriculture, which took the long-term view that fish stocks had to be preserved however hungry people were, and he was forced to withdraw his instructions.[44] The German authorities were also concerned by stock shortages, not least because they allowed ordinary soldiers to fish, and the issue of security came into play too. In 1942 the Feldkommandant of Angers required the prefect, notwithstanding the decrees of the French Ministry of Agriculture, to issue a regulation prohibiting night fishing from or near bridges, saying that the prefect of Indre-et-Loire had already obliged.[45] Such restrictions did not apply to German soldiers, who did not care for the traditional art of rod and line but blew the fish out of the water with grenades from motor-boats. One veteran of the French occupation of the Palatinate after 1918 said that French soldiers doing the same thing there had been punished by their commanding officers and that this 'vandalism' and 'piracy' must stop. Prefect Roussillon wrote to the Feldkommandant to protest, but received no answer.[46]

The Germans had no objection to sporting activities which involved no possible security risk, whereas the Vichy authorities might be more difficult. Horse-racing continued as a sporting and social event, as we saw at Chinon. The POW support committee of the small town of Noyant planned a race meeting in the summer of 1943, to which the German authorities agreed. But for reasons best known to itself the Ministry of Agriculture decided that henceforth race meetings in Maine-et-Loire would be permitted only at Angers and the downstream scenic centre of Rochefort-sur-Loire, and turned down the request from Noyant.[47]

Every spring and summer saw a rash of local cycle races: three times around Angers on 2 March 1941, sponsored by *Le Petit Courrier*, Angers to Saumur and back on 22 May 1941, organized by the Angevin Pedal Club, and the Grand Saint-Léonard Prize on 1 June, awarded to the winner of seven circuits of the village of the same name. As far as these harmless cycle races were concerned, the German military authorities decided in May 1942 that they had no interest and that French prefects should grant permission.

The only thing that stood between the French and their enjoyment of football was occasional German crassness. The ironmonger who ran the Saint-Pierre *patronage* in Nantes complained that their first championship match against an Angers team had to be called off because the Germans had requisitioned their football ground.[48] But the Parc des Sports at the Malakoff Stadium in Nantes seems to have been a veritable mecca of sport. On 7 December 1941 a rugby match between the Stade Nantais UC and the Paris Post Office workers was followed by an amateur football match between the Western League and the South-west League, both events attended by the prefect. In July 1943 a festival of gymnastics and physical education was held at the stadium, organized by the Anjou committee of the Gymnastic and Sporting Union of French Youth Clubs.[49] Meanwhile, at the Bessonneau Stadium of Angers on 27 June 1942, in front of the prefect delegate, police intendant, head of education and a crowd of 6,000, 1,500 athletes from all over Maine-et-Loire took the 'oath of the athlete' to Marshal Pétain.[50] Sport, and in particular athletics and gymnastics, corresponded to the Vichy ideal of a healthy mind in a healthy body and to the virtues of fitness, individual prowess and teamwork.[51]

The Vichy regime devoted a great deal of time and effort in providing structures for young people which would educate them in morality, duty and patriotism. Just as each department had a delegate of the Secours National, so also it had one from the General Secretariat of Youth which was supposed to coordinate and promote initiatives for young people. These delegates faced an uphill struggle, however. Teachers, clergy, Catholic youth organizers and even municipalities resented the advent of these cocksure newcomers on their patch, the more so because they suspected a hidden agenda of forging a single national youth movement along vaguely fascist lines. H. Biessy, Vichy's departmental delegate in Touraine, accused all these agencies of variously trying to sabotage his efforts. He tried to put in place a network of correspondents in each canton, a team of clean and energetic youth leaders on whom he could rely, but even where these were up to the task they resigned or were drafted for labour service in Germany. The only organization that offered support, he said, was the small Francist movement, which grouped young men of fascist inclinations, but Biessy was the first to confess that 'it is difficult to argue in favour of the educative value of such a movement when all they ever do is write on walls'.[52]

Nevertheless, the most difficult problem they faced was the attitude of young people and the alternative entertainments open to them. One of the manias of the Occupation was theatre-going and some of the plays put on raised the eyebrows of Vichy traditionalists. M. Goupil de Bouillé, a member of the administrative commission of Indre-et-Loire, objected to a play called *We Are Not Married*, put on at Bourgueil by the Charles Baret theatre company at the invitation of the lay youth club. Much of it took place in an artist's studio where a scantily clad model disported herself, and M. de Bouillé saw the whole thing as an apology for free love. 'Allow me to point this out in my capacity as departmental delegate of the Rural Family and president of the cantonal committee of family organizations,' he told the prefect. 'I am certain that you will not allow the Marshal's moralizing programme to be flouted in this way.'[53] The teacher responsible for allowing the play was duly reprimanded. On the positive side, the best way to promote moral and uplifting fare was to sponsor the classical theatre. A touring company called the Revival, directed by Christian Casadeus, spotted an obvious gap in the market. He secured the patronage of Ferdinand de Brinon, Vichy's ambassador in the Occupied Zone, and finance from the Education Ministry to bring the plays of Molière and Dumas to a string of provincial towns. He dreamed of reaching all audiences, with matinees for young people and private performances for workers organized by firms' social committees, but he still had to reckon with the fact that some municipalities were only interested in commercial productions that would maximize returns.[54]

Meanwhile, plays were produced on a vast scale by schools, youth clubs, Catholic youth movements, sports clubs and factory social committees, partly as entertainment, partly also to raise funds either for their own activities or for good causes like the support of POWs. Most of the plays, playlets and songs were comic, sentimental or harmless, but their content still had to be approved by the German authorities, which after mid-1942 meant the Sicherheitspolizei. The formality of the German police certainly created a rod for its own back: between August and December 1942 it processed 284 requests to perform plays and concerts in Indre-et-Loire alone.[55] Most of the hard work, to be fair, was passed on to the Propagandastaffel, which must have been intensely boring. In a large file of plays, songs and libretti which passed through its hands at Tours the only red pencil mark crossed out the phrase 'American chic' from a song about a moustache.[56] The Germans blew hot and cold when some French flags were draped on the stage for a performance of the unavoidably patriotic *La Fille du régiment* at the municipal theatre of Angers in 1942, but other political references eluded them altogether. The Jesuit Collège de Saint-Grégoire put on Péguy's *Jeanne d'Arc* at the municipal theatre of Tours in May of the same year. When Joan reached the phrase, 'We must boot the enemy out of France', it is said that the audience rose to clap while the Germans present only sat bemused.[57]

More sensitive than theatres from the German point of view were cinemas.[58] In this golden age of the cinema there were five cinemas with a total of 4,500 seats in Angers, six with 4,300 seats in Tours and nineteen with 11,500 seats in Nantes.[59] The largest cinemas had 1,000 seats and, teeming with young people on a Saturday night, could be a security risk. The German authorities required cinemas to register but they did not care what films were shown. Trouble tended to occur during the projection of newsreels which were basically German, Italian or Vichy propaganda. In the darkness the audience could express its opinion anonymously by cat-calls, stamping, coughing, applause and even shouting. The German authorities insisted that the French come down heavily on miscreants. They regularly closed or threatened to close cinemas where incidents had taken place, and where they prosecuted individuals the sentences were generally tough. For example, André Tallourd, a young carpenter arrested in October 1940 for a disturbance during a German newsreel at the Athenée cinema in Saint-Nazaire, was prosecuted by the French authorities only for drunkenness, whereas Roger Morel, a young optician of Le Mans, was sentenced by a German military court to two years in prison for applauding the bombing of a German hospital by the RAF.[60] After the outbreak of hostilities with the Soviet Union the Germans became even more tense. The Feldkommandant of Tours ordered newsreels to be shown in half-lit houses in order to expose demonstrators, and stern warnings to be issued to audiences about the consequences of subversive behaviour. In March 1943, after the audience at the 1,000-seat Majestic cinema of Tours had coughed all the way through footage of Pierre Laval making a speech in support of French workers going to Germany and laughed at a shot of a German soldier removing a 'No Entry' sign on the demarcation line, the German police arrested seventy young people and closed the city's cinemas for a week.[61]

Obviously the Vichy authorities could not sanction criticism of Laval, but the main concern of the Vichy establishment was not anti-German sentiments but immorality. Not all cinemas were at risk. In Loire-Inférieure, where the Church and Catholic family movement was strong, 60 per cent of cinemas were parish-based, owned by the Catholic *patronages* or youth clubs and generally called the Familia. The clergy leased their premises to travelling projectionists and retained complete control over what was shown.[62] Influencing what went on in commercial cinemas was more difficult. Jean Briand, president of the Jeunesse Ouvrière Chrétienne in Loire-Inférieure, complained in July 1941 that seven out of the ten films currently being shown in Nantes undermined the virtues of hard work, family dignity, female modesty or masculine pride. He had recently passed a suburban cinema on a Thursday afternoon, when the schools took a holiday, and witnessed the supervisor of an after-school club taking nine-year-old girls to see *The Maltese House*, 'a film as immoral as you can get, sadistic, humiliating of women, ridiculing marriage, preaching free love, and finishing with suicide'.[63] On a few occasions the Catholic lobby was able to influence the authorities. In 1942 Dr Yves Bureau, president of the Family Associations in Loire-Inférieure and a frequent lobbyist, prevailed upon the mayor of Nantes to ban admission to the under-twenty-ones to one particular film. He was concerned that when the film opened children as young as twelve had been to see it and quoted a survey which said that working-class youths under sixteen liked violence, and over sixteen sex. 'The cinema unhinges young people,' Dr Bureau observed. 'They spend a restless night after the film. The next day they do nothing but dream and talk about what they have seen. Some of them imitate gangsters and finish up before the juvenile court.'[64]

One of the points made by Dr Bureau was that censorship in the Occupied Zone was paradoxically far laxer than that in the Free Zone. Over 200 films banned in the latter continued to be shown in the former. This was because the German authorities had the upper hand, wanted no meddling in their censorship, and were more exercised by cat-calls in cinemas than by sex. When the French courts fined a cinema owner in Maine-et-Loire 6,000 francs for not having a permit, the German authorities said than the man was registered with the Propagandastaffel and ordered proceedings to be dropped.[65]

The same contrast between the German and Vichy authorities was clear when it came to dancing.[66] The Germans imposed a curfew for military reasons and from time to time gave permission to hotels or restaurants to stay open late for a wedding. But in June 1941 they formally ceded responsibility for the supervision of dancing to the French authorities, who were more than keen to exercise that power. When the Kreiskommandant of Cholet issued a spate of licences to hoteliers and café owners allowing weddings and other family parties to continue beyond the curfew, he received a rap on the knuckles from the subprefect who made it clear that the business of the Germans was only closing times, while permission to allow the dance or not attached to French sovereignty.[67] French policy, introduced during the war of May–June 1940 and developed by Vichy, was that so long as France was in mourning for its defeat and the absence of its loved ones in German POW camps, concentration camps or German factories, modesty and decency should be cultivated and dancing banned.

There was a brief window after the Armistice when it was assumed that dancing would be allowed to revive. Owners of cafés, restaurants and hotels were keen to re-open their dance floors and boost their clientele. The Vichy authorities, however, reiterated that public dancing was prohibited. In Touraine there was a wave of petitions, from 'a young woman who loves dancing', denying that balls were 'places of debauchery but somewhere one can have fun gaily and freely, without another thought', from a group of 'young people who want to make the most of being twenty', and from fifty youths who, taking the altruistic tack, said, 'We are working with all our heart and with all our strength for the speedy recovery of our country. We hope that you will understand us and reward our labours by allowing the dance floors to re-open very soon.'[68]

For a while the Vichy authorities were prepared to allow private dances. In April 1941 prefect Chaigneau of Indre-et-Loire was giving permission for dances at marriages on the grounds that 'if a dance takes place at a private house it is impossible to prohibit it'. But two months later, after a so-called private dance in the village of Reugny was crashed by 300 people, he told the mayor that no more dances at all would be allowed.[69] Prefect Roussillon of Maine-et-Loire was moving in the same direction. In September he told Mireille Gense of Coutures, who requested permission for a dance at her wedding which would be 'an entirely family occasion and no more than the little bop [*sauterie*] usual on such occasions', that both public and private dances were formally prohibited 'for reasons of decency that you will readily understand'.[70] The following July Roussillon clarified his policy for the region.

Given the grave circumstances which require a dignified and reserved attitude from all French people and render it impossible to tolerate public behaviour which is misplaced merrymaking and flouts the country's state of mourning, it is decreed that on the territory of the five departments of the Angers region all public and private dances, noisy or rag processions, singing or licentious behaviour on the public highway, all music that can be heard outside, whether by loudspeaker, jazz band, gramophone or radio, are and remain forbidden.[71]

The effect of these regulations was simply to drive dancing underground. The craze grew, and the authorities noted a veritable explosion of dancing in the summer of 1943. Prefect Delegate Daguerre of Maine-et-Loire was obliged to reissue the ban, and told his mayors that even Marshal Pétain was concerned about 'the upsurge of clandestine dances, especially in the countryside'. He himself had observed the spate of dances, organized by café owners, hoteliers and private individuals 'in isolated houses, barns, and even on the main squares of certain villages or hamlets. I will not dwell', he added, 'on the shocking character of such merrymaking at a time when hardship afflicts so many families. Only too often women whose husbands are in POW camps are persuaded to dance, a scandalous state of affairs which demoralizes the prisoners who get wind of it.'[72]

The amount of clandestine dancing that went on is a fair indication of the limits of Vichy's National Revolution. Since it was clandestine it is impossible to quantify with any accuracy. Dances were raided by the gendarmerie who tried to make arrests and submitted reports. The gendarmerie of Vernantes on the Touraine border of Maine-et-Loire, for example, unearthed four clandestine dances involving up to eighty people there and in the neighbouring commune in the Christmas–New Year period 1943–4 alone.[73] But what they discovered represented only the tip of the iceberg. A well-dressed young man picked up on the road at Chanceaux, just north of Tours, early one morning in June 1943 turned out to be an agricultural labourer who had just slept over at a dance and had been to one the previous Thursday and another the Sunday before that. 'They take place nearly every Sunday,' he said, reeling off the names of the farms, 'either at La Boulas, or at La Hardinière, or at les Rentries.'[74] As for André Roussel of Bléré, he asserts that he and his friends were never caught by the gendarmerie. Undeniably there was a complete subculture of clandestine dancing, which has left little trace in the records.

This dancing was first and foremost an expression of youth culture. Of course it may be seen as a political statement in that it was banned by the Vichy authorities, but breaking the curfew can scarcely be called resistance. The Occupation nourished political awakening, but it also stimulated political indifference, escapism and hedonism. The young people born in the aftermath of the Great War were not prepared to see their youth ruined by another war. Opportunities for amusement in the countryside were limited. 'Just when the return to the land is being preached,' two young men told the prefect of Indre-et-Loire, 'all entertainment is being totally abolished. Can peasants go to the cinema? Do they play *boules* or cards at their age? Of course not. That is why we are asking you to permit dancing at least for a few hours on Sunday afternoons.'[75] At its most basic, dancing was the obvious release for young people who worked in the fields, shops or workshops six days a week. Sometimes it was part of the ritual observed by twenty-year-olds about to leave on military service or, when that was suspended under the Occupation, about to go to Germany as labour conscripts under STO, or to celebrate their return. The frenzy of dancing increased at Christmas and the New Year, but also around 14 July which was traditionally marked by dancing in the streets yet was a commemoration heavily discouraged by Vichy. Although the sale of food and dancing were strictly banned at parish patronal festivals or *kermesses*, they were generally tolerated by mayors, and the derisory level of fines made the gendarmerie virtually powerless.[76]

Dancing, food, drink and money went easily together. André Roussel argues that drinking did not take place at clandestine dances, although afterwards the dancers sometimes retired to drink in an isolated limestone cave and once he had to bring a legless friend home in a wheelbarrow. If dances took place in barns or farmhouses, the parents or uncles of the dancers were generally involved and often took the opportunity to earn some money. Dancing was a good cover for black market activity. As the gendarmerie of Longué, near Saumur, surprised a clandestine dance in a barn, over 100 young people scattered, leaving a table groaning under bottles of wine and a 50-litre barrel, drunk to the last few litres. The owner, Auguste Josselin, aged seventy, confessed that he had organized the dance with his thirty-one-year-old son Maurice, charging the boys an entry fee of 20 francs, the girls 10 francs, and selling wine for 40 francs a bottle. The gendarmes were delighted to charge him not only with organizing a prohibited dance but with selling liquor without a licence.[77]

One representative of the Vichy regime thought that clandestine dances, put on with the consent of their parents, was just another example of how spoiled the young farmers were in Touraine. On the one hand, he said, were the disinherited class of agricultural labourers, woodcutters and carters, on the other the sons of winegrowers and farmers who were often only children destined to inherit a very profitable concern. 'The child has no respect for old age, infirmity or suffering,' he argued. 'Religion and Country are for him vague notions which disappear under the weight of egoism and the increasing desire for comfort. From children who are never denied anything we get a youth which thinks only of pleasure and of every pleasure: new clothes and clandestine dances more numerous than ever.'[78]

Let the last word be left to the curé of Nouzilly, 10 kilometres north of Saint-Pierre-des-Corps. One night in April 1944, as the Allies bombed the railway yards as part of their campaign to destroy the German military infrastructure before a seaborne invasion, his parishioners were dancing at a wedding which gradually sucked in more guests and went on all night. Did they rush to join the emergency services? Were they encouraged to join the Resistance? They came out of the dance to watch the fireworks in the night sky and then went back to dance until dawn. 'While unfortunate victims were dying under the bombs,' bemoaned the curé, 'these ignoble people continued their insanity. Where is this mentality going to lead us? To certain perdition.'[79]

Associative life and civil society thus flourished under the German Occupation more than has often been imagined. Sometimes it was encouraged by Vichy, through the Secours National or its various attempts to organize, educate and moralize young people. Just as often, however, it was an expression of youth subculture that challenged the 'boy scout' morality of the regime. Sometimes, as with hunting, handpicked Frenchmen and Germans enjoyed themselves together, but hunting for ordinary people was illegal and no different from poaching. Theatre and cinema newsreels could be used as vehicles for anti-German statements, but much sport and entertainment went on that did not have a political spin. The range and variety of camaraderie and merry-making demonstrated eloquently that much of ordinary French life continued under the Occupation.

7. DEMONSTRATORS

Liberation came early to Loches in southern Touraine. On 12 July 1940, to be precise. The German troops who had occupied the town three weeks before left, and there was a riot as people tried to get their hands on petrol stocks left behind before the French gendarmes arrived. By the afternoon everything was ready for the theatricals, and the inhabitants hung tricolour flags from their windows as General Mouton led the 32nd Infantry Regiment of the Armistice Army into the town. The soldiers were drawn up in the main square, the French flag was run up, medals were awarded and a wreath laid at the war memorial. 'Loches is no longer occupied!' ran the headline in the local paper.[1]

The reason for the liberation was not armed struggle but diplomacy. It was discovered that under the fine print of the Armistice, Loches should be in the Free Zone, and after consultation at the Armistice Commission in Wiesbaden, German forces withdrew. This incident betrayed some of the confusion of the early days of the Occupation, but it was a confusion that did not last for long. People, goods and even letters were not allowed to cross the demarcation line without permission from the Germans, although the flow could be turned on or off like a tap in order to put pressure on the government at Vichy. In the early days, when the German military was in control of the border, things were often quite relaxed. La Haye Descartes, right on the line, became a kind of frontier town. French and Germans mingled in the cafés. On one occasion the French stood up to sing the *Marseillaise*, took the Germans' revolvers and would not return them until they had stood up to sing too, fists in the air. On another the barn of a saddler called Théo caught fire, but it was on the wrong side of the line and the Germans would not let him through without a pass. Théo was so abusive that they gave in, and French and Germans put out the fire together. Then Théo opened a barrel of wine on the pavement and the local vet remembers seeing 'French and Germans returning arm in arm to La Haye, singing with the saddler who was still abusing the Germans, reminding them of Verdun where he had fought and of their defeat in 1918.'[2]

In February 1941 things were tightened up. The military on the line were replaced by professional customs men who had dogs and motorcycles and took their job extremely seriously. One person was shot that month, but the usual penalty for anyone caught crossing the line was a month's imprisonment in Tours.[3] Many who crossed the line were making a bid for freedom: men who managed to escape from POW camps when they were still located in France, others who wanted to continue the fight by joining the Armistice Army in North Africa, or Jewish families fleeing persecution. In January 1941, when Franco-German relations were going through a bad patch, a rumour spread that the Germans were about to conduct a census of all men between the ages of eighteen and forty-five, with a view to holding them hostage, and there was a rush for the line before the idiocy of the rumour was exposed.[4] It should not be forgotten, however, that just as many people wished to cross the line the other way, *into* Occupied France. There were refugees who had fled before the German armies in 1940 and were not allowed back into the so-called Forbidden Zone of north-eastern France.[5] There were soldiers who had been demobbed in the southern zone and wanted to get back to their families. There were young men whose applications to join the Armistice Army had failed and who fetched up penniless in Tours, treating the prefecture as a kind of consulate.[6] Finally there were businessmen who wished to visit the Paris Trade Fair in September but did not want then to find themselves stranded. These came, not walking long-distance from Marseille, but in coaches from Châteauroux which made regular trips right up to the line.[7]

In theory most of them could make the journey legally with a pass or *Ausweis*. But these were difficult to obtain from the German authorities and deliberately rationed. *Frontaliers* living on the line found it easier to obtain passes, as did professionals such as priests, doctors, midwives and vets. This explains the extraordinary activity of André Goupille, the vet of La Haye Descartes, who had a high reputation among the line-crossing fraternity as a reliable contact and received a large postbag of letters from satisfied clients. One father from the Pas-de-Calais who sent money to his daughter in Toulouse via Goupille told the vet and his wife 'how sweet it is in our distress to find sympathetic hearts which beat not only in time to ours but above all especially in a Christian way, which is much rarer at the present time'.[8] But for every angel like Goupille there were a dozen con men like Roger Audebert, a mechanic from Tours who gave up his regular job for the more lucrative one of *passeur*, asking 200 or 400 francs per person (Goupille said the standard rate was 50 francs per head) and then not even taking them to the line but dropping them short, so that many had to turn back. Whereas Goupille was arrested by the Germans in January 1942 for passing letters and spent five weeks in prison, Audebert was arrested as a swindler two months earlier by the French police at Loches and interned.[9] Goupille was always quick to thank the farmers near the line who kept him informed about the position of customs men. But his task and the chances of his clients were not helped by the odd black sheep like Sidonie Bichet, a farmer's wife from Courçay, who was said by other farmers in the village to have scanned the demarcation line from the top of her house with German binoculars, shouting if she saw anyone suspicious to her daughter who would then cycle to the nearest customs post. Her husband was a POW in Germany and she even took one of the customs officers, Herr Walter, nicknamed 'Fil de Fer', as a lover.[10]

The vast majority of French people who fell under the German Occupation of course stayed put. Family ties, jobs, studies, friendship or community networks gave them no alternative. The Occupation, as we have seen, contracted the horizons of most people and rooted them even more firmly in their localities. Survival and sociability, bread and circuses, became their main obsessions. That said, they had to habituate themselves to the presence of the Germans, in their streets, in their places of entertainment, even billeted in their homes. Some worked for the Germans, traded with them, flirted, slept with or informed them; others made sure that they had as little to do with them as possible. The vast majority of course resented their presence, but were powerless to do anything about it.

Some angry and fearless young people, in the immediate aftermath of the Occupation, refused to see it as definitive and, perhaps taking de Gaulle's appeal of 18 June at face value, dreamed of resistance. In the autumn of 1940 the eldest son of Louis Ancelin, the magistrate of Saumur who had 'saved' the town in tense negotiations with the Germans, led a group of youths between the ages of sixteen and nineteen who met in secret in the surrounding countryside to set up a 'clandestine militia'. They had found some weapons abandoned by the retreating French army and planned to attack the Germans in the rear when they retreated, which they imagined would be fairly soon. When Subprefect Robert Milliat got wind of this escapade he summoned Procureur Ancelin to his office. The magistrate was 'extremely annoyed' and promised to 'admonish his son severely'. Milliat then called in young Ancelin and his group and warned them that their activities were not only useless but dangerous, exposing their families and the populations of the Saumurois to 'terrible reprisals' from the Germans. While young Ancelin was sent away to board at a college in Cholet, Milliat reported to the prefect that he feared the youths were being manipulated by English agents. The prefect, for his part, veered between verdicts of childish behaviour and a foreign plot before settling on the reasonable theory that 'We are looking at impetuous young people who are irritated by the oppressive atmosphere of the Occupation.'[11]

Young people soon learned that any kind of military resistance was out of the question. Not only was the balance of force totally stacked against them, but the German strategy of massive reprisals was a powerful disincentive. One alternative was to draw on the battery of commemorations and festivals around which the identity of the Republic and nation was constructed: 14 July, Armistice Day, or Joan of Arc Day. The Germans, exercised by the needs of military security, banned processions, parades, badges and tricolour flags in the Occupied Zone. They also held the Vichy authorities responsible for maintaining order as a condition of involving them in indirect rule. Some kind of symbolic gesture on these key anniversaries, however, was a way for French people to reach for a moment beyond their narrow communities or material concerns and re-create the identity of the Republic and nation. On some of these occasions the Vichy authorities would be holding their own ceremonies, within the limits of the German law, in order to broadcast the regime's values of Family, Work and Fatherland. The strategy of protesters was thus to defy German bans as far as they dared, and to subvert or reclaim official ceremonies for an alternative set of values: Gaullist or communist. At the end of the day it took very little to make a patriotic statement: a tricolour buttonhole, a slogan or sign chalked on a wall, a wreath laid with a message. Such gestures were a nod and a wink to every other patriot, weaving the gossamer of the French Republic and nation together in a virtually invisible way. Similarly, only a minimum of imagination was required to jolt the leaden message of Vichy ceremonies and put a more playful one in its place. The battle for hearts and minds took place in a world of codes and symbols. But the symbols were supercharged and the stakes were high. By the end of the Occupation it was as easy to be arrested for a buttonhole as for a bullet.[12]

Traumatized by defeat, and four days after parliament voted full powers to Marshal Pétain who promptly abolished the Republic, few French people in 1940 were in a mood to mark 14 July, that celebration of the republican nation. Even in the Free Zone, at Loches, there was only a 'sad' little ceremony at the cemetery, where the mayor and municipal council laid a wreath in honour of the dead of two wars.[13] In the Occupied Zone the German high command prohibited the flying of the national flag or the singing of the *Marseillaise*, and in Loire-Inférieure the prefect decided that although there would be a public holiday, no ceremonies would take place.[14]

By Armistice Day on 11 November some of the shock had worn off and the French were beginning to chafe under five months of occupation. Edmond Duméril, interpreter at the prefecture of Loire-Inférieure, noted that the Germans had 'an extraordinary fear of demonstrations', and the twenty-second commemoration of their own defeat in 1918 was more than they could stomach.[15] No ceremonies were allowed, not even religious services, nor was the laying of wreaths at war memorials, even by isolated individuals. Even more than the generation that had fought the war, it was the young people who wished to express their outrage. In Paris, students openly defied the ban by processing down the Champs-Élysées, where German military paraded daily. Many arrests were made, and students sent before courts martial received prison sentences.[16] The movement also spread to the provinces. In Nantes, university students made common cause with the the students at the Lycée Clemenceau and the Lycée de Jeunes Filles, and tried to organize a school strike on what was to be a Monday. Attempts were made to lay wreaths at the imposing war memorial close to the prefecture, but the way was barred by French municipal police and the Feldgendarmerie. Scuffles broke out on the steps of the Théâtre Graslin, where some students started to chant the *Marseillaise*. They had their identity cards confiscated and had to go to the Kommandantur to retrieve them.[17] Most spectacularly, the previous night a university student, Michel Dabat, and a sixteen-year-old schoolboy, Christian de Mondragon, climbed the tower of the cathedral and tied a tricolour flag to the lightning conductor. The next morning huge crowds gathered to gawp and pass comment as firemen struggled to find a way to bring the flag down, news of the exploit spread 'like a powder-trail', in Mondragon's words, all over Brittany, and was even greeted as an act of resistance by the BBC.[18]

The Feldkommandant of Nantes promptly called for the Lycée Clemenceau to be closed down. Prefect Dupard had a difficult task to persuade him to change his mind and then summoned the headmaster to impress on him the need to restore discipline and combat Gaullist propaganda. On the positive side, he told the Interior Minister, the only group susceptible to Gaullist propaganda were the students, and 'everywhere I have been able to satisfy myself that the immense majority of the population venerates Marshal Pétain, approves his decisions and is infinitely grateful for his efforts'.[19] Even the students were not uniformly Gaullist. Mondragon recalls that as he asked around among his friends for a flag some offered help, others immediately made themselves scarce, and a third group asked him what he wanted it for. He says he expected the whole town to be decked with tricolours, and only wanted his to be the highest.

The protesting students may have been a small minority, but they certainly unsettled both the German and Vichy authorities. The absence of a commemorative excuse did not deter them. Early in 1941 a graffiti campaign of anti-German slogans began in Angers, targeting buildings occupied by the Germans. Under pressure from the Feldkommandantur Prefect Roussillon published an 'appeal to the population', especially young people, saying that if the daubing did not stop 'there would be regrettable consequences for the population at large, notably collective reprisals'.[20] On the night of 13 March, however, a new campaign began – the 'V' sign for victory, often accompanied by the cross of Lorraine which had become dear to Lorrainers after their annexation in 1871. The Feldkommandant of Angers immediately saw this as Gaullist propaganda and ordered the owners of buildings where these signs had been daubed to remove them at once; Roussillon was instructed that the French police must work closely with the German police to track down the culprits.[21] But the campaign spread. The police commissioner of Saumur reported that 150 'V' signs had had to be erased in his district. Meanwhile the craze spread to Nantes, where 'V' signs and Lorraine crosses appeared from 23 March, first in chalk, then in paint. The speed with which they appeared, said the police chief, is explained 'not only by the ease with which they can be drawn but by the rebellious attitude [*l'esprit frondeur*] of young people who are convinced that they will not be caught'. The police doubled their surveillance, arresting three students painting graffiti on the prefecture and charging them for defacing a public monument, then catching three adolescents drawing a 'V' on a shop front and sending them home with a caution.[22] The night of 29 March, however, was particularly bad. Feldkommandant Hotz told Prefect Dupard that 'V' signs had appeared all over Occupied France the previous night, 'clearly in response to a single order from the enemy. 'This anti-German propaganda', he insisted, 'cannot be tolerated in any way'. He held the prefect responsible for removing all the signs within forty-eight hours, on pain of severe reprisals. Prefect Dupard duly sent orders to subprefects, the police and the gendarmerie to complete the clean-up operation by 2 April at noon. He told the mayor of Nantes to mobilize teams of unemployed with buckets, the head of education to instruct head teachers to lay down the law in their schools, and other mayors that 'such goings-on are nothing to do either with courage or with patriotism. It is not by drawing on buildings that the French will contribute to national recovery.'[23]

This circular from Prefect Dupard admirably illustrates the gulf of understanding between the Vichy regime and the young patriots. For Vichy the National Revolution was intended to restore a moral order to wash away the sins which had brought about the catastrophe of 1940, including the disobedience and hedonism of youth, but renewing the war against Germany was not part of the agenda. For some young people the restoration of national dignity could only come about through a patriotic upsurge, brushing aside the old elites who were themselves to be blamed for the failure of 1940. This divergence of approaches was clearly evident in the commemorations of May Day and Joan of Arc Day in 1941.

May Day, since the 1890s, had been the day on which the labour movement flexed its muscles, demonstrated proletarian solidarity and stated its demands.[24] Now the Communist Party had been dissolved, the labour movement was losing members, and class conflict was to be replaced by class harmony. The Germans took no chances, banning all meetings and processions, but the Vichy government was also worried that the Communist Party would try to stage a come-back, spreading tracts, sabotaging industry, organizing demon-strations and even launching a general strike. To combat this, security was tightened up and Marshal Pétain was to broadcast reassuringly to factory workers at 5 p.m. Not only was work the first element of 'Travail, Famille et Patrie', but 1 May also happened to be St Philip's Day. There were some incidents. When May Day dawned in Nantes a red flag, decorated with the hammer and sickle, was discovered flying from the flagpole at the war memorial.[25] One communist tract picked up denounced attempts to appropriate May Day by 'Philippe Pétain, that senile old man and pretender to the throne', but was no more complimentary to de Gaulle, who was accused of wanting to drag the French into 'an imperialist war for the benefit of Anglo-Saxon capitalists'.[26] Leaflets and bills called for a general strike but work continued as normal: Prefect Dupard was with the workers of the Ateliers et Chantiers de la Loire to hear Pétain's speech, while the subprefect of Saint-Nazaire visited the SNCASO aeronautics firm.[27]

In Angers, the Employers' Federation of Anjou organized a 'Festi-val of Work and Social Concord', the high point of which was a Mass celebrated in the cathedral, presided over by the bishop and attended by all the town's dignitaries. In his address Canon Pinier of the Catholic University of Angers reminded the congregation that 'the maxim of social concord, which is so necessary to build a harmonious city, is also a law of the gospel'.[28] In the afternoon there was a large sporting event at the stadium, and the police were delighted that the 'extreme left-wing' Églantine sports club of Trélazé had attended and that there had been no incident.[29] What became clear, however, was that the Gaullists too tried to appropriate May Day. The order from the BBC was that at 6.30 p.m. people should make their way into the town hall in silence, wearing tricolour ribbons or rosettes if they so wished. Eye contact alone would carry the message of mutual recognition and hope. Moving singly or in groups of two or three, it was a demonstration that was not a demonstration. In Nantes those on the move were young people and women taking advantage of the closure of shops and schools, so that the scene looked 'exactly like what happens in the rush hour in the city centre. Nothing was said, there were no shouts,' reported the prefect, with the result that neither the French nor the German police intervened.[30] In Angers also it was remarked that the crowd was made up of young people, mostly students, four of whom with tricolour ribbons were taken to the police station to check that they were not communists. It soon became clear, confessed the police chief, 'that these young students belonged to Catholic families and were in no way communists. They told me that they were royalists and that they had come to the demonstration that was due to take place before the Town Hall for purely patriotic reasons.' Not communists, not even really demonstrators, certainly smarter than the police, they were released.[31]

Maybe the Vichy authorities cursed the plethora of public holidays in May, for within ten days they had to deal with Joan of Arc Day. No doubt Joan of Arc was easier to handle than the festival of labour: canonized in 1920, declared a national heroine in 1921, she was the official as well as the Catholic patron saint.[32] The only danger was that she would be portrayed as a military heroine who expelled the enemy from French soil. Wary of this, the German authorities banned all processions, although they permitted the laying of wreaths at the foot of statues of Joan of Arc, which were part of the public furniture of most French towns. Church services were held, attended by Vichy officials and notables, which presented Joan as an inspiration to moral rearmament rather than to military glory. In Angers cathedral, Mgr Costes underlined Joan's 'superhuman energy' and 'incomparable purity', and invited the faithful 'through the intercession of Joan of Arc, to pray for the courageous energy and austere practice of purity which are necessary to rebuild our dear country'.[33]

The authorized version of bishops and prefects did not however go unchallenged. At Bléré, on the demarcation line, during the night of 10–11 May preceding Joan of Arc Day a swastika flag was removed and a tricolour bearing a Lorraine cross hoisted to the top of a poplar tree. The Feldkommandant was clear that the perpetrators must be young Gaullists, although the mayor argued that the culprits must have come from outside the commune, probably from the Free Zone.[34] During the afternoon following the official wreath-laying in Angers many private individuals discreetly laid wreaths with messages such as 'Protect France', 'Ever faithful to Saint Joan, the country's liberator', and 'Boot them out'.[35] A secret Gaullist organization in Nantes called the Sons of France left the first wreath by the statue of Joan of Arc, a huge one with a patriotic banderole, which officials in vain tried to cover up with their smaller wreaths.[36] Crowds also carried wreaths to the graves of six British airmen in the cemetery of La Gaudinière, outside Nantes, who had been buried the day before. The Feldkommandantur considered this anti-German provocation, and told the prefect as much. The cemetery was closed, but a crowd of fifty young women, arriving with their wreaths at 6 p.m. to find the gates shut, began to shout 'Long live de Gaulle! Down with the Boche!' until French police moved them on.[37]

It was becoming clear by the summer of 1941 that the dissident network included not only male students from the faculties and secondary schools but also female students and women from outside the education system. The female fans of British airmen who made their mark at the cemetery of Nantes were not an isolated example. Gisèle Neau, a girl of eighteen from the outskirts of Saumur, was prosecuted for her part in the 'V' sign and Lorraine cross campaign and fined 10 francs, although her father was held civilly responsible as she was a minor. A thirty-seven-year-old Saumur housewife, Jeanne Barbault, was sent before the public prosecutor for distributing tracts written in pencil attacking Marshal Pétain and Prime Minister Darlan, as was a widow, Jeanne Brouiel, who had been to a photographer in Saumur to order 100 prints of General de Gaulle.[38] The opposition movement was also spreading from towns to villages and from middle-class secondary school students to working-class students of the Écoles Primaires Supérieures (EPS). After 'V' signs appeared during the night of 17–18 June 1941, the first anniversary of de Gaulle's appeal, on French and German road signs, the road itself and on the embankment wall of the riverside village of Les Rosiers-sur-Loire near Saumur, the trail led to three local lads aged fifteen, sixteen and twenty-one, 'all belonging to honourable families, the fathers of two of them wounded and decorated in the 1914–18 War'. Meanwhile, at the EPS Chevrollier in Angers pupils were using the official portraits of Marshal Pétain for target practice, firing at them rubbers, chalk and balls of papier mâché.[39]

The German invasion of the Soviet Union and the consequent launch of a campaign of terror by French communists dramatically raised the stakes as far as demonstrations were concerned. For a long time these had been considered by the authorities to be little more than schoolboy pranks, rebellious but good-natured and not a major security risk. In March 1941 the Feldkommandant of Tours reported that he did not think any more sinister organization stood behind the Gaullist supporters who were just 'small groups of young intellectuals without particular significance'.[40] On 20 October 1941, however, the Feldkommandant of Nantes was assassinated by a hit squad which was thought to be either Gaullist or communist, and the Germans responded swiftly and brutally with mass executions, a subject we shall return to in Chapter 11. From this moment demonstrations were much more difficult to organize and much more risky to take part in.

For 11 November 1941 the German authorities prohibited all meetings and demonstrations, allowing only religious services and wreath-laying. Particular attention was paid to student activity, given what had happened the previous year. In Angers a wreath with the dedication 'To those executed by firing squad at Nantes and Bordeaux' was found by police at the foot of the war memorial at 10.30 p.m. on 10 November and quickly removed. Also strewn around were small bills reading 'May all our glorious dead of the 1914–18 and 1939–40 wars protect our allies. A group of 38 young women of France'. Regional Prefect Roussillon was satisfied that the clampdown had worked, reporting that 'the greatest calm prevailed that day and the orders given by the Communist Party had no effect whatsoever'.[41]

The extent to which both French and German authorities were prepared to go to head off unrest was well illustrated by the events of 1 May 1942. The attempt by employers and the Church to hijack May Day continued, with the bishop of Angers telling a congregation of employers, managers, foremen and workers that the Labour Charter was the embodiment of social justice, to which religion brought the 'indispensable support' of 'a restoration of moral values' in the workplace.[42] Marshal Pétain again spoke to the workforce on 1 May (a Friday) at 5 p.m., and two firms at Tours were reprimanded by the prefect when it was discovered that they had not broadcast the Marshal's words, on the grounds that they had no radio set.[43] Much more serious was the punishment meted out to three young communist militants who were picked up by French police in Tours while painting graffiti the night preceding 1 May. A demonstration calling for their release was hastily called outside the Hôtel de Ville of Tours at 6 p.m. on 1 May, but to no effect. This time the culprits were not just exuberant students but linked to a wider movement, and the French police used torture to expose the trail that led to two young communist leaders. Instead of acting autonomously, the French police handed the five young communists over to the Gestapo, with tragic consequences that will be followed in Chapter 12.

Despite or even because of harsher repression, sacred commemorative moments for France and the Republic continued to be a focus for opposition to the Germans and to the Vichy authorities who were increasingly seen to be their collaborators rather than a 'shield' to protect the French people. Pierre Laval's government was extremely concerned that 14 July 1942 would become the occasion of mass demonstrations by Gaullists and communists, and demanded tight security and brutal discipline if necessary. At Trélazé, the slate-quarrying suburb of Angers, tracts were found denouncing concentration camps as new Bastilles, the execution of patriots, the persecution of the Jews as a revival of the wars of religion, the peasants subject to the *taille* and the *corvée* (poll tax and forced labour) as before 1789, robbed of their produce by the Vichy government for the benefit of German troops, 'that new race of seigneurs'. In Saumur, in M. Boiron's café, the orchestra suddenly struck up the *Marseillaise* at 4 p.m., and the clientele inside and out sang with a will, despite the presence of three or four German soldiers, until the police intervened and Boiron lost his licence for the weekend.[44] In Loire-Inférieure, the prefect reported that the attitude of the population was 'very dignified', although three communists had been arrested distributing tracts at Trignac, which led police to a communist cell at Saint-Nazaire, where three more arrests were made.[45]

Unlike in the Free Zone, where 14 July 1942 was the occasion of an outburst of criticism of the regime, in the Occupied Zone the machinery of repression made demonstrations extremely risky. After its relative failure Prime Minister Laval fully expected the communists to try to redeem themselves by promoting demonstrations on 20 September 1942, the 150th anniversary of the battle of Valmy.[46] This was the day on which the citizen-soldiers of France routed the Prussians who had invaded to put the French king back on the throne and prompted the Convention parliament to depose the king and proclaim a republic. There was certainly a good deal of communist propaganda in evidence. In Nantes the police found hundreds of tracts leading up to the anniversary and bills inviting people to demonstrate on Sunday, 20 September, at 6.30 p.m. on the place du Commerce. 'Let us show the enemy that we are prepared to fight to liberate the country's soil. Out with the Boche. Death to Hitler the murderer. Death to the traitors. Down with Pétain. We will have another Valmy. Bread and weapons.' Another tract produced by the communist-run Popular Women's Committees appealed to women working for famine wages for the German war machine to join 'housewives, wives of POWs and Catholic women' in the same demonstration, 'as at Valmy the people rose up against the coalition of kings'.[47] At Segré in Maine-et-Loire a tract of the communist youth movement was found instructing young people to parade in front of their town halls, lay wreaths at war memorials, and wear red, white and blue. 'On 20 September the soldiers of the Revolution crushed Brunswick's Prussian hordes at Valmy,' it read. 'On 20 September 1942 the young people of Maine-et-Loire will join the young people of France to demonstrate their invincible spirit of struggle and their will to free the country from Hitler's hordes.'[48]

There is little evidence that the communist propaganda barrage gave rise to much actual demonstration, but revolutionary and patriotic symbols summoned up sentiments of solidarity and widened the gulf between government and people. Very little was needed in this universe of historical signs to express commitment one way or the other. School students loyal to Marshal Pétain wore the *francisque*, the tricolour axe and fasces that was the symbol of the Vichy regime. Although the German authorities formally banned all badges under their ordinance of 28 August 1940, in practice they did nothing to punish wearing the *francisque*, and Regional Prefect Donati was all in favour of it.[49] In the spring of 1943, however, a craze spread among opposition students, and from them to young workers, of wearing badges made from 50-centime, 1-franc or 2-franc coins, on which the head of Marianne, symbol of the Republic in her Phrygian bonnet, was etched. The prefect of Loire-Inférieure ordered the police to clamp down and two apprentices, a plumber and butcher aged sixteen or seventeen, were stopped by the police in Nantes.[50] More sensationally, Benjamin Decure, an apprentice mason aged sixteen, was set upon on 1 May 1943 by two collaborationist Francists who tore the Marianne badge out of his buttonhole. Calling for reinforcements, they then went to his home armed with coshes, beat up the apprentice and his father and slapped his mother.[51] As divisions within the French population intensified, badge-wearing, at once discreet and provocative, was defining the loyalties of the young people of Nantes.

Demonstrations in 1943 and 1944 showed that the authorities were failing to make the art of commemoration work for them and consequently losing the affections of the population. Labour Day was moved to the nearest Sunday in order to avoid any disruption of work. At Tours the municipal theatre was already booked for another event on 2 May 1943, so the ceremony was moved to the Majestic cinema. The award of medals to deserving artisans or wives of artisans who had taken over from their POW husbands was undermined by the omission of representatives from artisans' organizations from the guest list, by the failure of the medals to arrive from Marshal Pétain's private office, and by the inability of four of the prize-winners to turn up because of bad weather or poor transport.[52] When Labour Day came round in 1944 there were fears that the Communist Party would try to launch a general strike and factory occupations, as in 1936, with the backing of workers' militias. Orators were instructed to take an aggressive line, echoing the sentiments of the national-socialist Minister of Labour, Marcel Déat, to be broadcast from the Palais Chaillot in Paris.[53] At Tours the event took place in the Majestic cinema, but was interrupted by an air-raid warning which emptied the audience of the many people attached to the civil defence corps. The few who were left included the presidents of the Chamber of Commerce and Chamber of Trades who were shocked by the rabid speech of one of Déat's emissaries in support of the New European Order and the counter-insurgent

Milice.[54] Of the working classes all that can be said is that they were a long way from strike action but totally alienated by Vichy's desperate line.

With Labour Day the Vichy regime still thought in terms of appropriation but there was no sense in which the commemoration of 14 July could be made to work for the regime and it was therefore met only by repression. The Laval government was almost in a state of panic about the way in which the day might be exploited by communists. In the event all that was apparent was dissident gestures, but no outright resistance. In 1943 Laval told regional prefects that all demonstrations were banned, that anyone planning 'an anti-national action' should be interned, and that if necessary order should be maintained by declaring a state of siege under a law of 1849. The word from the communist-led Front National was that people should come on to the streets at 7.45 p.m., a later time than usual, to merge with those going out for the evening to the theatre or cinema, walking alone and not in any organized way. In Angers it seemed only that the evening crowd was larger than usual, some of them wearing a little tricolour ribbon or bouquet.[55] In Nantes about 3,000 people processed in the town centre and at 8.30 p.m. about 150 of them struck up the *Marseillaise*. These were dispersed by the police, and only one man, a drunk, was arrested.[56]

For 14 July 1944 the discrepancy between what the government feared and what actually transpired was even greater. Laval warned of a possible insurrection and told prefects and police chiefs that if demonstrations looked like turning into risings they should not hesitate to open fire. What actually happened was that the dog did not bark. For five or six weeks since the Normandy landings the real action had been elsewhere. A flower-seller at Joué-lès-Tours doing a trade in red, white and blue flowers was told to pack up his wares and go home. In the afternoon in Tours young women with tricolour ribbons and young men with tricolour buttonholes were asked to remove them. At Château-Renault a tricolour flag flew all day from the town hall.[57] In Angers there was even less activity. 'Instructions issued by dissident forces', reported the police chief, 'have had no effect on the Angevins, who have a horror of all violence.'[58] These demonstrations may either be dismissed as childish pranks of little consequence or given the status of a kind of 'pre-Resistance' that led on to more decisive acts. Jacques Maurice, recalling the 'V'-signs and tricolours that were painted at Azay-le-Rideau on 14 July 1941 claims that 'by such demonstrations we learned to fear our German masters less and toughened ourselves for the future. Many future Maquisards started this way.'[59] Such claims, made in retrospect, may be a little extravagant. Symbolic gestures contributed little to the downfall of the German Occupation. Their importance was else-where, as subtle and imaginative ways by which the French were able to recognize each other in the construction of a patriotic universe. Sometimes the demonstrators were caught and punished but the object of the exercise was not to break the laws laid down by the German authorities or Vichy but to tease and subvert official legitimacy. They were a manifestation of the strategies resorted to by French people to preserve their dignity and express their faith in the future.

8. TRIMMERS

Early in 1942 a group of teachers at the Medical School of Tours sent a long report to the prefect of Indre-et-Loire to complain about their director, Dr Paul Guillaume-Louis. They accused him of 'directorial autocracy', corruption and favouritism. Since taking over the School in 1928, they said, he had flooded it with Romanian, Yugoslav, Armenian and Greek students, most of whom were Jews. On the strength of this expansion, they alleged, he had obtained a decree from his 'great friend' Camille Chautemps, the Radical Party boss of Touraine, upgrading the School to full degree-giving status in 1938. This led to his being promoted commander of the Légion d'honneur and having a self-congratulatory bust of himself placed in the School when the new buildings were opened in 1938 by the Jewish Minister of Education, Jean Zay. The expansion of the School created a plethora of jobs which, they argued, he had given to his 'comrades', such as Émile Aron, Freemason, socialist and Jew, appointed professor of physiology in 1936. When the Vichy regime deprived Aron of his chair, Guillaume-Louis gave him a job in the teaching hospital, of which he was an administrator, until this trick was exposed by the collaborationist paper *Je suis partout*. 'The presence of Dr Guillaume-Louis as director of the Medical School of Tours', they concluded, 'is a sure guarantee of the reign of favouritism, arbitrariness, immorality and cronyism, for the benefit of a certain mafia most of whom belong to the Demophiles masonic lodge. We request the immediate dismissal of this extremely dangerous person who embodies opposition to the principles of the National Revolution.'[1]

This attack on Guillaume-Louis found favour with the Vichy regime because it highlighted vices that were identified with the Third Republic that had led France to defeat in 1940. The Third Republic was seen as the 'Republic of comrades', a radical and socialist mafia linked by Freemasonry, and Protestant, Jewish or anticlerical rather than Catholic, looking after its own and excluding others from the honeypot of jobs, privileges and honours. It was a mafia that had acquired a tentacular grasp on power, colonizing the administration, controlling the press, and using both to manipulate elections and dominate representative institutions. Guillaume-Louis himself was not only the medical supremo in Indre-et-Loire who had examined the brain of the writer Anatole France after his death for physical manifestations of genius but also mayor and *conseiller général* of the small town of Montbazon, south of Tours. This mafia's grasp on power made it extremely difficult to shift, even by the authoritarian Vichy regime. Moreover, so long as a politician was willing to 'rally' to the new regime, and put away regrets for the 'Ancien Régime' of the Third Republic, Vichy saw the advantage of keeping him on, because his influence over those who had elected him had been demonstrated and he was probably the best person to bring them into line. Thus Guillaume-Louis had been confirmed as mayor of Montbazon in 1941 and, when the elected *conseils généraux* were replaced by small, appointed administrative commissions to advise prefects, he was included on that of Indre-et-Loire.

Given the changeability of the international situation and the difficulty of forecasting which regime would be in power a year or so down the road, however, it was better not to cosy up too closely to Vichy. The dismissal of Guillaume-Louis from the Medical School, following the hostile petition of the teachers, was a blesssing in disguise. Had he continued to take part in Vichy's institutions much longer, it is likely that he would have been purged from the *conseil général* when it was revived in 1944, sharing the fate of Mayor Mattraits of Chinon. A short period in opposition was enough to give a gloss of 'Resistance' to a notable who had to begin with been endorsed by Vichy. In the event Guillaume-Louis was not only included on the 1944 *conseil général* but also triumphed in the elections of 1945 when other radicals were routed in Touraine, and became president of the new assembly.[2]

Navigating the treacherous reefs of Occupied France, it was generally less advisable to embrace the Resistance decisively than to trim one's sails to the changeable gusts of wind. The case of Guillaume-Louis illustrates moreover that political survivors were just as common as political casualties. This may be explained in part by the chameleon skills of France's trimmers and the way in which they spun webs of power and influence that were difficult to dismantle. It may also be explained by the contradictions of a regime which, while hammering the reactionary and moralizing ideology of the National Revolution for all it was worth, did not have the clout to carry through a root-and-branch purge of the political class.

The reform of institutions in a formal sense was decisive. Days after Marshal Pétain was voted full executive, legislative and constitutional powers on 10 July 1940, he suspended Parliament indefinitely. Then on 12 October the *conseils généraux* were abolished. These measures did away with the elective assemblies that had been conquered by the Left since 1936. Parliamentary elections due to be held in 1940 and postponed because of the war, however, would undoubtedly have given victory to the Right. A deeper reason for these radical measures was therefore the abolition of representative institutions which were seen to have weakened France at a time when its international competitors were going over to tougher, more authoritarian regimes, and led it down the slippery slope to defeat. The National Revolution planned by Vichy was to be driven from above, by bureaucrats and technocrats who would not have to be answerable to meddling and self-serving politicians.

Politicians were sent back to their constituencies to graze. They were deprived of access to ministers and prefects which under the Third Republic had enabled them to obtain subsidies, contracts, favours, exemptions and honours for their constituents, either individually or collectively, in order to sweeten their clientele with a view to the next elections. No longer did they have what was called *le bras long*, that ability to influence those in power that made them invaluable to their own supporters. And yet the Vichy regime was unable to drive away the politicians of the Third Republic simply by shutting off their access to the central government. These politicians were only figures of national significance because of their local power-bases. They were not career politicians who lived 'off' politics but notables who lived 'for' politics, wielding influence in the local community by virtue of their family, wealth, profession and connections.[3] Before they became deputies or senators they followed a *cursus honorum*, starting as mayor of their commune, then *conseiller général* of their canton, which served as both a political apprenticeship and a means of making important political contacts and alliances. The ownership of a local newspaper was also indispensable. This was less a business enterprise than a political mouthpiece for the local politician, a public relations exercise and an electoral tool.[4]

In some urban pockets, of course, socialist or communist politicians emerged on the back of the labour movement and mass parties. Nantes, as we have seen, was controlled by a Socialist Party machine under Deputy-Mayor Pageot, while in Tours the socialist Ferdinand Morin, deputy since 1914, took the town from the radical Camille Chautemps in 1925 and made it his fief through municipal socialism. The railway suburb of Tours, Saint-Pierre-des-Corps, went communist in 1920 when a railway strike was abandoned by the moderate CGT national leadership, leading to 2,500 dismissals, and communists split from socialists at the Congress of Tours. Since then the town had been run by the aptly named Robespierre Henault, a railwayman who had lost an arm in an industrial accident, and by a council of young workers of the Paris–Orléans Railway Company who were often foreign to the town.[5] Otherwise there were two basic models with which politicians in the Loire valley tended to identify.

East of Angers, in the Saumurois and Touraine, radical politicians such as Léon Courson, mayor of Noyant and deputy of Chinon, or Paul Bernier, mayor of Mouzay and also a deputy, held sway. They were landed, involved in the liberal professions or commerce: Courson was a pig merchant. They were often connected by membership of Masonic lodges which were non-religious if not anti-religious, and affiliated to organizations such as the League of Rights of Man, founded during the Dreyfus Affair, or the Education League, whose mission was to undermine the Catholic Church's control of the school system and entrust it to the secular state.[6]

West of Angers, in the Mauges and Loire-Inférieure, politics was run by noble, landowning families who, far from having been swept away by the French Revolution, extended their influence over their local constituents in the modern age through agricultural organizations, the defence of the Catholic Church and Church schools, and cultivating the memory of the Vendean uprising against the French Revolution. Deputies of Loire-Inférieure like Marquis Henri de La Ferronnays and Jean Le Cour Grandmaison pursued careers in the army or navy before virtually inheriting their fathers' seats (in 1907 and 1919 respectively) and promoting agricultural unionism as a tool of conservative hegemony. The senators tended to have more professional or academic credentials: Louis Linyer was a brilliant barrister at the Nantes Bar, François de Saint-Maur was professor at the Angers Law Faculty, while Gustave Gautherot was professor at the Catholic Institute in Paris. As conservatives they dominated the *conseil général*, of which Henri de La Ferronnays was president from 1931. The binding force and mass base was provided by the Catholic Association of Family Heads of the Diocese of Nantes, under the auspices of the bishop, with sections in every parish and a membership of 20,000 in the 1930s. It was linked to the National Catholic Federation of General de Castelnau, set up after the Right lost power to the radicals in 1924 to fight what was seen as a Masonic conspiracy to de-Christianize France. Henri de La Ferronnays acquired a martyr's crown and boosted the movement in 1925 when he demanded that radical Prime Minister Herriot withdraw his denunciation of an alliance between the Catholic Church and bankers, for which the Marquis was himself expelled from the Chamber of Deputies.[7]

Before it could settle its score with politicians the Vichy administration had to put its own house in order. Unreliable prefects were purged in the hot summer of 1940. Fernand Leroy of Loire-Inférieure was sacked because he was deemed ineffectual, because he had been appointed by the Popular Front, and because he was rumoured to be a Jew – which was incorrect, although he was married to one.[8] The new model Vichy prefect was to be altogether more decisive. 'You have been functionaries,' the Interior Minister told them, 'now you will be leaders.'[9] Philippe Dupard, a man of huge presence who took over as prefect of Loire-Inférieure, quickly got rid of Leroy's chef de cabinet and secretary-general, the top two posts in the prefecture, removed the police chief of Nantes on the grounds that he had once been a Freemason, and sacked the subprefect of Saint-Nazaire for being in the pocket of the socialist municipality.[10] Jean Roussillon, who took over as prefect of Angers, was dynamic, ambitious, outspoken, but also difficult, moody and irascible. He was seduced by the idea of 'direct administration', whereby the prefect would relate directly to those he was responsible for instead of finding local politicians in his way, and planned monthly meetings with mayors in each *arrondissement*.[11] He was determined to break the back of the politicians of the Third Republic and carve out his own empire. But he would soon find that the 'Ancien Régime', as he called it, would not lie down so easily.

Some deputies, as it happened, gave little trouble. Roussillon described Émile Pérein, radical–socialist deputy of Angers, as a 'colourless figure' who had still not made contact with him six months after his appointment. Robert de Grandmaison, centre-Right deputy for Saumur, was 'by far the most intelligent parliamentarian in the department, and also by far the most keen to meddle in his constituency'. He was said to have burst into the office of the mayor of Saumur before a council meeting and attacked Marshal Pétain as 'an old man . . . old, very old', and 'entirely in the hands of the Germans'.[12] Gaston Moreau, deputy-mayor of Baugé after defeating a radical–socialist against the swing in 1936, was described as a 'curious person who would have interested Balzac. He is unstoppably talkative, which creates the illusion of hyperactivity. Dreams of playing a role in the Baugeois.' In pursuit of this role he held weekly surgeries of the mayors in his canton to examine the prefect's circulars and listen to their grievances. Roussillon was concerned that his circulars were being 'discussed and interpreted' by lowly mayors and that Moreau was still behaving as a deputy, finding a new way to weave local contacts and create debts that would be recalled if ever elections returned.[13]

These were only pinpricks compared with the real thorn in Roussillon's flesh, Anatole Manceau. Manceau was senator for Cholet, a liberal who had been elected in 1925 against Léon Daudet of the dynamic royalist movement Action Française, who attempted to parachute into the seat from Paris.[14] Now that the Senate was suspended, Manceau returned from Vichy to his local power-base. He was president of the Chamber of Commerce of Cholet which, in the absence of the *conseil général*, took on more importance as a tribune. Above all he was the owner of *Le Petit Courrier*, the biggest newspaper in the department. Relations between Roussillon and Manceau began well. In November 1940 the former visited Cholet where a new subprefect was taking over, and met the mayors of the *arrondissement*. He was welcomed by Anatole Manceau who told him of the magnificent activity of the local textile and shoe industry. Roussillon adopted *Le Petit Courrier* as the official newspaper of the prefecture, in which important public announcements would appear.

But there the cooperation stopped. Manceau was keen that in return for his 'official' status he should have privileged access to the prefecture and a certain influence there. For Roussillon this went against the new doctrine of Vichy, that former parliamentarians should expect 'a courteous reception, but no more'. The old days, when prefects were at the beck and call of local deputies and senators in order to distribute jobs and favours and 'make' elections, were finished. Manceau felt left out in the cold and took his revenge by publishing in *Le Petit Courrier* an editorial written by a hostile Paris journalist, Jean Luchaire, which had appeared in *Les Nouveaux Temps*. Roussillon riposted by suspending *Le Petit Courrier* for twenty-four hours on 1 December 1940. Manceau replied by proxy with an article in *Les Nouveaux Temps* arguing that France was collapsing into 'so many fiefs, ruled at the whim of prefects. This was the desire neither of parliament, nor of the Marshal.' Meanwhile Roussillon was given a rap over the knuckles by Feldkommandant Kloss, who told him that he had no right to censor a newspaper without reference to the German authorities.[15]

Roussillon did everything he could to undermine Manceau's power-base. He tried to abolish the Cholet Chamber of Commerce on the grounds that one chamber of commerce per department was enough (Maine-et-Loire had three), but Manceau saved it. Manceau was included as a member of the new municipal council of Cholet in April 1941, and was undoubtedly behind the pantomime of 24 June, when the council passed a unanimous vote of confidence in Marshal Pétain but divided 50–50 on a following vote of confidence in the autocratic then prime minister, Admiral Darlan. Roussillon stormed down to Cholet and reconvened the municipal council in the prefecture where he lectured them and forced them to take a new vote, on pain of collective dismissal. The only councillor to be dismissed was predictably Manceau, for insulting Admiral Darlan. Roussillon complained that even if Manceau 'had lost his mass appeal he was still in touch with what remains of his old electoral organization, through personal and often friendly contacts with mayors and other local figures, and is only too often an agent of demoralization and anti-government propaganda'. In exasperation he took the extraordinary step of replacing Manceau on the municipal council by a cleric, the Abbé Douillard, archdeacon of Notre-Dame de Cholet, on the grounds that Cholet had been the capital of the Vendean rising against the French Revolution in defence of Church and King in 1793, and it was good to keep the Church sweet.[16]

Manceau had no mind to let Roussillon off the hook. In the Cholet Chamber of Commerce and at private dinners he continued to criticize the prefect and Darlan, and now began to suggest that the ageing Marshal Pétain was losing his memory, was no longer capable of governing France, and had even fallen prey to Action Française to the extent of declaring the royal pretender, the Comte de Paris, his successor.[17] Le Petit Courrier published pieces giving credence to the rumours circulating that the vitamin-enriched biscuits distributed to schoolchildren by the Secours National had been contaminated by the tuberculosis bacillus.[18] The prefecture demanded that the paper publish a communiqué dismissing the rumours and accused the paper of an 'anti-national campaign and an attitude contrary to the public good'. Manceau refused to do this, and instead published parts of his angry correspondence with Roussillon which showed the prefect in a very bad light. Roussillon then refused to send any of his communiqués to Le Petit Courrier for a fortnight, hoping to bring it to heel, but Manceau blocked him, using his influence with the Propaganda-staffel to persuade them to ban all other local papers from publishing the prefect's communiqués, so that the prefect was reduced to writing directly to hundreds of mayors. To complete the victory, Manceau hired the local branch of the collaborationist Mouvement Social Révolutionnaire to step up their attacks on Roussillon as an incompetent prefect who was incapable of checking Gaullist propaganda or the black market and whose own civil servants were involved in it. In the end Roussillon was summoned by General Matthaei of the military administration of Bezirk B in Angers, to give an account of himself.[19]

The dogfight between prefect and politician demonstrated that the authoritarian Vichy regime did not have it all its own way. It abolished parliament and conseils généraux and its officials were advised to adopt an authoritarian style and haughty attitude towards politicians who returned to their constituencies. This, however, was to reckon without the surviving local power-base of politicians and their skill in manipulating a political system which the German presence had made more complicated. Even if the Senate no longer existed Manceau was able to use his prestige as a senator and the political connections that had put him there. The presidency of the

Chamber of Commerce of Cholet gave him authority over the industrialists who ran the town and the ability to persuade the municipal council to vote in large numbers against Admiral Darlan. Above all, as a press baron he was able to hold the prefecture, which had no official mouthpiece apart from his own *Petit Courrier*, to ransom. Throughout he played a double game, protesting his loyalty but constantly sniping. Loyal to Pétain he might just have been, but he had no time for Darlan, and even while acknowledging this vote he was spinning webs around the German authorities and collaborationists of the worst odour to bring down the prefect who had snubbed him. A year or so later it was Roussillon who left the scene, not Manceau.

In order to drive through the National Revolution it became clear that Vichy would have to pay as much attention to power in the localities as to power in the centre. Municipal councils and mayors had been elected in 1935, on the same wave that had brought the Popular Front into government in 1936. Municipal elections due in 1941 would, like national elections, have registered a shift to the Right, but that was beside the point. Vichy wanted to gain full control of local government, abolishing the local democracy that had finally been consecrated by the Republic in 1884. Some authoritarian measures had already been taken before 1940. The communist municipality of Saint-Pierre-des-Corps was dissolved in October 1939 as part of the clampdown on communists after the Nazi–Soviet pact and replaced by an appointed 'special delegation', while a Vichy prefect interned former Mayor Robespierre Henault early in 1941.[20] A law of 16 November 1940 allowed the Interior Minister and prefect between them to appoint mayors and municipal councillors in towns defined as having a population of over 2,000. Villages (under 2,000) were not expected to give any trouble and would remain under the regime of 1884, although no elections would be held during the war and existing mayors and councillors would simply be carried over.

This catch-all law gave Vichy the opportunity to go through local government with a toothcomb and purge its political enemies. Some difficult left-wing mayors were unceremoniously removed. Mayor Pageot of Nantes, who exasperated the Germans as well as the French administration by his bombastic and misplaced patriotism, was replaced by Gaëtan Rondeau, a sixty-eight-year-old former lawyer and top municipal administrator of Nantes, who was described as 'very courteous, intelligent and cultivated, upright and honest, with a perfect understanding of the cogs of the municipal machine'. His right-hand man (*adjoint*), Abel Durand, sixty-two, was professor at the Law School of Nantes, a practising Catholic and departmental delegate of the Secours National, 'combining intellectual qualities of the first order with great energy in the community which he devoted to agencies of social relief'.[21] The other nuisance in the region was Robert Amy, radical–socialist mayor of Saumur. He was seen to have been insufficiently plucky when the Germans arrived – all the credit going to Procureur Ancelin – and was generally considered the prime mover of radicalism and freemasonry in the Saumurois. He and his council were replaced by an appointed special delegation under a lawyer, Maître Baudry, until Subprefect Milliat judged that the latter had not sufficiently changed his spots. Baudry, he reported, 'has remained a man of the Left, if not *the* man of the Left, and I use these words in the old-fashioned sense, given that at the present time we are not supposed to remove those who have rallied to the Marshal's policies'.[22] Baudry was duly replaced by a barrister and acting police chief, René Drouart, which seemed a splendid idea until he was caught up in a sex scandal.

The subprefect's comments showed that he had fully imbibed the instructions of the Ministry of the Interior. Clearly 1940 was a new chance for the Right, displaced in 1936 and arguably on the ropes from as long ago as 1877. For Charles Maurras, leader of the royalist Action Française, 1940 was a 'divine surprise' that would simply ring out the Left and ring in the Right. For others, ministers at Vichy, however, things were more complex. Civil strife had to be replaced by national unity, which meant winning over former political enemies to the new project. In his long circular to prefects in January 1941 Interior Minister Marcel Peyrouton therefore said that the object of the combing of municipalities was not a 'massive replacement' of mayors and councillors but only the removal of those who were demonstrably hostile to the regime. Old political rivals should be forgiven 'if their rallying to the new politics is complete and sincere and gives no sign of *arrière-pensée*'. New appointees should not just be 'reactionaries': 'the new order is not supposed to be a sort of *Moral Order* [his italics, referring to a period of reaction in the 1870s] or a revenge for the events of 1936'. Those required were 'people of indisputable morality both in their public and private life and of absolute devotion to the policies of the Marshal's government'.[23]

One of the striking features of municipal politics under Vichy was thus the survival of some left-wing mayors. They indicate that what mattered was open endorsement of the regime and tested authority over the local population. At Tours Ferdinand Morin, who had endeared himself to the townspeople by his courage as the Germans began to bombard the city in June 1940 and to the regime by his vote as deputy of full powers to Marshal Pétain at Vichy, was confirmed as mayor in March 1941. At the ceremony Prefect Chaigneau said that 'the choice made by Marshal Pétain summoning you to head the municipal administration has had the most gratifying repercussions among the population, if I trust to the flattering commentaries that followed the appointment'.[24] He had already told the minister that 'In Touraine, which is very calm and balanced and people have a solid common sense, the replacement of M. Morin at the town hall of Tours by somebody else would not be understood. In the present climate his dismissal would be considered a psychological error which I simply could not commit.'[25] Although elections had been abolished, it was as if a phantom plebiscite had been held and delivered a resounding verdict: Morin must stay.

Even more surprising, at the other end of the region in the port of Saint-Nazaire, the socialist François Blancho was confirmed as mayor. Orphaned, a worker from the age of thirteen in the Penhouët shipyard, trade unionist, socialist, mayor and deputy of the port by the age of thirty-five in 1928, Under-Secretary of State for the Navy between 1936 and 1938, and as such the boss of Darlan, then commander-in-chief of the French navy, he was superficially the very politician who was anathema to Vichy. When he was reappointed mayor in March 1941 the departmental Taxpayers' Federation expressed outrage to Marshal Pétain that one of 'the demagogues "who did us so much harm", to use your own expression' was still in business, not least because Blancho was also 'one of the great artisans of the disorganization of the naval arsenals who preached holidays and disarmament while the Germans were rearming relentlessly'.[26] On the positive side, however, Blancho had voted full powers to Marshal Pétain, he was the acknowledged leader of the working class in an essentially working-class town who had kept

Saint-Nazaire a socialist fief in the face of the communist challenge and had played a moderating influence in labour disputes.[27] Rather than being dismissed, he resigned in May 1941 in protest at Admiral Darlan's uncompromising attacks on the record of the Third Republic. 'Orphan from a very young age,' he said at the Liberation, 'I owe everything to the working class whose sufferings and hopes I have shared . . . I cannot accept that our fellow workers might have to be ashamed of the man who was for so long their spokesman.'[28]

The resignation of Blancho, followed by the socialist councillors, highlighted the difficulties faced by Vichy in running a town in which class divisions were so clear. The unenviable task of the subprefect of Saint-Nazaire, in his own words, was to 'find a man who was not branded politically but who was converted to ideas of social progress and who, even without the support of the socialists, could win over some workers to serve. He should unite under his leadership all men of goodwill belonging to all classes of the population and representative of all the currents which are loyal to the government.'[29] For the new mayor he hit upon Pierre Toscer, a man of the same age as Blancho who had started work as a fitter in the Ateliers et Chantiers de la Loire. There, however, their paths diverged as Toscer had obtained a technical training at the Arts et Métiers, become an *ingénieur*, then inspector of technical education in Loire-Inférieure and finally manager of the Chantiers Loire Saint-Denis. He was seen to be the candidate of the shipyard employers, but as a self-made man he was respected by the workers and had qualities that transcended the lines of class struggle: a local man, a veteran of 1914–18 with the Croix de Guerre, a father of four, a practising Catholic (with one brother a priest and a sister a nun), significant in what was after all a Breton port. No doubt in the light of this appointment Interior Minister Pierre Pucheu, a technocrat rather than a reactionary, told prefects that if mayors and municipal councils were to be replaced, the new council should 'correspond as much as possible to the general physiognomy of the town'. In former socialist or communist towns it was 'a particularly bad idea to hand over the control of municipal business to elements which were the very opposite of the previous party', and especially to those who had previously been defeated in local elections. This would be interpreted as a 'provocation which would alienate the population from the new administrative set-up . . . a revenge of past struggles and a disregard of public opinion'. In working-class towns notables should be avoided and the ideal choice would be a worker who had the respect of his comrades, whether in the trade-union movement or not, 'who seems to you to have consciously rallied to government policy'.[30] Unfortunately the Vichy regime would discover that these 'rallied workers', worth their weight in gold, were an increasingly rare commodity, and 'pseudo-workers' such as Toscer found it difficult to maintain a stance of class neutrality when demands for labour for the Reich began to bite in 1942.

Of course, working-class towns such as Saint-Nazaire were atypical in western France. The main problem faced by the Vichy regime was not bridging the class divide but being sure that mayors and councils that had ostensibly 'rallied' to the government were not in fact playing a double game and behind appearances resisting the new order. The occasional mayor, such as M. Chatelain of La Gâvre, was silly enough to be arrested by the Germans: they raided M. Chatelain's house and discovered a photo of General de Gaulle and extracts from his broadcasts. He went to prison for seven months, after which he was persuaded to resign by the Vichy authorities.[31] Most mayors, however, were more discreet and criticisms of them were often no more than hearsay. Of François Servant, a lawyer and mayor and *conseiller général* of La Haye Descartes on the demarcation line, it was said that though his family was religious he belonged to Masonic Lodges in Chinon and Châtellerault, that he was an active radical–socialist who had supported strike action in 1936 and that his loyalty to Marshal Pétain was 'wholly superficial': he was an Anglophile, hostile to Franco-German collaboration.[32] Yet it was often difficult to remove these local notables, partly because their influence was entrenched and valuable, partly because they gave the administration just as much loyalty as was necessary while otherwise playing a very long game and keeping their options open.

Even in Indre-et-Loire, that bastion of radical–socialism and anti-clericalism, only 36 per cent of mayors were replaced by Vichy.[33] One good example of survival was Dr Tardif, mayor and *conseiller général* of Longué, near Saumur, who had run against Manceau and Daudet in the senatorial elections of 1925. He was a hard-bitten radical–socialist and anticlerical, the quintessence of the Third Republic, and Subprefect Milliat would have been delighted to persuade him to resign or dismiss him if he put a foot wrong. But

Tardif refused to resign, 'preferring to be replaced in a way he could glorify later and present himself as a martyr of the Ancien Regime'. While 'there are doubts about the genuineness of his current commitment to the Marshal's ideas', Milliat reported, Tardif had moderated his extreme views and was now proposing to name a street in honour of Marshal Pétain, happily leading off 'our beautiful Verdun square'. 'Either this man is sincere,' wrote Milliat, 'or he is a fine Jesuit . . . even at his ripe age the old radical fighter is diabolically intelligent.'[34] A year later the prefect delegate described Tardif as 'an old fox, an old boar, unshakeably attached to the past', but just as unshakeable, it seemed, in his *mairie*.[35]

Just as important as political loyalties in the evaluation of mayors, as the circular of the Interior Minister made clear, was public and private morality. This proved the downfall of the head of the special delegation of Saumur, which replaced the elected council, René Drouart. The trouble started early in 1943 when in his capacity as a barrister he defended a gypsy girl accused of stealing money from the old lady who employed her, in the course of which he impugned the integrity of the police. Since he had until recently been in charge of the municipal police force, this upset local police and magistrates. He was then accused of having a mistress, a dressmaker whose seventeen-year-old son was employed at the town hall, and stepped down provisionally as mayor to bring a libel suit against his accuser. On the night of 5–6 April 1943 a handwritten poster was plastered on the walls of Saumur. It read, 'Your mayor M. Drouart is dismissed. Why? Because of a public scandal of concubinage. And this man has the nerve to judge and preach morality. Drouart, you are just a bastard.'

Drouart had his supporters, such as the author of an anonymous letter to the prefect, which claimed to unveil the hypocrisy of the town fathers.

Is our captain of gendarmerie who is constantly with his girlfriend in the rue Beaurepaire sacked for this much? And our engineer M. Bouvy who is busier with M. Gouin's wife than with what ought to be his own business, is he placed on the Index? As for the president of the Chamber of Commerce, M. Pichard, commonly regarded as God, his mistress is real enough for him; he had the house she lives in built for her. This liaison is public knowledge in Saumur, and goes back a long way before the events [of 1940].

Have these grand seigneurs got rights while everyone else has duties? As for the curé of Saint-Nicolas, he prefers men to women. His mistress is called M. Bernon and lives not so far from you.

The point about Drouart, however, was not that his immorality was exceptional but that he lost the confidence of those who mattered in Saumur. His four deputies (*adjoints*) at the town hall, who included a retired major and a retired captain, together with a number of other councillors, threatened to resign collectively if the prefect did not sack him within a fortnight. The decision was not one which came from a sanctimonious administration but from an outraged corps of notables. They obliged Drouart to write a letter of resignation which the prefect then accepted. Vichy could not dictate or fail to act in the teeth of local opinion, and the conduct of local affairs was always a matter of negotiation between the two.[36]

The influence of local notables was felt not only in the towns but also at regional level. It made its mark during the great debate of the spring of 1941 about whether Vichy was going to continue running France as a centralized state, which had been the model since the Revolution and Napoleon, or whether it would relax the vice-like grip of the centre and devolve more power to the provinces or regions. The argument in favour of decentralization was that centralization had repeatedly allowed revolutionaries who seized power in Paris to impose revolution on the rest of the country; to decentralize would insulate the provinces against revolution. It would also undermine small movements in some parts of France, which believed themselves to be ethnically or historically distinct – such as Brittany or Flanders – and who wanted even greater autonomy. The argument against decentralization was that to resurrect the provinces was to resurrect the influence of the pre-revolutionary élites with their local power-bases and to run the risk of the disintegration of the state. After all, if the revolutionaries and Napoleon had fashioned the centralized state, the restored monarchy had seen no reason to melt it down. The Vichy regime was indeed torn two ways, between an urge to decentralize in order to break the power of left-wing governments which had cynically used the state machine to impose their ideology, and a fear that with the weakening of the French state under the German Occupation this was scarcely the moment to weaken what state power existed.[37]

In the absence of a parliament Vichy set up a Conseil National, a consultative body of notables to advise on constitutional matters.[38] One of its commissions – on which sat Jean Le Cour Grandmaison, former deputy of Loire-Inférieure and vice-president of the Fédération Nationale Catholique – examined the issue of administrative decentralization and proposed a network of governors who, above the heads of the prefects, would superintend a grand strategy for the regions and be advised by regional councils in which not only territorial but also economic and spiritual interests would be represented. In some sense they would build on the economic regions established in France after 1917, but would bring in notables involved in family, social or religious issues. It marked a step down the road away from representative democracy and towards the corporative state in which, under the aegis of the government, not abstract individuals but the concrete interests of 'real France' would be represented.

Decentralization was not simply decreed from on high but was the subject of a great deal of local jockeying for position. As early as August 1940 the bishop of Nantes received a visit from Hervé Budes de Guébriant, president of the Chamber of Agriculture of Finistère, who told him of the Vichy government's plans to set up a province of Brittany in order to undermine the Breton nationalists who had just set up a Breton national council at Pontivy and announced the creation of a separate Breton state. Guébriant thought that he was firm favourite to be governor of Brittany and wondered whether the bishop saw a place for Nantes within it.[39] Whether Nantes and Loire-Inférieure were a part of Brittany was a matter of long and heated debate. The Archaeological and Historical Society of Nantes and Loire-Inférieure, 600 strong, reminded the prefect that Anne of Brittany, whose marriage to Louis XII in 1499 had marked the union of Brittany and France, had been born in the ducal château of Nantes and that Nantes was the capital of Brittany, never to be separated from it.[40] Meanwhile, a movement of collaborationist Breton nationalists called the National Socialist Youth targeted Loire-Inférieure with their propaganda. In December 1940 tracts called for the destruction of a French state in hock to authoritarian prefects and Masonic politicians, in February 1941 graffiti such as 'Free Brittany' and 'Neither Albion nor Mariâne. A Breton government' appeared, while 'Down with Rondeau' was scrawled on Nantes town hall in May.[41]

The debate over the future of Brittany showed that there was far from being a consensus in the city of Nantes. Paul Brossier, president of the Chamber of Commerce of Nantes, and Abel Durand, professor of political economy at the Law School, *adjoint* to Mayor Rondeau and an expert on regional questions, advanced the counter-argument that to reconstitute the five departments of Brittany would be a backward-looking revival of an *ancien régime* province, an unforced concession to the autonomists and disastrous from the economic point of view. The capital of historic Brittany would inevitably be Rennes, not Nantes. They proposed a region whose 'spinal column' would be the departments of south Brittany (Finistère, Morbihan, Loire-Inférieure) and the Vendée, which had been linked since 1919 in an economic region, which basically federated a number of chambers of commerce,[42] and served as an agricultural hinterland for Nantes. The two north-Breton departments of Ille-et-Vilaine and the Côtes-du-Nord might be added, but to check autonomism Brittany would then be drowned in a larger 'Armorican region' including the Mayenne, Sarthe and Maine-et-Loire. The capital of this region would necessarily be Nantes with its sea-port, communications and population of 200,000, twice the size of Rennes. Prefect Dupard was won over to this school of thought, met Admiral Darlan in March 1941 and put presssure on Jean Le Cour Grandmaison, sitting on the key commission.[43]

While Nantes was fighting the pretensions of Rennes, Angers was fighting those of Nantes. Competition between regions generally articulated competition between major cities whose status as a regional capital was at stake. In May 1941 a delegation went to Vichy from Angers, led by two splendid aristocrats, Vicomte Jacques de la Grandière, another member of the Conseil National, and Comte Joachim du Plessis de Grenadan, dean of the Law Faculty of the Catholic University of Angers, whose name, said Prefect Roussillon, was 'synonymous with chivalric impartiality and generosity as well as with fidelity to the national and religious principles to which he has devoted his life'.[44] They argued that Anjou had nothing in common with Nantes, 'whose political influence stops virtually at its suburbs and has only the usual, anonymous force of attraction of any large port'. Nantes represented evil: urban anonymity, trade and socialism. Against it Anjou must seek an alternative alliance with Maine, now the Mayenne and Sarthe departments. They had similar economies based on grain, cattle, textiles and shoes and had a natural capital in Angers, whose magnificent royal house had ruled at various times England, Provence, Naples and Sicily, Poland and Hungary. With its cathedral, Catholic University and Appeal Court it was 'the Athens of the West'. Implicit was the argument that Anjou–Maine would be a bastion against the modern world, dominated by the landed nobility, the Church and the liberal professions, still in the *ancien régime* in spirit if not in fact.[45]

Neither Angevins nor Nantais had much to say about the Tourangeaux, who did not figure in their regional plans, and the Tourangeaux repaid the compliment by planning to split Anjou and annexe half of it. Ironically there were strong economic links provided by the fifth economic region, which grouped the Chambers of Commerce of Lorient, Nantes, Angers, Saumur, Tours and Le Mans, while the Assembly of Chambers of Commerce of the Loire basin included those of Saint-Nazaire, Nantes, Angers, Saumur, Tours, Blois and Orléans. Both met fairly regularly, at least in the early part of the Occupation, essentially to lobby government to make the Loire navigable and to improve rail communications from the Loire valley to Lyon.[46] These links, however, did not seem to feed into political thinking when it came to the debate on regions. The Chamber of Commerce of Tours produced a glossy brochure entitled 'Tours, Provincial Capital', in which it was argued that Tours was a turntable of communications, an archbishopric, the historic centre from which Louis XI had created the unity of France, and the seat of national government when Paris was evacuated in 1870 and 1940. The extent of the province was not clear, but it aimed to take a chunk of Maine-et-Loire on the grounds that that department was not a unity. Within Maine-et-Loire, it argued, the Saumurois was really an extension of Touraine and ought to be absorbed by it, while the department west of Angers was more feudal and had more in common with Loire-Inférieure. 'Nothing in the government plan', it concluded, 'requires that a department has to belong as a whole to one of the regions being created.'[47]

As it happened, there was nothing in the government plan either which required any of the lobbies of provincial notables to be satisfied. Vichy's law of 19 April 1941 ignored the recommendations of the Conseil National and set up not provincial governors but regional prefects. These were to be drawn from the existing corps of prefects, and in the department where a regional prefect was created, his departmental responsibilities would be carried out by a so-called prefect delegate. The purpose of the reform was not decentralization to please regionalists but the concentration of administrative power at a regional level to deal more effectively with the challenge of the German military administration and the problems of communicating with Vichy. Prefect Roussillon reported from Angers that since 1940 'the prefects in the Occupied Zone had been completely cut off from the government and thrown back upon themselves, without advice or instructions, able to correspond to Vichy only via the tenuous and theoretical link of the Délégation Générale'. This had resulted in 'an incoherent autarky of each department and different interpretations of government orders from prefect to prefect'.[48] A regional prefect, he said, would be able to impose a certain order and consistency on a group of neighbouring departments. Meanwhile, the location of the regional prefectures took account of the design of the German military administration, and since Angers was the base of Bezirk B, which controlled south-west France, it was clearly logical to make Angers the capital of a region. The exact contours of the regions were published in July 1941: that of Angers included Maine-et-Loire, Loire-Inférieure, Indre-et-Loire, Mayenne and Sarthe. Roussillon, predictably, was promoted regional prefect for Angers and given Pierre Daguerre, formerly subprefect in Dieppe, as his prefect delegate for Maine-et-Loire.

Immediately there was an outburst over the configuration of the regions. The Nantais in particular was aghast to have been upstaged both by Rennes, which became the regional capital of a Brittany which excluded Loire-Inférieure, and by Angers, the regional capital to which they were now beholden. Mayor Rondeau exploded in the press and Brossier's protest, endorsed by the Chamber of Commerce at this slight to 'the uncontestable and uncontested metropolis of the West', was forwarded to Vichy. Students from the Law, Medical and Commercial Schools, together with the Arts Faculty of Nantes, staged a one-day strike. At a reception in honour of the regional prefect of Angers, one Breton mayor refused to drink the toast, saying, 'Here, *Monsieur le préfet*, Muscadet and Anjou wine are not drunk from the same glass.'[49] A year later, when steps were being taken to set up a Breton Consultative Committee at Rennes, which would draft a Charter of Brittany, rumours began to circulate that Loire-Inférieure would become part of the regenerated Breton region, under Rennes. This might have satisfied some regionalists but not the city fathers of Nantes. Immediately Brossier and Rondeau penned a letter to Laval, demanding that Nantes be made the capital of the vast Armorican region envisaged in 1940, or the capital of a little region including Loire-Inférieure and the Vendée, currently attached to the Poitiers region, or a free city. On no account, however, would they accept subordination to Rennes.[50]

The notables' noses were also put out of joint by the administrative concentration which put more power in the hands of prefects and gave back none of the influence that notables had wielded in the *conseils généraux*. The *conseils généraux*, which under the Third Republic had become representative assemblies between thirty and fifty strong, with which the prefect was bound to reckon, were replaced by truncated administrative commissions of between seven and nine. As far as their social composition went, however, prefects generally understood that it made sense to include the most influential members of the *conseils généraux* on the commissions rather than to indulge in social engineering. Prefect Roussillon, for example, pointed out that the *conseil général* of Maine-et-Loire 'was always patriotic in spirit, hardly prey to political agitation or demagogic excess'. Out of thirty-four councillors there were only eight radicals or radical–socialists and no socialists at all; 55 per cent were large landowners, 45 per cent noble and 47 per cent were over sixty years old, and Roussillon proposed to take seven of the nine new commissioners from the old *conseil général*. Here, however, he came into conflict with the Interior Ministry which, as with mayors, was not content to hand the baton to reactionaries but determined to widen the field from which councillors were drawn. Prefects must include representatives of other groups, including fathers of large families, skilled workers and younger men. Roussillon was forced to drop several ageing nobles, to include two industrialists, both aged thirty-eight and respectively fathers of six and ten children, and to bring in Daniel Cadeau, a worker from the Bessonneau factory in Angers, who was described by the local press as 'kind, simple, paternal, in his modest dwelling which was yet clean and as if perfumed by family virtue'.[51]

Despite the stand-off between central and local government over the administrative commissions the notables in place survived quite well. Victor Bernier, mayor of Angers, president of the *conseil général* of Maine-et-Loire in 1940, became leader of the department's administrative commission in 1941. Marquis Henri de La Ferronnays, president of the *conseil général* of Loire-Inférieure in 1940, was there to reply to the speech of Prefect Dupard at the opening session of the administrative commission, pledging loyalty to Marshal Pétain and to 'the three notions at the foundation of the new state: Work, Family, Country'.[52] As for Indre-et-Loire, councillors who were also deputies, such as Léon Courson and Ferdinand Morin, were not carried over, but the radical–socialist *conseillers généraux* were still there in the shape of Paul Guillaume-Louis, as we have seen, and François Servant, mayor of La Haye Descartes, whose 'rallying' continued to be under scrutiny.[53]

In the long run who survived politically was less important than where the power lay. The administrative commissions met monthly in Indre-et-Loire, on a Saturday afternoon in the prefecture, and three times a year in Loire-Inférieure for no more than a day. Chaired by the prefect, there was little input from the floor. At Tours the three former *conseillers généraux*, Guillaume-Louis, Servant and André Gouin, banker and mayor of the Tours suburb Fondettes, became slightly more vociferous under the new prefect, Tracou, but Jean Goujon, a garagist and member of the Chamber of Trades, said nothing in two years. It may be that all references to politics were excised from the minutes: the business they dealt with – subsidies, scholarships, school buildings, church towers, doctors' fees, local roads, railway timetables, sewerage – was essentially routine and parochial. There is a strong sense of the First or Second Empire, when for most of the time liberal democracy was heavily censored.[54]

This was a reflection of a concerted drive by the Vichy regime to have done with the corrupt and self-serving reign of the politicians and to increase the authority and prestige of public officials. All French prefects were summoned to Vichy on 19 February 1942 to take a solemn oath to Marshal Pétain and to demonstrate that national unity overrode the division between Occupied and Free Zones. Interior Minister Pierre Pucheu, who orchestrated the ceremony, announced that with the suspension of France's decadent political institutions prefects were now 'the political guides of opinion, the intellectual and moral leaders of those they administer, they have the duty in a word to aspire to the role of real spiritual chiefs'.

He was, he said, continuing the work of his friend and predecessor at the ministry, Admiral Darlan. 'Your government no longer wants to know parties or partisans of the past. It sees in France only French people,' he concluded, all of whom had to follow the Marshal on the path he had traced.[55]

All this was music to the ears of Jean Roussillon, who now had a reason to assert his authority over the other prefects of his region in his mission to destroy the *ancien régime* of parliamentary intrigue. Pierre Daguerre, prefect delegate of Maine-et-Loire, noted that Moreau, the deputy-mayor of Baugé, with his eye on future elections, was having his photograph included in parcels sent to POWs, while Robert de Grandmaison, 'obsessed by his electoral fief' in the Saumurois, was 'worried about a diminution of his rights of suzerainty'. 'It is vital', he reported, 'that the prefectoral administration replaces parliamentary activity which is seeking to survive.'[56] The Baugeois and Saumurois were to some extent an extension of Touraine, which was the real problem. The new prefect, Jean Tracou, a naval man who had headed Admiral Darlan's office, shared all the political prejudices of his master Roussillon, who was well pleased with him. He warned of the

> *attentisme* of the supporters of the old politics. They do not believe that 'the Pétain experiment' will last or succeed. They laugh at the label of 'ralliés' which has sometimes been given to them too generously and allowed them to keep their positions of command. Confidently they await the return of the old system. From the beginning of the century the department has been the finest example of a 'rotten borough' of left-wing parties that the parliamentary regime has produced. As before it is richly larded with Freemasons, sympathizers of Freemasonry, creatures of the Chautemps dynasty and supporters of the Popular Front. A timid purge has affected only the small fry, without importance. The bosses are still in place. In no way have they rallied to the Marshal's government. Quite simply, they are prudent and waiting.

The cancer, said Tracou, went as far as the administrative commission, which was controlled in his opinion by Dr Guillaume-Louis, 'the grand elector, liegeman and close friend of Camille Chautemps' and François Servant, 'the rural grand elector, client of deputy Bernier, and himself the declared enemy of the government'. Meanwhile Ferdinand Morin, mayor of Tours, despite his courage in 1940, was 'one of the most remarkable representatives of the previous regime', anti-militarist, anti-religious, a 'mediocre administrator' whose only concern was to cultivate his electorate.[57]

To confront the issue Roussillon went to Tours and made a major speech at the prefecture to the heads of administrative departments, notables and the press. He underlined the goals of the National Revolution and made clear 'the intention of the new administration no longer to tolerate the failings of the past and to complete the break with unassimilable elements of the *ancien régime*'. How easy it was to uproot this regime was another question, and Roussillon told Pucheu that 'The department of Indre-et-Loire is one of those where, in the past, under the influence of the likes of Chautemps, Bernier and Morin, radicalism and freemasonry have thrust their deepest roots and larded the public services with their clients.'[58] Some 'improvements' were made. As we have seen, Guillaume-Louis was denounced by a faction of his own staff, lost his directorship of the Medical School and dropped from the political scene. Laval's police chief, René Bousquet, was keen to intern a few leading 'Gaullists' in each department to 'encourager les autres'. Prefect Tracou suggested Robert Chautemps, a forty-eight-year-old lawyer and cousin of Camille Chautemps, who was regarded as amoral and dissolute. 'Too clever to express his opinions openly, he acts deceitfully and by denigration in private, an ironic and sarcastic mind which uses every opportunity to criticize the Marshal and M. Laval'. Another suggestion was Charles Dubourg, a printer and former *adjoint* of Morin on the municipal council of Tours. Though he claimed to be a friend of Laval, he was 'constantly in the cafés of the market quarter, stirring up discontent among café owners and traders'.[59] His arrest, moreover, helped to bring down Morin, who was prevailed upon to stand down as mayor of Tours in December 1942.

The idea that the notables of the Third Republic could simply be purged, however, remained a dream. The tentacles of their clientage system spread too far, as the Vichy prefects in their more lucid moments appreciated. More important, however, was the fact that they *were* the notables, and without their cooperation no regime could function. The Vichy model of direct administration, with prefects and subprefects cutting out the political middleman and making regular tours to meet rural mayors, was impossible to sustain in practice. Besides, the invisible hand of the local politicians, grand electors who had built their careers on cultivating mayors, school-teachers, shopkeepers, café owners and the like, was always there, and in the last resort Vichy simply had to negotiate. Vichy was caught in an impossible contradiction, wanting to make government more autonomous and to destroy the remnants of parliamentarism, but needing to find a broad popular base which even in a democratic system was mediated by notables.

This contradiction soon became obvious in the functioning of the administrative commissions. Interior Minister Pucheu, so keen to energize and even politicize the prefectoral corps, also realized that the truncated and powerless commissions sitting beside them occasionally had no purchase on the country at large. In December 1941 he therefore declared that 'the moment has come to associate the representatives of the *pays réel* closely to the work of the government'. The commissions were to be enlarged from seven or nine to fifteen or twenty-five individuals, 'not resembling assemblies of notables but corresponding to the social composition of the department, representatives of the liberal professions, of rural populations, of the working class and of the economic interests of the region'. For the administrative commission of Loire-Inférieure Prefect Dupard proposed a shoemaker who also taught for the Chamber of Trades, a fitter and boilermaker who were shop stewards at the Chantiers Dubigeon and also on the Nantes municipal council, and a turner at the Chantiers de Penhouët at Saint-Nazaire, who was secretary of the Catholic engineers' union. He also, however, proposed Pierre Toscer, mayor of Saint-Nazaire, the director of the Chantiers de Bretagne, and Yves Bureau, professor at the Medical School of Nantes, father of eight and a lobbyist on family issues.[60] On the administrative commission of Indre-et-Loire the silent worker Goujon was joined by André Garantie, secretary of the Bourse du Travail of Tours, municipal councillor and supporter of the Labour Charter, by Émile Oudin, a Catholic railway unionist and president of the Catholic unions in the department, and by Charles Vavasseur, member of the Conseil National, mayor of Vouvray and producer of the local sparkling wine.[61]

The enlarged administrative commissions had not met, however, before the government of Pierre Laval planned an even more radical reform. While adopting a new collaborationist and authoritarian line in one way, turning France into much more of a police state,[62] he also realized as a veteran politician of the Third Republic that if bridges to the political class were not built, the regime was doomed. 'Deprived of all decision-making powers and all right of initiative,' wrote one official of the Ministry of the Interior, 'the administrative commissions give the prefect only a platonic and ineffectual support.'[63] The answer, extraordinarily, was found in the return of the *conseils généraux* or something very close to them, called departmental councils. At a meeting of regional prefects of the Occupied Zone in May 1942, Laval's acolytes Georges Hilaire of the Ministry of the Interior and police chief René Bousquet explained Laval's view that the departmental councils would be made up of one councillor per canton, as were the *conseils généraux*, except that they would be appointed, not elected. Obviously councillors would have to have 'rallied' to Marshal Pétain and his government but, stated Hilaire, 'only those who belong to condemned milieux – Gaullists, communists, warmongers – would be excluded. Socialists who had rallied would not be left out.' The 'idea of social representation' used in appointments to the administrative commissions would be a factor but what really mattered was an individual's 'influence over opinion' and 'the maximum authority in the local environment'. A reliable gauge of this influence and authority was having been elected as mayor or *conseiller général*, and this meant in effect a return to the rule of notables. The typical candidate would be the mayor of the main town in the canton. Inevitably this would prejudice the chances of workers' representatives who had been accommodated on the commissions, but Bousquet pointed out that 'the aim was *the constitution of a political assembly* [my italics], to be recruited according to political not occupational criteria. It was quite different from the representation of the Corporation Paysanne and the Charter of Labour which was done on an occupational basis.'[64]

And so it came to pass that under the law of August 1942 all notions of corporative representation were brushed aside. When the furriers' organization in Indre-et-Loire argued that each occupational family under the Charter of Labour should be represented, it was told that being a municipal councillor was a minimum qualification.[65] Labour representatives were now considered much less attractive. Jean Goujon, the garagist who had sat silently on the administrative commission at Tours, was not included on the grounds that he 'had no credit with the working class. A decent chap, who represents nothing.' On the political front the opportunity was taken to weed out those who, though mayors of the main town in the canton, failed the fidelity test. Out finally in Indre-et-Loire were the drunken demagogue Dr Labussière, Ferdinand Morin, whose days as mayor of Tours were numbered, François Servant, described as being 'at the forefront of pre-war electoral struggles', and Paul Guillaume-Louis, 'considered the standard-bearer of Masonic, Gaullist and anticlerical sectarian elements in the department'.[66]

There was however no automatic blacklisting of parliamentarians, according to the early rhetoric of Vichy. In his proposals to the Ministry of the Interior, Prefect Tracou of Indre-et-Loire took into account 'the political situation of the department, as it appears from the legislative elections of 1936 and cantonal elections [to the *conseil général*] of 1937, in which radicals and socialists had done well'. Although the new councillors were not elected, the understanding was that the 'dosage' should reflect the balance of political opinion. Robert de Grandmaison was finally admitted to the council in Maine-et-Loire, on the grounds that he was the dominant radical figure in the Saumurois. He was delighted to return to house-to-house campaigning, only to find, reported Prefect Daguerre with some ironic pleasure, 'that he did not find the support he hoped for. In fact he even had some rather scathing rejections.'[67] René Tardif was considered since 'although he was very attached to his political ideas he seemed to have rallied to the government ... his former colleagues of the Conseil Général appreciate his strong and lively intelligence'.[68] In the end, however, he was thought too unreliable and dropped. Gaston Moreau, mayor and former deputy of Baugé, was kept out initially because he had attended a meeting of the collaborationist Jacques Doriot in Angers and was suspected of being Doriot's candidate for prefect in the event of an extreme right-wing coup. But he was also thought to be too subtle a politician to commit himself irrevocably to the fascists and had to be included when the first choice for the canton died.[69] In Loire-Inférieure, finally, the socialist deputies Pageot and Blancho who had demonstrated their unreliability and had in any case moved to the Free Zone were excluded, and Jean Le Cour Grandmaison, also in the Free Zone, was left out, but otherwise the cohort of aristocrats and their academic allies were back: the Marquis de La Ferronnays, Hubert de Montaigu, Gustave Gautherot and Louis Linyer.

In many respects the departmental councils were the *conseils généraux* resuscitated, and contemporaries were only too aware of this when they finally met in the spring of 1943. At the opening of that of Loire-Inférieure Prefect Dupard praised the old *conseil général*, which had 'always preserved the ancestral traditions that are the basis of French greatness', and paid especial homage to its last president, the Marquis de La Ferronnays. Taking up the theme, the new president of the departmental council, Ricordeau, mayor of Saffré and barrister at the Nantes Bar, said that the Council 'is a continuation of age-old institutions': the provincial assembly of the *ancien régime* (pre-1789 style), the departmental councils of the Revolution, and the *conseils généraux*, which were variously appointed or elected.[70] In Maine-et-Loire, at the opening of the council, Jean Roussillon announced likewise that 'the new assembly is, in essence, only a reproduction of the old one', even to the extent that the mayor of Angers, Victor Bernier, president of one, was also president of the other.[71] For one local paper the *ancien régime* comparison was full of revolutionary foreboding. The list of councillors, it announced scornfully, 'gives us a taste of the past: that of Louis XV and [his wife] Marie Leczynska . . . Everywhere names with handles, conservatives, monarchists, national republicans . . . the new Parlement is born. The registers of grievances will follow.'[72]

The continuity between *conseil général* and departmental council was greatest where the traditional élites still held sway in 1940. In Indre-et-Loire, for example, the 'rotten borough' of radicalism, only five of the twenty-four seats (21 per cent) were filled by former *conseillers généraux*. In Loire-Inférieure, split between conservatives and socialists, the proportion was seventeen out of forty-six (37 per cent). In Maine-et-Loire, which apart from the Saumurois was dominated by the Right, twenty-one of the thirty-two members of the new departmental council (62 per cent) were carried over from the old *conseil général*, offering clear proof of the adaptability of the local notables to the pressures of the Occupation.

Just as significant, however, were the limits set to the bridge-building between the new departmental councils and the public at large. As the Occupation wore on and the fortunes of war changed, adaptability came less to mean changing one's spots to fit in with the new regime than holding back as the odds against the durability of the 'Pétain experiment' shortened. *Attentisme* may have been a dirty word invented by Vichy but it corresponded to a calculation that it would pay not to be too compromised by association with the regime the day the Americans landed. This reluctance to serve was already apparent in the failure to fill all the places on the departmental councils. That of Maine-et-Loire was complete, but there had been great difficulty finding candidates to sit for the radical Saumurois. Six cantons out of twenty-four were without representation in Indre-et-Loire, including the bases of Guillaume-Louis and Servant, although numbers were made up by two workers – Garantie and Oudin – carried over from the administrative commission. Most worrying, ten of the forty-six seats on the Departmental Council of Loire-Inférieure lay fallow. The gaps multiplied as a result of resignations as the fortunes of Vichy faltered. Garantie, sensing rather late that the labour movement had long been moving in the opposite direction, resigned from the departmental council and from the municipal council of Tours in January 1944. Absenteeism increased as many who remained formally members stayed away. At the second session of the Council of Indre-et-Loire there were four absentees, while in June 1944 only six of the nineteen councillors turned up and, for want of a quorum, the meeting was postponed until 8 July. On that day President Vavasseur spoke of the suffering into which the country had been plunged and the Council bravely adopted a motion appealing 'to all French people to gather around Marshal Pétain and work together for the uplifting of our dear country'.[73] Loyal this minority was, but it was a small group of notables who had now lost all influence and authority, twisting in the wind.

Many if not most of the members of the departmental councils were mayors, who were experiencing their own conflicts of loyalties. At the beginning of the Occupation Vichy enjoyed a certain luxury as to who to confirm and who to remove, particularly in the large towns, while expecting that rural communes would look after themselves. Increasingly, however, rural communes began to present problems. Even in the conservative, Catholic Mauges the subprefect had to investigate Comte Hubert d'Anthenaise, accused in *Je suis partout* of 'leading a ceaseless and perfidious campaign against the Marshal's government' and of telling people that the population of Anjou was going to be deported to Upper Silesia.[74] This turned out to be a libel by a rival in Action Française, but at Montfaucon-sur-Moine the problem was real enough. The mayor resigned in 1941, the municipal council was dissolved, and a special delegation was appointed under a former mayor to look after the commune. But the commune remained totally divided between factions, the leader of one of which was placed under house arrest in the summer of 1944.[75]

Incidents such as these obliged the government to extend the powers it had to replace elected mayors, *adjoints* or municipal councils by appointed special delegations. But as with representation higher up, the government was torn between taking a tough line to ensure loyalty to Pétain and the Vichy government and not alienating support that was increasingly difficult to count upon. When Pierre Laval returned to power he ordered all busts of Marianne to be removed from town halls and schools, but also urged prefects to use their powers to interfere in municipal politics sparingly. There was the danger that local councils would 'become discouraged or lose their authority', and if new delegations were appointed care must be taken to represent the local population as broadly as possible.[76] The obvious way out of the contradiction was to work closely with local government and energetically rally support. Prefect Daguerre told the mayors of Maine-et-Loire that they must 'think in common, act in common, obey in common' because, according to the best teaching of Vichy, a house divided against itself could not stand. After his third tour of the department in March 1943 he said that he had criticized those who had fled the country and asserted that 'those who have stayed at their posts with some risk, since the Occupation, have no lessons in patriotism to take from those who ran away'.[77]

Many prefects and subprefects were as diligent as they could be in their meetings with groups of local mayors. More seductive was the ritual of an introduction to Marshal Pétain himself. In October 1943 eight mayors from each department in the Angers region were selected to make the trip to Vichy. These included mayors of large towns – Nantes, Saint-Nazaire, Angers, Cholet, Saumur and Tours, but also smaller communes. Dr Guillaume-Louis, mayor of Montbazon, was rather surprisingly invited, but replied that while being 'very touched' was unable to accept because of 'pressing professional obligations at Tours'. Since he was no longer director of the Medical School we may conclude that he felt that at this stage in the Occupation it would be unwise to have his picture taken shaking hands with Marshal Pétain. The Touraine delegation went bearing gifts: an 1884 magnum of Vouvray, two bottles of Bourgueil and two of Montlouis (communes of two of the mayors), leather from the tanning factory of Jacques Hervé, mayor of Château-Renault, fruit from Athée-sur-Cher, where Rémy Poitevin was farmer and mayor, and books from the publisher Mame of Tours. At the ceremony the eighty-seven-year-old Marshal showed that he had lost none of the art of conversation. He spoke to the mayor of Tours about his visit to the city in October 1940 after meeting Hitler at Montoire, to the Comte de Tristan, mayor of Chambon, who had only recently been released from a POW camp, about life in Germany, to Mayor Hervé about leather, to Mayor Boutet of Bossée, a farmer, about milk and butter, and to mayor Reneuve of Montlouis, a pig-farmer, about pig-killing.[78]

It is significant that the mayors from Touraine included none of the familiar radical bosses. These were already thinking of rallying according to their own rules, reviving the Association of Mayors of Indre-et-Loire. Founded in 1919, it had been in eclipse since 1939 but Gounin, a wealthy shoe manufacturer and radical–socialist mayor of Amboise, was keen to relaunch it. The problem for the administration was that it was a fief of radical mayors, and although Gounin was 'by a long way the most active and intelligent member', it would be unwise to put him at the head of it. Anticlerical, possibly a Freemason, and pro-Popular Front, he was ostensibly loyal to Vichy but 'the sincerity of his conversion is questioned by many of his adversaries and his spirit of intrigue makes him quite redoubtable'. As a compromise Prefect Tracou suggested resurrecting the association under Vavasseur of Vouvray, a good Pétainist who was due to be president of the departmental council. But Regional Prefect Roussillon would have nothing at all to do with it, arguing that it was a subversive vehicle of radical mayors of the Third Republic. This was not the moment, he asserted, 'to recycle people who only recently had a fierce part in local electoral struggles on the political circuit, and to re-establish an organization which would be at best a useless intermediary and at worst a screen between the administration and the people'.[79]

With or without such associations, however, mayors were in the nature of things intermediaries between the administration and the people. They could choose to act as transmission belts relaying official instructions or they could act as screens or buffers to protect local people from official pressures. As the Occupation progressed, those pressures intensified. Mayors were held responsible for delivering quotas of grain, milk, butter or livestock. They were held responsible for delivering quotas of labour for Germany. They had on their backs not only the Vichy administration but the Germans, and the more demands were made, the more angrily local populations reacted, making the position of the mayors in between almost untenable. In November 1942, with the implementation of the *Relève* to exchange workers for POWs, a rash of mayors in the Châteaubriant area resigned. They had been insulted, molested and even received death threats from workers who had been chosen to go to Germany or because their own sons had mysteriously not been chosen.[80] Jacques Hedouin, a Vichy-appointed mayor of Vernoil-le-Fourrier on the Anjou–Touraine border, refused to hand over wheat that had been requisitioned on the grounds that he needed it to feed the local population before the new harvest came in. Accused of 'communal autarky', he argued that he had always 'defended his commune without any ill-will and certain of having done my duty', and promptly resigned.[81] Of 282 mayors in Indre-et-Loire thirty-seven resigned in 1942 and twenty-seven in 1943, the typical mayor being a farmer aged over sixty.[82] Defending the interests of one's commune might win the loyalty of the locals but infuriated the Germans, who as their situation deteriorated demanded ever more foodstuffs, labour for Germany, and labour for local defences. In the first two months of 1944 alone they arrested twenty mayors or their secretaries in Touraine. Squeezed between Vichy and the Germans on the one hand and an increasingly frightened and hostile population on the other, mayors were increasingly siding with the local population. The loss of mayoral support compounded the loss of support on the departmental councils. The notables finally turned their backs on Vichy and without the notables Vichy could not survive.

The vigour of local government, set alongside the flourishing of trade unions, peasant organizations, charities and cultural associations, confirms that civil society, despite the difficulties it faced, was in no sense eclipsed under the German Occupation. It also demonstrates that the authoritarianism of the Vichy regime was limited by its reliance for effectiveness on the influence of local notables who ran municipal and departmental councils by virtue of their family connections, professional status or private wealth. Vichy was unable to purge local government of its ideological enemies even if it wanted to. Against the grain of their subsequent brutal reputations it was Interior Minister Pucheu who advised that local government must reflect the political makeup of the locality, while Prime Minister Laval wanted to bring back the political class as a whole through a revival in all but name of the *conseils généraux*. What was required of local notables, independent of their political affiliation (unless they were communists) was express loyalty to the Vichy regime. Some were happy to do this emphatically, others paid only lip service while waiting for times to change. These were the trimmers who, as we shall see, ensured a peaceful transition to the new republic in 1944. Their pivotal role between Vichy and the people calls into question the distinction that has gained some authority between the Vichy regime on the one hand and the French on the other. The most one can say is that the task of mediation became more and more difficult as pressure from the Germans for labour and resources increased, and that increasingly local administrators were either siding with the local population against the authorities, passively if not actively, or using resignation as the obvious exit from their dilemma. By 1944 the Vichy regime in Occupied France had lost its anchor in the local community.

9. SAINTS

Four days before the Allied landings in Normandy, in the early evening of 2 June 1944, a large crowd, headed by the bishop of Nantes, the mayor and his council, waited on the outskirts of Ancenis, a market town on the Loire at the gateway between Anjou and Brittany.

> There were thousands of people, reciting the rosary, singing familiar anthems, offering to heaven the supplications of the *Pace Domine*. Children from the schools and catechism classes, pupils from the Institution Saint-Joseph, the Petit Séminaire of Guérande, the Enfants-Nantais Day School and the Joliverie who had been evacuated [from the coast] to the Ancenis area, young men and women of Action Catholique, nuns of every order and every habit, were drawn up in the beautiful green setting of the Hospital courtyard. Then behind the surplices of the choristers and priests appeared the white vision of the Madonna. What a moving moment it was finally to behold the Virgin who had already travelled halfway across France and was now here to spread her blessings among us.

The statue of Our Lady of Boulogne, carried in her boat, was welcomed by Mgr Villepelet, who warned her nevertheless that she would travel 'the path of suffering' across the diocese, greeted by the families of prisoners of war, evacuees, disaster victims, the ruins of Nantes and Saint-Nazaire. Taking words from the mouth of Joan of Arc, he said that

> there always was great distress (*grande pitié*) in the diocese of Nantes. Has this beautiful jewel of Christianity been cast into the crucible of suffering in order to throw up ever brighter flames? We

accept the will of your Son. But we ask you to bind our wounds and dry our tears. You, whose eyes have cried so much, understand us. Bring the comfort of your maternal tenderness to our unspeakable grief. Share with us our way of the cross, and as you advance bring forth under your feet joyful days, dawns that herald peace. *Prospere procede et regna!* In your splendour and majesty, proceed and reign.[1]

This rapturous welcome for a statue of the Virgin Mary was replicated in a thousand towns and villages towards the end of the Occupation. To make this possible four identical statues had been made and sent off on their own itineraries, assuaging the hungry faithful. The reception of Our Lady of Boulogne suggests a piety and fervour that might be thought uncommon in the mid-twentieth century which was, after all, supposed to be a period of secularization.[2] People were only too willing to accept the Catholic version of events, that war, defeat and Occupation had been visited on the French for their sins: their materialism, selfishness, pleasure-seeking and turning away from God. Salvation would come only through prayer, repentance, a return to the paths of righteousness. God would offer his protection again, but the Almighty could only be approached by mere humans through the intercession of the saints, and above all of the Virgin Mary.

For the bishop of Nantes and his flock appeals to Providence were the traditional and obvious way of responding to catastrophe. Four years earlier, in May 1940, as German forces swept into France, Mgr Villepelet promised that like his predecessor, who during the German invasion of 1870 pledged to build a new church to bear witness to the protection of Nantes by the Sacred Heart, he too would build a new church dedicated to Mary the Mediator should the city of Nantes be saved. Saved it was from the bombardment suffered by Tours, Saumur, Angers, Rennes and Bordeaux, but his prayers for the protection of France had not been answered, and the causes for this had to be sought.[3] Speaking on 16 June 1940 to the Federation of Young Christian Women of Nantes as the Germans advanced towards the city, the bishop was in no doubt what the causes were. France had been defeated not by military superiority nor even by social strife but by dechristianization and sin. 'France has driven Christ from the law courts and schools,' he proclaimed. 'She has expelled the religious congregations. She has systematically and deliberately destroyed all faith in the souls of too many of its children. She has tolerated vice, immorality and wrong. She has undermined the family by divorce and suppressed the birth rate.'[4] The remedy to this disaster was also plain. The French must return to the ways of God, by prayer, repentance, reparation, even sacrifice. All those with the power to intercede – angels, saints, the Virgin Mary – must be mobilized. Eventually God would be placated and restore the hand of protection to France.

In one way the defeat was already a start. It had cleared from power the republican politicians, manipulated by Freemasons and Jews, who for seventy years had pursued their work of dechristianization. The new regime under Marshal Pétain was thus to be welcomed. Following a meeting of the cardinals and archbishops of the Occupied Zone on 28 August 1940 all dioceses recommended three rules of conduct to the clergy and faithful, which were published in October: '1. Absolute loyalty to the legitimate power in France; 2. The greatest spirit of order and exact discipline in relations with the Occupation authorities; 3. The greatest discretion in things said, either in public or private.' One of the archbishops, Mgr Gaillard of Tours, immediately had the occasion to put these rules into effect on 25 October 1940, when, following his meeting with Hitler at Montoire, just to the north of the diocese, Marshal Pétain, accompanied by Prefect Vernet and Mayor Morin, visited him in his palace. Pétain praised the archbishop's conduct during the bombardment of the city by the Germans and in reply Mgr Gaillard 'guaranteed the confident admiration and perfect loyalty of the whole diocese, clergy and faithful, with respect to the Marshal and his government, as well as the constant prayers that would rise from Touraine to call down heavenly assistance for him'. Evidently moved by his experience, in January 1941 Mgr Gaillard told the faithful that 'French citizens are not only the friends but the subjects of Marshal Pétain', who was no less than 'God's representative'. Within days, however, the assembly of cardinals and archbishops of the Occupied Zone meeting in Paris were in fact moderating their language, replacing loyalty to the 'legitimate power' to loyalty to the 'established power' (15 January 1941). Obedience was still required, but already (except perhaps for star-struck Mgr Gaillard) Vichy had lost a little of its aura.[5]

No particular ideological revolution was required here. The

Church always rendered unto Caesar what was Caesar's. But the Vichy regime made it easy by reversing much of the anticlerical legislation that had been passed since 1870. Religious instruction could be given in state schools for the first time since 1882. State subsidies could be made to private Catholic schools for the first time since 1886. Religious congregations that had been driven out of France under legislation of 1901 and 1904 were allowed to return.[6] The Masonic lodges, which were seen by Catholics to be at the origin of this anticlerical offensive, were dissolved.[7] Relations between Church and State, which had been virtually non-existent under the Third Republic, were rebuilt. 'How times have changed!' exclaimed Mgr Villepelet as Prefect Leroy and his Jewish wife were replaced by Prefect Dupard, who asked him to confirm his twins and invited him to dinner at the prefecture, and two years later organized a huge wedding for his daughter in the cathedral.[8] Mgr Gaillard instructed his parish clergy to meet the 'temporal authorities' – mayors, school-teachers, tax collectors, delegates of the Secours National, Youth and Sports – and reserve them places in church, so that when he appeared on a pastoral visit, or for Joan of Arc Day or Mother's Day, he might be introduced by name.[9]

The Church did not have it all its own way. Vichy was not a clerical regime and ministers changed so fast that the promises made by one were rarely kept by the next. Rector Vincent of the Catholic University of Angers lobbied hard to obtain official recognition, state subsidies and degree-giving powers for the 'Catho', only to find, as he put it, that the Education Ministry was still staffed by 'militant secularists if not Freemasons', who frustrated him at every turn.[10] In spite of such setbacks the Catholic Church remained an extremely powerful institution and was becoming even more so. Given that under German military administration and cut off from Vichy the state was a shadow of its former self, it could be argued that the Catholic Church, rather on the Irish or Polish model, was the strongest French institution in Occupied France.

Included in the Church were not only the hierarchy of bishops and priests, but the religious congregations, especially those of women, who had weathered the anticlerical onslaught of the turn of the century and had a powerful role in hospitals, charities and church schools. In 1943 there were 14 female religious congregations in Angers, from the Carmelites to the Little Sisters of the Poor, 16 in

Tours and 17 in Nantes.[11] Most parishes had a *patronage* or youth club, the object of which was to provide wholesome recreation for young people, and the Catholic Scout movement was far more developed than its secular rival, the Éclaireurs. The interwar period saw the development of Action Catholique which, under the control of the clergy, developed different branches to colonize different constituencies: Jeunesse Étudiante Chrétienne (JEC), the Jeunesse Agricole Chrétienne (JAC) and the Jeunesse Ouvrière Chrétienne (JOC), which was said to be expanding in Tours as fast as the Communist Youth was declining.[12] Mobilized against a new threat of anticlericalism from the Cartel des Gauches government of 1924–6 was the National Catholic Federation of General de Castelnau and its affiliated branches, which included, as we have seen, the Catholic Association of Family Heads of the Diocese of Nantes and the Catholic League of Anjou, under Vicomte Palamède de la Grandière.[13] For both the baptism of fire was a demonstration in March 1925 against Freemasonry, attended in Angers by an estimated 50,000 people.[14] Inevitably there were women's organizations which paralleled those dominated by men, such as the Patriotic League of French Women in the diocese of Nantes, headed by the Marquise de La Ferronnays. Far from being out of touch, the Church was always quick to put the latest technology to use. The Catholic press included a weekly diocesan magazine and parish magazines for most parishes and the Association of Family Heads of the Diocese of Nantes promoted local Catholic radio, while 60 per cent of cinemas in Loire-Inférieure were controlled by Catholic *patronages*.[15] Admittedly, the influence of the Church was not equal in all parts of the region, as measured by the rough indicator of what proportion of the adult population attended Mass on a Sunday. West of Angers, at the turn of the century, the proportion was over 90 per cent in the diocese of Nantes and the *arrondissements* of Cholet and Segré. East of Angers, by contrast, the figure was 58 per cent in the *arrondissement* of Baugé and 48 per cent in that of Saumur at the turn of the century, and 18 per cent in the diocese of Tours in 1936–9, falling to 11 per cent in the canton of Bléré and 8 per cent in that of Château-la-Vallière. In what was historically the Vendée the grip of the Church was thus immovable, whereas east of the river Layon the challenge of anticlericalism and religious indifference was far stronger.[16]

Despite its stronger position vis-à-vis the Vichy state, however, the

Catholic Church had much to fear from Nazi persecution. Having liquidated all opposition parties, the Third Reich began to attack the press, schools and youth movements of the Catholic Church in Germany on the grounds that what was formally religious practice concealed political opposition to the regime.[17] In France the main concern of the German military authorities was with anything that might be construed as a threat to the army. Their initial position on occupying France was nervy and intolerant. It soon emerged, however, that German regulations concerning the Church were confused and unevenly applied, and that a headstrong bishop could on occasion force his adversaries to climb down.

When the Germans arrived in Nantes they forbade bell-ringing, lest it be used as a call to arms. After a month, however, they relaxed the ban, in time for the bells to ring for the feast of St Anne, patron saint of Brittany.[18] German officers went to the printer of *La Semaine religieuse* of Nantes, having heard a story that the bishop had written a fiercely patriotic pastoral letter, and the Kommandantur asked the bishop to stop 'all attacks on the German army and all propaganda agitation by the clergy among the population by spoken or written word'. It required *La Semaine religieuse* to be submitted for censorship prior to publication and tried to stop 'politics' infiltrating the magazine in the shape of prayers for POWs and letters from priests in POW camps.[19] Purely religious processions were generally permitted, but there was some confusion over what 'purely religious' meant. Funerals were sometimes used as an excuse to drape a tricolour flag over the coffin, and that was banned. Traditional processions to cemeteries and graveside speeches on All Saints' Day, 1 November, were prohibited throughout Occupied France because since the Great War it had become a prelude to Armistice Day, which commemorated victory over Germany in 1918 and was very popular with veterans. Only prefects and mayors were allowed to lay wreaths on behalf of the French people. But while the Feldkommandant of Nantes enforced the ban rigidly, that of Angers permitted processions that were 'purely religious'. Such was the confusion that some mayors in Loire-Inférieure formally dissociated themselves from processions led by the parish priest lest they should get into trouble, while in Nueil-sur-Layon in Anjou the priest and mayor were both arrested by the local gendarmerie on the grounds that they were violating the ban.[20]

Another target of German repression were Catholic youth movements such as the JAC and JOC, which fell under the ban of 28 August 1940 prohibiting all uniformed movements. In Nantes a Jocist wearing the movement's badge was arrested and interrogated at the Kommandantur.[21] At Angers Feldkommandant Kloss complained that 'a large number of young people, accompanied by clergy, have recently been going on trips to the country, either by bicycle or on foot. These trips are more than purely religious and thus cannot be allowed.' General Neumann-Neurode reported that the surveillance of banned Catholic youth organizations was extremely difficult. The clergy were trying everything to regroup the Catholic youth in sports clubs. In the spring of 1941 there was a region-wide scare that the JAC was continuing to function illegally, and prefects were put under pressure by the German authorities to ensure that all meetings that were not 'purely religious' were prohibited. This stipulation was incomprehensible to some local clergy. The curé of Champtoceaux, for example, said that young people had been meeting for the last few months but 'do not belong to any organization. The meetings are to instruct them in agriculture and religion. There has never been any question of talking politics, and we are totally comitted to obeying the orders of the Marshal.' A French cleric, used to a tradition where many associations were required to eschew politics, could not see the thrust of a ban that was determined by reasons of military security.[22]

One of the reasons why the Germans had difficulty enforcing their restrictions was the stubbornness of the French clergy. True, some clergy were easier to intimidate than others. Mgr Costes had laboured under the shadow of the previous bishop of Angers, who was ninety when he eventually died in 1940, so that Costes was somewhat fragile when he took over at the age of sixty-seven. The adjective most frequently used of him was that he was good. 'He never tired of being good,' his funeral orator later declared. In August 1940 Costes told his clergy never to comment from the pulpit on current affairs, and to deal only with religious and moral issues. 'Repentance, courage, dignity in the face of adversity, conscientious work, prayer, trust in Providence, confidence in the inexhaustible goodness of God, effort to the point of sacrifice, limitless love of those who are wounded in their body or soul', all these were what they should aim to preach. So timorous was he that he cancelled the main Mother's

Day service in Angers 1941 because he thought – owing to a mistranslation – that the Germans had banned it, and subsequently had to apologize shamefacedly to his flock.[23]

Mgr Villepelet, bishop of Nantes, was made of sterner stuff. Ten days after the Germans arrived in Nantes he received a telephone call from the town hall to say that the Kommandantur had requested the use of the cathedral for a service the following Sunday. For Villepelet, the holding of a Protestant service in the cathedral was a 'scandal' that must be prevented at all costs. When the German Protestant pastor turned up to make the request in person Villepelet flatly refused, saying that 'it is not a question of nationality but a religious issue'. But when the German Catholic chaplain, whose superior – the bishop of Paderborn – Villepelet happened to know, asked a month later if the cathedral could be used for Catholic services, which had already taken place, he said, in Angers, Villepelet played for time by saying that he would have to consult the papal nuncio. The climax came at Christmas 1940, by which time it became clear that the cathedrals of Tours and Bourges had been used for Protestant services, a swastika flag hanging from the pulpit. Villepelet was visited by the ordnance officer of Feldkommandant Hotz who demanded use of the cathedral for Christmas Eve. The bishop again refused, at which the colonel, 'cold and impassive', threatened to requisition it. Villepelet reiterated that 'the cathedral is the personal church of the bishop; I cannot allow a Protestant service to take place there, under my eyes'. He offered them the church of St Donatian as an alternative, but the colonel riposted that the German military would regard this as a slight. The following day, however, the colonel returned with a Protestant pastor and conceded that St Donatian, with its twin towers, had a cathedral-like façade, so honour was saved. The cathedral was preserved for the diocese and Christmas Eve saw a gathering of the Catholic faithful as never before, with people clinging to every possible perch, the doors open on to the crowds left outside, and nearly 3,000 communion wafers were exhausted long before everyone was satisfied.[24]

With time the German military became a little more discerning about what kind of activities might constitute a security risk and what would not. In April 1941 they decreed that traditional religious processions would be able to take place without permission being sought, so long as they were informed in good time. This meant that the Fête-Dieu or Corpus Christi processions of June 1941 were staged with especial splendour. 'This year,' declared Mgr Villepelet, 'because of the situation we are going through, our prayers will be still more plentiful and more fervent. You will pray for France, for your dear war dead, for your prisoners, for the peace of the world.' The procession through the streets of Nantes of the Holy Sacrament on its dais of velvet embroidered with gold brought together Church and state in a public display of solidarity. Led by the curés, choir school and seminarists, the Host was followed by Mgr Villepelet, his vicars-general, archpriests and canons, notables such as Jean Le Cour Grandmaison of the Conseil National, Paul Brossier, president of the Chamber of Commerce, the municipal council and members of the former *conseil général*, girls who had taken First Communion in their tulle veils, carrying lilies, roses and gladioli, children from the church schools and parishioners with their banners.[25] Purely religious, and for that reason the only kind of procession the German military were prepared to tolerate, the stylized expression of ecclesiastical magnificence nevertheless had a resonance in the community that was more than simply religious.

The art of the Catholic Church under the Occupation was to sustain the widest variety of Catholic activity, beyond traditional religious services and processions. In the diocese of Nantes the Catholic Association of Heads of Families remained active, with annual retreats every January, taking advantage of the Vichy law of December 1942 which set up family associations in each commune to seize control of them. Its new president in 1941 was Dr Yves Bureau of the family movement, who used it as an additional platform for his campaign against immoral plays, films and dancing.[26] More delicate were the manoeuvrings of the JOC, which was officially banned but, like the scouts, continued to meet clandestinely or in other guises. Père Salmon, chaplain of the Touraine JOC, recalled that 'we met in places that were carefully blacked out and as the hour of curfew drew close we stopped the study group so that no one was arrested on the way home by German patrols. For retreats we went to Cormery in small groups so as not to attract attention, since the demarcation line was close by.' He remembers the dramatic meeting in 1943 when the executive had to decide what line to take over STO, the requisition of young men for labour service in Germany. In the end they decided to leave the decision as to whether to go or refuse to go to the conscience of those involved. Those who went would give spiritual support to young French workers but their ambitions would not stop there. 'If we meet young German workers over there,' they resolved, 'we will make them into Jocists, and plant the Jocist cross in the place of the swastika.'[27]

Refusing to go to work in Germany was often seen as a token of resistance, but the notion of resistance in the case of the Catholic Church has to be put in context. The defence of the Catholic Church as an institution was in itself a 'politics of presence' that offered a guarantee against the Nazification of France and the French.[28] There were clergy who became more involved in Resistance activities, reaching out to those in overlapping institutions, such as the armed forces, or simply to their brothers, Christian or otherwise. Canon Robin, dean of St Martin's Cathedral, Tours, had served as an army chaplain and briefly been a POW in France in the summer of 1940. He would regularly shelter escaping POWs, employing them in the gardens or cellars of the cathedral for a few days, before passing them to other contacts: Captain Morel of the Tours gendarmerie, and a cluster of agents along the demarcation line, including Abbé Lacour, curé of Athée, Abbé Lhermitte, curé of Esvres-sur-Loire, Abbé Péan, curé of Draché, Abbé Roussel and André Goupille, respectively curé and vet of La Haye Descartes. Those they helped diversified from POWs to Resistance workers and Jews. The casualty rate of these agents was extremely high. Canon Robin survived to become bishop of Blois but Captain Morel was deported and executed in Cologne in 1943, Abbé Lacour and Abbé Lhermitte were deported in 1944 and never returned, Abbé Péan was arrested after saying Mass in February 1944 and was tortured to death by the Gestapo in Tours.[29] Some clergy belonged to established Resistance networks. In May 1942 Père de La Perraudière and Père de Solages of the Jesuit Collège Saint-Grégoire of Tours both put on Péguy's controversial *Jeanne d'Arc* in the college, as we saw in Chapter 6, and said a private Mass in the Carmelite convent for the five young communists who had been executed by the Germans outside the city on 16 May.[30] They were members of Ceux de la Libération, which was closely linked to Libération-Nord, a larger network that grouped both Christian democrats such as Anne-Marie Marteau of the Modern Girls College at Tours and socialists such as the former deputy of Tours, Jean Meunier. Père de La Perraudière was arrested when the Gestapo decimated Libération-Nord in September 1943 and died in Dachau in April 1945, while Père Solages fled south and became chaplain to the Maquis in the Tarn.

To a large extent these clergy took their cue from those around them. The German authorities in Cholet reported that 'with few exceptions, the clergy articulate the mood of the people against us'. One priest had told a meeting of young people that the air attacks on industrial targets in Paris, of which Vichy made such intense anti-British propaganda, were not necessarily the work of the British. Another told peasants from the pulpit that they did not have to obey the bishop's orders to deliver grain, because it would only be passed on to the Germans.[31] For the Vendean population of the Mauges who had risen up against the French Revolution in 1793 and experienced triumph, defeat and savage repression, the local Resistance hero was Dom Sortais, abbot of the Trappist monastery of Bellefontaine. A veteran and former POW, he was said to have hidden British airmen and STO dodgers in the monastery, and frequently declared from the pulpit that the French owed nothing to the Germans, not even obedience.[32] He incarnated a Catholic and conservative resistance to oppression that was the very essence of the Vendée.

These clergy, with their roots in local communities, did not act with the approval of the hierarchy. Bishops, as we have seen, co-operated with the state authorities to urge peasants to deliver their quotas of milk and grain. Archbishop Gaillard of Tours wrote severe and dispproving letters to Abbé Péan, nicknamed 'Péan le fou'.[33] Mgr Villepelet agreed to hold a solemn funeral in his cathedral for M. Le Bras, a Nantes judge involved in the business of repression, who had been shot dead by three 'terrorists', as he called them, who walked into his office.[34] For the upper clergy communism, which fired so much of the Resistance, was regarded as just as bad as Nazism, if not worse. To assess the contribution of the Catholic Church to Resistance or collaboration, however, is largely to miss the point. For the Church salvation would come not by force of arms but by divine intervention. The way forward, according to this world view, was to return to the way of God. Defeat and Occupation had been sent as a punishment for the sins of the French people; liberation and peace would come from Providence, once the French had shown themselves once more worthy of God's protection. The main business of the Church under the Occupation was therefore to step up prayer, repentance and renewal, to call upon the Virgin Mary and the saints to intercede with God. This was in no sense just spiritual abstraction. Through saint cults and pilgrimages the Church used its spiritual leverage to offer protection and hope to local populations who traditionally dedicated their prayers to specific saints and their local shrines.

Religious devotion in the diocese of Tours centred on the cult of St Martin, bishop of Tours in the fourth century, who famously gave his cloak to a beggar and was beheaded in 397. His head was placed in a separate reliquary in 1323 and was exhibited every 1 December until the Revolution.[35] Moribund since then, the ceremony of exhibiting the head of St Martin was revived by the archbishop of Tours under Vichy. On 30 November 1941 a procession of choirboys, seminarists, students of the Jesuit college of Saint-Grégoire, schoolchildren, nuns, womenfolk, the archbishop and his vicars-general, notables such as René Feld, secretary-general of the prefecture, and André Gouin, banker and leading conservative politician, bore the holy relic to the cathedral, where 3,000 people were seated. The following year Mgr Gaillard decided that in view of renewed enthusiasm for the cult of St Martin, the date of his ordination, 4 July 370, would be marked by a great procession of his relics along the banks of the Loire to the monastery of Marmoutier. 'We are not asking St Martin for the miracle that will save us with no effort from ourselves,' the archbishop announced at the monastery, 'we are rather asking for the faith of former times – religious faith to begin with and then its constant companion, patriotic faith – and with that faith the disciplined energy that will make us the true artisans of our salvation'.[36]

In the diocese of Angers the greatest enthusiasm was for the Marian cult, which had taken off after the defeat of 1870 under the great nineteenth-century bishop of Angers, Mgr Freppel. Every year on 8 September, date of the Nativity of the Virgin Mary, not one but three pilgrimages to Marian shrines took place. The first was to Our Lady of Béhuard, a shrine on a small island on the Loire below Angers, where a chapel had been built and the Virgin solemnly crowned in 1923. The second was to Our Lady of Marillais, further down the Loire near Ancenis. The third was Our Lady of Gardes, a high point of the Mauges, whose chapel was serviced by the Trappist monks of Bellefontaine. Of the pilgrimage to Béhuard of 8 September 1942, presided over by Mgr Costes, a reporter noted that 'many good people whom we met on the island had come impressive distances on foot. While the humble faithful recited their rosary as they walked, more educated people found themselves remembering the fine prayers of Louis Veuillot [an influential Catholic journalist in the nineteenth century] said on the road to Our Lady of Lorette or those of Charles Péguy as he made his pilgrimage from Paris to Chartres.' So great was the crush to take communion that young people arriving on foot were still queueing for it at 2 p.m.[37]

The Angevins, particularly those of the Mauges, also defined their Catholicism by reference to the Vendée, when the west rose in defence of Church and King against the persecutions of the French Revolution and experienced triumph, defeat and savage repression. The year 1943 was remembered as the 150th anniversary of the rising, not least by the Church which seized the opportunity to extend its influence. In March 1943 Mgr Costes said a solemn mass in honour of the statue of Cathelineau, one of the great leaders of the Vendean rising of 1793, known as 'the saint of Anjou', at Le Pin-en-Mauges. This statue had been pulled down after the Revolution of 1830 but was now ceremonially restored to its plinth. The following June the nearby commune of Bourgneuf-en-Mauges was solemnly dedicated to the Sacred Heart of Jesus, the symbol under which the Vendean army had fought, 'to beg forgiveness for all the faults committed by France ... and to ask him to continue his protection of the commune in the trying times we are living through'. In February 1944 Mgr Costes said Mass at Le Loroux Béconnais, north of the Loire, in honour of the local curé, Noël Pinot, who was guillotined for his beliefs at Angers 150 years previously and was locally considered a martyr. Finally, on 16 April 1944, Mgr Costes was at the so-called Field of Martyrs outside Angers, remembering the 2,000 women and children who were shot there by revolutionary forces between 12 January and 16 April 1794, asking the assembled faithful to pray to hasten the process of their beatification at Rome.[38]

In the diocese of Nantes suffering was not history but actuality. One of the great shrines of the city was Our Lady of Bon Secours, revered since about 1450 for protecting sailors from the sandbanks of the Loire, whose statue and sanctuary were in the Église de la Sainte-Croix. Mgr Villepelet took refuge with other clergy and nuns in the cellars of the Catholic college during the Allied air raid of 23 September 1943 and remembered emerging to see 'an immense brazier throwing gigantic flames skywards, a scene from the Apocalypse'. Miraculously, the statue was saved from the burning church of Sainte-Croix and moved to the cathedral sacristy, where it became the focus of nine days of pilgrimage and thanksgiving the following November.[39] Other shrines beloved by the Bretons were dedicated to St Anne, mother of the Virgin Mary and patron saint of Brittany, whose feast day was celebrated on 26 July. Every year a *pardon* or religious festival was held in Nantes for Breton-speaking emigrants to the big city. At that of 1941 Mgr Villepelet prayed to St Anne for 'the end of our present sadness and the dawn of better days'. There was another shrine to St Anne at Vue, south of Nantes, although the main celebrations took place at St Anne d'Auray, in the Morbihan, and was traditionally attended by the five Breton bishops of Rennes, Quimper, Saint-Brieuc, Vannes and Nantes.

While the clergy spoke of repentance and reform, some young people began to use pilgrimages as a cover for political demonstration. At the pilgrimage to Vue on 26 July 1942, for example, it was discovered by the Feldkommandantur that hundreds in the procession of 5,000 young people were wearing 'Gaullist' insignia in red, white and blue, sporting the cross of Lorraine.[40] In such ways 'purely religious' ceremonies could be infiltrated or subverted in order to convey a political message.

All these pilgrimages, however, were but a foretaste of the great event of the spring and summer of 1944, the Return of Our Lady of Boulogne. Said to have entered the port of Boulogne miraculously in 636, in a ship sailed by angels, the statue and the three copies made of it were the centrepiece of a Marian congress held in Boulogne in 1938 to mark the 300th anniversary of the dedication of the Kingdom of France to the Virgin Mary by Louis XIII on learning that he had an heir. The statues was taken secretly over the demarcation line to Le Puy, where another Marian congress was held on 15 August 1942, and thence to Lourdes. In the meantime the French bishops endorsed the papal consecration of humanity to the Immaculate Heart of Mary, and a Grand Return for the four statues was planned to start in March 1943. Of the four routes from south to north, one went from Bordeaux to Angers and Nantes and a second went from Lourdes to Poitiers and Tours. As the processions went from town to town and village to village, streets were decked out in garlands, and the faithful came forward to confess to the missionaries who accompanied the statues. The Grand Return to Boulogne was supposed to signal the Grand Return of the French people to God, which in turn would bring salvation. The redemption of France was not a military question but a spiritual one. As *La Semaine religieuse* of Nantes said, 'to obtain an end to the fighting we must first establish our peace with God'.[41]

One of the statues entered southern Touraine from Poitou on 17 May 1944, received by Archbishop Gaillard and 150 faithful. Particular enthusiasm was manifested at Richelieu, where the procession grew to 2,500 strong, 500 took communion and thirty-seven sick were lying in the church to receive grace.[42] The statue moved on to Loches and Chinon before reaching Tours on 24 June, and on into the less Catholic north and east of the department in July. Abbé Jacques Ménard, who had just graduated from the seminary of Tours to his first cure of souls at Athée, following the arrest of the Abbé Lacour, said it was 'a *pays* given to the devil'. As the cortège crossed the nearby village of Dierre, 'the little Kremlin', he recalls, stones were thrown at it.[43]

The reception of the statue that progressed through the dioceses of Angers and Nantes was quite different. It entered the diocese of Angers on 12 March 1944 from the Vendée to be greeted by Bishop Costes and an array of churchmen, the local mayor in bare feet, carrying a cross, 'a huge meditative crowd' and 'kilometre upon kilometre of garlands, flowers and triumphal arches'. A ceremony was held at a column erected in honour of the Chouans, who had fought the battles of the Vendée. On 16 March the procession was met at the outskirts of Cholet by Mayor Darmaillacq at the very spot where four years previously he had negotiated with the Germans that the town be spared. This time he was there with the municipal council and a crowd of 15,000: 'the whole town was there', reported *La Semaine religieuse*.[44] On 14 April Our Lady, her float dragged by young militants of Action Catholique, barefoot, reached Angers where she was met by Regional Prefect Donati and municipal councillors such as Charles Poisson, who fell to their knees. The statue was installed in the cathedral where 20,000 faithful came to pay their respects, first children, then women, then in turn pupils, young ladies and men, in an elaborately choreographed rota.[45]

The Liberation of France did not take place miraculously, and ironically the passage of Our Lady of Boulogne coincided with some of the worst Allied bombing of the war. Angers suffered its first attack on the night of Whit Sunday, 28 May 1944. Bombs aimed at the station killed many Angevins who took refuge in the church of St Laud and destroyed the bishop's palace. Mgr Costes would undoubtedly have been killed had he been there and not at Béhuard, where the statue was resting that night. On 15 June Nantes suffered an air attack that seriously damaged the cathedral and killed an archpriest. The miraculous statue of Our Lady of Bon Secours was feared destroyed, but firemen pulled it from the ruins six days later, its face intact, and restoration seemed possible.[46] Even before the attack the prefecture had forbidden children from taking part in the procession, lest it was machine-gunned from the air. Mgr Villepelet decided that Our Lady of Boulogne could not be housed in the cathedral, nor even in another city church, and the statue was hurried through the streets, gathering a thin crowd of two or three thousand, and taken to the grotto of Our Lady of Lourdes at Le Pont-du-Cens. There a crowd of 20,000 did gather for an evening service in the open air, described as a 'veritable apotheosis' by La Semaine religieuse. Mayor Orrion of Nantes was there, carrying a crucifix, as was Ricordeau, president of the departmental council. 'You yourself have wanted to be the Great Missionary of France,' Mgr Villepelet told Our Lady of Boulogne, 'at a moment when the return of peace is linked to the return of souls towards God.' And there the Grand Return ground to something of a halt, as the bishop of Vannes thought his diocese 'too disturbed by terrorism and the Maquis' as well as being vulnerable to air attacks. 'People are not in the right frame of mind', he said, to welcome the statue, which therefore remained for the time in the diocese of Nantes, cared for by the Sisters of St Gildas.[47]

The story of the Grand Return of Our Lady of Boulogne resembles a medieval epic that has wandered into the secular age of the twentieth century. It seems incredible that people should be praying for the deliverance of France to four plaster statues of the Virgin Mary when the future of Europe was being settled by arsenals of modern technology. And yet this was an understandable response precisely because ordinary people had no control over the battles being fought over them and inflicting mounting casualties on French citizens. Collective prayer to the Virgin Mary and other saints and martyrs served the purpose of bringing down divine protection to local communities which felt deprived of more immediate sources of defence. This devotion, mediated by the Catholic Church, was also part of the Church's strategy to ward off foes whose cohorts seemed to be multiplying: Nazi paganism was in retreat, only to be replaced by Anglo-Saxon materialism and Soviet communism. The Church had successfully safeguarded its interests under Vichy and during the German Occupation; now it needed to meet the challenges of liberated France. Some clergy, as we have seen, distinguished themselves by Resistance activities and earned themselves a role in the liberation committees that sprang up in the summer of 1944. Dom Sortais, we shall see, was recruited to the local liberation committee at Cholet, while the Jesuit Père de La Perraudière, though a deportee who was never to return, was included on the Departmental Liberation Committee of Indre-et-Loire which had a strong contingent of Christian Democrats such as the Tours schoolteacher Anne-Marie Marteau.[48] Such people were able to continue the defence of the Church's interests either through traditional conservative politics or through a renascent Christian Democracy that was one of the outstanding features of the Liberation.

10. SINNERS

Just before the arrival of the Germans in 1940 stories circulated in the small town of Bléré that lights had been seen flashing on and off in the château of a Hungarian landowner in the commune. Local wisdom had it that this was a signalling system set up to send information to the enemy. The mayor of Bléré and the gendarmerie visited the château and reported that the flashing lights were no more than the light on a staircase being switched on and off. After the Occupation, however, the demarcation line ran right through the Hungarian's estate, which only served to fuel local rumour and keep up the stream of anonymous letters to the prefecture. The Hungarian, named Strausz, was a former agricultural chemist and theatre producer who had married a Frenchwoman of a highly respected family, Mlle de Berly, in 1934 and called himself Strausz de Berly. He moved into the château of Fossambault in 1937 and farmed the property. He spoke German, which enabled him to persuade the Kommandantur to grant special passes to the local inhabitants because they needed to cross the demarcation line on a daily basis. But far from endearing him to the locals, his contacts with the Germans rendered him even more suspect. In December 1940 he was publicly accused of spying by his cleaning lady and summoned to appear before the JP of Bléré. The cleaning lady admitted that she had lied and the police inspector investigating the case said that Strausz had been slandered, 'because his wife is deeply patriotic and would never have allowed her husband to become involved in spying'. Shortly afterwards the demarcation was moved slightly north, so that the whole of Strausz's property was located in the Free Zone, and no more was heard of the case.[1]

What is suggested by this spy mania is an intense suspicion of foreigners that war, defeat and occupation only served to heighten. The war saw an obsession with 'fifth columnists' who were infiltrating and passing secrets to the enemy, and anyone who was marginal or different was a likely suspect. Although married to a Frenchwoman of good family, farming the land and playing the seigneur, the Hungarian was regarded as an interloper and traitor. How much more difficult for those without local ties to rise above the suspicion and fear of local communities, for whom the weapon of denunciation was always to hand. In this instance the notables and authorities, who no doubt moved in the same circles as Strausz and his wife, did not give credence to the gossip of the community. Had they done, as both Vichy and the German authorities did in other cases, the outcome would doubtless have been very different.

War and Occupation saw the progressive exclusion from the local and national community of travellers, foreigners, Jews, communists and Freemasons. On the eve of the German offensive, in April 1940, the French republican government prohibited what it called 'nomads', defined as those 'without home, or country or proper occupation', from travelling the country. These gypsies were seen to be a risk to 'national defence and the protection of secrets' and were to be interned. The French government distinguished them from *forains*, defined as travelling traders and artisans, who 'for the most part had honourable reputations'. The German military, however, made no such distinction and in November 1940 banned travelling traders too.[2]

Any foreigners, as the case of the Hungarian Strausz shows, were liable to persecution in wartime. Most vulnerable were foreign Jews, who accounted for 70 per cent of the Jewish population of 300,000 in France before the war. In the gentile imagination they already suffered from being nomadic and immigrant, to which all the traditional prejudices heaped on Jews had to be added. They had come in waves: Russian, Romanian and Polish Jews after pogroms in the 1880s, Baltic, Hungarian and more Romanian and Polish Jews after the formation of the new national states of eastern Europe following the collapse of the Russian and Austro-Hungarian empires in 1917–18, and German Jews after the triumph of the Nazi party in 1933.[3] Among the German-Jewish refugees were the interlocking families of Abraham, Rothschild, Grumbacher and Meier who fled to France in 1934. Rather than live in Bléré, they bought the abandoned estate of Sainte-Radégonde in the village of Chênehutte-les-Tuffeaux near Saumur, and began to farm it. Though they were hard-working and discreet, they stood out as an exotic little colony in the Garden of France and were repeatedly denounced to the authorities for spying. In 1939, with the outbreak of war, the four fathers were rounded up and interned as a security risk, leaving only the patriarch Albert Abraham and his wife Lina, both aged seventy-three, their three daughters, Selma Rothschild, Fanny Grumbacher and Martha Meier, and daughter-in-law Erny Abraham, with their nine children aged twelve to nineteen.[4] Other Jews who left Germany later, in 1939, wanted only to get out of Europe. Over 500 German Jews armed with visas for the United States left Saint-Nazaire in May 1939 on the *Flandre*, only to be turned back from Havana and forced to return to Saint-Nazaire. There the neediest were looked after by the Jews of Nantes, through their Refugee Assistance Committee.[5]

In October 1940, after the Germans ordered a census of all Jews in the Occupied Zone, there were 736 Jews in Loire-Atlantique, overwhelmingly in Nantes and Saint-Nazaire, 314 (43 per cent) of them foreign, particularly Poles (93), Germans or Austrians (73), Romanians (30), Turks (27) and Russians (24). In Maine-et-Loire there were many fewer Jews, 231 French and 57 foreign. These included the Sternchuss family of Angers, for example, composed of two Polish grandparents, their son David born in Warsaw in 1893 and his young wife Regina born in Budapest in 1913, both described as of 'indeterminate' nationality, and their five children born in Angers between 1931 and 1940.[6] In Indre-et-Loire there were 372 French Jews, 46 children of foreign Jews registered as French, and 185 foreign Jews, half of whom were Polish.[7] This number, however, was soon to be increased. Many foreign Jews who had settled in the main cities of eastern France, Nancy, Metz and Strasbourg, were advised by the French government to evacuate to Bordeaux when fighting broke out in May 1940. When the Germans occupied the Atlantic coast, however, they decided that the foreigners crowded there were a security risk. Alsace-Lorraine had been annexed by Germany, and foreigners were forbidden to return there, so in December 1940 a riff-raff of 300 foreigners 'of all social conditions, nationalities, and religions, mingling priests, nuns, intellectuals, workers, prostitutes and about 120 gypsies' were processed there and divided into foreign Jews and Polish Catholics. The Catholics were sent to the relatively open camp of La Lande, at Monts, south of Tours, and gypsies and other travellers were put behind barbed wire in the camp of La Morellerie, at Avrillé-les-Ponceaux, near Langeais.[8]

In the demonology of Occupied France communists were second only to Jews. For the Germans 'Judaeo-Bolshevik' was often run together as the compound most dangerously opposed to the Third Reich. In France communists were seen as a fifth column, controlled by Moscow, now building the Popular Front to drag France into a disastrous war with Germany, now allying cynically with Germany under the Nazi-Soviet Pact to leave France totally exposed to Hitler. The French government replied by dissolving the French Communist Party in September 1939 but the communists continued to be feared as a clandestine movement that could strike at any time. The Nantes police reported in October 1940 that

> It is certain that the ex-communists have not disarmed but are continuing their disastrous propaganda under the cloak. At the moment I am having the Café d'Alsace in the rue Jamin watched. It is run by an Abel Detée whose clientele consists of a certain number of individuals who belonged to the ex-Communist Party or who subscribe to extreme views. Five or six of them meet frequently to discuss politics, sometimes for several hours. One of them is Paul Gautier, a boilermaker, living at 6, rue de Bourgneuf, who is suspected of having distributed copies of a tract called *Workers and Ordinary People of France*.[9]

A month or so later, with no let-up in the leaflet campaign aimed at factories in the Nantes–Saint-Nazaire area, the police launched a series of raids and interned thirteen communists. This only provoked a graffiti campaign in January 1941, with 'Power to Thorez!', 'Soviets everywhere!' and 'The USSR will win!' daubed in red paint, particularly in the Barbin district of the city which was worrying the police. More raids in Nantes followed, but with the German invasion of Russia in June 1941 things threatened to get out of hand. To cut off the slogans movement thirty-four communist militants were arrested and interned in the camp of Choisel near Châteaubriant, once used by POWs but now given over to holding communists from all over France.[10]

The police had their favourite communist suspects from before the war, but the picture was changing quickly as young people became involved and new tactics were tried. When copies of a tract called *L'Avant-Garde* began to inundate letter boxes in Tours and Saint-Pierre-des-Corps, the prefect reported that 'we are faced by a new occult organization, difficult to catch at work because of the blackout in the streets and the speed of the operation. It nevertheless appears that these tracts have been brought from Paris by railway workers.' They may have been brought by railway workers, but they were distributed by youths such as the two boys of Tours Higher Primary School, one of whom carried a revolver. The prefect realized that the PCF in Touraine was being revamped with 'very young people unknown to the police', 'young fanatics pushed forward by former militants who organize them while remaining in the shadows'.[11]

Another feature of the secret communist movement in the region that exercised the authorities was the fact that it was not confined to urban or industrial areas but appeared in a few rural pockets too. In Maine-et-Loire the slate quarryers of Trélazé outside Angers was a centre of communist agitation, but so was the village of Turquant near Saumur. Bléré and the surrounding villages in the valley of the Cher, down the tracks from Saint-Pierre-des-Corps and close to the demarcation line, such as Dierre, nourished communist activity, as did the Loches area in the unoccupied part of Touraine. The communist schoolteacher of Dierre, M. Delanoe, was moved to another village, but the post of secretary of the *mairie* was then taken by Gabriel Bouffault, who found his twenty-one-year-old son Robert a job in the *mairie* of Bléré, even though both of them had been expelled from the Orléans area for communist activity. Gabriel was particularly friendly with Henri Berthelot, the rural policeman of Dierre, from whom he managed to get a demarcation line pass for locals. The police were concerned that the three of them could 'pass at will from one zone to the other, serving as liaison agents between the communist and anti-governmental elements of both zones'.[12] Meanwhile, in the Free Zone, the Loches area was a hive of communist activity. Secretaries of *mairies* such as Georges Moreau, aged seventy-five, of Montrésor, Marceau Begasset of Saint-Senoch, whose wife the postmistress was just as dangerous, were joined by postman Alexandre Buret of Le Petit-Pressigny and artisans such as shoemaker Camille Pingault of Le Grand-Pressigny and Raymond Gabillet, a blacksmith of Perrusson. It was not industrial workers but state employees and artisans who were the prime movers of communism in the Loches area and, though few, they enjoyed wide support among the population.[13]

Jewry and communism were suspected as occult and tentacular organizations that were working insidiously and indefatigably against Vichy and the Germans. One other organization was regarded in the same way: Freemasonry. Freemasonry was seen to be the secret network of radical republicanism that had insinuated its members into positions of power and influence in the Third Republic, primed anticlerical attacks on the Catholic Church and its school system, opposed militarism and greatness and generally led France down the slippery slope to defeat. Under laws of 13 August 1940 and 11 August 1941 Masonic lodges were banned and Masonic officers discovered in high places were ruthlessly 'outed', having their names exposed in the *Journal officiel* and the press. *La Dépêche* of Tours and *Le Petit Courrier* described a long list of Masonic dignitaries that appeared in the *Journal officiel* of 15 August 1941 as 'highly instructive'. There were seventeen Blochs, eleven Cohens and various Blums, Blumenthals and Blumenfelds, a tempting convergence of Freemasonry and Judaism. Also named was Camille Chautemps, radical boss of Touraine and former prime minister. 'French people will be stupefied to see this long list which brilliantly demonstrates the network woven by Masonry in all branches of national activity in order to secure its disastrous domination of the country.'[14] The corollary of this exposure was that any Freemason who was employed in the public service would immediately be dismissed. In this respect, declared Interior Minister Pucheu, 'Masonic dignitaries are assimilated to Jews'. Freemasons holding any of the offices listed in article 2 of the Statut des Juifs of 2 June 1941 would lose their jobs.[15] In the new Vichy order neither Masons nor Jews could hold any position of influence or authority. Whether after this they would be treated in the same way remained to be seen.

All of these groups – gypsies and travellers, foreigners and Jews, communists and Freemasons – were excluded from national life as the price of national redemption. National unity as it was conceived by Vichy was founded on the persecution of such elements whose sins were held to be responsible for France's ills and had to be purged so that France could be whole once again.[16] All were punished, some brutally, some with more discretion. Of course the extermination of the Jews after 1942 was in a class apart. But until 1942 it is interesting to examine the process of marginalization and exclusion in a broad context, in order to search for similarities as well as differences. Were some kinds of punishment saved for one group rather than another, and were they meted out with equal efficiency and effectiveness?

The first stage of the purge was to dismiss Freemasons and Jews from positions of power and influence. Neither were permitted to remain as public servants, and salaried public servants were required to sign declarations – on pain of dismissal and loss of pension rights – that they were not Freemasons or Jews. If a public official were found to be a communist he would certainly be dismissed, and this would be the least of his pains. The same went for elected as for appointed officials. Robespierre Henault, the communist mayor of Saint-Pierre-des-Corps, was not only dismissed as early as 1939 but suffered a period of internment in 1941.[17] Camille Aron, mayor and councillor-general of Le Boulay in Touraine, was a winegrower and great supporter of farming: founder-president of two local mutual aid associations to insure cattle and protect against fire damage, member of the Chamber of Agriculture of Indre-et-Loire and secretary-treasurer of the regional Crédit Agricole. He was also president of the League of Rights of Man in the department and Jewish. As a result he was required to resign as mayor and councillor-general, and though the municipal council asked the government to make an exception given his 28 years' service as mayor to the commune, agriculture, and the poor, it was in vain.[18]

The punishment of Freemasons seems to have been less systematic than that of communists and Jews. True, the lay public school system, which was fairly well riddled with freemasonry, especially in radical and anticlerical areas like Touraine and the Saumurois, was dealt a heavy blow. André Moreau, *instituteur* of Vernoil-le-Fourrier on the Saumurois–Touraine border, was dismissed from his teaching post as a Freemason in October 1941. The prefect then discovered that as secretary of the *mairie* Moreau was 'the effective mayor of the commune which did nothing without consulting him and was even proposing to petition against the disciplinary measure I have just ordered'.[19] He was duly removed as secretary of the *mairie* as well. Two members of the municipal council of Tours, one of them an *adjoint* to Fernand Morin, a civil engineer, president of the building employers' federation and chevalier of the Légion d'honneur, were also exposed as Freemasons and dismissed. But other Freemasons were harder to shift, generally for the reason for which Vichy disliked them, namely, their influence and connections in the Third Republic. Some mayors in Touraine who were reputed to be Freemasons, such as Émile Gounin of Amboise and François Servant of La Haye Descartes, managed to hold on to their *mairies*. M. Déré, director of the Hospital and Hospice of Saumur and officer of the 'Perseverance' Grand Orient Lodge in the town, remained because by some accident his post was not one of those which Freemasons were prohibited from holding under the law of 11 August 1941. It was said that he had '*le bras long*, that he knows too many secrets and can't be touched'. Though the lodge was officially dissolved, Déré gave it a phantom existence by continuing to hold meetings of up to seventeen members, including ex-Mayor Robert Amy, at the hospital. When the concierge reported Déré to the police, he demonstrated his influence by having her taken to court and evicted. She was left to meditate on the conundrum 'I have always done my duty but have to bow to M. Déré who was an official of the Perseverance Lodge of Saumur'.[20]

Even more telling as an example of influence was the case of Michel Legeron, a police commissioner who was transferred from Bordeaux to Angers in 1940. When he was exposed as a Freemason in 1942 Prefect Roussillon dismissed him forthwith, only to receive a scalding riposte from Secretary-General of Police René Bousquet, who said that the administration of the national police service was his responsibility and the prefect's order was thus null and void.[21] This champion of a Masonic policeman was of course the same Bousquet who four months previously, in conjunction with the SS, had organized the mass round-up of foreign Jews in Paris.

The occasional communist functionary seems to have been able to hold on to his position. The mayors of Dierre and Bléré were summoned by Prefect Tracou to be instructed to dismiss Gabriel and Robert Bouffault, respectively secretary of the *mairie* of Dierre and employee of the *mairie* of Bléré. The mayor of Dierre said he would sack Bouffault *père* when he had found a replacement; the mayor of Bléré simply failed to attend the meeting.[22] Other communists were less fortunate. Marceau Begasset lost his job as secretary of the *mairie* of Saint-Senoch, near Loches, and his wife was also dismissed as postmistress. He was then reported by the police for frequenting café owner Abraham Crespin, who was known as a former communist, and for ceaselessly criticizing the mayor. The prefect of Indre, who was in charge of the non-occupied part of Indre-et-Loire, duly ordered his internment.[23]

At the other extreme was the case of Claude Millot, an employee of the Indirect Tax Office at Nantes. Investigated as a suspected communist late in 1940, he was said by his boss to have once been the secretary of the Chantenay cell in the industrial suburbs but was no longer active. Regional Prefect Roussillon was not convinced and ordered the Sûreté to reopen the dossier. This time the Sûreté confirmed that Millot was politically retired, but it was still decided that he would be transferred to Le Havre. At this point Millot went underground and he was arrested by the Sûreté in August 1942. Now it was argued that he was the 'intellectual' behind the terrorist wing of the Communist Party in the Nantes region. He was handed over to the Germans, who tried forty-one other suspected members of the terrorist wing by court martial in January 1943, and was one of the thirty-seven subsequently shot.[24]

Communists in the public service were considered a security risk by both the French and the German authorities and were thus liable to the most extreme sanctions. Jews were considered, at least at the beginning of the war, less as a security risk than as an evil cancer which explained France's present predicament. While the Germans wanted above all to exclude them from economic life, the French wanted to exclude them from public life and influence. Vichy's Statut des Juifs of 3 October 1940, developed by that of 2 June 1941, removed Jews from employment in the public services and the media and subjected them to strict quotas in the liberal professions. Just as significant as the substance of the measures, however, was the way they were implemented. The law was applied suddenly and brutally to individuals who had been excellent public servants and were fully integrated into the French national community. Of the 2,000 employees of the municipality of Nantes, only three individuals declared that they were Jewish: Eva Dreyfus, who had been an army nurse in 1918, Marie Faigenbaum, who was only eighteen, and Jean Sofer, a naturalized Romanian in the police service. Sofer visited the head of personnel to say that he was 'on good terms with the Occupation forces and counted on the goodwill of the administration not to throw him on to the street'. 'Unfortunately,' added the head of personnel in his report, 'the law is the law,' and Acting Mayor of Nantes Prieur, a socialist, noted in the margin, 'Alas, yes.'[25] All three were dismissed as the administration took refuge behind the black and white of the regulations.

If the law had been applied according to clear bureaucratic rules, that would have been at least a step in the right direction. Only too often, however, French and German authorities cynically ignored the rules that they had invented for themselves. The rules defining Jewishness were admittedly contradictory. Built into the legislation was a tension between Judaism as religion and Jewishness as question of race. The German ordinance of 27 September 1940 which imposed a census of all Jews in France, defined a Jew as someone who belonged to the Jewish religion or had at least three Jewish grand-parents. The Statut des Juifs said nothing about religion and defined a Jew as someone with three Jewish grandparents, or alternatively two Jewish grandparents if their spouse was Jewish.[26] Many Jews in France did not practise their religion or had converted to Roman Catholicism but this made no difference in practice as far as the German authorities were concerned. The Feldkommandant of Tours told the prefect that he must issue identity cards stamped with the term 'Juif' or 'Juive' to Jews who had been at some point baptized in the Catholic faith. 'Baptism', he declared, 'has no effect.'[27]

Nor did such niceties make much difference to Vichy officials. When twenty-year-old Pierre Terrier, an interpreter at Saumur town hall, was dismissed on instruction of the German authorities who had learned of his Jewish background, inquiries began into the Jewish nature of his mother, Marcelle Terrier *née* Geissmann, who kept a haberdashery and hosiery shop in Saumur. Mme Terrier told the Saumur police that she was not Jewish because neither she nor her parents had ever practised the Jewish religion; 'she persisted with this simplistic solution and the impossibility of proving her ancestry', said the police commissioner, because her parents had been born in Mulhouse, Alsace, which had now been annexed by the Germans. Subprefect Milliat asked the Kreiskommandantur at Saumur whether they could look up her racial origins in Mulhouse, but the Germans replied roundly that it was up to Mme Terrier to provide proof of her non-Jewishness, and that within three weeks. Prefect Roussillon told Subprefect Milliat that 'whether an individual practises or does not practise the Jewish religion need not be taken into account', and Milliat later came round to the view that Mme Terrier was Jewish. The only evidence she had offered to the contrary was the testimony of several rabbis who said that her parents did not practise the Jewish religion, 'which has obviously nothing to do with the question of race', said Milliat, just as the fact that 'recently she has been ostensibly going to Mass' was completely irrelevant.[28]

Since the Revolution French citizenship had been based on the idea that membership of the French national community was an act of will, underpinned by a readiness to assimilate French language and culture and to fight and shed blood for the *patrie* if necessary. Religion was regarded as a private matter and ethnic origin was not considered a definition of Frenchness. The emancipation of the Jews at the Revolution meant they could acquire full citizenship, become educated and assimilated, practise their religion or not as they liked, and defend the home of the Rights of Man on the battlefield. The Statut des Juifs gave some grudging recognition to this. Exceptions could be made, allowing Jews to remain in the public service or professions if they had been decorated in the 1914–18 or 1939–40 Wars, had been awarded the Legion of Honour for military reasons, or had made a significant contribution to the French state in the fields of science, arts or letters. Whether or not these exceptions were granted in practice, however, was another matter.

René Ross was dismissed under the Statut des Juifs from his teaching post at the École Pratique, or technical college, of Saint-Nazaire in the autumn of 1940. His family came from Alsace and both his grandfathers had been wounded in the war of 1870. When Alsace was annexed by Germany in 1870, his grandfathers opted for French citizenship and moved to France. René was born in Béziers in 1891, was educated at the École Supérieure d'Électricité and published papers on electricity and ballistics. He had a glorious military record, winning the Croix de Guerre and the Croix du Combattant in both 1914–18 and 1939–40 and receiving the Légion d'honneur for military services. He joined the Socialist Party (SFIO) in 1914 but was a moderate. He disapproved of the factory occupations in Saint-Nazaire in 1936 and left the SFIO for the Radical Party, for which he was a regional delegate. Though Jewish, he converted to Protestantism in 1938. He qualified for exemption under the Statut des

Juifs because he met not one but all four of the military and scientific criteria. And as he wrote to Marshal Pétain, 'I had the honour and pride to serve under your orders at Verdun ... I appeal to your exalted sense of justice.' Ross gained the support not only of the director of the École Pratique but also of the head of education in Loire-Inférieure and even Prefect Dupard, who was no soft touch. To no avail. The Conseil d'État ruled that although Ross's scientific publications were 'remarkable', they did not have the necessary brilliance to merit exemption, whatever that meant. His military honours evoked no patriotic recognition and his conversion to Protestantism was simply not considered. In December 1941 Ross appeared on a list of Jewish hostages against whom reprisals would be taken if terrorist attacks continued. He wrote angrily to the prefect protesting at any suggestion that he might be the accomplice of murderers who shot German soldiers in the back. He had fought the Germans for six years, he said, but always 'face to face'; he was 'as French as anyone else'. But definitions were shifting. To be a citizen, totally assimilated and a patriot was now not enough to qualify as French. Jewish blood disqualified, and the exceptions written into the Statut des Juifs to give weight to services rendered in patriotic blood were not worth the paper they were written on. On 18 January 1942 René Ross was arrested by the Germans.[29]

Losing their employment in the public sector was only one part of the persecution meted out to Jews. Their private businesses and other property was also confiscated. While the French authorities were more interested in eliminating Jews from positions of power and influence, the Germans wanted to destroy their place in the economy. The German ordinance of 27 September 1940 which imposed the census also required all Jewish businesses to put up a yellow sign in the window saying *Jüdisches Geschäft/Entreprise juive*. A second ordinance on 18 October 1940 defined a Jewish business as having one Jewish associate or partner or, if it were a limited liability company, one in which a third of the directors or shareholders were Jewish. These were to be placed under the management of an Aryan administrator and were now to display a red notice. To close even more loopholes, a third ordinance on 26 April 1941 stated that no one in a senior position in a business or having contact with the public, such as a shop assistant or an artisan who sold his goods in his shop, could be Jewish.[30]

There were many business equivalents of René Ross who obediently put up their yellow sign but appended to it some remark to the effect that they were war veterans, and had been wounded or decorated. The German authorities were incensed by this practice, and ordered it to stop. Prefect Dupard, meanwhile, was anxious that such signs would be a red rag to anti-Semites and provoke a wave of window-breaking; he instructed the police to keep a close watch on Jewish businesses.[31] The Germans were also impatient to see all the signs put up by the deadline of 1 November, and keen to winkle out businesses that were Jewish but had not declared themselves as such. Again Dupard tried to offer some protection to the businessmen of Nantes, telling Dr Rheinfels of the Feldkommandantur, for example, that Petrus and Einar Mosesson were not Jews but Swedish Protestants, while the forebears of Raoul Leclerc, manufacturer of car radiators, were 'pure Aryans, belonging to old French and Catholic stock from the west of France'.[32]

It may come as something of a surprise that when it came to the 'Aryanization' of Jewish businesses, the French public could be a good deal more anti-Semitic and mercenary than the French administration. The labour inspector of Maine-et-Loire, Lehlmann, refused to organize a census of Jewish employees in private firms with a view to dismissing them, saying that his job was to protect workers.[33] By contrast Édouard Laraia, who owned the Café de la Ville in Saumur, saw the opportunity of dealing with a rival by complaining to the subprefect that 'the Jew Lazare Schnerb' had not yet put up a yellow sign on his Hôtel-Bar Budan. Asked by the police what proof he had that Schnerb was Jewish, Laraia could only reply that when he had called Schnerb a 'dirty Jew' he had not replied. The police reported that it would be necessary to ask Schnerb directly whether he was Jewish, but that he was currently in Pau.[34]

In larger firms, which ran the risk of being Aryanized if they had a Jewish partner, non-Jewish partners regularly turned on their Jewish partners and forced them out. In Nantes the Société Parisienne de Confection was 92 per cent owned by the Galeries Lafayette, itself a Jewish company, and three of its directors – Bernheim, Blum and Meyer – were also Jewish. Bernheim and Meyer resigned and Blum, who refused to go, was dismissed by an extraordinary meeting in October 1940. Meanwhile, nearly 60 per cent of the Société's shares were bought by the Crédit Commercial de France. Instead of waiting to be Aryanized, businesses promptly Aryanized themselves in order to avoid complications.[35]

Aryanization involved the appointment of non-Jewish provisional administrators to manage and ultimately sell Jewish businesses. Those who participated gave a clear and material sign that they were prepared to make themselves rich on the backs of the Jews. The Chamber of Commerce of Saumur proposed the notary Louis Raimbault to manage the few Jewish businesses in the town; the Chambers of Commerce of Angers and Cholet were reluctant to become involved, but mainly because they saw that the best option from their point of view was to give the Jews a little more time to liquidate their own businesses and release scarce stocks on to the market.[36] Some of the fine flower of the Catholic elite did not hesitate to seek or recommend appointment. In Angers, for example, Vicomte Palamède de la Grandière, senator and stalwart of the Catholic League of Anjou, wrote to his 'dear friend' Xavier Vallat, head of the Commission Générale aux Questions Juives (CGQJ), to recommend a client as an administrator (unsuccessfully as it happened). The task of administering Jewish businesses in Angers essentially fell to the very Catholic Charles Poisson, appropriately enough a bankruptcy lawyer, who took over four firms – mainly ladies' fashions – in the spring of 1942, and his cousin Pierre Poisson, who was in charge of seven.[37] When it came to selling off the businesses there was no shortage of takers, crowding like vultures for easy pickings. The prefect of Loire-Inférieure had a very full postbag. The Federation of Furriers wrote asking to dismantle the fur trade in Loire-Inférieure and shift the stock to Paris. The Organization Committee of the Leather Industry wanted to take over all the tanneries and shoe and leather-goods factories. Individuals also wrote in. Marcel Bourguignon of Brest wanted a shoe, fine leather, shirt or souvenir shop. Eugène Hue of Paris wanted only a shirt business. M. Hincelin of Drancy wanted an electrical business, while Mme Richard of Paris was looking for any hotel, boarding house or shop in the Nantes–Saint-Nazaire area. She was put in touch with Gabriel Hervouet, the provisional administrator in Saint-Nazaire, for hotels were still up for grabs. Most inquirers, however, were disappointed: the businesses had already been sold.[38] The details of the process of Aryanization provide hard evidence of the anti-Semitism of at least a proportion of French people, including the wealthy and privileged, a conclusion that goes against the grain of some recent writing, which tends to blame the Vichy regime while exculpating the people.[39]

The relentless persecution which gradually closed down opportunities for Jews to make an honest living drove them into poverty, clandestine activity and despair. After the German ordinance of 26 April 1941 only artisans and workers who had no contact with the public were allowed to continue. On the estate of Sainte-Radégonde at Chênehutte-les-Tuffeaux Marion Abraham and Sédi Grumbacher were permitted in June 1941 by the German authorities to continue working as seamstresses for a Mme Drais in Saumur, while Ernest Meier was authorized to work for his parents as a farmhand. In Angers, however, David Sternchuss, an artisan tailor with five children, was told to finish his current orders by the end of August 1941 and to accept no new ones.[40] Some Jewish entrepreneurs tried to find ways around the throttling restrictions. M. Katz of Angers, whose jewellery business had been sold in March 1941, continued to work from home, until he was found out and told by the secretary-general of the prefecture that if he continued to work 'he would risk punishment, including internment in a concentration camp'.[41] The clandestine economy worked best when non-Jews were economically dependent on Jews rather than rivals. Adrien Geismar was a Jew who had taken over the running of the shoe factory of Francis Chené at Saint-Florent-le-Viel in the Mauges in 1936 when it was on the verge of bankruptcy and totally rebuilt it. In June 1941 Chené told the authorities that Geismar was a 'commercial technician specializing in the receipt, inspection and use of raw materials necessary to the factory', without contact with the public. Prefect Roussillon accepted this formula but the Paris-based police specializing in Jewish Questions reported that 'Francis Chené is always present but the business is run financially and commercially by Geismar', who was even trying to take over a shoe factory in a neighbouring village.[42] Systematically and ruthlessly, the German and French authorities expelled Jews from the economy, and when they resorted to the black market, clamped down on them as criminals. In April 1941 Vichy asked prefects to intern a number of foreign Jews 'known for their anti-national attitude, who had entered the country illegally, particularly after 1 September 1939, and whose absence of resources makes them a burden on the national economy'. No reason was given, and it can only be assumed that it was to intensify the climate of fear. Prefect Dupard reviewed a number of victims in his bailiwick. He passed over the Horowitz family who had come from Berlin in 1939 and were living off their own resources while they waited for a US visa to enable them to join their daughter in Cleveland, Ohio. Likewise he passed over Dina Garber, a Russian Jew who was living with her son on a small pension after her business was closed down. In the end he decided to intern a Portuguese Jew, Michael Fresco, and a Constantinople Jew, Isaac Hodara, former vanilla traders who now sat around in the cafés of Nantes 'exchanging large sums of money, the origin of which is unknown given that they have no occupation, so to speak'. To make up numbers he also interned the Lithuanian Jew Mordacheff Gruseka who since the closure of his business had been living with his mistress, Mme Augureau. No bad reports had been received about him, although he had recently been fined a paltry 50 francs for complicity in the receipt of stolen goods.[43]

'France was not a gulag,' asserted Abbé Jammoneau, who was secretary to the bishop of Nantes under the Occupation, when I met him in 1997.[44] For those excluded for their sins from the national community, however, experience of life in a camp was a fact of life. In December 1940, as we saw earlier, the gypsies and travellers put on trains from Bordeaux to Tours were kept behind barbed wire at La Morellerie, near Langeais, while the foreign Jews and Polish Catholics were housed at the La Lande camp at Monts, outside Tours, which had originally been built to house Vietnamese workers at the Ripault munitions factory. There the regime, organized by the prefecture, was initially fairly liberal. Some inmates were even allowed to live outside the camp, in the village of Monts or in Tours, so long as they reported once a week to the Kommandantur. They bathed in the Indre and went on walks and bicycle rides in the countryside, not least to collect supplies from farms to augment their meagre diet. There was no love lost between the Catholic Poles and the Polish Jews. The Catholic Poles who worked at the Ripault factory protested that they were ill done by, given that there were nearly 500,000 Poles living free in France and they only had the misfortune of being refugees. 'We are not political detainees,' they said, 'and never have anything to do with the Jews.'[45] The Jews fell back very much on their own devices, receiving gifts from Jewish communities in Bordeaux, Angoulême and Poitiers, and medical aid from a Jewish charity in Paris. A school and nursery were opened, the children had dancing lessons, the adolescents courted and some marriages were celebrated.[46] Jérôme Scorin, a young inmate of the camp, recalls that the Jews did terracing work inside and outside the camp and helped neighbouring farmers thresh wheat in the summer of 1941. Prefect Chaigneau, on the other hand, reported that the Jews alone did not take part in horticultural work, 'demonstrating once again that if the Jew excels in commerce with very few exceptions he does not want to do manual work', and preferred the black market.[47]

All this changed in October 1941. The German authorities decided to reorganize their camp system. Foreign Jews were to be moved to the camps of Pithiviers and Beaune-la-Rolande in the Loiret, which were already filling up with foreign (mainly Polish) Jews arrested in Paris, while La Lande would be used to hold 500 communists from the Paris region. In the event it was decided that only adult males would be sent to Pithiviers, a 'stupefying decision' which would break families up. On the day the buses came panic swept La Lande as the men were marched out. There were heart attacks and a miscarriage. A doctor certified thirty-eight men as unfit to travel, and forty-five (including Jérôme Scorin) escaped. The German authorities were furious, pointing out that the bid for freedom of 'these individuals from international nomadic tribes' should have been predicted and suggesting that 'the mass escape had been tacitly and silently tolerated by the French authorities'. They demanded the punishment of those responsible and the erection of barbed-wire fencing around the camp. The barbed wire was obtained from the La Morellerie camp, which was dismantled, and the gypsies and travellers moved to a new camp at Montreuil-Bellay, inside Maine-et-Loire. This had been used before the war to house Spanish republican refugees working at a local munitions factory and after the war was lost as a POW camp for French soldiers. By April 1942 there were over 1,000 gypsies and travellers at Montreuil-Bellay, brought in from all over the west of France. Once the barbed wire had gone up around La Lande, meanwhile, it was decided to bring the men back from Pithiviers. 'Knocking down the gates, jostling the gendarmes who this time allowed themselves to be totally overwhelmed, great throngs of women and children threw themselves at the doors of the coach. That December, when even the sun wanted to play a part', wrote Prefect Tracou with some emotion, 'was and will remain for many,

I am convinced, the finest day at the camp of La Lande.'[48] The rejoicing was brief, however, because for the 300 foreign Jews held at La Lande the camp turned out to be an antechamber of Auschwitz.

Foreign Jews were interned merely because they were foreign Jews. They had sinned collectively against France and indeed Christendom, and there was no sense that they should undergo due process of law to establish individual guilt. With the communists there was still the notion that they had sinned individually, although the legal process that offered protection became more and more arbitrary. When Raymond Gabillet, the blacksmith of Perusson, was arrested in October 1941, General Mouton, who commanded French forces in the Indre and the unoccupied part of Indre-et-Loire, told the prefect at Tours that he preferred internment to trial because he regarded the procureur de la République at Loches as 'feeble', and that if Gabillet were acquitted by the courts, people in Loches would think that Vichy was not serious in its anti-communism.[49] The wobbliness of the ordinary courts was one reason why Vichy invented 'special sections' of its Appeal Courts to deal promptly with communists. These were perfectly capable of meting out harsher punishments than German military tribunals. The student from the Higher Primary School of Tours who was caught distributing tracts and possessing a revolver, for instance, was given one year in prison by the German military court but five years' forced labour from the Section Spéciale of Orléans, with six months for his friend.[50] The Section Spéciale of Angers sentenced Pierre Brocheteau, a thirty-five-year-old tax clerk, to five years in prison for leading a group of peasants of the Baugeois in a farmyard rendering of the *Internationale*.[51] Some communists, such as Désiré Gauchais, a blacksmith of Turquant near Saumur, who was found to be storing piles of subversive tracts, was interned in Fontevrault prison and then sentenced to five years' imprisonment by the Section Spéciale of Angers.[52] Others were simply interned without further ado. The magic of the internment was that it was an administrative decision, not a judicial one, taken by a prefect not by a court, however arbitrary it might be. Increasingly communists, like Jews, became the victims of internment decisions, without further legal process.

Over a period of three weeks in May 1941 over 200 communists arrived at the camp of Choisel outside Châteaubriant. They came from both small local centres like Le Croisic on the Breton coast and Laval and large centres such as the former abbey of Clairvaux, Poissy, or La Santé prison in Paris. The population of Châteaubriant was curious but in no way sympathetic. While traders relished the idea that business would expand with the size of the camp, ordinary citzens feared that there might be additional pressure on scarce foodstuffs. It was not that the camp had previously lain empty. Until January 1941 it had been a POW camp under German control, from which a stream of escapes had been organized by the prisoners' support committee of Nantes.[53] Since then it had been used to house over 300 gypsies and travellers, together with a few score 'undesirables' or common-law criminals from Nantes or Paris: gangsters, pimps and black marketeers. The 'undesirables' tried to make overtures to the communists, but were cold-shouldered. The communists considered themselves 'a class apart, a caste that could revolutionize society'. Although surrounded by barbed wire, the camp was not totally secure. On 19 June 1941 escapes were made by four gypsies, four 'undesirables' and five communists including Fernand Grenier, deputy of the Parisian suburb of Saint-Denis, Eugène Hénaff, secretary of the CGT union of unions of the Paris region, and Léon Mauvais, a member of the Central Committee. Security was tightened, the number of gendarmes increased to sixty-five and the barbed wire fence raised to 3.5 metres. The gypsies and travellers were removed to another camp at Moisdon-la-Rivière and replaced by communists, who numbered 564 in September 1941. Internal discipline was increased, with roll-calls, unannounced searches, curfew and censorship of correspondence. It was impossible, however, to isolate the camp totally from the outside world. News of the German invasion of the Soviet Union filtered through at 7 a.m. on 22 June 1941 from the radio of someone living near the camp. 'The first reaction was stupor,' reported the camp governor, 'the second delirious joy but since then there has been anxiety because the internees learn only of German victories.'[54] The internees would have much more to be anxious about in the coming months. The entry of the Soviet Union into the war triggered a campaign of communist attacks on the Occupation forces in France, and the Occupation forces responded with a strategy of massive collective reprisals. Under this strategy, it was announced in September 1941 that all communists interned by the French authorities, for whatever offence or none, were designated hostages who could be taken out and shot if reprisals were ordered.

Whereas in many ways, as we have seen, the Occupation drew communities together in a common enterprise of survival, it is also clear that the need to blame someone for the ills that had befallen France defined communities narrowly against outsiders. Mysterious international movements or groups were singled out for blame as fifth columnists and traitors. Freemasons, communists and Jews were liable to lose their jobs and, in the case of Jews, their businesses. Communists and Jews who had become uprooted from their homes were liable to be interned. Influence counted for more than the rule of law. Thus Freemasons who should have been drummed out of office often managed to cling on by virtue of the connections they had, but Jews who might have retained their employment even under the laws Vichy made for itself were sacked. Most serious of all, there is much evidence, particularly from the process of Aryanization, that gentiles were quick to dump Jewish partners, only too happy to take over their businesses. The debate about the anti-Semitism of the Vichy regime has long been settled but there is also firm evidence for the anti-Semitism of at least a proportion of French people.

11. MURDER

It was still dark at 7.30 on the morning of Monday, 20 October 1941, in Nantes when two German officers, having taken coffee at the Café du Nord, crossed the cathedral square on their way to work. As they entered the rue du Roi Albert, leading off the square, two young men emerged from the shadows and quickened their pace behind them. Two shots rang out. One of the officers exclaimed, '*Die Schuften!* (The bastards!)' and fell forward on to his face. As the second officer crouched over him, shouting for a doctor and a telephone, the two men dashed through the maze of narrow, ill-lit streets that surrounded the cathedral, jumped on to a tram which kindly slowed down for them on the rue de Strasbourg, and disappeared.[1]

Fifty years later, one of the assassins argued that his deed was 'an act of war' which 'unleashed armed resistance in the West of France'.[2] The local population, it might be imagined, would have been delighted to be rid of a member of the Army of Occupation, the more so because the victim, as it turned out, was Lieutenant-Colonel Karl Hotz, the Feldkommandant of Nantes. And yet this was far from the case. The immediate fear of French authorities and citizens alike was that the Germans would inflict savage reprisals on the population, which they did. The authorities particularly regretted the assassination because, as we saw in Chapter 2, the mayor and prefect had a good working relationship with the Feldkommandant. Hotz was especially appreciated by Edmond Duméril, interpreter at the prefecture, who noted in his diary, 'I have lost a sure support with the Germans. He was a just, intelligent man who was in no sense a Hitlerian, a friend of the French and particularly considerate towards me, linked to him almost daily for over fifteen months as I was. Will the Nazis replace him by some odious Prussian sabre-rattler?'[3]

The immediate concern of the French authorities in Nantes was how to limit the wrath of the German military that would imminently be brought to bear. The mayor, Gaëtan Rondeau, went at once to the Feldkommandantur to present his condolences, particularly to Captain Wilhelm Sieger, who had been walking with Hotz when he was shot. He declared that for the Nantais Hotz was 'just and good' and made clear that the assassin could not possibly be a Frenchman. He added that as mayor and head of the municipal police, he was at the disposal of the German authorities as a hostage. He got an icy reception and was told that the matter was far too serious to be resolved locally; decisions would be made in Paris and Berlin. At 10 a.m. the prefect, the corpulent M. Dupard, arrived to present his own condolences and returned at midday to present those of Vichy's ambassador in Occupied Paris, Fernand de Brinon. Dupard's position as guarantor of the security of the Occupation forces was even more delicate. At 6 p.m. he was arrested by the Geheime Feldpolizei or secret military police and held overnight in the Lafayette Prison while his offices were searched.

The message of the French authorities to the people of Nantes, alerted by poster, was that the killing was a heinous act and that the culprits must be found. Everyone understood the desperate situation that would otherwise arise. The prefect's appeal paid homage to the 'intelligent understanding' of Colonel Hotz and urged the people to 'maintain the unity of the fatherland in loyalty, order and dignity' by finding the guilty men. The appeal, issued by the mayor and municipal council, which met in emergency session at 5 p.m., was even more explicit. They called the colonel 'just, good and welcoming', expressed their indignation at the 'cowardly assassination', and called on the Nantais to demonstrate their own condemnation of the 'odious crime' by helping to find the assassins.[4]

The citizens of Nantes reacted as they were supposed to, sending messages to the town hall and prefecture which were generally forwarded to the Feldkommandantur as evidence of their goodwill. One anonymous message on 21 October said that 'in the circumstance there is no longer victor and vanquished but a defenceless foreigner who has been the victim of a cowardly attack within the walls of the city of Nantes. No Frenchman worthy of the name can remain indifferent to such a savage act, the honour and reputation of France itself being at stake.' Similar condemnations of the murder came from the 350-strong Union of Retailers, the Employers' Associations of Loire-Inférieure, and the coordinating committee of the War Invalids of Loire-Inférieure.[5] The principal newspaper of the city, *Le Phare*, mixed its condemnation with clarification as to who the culprits might be.

> All good French people, all those who have a sense of honour, are outraged and have poured scorn on the criminals who acted under cover of darkness, shot from behind and ran away. THE ASSASSINS MUST BE FOUND ... They belong to the small but fiercely active clan of agents paid by London and Moscow and who, to cite General von Stülpnagel [Military Commander in France] himself, 'have only one goal: to sow discord between the occupying power and the French population'. He who shoots German soldiers who are only doing their duty here, in the back, is not a patriot but a cowardly murderer and the enemy of all respectable people ... Lieutenant-Colonel Hotz was a great soldier with a magnificent past. Since his arrival in Nantes he has always demonstrated qualities of tact, fairness and generosity in his difficult task. We bow before his body, expressing here the sentiment of all French people worthy of the name.[6]

Le Phare was on the right track when it surmised that the assassins of Colonel Hotz were in the pay of London or Moscow. Communists in France, who had been disoriented by the Nazi–Soviet Pact in 1939, found their revolutionary and patriotic instincts once more coming together after the German invasion of the Soviet Union in June 1941. They sought to exploit the massive transfer of German soldiers to the Eastern Front by launching an armed struggle against the occupying forces in France. On 21 August 1941 Gilbert Brustlein, a young Alsatian living in Paris, was at the Métro station Barbès-Rochechouart, when Pierre Georges, alias Fabien, a veteran of the International Brigades, shot the naval adjutant Alfons Moser. The Kriegsmarine demanded the execution of six hostages by way of reprisal, and to keep control of the situation the Vichy government agreed to set up a Cour Spéciale, which condemned six communist leaders to death. The cycle of attack and repression intensified, so that by the end of September fifty-eight hostages had been guillotined or shot. At this point the communist leadership decided to switch the campaign to the provinces, and commando groups were sent to Bordeaux, Rouen and Nantes.[7] The Nantes commando team consisted of Gilbert Brustlein (twenty-two), Marcel Boudarias (seventeen) and another former member of the International Brigades, Spartaco Guisco (thirty-one). Brustlein and Boudarias took the train to Nantes on 16 October, independently of Spartaco, and dined regularly over the next few days at the Boîte à Sardines restaurant, rue Paul Bellamy. In the early hours of 20 October the three set explosive charges on the railway line at the western exit from Nantes, hoping to catch a trainload of German soldiers, then Brustlein and Spartaco walked into the centre of town in search of their prey. In the attack Brustlein fired two shots at Hotz but Spartaco's revolver, aimed at Captain Sieger, jammed. As the Germans sealed off the town and began extensive searches, Brustlein and Spartaco left the town by the north and then separated. Brustlein walked north and slept in a haystack before boarding the train from Rennes to Paris.

The assassination of the Feldkommandant of Nantes may have been intended to trigger armed resistance but in the short term it set in train a strategy of repression that had been devised in advance by the highest German military authorities. On their arrival in France the Germans had instituted a hostage policy, keeping notables in a hotel overnight on a rotation basis as a guarantee against misbehaviour. What was now planned was something completely different. On 16 September 1940 Field Marshal Keitel, Chief of the Wehrmacht High Command (OKW), issued a circular to the effect that communist insurgency constituted a danger to the German war effort and that the Führer had ordered that the severest measures must be taken to crush it in the shortest time. Accordingly the assassination of one German soldier must be answered by the execution of 50 to 100 communists and 'the manner of the execution must increase the deterrent effect' (*die abschreckende Wirkung*). In response to this General Otto von Stülpnagel, Military Commander in France, issued orders that all those held by the French authorities for communist or anarchist activities were now considered German hostages and could not be released without his consent. The head of each German military region was to draw up a list of 150 communist hostages, rising to 300–400 in Greater Paris.[8] When the news of the assassination of Hotz reached the Führer's headquarters at 10.30 a.m. on 20 October, Keitel proposed that 100–150 hostages be shot and a reward of 1 million gold francs offered for information leading to the capture of the killer, so that the French would plead with London (he made no mention of Moscow) to refrain from future assassination orders. Stülpnagel was keen to retain some control of the crisis, to take national and local circumstances into account. He accepted 100 executions but fought for three days' grace to allow time for the murderer to be found. Hitler ruled at 2 p.m. that fifty hostages were to be shot at once and a further fifty in forty-eight hours, should the criminal not be found.[9]

If communist hostages alone had been executed, local opinion at Nantes might have found the reprisals less difficult to bear. These were essentially outsiders, 564 of them held in the Choisel camp at Châteaubriant, 40 miles away. But there was a tension within the German military occupying France between those who wished to punish communists alone and those who wished to enforce good behaviour by executing a far wider spectrum of the French population. This placed at risk a local stock of non-communists, namely the veterans of a prisoner support committee who had organized the escape of scores of POWs from makeshift camps, including that of Châteaubriant, before POWs had been sent to Germany.[10] The ringleaders, including Léon Jost, decorated with the Légion d'honneur, lawyers Alexandre Fourny and Fernand Ridel, an outspoken level-crossing keeper, Marin Poirier and a secretary, Marcelle Litoux, were arrested in January 1941 and sent for trial by a German court martial the following July, with Edmond Duméril pleading for the defence, which had to be in German. The Germans were torn between a strict application of martial law, echoing the treatment of Edith Cavell in the First World War, and the need to placate French opinion to ensure the success of the policy of collaboration. Six, including Jost, Fourny and Ridel, were sentenced to three years in prison for intelligence with the enemy, while Poirier got four and a half years. The defence appealed but in August the communist campaign of assassination took off. Poirier was again defended before the German court martial by Duméril but was sentenced to death explicitly to intimidate (*abschrecken*) the French population. Despite pressure applied by Duméril and French magistrates on Hotz, the latter was unable to prevent the execution of Poirier on 30 August, but asked Duméril to send his condolences to the widow.[11] Jost, Fourny and Ridel, in a Nantes prison, were now sitting targets.

On 21 October 1941 Otto von Stülpnagel announced the German decision on blood-red posters pasted all over the Occupied Zone.

Cowardly criminals in the pay of London and Moscow shot the Feldkommandant of Nantes (Loire-Inférieure) on the morning of 20 October 1941. To date the murderers have not been arrested. To expiate this crime I have ordered that fifty hostages will be shot in the first instance. In view of the gravity of the crime, fifty more hostages will be shot if the guilty parties are not arrested before 23 October at midnight. I am offering a reward totalling 15 million francs to inhabitants who contribute to the arrest of the culprits.[12]

Controversy has centred in the question of the hostages on the extent to which the Vichy government was the powerless victim of events and how far it was actively involved in the repression. Certainly national and local government were eager to catch the perpetrators. To this effect the city of Nantes offered a reward of 200,000 francs and the French government a further 500,000 francs for information leading to the arrest. As for the choice of hostages, the French Ministry of the Interior, headed by Pierre Pucheu, had been involved from the announcement of the German hostage policy in nudging the Germans towards placing particularly dangerous communists at the front of the firing line. One of Pucheu's envoys, Chassagne, made several visits to the Châteaubriant camp in order to inspect the register of internees and prepare lists. When, on 20 October, immediately after the assassination, the Kreiskommandant of Châteaubriant, the Pomeranian Captain Kristukat, demanded the register of internees from the French camp commandant, Pucheu and Chassagne immediately went into action in conjunction with the subprefect of Châteaubriant, Bernard Lecornu. After frantic telephoning they drew up a shortlist of sixty names, copies of which Lecornu took to Kristukat and Pucheu to Stülpnagel. The final decision was made at the regional level by the Abwehr or military counter-espionage of Angers. They were concerned that the executions should be a lesson not just for the Communist Party but for Nantes and the west of France as well. The twenty-seven names from the Châteaubriant camp were all those of communists, including a parliamentary deputy and Guy Môquet, the seventeen-year-old son of a second deputy, three local politicians, three trade-union leaders and five teachers. Three of the eighteen on the Nantes list were also communists but the majority was accounted for by the six veterans' leaders, including Jost, Fourny and Ridel, two young resisters linked to London, Jean-Pierre Glou and Jean Grolleau, Michel Dabat, who had raised the tricolour on the cathedral on Armistice Day 1940, and a farmer who had been sentenced to death for not handing in his hunting rifle. Six names were added from Nantais held at the Fort de Romainville in Paris.[13]

Much was at stake at this tense moment of the Occupation when so many lives were in the balance. The policy of collaboration followed until then presupposed that the German military would allow French authorities some autonomy in decision-making, so long as they guaranteed the security of the Wehrmacht. The beginning of armed resistance called all this into question. The practice of indirect rule that had functioned effectively for eighteen months seemed on the point of breakdown. A struggle took place between the supporters of direct confrontation, namely the communist commandos and the staff of Hitler's headquarters behind the Eastern Front, and the supporters of accommodation and compromise, that is, the German military in France and the local and national French authorities. The former were reluctant to take decisions in a purely military light but paid attention to the wider political context. The latter held on to the shred of hope that their claim to deliver local loyalty still counted for something and that they might yet be able to influence German decisions.

There was some desperate last-minute negotiation when the names of the hostages became known to French officials on 22 October. Subprefect Lecornu tried to persuade Kristukat to remove the names of seventeen-year-old Guy Le Môquet and two others who were due to be released, but Kristukat would only agree if Lecornu provided three substitutes, so he abandoned the bid. In Nantes Duméril dashed between the Abwehr, Gestapo and Feldkommandantur and managed to have Ridel and one other removed from the list of hostages. Stülpnagel, for his part, was prepared to see the list reduced to forty-eight hostages without the substitution of new names.[14] At 3 p.m. Prefect Dupard and Mayor Rondeau joined forces with the bishop of Nantes, Mgr Villepelet, to send an address to Marshal Pétain to ask the Germans for clemency, but by that time the executions were under way.[15]

Towards noon on 22 October Catholic priests were summoned to the prisons of Lafayette and Les Rochettes in Nantes to inform the hostages of their fate, giving them two hours to write to their families. As the hours passed a reprieve seemed possible, but at 4 p.m. German soldiers arrived to take the sixteen hostages to the firing range of Le Bêle, outside Nantes, where they shot them in groups of three or four. At Châteaubriant, the French gendarmerie were brought inside the wire and ordered to fire without warning on any internee who refused orders. At 11.30 a.m. Kreiskommandant Kristukat arrived with eight Feldgendarmes carrying automatic weapons, and asked for the twenty-seven designated hostages to be handed over. They were led to an empty hut where Subprefect Lecornu announced their fate. The curé of Saint-Nicholas church refused to minister to atheists so another priest had to be found. The hostages told him that the Communist Party was to have its martyrs like the early Christian Church, and that they were happy to die to make France a better place. At 2.30 p.m. the SS arrived in a lorry and drove the hostages away. They were taken through the centre of Châteaubriant, singing the *Marseillaise*, much to the consternation of the townspeople, on their way to the quarry where stakes had been erected. They were shot in three batches of nine, shouting '*Vive la France!*' before each volley.

No Frenchman was present at the executions. Nor were the names of the victims known until they were published in the papers on 23 October. The father of one of the Nantes victims, Michel Dabat, choked on his morning coffee when he learned that his son had been shot. The brother of another victim, Jean Grolleau, could not refrain from calling two Germans travelling on the same tram 'bastards', and was promptly arrested.[16] The ambivalence of the public was pinpointed by one police report which said, 'The population openly condemns the act of the assassin [of Hotz] and hopes that the search is successful. But the punishments inflicted by the German authorities have sown consternation everywhere. No one accepts that the act of a criminal on the run should be paid for by such a large number of human lives.'[17]

Immediately battle was joined to obtain a reprieve for the fifty more hostages who were destined to be executed if the killers of Hotz were not found by midnight on the 23rd. A number of fresh arrests had been made, including that of the socialist former deputy-mayor of Saint-Nazaire, François Blancho, who had resigned from the town hall after disagreement with the government of Admiral Darlan. Marshal Pétain drafted a message to Hitler saying that he was ready to go to the demarcation line and surrender to the Germans as the one and only hostage, but he was dissuaded by his ministers, led by Pucheu. Instead he made a broadcast to remind French people that the Armistice by which they had laid down their arms still held and that they had no right to shoot Germans in the back. Only continued collaboration with the Germans could make the Occupation tolerable, he said; the foreigners who had ordered the killing of Hotz wanted only to hurt France and had no concern for the grief it caused 'our widows, our orphans, our prisoners'. 'Frenchmen,' he said, 'your duty is to stop the slaughter . . . I appeal to you with a broken voice: Do not allow any more harm to be done to France.'[18]

Marshal Pétain was not the only person to offer himself as a sacrificial lamb. Mlle Paulette Benoîte, a teacher at the Nantes Conservatory, said that she 'belonged to a milieu in which young women, even at the age of thirty-eight, have no experience of public life'. She asked to be taken to the Kreiskommandant of Nantes to offer herself, for no other reasons than 'my private veneration of the Marshal and the simple calculation than my life is less useful than that of fifty men'. She spoke for some time with the Kreiskommandant, Major von Hasselbach, who deplored the execution of the veterans and believed that those in high places had no inkling of their status, but her offer was kindly refused.[19] The trio of prefect, mayor and bishop of Nantes made a personal call on the Feldkommandantur in the afternoon of 23 October. They were received by Lieutenant-Colonel Baron von und zu Bodman, the Kreiskommandant from Saint-Nazaire who was standing in for Hotz. The bishop warmed to him as a 'kindly man, Catholic and royalist' after his own heart. 'I will do everything that I can,' said the baron, 'and I am sure that there will be a measure of clemency. But it is not up to me.'[20]

Clearly the ultimate decision would be made in Paris or in Berlin, not in Nantes. Mayor Rondeau duly sent a delegation to Paris consisting of the assistant mayor, Abel Durand, and the head of the Nantes Bar, Maître Guinaudeau, who had been involved in the defence of the veterans' leaders in July. Their mission was to visit Vichy's ambassador in Paris, Fernand de Brinon. In his letter Mayor Rondeau warned of 'the unanimous movement of indignation at yesterday's horrible execution, which mixed together communist militants with the glorious combatants of the Great War . . . It has plunged our town into a painful stupor, a sort of moral darkness from which there is no telling what unstoppable emotions may arise if the volleys of a second execution ring out tomorrow.'[21]

Rondeau also used a connection dating back to his involvement in the Franco-German Committee in the 1930s. One of his associates on that committee was the president of the Groupe Collaboration and editor of the collaborationist *Gerbe* newspaper, Alphonse de Châteaubriant. He urged Châteaubriant 'in the name of our fraternal friendship and of our common efforts in the past to prevent a Franco-German war' to intercede with Abetz, the head of the German embassy in Paris and a former activist in their movement.[22]

The main strategy of the French authorities was to express their goodwill towards the Germans and continuing commitment to the policy of collaboration. They were also keen to show that the breakdown of order that had resulted in the assassination of Hotz would not be allowed to recur. Hotz's funeral, scheduled for Friday, 24 October, offered an invaluable opportunity to demonstrate that the practice of indirect rule was still working. The Germans made clear that the French police were expected to provide security at the funeral, and their effectiveness would be on trial. Over 1,000 police and 500 gendarmes were drafted in for the occasion from neighbouring departments and Paris, and in the end the crowd numbered 3,000. In his keynote speech the military commander of south-west France, General Neumann-Neurode, announced that 'starting from the principle that understanding between peoples and close cooperation between them is the first requirement in the new Europe, [Hotz] carried out his responsibilities in close collaboration with the French authorities'. Baron von und zu Bodman, now officially promoted Feldkommandant of Nantes, went even further, suggesting that it was precisely because of Hotz's championship of Franco-German understanding that he had been assassinated by English agents.[23] The French authorities were careful to endorse these sentiments, and the funeral cortège was followed by Regional Prefect Roussillon, Departmental Prefect Dupard and Mayor Rondeau, as well as by a number of French delegations including the Groupe Collaboration and the fascist Parti Populaire Français (PPF). Wreaths were laid by the prefect, the mayor and municipal council, the civil servants of the department, and the PPF.[24] The only notable absentee, watching from his window, was Mgr Villepelet. He adopted the convenient position that the service was a Protestant one, and that to attend the funeral was in some sense to endorse the execution of the hostages so closely linked to it. His absence did not go unnoticed, with one Nantais arguing that he should have tolled a mourning bell and said a requiem mass.[25]

The bishop of Nantes had his own agenda. The following day he sent a telegram to the archbishop of Paris, Cardinal Suhard, urging him to make personal contact with Hitler. Suhard later confirmed that he had received the bishop's telegram 'with some emotion' on Saturday the 25th and sent a telegram directly to Hitler that same evening. On the Monday Mgr Villepelet went to the town hall to urge the mayor and council to pray to the Virgin Mary to intercede, only to be met by a courteous refusal in the name of the religious neutrality of French politics. The bishop went on alone to the church of Sainte-Croix, where he took a vow before the statue of the patron saint of the city, Notre-Dame du Bon Secours, that if the second batch of hostages were spared, he and his successors would light a candle to her every year for fifty years.[26] The cream of the Breton military nobility was also active. Identifying with the Prussian or Bavarian military nobility as the same ruling caste, they maintained social contacts with them from early in the Occupation which were put to political use at a time of crisis. Thus the Marquise de Sesmaisons sent a wreath to Hotz's funeral, intervened to ensure that her friend Maître Ridel was not executed along with the other veterans on 22 October, and then persuaded the commander of a local Luftwaffe base and SS Haupsturmführer Ernst, to telephone Hitler's headquarters to insist that Franco-German collaboration would be sorely undermined by a second wave of executions.[27]

Most poignant of all the intercessions, however, was the petition submitted by thirteen of the twenty grieving families of the Nantes hostages. Organized by the father of the nineteen-year-old Jean-Pierre Glou, it 'accepted with courage and resignation the cruel loss that afflicts them' and expressed confidence in the Germans' 'feelings of humanity' to call off more executions. Mayor Rondeau called it 'a heroic gesture of French solidarity [which] honours the city of Nantes'. The petition was taken to the Feldkommandatur where Captain Sieger described it as 'precious to influence the higher authorities'. Baron voñ und zu Bodman announced that there was hope of a favourable outcome and actually missed his Sunday lunch to take the petition to General Neumann-Neurode at Angers for forwarding to Paris and Berlin.[28]

It is of course impossible to weigh the relative importance of these intercessions. From what is known about the responsiveness of the Third Reich to public opinion, it may be surmised that these pleas counted for little. Yet there was clearly a disagreement between the highest military authorities in Berlin and the military authorities in France. The closer to the local situation the German military were, the less happy they were with the policy of mass executions. In this equation the attitude of Otto von Stülpnagel, the head of the occupying forces in France, was central. He was in touch with the French prime minister, Admiral Darlan, and was himself a shrewd calculator of what was in Germany's best interests. As we have seen, he was keen in the immediate aftermath of the assassination to allow more time to catch the killers. In the afternoon following Hotz's funeral he sent a telegram to Hitler's headquarters warning of the dangers of applying savage 'Polish methods' to France.

I have stated my opinion that the great mass of the French population is foreign to these assassinations, which are much more likely to have been carried out by small groups of terrorists in the pay of England. I have clearly come to the view that because of the particular situation in France I am opposed to the mass execution of hostages. This must inevitably provoke increasing bitterness in the population and make future political rapprochement extraordinarily difficult if not impossible. Admiral Darlan said to me in my conversations with him that as a soldier he fully understood the harsh measures taken but he has persuaded me that the mass executions are doing exactly what England wants, stirring up the French against us and putting paid absolutely to a reconciliation of the two peoples (on the radio England is already gloating over these mass executions). Darlan's policy of collaboration would be compromised if it ceased to be understood by the French people.

I have myself warned enough against the use of Polish methods in France. I have acted with moderation, and staked my ideas and myself on this. The measures taken in Nantes were imposed on me from above. I was placed under the most intense pressure. I now wish to have a clear statement of intent from the Führer as to whether he wishes to inflict these draconian measures in the circumstances I have described and put up with the political consequences I have outlined that will undoubtedly follow. I must stress again most emphatically that in the long run these measures are not appropriate.[29]

Corroboration of von Stülpnagel's views comes from Ernst Jünger, man of letters, socialite and a similarly humane member of the German army in Paris. He observed that the mass execution policy had 'unnerved and profoundly shaken' von Stülpnagel. The General also saw that the contribution of French industry to the German war effort meant that relations with the French people must be as positive as possible and that, given the lengthening campaign on the Eastern front, 'it was important that German influence in Europe continued beyond the period when it was based on bayonets alone'. Finally, he feared that collective reprisals played straight into the hands of the Resistance, and that the cycle of terrorist attack, reprisals and resistance had to be broken.[30]

In the short term, Otto von Stülpnagel's telegram may have had some influence. Hitler made the final decision about the second batch of hostages in two stages. On Friday, 24 October he made a decision to grant a seventy-two-hour stay of execution, until 27 October at midnight. Then, on Tuesday, 28 October, the execution was postponed indefinitely. France was seen to be an area where occupation went smoothly and resistance was minimal. In other areas invaded more recently by the Germans and where their authority was more fragile, such as the Balkans and the Ukraine, the punishment of acts of resistance was much more savage. Thus the ambush of a German column near the Serbian town of Kragujevac provoked the execution on 21 October of 2,300 Jews and communists, while a series of bomb explosions in the city of Kiev, in immediate response to its occupation by German forces on 19 September 1941, led to the massacre on 29–30 September of 33,771 Jews at the ravine of Babi Yar.[31]

Although the French had been granted a reprieve, the menace had not been lifted irrevocably. Hitler ruled that the French would have to demonstrate not only in their words but in their deeds that their commitment to the policy of collaboration with Germany was genuine. In the event the cycle of terrorist attacks and mass reprisals began again in December, but this time outside Nantes. While the Nantais breathed a sigh of relief, Otto von Stülpnagel resigned in

February 1942 in opposition to the continuing policy of mass executions. This was less out of humanitarianism than because he took a long-term view of the conditions needed to ensure Franco-German collaboration and because he felt that, though closer to the theatre of events than Hitler's immediate staff, he was denied any flexibility in decision-making. He was duly replaced by his cousin, Carl-Heinrich von Stülpnagel, a former member of the Armistice Commission, who would have his own reasons for falling out with Hitler two years later.

How far the assassination of Hotz and the collective reprisals that followed contributed to French resistance can be examined in some detail in the case of Nantes. Although the incident was later presented by militants as the trigger behind the Resistance in the west of France, for the local population it served only to illustrate the madness of armed resistance and the benefits of avoiding reasons to upset the Germans. This was collaboration not in the later sense of supporting the German mission in an ideological sense, but in the original sense of maintaining good relations between French and Germans, whether at public or private level, in order to benefit all concerned.

The Germans, it will be remembered, offered a reward for information leading to the arrest of the assassins, and this reward was added to by the French government and municipality of Nantes. Patriotic solidarity might have kept clues about the perpetrators from the French and German authorities, but for some patriotism ordained that they should reveal what they knew, to avert mass executions and to underpin public order, and the size of the reward could not be sniffed at. Mme Marie-Louise Huau, the fifty-three-year-old owner of the Boîte à Sardines restaurant in the rue Bellamy, Nantes, noticed that the two young men who had eaten there in the days leading up to 20 October had not returned since. She reported this absence to the French police on 22 October and was interviewed by the Gestapo on 26 October. She recognized Gilbert Brustlein from a photograph shown to her and the French police had a lead on him by 4 November at the latest.[32] Mme Huau claimed her reward and eventually obtained 500,000 francs from the Germans, 100,000 francs from the prefecture and 80,000 francs from the town of Nantes. Spartaco and Bourdarias were executed by the Germans on 17 April 1942, although their involvement in the assassination of

Hotz was not known; Brustlein was never captured. Arrested and questioned after the Liberation, Mme Huau declared that she intended to give the money to a charity for POWs when the war ended. She did not know that the men she had denounced were patriots and was indeed convinced that she had saved the lives of the other fifty hostages. An alternative view, put by a local fishwife, was that Mme Huau boasted of the money she had earned by denouncing Hotz's killers, and struck fear into the inhabitants of the neighbourhood, who thought she might denounce them as Gaullists.[33]

It is possible that Mme Huau was the sole collaborator in a town full of Gaullists, but the way in which the city reacted to Gaullist propaganda after the hostages affair suggests otherwise. The reprieve of the second fifty hostages was interpreted locally as a victory for the policy of collaboration, in which the citizens of Nantes demonstrated that their good conduct since the assassination of Hotz had paid dividends. Mayor Rondeau announced that 'the attitude of the population of Nantes and that of the families of the victims, emotional as it was, weighed heavily in the recent decision of the German authorities'.[34] From London, General de Gaulle insisted that no one should shoot Germans until he gave the order, given the certainty of reprisals, but ordered a 'gigantic standing to attention' or 'French national strike' between 4.00 and 4.05 p.m. on 31 October, a wonderful expression of fraternity and a warning to the Germans of the threat surrounding them.[35] The German authorities made it clear that any such demonstration would be regarded as overt support for the assassins of Hotz. Prefect Dupard called his subprefects, service chiefs and other notables together on 30 October to 'ensure the failure of the demonstration called by the English radio', while Mayor Rondeau warned all municipal employees that any following of 'instructions given by foreigners' would entail severe punishment, even dismissal.[36] In the event some 70 per cent of the workforce in the biggest factory in Nantes stopped work for five minutes, and four people who halted on the highway in Nantes were asked to move on, but otherwise there was no response.[37] Most Nantais understood that to demonstrate was to provoke the Germans for no good reason.

The other key test of Gaullist opinion in Nantes was the response to the General's award of the Croix de la Libération to the city on Armistice Day, 11 November 1941. This honour, intended for individuals and communities contributing to the liberation of France and its empire, hailed Nantes as 'a heroic city which, since the capitulation, has opposed a fierce resistance to all forms of collaboration with the enemy . . . By the blood of its martyred children it has just borne witness before the whole world of the French will to national liberation.'[38] Fearing that to accept such an honour would antagonize the German authorities, Mayor Rondeau and his council decided not to acknowledge it. For his part de Gaulle interpreted this gesture as a snub for which he would make the city pay in the future. Although the old municipality was dissolved at the Liberation, the new mayor and council were unable to prevail upon de Gaulle to visit the city and make the award in person until January 1945, and even then he declined to stop at the town hall. Under the Occupation the population was scarcely converted to the gospel from London, seeing as they did the virtues of patient negotiation within the framework of the German presence. Public opinion in the department, the prefect reported in December 1941, had been transformed over the previous month. 'The painful events of Nantes and the excesses of the English radio have caused many people to ponder,' he said. 'Not only have a large number of those who had remained hostile to the policy of Marshal Pétain seen the necessity for all French people to rally round the Head of State, but even those who were privately champions of the Marshal but did not dare refute pro-English arguments are no longer afraid to speak out and denounce the activities of those who persist in criticizing everything the authorities do.'[39] Only the communists begged to differ. A clandestine paper attacked 'Pétain-the-defeat, Darlan and, in our department, Dupard and Rondeau-the-Boche, partisans of total "Kollaboration"' for using the death of Hotz as a pretext to massacre true patriots and for raising the hue and cry against his killer to cover up their own shameful involvement in the black market and prostitution.[40]

Although the assassination of Hotz and the mass executions that followed were not necessarily the trigger that launched the Resistance in the west of France, they were clearly a turning point in Franco-German relations. The crisis in Nantes and Châteaubriant had partially been resolved by desperate negotiations, but relations in future would be increasingly strained. On the first anniversary of the execution of the forty-eight hostages Edmond Duméril reflected that the brutality had 'killed eighteen months of our efforts to bring about the collaboration of the two peoples, in the opinion even of Kommandants von Hasselbach and von und zu Bodman'.[41] Military leaders who recognized the need for the tacit consent of the French population were brushed aside. The Germans now feared that terrorists were hidden in the otherwise peaceable population, and were no longer persuaded that the French authorities could guarantee the Wehrmacht against attack. The model of 'indirect rule' by which the Germans allowed the French authorities substantial discretion in return for maintaining public order was called into question. A new form of collaboration was introduced, based less on negotiation between Germans and French than on *Diktat*, the imposition of terms. The whip hand on the German side passed from the military authorities who were tough but fair to the secret police who were interested only in repression. This might have led to a head-on collision between Nazi dictatorship and French Resistance, and certainly there were now militants who believed that only violence would teach Germans lessons. On the other hand, peaceable local communities feared that violence they did not sanction and over which they had no control would only provoke savage reprisals against themselves. Thus violence drove wedges not only between French and Germans but also between resisters and communities.

12. TERROR

May Day was traditionally a moment when the labour movement made a show of strength, but under the German Occupation extreme caution was required. Unfortunately, on the night of 30 April–1 May 1942 three young Frenchmen – Robert Guilbault (twenty-one), André Anguille (twenty-two) and Robert Couillaud (twenty-six) were caught red-handed by two French police officers as they daubed anti-German slogans on the walls of Tours. The municipal police had received instructions from Commissaire Central Moracchini to clamp down on 'anti-national propaganda' and to make an example of any offenders. There had been a spate of terrorist incidents in Tours since the beginning of the year and, although painting graffti or distributing tracts was fairly anodyne, the first May Day since the entry of the Soviet Union into the war was bound to be a moment for the Communist Party to raise its profile and an opportunity for the authorities to capture its militants. The trio arrested were rather innocent communist sympathizers, but once they were in police hands the trail led to bigger fish: Maxime Bourdon (twenty-five), the organizer of Communist Youth in Indre-et-Loire, arrested on 4 May, and André Foussier (twenty-two), the leader of the Front National (essentially communist) students, arrested on 7 May.

Although the young men had been arrested by the French police, they soon found themselves in the hands of the Gestapo. How this happened was the subject of conflicting accounts. The young men told their parents that they were beaten by two officers of the Sûreté, Officer Euzenat and Inspector Bernard, on the orders of Commissaire André Maurice, who then telephoned the Gestapo and handed them over. The father of André Foussier made his own inquiries and came to the same conclusions about the responsibility of Maurice. The guilt of Maurice was substantiated after the Liberation by another police officer, who said however that he could not bring allegations against Moracchini because he was his 'hierarchical superior'.[1] Interviewed in October 1944, Maurice, since then promoted to head the Sûreté Nationale in Paris, said first that he had absolutely no memory of how the young men had been interrogated and how the Gestapo had got hold of them, then recalled that they had 'no traces of violence' on their bodies when he had interviewed them, and blamed a subordinate officer for alerting the Gestapo. Moracchini, interviewed in December 1944, by which time he was Secretary-General of Police for the Angers region, said that 'the unfortunate victims were not handed over willingly but snatched by force according to procedures dear to the oppressor'. This clashed somewhat with the memory of another officer who recalled on the night in question seeing Maurice 'swinging an enormous cosh as long as a walking stick' in front of three young men in handcuffs and Moracchini 'sitting in his armchair while a very merry German officer was patting his stomach and saying "good collaboration"; on the desk was a bottle and five or six glasses of white wine, full to the brim'.[2]

The consequences of being handed over to the Gestapo were lethal. Had the five young men remained in the hands of the French police they would have gone before the Procureur de la République and probably been interned; in the hands of the Gestapo they were brought before the military court of the Feldkommandantur of Tours on 14 May 1942 and sentenced to death. Prefect Tracou went to see Feldkommandant Kloss, who gave him a fair interview, and made urgent representations in Paris, but the appeal for clemency was rejected and the five young men were taken to the military Camp du Ruchard outside Tours on 16 May and shot. Although the executions were carried out in secret, rumours began to spread and with them shock and disbelief. 'Many people refuse to believe that the sentence has been carried out,' Moracchini told Tracou. 'There is a great deal of hostility in the working-class milieu and even those without ideological commitments are appalled.' Tracou relayed to the regional prefect news of an 'intense reaction of amazement which has still not calmed down'.[3] Unable to cope with the grief, André Foussier's mother committed suicide three months later. A huge crowd turned out for her funeral on 25 August. Returning home after the funeral, Foussier's father also killed himself. His burial three days later was, according to the account of communist militants who had escaped the net, 'a formidable and silent patriotic demonstration'.[4]

For the Tourangeaux the execution of five young men whose crime was scarcely more than vandalism was incomprehensible. What made it outrageous was that the French police had at best caved in to the Gestapo, at worst actively collaborated. For many French people these youths were patriots who happened to be inspired by the force that was putting up the staunchest resistance to the Nazis on the Eastern Front. As far as the Vichy regime was concerned, communists were as much their enemy as those of the Germans and their activities 'anti-national' as well as anti-German. What mattered for Vichy was to retain sufficient influence to negotiate with the German authorities on fair if not equal terms. Even over the hostage crisis in Nantes–Châteaubriant they had managed to persuade the Germans to spare a second batch of victims, and General von Stülpnagel argued successfully with his superiors that further terror would be against German interests. Unfortunately, the bargaining position of the French authorities was becoming steadily weaker, negotiation more difficult and compromise more unlikely. One reason for this was that as the campaign against the Soviet Union became bogged down, as communist resistance in Europe grew bolder, and as the Allies too began to inflict damage in the west, German reactions became angrier and more unpredictable. Another reason was that military administrators who favoured a more moderate approach were gradually moved on, and the German military administration itself became displaced in the spring and summer of 1942 by the secret police.

The tragedy of 16 May 1942 was not an isolated incident but followed a number of attacks on German installations and personnel. For a time, in Tours, the French and German authorities managed to limit the extent of collective reprisals, but their task was becoming harder and harder. On the night of 12–13 January 1942 a German train was derailed on the Paris–Bordeaux line near Tours and a bomb was thrown into the La Paix café, a Tours night spot frequented by German officers. It did not go off. Feldkommandant Kloss was minded to impose a collective fine of 1 million francs on the town, but Prefect Tracou managed to persuade him that the culprits were not locals at all but the Brustlein gang, and Kloss contented himself with ordering an 8 p.m. curfew for a fortnight. As he told Tracou,

'I do not see myself as a conqueror here; I want only to work in full agreement with you, and to facilitate your mission as Marshal Pétain's representative.'[5]

This understanding was severely threatened when a German sentry by the name of Kropiunik was shot outside a petrol dump in the rue du Hallebardier, Tours, on the night of 5 February 1942, and died a few days later. The German authorities arrested fifty hostages, ten communists and forty Jews, both foreign and French. For the first time in the region Jews entered into the German equation of collective punishment. Émile Aron, a doctor at Tours, was warned by his maid that the Feldgendarmerie were on their way to his house, and he managed to escape from a rear entrance, making his way over the demarcation line and thence to Switzerland.[6] Prefect Tracou, arguing that the death was probably the result of a brawl between Germans, managed to persuade the German authorities to release two teachers, on the grounds that they could not possibly have been guilty, along with two communists and eleven Jews on health grounds. Feldkommandant Kloss was convinced that the deed had been done not by a local but by a terrorist from outside, and tried to avoid any executions taking place. His superiors were prepared to show a little flexibility in the interests of Franco-German relations, but at the same time the penalty for killing even the humblest sentry needed to be made clear.[7] In accordance with German policy on reprisals, General von Stülpnagel might have ordered the execution of fifteen hostages, but satisfied himself with ten. In order to avoid the violent community response provoked by the shooting of high-profile veterans and local youths in Nantes, those selected were six communists sentenced to long prison terms, five by French courts and one by a German court, and held some way off in the former abbey-cum-prison of Fontevrault, where the execution took place on 21 February, and four Jews who had been interned by the French authorities.[8] The thinking now was that Jews as well as communists were beyond the pale of the local community, which would be less exercised by their execution than by anyone more integrated into it.

While this repression in Touraine was finely calibrated politically, at the other end of the region Allied involvement in an incident provoked a much more violent and arbitrary German response that pointed the way to what might happen in the future. On the night of 27–28 March 1942 a small British flotilla of commando launches escorted the torpedo boat *Campbeltown* unnoticed up to the port of Saint-Nazaire in order to destroy the floodgate of the immense dry dock which was due to receive the battleship *Tirpitz* for repairs, and if possible to damage the U-boat base as well. The *Campbeltown* jammed itself up against the floodgate and blew itself up with a delayed charge while the forces leapt ashore. In the fighting fifty-nine British commandos and eighty-five sailors were killed, while 109 commandos and 106 sailors were taken prisoner by the Germans, but that still left 252 crew unaccounted for. The Germans were convinced that they were being sheltered by the inhabitants of Saint-Nazaire, and distributed a poster to the effect that a further attack on the German army would result in a tenth of the population in the district where it happened being shot. During the night of 30 March a second delayed explosion rocked the port, and the Germans ran amok, shooting through doors and windows, throwing grenades into flats, breaking into houses to force the population on to the streets and continuing to shoot at them. In the carnage eighteen were killed and twenty-six seriously wounded. Twelve hundred people from the port district were then taken 'like a common herd', in the words of the bishop of Nantes, to the former POW camp at Savenay, 20 miles away, where they were held under the orders of a colonel sent from Angers because the local Kreiskommandant, von Trotha, was deemed to have forfeited too much authority. Fearing that savage reprisals might be taken, Mayor Tosca and Subprefect Lecornu of Saint-Nazaire raced to the camp by car, and tried the unorthodox tactic of thanking the colonel for saving the inhabitants of the port district from further risks at Saint-Nazaire, and offering to evacuate them out of harm's way to Le Croisic. Lecornu agreed to the colonel's condition that all papers should be checked, in order to flush out any British or Canadian servicemen in disguise, and was able to agree to the release of the civilians.[9] The incident demonstrated that the German authorities were not always in control of their subordinates in extreme situations and that negotiations, while they continued, hung by a thread.

Meanwhile, the Germans experienced in the practice of Franco-German cohabitation since the beginning of the Occupation were leaving the scene. In July von Trotha was promoted from Saint-Nazaire to Nantes to replace Baron von und zu Bodman, the distinguished Bavarian Catholic who had so impressed the bishop of

Nantes, while Colonel Kloss, whose flexibility had been much appreciated by the French authorities in Angers and then in Tours, left the region. Over the next two years there were five different Feldkommandants at Tours, making it impossible to develop a working relationship. Even before then Otto von Stülpnagel had resigned and the new Militärbefehlshaber, his cousin Carl-Heinrich, informed Ambassador de Brinon that from 1 June a High Commander of the SS and German police would be in post in Occupied France, and from that time all police matters that had previously been dealt with by the German military administration would be taken over by the High Commander of the SS and German police, Carl-Albrecht Oberg, who was Reinhard Heydrich's man in Occupied France for the integrated services of the state security police (Sicherheitspolizei, commonly known as the Gestapo) and security service of the SS (Sicherheitsdienst, or SD).

By this time Hitler had grown exasperated with the ineffectiveness of the Darlan government and German pressure was applied to Pétain to drop Darlan and bring back Laval, this time as head of government, in April 1942. As a guarantee of more serious collaboration, Laval appointed the thirty-three-year-old technocrat René Bousquet secretary-general of police. Bousquet held a series of meetings with Oberg and endorsed the principle of collaboration of the French and German police against the common enemy – anarchists, communists and terrorists – in return for having the German policy of reprisals against hostages ended and a certain autonomy ringfenced for the French police. He realized that communists interned by the French authorities for their own security reasons had been used for target practice by the Germans with disastrous results for Franco-German collaboration. He also realized that the numbers of Feldgendarmes and Gestapo that the German police could deploy in France was limited, and that some conditions might be attached to the collaboration of the French police. He was concerned above all to define a sphere in which French citizens arrested for crimes that did not constitute a threat to the Army of Occupation should be dealt with by the French police and the French judicial system, under French law. For Oberg, there were few gestures of opposition and resistance in Occupied France that did not threaten the Army of Occupation and as far as he was concerned the function of the French police was simply to act as executive agents of the Gestapo.

The so-called Bousquet–Oberg agreement of July 1942 outlining the parameters of Franco-German police collaboration was in fact the subject of very different interpretations on each side. At a meeting of regional prefects and regional Sicherheitspolizei/SD commanders on 8 August, Oberg praised the international police collaboration promoted by his late colleague Heydrich, recently assassinated by Czech partisans, and emphasized what the French police could do for German security. In his letter to prefects of 13 August, enclosing the definitive text, however, Bousquet emphasized that French police would not have to choose hostages, and that French citizens accused of crimes that did not threaten the Army of Occupation would be dealt with by the French system.[10]

How much autonomy the French police preserved would depend very much on the outcome of power struggles in the locality. The regional police chief in Angers, SS Hauptsturmführer Dr Hans-Dietrich Ernst, made clear from the start that he would tolerate no lapses in collaboration. Early in July he informed Regional Prefect Roussillon that Moïse Ossant, a police inspector at Saumur, had been sent before the military court of the Feldkommandantur of Angers for 'anti-German activity'. Asked to provide French staff for the Saumur Soldatenheim, he had proposed a team totally unfit for service. 'Of eleven women,' complained Ernst, 'three were visibly sick, one was pregnant, one was syphilitic and three others seemed to be prostitutes; only three could be employed.' The military court ordered preventive detention, a sentence which Ernst quashed, if only to demonstrate that even German military justice had to bow to the Gestapo, on condition that Ossant was transferred from Saumur.[11] A week later he produced his own version of the Bousquet–Oberg agreement which left precious little autonomy to the French police. He told Roussillon that he expected a daily report to be submitted to him, in German, on 'all incidents and phenomena liable to trouble public tranquillity, security and order' as well as 'isolated incidents out of the normal run of things'. He must be informed of what inquiries were taking place, and by whom, by a specially designated police chief. Special reports were required on any sabotage of German installations or attacks on members of the German army. Incidents in each department should be reported to the local SS. Given that this reporting system totally cut out the French police hierarchy, Roussillon made representations to Ernst. But the furthest he got was that incidents would be reported to the police superintendent at Angers for forwarding to the regional Sicherheitspolizei/SD.[12]

Some idea of the character of the departmental SS commanders may be gained from the case of Georg Brückle, head of the Sicherheitspolizei/SD in Tours. In his early thirties, Brückle was a native of Prague and spoke German with a Slav accent. He had a low opinion of the French police except of the crack Anti-Communist Police Section (SPAC), but had a good working relationship with Commissaire Joseph Boucherie whom he regarded as 'a man who may be trusted absolutely from a political point of view'. He managed to get Boucherie promoted to Commissaire Central of Tours, a post left vacant after the departure of Moracchini, the right man in the right place 'in order to guarantee an irreprochable and productive collaboration with the French police here'. This collaboration did not include French police arresting women servicing Germans as clandestine prostitutes, which sent him into a fury. Brückle himself, a regular at the Casanova night club, was reputed to have had 200 mistresses in Tours and the neighbouring area. One French woman, with whom he lived for a year, Colette Wetter, bore him a child and disappeared a few months later, no doubt for her own safety. The thirty-two employees of the Tours Gestapo had much in common with Brückle. Of twenty-nine men and three women, seven were born outside the 1937 frontiers of Germany: three Alsatians, two Sudenten Germans and two Romanians. One in three had a French mistress, and most were corrupt. The most feared was probably an Alsatian woman in her late twenties, Klara Knecht, who had been a secretary and interpreter at the Feldkommandantur before graduating to the Gestapo. Relations between the Gestapo and French people were not only sexual; plenty of informers gravitated around them for money or revenge. Among these were Antoine Devraud, a railway employee of Tours, and a Vietnamese, Phang Bang, domestic of Mme Hélène Bruneau, whose Resistance network based on her château south of Tours he betrayed.[13]

The picture that begins to emerge is that while French authorities were able to argue with and even to some extent to frustrate the demands of the German military administration, dealing with the Gestapo was an entirely different matter. In August 1942, for example, the Feldkommandantur of Angers asked the prefect to send him a list of all the mayors, municipal councillors, curés and primary school teachers in the department within four days; the prefect replied that this went against clear French government policy and asked, no doubt rather naïvely, for a 'formal guarantee that the list you request will not be used to select hostages'.[14] The following October the Kreiskommandant of Nantes, who was keen to monitor POWs who had returned on leave and even those who had been released definitively, wished to mobilize the French gendarmerie to undertake the task. This provoked protests from Prefect Dupard and from the local gendarmerie commander who smelled a whiff of hostage-taking.[15] With the Gestapo, however, orders were rarely disobeyed. When Dr Ernst became convinced that Catholic priests in the Mauges were stirring up anti-German feeling, he asked for them to be moved to different parishes. Admittedly Canon Douillard, archdeacon of Cholet, was first arrested to make the point, but neither Regional Prefect Roussillon nor Mgr Costes, bishop of Angers, put up any fight; indeed, Roussillon urged Costes to accept a 'benign punishment' for fear of provoking anything worse.[16]

The purpose of police collaboration, of course, was to facilitate the campaign against the common enemy, the communists. Bousquet's idea was that the more the French police demonstrated their effectiveness, the more autonomy they would achieve. This led them sometimes not to wait for orders but to take the initiative. In a massive operation in Nantes on 27 August 1942, for example, the Anti-Communist Police Section (SPAC) and the Nantes Sûreté rounded up 143 communists, forty-two of them Spanish republicans and 101 French. Of these, forty-one were identified as the authors of twenty terrorist attacks in the Nantes area. The most notable of them was Raymond Hervé, who, since joining the Special Terrorist Organization (OS) of the Communist Party in March had sabotaged the Batignolles locomotive factory, killed a suspect collaborator, thrown a bomb into the luxury Hôtel de la Duchesse Anne in Nantes used by the Germans, and stolen ration cards and money from various town halls and châteaux. Hervé was being interrogated by examining magistrate Le Bras in Nantes on 9 September when an armed group of his communists burst in, shot the magistrate dead and made good their escape.[17] This incident led to a massive round-up of suspects over the following two days, but without success. Then, on 15 September, the Spanish leader of the Nantes OS, Alfredo Gomez-

Ollero, was arrested in Saint-Nazaire, and the trail led to the arrest of more Spanish and French communists including Marcel Viaud, a Châteaubriant schoolteacher and member of the Party since 1934 accused of hiding terrorists on the run.[18]

The French administration was delighted by this campaign, which effectively destroyed the Nantes OS. Prefect Dupard noted that Fourcade, head of the Sûreté, 'had particularly excelled since June in the investigation [sic] of the Communist Party and its terrorist organization in Nantes. I request that M. Fourcade be promoted to principal commissaire as soon as possible . . . from the national point of view, his attitude cannot be faulted in the least.' Whether the success of the French police increased their autonomy in the long run was another question. At first things seemed to be going that way. Yves Bayet, secretary-general of the Nantes prefecture, reported that 'the anti-communist operation allowed the French police and administration to make direct contact with the SS. I was very happy to observe that not only did they collaborate closely with us to help us, but also handed over to us a certain number of communists whom they had arrested previously so that we could interrogate them and hand them over to the French courts.' Hauptsurmführer Ernst, visiting Nantes, personally thanked the prefect for the 'excellent work undertaken by the French police'. After the assassination of examining magistrate Le Bras and the subsequent arrests, the SS Police Chief Oberg made it clear that, while members of the communist youth and ordinary members of the PCF would be tried by French courts, members of the terrorist OS would faced a German military court.[19]

In the end the French police and administration, imagining that they were acting independently, in fact simply did the dirty work of the SS and then found matters taken entirely out of their hands. The French judicial system was totally sidelined, except in so far as the Assize Court of Loire-Inférieure was used as a stage for the court martial of Feldkommandantur 518, decked out in swastika flags. No fewer than forty-two accused were brought before military judge Dr Gottlob on 6 January 1943, for crimes running the gamut from assassination, sabotage and illegally bearing arms to small offences such as hiding stocks of ration cards. Edmond Duméril, who helped the defence because the trial was conducted entirely in German, noted that 'the Germans intended to conclude this trial by an apotheosis of justice in the shadow of the swastika. They were therefore without pity.' Such terror would be struck into the hearts and minds of the French population that they would in future neither engage in violence nor protect those who did. The verdict divided the defendants into 'assassins', 'guerrillas' (*francs-tireurs* or *Freischärle-lei*) and 'accomplices' but took the view that the will to commit a crime amounted to the crime itself and that 'this harsh period of war requires the harsh punishment of those who attack the German army or commit crimes in occupied territory. Those who do so risk their heads and must be eliminated.' Dr Gottlob acquitted two, sent three to prison and condemned the remaining thirty-seven to death. The judges hurriedly left the courtroom as the oldest defendant, a retired railway worker named Henri Adam, led the singing of the *Marseilla-ise*. In the days that followed the prefect, mayor and bishop of Nantes made representations for mercy on behalf of the condemned, but Prefect Dupard was so pessimistic that he requested a pardon for only ten of them. The time when negotiation might bear fruit was now passed. Nine of the condemned were shot on 29 January 1943, twenty-five more on 13 February, and the last three, tortured in order to extract information about other comrades, were finally executed on 7 May.[20]

Collaboration between French and German police and administration now meant that the former were used and abused, and greater collaboration between police forces meant decreasing enthusiasm of the French public for collaboration in a wider sense. The collaborationist *Phare de Nantes* toed the German line, denouncing as 'outlaws' and 'terrorists' those who 'called themselves patriots but in fact serve the interests of quite another country' and 'are ready at any moment to sacrifice the property and lives of French people'.[21] In his report to the Interior Minister, however, Prefect Dupard noted that 'these severe sentences have made a deep impression on public opinion, which tends to consider the perpetrators of crimes such as the murder of examining magistrate Le Bras, the theft of ration tickets, arson attacks on crops and buildings, or sabotage, as guerrillas and patriots'. He regretted that the accused had not been tried by a French court which would have handed down lesser sentences. But now that the German police had the upper hand the only solution was 'good anti-communist propaganda' which would impress on public opinion that terrorist attacks were 'the work of brigands and criminals, not that of patriots, partisans or guerrillas'.[22] Even René Bousquet realized that the balance of police collaboration and autonomy agreed with Oberg the previous August was not working. At a meeting of regional prefects and chiefs of the Sicherheitspolizei in April 1943 he protested that even when German military personnel and installations were not directly threatened, and where the culprits had been arrested by the French police, the Germans were citing the principle of the security of their army to take custody of the arrested individuals and send them before German military courts. Although Oberg reiterated that the division of responsibility as agreed in August 1942 would continue, clearly the Germans were now saying one thing, but doing another.[23]

The negotiations between Oberg and Bousquet which led to the collaboration of French and German police against the communists in the late summer of 1942 had already begun its task against the Jews in the high summer. The comparison of the persecution of communists and the persecution of Jews sheds a great deal of light on the attitudes of the French police and administration on the one hand, and of the French population on the other. Bousquet's concerns about the autonomy of the French police were not voiced at all in relation to the deportation of the Jews, and most of the detailed negotiations with the German authorities early in July 1942 were carried out by his deputy Leguay and the head of the Commissariat Général aux Questions Juives (CGQJ), Darquier de Pellepoix. The French police tried to safeguard French Jews while letting foreign ones go, but were otherwise enthusiastic stooges of the German police and keener than the Germans to have Jewish children deported with their parents. The initial reaction of the French population was one of indifference. Since the deportation was supposed to concern not French Jews but only foreign ones, there was little hostility to the removal of those who were regarded as unwelcome immigrants. Only when Jewish children began to be separated from their families and French Jews began to be caught up in the net, did any kind of hostile reaction take place.

On 30 May 1942 de Brinon sent a circular to all prefects in the Occupied Zone informing them that Oberg had published an ordinance the previous day that all French Jews over the age of six should wear a yellow star from 7 June, on pain of a fine, prison or transfer to a 'camp for Jews'. This discrimination, which had applied to Polish Jews from 1939 and German Jews from 1941, was intended to divide Jews from the rest of the national community and ascertain whether non-Jews showed solidarity or simply looked to their own survival. Many French Jews could not believe that this measure applied to them and asked the French authorities to obtain an exemption, but the authorities demonstrated impatience or indifference. Mayor Rondeau of Nantes wrote to Prefect Dupard to request exemption for Raoul Jacob, now seventy-six, who had apparently saved Aristide Briand, who as prime minister and foreign minister in the 1920s had promoted Franco-German rapprochement, from a communist plot to kill him in 1919. Dupard forwarded the request to de Brinon, only to be told that it was not in his power to grant dispensations and that he should address himself to Obersturmführer Marnitz, the SS chief in Nantes.[24] Georges Salomon, a salesman who said he did not practise his religion and was married to a Catholic, asked the prefect of Maine-et-Loire whether as 'the son and grandson of French citizens' from Alsace and a veteran of two wars, wounded in 1917, he really had to wear the yellow star. Prefect Delegate Pierre Daguerre, who was alleged to have protected Freemasons in his previous post as subprefect of Dieppe, clearly had little time for Jews. He told the mayor of Salomon's commune that 'if he did not wear the star from 7 June I will have to report him to the Feldkommandantur with a view to having him interned in a concentration camp'.[25] Subsequently he secured confirmation from the CGQJ that in defining a Jew the stricter French definition, which included Jews who did not practise any religion, was to be observed in preference to the German definition of a Jew as one who had two Jewish grandparents *and* belonged to the Jewish faith.[26] Some Jews, bowing to the law, chose to wear their stars with pride. In Saumur Rabbi Henri Lévy, a former army chaplain, wore his with his Croix de Guerre and Légion d'honneur, and as the traditional Fête-Dieu procession passed through the streets a priest left it to step on to the pavement and shake his hand. These gestures of solidarity were magnificent, but did not do anything to alter the course of events: on 18 July Lévy was arrested and deported.[27]

The round-up of Jews in Paris on 16–17 July 1942, known commonly as the *Rafle du Vel d'Hiv* because over 13,000 Jews were arrested and crammed into the Velodrôme d'Hiver cycle stadium, is well documented, as are the round-ups of Jews in the Free Zone the following month. Much less well known are the round-ups in the Occupied Zone outside Paris on 15–16 July 1942, which some books simply fail to mention.[28] No doubt the number of Jews there was relatively small – in June 1942 there were 387 (240 French, 95 foreign and 52 'evacuated from the coast') in Maine-et-Loire and 304 (105 French, 199 foreign) in Loire-Inférieure. Numbers in Loire-Inférieure had more than halved from 736 (422 French, 314 foreign) in October 1940, largely because of escapes to the Free Zone, although they had risen in Maine-et-Loire from 288 (231 French, 57 foreign) at the same time. And yet this region had its own concentration camp for foreign Jews at La Lande near the village of Monts, outside Tours, together with a work camp of foreign Jews mainly deported from Paris at Clefs, in woodland north of Angers, while resorts like La Baule on the Atlantic coast west of Nantes were notorious congregating grounds of Jews on the move. Most deportations to concentration and extermination camps in the east left via Drancy, an unfinished housing estate north of Paris. However, it was from Angers that the only convoy to journey directly from the French provinces to Auschwitz left on 20 July 1942 with a cargo of 824 Jews.

Debate has raged as to whether the Nazis or Vichy bore more responsibility with regard to treatment of the Jews. The French police were perfectly candid about their role in the deportation, which in the first instance was limited to foreign Jews aged sixteen to fifty, men and women, except those women who were pregnant or breast-feeding. A police official of Loire-Inférieure reported that 'gendarmes seconded to the German security police on 15 July accompanied German soldiers of the Feldgendarmerie who were organizing the arrest of Jews'. 'Following instructions received from the prefecture and at the request of M. Einfeld, the SS chief,' said Subprefect Bernard Lecornu, 'the Commissaire Central of Saint-Nazaire provided three police officers to guard the Jews', fifty-four of whom had been arrested.[29] On the evening of 15 July between 8 p.m. and midnight, and again on the 16th at 5 a.m., reported the Commissaire Central of Angers, 'my staff helped the German SD in the operations against the Jews'.[30] 'A detachment of gendarmerie alerted on 15 July at 4.50 p.m.', said Adjutant Barreau of the Gennes brigade, near Saumur, 'helped two German gendarmes guard and transport the persons arrested, without becoming involved in the details of the arrest.'[31] Among those arrested were the German-Jewish clan who owned the Sainte-Radégonde estate at Chênehutte-les-Tuffeaux, with the exception of the grandparents Abraham, in their seventies, and their daughter-in-law, Erny. The arrested Jews were taken to the Grand Séminaire in Angers, where they were joined by other groups of Jews transported from as far away as Le Mans and Poitiers. A contingent of 133 'healthy' Jews out of a total of 291 left the camp de La Lande for Angers on 16 July, leaving space for 200 Jews rounded up in Tours on 15 July to be housed there instead. Having been kept confined fifteen to a cell in the Grand Séminaire of Angers for several days, the whole contingent of 824 Jews was bused on to a train and sent off in the direction of Auschwitz.

While the responsibility of Vichy is now well established, there is still controversy about how ordinary French people reacted to these terrible scenes. Did they care? Were they shocked? Or did they simply close their doors and shutters and thank God that it was not them? Abbé Henri Richer, who came from an extremely Pétainist family and was a seminarist in Angers at the time, remembers a German soldier teasing a Jewish girl with a piece of cheese in the courtyard of the Grand Séminaire, and though he knew that the Jews were crowded fifteen to a cell, felt more sympathy for the German soldiers because of the heat.[32] 'Until now,' reported the Commissaire Central of Angers on 16 July, 'the vast majority of the public has remained fairly indifferent to the Jewish question, and continues to show reserve. Today, however, many are not hiding their sympathy for those who appear to be victims of persecution.'[33] Writing shortly after the 824 Jews held in the Grand Séminaire had been taken away and 'certain particularly painful details about the round-up had emerged', the prefecture of Maine-et-Loire noted that 'there is some concern that a current of pity may be provoked in favour of the Jewish race now seen to be martyrs, even among those who fully approved the protective measures taken by the government such as that restricting their access to public office'.[34] The subprefect of Cholet was less agitated, suggesting a discrepancy between private sentiments and public attitudes. 'Though the measure has been sharply criticized by people under their breath and troubles the conscience of most French citizens,' he reported, 'it has not provoked any manifestation of collective sympathy. The arrests have left the population rather indifferent and have not caused any unrest.'[35]

The French were generally more shocked by the manner of the

deportation than by the deportation itself, because the story that the Jews were being taken to labour camps in eastern Europe was widely accepted. In Angers, Jews were seen loaded on to cattle trucks, the doors of which were then locked, and parents and children had been separated.[36] Though Laval and Bousquet had insisted that children be deported with their parents precisely to avoid this kind of scene, the Germans at this point only wanted to remove healthy adults to keep alive the fiction of labour camps in the east, and decided that the children would stay. At Tours, in consequence, Prefect Tracou reported 'a violent hostility to the way the occupying authorities were going about things, especially with regard to small children abandoned to the most complete destitution'.[37] After the adults fit to travel were removed from the Camp de la Lande outside Tours, their sixty-five children were entrusted to other families in the camp, and were joined the next day by thirty-two more children who had not been found families after the round-up in Tours.[38] But the predicament of the children gave non-Jews a concrete opportunity to show some solidarity. The subprefect of Saumur was summoned by the Feldgendarmerie on the evening of 15 July, the day before the round-up, and told to find premises with the utmost discretion where children might be accommodated for two or three days. These should not be places run by nuns or priests, he was told, the understanding being that they were overly sympathetic or might have escape networks. Since the holidays had begun, the subprefect laid on the girls secondary school.[39] In Angers seventeen children had to be dealt with; two were housed with other Jewish families, three disappeared, and the rest were taken in by non-Jewish families. The five Sternchuss children of Angers – Nathan (eleven), Mina (nine), Lola (six), Simone (four) and Odette (two), were entrusted to a family friend, Mlle Frouin, at Château-Gontier, while their traumatized mother was interned in the lunatic asylum of Gennes.[40] This sympathy shown by non-Jews angered Gestapo chief Ernst who ruled on 24 August that Jewish children were no longer to be looked after by 'French families'. 'I will decide in all cases', he added, 'where Jewish chidren stay.'[41] Some non-Jews continued to show solidarity. Mme Lévy, who came from Lorraine, and was left at Beaupréau with her children aged one and five so long as she reported daily to the gendarmerie, failed to show on 4 September and was last seen pushing her pram towards Saint-Florent. It was assumed that she had been given a lift by a motorist to the station at Varades or Ancenis, and would try to join her husband in the Free Zone.[42] Other French people were less sympathetic, not least because the deportation left Jewish assets as ripe fruit for acquisition. Within two days of the round-up of 16 July, Dr Georges Barrault of les Ponts-e-Cé outside Angers approached the German authorities to take over the practice that a Polish Jew, Dr Gurwicz, had been managing for the widow of local practitioner Dr Béguin. He pointed out that Gurwicz was 'ethnically unqualified' to run the practice under the Statut des Juifs and had refused to wear the yellow star; in any case he was impatient to acquire the business as soon as possible to develop a *maison de cure*.[43]

Assistance from gentiles made it possible for some Jews to escape the round-ups. While 36 Jews were arrested in Angers on 15–16 July, 19 French Jews and 15 foreign ones managed to escape.[44] It is quite clear, however, that the condition laid down by Laval and Bousquet, and which by and large was observed in the Paris region, namely that only foreign Jews would be deported, simply did not stick in the Loire valley. Of the 36 Jews arrested in Angers on 15–16 July 1942, for example, no fewer than 15 were of French nationality. Of the 824 Jews finally deported from the Grand Séminaire of Angers on 20 July, 337 were Poles, 286 were other foreign nationals, and 201 were French.[45] The statistics on the Atlantic coast were even more telling. Of the 65 Jews arrested on 15 July 1942 in the *arrondissement* of Saint-Nazaire, for example, 52 were French. These included Armand Lévy of Saint-Nazaire, his wife, and daughter aged eleven. When his father-in-law, Lucien Bernheim, eighty, also a French citizen, heard of their arrest, he wrote to the prefect assuming it was an 'error' and requesting that they be released.[46] We do not have the reply of Prefect Dupard but Subprefect Lecornu later told him that *all* the French in his *arrondissement* had been arrested in July but that this was not a problem for the French administration. 'It is my opinion', he announced, 'that the question of principle concerning the arrest of French Jews should be put to the German authorities.'[47]

The position of the French administration seems to have been that, regrettable though it was, and irrespective of the fact that French police had been openly involved in the round-ups and arrests, responsibility lay entirely with the Germans. A barrister of Tours wrote to Prefect Tracou on behalf of his client, Mme Estelle Isakow, a local shopkeeper, and her daughter Paulette, who were both naturalized French but had been arrested and sent to the Camp de la Lande. Tracou replied bluntly, 'I regret to have to tell you that since these measures have not been taken by the French authorities, I have no means of improving their lot,' and he referred the barrister to the Sicherheitspolizei, 118 boulevard Béranger.[48] After an article appeared in Le Pilori about the number of French Jews arrested in Touraine and Regional Prefect Roussillon asked Tracou to comment, Tracou answered rather disingenuously that 'the French police have not arrested any Jews, let alone French Jews. Everything has been carried out by the German services.' He conceded that about sixty of the arrests had been of French Jews but these were Jews who had been brought to the attention of the German police for other reasons and were therefore suspect.[49]

By this time the Union Générale des Israélites de France started to put pressure on the prefecture of Angers to do something about the arrest of French Jews, in particular to order the release of those being held in the Camp de la Lande. It observed that the exemption of French Jews had been scrupulously observed in Paris and the department of the Seine, and demanded to know why the administration in the Loire area should be so careless. Prefect Delegate Daguerre took the official line that 'these police operations were carried out on the instructions of the SS and according to information that it alone possesses'. But he forwarded the complaint to SS chief Ernst and also wrote to Pierre Laval to say that his information did indicate that a large number of French Jews had indeed been arrested in his area. The prefect representing the Ministry of the Interior in Paris simply told him to sort this out with the local German authorities. By this time Dr Ernst had replied to Daguerre that 'The French Jews arrested during the operation against the stateless Jews had all rendered themselves guilty. For that reason they have been transported to labour camps in the east.'[50] Daguerre forwarded this reply to the Ministry of the Interior in Paris saying that he now considered the matter 'closed'. Again it appears that agreements made with the Germans were not worth the paper they were written on. But it also seems that, faced with a clear violation of the agreement, the French administration did not challenge the German high-handedness or question the emerging logic that all Jews were 'guilty' simply by dint of being Jews. Whether, as the reply of Prefect Tracou to Roussillon suggests, they were imbibing the German ideology, or whether they simply did not have the will to stand up to the Gestapo, the result was the same: in this part of the Occupied Zone at least, the distinction between French and foreign Jews amounted to nothing.

The progress of the deportations thus progressed unimpeded, in a very different way from the strife that surrounded attempts to deport French labour under the *Relève* and STO.[51] On 4 September 422 Jews – 145 men, 277 women and children – left the Camp de la Lande for Drancy. The only ones left were 78 children, 7 pregnant women, 10 very sick patients, 4 aged between seventy-one and eighty-three, and a Jewish doctor and student to provide some sort of medical service. By the end of October all the Jews had gone and La Lande took on a new function, as an internment camp for over 250 female communists.[52] On 7 October French police and gendarmerie chiefs were summoned to see Gestapo chief Ernst at Angers and told that following orders from Hitler and Goering all remaining foreign Jews, including children, the old and the sick, were to be rounded up 'without pity' on Friday, 9 October, at 7 a.m. and deported. They would be allowed to take two blankets, two pairs of shoes, underwear and washing things, but would have to hand over identity papers, ration cards, money, valuables and even keys to the SS. The operation would take place under the direction of the SS but, said Ernst, the SS were too busy themselves to make the arrests and manage the deportation, which would be up to the French police and gendarmerie. Naturally, said Ernst, French Jews would not be involved.[53]

The arrests, Prefect Daguerre later confirmed, almost with pride, were undertaken '*uniquely* by the French police'.[54] Thirteen were arrested in Angers, including the 5 Sternchuss children and their grandmother Rebecca, 34 were arrested elsewhere in the department, and 69 were brought from Tours. All 116, as in July, were housed in the Grand Séminaire of Angers until, on 16 October, they were taken in three coaches to Angers station, where they were put on a train to Drancy, escorted by 22 French gendarmes and 2 Feldgendarmes. Not only were the French police happy to play the leading role, they did not seem concerned that as usual French Jews were caught in the net. Of 116 deported, 40 were French according to the official lists and the number was probably 47 because some, like the Sternchuss family, were now cited as Polish whereas previously they had been recorded as French.[55] Among those in the contingent from Tours there were some extremely eminent French Jews, now all in their seventies, such as Albert Lipman, former first president of the Appeal Court of Tours, aged seventy-three, and his wife Berthe, from Lorraine, merchants David and Benjamin Aron who originated from Dole in the Jura, and David's wife Alice, born in Constantine, Algeria, and active in the Croix Rouge.[56] Alice and David Aron were in fact moved from Drancy to the Rothschild Hospital in Paris, and wrote to the prefect of Indre-et-Loire asking that since they were third-generation French, had lived in Tours for fifty-seven years and were 'highly respected in commerce', they be allowed to return to the town. The prefect replied to say that the German police prohibited their return, and David Aron died in the Rothschild Hospital the following month.[57]

While the French police and administration seemed to be hardened to the deportations, public reaction was becoming less ambivalent. Perhaps not too much significance should be attached to the gesture of M. Dupré, manager of the café opposite the Grand Séminaire of Angers, who submitted a bill for 12,220 francs for meals provided to the inmates between 13 and 16 October, since he had a living to make. Prefect Daguerre detected a growing concern among local people, not least because with the arrest of French Jews as well as foreign Jews the line between who was liable for persecution and who was safe was becoming blurred. 'There have been harsh criticisms of the deportation of women and small children, brought together in Angers from several departments,' he wrote, 'The population has not been indifferent to the removal of whole families, taken in lorries across the town to the railway station. People are saying everywhere, "Today, it's the Jews, tomorrow it will be the others." '[58] Gradually it seems that the pressure of public opinion was beginning to have an effect on the attitude of the French authorities. True, there were scarcely any more Jews in the region. After the round-up of thirty-eight Jews in his department on 9 October, Prefect Dupard reported that 'there are now no Jews, whether French or foreign, on the coastal stretch of Loire-Inférieure', which is the only place they had ever been anyway.[59] In June 1943 the Renseignements Généraux section of the police reported that there were no Jews left in Maine-et-Loire.[60] This omitted the sixty-four mainly Polish, Russian, and Turkish Jews at the isolated work camp of Clefs, north of Angers, but these were rounded up by the Sicherheitsdienst on 22 November 1943, and arrived at Drancy two days later.[61]

The persecution of the Jews was now virtually of academic interest, reduced to tracking down Jews on the run from Paris and elsewhere, and exposing Jews lying low under false identities. These were the concerns not of the prefectoral administration, the police or gendarmerie, but of the professional anti-Semites of the CGQJ. This outfit, sinister though it sounded, was in fact isolated and extremely ineffective. Its regional delegate in Angers from September 1942, Georges Gasseau, was a smooth talker but a career fraudster, who had no staff, failed to pay his office phone bills, plundered the properties of deported Jews and was finally dismissed in the spring of 1943. It had a file on 200–300 Jews in the region, but most of the bogus Aryans it tried to uncover were in fact genuine. It needed a network of paid informers but did not have the funds and discovered that public opinion was against it.[62] The police and prefectoral administration found it obsessive and interfering. For nine months, for example, it was determined to nail a certain Jacques Cohen or Coen, an antique dealer of Nantes, as a Greek Jew, black marketeer and Gaullist spy. The Nantes police insisted that the name was Coen, that he had a baptism certificate and had been married in a Catholic church, and was supported by the prefecture. The regional delegate of the CGQJ replied that it had medical evidence of Co(h)en's circumcision and that 'his baptism in the Catholic religion in no way changes his racial identity'. In the end the matter was decided by the Germans, who arrested him in April 1944.[63]

The deportation of the Jews ceased to interest the general public for one very simple reason, that the heavy hand of the Gestapo was now descending not only on Jews and communists but also on ordinary French citizens. The limited comfort brought by the sense that only the traditional Judaeo-Bolshevik demons were at risk was undermined by the fact that anyone suspected of opposition, let alone resistance, was liable to arrest and deportation. Among those who fell under suspicion were soldiers, notables, politicians, teachers, students, and eventually even bureaucrats and the police. The Gestapo terror also exposed division and treachery among French people. Just as in Germany the Gestapo was thin on the ground and relied on German citizens denouncing each other, so also in France, as we saw in Chinon, the French were only too happy to turn each other in.[64] Moreover, after the show trial of communists in Nantes in January 1943, trial even by the military court of the Feldkommandantur was a luxury of the past. The Gestapo acted secretly and those they arrested simply disappeared: they were first tortured to reveal their accomplices, then quietly shot on a nearby firing range or deported to Germany. The model of deportation without trial introduced for the Jews who, after all, had committed no crime, became standard practice for all other victims.

On 11 November 1942 German forces marched into the Free Zone and the Armistice Army, 100,000 strong, was disbanded. Some of the cadres of the Armistice Army formed a Resistance organization, the Organisation de la Résistance Armée (ORA), which after two years' obedience to Marshal Pétain, tended to be loyal less to de Gaulle than to his even more right-wing rival for leadership of the Free French, General Giraud. Giraudist opinion, it seems, was particularly strong in the region of Loches, the small town in the south of Touraine 'liberated' in July 1940 when the demarcation line was redrawn, but now once more occupied.[65] The 32nd Infantry Regiment, which had liberated Loches, immediately fell under suspicion. In January 1943 three members of the Gestapo, on orders from Brückle in Tours and apparently with the approval of Bousquet in Paris, called on the police superintendent of Loches to enlist his cooperation. They then arrested the recently demobilized commander of the 32nd Infantry Regiment, Robert Martin, and two other officers.[66]

Less than two months later a knot of influential individuals in the Angers region were arrested. One, oddly enough, was the regional propaganda chief, Michel Favre. Regional Prefect Roussillon was unable to extract the reason for his arrest from Gestapo chief Ernst but told Laval that 'it seemed to be connected with the arrest of several people belonging to PSF and royalist circles in Angers'.[67] He was able to secure the release of Favre but not of the head of the Secours National, Colonel François de Sauvebeuf. Sauvebeuf was also president of the Anjou federation of the Parti Social Français of Colonel de La Rocque, and had chaired a meeting in July 1942 when de La Rocque had attacked Gaullism and called for a 'good understanding' with Germany but made clear that France would not permit any amputation of her territory, a clear reference to Alsace-Lorraine, now ruled by a brace of Gauleiters.[68] More nationalist than fascist, the PSF was dissolved by SS chief Oberg in November 1943. Sauvebeuf made over the PSF office in Angers to the Secours National, then held a clandestine meeting in his house the following January. Arrested on 9 March 1943, he was sent to the transit camp of Compiègne the following month before being deported to Germany in January 1944. He was later joined on his voyage by his colleague on the Société d'Agriculture, Sciences et Arts of Angers, Henri de Champagny, mayor of Somloire, *conseiller général* of Vihiers, and of a chivalric, royalist, Vendean and anti-German temperament. Champigny provoked the anger of the Germans by encouraging peasants not to cooperate with German requisitioning of milk and butter, saying, 'What the peasants don't hand over, the Germans can't take.' As a result the Gestapo demanded that he resign as mayor, vetoed his membership of the *conseil départemental* that had recently been agreed by the Vichy authorities, and then arrested him.[69] He and Sauvebeuf were sent first to Buchenwald and then Flossenberg, where Champigny died after three weeks in March 1944 and Sauvebeuf the following October.[70]

The wave of arrests was not confined to right-wing notables but extended to teachers who tended to be on the other side of the political spectrum. Marie Talet, headmistress of the Collège Joachim du Bellay of Angers, was arrested in February 1943 along with two of her staff, allegedly having been denounced by the headmaster of the boys Lycée. This may have been because of their own beliefs or else because of the actions of their pupils, for which the Germans now held them responsible. Louis Brun, the headmaster of the Lycée Descartes in Tours, was arrested by the Gestapo after a Gaullist graffito was discovered in a pupil's desk and a half-rubbed-out '*Vive le . . .*' in the toilets.[71] The Tours police, who worked well with Gestapo chief Brückle, managed to secure the release of Brun, who was supposed to support the 'policy of collaboration', so long as he was moved to another post, but the Angers police had no such luck with Mme Talet, who was deported to Ravensbrück, where she died.

The arrest of key figures in the local community had a powerful effect on opinion. 'These arrests', reported the police superintendent of Angers, 'have been the subject of much conversation and create a certain fear in many circles. Increasingly, however, people no longer express their opinions, even to their friends.' In the absence of hard information rumour was rife. 'This week,' continued the superintendent, 'people say that six people have been shot, among them someone arrested recently.'[72] Prefect Daguerre noted that those arrested were very respectable and often extremely loyal to Marshal Pétain. They belonged to 'the most varied social milieux: shopkeepers, peaceable bourgeois, teachers from colleges and lycées, the headmistress of the Collège de Jeunes Filles who was universally respected. One day it's the chemist who goes to prison, the next it's a banker. Naturally these arrests are creating a special psychosis in public opinion which makes propaganda for Franco-German understanding difficult to sell'.[73] In Tours and Chinon, in the spring of 1943, the Sicherheitsdienst cast its net even wider, rounding up unsuspecting Frenchmen in cafés, cinemas, stations, even on the street. 'Admittedly,' said Prefect Tracou, 'most of them were released a few days later but these operations irritate the population and create a sort of terror.'[74]

Arbitrary arrests did little for the spirit of Franco-German cooperation, but the German authorities were becoming increasingly frustrated by the lack of cooperation they seemed to be getting even from French officials. On 30 June 1943 a stranded American airman called Goodman walked into the café of Jeanne Barthe, who decided that he needed equipping with identity and ration cards. Either naïvely, or because she had contacts there, she took the airman round to the town hall and prefecture of Tours where various employees and officials were willing to help, right up to the secretary-general of the prefecture, Charles Aubert. It seems that the operation was revealed to Commissaire Boucherie and Gestapo chief Brückle by Bernard Molas-Quenescourt, *chef de cabinet* at the prefecture, who was highly regarded in collaborationist circles and envious of Aubert's job. German records show that until this point Aubert had appeared honest and loyal but was now acting in a completely different way. Aubert and five other staff of the prefecture and town hall were arrested on 4 July and sent before the military court of the Feldkommandantur of Tours in September where Molas-Quenescourt testified against them. Aubert was sentenced to three years' imprisonment. Tracou, impressed by 'the considerable emotion produced in the whole department by these arrests', went to Paris to try to secure Aubert's release, but to no avail. Aubert was subsequently deported, and Molas-Quenescourt duly inherited his job.[75]

Increasingly, it was not just parts of the administration on which the Germans felt they could not rely, but elements of the French police. While most of the police continued to collaborate with the Gestapo, some individuals became disillusioned by their role, and became a prey to infiltration by Resistance groups which could benefit from armed, structured and highly mobile organizations. Inspector Jean Vairé of Nantes, for example, headed a group of the Sûreté of Nantes who belonged to the 'Hussards of Liberty' orchestrated since October 1942 by a Missouri-born, French-speaking RAF officer, Ted Wilkinson, who was an agent of the British Special Operations Executive (SOE) in the Loire area. Obliged to go underground in August 1943, Vairé was denounced by a peasant in the Sarthe and arrested by the Gestapo, by which time four of his colleagues in the Sûreté had been arrested too. Condemned to death, then deported, Vairé was repatriated in May 1945. In Angers a young officer of the Sûreté, Henri Robin, was arrested by the Gestapo on 31 August 1943. One colleague, Jean Martin, fled, but another, Gaston Cousseau of the municipal police, was tracked down. The regional prefect was informed that they had been 'forming Resistance groups and collecting weapons'. Robin and Cousseau survived Mauthausen and Neuengamme respectively. In Saumur, finally, the gendarmerie Captain Royer headed a resistance group which included police as well as demobilized officers and NCOs of the Armistice Army but was broken by the Gestapo in September 1943, with terrible consequences.[76] Learning of these arrests, the normally calm people of Anjou became anxious and fearful and started to talk about 'a reign of terror in the country, like that known to exist in Germany'.[77] The reign of terror created an unbridgeable gulf between the French and Germans, but also had a second result, to push together French people and even foreigners in their midst who had been separated until then by Vichy's practice of divide and rule. Henceforth everybody was at risk: they were all Jews now.

13. CONSCRIPTION

On Friday, 2 October 1942, the Ministry of Information delegate for Loire-Inférieure organized a meeting at the Batignolles-Châtillon locomotive plant in Nantes to drum up support for the *Relève* scheme by which French workers would go to work in German factories in exchange for French POWs who would be allowed to return home. Of the workforce of 2,400 about a quarter turned up. The manager announced that a quota of seventy-five workers and eight technicians had been imposed on the plant, and then introduced the speakers, who were a former POW and a former worker in Germany. Tillaut, who had returned under the scheme from two years in a German POW camp, was listened to in silence. But Lamothe, who had gone to work in Germany for six months, was greeted by shouts of 'Why did you bother to come back?', 'You should have stayed there!' and 'Traitor!' Tillaut, who tried to mingle with groups of workers, was chased out amid whistles and cat-calls and the party of visitors left hurriedly by car. Subsequently Tillaut wrote to the Ministry of Information official to say that he could no longer help. 'I went home after the Batignolles session much more depressed than I imagined . . . I have suffered cruelly from coming up against such a lack of understanding. I addressed the workers purely so that they could hear the voice of those who are waiting behind the barbed wire. In vain. I appealed to their generosity and they were not moved. You can see how distressed I am.'[1]

First thing on Monday morning, 5 October, the Nantes gendarmerie picked up copies of a tract in the suburban streets which were signed by 'the popular factory committees' and were clearly communist in inspiration. Addressed to the engineering workers, the tract explained that the *Relève* was to liberate not French POWs but

German workers who would then be sent to fight the Russians on the Eastern Front.

> The Vichy traitors and their stooges Dupard and Co. have agreed with Hitler to send men to Germany by force. You have already refused. Good. HOLD FAST. DO NOT GO. DO NOT LEAVE. Form a single bloc. Do not allow those who have been picked out to leave. Tomorrow it will be your turn. Go on strike. Fight if you have to to save your lives. Use every means possible to ensure that nobody goes. Show the invader and the traitors that you are not frightened, that you are decent people.
>
> Hitler will be defeated. Hasten his defeat. Don't work for him, you will only prolong the war. Stick together. NOT A SINGLE FRENCH WORKER FOR THE BOCHE.[2]

The following day, returning from lunch, the Batignolles workers were confronted by the list of those who had been selected to go to Germany. Immediately they downed tools. The management did not report the strike but convened the shop stewards and tried to negotiate a return to work. But the news leaked out and Prefect Dupard was summoned to the Feldkommandantur where von Trotha threatened to arrest the workers who failed to show. As it happened, two high-ranking Vichy officials, one representing the Ministry of Information and the other Laval, had come to Nantes to investigate the incident of 2 October. They persuaded the German authorities that if they lifted the threat of arrests they would talk to the shop stewards and those selected about the duty of going to Germany. The situation was defused and the workers went back after a strike that lasted three hours in all – a gesture that was more symbolic than anything else, but a courageous step taken in defiance of German orders.

The incident sheds a good deal of light on the issue of the *Relève*, which was negotiated with the Germans by Laval after he returned to power in April 1942 and sold to the French with the maximum of public relations spin available at the time. Sauckel, a former Gauleiter, then governor of Thuringia, and now with responsibility for recruiting labour for German factories by fair means or foul from all over German-occupied Europe, demanded from France 350,000 workers (of whom 100,000 were to be skilled engineering workers). Laval insisted that the right 'psychological ground' had to be prepared and was hoping for the release of one POW for every worker recruited. Sauckel, with Hitler behind him, was difficult to impress and it took Laval eight hours on 16 June simply to get Sauckel to agree to repatriate 50,000 POWs in return for 150,000 *skilled* workers.[3] Laval announced the *Relève* in a radio broadcast on 22 June during which he famously announced that 'he hoped for the victory of Germany because without that communism will take over everywhere'. Recruitment offices were opened in town centres and the authorities waited for the queues to form. They did not. By the end of July only 40,000 workers had left, only a quarter of them skilled, and a crossover of a departing train of volunteers and a returning POW train did not take place until 11 August at Compiègne, when Laval revealed for the first time the lopsided nature of the deal. It became clear to the Germans that waiting for volunteers would not begin to meet the quotas they needed, and an ordinance of 22 August 1942 gave them the powers to requisition labour. Ever eager to assert the autonomous role of the Vichy government between the German authorities and their prey, Laval issued a law on 4 September requiring all male workers aged between eighteen and fifty, and unmarried women aged twenty-one to thirty-five, to 'undertake all work that the government sees fit in the higher interests of the nation'.

Whether Vichy was acting as a brake on German demands or facilitating them is best examined in the local context. The *Relève* was an extremely unpopular measure which confronted head-on the interests of a French proletariat that had never been more cohesive and class-conscious. The comparison between the deportation of labour and the deportation of the Jews is instructive. The Jews, relatively few, dispersed among the local populations and isolated from the rest of society as refugees or bearers of the yellow star, were not able to resist and elicited no more than pity when they were rounded up. The workers, concentrated in large-scale plants up to 2,000 strong, firmly implanted in working-class communities, were able to show defiance and demonstrate solidarity. Moreover, whereas the French authorities acted promptly and efficiently to execute German orders when it came to rounding up Jews, when it came to sending workers to Germany they were confronted by industrial action and angry public opinion and were forced to acknowledge that the Vichy regime, though nominally authoritarian, relied in reality on tacit consent.

General Feldt, who had replaced Neumann-Neurode as head of Bezirk B, summoned all four regional prefects responsible for the west of France to deliver on Sauckel's instructions. As far as Loire-Inférieure went, 6,800 workers would have to be recruited by 12 November. Any worker who refused to sign a contract or accept one signed on his behalf by the Inspecteur du Travail would be treated as a saboteur. 'It is not a voluntary system', reflected Prefect Dupard, 'but scarcely disguised requisition.'[4] Torn between the formal constraints of collaboration and the anticipated wave of popular hostility, he cranked up the propaganda offensive. On 11 August 1942 the *Phare de Nantes* published a picture of Dupard reading a speech in support of the *Relève* under a portrait of Marshal Pétain, his large frame seated next to the Feldkommandant of Nantes and a rather bemused and frightened young man who was being congratulated as the 5,000th worker to leave for Germany. 'Bring home to the fields of peace those who left for the battlefields,' Dupard urged. 'It is my duty to emphasize the immense hope that the appeal of the government has inspired among our rural populations.'[5] The *Phare*, which was dedicated to the policy of Franco-German collaboration, tried to recruit other key figures for the campaign, but with little success. Mgr Villepelet, the bishop of Nantes, told the editor that he did not comment on political or even temporal issues, and even a follow-up visit by the Propagandastaffel failed to persuade him to change his mind.[6] More serious was the attitude of Gaëtan Rondeau, the mayor of Nantes. He also refused to give an interview to the *Phare* in support of the *Relève*, and told the regional delegate of the Ministry of Information that his office required reserve and discretion in order to maintain order and calm.[7] Since the execution of the hostages almost a year earlier, Rondeau had felt squeezed between the intensifying pressure of the Germans and the increasing panic of the local population. He did not feel that he could struggle against public opinion on behalf of a policy of collaboration in which he had less and less faith. He retired to his holiday property of Tiffauges in the Vendée and opted out of the collaborationist cause. He even sent his apologies to Marshal Pétain for not being able to attend a meeting of the Association of Mayors of France at Vichy at the end of August.[8] The case of the *Phare* interview was the last straw. Regional Gestapo chief Ernst told Dupard and Regional Prefect Roussillon that Rondeau would have to go; he had adopted a policy of 'neutrality' which amounted to following public opinion away from collaboration. Dupard tried to defend Rondeau and stalled for nearly two months, but at the end of September 1942 he visited Rondeau at Tiffauges and told him that the game was up.[9] Rondeau wrote a letter of resignation on 10 October, which was read to the municipal council on 20 October, and the council in solidarity resigned en bloc.[10]

While the fate of Mayor Rondeau was being decided, opposition to the *Relève* was spreading among the workers of Nantes. On 9 October 300 of the 1,100 workers at the Société de Mécanique Générale de l'Ouest engineering works, of whom half were women, went on strike in response to notice to leave served on a dozen young workers out of the firm's quota of sixty-two. The local SS chief arrived with three officers of the Feldkommandantur and demanded that the young men be arrested. Prefect Dupard argued that this would 'have very regrettable consequences among the workers' and his *chef de cabinet* convened the management and the Comité Social d'Entreprise to remind them of their duty. Again the crisis was defused, but three day later the Chantiers de la Loire (1,700 strong) and Chantiers de Bretagne (2,000) went on strike when they learned of the size of their quotas. Here the issue was settled by the management and the workers went back after half an hour. The situation that arose at the SNCASO aircraft factory at Château-Bougon on 14 October, however, was much more serious. A team of four German civilians, including a representative of the Heinkel factory in Rostock, where the enlisted workers were to be taken, arrived at the factory with ninety-five work contracts to be signed. The workers refused to sign, and the workforce of over 1,600 went on strike. The German view was that propaganda had failed and 'it is now up to the authority of the Wehrmacht to overcome all resistance (*Widerstand)*'. Despite the attempt of secretary-general of the prefecture Yves Bayet to negotiate, the Feldkommandant ordered a military occupation the next day. The workforce was filtered and twenty-four of the chosen workers were arrested and imprisoned in Nantes until they had signed. But many workers, scenting a trap, failed to turn up that day and seventy designated workers were not found. Furious, the Feldkommandant ordered the management to provide a list of 100 new workers to replace the missing seventy, and demanded their arrest. After hard bargaining and promises that the police were on the trail of the missing seventy, the prefecture managed to avoid any more arrests.[11]

The predictions of the prefecture that arrests would only serve to inflame the workforce proved correct. On 21 October strikes broke out in the Chantiers de Bretagne and Chantiers de la Loire, where lists of 100 and 150 workers respectively were posted. The prefecture was unable to calm the situation and the movement spread that afternoon to seven other shipyards and factories, including the Chantiers Dubigeon, the Compagnie Nantaise des Chargeurs de l'Ouest, the Anciens Établissements Joseph-Paris and the Entreprises Métropolitaines et Coloniales, involving over 5,000 workers, and the following day to the Société Nantaise de Fonderies and the SNCF workshops of Nantes-Blottereau.[12] The police intendant of Angers went so far as to call it a 'general strike'.[13] The effect of the strike movement in terms of municipal politics was also considerable. The new mayor of Nantes proposed to Laval by Prefect Dupard was Henri Orrion, aged fifty, holder of the Croix de Guerre from the 1914–18 War and president of the syndicate of wholesale druggists of the west of France, whose attitude, he thought, 'inspires the confidence of representatives of the German army'. Unfortunately, he did not inspire the labour representatives who had sat on Rondeau's council, and Orrion was unable to find any labour leader either within or outside the CGT unions to serve as municipal councillors. After frantic negotiations he managed to put together a 'special delegation' of ten men drawn from professional, business and administrative circles, of which he would be president, not mayor, to run the city. Technocratic rather than political, it might stand for efficiency, but it did not have the support of the working-class communities which played such a vital part in the political life of the city and indicated that the gap between the Vichy authorities and public opinion was steadily widening.[14]

The workers who were sent to Germany made their views quite clear as special trains left Nantes at the beginning of November. One trainload of workers was immobilized when the communication cord was pulled, and agitated families on the station platform had to be dispersed by the Feldgendarmerie shooting into the air.[15] As they were moved off the workers sang the *Internationale* and shouted 'Death to Laval!' and 'The stake for Hitler'.[16] The promises of the *Relève* looked distinctly threadbare as, in a fortnight when 1,000 workers left, only seven prisoners returned to Nantes. For all his public campaigning, Prefect Dupard was forced to admit in private that 'the *Relève*, in the original formulation conceived by the government, has indeed been a failure'.[17]

The Germans, fighting for their lives on the Eastern Front, became increasingly impatient with the shambles of the *Relève*. Between 1 June and 31 December 1942 the *Relève* had furnished 240,000 workers for Germany, 135,000 of whom were skilled, mostly from the Occupied Zone and the industrial areas within them. Now Sauckel decided on a 'second action', which would recruit 250,000 workers, of whom 150,000 would be skilled, in half the time, by 31 March, and the same again by the end of June. To ensure that French interests and sovereignty were respected, as far as they could be, Minister of Industrial Production Jean Bichelonne, another acolyte of Laval, published the law on the Service du Travail Obligatoire (STO) on 16 February 1943. This established labour service in Germany as an alternative to military service, which was clearly suspended, and was to apply in the first instance to those born in 1920, 1921 and 1922.[18] It was a powerful project, but unlike the deportation of the Jews it failed to work.

To begin with, German demands for French labour in Germany clashed with their own demands for French labour to work in France, either building coastal defences for the Todt Organization, or working in factories specially assigned to production for the war effort. A German circular of 7 October 1942, for example, demanded 100,000 additional workers, especially from the building trade, to be provided by the French administration. The quota for Indre-et-Loire was 1,000, driving Prefect Tracou to protest to the Minister of Labour that German demands for labour were 'absolutely out of proportion with the available workforce' and to remind the Feldkommandant that 'a real effort is already being made to send workers to Germany'.[19] Two months later the Feldkommandant told Tracou that the labour supply for Todt had been 'inadequate so far and catastrophic this week' and instructed him that the full quota must be delivered by the end of the following week. In a vain attempt to square the circle, the Inspecteur du Travail admitted to Tracou that in consultation with the employers in the construction industry he was illicitly moving workers from protected factories to supply Todt.[20] The protected Rüstung- or V-Betriebe of course also had their own claims on the French labour force, and those who worked for them could not in theory be recruited for STO. They constituted an excellent refuge for workers who did not want to be conscripted for work in Germany, and even the German military authorities with an interest in these factories were keen to protect them from the STO recruiters. An official of the Feldkommandantur of Nantes was delighted in March 1943 that there were now eighty-eight V-Betriebe in the department, with another thirty on the way. Initially, he said, they had been able to protect their labour force but they had been 'severely affected' by the second Sauckel action and recently most of the V-Betriebe had been forced to surrender workers. 'This double use of V-Betriebe', he concluded, 'provokes a good deal of irritation and much unrest.'[21] Increasingly, however, Sauckel found himself pitted against Armaments Minister Albert Speer, who believed that it would be more beneficial to keep French workers working for the German war machine in France. From the autumn of 1943 Rü-Betriebe and V-Betriebe were combined as Speer- or S-Betriebe, whose workforces would be immune to deportation. In November 1943 Oberst Keil, head of the Rüstungskommando of the Le Mans region, called meetings of French factory bosses in Le Mans, Angers and Tours to announce that the elevation of forty-two of the seventy Rü-Betriebe to S-Betriebe would undoubtedly induce the *réfractaires* back to work.[22]

German labour demands were thus contradictory and often counterproductive. In the haste to extract quotas they were also arbitrary, riding roughshod over categories of exemption that had been agreed with the Vichy government. This arbitrariness, however, was at times undermined by the corruption of their own officials, for cutting across the general German interest, which was to milk the French economy, was the self-interest of particular Germans who made a profit from selling individual exemptions. The STO was in lieu of military service from which categories such as former POWs and demobilized members of the Armistice Army – unless they happened to be metalworkers by trade – were exempted, but the German authorities were impatient with such niceties. The Inspecteur du Travail of Indre-et-Loire reported that his service could 'only *strive* to obtain the respect of rules, the application of which is subordinate to the interpretation of local German authorities'.[23]

Arbitrariness might be efficient, but the other face of it was corruption. How corrupt the German administration was is difficult to ascertain, for the evidence is anecdotal, but two examples suggest that rogues were not rare. Sonderführer Hermann Brüning, the son of a Koblenz banker whose sister had married a rich Parisian, was already used to an easy life when he came to Nantes in the summer of 1942 to work for the employment service. He spent a lot of time and money in the Chez Elle bar of the Hôtel de Paris, in the company either of women or directors of German firms who came to prospect for labour. A colleague became suspicious when an anxious Frenchman visited the office one Sunday wishing to speak to Herr Brüning and let slip that he would offer him 10,000 francs to get off labour service in Germany. Further inquiries revealed that it was common knowledge in the cafés and bars of Nantes that Brüning took money to protect workers from labour service. He was sent before a German military court in April 1943 and sentenced to four months in prison and loss of rank.[24] Xavier Hupfer, a Lorrainer from Metz, interpreter for the economic services of the Feldkommandantur of Angers, took money for issuing certificates not only to farmers to exempt them from STO but to industrialists who wanted their factories classified as S-Betriebe in order to protect their workforce. He was brought low by his arrogance, arguing that to avoid STO 'in France three-quarters of the population are peasants and the rest sick', by bringing the shoe industry of Cholet to a virtual standstill by failing to process classification documents, and finally by announcing, 'It's not the prefecture that's in charge but the Feldkommandantur, and the Feldkommandantur is me.'[25]

One of the problems with labour service was that, even according to the rules, the burden did not fall equitably on all sectors of the population so that those who felt penalized were more likely to put up resistance. The *Relève* fell solely on workers, who were supposed to take over the sacrifice of the soldier-peasants in the POW camps, but they did not necessarily see it like that. The workers of the Nantes–Saint-Nazaire area resented the fact that the peasants were exempt, the more so because they were seen to be fleecing the working classes by selling their produce at inflated prices.[26] In Anjou Prefect Daguerre even spoke of a 'class struggle' with the workers, complaining that they alone shouldered the burden of labour service.[27] Another issue was the generation gap. Although it made sense for younger workers without attachments to leave home, in practice they often opted for a protected factory or the Todt Organization, leaving heads of families liable to be sent to Germany. Many of these inequalities were supposed to be ironed out by the STO, which imposed labour service on young men of military age, between twenty and twenty-two. Unfortunately, like universal miltary service, it was never quite universal. One privileged category were students, who were granted exemption until further notice. The workers of Nantes–Saint-Nazaire now transferred their anger with cosseted peasants to cosseted students who, because secondary and especially higher education demanded money and leisure, were essentially middle class. Prefect Dupard thought that the students might have been excused until 1 June, by which time they would have taken their exams, and then been liable to go. As it happened, he said, the measure looked like an additional privilege for the bourgeoisie, 'which until now has not suffered much from the war and occupation'.[28] These exemptions were abolished by the summer of 1943, and Prefect Tracou of Indre-et-Loire reported that this equitable measure had been welcomed by the workers, who now saw 'not only their friends leaving but also peasants, students and functionaries'.[29]

The strategy of Laval was always to insert the French government and administration between the German authorities and the French population, in order to preserve French sovereignty. Whether this made the burden of the Occupation lighter is open to debate. Vichy was officially committed to the policy of collaboration and thus in one sense legitimated and facilitated German rule. But the more burdens were imposed on the French people, the more popular discontent increased, and the more the French administration found itself impossibly squeezed between its German masters and a rising tide of popular anger and fear. The STO was the single most important factor which demonstrated to the French people the perniciousness of collaboration. What it meant in reality was the subject of swelling myth and rumour. One myth was that it was 'disguised deportation'.[30] Just as the Jews had been told that they were being sent to labour camps in the east, so the same story was being fed to French workers, who were in fact being sent to 'another destination'.[31] Another story was that workers were going to service German armies at the rear on the Eastern Front or even to fight alongside German soldiers against the Russians.[32] Even if things were as they were told, and they would be working in German factories, the Allied bombing of German cities made this extremely hazardous. Workers who had been evacuated from Hamburg where their factories had been destroyed returned to Tours in the late summer of 1943 and reinforced fears of the holocaust being inflicted on the cities of the Reich.[33]

The French authorities tried to steer an increasingly tricky course between German demands and popular resentment. Prefect Dupard, summoned to a meeting at the Feldkommandantur of Nantes on 8 March 1943, was told by a representative of Sauckel that the French police were, under instructions from Laval, 'responsible for the departure of French workers to Germany'. Dupard replied that his interpretation of the STO regulations was that the French police were responsible for arresting conscripts who failed to appear, but not for sending them to Germany.[34] Whereas the French police seem to have acted efficiently and with alacrity when rounding up Jews, their attitude to STO was altogether more relaxed. The account by Mayor Darmaillacq of what happened in Cholet may suffer a little from special pleading after the Liberation, but even if it were only partly true it would be significant. Darmaillacq asserted that when the young men were conscripted for STO and many reported sick, he did not send the police to visit them at home. When he did have to send the police to check on certain queries, to satisfy the prefecture, he reported that everything was in order. Some individuals were even said to have gone to Germany, whereas in fact 'they were walking quite openly around the town'. The town hall, he said, never became involved in choosing who had to go, and when some failed to report to the station after a period of leave to return to Germany, he did not send the police after them.[35]

Mayors played a crucial role in issues of labour recruitment, whether for Todt or STO. Still subject in rural areas to pressure from the Germans, they were even more so to pressure from local inhabitants, whom they knew and who looked to them to protect their interests. Mayors in Touraine, faced with a demand to find workers for the Todt Organization in February 1943, sent in such replies as 'the commune is essentially agricultural and no workers live here', or simply, 'I am unable to choose anyone.'[36] There were risks in reacting too energetically on behalf on the local population, and risks for not reacting strongly enough. The Marquis de Lussac, mayor of Sainte-Catherine-de-Fierbois, confronted the German authorities in front of thirty men summoned for Todt work. When he failed to have the village baker released, he went into a tirade against the 'veritable slave trade' that was being practised. Brückle's Sicherheitspolizei were summoned from Tours and the mayor was arrested. He was sentenced to five years' imprisonment by the military court of Tours and Prefect Tracou was required to dismiss him as mayor by the German authorities in Angers.[37] M. Forest, the mayor of Marçay, aged seventy-two and himself the father of a POW in Germany, who was alleged to have provided ration tickets to STO dodgers working illicitly on farms in his commune, was arrested on Brückle's orders and held hostage until other mayors provided him with lists of STO dodgers working in the region, a crisis that the prefect was not able to resolve for nearly three months.[38] Further west, in the *arrondissement* of Châteaubriant, mayors were threatened with violence if they seemed to be doing the bidding of the authorities. The mayor of Soudan received a death threat from one individual who had been selected, that of Nozay had his house daubed with insults after he failed to include his son on the list of those who would go, and the subprefect complained of a 'general tendency of resignations' of rural mayors who could not cope with hostility on all sides.[39]

The dilemmas caused by STO afflicted not only local mayors but also the higher administration. Just as the *Relève* broke the career of Gaëtan Rondeau, mayor of Nantes, so STO proved the undoing of the regional prefect of Angers, Jean Roussillon. The German authorities were no longer prepared to waste time negotiating or massaging French sensibilities. They now wanted their demands met in full, immediately and with no quibbling. The German authorities were impressed by Roussillon's skill and competence, but began to find him secretive, opportunistic, 'smooth as an eel'. Although he was officially anti-British and anti-communist he was opposed to the collaborationist parties and told the president of Collaboration that he would not publish articles in the press in favour of STO which he regarded as a 'slave trade'. He had apparently told the police not to make notes of anti-German slogans shouted by STO conscripts as their trains left and had done nothing to bring anti-German officials under control. 'So long as the regional prefect remains in Angers,' concluded the report, 'the work of collaboration will have no luck.'[40] Roussillon was removed from office in July 1943 and was happy to pose as a victim. 'The Americans will soon come and sort things out,' he is alleged to have said, although he did not manage to endear himself to the Free French who saw him as a 'complete collaborator' and a man without conscience.[41]

The episcopate as well as the civil administration wobbled over STO and was forced to reconsider its doctrine of blindly rendering unto Caesar what was Caesar's. The long delay before the bishops responded to the round-up of Jews, and the fact that powerful protest came only from two bishops in the Free Zone, the archbishop of Toulouse and the bishop of Montauban, have been well documented.[42] Under pressure from the Christian faithful, the reaction of the episcopate to STO was more positive, and indeed more assertive in the former Occupied Zone, but the opportunity for bold intervention was again passed by. The first reaction of Cardinal Liénart, archbishop of Lille, was 'Accept it, it would be cowardly shirk it'. Within a week, under pressure from industrial workers mediated by the Jocist movement, he announced, 'To get out of it is not a sin. I am not going to advise you to go. It is a question of force.'[43] The Assembly of Cardinals and Archbishops drafted an official message along these lines that was to be read out by all bishops on Easter Day. Mgr Gaillard, archbishop of Tours, asked his bishops to come and fetch a copy, which must remain absolutely secret until then. It claimed to discuss not the politics of the question but the religious and moral dimension, but what was central was the same ambiguity.

> We cannot, our dearest brothers, make it an obligation of conscience to submit to the requisition. Does it follow that we are advising you to shirk from it? No! We are confronted by a force that the French authorities are trying to make more humane. We ask the Christians who will be going to give the ordeal its full redemptive value for the salvation of our country and wherever they go to console, support and comfort their comrades in work.[44]

Even this message was thought, on reflection, by Cardinal Liénart and Cardinal Suhard, archbishop of Paris, to be too outspoken. Mgr Villepelet learned that Suhard thought the text too tragic for Easter Day, that Pétain had wanted changes, and that Laval had indicated that it would undermine his negotiations with the Germans. Rather than risk exposing individual bishops to German reprisals, it was agreed that only Cardinals Suhard, Liénart and Gerlier of Lyon would sign the text, taking full responsibility, and that it would be read out on Joan of Arc Day, 9 April. Even this was an event in Nantes, where Mgr Villepelet read the message from the pulpit in front of the mayor and prefecture officials, and the Propagandastaffel telephoned to ask for the text.[45] In Angers, reading the message was probably the bravest thing the meek Mgr Costes did under the Occupation, although the text relayed by Regional Prefect Donati concentrated on the inhumanity of separating young people from their families and the inhumane conditions they had to endure.[46]

The Church, of course, was not the only body defining a position on STO, nor did it necessarily command the most attention. The Sicherheitspolizei of Nantes warned the prefect that they had received intelligence about a communist-inspired strike scheduled for 19 April 1943 between 11.45 a.m. and midday in the Paris region, and demanded that all police and gendarmerie be placed on full alert.[47] In the event nothing happened, but on the eve of 1 May communist tracts were picked up in the streets of Nantes and Tours, calling on the workers variously to strike, demonstrate, refuse to go to Germany, sabotage German factories and form groups of guerrillas.[48] Demonstrations there were, as conscripts were rounded up and sent off with ever more urgency to meet the deadline of the third Sauckel action at the end of June. On 21 June, for example, a train carrying many railway employees from Nantes halted at Angers Saint-Laud station. The carriages had been daubed with slogans such as '*Vive la classe de 1942!*', '*Vive les cheminots!*', '*Vive la France!*' and '*Vive de Gaulle!*' As the train was on the point of leaving, about 100 conscripts in the front carriages struck up the *Marseillaise* and the whole train began hurling insults at German soldiers stationed on the platform. Fourteen young men were detained by the gendarmerie, and the train was delayed by nearly an hour.[49]

Those who actually left on the trains for Germany were only a minority of those called up, but the rate of draft-dodging varied considerably from area to area. Figures for the second Sauckel action of January–March 1943 show that in Indre-et-Loire 89 per cent of the quota of 2,450 reported for duty. 'There is more resignation than revolt,' reported Prefect Tracou, putting it down to 'the calm temperament of the Tourangeaux'. He added, however, that they were worried that by doing their docile duty they would be considered mugs/suckers (*poires*).[50] In Maine-et-Loire 84 per cent of the quota of 2,700 reported, but there was much more recalicitrance in Loire-

Inférieure, where only 50 per cent of a quota of 4,000 found its way to Germany. The result for the third Sauckel action in Loire-Inférieure in April–June was even worse. For a quota of 3,650 imposed on the department, only 1,324 (36 per cent) actually left on STO. Since 400 young men were in fact tranferred from the Todt Organization the real total was 924 (25 per cent). The number of draft dodgers (*réfractaires*) was calculated as 1,130. Curiously, the highest rate of refusal was not in the *arrondissement* of Nantes, where the strikes against the *Relève* had concentrated (40 per cent), nor even in that of Saint-Nazaire (60 per cent), but in the *arrondissement* of Châteaubriant, in the deep Breton interior, where it was 80 per cent. The main enemies of STO were the peasants who, in the summer of 1942, when the 'class of 1942' was conscripted, were effectively summoned for the first time. In this region of isolated farms and *bocage* it was easy to find illicit agricultural work and be fed without the need for ration tickets. The local farmers were delighted to find a new source of labour and were extremely sullen and obstructive when the gendarmerie made inquiries, which was rare.[51]

For many historians, and even for Laval in his negotiations with Sauckel, STO dodgers fed directly into the Resistance. This is a myth that dies hard. For the vast majority of *réfractaires*, the purpose of dodging STO was to increase their chances of survival, and joining the Maquis was only one of their options. In the Mauges commune of La Pommeraye a dozen young men went on STO but two tried (unsuccessfully) to flee to the Spanish frontier and many simply went to ground locally, one emerging at the Liberation to hoist the tricolour on to the church spire. The collective history of the village makes no mention of the Maquis.[52] Near Segré the son of the stationmaster of La Ferrière-de-Flée hid for most of the duration in a concealed room above the station, receiving his ration tickets from the daughter of the *secrétaire de mairie*, and having lunch regularly with his family.[53] If there was any political dimension to opposition to STO in this part of western France, it was a rerun of the Catholic–Royalist Vendean uprising of 1793, protesting against military conscription into the armies of the Republic to go and fight on the Eastern Front for a cause in which they did not believe. This equivalence is reinforced by the fact that the most anti-STO area of Anjou was the Mauges, the Angevin Vendée. As early as 1942, the German commander in Cholet reported that the local population was 'particularly attached to their family and home (*Heimat*) and can be taken from them only with great difficulty'.[54] On 28 June 1943, at the high point of the deportation of the class of '42, when 428 youths left Angers station, 335 of them peasants, the song of La Jeunesse Agricole Chrétienne was more in evidence than the *Internationale*, and the slogans daubed on the carriages included 'Vendée, cabbage eaters' as well as '*Vive de Gaulle!*'[55] The *arrondissement* of Châteaubriant, which was the most hostile area to the draft in the whole region, was described by the prefect as a 'theatre of terrorism' and it threw up the Maquis of Saffré in June 1944.[56] Whether these Maquisards were always the heroes of later legend, however, was open to question. Here, and spilling into adjoining cantons of the Breton interior such as Guéméné-Penfao, Saint-Nicolas-de-Redon and Saint-Gildas-des-Bois, was a veritable Wild West in which masked and armed gangs roamed, taking ration books from *mairies*, cigarettes from tobacconists, and money, food, radios and old weapons that had not been handed in from isolated farmhouses. On 19 May 1944 ten or eleven individuals, one of whom said he had escaped from prison in Vitré, took 33,000 francs, silver and a radio set from the Rousseau family, who were tailors near Saint-Nicolas-de-Redon, and also shaved the wife's head. Four days later a gang speaking the local *patois* robbed a farmhouse in the neighbouring commune. Again they took money, food, clothing and documents, and in the absence of the husband shaved the wife's head.[57] Of course, shaving women's heads for 'horizontal collaboration' was a commonplace at the Liberation,[58] but it is debatable whether such gestures, when accompanying armed robbery, merited the accolade of Resistance.

As the recruitment of labour became more and more difficult, the German authorities required and resorted to ever more desperate measures. One new tactic was the establishment of mixed Franco-German 'combing commissions' which summoned employers to see if any more labour could be extracted from their firms. That in Nantes, which sat at the German recruitment office in the rue Sully, met for the first time in February 1943 but became especially active a year later, meeting four days a week. On 7 March 1944 M. Merlant of the food-processing firm Maison Amieux was summoned before the commission. He protested that his small firm had already provided five men for the Todt Organization and twelve for STO, and cited a German circular of 2 February issuing instructions to the effect that for obvious reasons the food industry should be protected. The commission told him that this instruction had now been over-ruled, and the deputy director of the Commissariat Général à la Main d'Œuvre (CGMO), the French labour department, reported to the prefect that 'employers are becoming more and more indisciplined in front of the combing commission and the proportion of employers who do not appear is now higher than that for employees'.[59] It appears, however, that the director of the CGMO, Viennot, who sat on the combing commission, was playing something of a double game. General Feldt wrote to the new regional prefect, Donati, to complain that the poor recruitment figures for Loire-Inférieure were made worse by Viennot seeking to protect young workers by moving them to S-Betriebe 'behind the back of the Feld-kommandantur and contrary to instructions from higher authorities'.[60]

One of the structural problems with the labour recruitment system was that German officials with responsibility for S-Betriebe had a preference for younger workers, who were thus protected from STO, leaving older married workers to be sent off to Germany. In February Regional Prefect Donati visited the Hesse-Nassau region of Germany, where the bulk of STO conscripts from the region were working in towns such as Frankfurt, Darmstadt, Wiesbaden and Mainz. His main purpose was to report back favourably on the conditions enjoyed by French workers, and he told the press on his return that they were well housed and well fed, each camp having a French chef. His main criticism, also delivered to the press, was that he had come across fifty-year-old Frenchmen who were war veterans and heads of families, now doing another stint of duty while too many young men, who had suffered from neither the war nor the defeat, were enjoying the easy life in protected factories back home. His postbag began to fill not only with letters from French wives demanding their middle-aged husbands back, but with letters from workers in Germany who disagreed with his analysis of their conditions. One worker in Lübeck, who told Donati that he had read his account in the *Écho de Nancy*, reported that they lived in cold huts, with 150 men to one sink, worked twelve hours a day with only soup to eat, and had totally inadequate shelter from air raids. In reality Donati was well aware of the situation. 'I was struck', he wrote to Laval, 'by the bitterness, even the violence of their words.' They felt duped and abandoned, waiting in vain for 'la relève de la *Relève*', and realizing that those who had not done their duty in respect of STO were doing very nicely. 'It is a veritable army of discontented people who will return to France as soon as peace comes to swell the ranks of the communists.'[61]

Such was the pressure in the last months of the Occupation that no concessions were made to anyone, not to fathers of large families nor even to women. The collaborationist Marcel Déat became Minister of Labour and the rumour spread that he was going to order 'massive deportations' of labour.[62] A law of 1 February 1944 required the registration for labour service not only of men aged sixteen to sixty, but of women aged eighteen to forty-five. The threatened conscription of women violated a fundamental taboo and provoked a violent response from families, communities and the Church. 'Family life is still very solid and united in Anjou,' reported an official of the Ministry of Information. 'You will never persuade a father to accept that his daughter, even aged twenty-five, will go to work a long way away, beyond his supervision and control.' Given the danger of mixing women of different backgrounds and education, he predicted 'a very lively resistance, not only from ordinary citizens but also from certain mayors, to the registration of women'.[63] The Church's Assembly of Cardinals and Archbishops, which had previously maintained a cautious and ambiguous line on STO, came out strongly to condemn 'a serious attack on family life and the future of our country, on the dignity and moral susceptibility of women and on their providential vocation'.[64] In a word, their immortal souls were at risk.

The final step was to use on idle French youths the same method that had been used on the Jews: the round-up. As early as the summer of 1943 French police had raided cafés and cinemas in Nantes to check the papers of young men who might be shirking STO, and that September the Germans simply arrested 300 SNCASO workers at the Château-Bougon airport outside Nantes, which had been bombed, and whisked them away for Todt work at Cherbourg.[65] The main season for these raids, executed by the French police on German instructions, was the following spring and summer: 16 March and 6 April 1944 in Angers, and 19 May, 12, 13, 14, 18 and 21 June in Nantes. The haul rarely corresponded to the effort put in. The raid of Friday, 19 May, in Nantes involved 56 officers who arrested 370 young men. Of these 66 were detained of whom 42 were released after their papers were found to be in order. This left a residue of 18 who were selected to go to Germany and 6 to work for the Germans in France. The director of the CGMO (the former deputy, who had replaced the unreliable Viennot) reported that 'this first operation was a great disillusion for the local German authorities who expected a much bigger result and are especially disappointed not really to have detected the shirkers'. Although the Feldkommandantur had given them only six hours' notice before they went into action at 5.30 p.m., he admitted that by no fault of his own department there had been 'indiscretions' which rendered the operation 'almost impossible'.[66] If the leaks were not the fault of the labour department, they may well have been perpetrated by the police, who were clearly now operating by different rules than when rounding up Jews two years earlier. The operations were becoming increasingly fruitless. During the raid on twenty-five cafés around the main railway station in Nantes on 18 June 250 youths were checked but only three in the classes of 1940, 1941 and 1942 discovered; they were released after their situation was seen to be in order.[67] The plain fact was that young men who were not in order did not hang about cafés and cinemas in town centres on summer weekends, since the raids seemed to happen with predictable regularity. It is also the case that it was scarcely in the interest of the French police or administration to be too tough on young people for the benefit of the Germans during those weekends in June 1944 when the Normandy landings had taken place and the Allies were on their way.

The deportation of French labour was the single most important factor which alienated the French population from the German authorities and those Vichy authorities which were seen to be relaying their demands. Strikes against recruitment for the Relève, demonstrations of STO conscripts in railway carriages bound for Germany or simply disappearing into a clandestine existence, were different ways of expressing that opposition. Local authorities, squeezed between German demands and the discontent of the population, were placed in an impossible predicament. If they assisted in the business of labour recruitment they alienated their local constituencies, while if they obstructed the draft they faced dismissal as the Germans interfered increasingly in the make-up of the administration. Mayor Rondeau of Nantes and Regional Prefect Roussillon of Angers were removed by Vichy under pressure from the Germans for non-cooperation over the *Relève* and the STO respectively. The contrast in the attitude of the French administration to the deportation of French workers on the one hand and the deportation of Jews is nevertheless instructive. Admittedly Jews in France were often immigrants, widely scattered or already interned, making them vulnerable, whereas industrial workers and peasants, sustained by their own communities, could successfully go on strike or disappear into the countryside. The degree of opposition shown by French authorities – even the Church – to the deportation of labour, compared with their lack of action when it came to protecting Jews, suggests a double standard that throws at least some light on the question of French attitudes to the threatened Jewish population in their midst.

14. DISINTEGRATION

'How can a people as civilized as our former British allies be seized by such a fury of destruction, devastation and death without in the least advancing their military cause?' asked *Le Courrier de Saint-Nazaire* after British planes bombed the port in February 1942, killing eighteen and injuring thirty-two people.[1] Following another British raid the following May on nearby Nantes, the Kreiskommandant, Major von Hasselbach, prohibited military music in the soldiers' clubs and closed cinemas to German soldiers, as a mark of respect to the victims. To his surprise, however, on the evening of the funeral, all trace of mourning evaporated as the French crowded into the bars and cafés of Nantes and gave themselves over to loud music and laughter.[2]

These contradictory reflections shed interesting light on the predicament of French and Germans as, more than two years before the Normandy landings, the Allies began to attack the military and industrial infrastructure that underpinned the German war effort. Since most of the shipyards and factories of the Saint-Nazaire–Nantes conurbation were working for the Wehrmacht, the Luftwaffe and above all the Kriegsmarine they were considered legitimate targets for Allied bombers. Inevitably, and especially when American planes bombing from high altitude joined the campaign, French civilians as well as German military suffered casualties. To some extent this brought French and Germans together in a common suffering. Certainly Vichy propaganda was keen to exploit the raids to discredit perfidious Albion. Paradoxically, however, the French experienced some joy as the bombs rained down: each one inflicted damage on the German war machine for which they were obliged to work and brought closer the long-awaited moment of their liberation.

True, the bombing raids of early 1942 were pinpricks compared with what was to come later. The first target was Saint-Nazaire, which was attacked repeatedly in November 1942 and February 1943. Serious damage was inflicted on the Penhoët and Loire shipyards, the Saint-Nazaire foundry, the electricity works and the nearby oil-refinery of Donges.[3] On 9 November 186 people were killed, on 16–17 November 78, on 16 and 28 February respectively 27 and 17.[4] The attack of 28 February 1943 was described by Prefect Dupard as 'the most violent attack undertaken by Allied aircraft on a French town', turning Saint-Nazaire into 'a huge brazier', destroying three-quarters of the town and driving out the 12,000 people who still lived there. Such was the tragedy that the town was visited by M. Ingrand, representing the branch that the Vichy Ministry of the Interior was permitted to keep in Paris, and Colonel Bonhomme, aide-de-camp of Marshal Pétain and his official representative.[5]

Measures to evacuate children had been taken since the spring of 1942. Children were sent to colonies hurriedly established in châteaux and other vacant buildings along the Nantes–Angers railway line by municipalities, parishes and Catholic charities, lay school organizations and the Comité Ouvrier de Secours Immédiat (COSI) run by Marcel Blanchard, the pro-Vichy labour leader of Saint-Nazaire.[6] Ironically, most of them were brought back to their families in October 1942 on the grounds that the bombing had eased off, and had to be evacuated again after the attacks of November. After the inferno of February a distinction was drawn between industrial and Todt workers who were forced to stay despite the total inadequacy of air-raid shelters, and who downed tools for this reason after a further attack on 30 March, and those tactfully deemed 'useless for economic life', such as children, women and the elderly, whose evacuation to the interior of Loire-Inférieure or to Anjou was to be organized. The evacuations of 1943, virtually unknown in comparison with the 'exodus' of 1940, sheds interesting light on the relationship between very different French communities, suddenly forced to live cheek by jowl with each other. 'Suffering draws together,' said Mgr Villepelet at the funeral of the victims of the Saint-Nazaire air raid of 16 February 1942, but it seems that there were limits.[7] After all, the population of Saint-Nazaire was urban, poor and anticlerical, that of the host communities rural, prosperous and Catholic. Anne Curet, evacuated at the age of twelve, recalls that 'the peasants were generally welcoming and even generous', and that a barter economy grew up, sewing in exchange for flour or butter, work in the fields for a meal, tobacco tickets for groceries.[8] On the other hand, at Rochefort-sur-Loire, evacuees complained that they were being ripped off by the local growers who were asking 10 francs for a kilo of potatoes normally sold for 4 francs.[9] The owners of the pink-stuccoed Château de la Madeleine, overlooking the Loire at Varades, complained that the children of the COSI colony were running wild and breaking windows.[10] Villages in the Vendean Mauges on the other side of the river were reluctant to welcome outsiders. The mayor of Tilliers could find only one family willing to look after a child, who would have to be 'a girl of five or six years old', while the mayor of Jallais told the subprefect of Cholet that he was receiving some children from the Catholic school of Le Pouliguen, run by the same order of nuns as in the school in his own seaside village, next to La Baule.[11] By August and September 1943 the Nazarean evacuees were becoming organized, and holding public meetings about their needs for food, wood and coal in Cholet with the subprefect and in Angers with Prefect Daguerre, who claimed that as a former subprefect of Dieppe he knew about air raids too.[12]

By then the Allied bombers had started on the industrial suburbs of Nantes. On 23 March 1943 an air attack badly damaged the Batignolles locomotive works, which had so dramatically opposed the *Relève* the previous October. A huge crowd, mainly of factory workers, attended the funeral for the victims at the cathedral. Their anger was aimed at the management for not providing enough air-raid shelters rather than at the British, whose skill in targeting all twenty-four of their bombs on the factory itself they rather admired.[13] Subsequently the works was moved away from the coast, but only as far as Cholet. On 4 July the SNCASO and Heinkel works at Château Bougon were hit, and casualties were heavy. The grief of bereaved families was compounded by the dishonesty of the under-takers of Nantes, who charged the likes of young Marcel Maringue 6,000 francs in advance to bury his father and mother-in-law, whereas the cheapest option was said to be a mere 213 francs.[14] Even more anger was directed against the Germans. Although 90 per cent of the plants' capacity was restored within ten days, the Germans decided for security reasons to relocate the Heinkel factory in the Toulouse area and to remove the SNCASO machine tools to

Germany. The French manager of SNCASO, M. Gon, announced that he would cede only to force, so on 30 July force arrived in the the shape of a German detachment which loaded 182 machines into thirty railway wagons.[15] Since the aircraft workers were now unemployed, the German authorities ordered the French police to round them up and send them to work for the Todt Organization at Cherbourg, for a spell of six or seven weeks, it was said. On 14 September at 8 a.m. sixty police arrived at the airfield with twenty lorries and rounded up 220 workers, who were taken to the station and loaded on to a convoy.[16]

The most terrifying and destructive raids, however, hit the city of Nantes on 16 and 23 September 1943. On 16 September at 4 p.m. 160 aircraft dropped 1,000 bombs on Nantes and its suburbs, only a quarter of which hit the military targets of the Chantiers de la Loire and Chantiers de Bretagne, sinking six ships, the Chantiers Dubigeon remaining unscathed. The civilian population was unprepared. There had been a vast number of alerts, many of which had been false alarms, and when raids had taken place the bombs had been accurately targeted. Many did not even bother to take shelter in their cellars. The casualties were horrendous: 812 dead and 1,785 injured. A week later, on 23 September, there were two raids. About sixty British planes attacked at 9 a.m., dropping 500 bombs. This time the civilians were ready, the targeting on the port area was more accurate, and the casualty figures were forty-five dead and 110 injured. But that evening at 7 p.m. there was a second raid by an American force of 150 planes striking from high altitude, many of the 650 bombs falling on shopping and residential areas. Again the Chantiers Dubigeon were spared but 150 people were killed and 200 injured.[17] Subsequently the figure of 1,000 dead rose to 1,300. A wave of panic swept the city and 100,000 people, half the population, fled into the countryside. A thousand buildings had been destroyed or made uninhabitable, 20,000 were homeless. Post, telegraph and telephone services went down and gas, water and electricity supplies were gravely affected. A third of butchers, bakers, grocers and greengrocers were out of action, and the Ravitaillement offices were hit, leaving people without ration cards for essentials for several days.[18]

The Germans had lost forty soldiers and railwaymen, 100 German firemen helped to bring the fires under control, and Feldkommandant von Trotha attended a joint Franco-German funeral with the new Prefect Édouard Bonnefoy, on 19 October.[19] Dr Baessler of the Feldkommandantur suggested that the mutual suffering had improved relations between the two peoples. 'Perfect strangers talk to you on the street,' he said, 'and express their contempt for the English and Americans. People greet you politely and in a friendly way both in public and at home.' On the other hand the raids only increased the pressure on the Germans to maintain the momentum of their war production, and no concessions could be contemplated. 'It is of the greatest importance to keep the workforce in Nantes,' declared the Feldkommandantur the day before the second raid, but the workforce left with the rest of the population and Allied leaflets dropped on the area warning of the use of delayed-action bombs did nothing to hasten their return. 'Systematic work is as good as impossible,' complained the German labour office a month later, insisting that the first priority was to ensure that 'workers who have left are brought back to the Rü- and V-Betriebe as quickly as possible', the current manning level having fallen to 20 per cent, while the second was to force the return of food retailers. After tough negotiations with Prefect Bonnefoy it was announced that shopkeepers who did not return to the city by the end of October would lose their licences, and workers their ration cards.[20]

The population of Nantes was in no sense eager to return. On 1 October 1943 80,000 of them were classed as evacuees in their own department. Maine-et-Loire had 10,500 evacuees, including 5,000 from Saint-Nazaire and 2,600 from Nantes. Evacuees from Nantes were not in fact supposed to go to Maine-et-Loire but to other designated departments, such as the Vienne and Deux-Sèvres. Some workers from factories like the Batignolles were moved to Cholet, where the textile and shoe workers were generally docile, bringing with them their traditional 'trade-union activity' and 'political ferment'.[21] Meanwhile evacuees from Lorient, a naval base further west along the Atlantic coast and just as badly bombed as Saint-Nazaire, were detailed to go to Indre-et-Loire. Of the 11,600 evacuees there on 1 October, nearly 6,000 came from Lorient.[22] As in Maine-et-Loire, there was a balance of welcome and hostility. The ground had been prepared by the Secours National which produced a poster headed 'With Open Arms' showing a peasant leaving his pitchfork to greet a woman and two children, one in her arms, with the slogan,

'Any French person, anywhere in France, must feel part of a family'.[23] Most of the evacuees were indeed women and children, the men having stayed in Lorient to work, or returned. Among the male evacuees masons, plasterers and roofers were immediately snapped up for work, but many were sailors, dockers or arsenal workers, unfit for some reason or another, reluctant to work on the land despite the demand from farmers, preferring to idle around and spend their benefits in the bars and cafés.[24] Concerns were also expressed by the gendarmerie that 'some communist elements had slipped in amongst them'.[25] The Lorient refugees were also prepared to fight for their rights. On 24 March 1943 they held a meeting at the Café de l'Entr'acte at Tours, convened by a wine and spirits merchant named Poulain, to demand among other things entitlement to an urban food ration which they had had to surrender on arriving in a Touraine village, action against the high prices demanded by traders, and a good supply of potatoes to be transported from the Morbihan.[26] The prefecture was happy to dismiss Poulain as a rather dotty megalomanic and have nothing to do with him, but then found that the power of the Breton press was behind the Lorientais. After the mayor of Dierre closed the soup kitchen frequented by the twenty Lorient evacuees on the grounds that they now had their ration cards and could manage on their own, *L'Ouest-Éclair* attacked the insensitivity of the Touraine communities. This provoked Prefect Tracou to defend the honour of the Tourangeaux. He asked his opposite number, the prefect of the Morbihan, to have words with the editor of *L'Ouest-Éclair* who, he said, 'by setting the population of Touraine against that of Indre-et-Loire, is creating a climate from which in the end only the unfortunate Breton refugees will suffer'.[27] We have already seen that in matters of food supply rural communities tended to turn in upon themselves as the pressure to share increased. The same pattern emerges with the treatment of evacuees: despite exhortations to solidarity, what predominated was suspicion and hostility.

Touraine and Anjou were lucky in that for a long time they were not the target of Allied attacks. They were both less industrialized than the Atlantic ports of Lorient, Saint-Nazaire and Nantes and less geared into the German war machine. Even so, no part of France was without its Rüstung- and Speer-Betriebe and at Monts, south of Tours, close to where the Jews had been interned in the Camp de la

Lande, the Ripault ammunition factory which had lain fallow since the Armistice was recommissioned by the Germans in October 1942 to make torpedoes, shells and other high explosives. A year later, however, on 18 October 1943, the factory was ripped apart by a massive blast which was heard 100 kilometres away and shattered windows in Tours, 11 kilometres away. At the time 1,100 workers of the 2,000 employed, a high proportion of them women, were present. Of these 72 were killed, including 19 who 'disappeared', 140 were seriously injured and 500 were less seriously hurt. To begin with it was thought that the factory had been bombed or sabotaged, but it then emerged that gun cotton being unloaded was not damp enough and had ignited. The accident was a result of the pressure under which war production was operating. Despite pressures to restart production, the factory had to be totally rebuilt and production did not begin again until March 1944.[28]

By this time Allied bombers had turned to Tours and its railway and industrial suburb of Saint-Pierre-des-Corps, which were a central part of the French communications network, linking Paris and Bordeaux. Having inflicted severe damage on German war production itself, the Allies turned next to the transport system that supplied that machine with materials and fuel and would facilitate the movement of troops to a future Allied invasion point. On 14, 15 and 18 February 1943 the railway stations of Tours and Saint-Pierre-des-Corps, along with the CIMT railway workshops, were bombed. From the beginning of 1944 the US Air Force regularly attacked the Tours airfield at Parçay-Meslay and the Liotard factory at Saint-Pierre-des-Corps which made aircraft engines. On the night of 10–11 April the RAF returned to destroy the marshalling yards of Saint-Pierre-des-Corps with incendiary and delayed-action bombs. One eyewitness subsequently described the station as 'a mass of tangled ironmongery, and were it not for the tunnel one might suppose that it had never existed. The warehouses where the rolling stock was kept have been completely destroyed. All that remains are a few sections of wall left standing as if by a miracle.'[29] Eighteen people died, and another eleven were killed by delayed-action devices a few days later. The Rüstungskommando was relieved that the railway bridge over the Cher was still intact, but the bombers returned on 20 May to destroy that too, snapping communications with Bordeaux and Le Mans. Unfortunately a great deal of damage was also done to Tours itself, with 143 people killed, the archbishop presiding over their funeral in a cathedral that had itself been damaged in the attack. The gossip among locals was that the English were systematically bombing the towns that Joan of Arc had passed through.[30] Ironically the regional Rüstungskommando had moved for greater safety from Le Mans to Angers on 15 May, for on Whit Sunday, 29 May, Angers was subject to its first major attack. The Saint-Laud railway station was severely damaged, along with fifteen locomotives and 100 wagons. Enormous damage was done to the Bessonneau factory, currently working on a German order for 670 nine-man tents.[31] Again, civilian casualties were very high, with 230 killed in the station district, many of whom had taken refuge in the local Saint-Laud church. The episcopal palace was destroyed, although as luck would have it the bishop, Mgr Costes, was away on pilgrimage.

The destruction of rail communications threw the German military machine into chaos on what turned out to be the eve of the Normandy landings. In desperation they fell back on road transport, which involved the sudden and brutal requisition of lorries. This time it was Touraine, at the hub of the communications network, that suffered particularly. In February 1944 the Feldkommandantur of Tours demanded forty petrol- or diesel-fuelled lorries, which were extremely few and far between, and 300 charcoal-fuelled ones (*gazogènes*). The new prefect of Indre-et-Loire, Musso, told Regional Prefect Donati that this amounted to over a third of the 930 lorries authorized on the department's roads, and that since those of the Rü- and S-Betriebe would be protected, the full burden would fall on the domestic economy and particularly food supply. The secretary of state for Industrial Production was not inclined to take a tough line, telling Donati that if any new requisition took place he could ask the German authorities not to include vehicles from 'priority businesses'.[32] In the Saumur area the Germans requisitioned not only lorries but also 500 cars, carts and horses which were urgently needed for work in the fields.[33] Back in Tours, at the end of March, the police and gendarmerie handed all cyclists a German order to the effect that their bicycles were to be requisitioned the following day; this led to a haul of no fewer than 1,500 machines allegedly not needed for professional use.[34]

One of the main casualties of the breakdown of railway communications was coal supply, which fuelled the electricity stations. In turn the electricity generated powered the factories working for the German war machine. Electricity output was also reduced by direct air attacks on generating plants and the sabotage of power lines, notably those coming from the hydro-electric plants of south-west France. The failure of the electricity supply is an unsung story of the German Occupation but possibly the single most important reason why the German war machine in France collapsed.[35]

In January 1944 the Rüstungskommando of Le Mans, which had responsibility for all of this region apart from Loire-Inférieure, reported that because of coal shortages and the sabotage of pylons, supplies to the Rü-Betriebe would be reduced to 75 per cent of their supply in November 1943 if they had low-tension connections, to 60 per cent if they had high-tension connections, and to 50 per cent if they were non-mechanized. By March the current had dropped so much that only 10 per cent of Rü-Betriebe were working non-stop and all of the generating stations closed at weekends. A certain number of key factories were being privileged for supply, such as the ammunitions factory of Le Ripault, which had just gone back into production after the explosion, and the Bessonneau factory in Angers, shortly to be bombed.[36] After the begining of May, Oberst Keil of the Rüstungskommando reported, no more coal had been imported into the region and what supplies the Rü-Betriebe possessed had to be switched as a priority to the generating stations. By the end of June 1944 the electricity supply had fallen to 4.3 per cent of what it had been in June 1943, and even the most important Rü-Betriebe were receiving only 2,500kWh a day, about 2.2 per cent of their normal consumption. At the same time the Rüstungskommando of Nantes reported that 'in a few days there will be no more coal supplies left, and the electricity works will come to a complete standstill. A regular delivery of coal is *urgently* awaited.' Meanwhile, Keil was cutting his losses and arguing that now that war production had collapsed in France, the most important task was to remove as much equipment as possible back to the Reich, although he was worried about how far east of Tours it would get, given the transport problem. This report was dated 6 June 1944, which suggests that even as the Allies were landing on the beaches, some German military were already thinking in terms of retreat.[37]

If one reason for the collapse of the German Occupation was the damage inflicted by the Allies on its military–industrial base, another was the growing difficulty of maintaining the policy of collaboration with the Vichy administration. The success of the Occupation had relied on collaboration between French and German officials, on both a formal and an informal basis. The isolation from Vichy of French administrators in the Occupied Zone meant that paradoxically they were reliant on the German military to reinforce their authority, and they had the leverage to negotiate with the German authorities and reach compromises. The German authorities, however, became increasingly dissatisfied with the ability of the French administration to deliver public order, and resorted to a form of collaboration characterized by *Diktat* rather than negotiation, and run by the secret police instead of the military. Pressure on the French population intensified, with increasing numbers of arrests, deportations and executions, inflicted on wider and wider sections of the public which grew more and more anxious, fearful and alienated. The worse the war went for the Germans, and the more likely an Allied victory appeared, the more the Germans stepped up their demands and increased repression, and the more local communities withdrew their cooperation and demanded protection from their leaders and administrators. French officials became squeezed in a vice, forced to choose between collaboration and resistance. One escape from an impossible choice was the *double jeu*, appearing to cooperate while in fact offering resistance. This was, however, a perilous game, in which success was a rare commodity.

After the dismissal of Jean Roussillon under German pressure for unsatisfactory collaboration, a new regional prefect of Angers was appointed in August 1943. Charles Donati was an *inspecteur des finances* and former director of a bank at Strasbourg before its annexation in 1940 suggested a career in the Vichy administration. He was keen to establish good relations with local notables, who were invited in force to his installation in Angers on 9 August 1943, deputies and senators as well as members of the Conseil National and departmental councils, mayors, magistrates, generals and churchmen.[38] Plain-speaking, he told a meeting of the Angers Chamber of Commerce that there was 'at the present time a deep schism between the government and opinion'. This 'distrust and hostility', he continued, was not deserved because Marshal Pétain was 'not a usurper but a legitimate leader', invested by parliament, and was 'indisputably the greatest Frenchman by virtue of his military past, the glory that he evokes, his perfect success in all domains and the heroism that he demonstrates on a daily basis, even though he is in his eighty-eighth year'.[39] The German authorities liked Donati because he was a First World War veteran, who had lost his right arm in the trenches, and was an efficient, decisive administrator. They noted that he had sent his son on STO and that if there were to be a definitive Franco-German collaboration, he would be an active collaborator.[40] This did not mean that he was a pushover. The Germans preferred effectiveness to supineness, and in December 1943, for instance, Donati sent a strongly worded letter to General Feldt, head of the military administration of Bezirk B, to demand the return of buildings in Angers requisitioned by the Germans but essential for the proper functioning of the French administration.[41]

Another decisive prefect with whom the Germans were pleased to do business was Édouard Bonnefoy who, also in August 1943, replaced Dupard as prefect of Loire-Inférieure. Dupard, reported the Feldkommandantur of Nantes, promised much but delivered little, whereas Bonnefoy, formerly prefect of the Mayenne, was 'considerably younger, more skilful and a more diligent official. He prefers to communicate orally with mayors and others who have to execute his orders. Altogether there is now much more life in the French administration.'[42] 'We have a leader at last, a real leader,' noted Edmond Duméril, who saw Bonnefoy as 'deeply patriotic, understanding the capital importance of dialogue with the Germans'. To defend French interests, it was necessary to be well informed and to negotiate. Duméril was also delighted to do business with Dr Baessler, who was in charge of the German civil administration at the Feldkommandantur, and thought that 'he could be for me what Dr Hotz was in 1940–1'. From Leipzig but of Swiss origins, Baessler was 'an intellectual, humane, considerate, in no sense a Nazi. He knows that his country is bound for disaster, he will try to moderate the draconian orders he receives and if possible temporize. He will be our firmest ally in the struggle of the French administration with the new Feldkommandant, the terrible general who came from Russia in the tragic autumn of 1943, General Reinhardt.'[43]

In his first month Bonnefoy took on the Gestapo, obtaining a reprieve for four out of fifteen 'terrorists' sentenced to death by a German military court and ensuring that twenty-seven communists arrested by the French police went before a French rather than a

German court.[44] He criticized the Gestapo for giving orders directly to French police rather than going through the prefecture.[45] When General Reinhardt took over as Feldkommandant of Nantes from von Trotha in November, with a reputation for cruelty gained on the Eastern Front, Bonnefoy opposed his demands for 2,000 peasants to help with defence work, on the grounds that conscription for military activity violated article 52 of the Hague Convention of 1907. He was prepared to argue his case publicly when Reinhardt summoned French officials to a meeting in the Château des Ducs, Nantes, just before Christmas 1943.[46] Unfortunately for the Loire-Inférieure, Bonnefoy was appointed regional prefect of Lyon at the beginning of 1944.

While Donati and Bonnefoy perfected the art of tough negotiation, other prefects were weaker in their handling of the Germans and acquired a reputation for not doing enough to protect French citizens. In January 1944 Prefect Tracou of Indre-et-Loire was appointed head of Pétain's private office and secretary-general Molas-Quenescourt followed him to Vichy. He was replaced at Tours by Ferdinand Musso, formerly prefect in the Jura, who had something of a complex about his association with the Third Republic. In 1940 he had headed the office of Minister of the Interior Georges Mandel, once revered as the natural successor of Clemenceau but now reviled as a Jew who had brought France to the brink of destruction and was shortly to be assassinated by the Milice.[47] When he arrived in Tours Musso was put under intense pressure by the Groupe Collaboration to explain himself and he reacted by overcompensation, bowing to the pressure of the Germans and French collaborationist groups rather than putting up a fight. On 21 June 1944, for example, Feldkommandant Boehmer demanded 850 men at once from Tours and surrounding towns to assist with clearing débris at Tours station and the Parçay-Meslay airfield. Such work carried a physical risk from delayed-action bombs and further raids and was precisely the sort of demand that Bonnefoy would have challenged under the Hague Convention. Musso by contrast appeared in public at the Hôtel de Ville with Colonel Boehmer to urge greater efforts in meeting labour demands, and when only twenty-three of the fifty men conscripted in the rather left-wing town of Bléré reported for duty, he sent the police to arrest them.[48] Events finally caught up with Musso because he was the only prefect in the region to be sent for trial after the Liberation.

It was of course possible to resist with a little too much energy, in order to maintain authority over local populations, and even to send out a signal to the Free French based in London, then Algiers, that one was a candidate for office when the German Occupation and possibly Vichy came to an end. This tactic, however, ran the risk of forfeiting the confidence of the Germans, who were increasingly intolerant of any disloyalty in the French administration. Officials who wanted to survive needed to play a double game, giving the appearance of loyalty while working in the dark to protect French interests and even open an insurance policy with the emerging Resistance. As Prefect Tracou told the municipal council of Tours in December 1943 when the new mayor was invested, 'Present circumstances impose on all of us a very simple rule: work hard and say nothing. If you find that too absolute then work hard and say little.'[49] What an official's objective opinions or conduct were did not really matter. German files repeatedly confess that they did not know what the political opinions of such and such were. Everyone wore a mask and engaged in bluff and double bluff. The danger was to be unmasked, and here collaborationist groups who genuinely believed in a Franco-German crusade against communism were a greater menace than the Gestapo.

A model performer in the art of pretence, as we have seen, was the conduct of the subprefect of Chinon, Paul Cay.[50] Felt by Musso to be suspect, he was ordered early in 1944 to the isolated prefecture of Villefranche-de-Rouergue in the Aveyron, but went to ground in the Loire region and resurfaced to become secretary-general of the prefecture of Indre-et-Loire at the Liberation. Less skilful for different reasons were Marcel Saissier, who was Donati's prefect-delegate at Angers in succession to Pierre Daguerre, and Yves Bayet, secretary-general of the prefecture at Nantes. Like Daguerre, Saissier had also been subprefect of Dieppe and came to Angers with a similar reputation for protecting Masonic officials. He became the victim of a hostile campaign in the collaborationist Paris paper, *Je suis partout*, which accused him of being tough on Vichy loyalists and soft on Masons, Gaullists and communists. Although the Germans' own information suggested that he could be trusted, they could not take any risks and in the light of the collaborationist accusations ordered his arrest.[51] Meanwhile, the Germans at Nantes saw Secretary-General Bayet as 'the most honest collaborator in the prefecture, combining with his courteous demeanour an energy and exceptional diligence in the conduct of his office'. He had been an active promoter of the *Relève* and was said to have attended torture sessions administered by the anti-communist police squad. This fanaticism may have been explained, as in Musso's case, by a past he had to live down, for his father was Albert Bayet, who had been an ardent campaigner at the turn of the century for the wrongly imprisoned Jewish army officer Captain Dreyfus, was president of the anticlerical Ligue de l'Enseignement and had been dismissed from the Sorbonne by Vichy as the quintessence of everything it hated about the *camarades* of the Third Republic. Bayet went absent without leave around the time that Prefect Bonnefoy was appointed to Lyon. Some said that he had fled to Paris because of his links with the Resistance and his fear that he was about to be found out. Others argued that he disappeared because he had received death threats from the Resistance.[52] In the event, his insurance policy with the Resistance was not convincing enough. He failed adequately to demonstrate that his collaboration had masked a genuine commitment to the Resistance and he was sent for trial at the Liberation.

As hopes and anxieties about an Allied landing in France increased, so the Germans clamped down on any sign of disloyalty. At Nantes Prefect Georges Gaudard, who moved from Besançon to replace Bonnefoy, initially made a good impression on the Feldkommandantur, although they noted that he preferred to deal with them in writing rather than, like his predecessor, face to face.[53] The report on Gaudard drafted for the Free French, however, said that he was a veteran of 1914–18 with 'excellent patriotic sentiments' and 'very hostile to the Germans'.[54] The Free French may have thought this because Gaudard refused German orders to offer rewards to French people to denounce 'terrorists' unless, he conceded, a serious crime had been committed.[55] Although he thought he had agreed this with Dr Baessler at the Feldkommandantur, higher German authorities decided to have a general clampdown on suspect prefects. He was one of fifteen French prefects to be arrested on 14 May, as he was about to lay a wreath at the statue of Joan of Arc. Bonnefoy was arrested at Lyon in the same offensive and was deported to Germany where he died.[56] Gaudard was released and survived in post for the rest of the Occupation, until the Americans appeared in Nantes. He then tried to persuade the Americans to confirm him as prefect, instead of his secretary-general, Louis Ottaviani, who had been selected to become Liberation prefect by Michel Debré, the future Commissaire de la République. Before Debré came in person to Nantes in August 1944 it looked as though he might indeed pull off the coup. More successful in the long term was the head of Gaudard's office, René Tomasini, who was arrested by the Germans on 10 May 1944 but resurfaced at the Liberation as the head of Debré's office in Angers.[57]

Arrests were not confined to prefectoral officials. Mayors, within the local context, also had to tread the tightrope between satisfying German demands and providing as much protection as possible for local inhabitants. Again, the key to survival was to give nothing away. One example not to follow was that of Dr Jean Robin, mayor of Saint-Pierre-des-Corps, who had played a crucial role in ensuring the loyalty of a predominantly communist town. In August 1943, however, during a fund-raising event for POWs, he unveiled a commemoration stone that bore not only the names of the war dead but also those of bomb victims and of four communists who had been shot by the Germans. He was arrested the following day by the Sicherheitsdienst.[58] Symbolic gestures, albeit to maintain the morale of a local community, might be avoided, whereas fighting to protect its real interests was a necessity for a good mayor. About twenty mayors or *secrétaires de mairie* were arrested in Touraine during the first two months of 1944 alone, mainly because the Germans regarded them as insufficiently cooperative over the delivery of food-stuffs, livestock, labour or vehicles.[59] Some mayors such as Victor Bernier of Angers, it is true, were past masters of finding precisely the right line. Regional Prefect Donati was told by the Sicherheitsdienst soon after his arrival in Angers that seventy-five-year-old Bernier was 'likely to exercise an influence dangerous for the occupying forces'. Donati nevertheless told Laval that the Germans had never made a formal complaint against Bernier, who was held in high esteem by the Angevins for his courage in June 1940, and that his dismissal would provoke a municipal crisis and 'great emotion among the population'. A compromise was found in March whereby Bernier continued nominally as mayor but no longer came to the town hall to discharge business, which would be done by one of his deputies (*adjoints*).[60] This solution satisfied the Germans while maintaining the honour of the French administration, and was incidentally an ideal position from which Bernier could reassert himself as mayor after the Liberation.

Such fancy footwork for a prominent mayor was a rare event. Local notables found it more and more difficult to bridge the gap between increasing German demands and brutality and the growing anger, frustration and fear of their communities. One by one bridges snapped as notables decided that to keep faith with the Germans or Vichy no longer brought any advantage. This was the main reason why the *conseils départementaux*, set up in the autumn of 1943, came to very little.[61] In Loire-Inférieure, as we have seen, only thirty-six of the forty-six seats were ever filled. Previously solid Vichy notables lost sympathy with the Laval government and ceased to be active. Louis Linyer, who had been injured in the air raid of 23 September and was out of sorts with the Vichy government, went into virtual exile on his Vendean property and now lived mainly in fear of revolution. Dutertre de la Coudre, mayor of Machecoul, continued to admire Pétain but was opposed to Laval and thought that Darnand's Milice, which was trying to wipe out resistance, was far too violent. He was said to be 'tired and disgusted by politics, which he now wanted to give up, both as deputy and mayor'.[62] In the *arrondissement* of Saumur, Subprefect Trémeaud experienced great difficulty in finding a list of local notables suitable or willing to sit on the *conseil départemental*. Gaston Moreau, for example, was regarded as too collaborationist, while Édouard Tardif, the old radical–socialist, was seen as the leader of a covert opposition in the area.[63] Ironically, Subprefect Trémeaud was regarded by the Germans themselves as suspect for failing to appear at a Christmas party they organized in 1943, and he made the transition easily to the new regime in August 1944.[64] In Indre-et-Loire no representatives for the *conseil départemental* could be found for six out of the twenty-four cantons, with obvious foot-draggers being François Servant of La Haye Descartes and Dr Paul Guillaume Louis of Montbazon. Others did not stay for long because they wanted to keep faith with their constituents. This was the case of the labour leader Garantie, who had been a key figure in bringing workers over to Vichy's Charte du Travail but now saw that his base was turning away from him. He resigned early in 1944 both as secretary of the *conseil départemental* and as muncipal councillor of Tours.

In Touraine the resignation of mayors was a serious problem.

There were thirty-six resignations in 1942 and twenty-seven in 1943. Two-thirds of these were farmers or winegrowers and two-thirds were over sixty, which suggests that the stress of being squeezed between German demands for foodstuff and livestock and the frustration of their communities may well have been a factor. Another decisive factor was that their sons had been recruited for STO, which destroyed what degree of loyalty they had for the regime. These 'personal' reasons accounted for 15 per cent of cases, political reasons for 24 per cent, administrative reasons for 12 per cent of cases, of which half were asked to resign, and health and age reasons given (rightly or wrongly) for 40 per cent of cases.[65] In 1944, as pressure from the German authorities increased, matters became even worse. 'There is a certain panic in the municipalities,' warned Prefect Musso, 'and resignations are multiplying. No one wants to remain mayor any more, and no one agrees to become one.'[66] By May Musso himself was in a state of panic, reporting that 'resignations are raining down' as arrests of mayors by Germans increased, and that the risk now attached to exercising the office was making it unworkable.[67] More and more mayors were siding with their angry communities against the Germans and against a Vichy administration that was increasingly unable to protect them.

The pressure on mayors, as with officials, was to maintain a semblance of loyalty to Vichy and the Germans while in practice cooperating as little as possible in order to keep faith with the communities they represented. Foot-dragging in the face of German demands was not the same as Resistance, which was limited in the Loire region for geographical reasons as much as anything else. Some parts of the country, such as the Massif Central, the Alps and Brittany, which had the protection of mountains and forests, sustained a Maquis more readily than the Loire valley which was flatter, more agricultural and with better communications. 'There is no solitude in Anjou,' reported the local head of the Organisation Résistance Armée, 'no isolated shelter or defensible hiding places. A countryside divided by hedges but also criss-crossed by good roads ready-made for pursuit ... Such factors ensured that in this department the Resistance did not take the form of a Maquis.'[68] Michel Fourré-Cormeray, who became prefect of Maine-et-Loire at the Liberation, reported that while there were few collaborators in the department, 'most of the inhabitants did not join Resistance movements, were totally ignorant of what we were doing for four years and remained fairly attached to the mystique of the Marshal'.[69] Michel Debré, who as Commissaire de la République at Angers appointed Fourré-Cormeray, said that the region was 'defined neither by pronounced collaboration, nor by resolute resistance'. 'The château owners', he continued, 'have their sons with de Gaulle and the portrait of Pétain in their sitting rooms.'[70]

Loyalty to Marshal Pétain was a powerful and durable sentiment, which coexisted perfectly well both with hostility to the Laval government and indeed with hopes placed in General de Gaulle.[71] Early in 1942 the Angers police reported that 'the person of Marshal Pétain remains in general above criticism. It seems indeed that his prestige is greater than ever. The population admires his courage and the strength of his character, and seems to accord him even more confidence since it has learned that he is as far as possible defending the independence of the country.'[72] It was a sentiment that permeated most classes of society. That the nobles of the west of France revered Pétain is not surprising, but a selection of twenty-four letters addressed directly from Angevins to him in 1943–4 suggests that the weakest and most vulnerable in society above all regarded him as an arbiter and redresser of wrongs: three letters were from widows, two from wives of POWs, five from heads of large families, others from evacuees or those who had suffered bomb damage.[73] Overwhelmingly they saw him as a source of appeal when the administration had failed to address their needs. One typical request was from a woman of Saumur whose request for shoes for her husband had been blocked by the bureaucracy for over a year. 'Where, I beg of you, Monsieur le Maréchal, does one have to go to get shoes?'[74]

Pétain, to be sure, was increasingly a figurehead, while power was concentrated in the hands of Laval, the head of government. Laval was regarded as responsible for labour conscription and other burdens inflicted on the population. Even less popular were the small groups of collaborationists who campaigned for closer relations with Germany and tougher measures against communists and Gaullists. In the summer of 1943 a number of notables of Groupe Collaboration in Nantes received parcels containing little coffins in each of which were placed a miniature axe and rope. The blue-shirted Francists of Marcel Bucard, as fascist a party as France ever saw, tended to recruit young men of a thuggish disposition and were even less popular. At a *kermesse* organized by the municipality of Nantes in May 1943 a group of thirty of them were insulted by a man shouting '*Aux chiottes*, Bucard!', ('Dump Bucard!') The Francists replied by making a fascist salute, which provoked a riot in the crowd of about 1,000, controlled only with difficulty by the French police. Interestingly, reported the superintendent, no hostile words were directed at the German military, which did not intervene.[75] On other occasions the Francists went on to the offensive, but with no happier results. Later that May six of them arrived in the small Touraine town of Sainte-Maure to sell their paper. They found no takers and became involved in scuffles with local youths. Three weeks later they returned with German police in plain clothes and after some fighting four local youths were arrested by the German police for ripping down Francist posters. The gendarmerie reported that 'these incidents have disgusted the population of the region' which was 'essentially agricultural and peaceful' and created 'much turmoil/effervescence'.[76]

The fact that individuals and communities were opposed to collaborationists did not mean that by the same token they were great supporters of the Resistance. Those who wished to avoid STO had to go to ground, as we have seen. Some simply lay low close to home, some found work in isolated farms or in rural industries. Most, however, needed money and ration cards and, as we have shown, took to raiding *mairies*, post offices, tax offices, tobacconists, traders and prosperous farmsteads.[77] Vichy propaganda spared no effort to depict these groups not as patriots but as 'bandits' and 'terrorists', the modern version of the highway robber or the 'great companies' of the Hundred Years War. Unless the capacity of Vichy for self-deception was complete, this negative image of the Maquis seems to have made some impression. 'Many', Prefect Tracou relayed to Laval in one of his last reports from Touraine, 'see in all this signs of latent anarchy, the foretaste of civil war. Such a possibility terrifies many people and has changed what was originally sympathy for the *réfractaires* and members of "Resistance organizations" into disapproval and fear.' As a result, the articles of Jean de Corbigny in *La Dépêche du Centre*, usually unpopular because of his tough line against the Resistance, which he saw as no better than anarchy, acquired a cult following in Touraine.[78] The Nantes bourgeoisie, confronted by this approaching violence, became attentive listeners to the ferociously anti-communist broadcasts of the Minister of Information, Philippe Henriot.[79] The Renseignements Généraux in Angers reported in the spring of 1944 that the murder of police at Saint-Laurent by 'Judaeo-communist bandits' had seriously alienated the population, but that the arrival in Anjou of 'undesirables' of the Milice to deal with 'terrorists' was no more reassuring.[80] Even after the Normandy landings the German military command in Angers took the view that the peaceable inhabitants of the region 'opposed terrorism in all its forms', because they feared an eruption of the civil war much more evident south of the former line of demarcation.[81]

Whether the Resistance was regarded as patriotism or as terrorism, the least that can be said is that it was an extremely perilous exercise. This was not only because of the collaboration of the French and German police but because of the constant danger of denunciation or even carelessness. In June 1943 seven armed men – a schoolteacher, four teacher-trainees (*normaliens*) and two farmers, father and son, attacked a Saumur bank manager and burgled the town hall of Vern d'Anjou north of Angers in order to obtain money and ration tickets for STO dodgers in the vicinity. Stopped by three Feldgendarmes, they shot two but the third got away and raised the alarm. One of the *normaliens* abandoned his bicycle by the side of the road, which unfortnately had a list of other teacher-trainees who belonged to the communist FTPF in the saddle-bag. Fifteen teacher-trainees were duly arrested by the French police and handed over to the Germans. The seven who had taken part in the raid and one other teacher were executed at Belle-Beille firing range outside Angers and ten others were deported, of whom three died in camps.[82]

Arguably these were mainly naïve and reckless young men and more mature resistants who watched their step were more likely to survive. This was the case to some extent, although denunciation or being named by a comrade captured and tortured by the Gestapo remained a high risk. Jean Meunier, formerly socialist deputy of Indre-et-Loire, returned from a spell as a POW in Germany to run his printing business in Tours, but through Émile Aron, the dismissed Jewish medical professor who had taken refuge in the Free Zone, he became involved in hiding agents, collecting money for the families of arrested communists and printing false identity papers. He forged links with like-minded socialists such as Pierre Archambault, and Catholics such as the schoolteacher Anne-Marie Marteau and the Jesuit Père de Solages. This group, called CND-Castille, was linked to the wider Libération-Nord movement and turned out to be the embryonic Comité Départemental de la Libération (CDL) in Touraine. But this was not before the Gestapo struck in October 1943 and by arrest, torture and more arrests smashed the Libération-Nord movement in the area.[83] Similar blows were suffered by the Resistance network centred on the gendarmerie of Saumur and Montreuil-Bellay led by Captain Royer, rounded up by the Gestapo in September 1943, and by Victor Chatenay's Honneur et Patrie network based in Angers. In Loire-Inférieure the Armée Secrète movement, closely linked to Libération-Nord, was run by General Audibert, formerly an official of Colonel de La Rocque's Croix de Feu and in constant conflict with a communist militant named Bernier. Both Audibert and Bernier were arrested in January 1944 and deported. The organization was taken over by a certain Daviais, who turned the AS into a unit of the Forces Françaises de l'Intérieur (FFIs), drawing heavily on STO *réfractaires*, in March 1944. Daviais was also head of the future CDL but was betrayed and arrested in April. 'It was a disaster,' says one historian, 'They had to start again from zero.'[84]

Where the paths of close-knit Resistance groups and STO *réfractaires* crossed, Maquis began to form. These were commonest in Brittany, which was more isolated and forested and already, as we have seen, a lair for STO dodgers. The Maquis of Saffré was an expression of youthful enthusiasm that came into violent contact with German forces which became more violent the more they saw defeat staring them in the face. It traces its history to December 1943, when it was set up by Briac le Diouron, code-name Yacco, and Abbé Ploquin, curate of the nearby village of Bouvron. It was totally unarmed except for one machine gun that was used for training purposes and shared with neighbouring groups, and unstable, constantly dissolving and re-forming in different places at different times. It had no real purpose until after the Normandy landings, when it got wind of an arms drop that was to occur over the forest of Saffré on 29 June. Its amateurism was exemplary. It set up camp in the forest on 17 June and had a picnic 150 metres away from a German sentry who fortunately did not spot them. On the Sunday, however, they were seen by locals out for a walk in the woods who asked them, 'What are you doing there? We promise we won't tell the Boche.' They decided to strike camp and returned to Bouvron, where the Maquisards chatted freely in the cafés about their exploits.[85] They went back to the forest on 22 June, 300 or 400 strong, but either because of their indiscretion, or because of a betrayal, they were surrounded by German forces and attacked on 28 June. The Maquisards lost twenty-three dead and thirty were taken prisoner. These were taken to the Château de la Bouvardière outside Nantes and tried by a military court the following day as illegal *francs-tireurs*, although they had precious few weapons. Twenty-seven of them – of whom five were aged under twenty and the oldest was twenty-six – were shot in the park of the château between 11 p.m. and midnight on 29 June. According to one account they died singing the *Marseillaise*. Three Maquisards were kept back for further interrogation and shot two weeks later; only the Abbé Ploquin was spared, and deported instead. In the following repression at least sixteen other Maquisards were tracked down and executed in the surrounding area, and farms set ablaze.[86]

Heavily outgunned, Maquisard groups tended to avoid any direct confrontation with German forces. A more common tactic was to ambush and snipe at them as the Allies advanced and they retreated chaotically towards the east. In so doing, however, Maquisards greatly endangered surrounding communities, which were accused by the Germans of harbouring terrorists and subjected to ferocious collective reprisals. The legendary massacre at Oradour-sur-Glane on 10 June was one of many incidents which either ended in tragedy or saw tragedy narrowly avoided.

In this region the critical month was August 1944, as the Allies advanced towards the Loire and the Germans pulled out of Bordeaux and Nantes and drove for the frontier. The Germans knocked out their huge factories at Nantes, crossed the Loire to the south on 11 August, sabotaging the bridges as they went, and headed towards Cholet and the east. General Reinhardt got as far as Bourges where his car was blown up by a mine planted by Maquisards on 1 September, and he was killed.[87] Germans began to leave Angers from 5 August, seizing bicycles from their French riders and killing if they had to. 'You must be really afraid and in a hurry to leave if you have to steal our bicycles,' the manager of the Rally garage at Angers told a dozen German soldiers, before they shot him.[88] Further north, at Segré, American forces arrived on 5 August but withdrew the following day, and the Germans returned. Convinced that the town was harbouring terrorists, they took sixty hostages and set fire to the town with incendiary grenades. The subprefect, mayor and arch-priest kept up a constant dialogue with the young German officer in charge, seeking to defuse a catastrophe of Oradour proportions, and the Germans eventually withdrew on 7 August.[89] Disaster was also narrowly avoided at the small village of Toutlemonde outside Cholet, where two Maquisards were surprised by Germans with a vanload of weapons, tortured and shot. The young men were not local at all, but worked for the Batignolles factory that had been evacuated to Cholet. Under torture they confessed that the weapons were for 'tout le monde', and the Germans entered the village on 7 August and took the mayor, curé and sixty other men hostage in the schoolroom. The following morning the Gestapo arrived to interrogate them and threatened to shoot twenty-one of the hostages, including the mayor and curé, if the 'terrorists' were not handed over. Fortunately the matter was defused by an Alsatian interpreter employed by the Batignolles works, who was able to explain in German the linguistic confusion that had brought the village to the brink of disaster.[90]

One village where disaster was not avoided, however, was that of Maillé, in Touraine. By mid-August the Allies had reached the north of the department, but the Germans still held Tours and the Loire and retreating forces were moving up into the region from Bordeaux and Poitiers. On the evening of 24 August a group of Maquisards ambushed a retreating convoy near Maillé, provoking a German unit covering the retreat to surround the village, which they believed to be a terrorist lair. The following day they began to massacre the inhabitants systematically with machine guns, grenades and bayo-nets, set fire to the buildings, and then bombarded the village from a distance so that the emergency services were unable to enter it until the day after. There, according to Jean Meunier, president of the CDL, they discovered

> 126 bodies, mutilated, cut to pieces or burned . . . the body of a two-month old baby was found, its head smashed, lying on that of its mother, who had had her throat cut and guts torn out. A pregnant woman had been bayoneted in the bed where she lay. Another baby in a cot had been shot in the head at point-blank

range. A man and woman who had died in the flames had embraced each other so tightly that they looked as though they had melted together.[91]

Whole families had died, mainly women, childen and old men, because most of the men had been away working in the fields. For the Tourangeaux it was a massacre of the innocents, a typical German atrocity which confirmed their fundamental barbarism. Of the 126 victims, 37 were under ten, 18 were aged eleven to twenty, and 16 were over sixty. Roger Confolent lost his wife and all seven children. Serge Martin, staying with his grandparents that day, lost his parents and three younger siblings, aged nine, five and six months.

Hearing the news, Prefect Musso went straight to the Feldkommandantur of Tours on 26 August to protest. Lieutenant Colonel Stenger promised an immediate inquiry and that the guilty would be sent before a court martial. The guilty man turned out to be a Lieutenant Schiler or Schleuter, who claimed that Maillé was sheltering terrorists and that he had been acting on orders. In a difficult interview on 28 August Prefect Musso denounced an 'act of terror which no French person would ever have committed, even under orders', and which was particularly unjustified in Touraine, whose population had suffered four years' Occupation 'with the greatest calm and perfect dignity'. Feldkommandant Stenger pointed out that three Germans had been wounded the previous night and weapons had been found in two or three farms at Maillé, but that German orders were to punish aggressors and their accomplices, not the innocent. He apologized to the victims and their families and again said that he would happily see the culprit shot, but the lieutenant had disappeared from the scene and was sentenced to death *in absentia* by a French military court in Bordeaux in 1952.[92] The atrocity was unpardonable, but the deed of an army in panic, caught in a race against time by the advancing Allies and harried by Maquisards, in which German units, out of contact with their superiors, themselves behaved like terrorist bands.

Popular discontent and anxiety, fuelled by labour conscription for the German Reich, were increased by Allied bombing raids which devastated ports and cities and drove large numbers of people into the countryside. The German war machine was undermined not only by bomb damage to plant, communications and power supply, but by the flight of the labour force from targeted areas and its reluctance to return to work. Meanwhile, the French administration, on which the Germans had relied to relay orders, became less and less cooperative. Unreliable officials and mayors were dismissed, but sanctions tended to produce only the semblance of cooperation rather than the real thing. Resistance networks developed among figures in key positions, and STO *réfractaires* organized Maquis here and there. These groups, of course, remained small minorities in an environment shaped by fear of anarchy and fear of reprisals. Most French people simply kept their heads down and waited for Liberation to come from the only likely source: an Allied invasion.

15. LIBERATION

Early in the sunny evening of 10 August 1944, as the last German defenders abandoned Angers and the first Americans crossed the Pont de la Basse-Chaîne opposite the medieval château, Michel Debré, *maître des requêtes* at the Conseil d'État, approached the gates of the prefecture and flashed his identity card at the police on guard. Thirty-two years old, a graduate of Sciences-Po – Paris's LSE – and the Cavalry School of Saumur, briefly a POW in 1940, he joined Vichy's Conseil d'État at Royat, near Clermont-Ferrand, to which it had been evacuated. From 1943, however, he had a second identity, code name Jacquier, member of the Comité Général d'Études which selected prefects and Commissaires de la République who would take power at the Liberation, preventing both a deal between Vichy and the American forces and a communist revolution. He had left Toulouse on 5 August, travelling by train and bicycle, and linked up with André Trémeaud, subprefect of Saumur, who took him in his car to Angers on 8 August. Two days later, inside the prefecture, he came face to face with Regional Prefect Donati and announced that he was taking over as Commissaire de la République for the Angers region in the name of General de Gaulle. According to Donati's daughter, a girl at the time, Debré shook hands with her father, a handshake that was of capital importance because it symbolized the continuity of the French state across the Liberation.[1] Donati asked only to stay the night at the prefecture, in order to pack his bags. Debré then sat at behind the large desk and later recalled, 'I had become the state.'[2]

Commissaire Debré then sent for the new prefect, Michel Fourré-Cormeray, auditor at the Cour des Comptes, who was waiting in the café opposite. He also confirmed in office the secretary-general, Gey, the subprefect of Saumur who had acted as his chauffeur, Trémeaud, and the subprefect of Segré, Fouet, who had saved his town from disaster a few days earlier. As head of his office he took René Tomasini, who was doing the same job in the prefecture of Loire-Inférieure and was incidentally a friend of Maurice Papon.[3] Moracchini, Commissaire Central at Tours, was made secretary-general of police for the Angers region. The administrative continuity between Vichy and the Liberation was thus extraordinary. What emerges from the German archives, moreover, is that the transfer of power between the retreating Germans and the French authorities was fairly amicable also. The previous day Donati had said goodbye to the German regional commander for Bezirk B, General Feldt, expressing his regrets and declaring that four years of working together with the German military administration had taught him 'that the Germans are not the enemies of the French, but their friends'.[4] Despite the increasingly threadbare nature of collaboration at the end of the Occupation, the protection of state power against communist subversion was a powerful reason for cooperation between French and Germans.

In about a quarter of French departments the handover of power at the Liberation lasted for less than a week, and where the departure of the Germans was followed quickly by the arrival of the Allies there was little violence.[5] Maine-et-Loire was certainly one of these. Rather different was the case in Indre-et-Loire, where the Americans liberated the north of the department and Debré invested a provisional prefectoral administration under Pierre Archambault at Neuillé-Pont-Pierre on 18 August, while the Germans retained the department south of the Loire including Tours and maintained Prefect Musso in office. The Germans blew up the bridges across the Loire on 22 August, the telephone exchange on the 28th, then the bridges over the Cher as they left on 31 August. In what looked very much like a revolution on 1 September, Jean Meunier, president of the CDL, went to the Hôtel de Ville to take over as mayor from René Guerrier and then to the prefecture to arrest Musso and install Robert Vivier as the new prefect.[6]

A closer look, however, suggests that the revolution was of the palace variety. Jean Meunier was a Third Republic socialist deputy who had been groomed to succeed the socialist deputy mayor of Tours, Ferdinand Morin: Morin had voted full powers to Pétain in

1940 and was barred from a comeback; Meunier had not, and found the doors open. Paul Cay, appointed secretary-general of the prefecture, had been subprefect of Chinon until early in 1944. Prefect Vivier and Meunier were both Freemasons, which was the traditional way of making political connections under the Third Republic.[7] Vivier had in fact been Inspecteur d'Académie under Vichy until 1942; since his office had been in the prefecture he described his new appointment as simply moving downstairs. In 1977 the historian Henri Amouroux alleged in *Quarante million de Pétainistes* that as Inspecteur d'Académie Vivier held a school competition for the best essay on the life and ideas of Marshal Pétain. His son, Jack Vivier, forced Amouroux to withdraw the passage on threat of legal proceedings, and told me that his father was kept away from the visit to Tours in 1941 of Youth Minister Lamirand on the grounds that he was 'already suspected of hostility to the Vichy regime' and declared that his father was 'a pure and absolutely honest resistant' who listened to the BBC every evening and 'was a visionary like de Gaulle'.[8]

Astute though the work of Debré and the other Gaullist officials was, it was in a sense an unnecessary complication in the transfer of power. It would have been even more simple for the Americans simply to endorse the Vichy authorities in place. After all, many if not most of them were by now playing a double game, negotiating with the Germans on one side and secretly protecting the Resistance on the other. This was certainly the plot in Nantes, where Debré's chosen candidate, Secretary-General Louis Ottaviani, panicked and told Prefect Georges Gaudard of the plan. Gaudard won the confidence of the American colonel in charge of the city and published an appeal for calm, completely wrong-footing the local Resistance. Debré was forced to go to Nantes on 15 August to rapidly build up a power-base in order to impose a prefect of his choice. The candidate he had in mind was a lawyer, Alexandre Vincent, who had worked for the Secours National and had no obvious links to the Resistance. He solicited the support of the departmental FFI leader, Colonel Félix, whose brother he had known at the Cavalry School of Saumur. He lectured the American colonel on the legitimacy of de Gaulle and the fact that Vichy was now finished. He asked the Comité de Libération, which had a lively communist group and rejected Vincent because he had once made a speech to the Groupe

Unveiling the statue of Vendéen hero Jacques Cathelineau, Le Pin en Mauges, March 1943. The collapse of the anti-clerical Third Republic gave the Catholic conservatives of the Vendée the opportunity to renew the cult of local heroes who had opposed the French Revolution.

Notre-Dame-de-Boulogne at Saint-Florent-le-Viel, Anjou, May 1944. The tour of France by three different statues of Our Lady of Boulogne resonated with the sense of guilt and desire for redemption of the Catholic faithful, who greeted the procession at every stage.

The body of the Feldkommandant of Nantes, Lieutenant Colonel Hotz, October 1941. The killing of the Feldkommandant by a communist hit-squad from Paris led to the execution of forty-eight hostages, including local notables as well as interned communists, although desperate negotiations averted the execution of a second batch of victims.

Funeral of German soldier shot in rue du Hallebardier, Tours, February 1942. The death of this ordinary German soldier led to reprisals as well, though the Germans targeted Jews and communists in order to minimize the alienation of local communities.

Rue du Calvaire, Nantes, after the Allied air raids of September 1943. Allied bombing of military installations was not as accurate as it might have been, and Vichy made a good deal of propaganda capital out of civilian casualties.

Mgr Costes and regional Prefect Donati comfort mourners after the Whitsun air raid on Angers, 1944. The rapprochement of Church and state under Vichy is admirably captured by this poignant scene following an Allied air raid which hit a church close to the railway yards of Angers that were the main target.

Michel Debré as commissaire de la République, Angers, August 1944. De Gaulle's representative (and future prime minister) at his desk in the prefecture of Angers. Debré consciously embodied the new legitimacy although, like many officials at the Liberation, he had also served Vichy.

Maillé (Touraine) after the massacre of 25 August 1944. German reprisals became much more arbitrary in the summer of 1944, as ill-disciplined units wreaked vengeance on communities suspected of harbouring 'terrorists'.

The liberation of Angers, 11 August 1944. Debré is No. 1, Mayor Bernier No. 4. The wizened Mayor of Angers, who had 'saved' it by concluding a truce with the Germans in June 1940, welcomed the Americans four years later.

The liberation of Tours, 1 September 1944. Jean Meunier (with armband) and Robert Vivier (second from left) climb the steps of the Hôtel de Ville. As the Germans finally left the north bank of the Loire the new mayor and prefect took charge in a neatly staged transfer of power.

Le Coz and his Maquis. The forgettable face of the Resistance: Le Coz (third from left), whose maquis band controlled the Loches area of Touraine in the summer of 1944, was subsequently shot as a common criminal.

Jacques Chombart de Lauwe/Colonel Félix. The divided face of the Resistance: while Colonel Félix commanded the Resistance forces in the Saint-Nazaire area, his alter ego Chombart de Lauwe orchestrated the transition of the Right in southern Brittany from Vichy to the Fourth Republic.

General de Gaulle lays a wreath at the monument to the Marquis de Saffré, June 1950. The unveiling of monuments in the years after the war was central to the construction of the story of the Resistance. The presence of de Gaulle, out of power between 1946 and 1958, conferred a necessary legitimacy to local resistance groups.

Country children near Angers sing the 'Marseillaise'. The Normandy landings were an eternity in coming and eagerly greeted, although as Violette Lemasson, one of the girls pictured here, told me, 'we never went hungry' during the Occupation in her small village.

Surrender of the German forces of the Pocket of Saint-Nazaire at Bouvron, 11 May 1945. Despite the well-known photos of the liberation of Paris in August 1944 many parts of France were not liberated until much later. The Germans holed up in the Pocket of Saint-Nazaire did not surrender until after the collapse of the Reich.

Gilbert Brustlein (seventy-two) revisits the rue du Roi-Albert, Nantes. Fifty years on: Brustlein, who fired the shot that killed the Feldkommandant Hotz on 20 October 1941, returned to a hostile reception at the scene on 20 October 1991. Only for the sixtieth anniversary, on 20 October 2001, was any kind of reconciliation possible between Brustlein and the familes of the hostages who had been executed in reprisal for his act.

General Leclerc greeted by the Curé and Mayor of Grugé l'Hôpital and the Subprefect of Segré (Anjou), September 1946. General Leclerc returned as a local hero to the small commune in Anjou where, in 1940, he had been issued a pass to the Free Zone.

Grugé l'Hôpital (Anjou), unveiling of a statue of General Leclerc, 1980. By erecting this statue of General Leclerc the village, which had an uncommonly quiet Occupation, solidified its association with a hero of the Free French.

Unveiling of a new plaque at Camp de la Lande, December 1995. The original plaque marking the internment camp made no mention of the Jews held there; it took three years' campaigning to rectify this omission. Serge Klarsfeld is on the prefect's left.

Students from the College of Monts at the unveiling of the new plaque at Camp de la Lande, December 1995. According to some Resistance leaders, the Resistance has now been replaced by the Holocaust as the dominant memory of the Occupation period, especially among young people.

Collaboration, to broaden itself out and proposed the Marquis de Sesmaisons. He went to see the bishop, Mgr Villepelet, who thought Gaullism 'diabolical' and still had a portrait of Marshal Pétain hanging in his office, to assure him that the new regime wanted to collaborate with the Church and to ask him to nominate a cleric to sit on the CDL, which Villepelet refused to do. Even Mme de Sesmaisons, sent by Debré, could not bring him round. Villepelet was prepared to render to Caesar what was Caesar's, but not a centime more. Squeezed between the Pétainist establishment who wanted to stick with Gaudard or even have Bonnefoy back 'if he were free', and the communists in the local Resistance, Debré was forced to pretend that Vincent would only be a temporary appointment.[9]

Prefects and police commissioners did not have a free hand at the Liberation, but had to do business with the Comités de Libération that sprang up at departmental, *arrondissement* and local levels, mirroring the Conseil National de la Résistance. The CDLs were the assemblies both of local Resistance movements, in so far as they existed, and of political parties, trade unions and other pressure groups emerging or re-emerging after the Occupation. In some sense they acted as a 'dual power', reminiscent of revolutionary situations, putting pressure on the administration to be more ruthless in the purge of collaborators, but how independent they were depended on local circumstances.[10] Some prefects had strong personalities and were highly regarded by the committees, others were less so. The influence of a CDL might be explained by its radicalism, but alternatively radicalism might make it less representative of local opinion. Committees in fact had an ambivalent profile, both to articulate Resistance demands for a brave new world, and to represent a broad church of opinion that was more inclined to let bygones be bygones. There was a growing sense that a fair balance had to be maintained between Right and Left, reflecting the political complexion of the constituency. The more traditional parties were represented, however, the more the hardline resistance was swamped, and the more the opinion was expressed that the Resistance had had its day and it was time to return to party politics.

At one end of the spectrum, the CDL of Indre-et-Loire had a high level of coherence, with thirteen of the twenty-two members belonging to Libération-Nord, and another two to Ceux de la Libération.

Politically the complexion was both socialist and Christian democratic, but the two had worked effectively together in the Resistance.
The president of the CDL, Jeun Meunier, was also the new mayor
of Tours and the kingmaker in the department: Prefect Vivier was
his man rather than the other way around. The CDL set up and
controlled the main organ of the local press, *La Dépêche du Centre*.
Only in February 1945 did the communist/CGT/Front National
minority (a minority of three) start to cause a nuisance. Supported
by the communist *Voix du peuple*, they attacked M. Vareilles of the
CIMT, the employers' representative on the CDL, for having put
pressure on his workers to do STO in Germany, and they tried to set
up a local liberation committee for Tours alone. In both cases, however, Meunier used his majority in the CDL to stifle them.[11]

In Loire-Inférieure the communist/CGT/Front National alliance
was more powerful.[12] Auguste Péneau, who had led the trade unions'
opposition to the Labour Charter in the department,[13] was president
of the CDL, Bernier of the Front National a vice-president, while
Kléber, the communist representative, was an extremely effective
member. The original committee of seventeen was enlarged in the
autumn to include various communist front organizations, such as
the Mouvement National des Prisonniers de Guerre et des Déportés
(MNPD) and the Union des Femmes Françaises (UFF). The main
counterweight to the communists was the Marquis de Sesmaisons,
mayor and *conseiller général* of La Chapelle-sur-Erdre, secretary of
the Chambre d'Agriculture, and one of the few representatives of the
formerly hegemonic nobles in the department not compromised by
collaboration. Deeply conservative, his Resistance profile was guaranteed by his wife, who had battled with the Germans on numerous
occasions, became president of the Comité des Œuvres Sociales de la
Résistance (COSR) and was awarded the Légion d'honneur and
Croix de Guerre, and by his eldest son Jean, a graduate of Saint-Cyr
who had been deported.[14] This weakness of the Right on the CDL
rather undermined the position of Prefect Vincent, who was considered by the communists to be a Pétainist and narrowly survived a
vote of no confidence in March 1945 by eight votes to eight, with
one abstention.[15]

Much more influential was the conservative and Catholic lobby in
the CDL of Maine-et-Loire. Whereas in Indre-et-Loire 13 of the 22
members of the CDL were affiliated to Resistance organizations and

in Loire-Inférieure the proportion was 6 out of 17, in Maine-et-Loire the tally was only 3 out of 20.[16] The CDL had scarcely any history before the Liberation, and the original nucleus that met on 12 August 1944, two days after the liberation of Angers, was only seven strong. Michel Debré was keen on having the Christian Democratic former deputy Albert Blanchoin elected president; in fact the election was won by Le Tetour, a civil servant with the Vichy price-control office, and affiliated to Libération-Nord. Blanchoin, however, won the struggle to control the *Courrier de l'Ouest*, which took over from *Le Petit Courrier*, discredited as the official Vichy newspaper, and at the end of August Le Tetour had to be persuaded not to resign.[17] Le Tetour himself realized that the CDL would have to broaden its membership to become more representative of Angevin opinion, and commissioned René Le Bault de la Morinière, who had played the double game by accepting a Vichy nomination as mayor while joining Libération-Nord, to prospect in the Mauges. Le Bault, whose great-grandmother had been drowned by the revolutionary proconsul Carrier in the infamous *noyades de Nantes* of 1793, did not want the CDL to become like 'the revolutionary committees of public safety'. He swam across the Loire where the bridges were down to recruit Bernard Pellaumail, a leading Cholet industrialist, Canon Douillard, archdeacon of Cholet, and a conservative senator, Vicomte Palamède de la Grandière, one of the founders of the Ligue des Catholiques d'Anjou who, Le Bault told me with a wink, would have voted full powers to Pétain in July 1940 if only he had not missed the train to Vichy.[18] He also recruited Dom Sortais, abbot of the Trappist monastery of Bellefontaine, a former POW who had preached against the Germans in the churches of the Mauges and hidden many on the run from the Germans, for the liberation committee of Cholet. A soldier-monk, Catholic and patriotic, he was the ideal candidate to maintain harmony in the Vendée, and his biographer claims that because of his influence no woman had her head shaved for collaboration in Cholet.[19]

The only drawback to this balancing of Left and Right on the CDL was that the committee became divided into two opposing factions.[20] One row broke out over the inclusion on the CDL of Charles Poisson, who had made money as an administrator of Jewish properties in Angers under the the Aryanization laws. There was another row when it was discovered that Palamède de la Grandière had sat on the editorial board of a collaborationist newspaper, *Le Maine-et-Loire*.[21] The final row erupted in March 1945 when a communist proposed that in the forthcoming municipal elections, when women were to vote for the first time, the vote should be denied to cloistered nuns. This led to the resignation of the eight-strong Catholic lobby, including Le Bault de la Morinière, Palamède de la Grandière, Canon Douillard, Pellaumail, Poisson and Blanchoin, on the grounds that even 'the worst prostitutes' had the vote and the CDL 'clashes too often with the opinions of the great majority of the fellow citizens it claims to represent'.[22]

The task of notables, state officials and indeed the military at the end of the Occupation was to ensure their dominance and to keep the insurrection and anarchy surrounding the transfer of power to a bare minimum. One of the main challenges was to bring under control the FFIs which had mushroomed after the Normandy landings and especially after the Liberation, less to fight the Germans than to settle accounts with collaborators. These were a conflation of the Maquis and other Resistance movements, supplemented by volunteers from the towns, led sometimes by former officers of the Armistice Army but just as often by amateurs with chutzpah. One idealized view of the FFIs is that they were bands of merry men Robin Hood-style waving sten guns and devoted to freedom and social justice.[23] A more realistic view is that they were a modern version of Richard Cobb's *armées révolutionaires*, arresting, humiliating and sometimes killing collaborators, informers, black marketeers, girlfriends of the Boche and other enemies of the Resistance, little different from the bandits denounced by Vichy except that they wore armbands to indicate their military status and sometimes left receipts for provisions, cars and other consumer durables they requisitioned. In the four departments of Brittany adjoining Loire-Inférieure, Luc Capdevila has calculated that in what he calls the 'period of republican disorder' which climaxed in August 1944, FFIs and the like were responsible for two-thirds of the murders and summary executions of alleged collaborators and three-quarters of the head-shavings of women said to have slept with Germans.[24]

Once the Germans were safely on the run, all sorts of would-be resistants joined the FFIs, many of them extremely dubious and violent men. The FFIs also turned out to be an admirable refuge for collaborators seeking to recycle themselves as patriots. In order to control and discipline an unwieldy irregular force it seemed obvious to appeal to men with military training, but the former Armistice Army was by definition staffed by Pétainists. Lieutenant Colonel Eynaud, appointed FFI chief in Maine-et-Loire, had no record of any Resistance activity, made no bones about voicing Pétainist and anti-republican opinions, and said that his forces were really there to take on the communists. The CDL of Maine-et-Loire refused to recognize him in September 1944 and within a fortnight persuaded Commissaire Debré to dismiss him.[25] In Indre-et-Loire Major Balzac, who had a good Resistance record and commanded the FFIs in the south of the department, was somehow displaced as commander of the FFIs in the whole department by the Vicomte Major de Champmesle, a monocled graduate of Saint-Cyr, until it was discovered that he had been cashiered from the 32nd Infantry Regiment in 1937 for announcing in uniform at a public meeting that he would 'rather see Hitler at Bourgueil than communism in Paris', and that his FFI headquarters at Bourgeuil was like an eighteenth-century salon, presided over by the Duchesse de Talleyrand-Périgord, and swarming with royalists.[26]

An FFI leader who had been rejected by the Maquis of the Armée Secrète in the Loches area, run as it was by former officers of the Armistice Army's 32nd Infantry Regiment, was bound to acquire the popularity of a local hero. This was what happened to 'Dr Jean', alias Jean-Marie Scoarnec, Georges Dubosq and Captain Le Coz, who claimed both to have been in the Foreign Legion and to have escaped from Drancy, where his wife and children had died. Rejected by the Vichyssois officers, he organized his own Maquis drawn from young people of a wilder disposition who in the high summer of 1944 delighted in Le Coz's passions for staying in châteaux, taking fast cars, and picking up women. But Le Coz was also a killer, who assassinated Dr Abribat, leader of the local Légion Française des Combattants, members of the counter-insurgency Milice and other collaborators. His Maquis liberated Loches on 16 August 1944 and in front of a crowd of 2,000 on the main square he shot the local police chief who wanted them to go easy on purges. The Germans retook the town a week later and it took the 32nd Infantry Regiment to liberate it for good on 6 September. Meanwhile, Le Coz pursued a veritable reign of terror in the region as it was discovered that he was no hero but a common criminal and Nazi informer who had turned to the Resistance to save his skin. 'He is nothing more than a highway robber,' said the Liberation Prefect Vivier, 'he pillages farms, demands ransoms, murders, arrests arbitrarily, tortures and issues death threats . . . he is an inveterate alcoholic and sadist who while pretending to fight the Germans turns his weapons against Miliciens and collaborators.'[27] Vivier described the 100-strong Maquis as 'a veritable bandit business' and Le Coz himself as a 'terrorist pirate, murderer and executioner', responsible for nineteen of the thirty-one summary executions in the department.[28] Eventually, in October 1944, Le Coz was seized by an undercover police operation, tried by a military court a year later and shot.[29]

The problem of unruly FFIs was compounded by the fact that in the Nantes–Saint-Nazaire area the Liberation took not weeks or months but a whole year. Once they had liberated Nantes the Allies turned east, leaving 25,000 Germans in the naval and U-boat base of Saint-Nazaire contained behind a thin line of military and FFIs but in no hurry to flush them out. The French authorities were indeed concerned that if the Americans took the offensive they would put at risk the lives of the 125,000 French people still under German Occupation in what became known as the Pocket of Saint-Nazaire. This was one of a number of pockets on the Atlantic coast, along with Lorient, La Rochelle and Royan, where the Germans remained ensconced until the end of the war in Europe. The Americans let off their big guns at church steeples which were being used as German lookout points, while the embattled frontier, only a few miles from Nantes, became even more of a Wild West in which FFIs roamed at will, occasionally engaging in a skirmish as the tired Germans tried to break out, but often – and to the despair of the local authorities – drinking, womanizing, looting farms and villages on the frontier, hijacking vehicles, having fatal accidents with firearms or selling them to racketeers behind the lines, in the luxury restaurants and brothels of Nantes.[30]

The commander of the FFIs on the Saint-Nazaire front, code name Colonel Félix, was an ambitious and rather authoritarian character with jet-black hair and a somewhat haughty gaze. His career sheds a great deal of light on the Liberation, and how it was as much about negotiating the postwar political settlement as it was about recovering French territory. In particular it demonstrates how many of those who came to political prominence after the Liberation in fact joined the Resistance extremely late, and for no other reason than to prevent any revolutionary outcome. Felix, whose real name was Jacques Chombart de Lauwe, was an adventurer of Flemish origin who married into a rich Franco-Irish family, the Fitzgeralds of Leinster, and with his new fortune bought an estate at Herbignac in the Parc de Brière, now within the Pocket, to indulge his passion for hunting. From his estate he provided charcoal to fuel the lorries delivering the collaborationist Nantes daily, *Le Phare*. In June 1944 he tried to get the paper's editor and owner, son and father-in-law team René Bentz and François Portais, to hand over the paper, threatening that if they did not, his all-powerful friends would have the paper closed down. In the event *Le Phare* was closed down at the Liberation for collaboration, at which point Chombart de Lauwe tried to obtain control of its presses for a new paper he was launching, *L'Avenir de l'Ouest*.

Meanwhile, as Colonel Félix, Chombart de Lauwe managed to take command of the FFIs in Loire-Inférieure, becoming involved principally in order to stop the communists doing so. 'If he hadn't been there,' said his brother-in-law Pierre de Montalembert when I interviewed him in 1999, 'completely mad FFIs would have done all the stupid things possible that you can imagine. The people of Nantes realized that they were lucky to have someone sane at the head of the Resistance in Nantes and the region. People were reassured that it wasn't run by a *voyou* [thug], which at the time was very rare.'[31] Others had a rather different view of the methods of Colonel Félix. The CDL complained that the arrests it ordered were not being executed by the colonel, who in turn argued that he recognized only the authority of the prefect.[32] Meanwhile Prefect Vincent protested to Colonel Félix that his FFIs had threatened to shoot three gendarmes and had arrested seven police officers in Nantes. When a mayor declared that 'several times I was marched off by the Germans between two bayonets but this is the first time that I have suffered this from the French', Vincent told Colonel Félix that such incidents were discrediting the FFIs as a whole in the eyes of the local population.[33] Even Mgr Villepelet, who knew the colonel as a member of his diocese but hated 'the rule of the armband', remonstrated with him for the arbitrary arrest of one of his curés and refused him a chaplain to serve the FFIs.[34]

By October 1944 evidence about the political machinations of

Colonel Félix in his capacity as Chombart de Lauwe started to come to light, posing a threat to his Resistance credentials if not his military effectiveness. His military superior, General Hary, commander of the Fourth Military Region based at Angers, took the view that the row over the *Phare de Nantes* was a purely political matter that should be dealt with privately, that Colonel Félix had heavy military responsibilities on the Saint-Nazaire front and that he would 'forbid anything that might diminish Colonel Félix's authority'.[35] This was the same general who in 1945 regretted that 'too many so-called FFIs have behaved like veritable bandits and considerably discredited the Resistance'.[36] Discredited or not, the cat's life in the Resistance of Colonel Félix endured just long enough, as we shall see, for Chombart de Lauwe to secure the political legitimacy necessary to refloat the right wing in Brittany, the traditional dominant force but compromised by its Pétainism.

One of the influential accounts of the purges at the Liberation was that they were anarchic and savage, driven through by communists in order to destroy their political opponents.[37] It is true that in some parts of France the Liberation saw a violent *règlement de comptes* by opposing factions, with lynchings, kangaroo courts and summary executions. It was one of the priorities of the new government to bring such disorder under control, if necessary by interning those at risk from popular justice. A regular system of justice was put in place, with military courts at work in each region almost at once, then – in each department by the autumn – Cours de Justice for what were deemed criminal cases of collaboration and Chambres Civiques for cases of 'unworthy conduct'. Clearly there were conflicting views about what actions perpetrated under the Occupation needed to be tried and punished and what bygones could be allowed to be bygones. As Michel Debré asked an angry meeting in Cholet early in 1945 after a prisoner was freed, 'Who, in this room, has done nothing worthy of blame from the patriotic point of view since 1939?'[38] Justice, moreover, was not a shining sword that cut through all other circumstances. The brave new order demanded by those who had made sacrifices to the Resistance had to be set against the need to preserve public order and the authority of the state, the continuity of traditional ruling groups and the integrity of local communities, each or all of which risked being compromised by too violent a purge. Hence at the end of the day there was just as much complaint about lack of justice, cover-ups and the support of friends in high places as about excessive purges.[39]

The judicial cause célèbre in Loire-Inférieure was undoubtedly that of the Marquis de La Ferronnays, mayor of Saint-Mars-la-Jaille, who controlled opinion in his fief through his local paper, Le Journal d'Ancenis, and as president of the conseil général was the unchallenged leader of the Right in the department. After the Liberation his arrest was requested by the liberation committee of Ancenis, which was astounded to see Madame la Marquise presenting a flag to the first battalion of the FFIs at Saint-Mars, and taken up by the CDL. On the CDL the hardliners were led by the communists Bernier and Kléber, the soft-peddlers by the Marquis de Sesmaisons. The hardliners argued that although the Marquise de La Ferronnays was of Jewish descent she had been a fervent apostle of collaboration, while the marquis had effectively manipulated the prefecture of Nantes under the Occupation, helped to choose the fifty hostages of Nantes and Châteaubriant, personally selected men from his village for STO, and even had stakes knocked into his fields to prevent Allied planes from landing. De Sesmaisons rejected these allegations as totally unfounded and argued that the heroic war record of the marquis in 1914–18 alone guaranteed the uprightness of his character. Bernier retorted that plenty of veterans of 1914–18 had behaved badly under the Occupation, and argued that rather than hesitating because they were dealing with someone so important they should take the view that 'you cannot condemn Pétain and Laval without condemning M. de La Ferronnays'.

Against the will of Prefect Vincent, the CDL ordered the arrest of the marquis, which was carried out on 4 October by FFI Captain Saint-Roch. His group analysed all the editorials of the Journal d'Ancenis, which contained such statements as 'the victory of Germany is necessary to spare Europe the horrors of a communist invasion' (10 July 1942). The editorials were actually written by Tony Catta, who also edited the Souvenir Vendéen, but the Resistance argued that the marquis, as owner, must take equal responsibility. In the pre-trial period there was a clear division between the CLL of Ancenis, the FFIs and the Front National on the one hand, who saw the marquis purely and simply as a collaborator, and on the other the veterans of his old regiment, who 'considered their former colonel incapable of doing any wickedness under the Occupation', and the stalwarts of the local community at Saint-Mars who affirmed 'that he was not a collaborator but simply a supporter of Marshal Pétain'.[40]

The marquis, in the end, eluded justice. A sick man, aged sixty-nine, he was rapidly moved from prison to a clinic run by Augustinian nuns. In February 1945 a noisy congress of local liberation committees in Loire-Inférieure met to demand a speeding-up and toughening of the purges, which it said were being deliberately frustrated by the bureaucracy and judicial system. It complained in particular that no important figure had yet appeared before the Cour de Justice and called for the resignation of Prefect Vincent, whose appointment in any case was supposed to have been temporary.[41] Early in 1946, however, still untried the Marquis de La Ferronnays died. On the day of the funeral, celebrated by the bishop of Nantes and attended by the *fine fleur* of the nobility of the west of France, Colonel Félix/Jacques Chombart de Lauwe wrote in his paper that 'though I, from June 1940, chose another path and rallied to General de Gaulle [in fact he did no such thing until June 1944], I bow respectfully to the memory of M. de La Ferronnays in the hope that everyone might have a sense of duty as strong as his'. He denounced the ill-treatment to which the marquis had been subjected, defended his obedience to Marshal Pétain and argued that the motto 'Work, Family and Fatherland' was a good deal better than what might be that of the present government: 'Anarchy, Vengeance, Social Decomposition'.[42] In a world supposedly divided between Resistance and collaboration this intervention is puzzling at the very least. When I put this to Pierre de Montalembert, sitting in his salon in front of a shrine dedicated to his ancestor, the great nineteenth-century liberal Catholic, he smiled: de La Ferronnays was no enemy of Chombart but, in the loose way in which the Bretons formulate kinship ties, his 'uncle'. It becomes clear that the most important thing for the likes of Chombart and de Montalembert at the Liberation was to restore the unity and dominance of the French elite, momentarily divided by the Occupation, but which now needed to pull together to prevent a communist takeover.

The most famous purge trial in Maine-et-Loire was that of Anatole Manceau, senator, president of the Cholet Chamber of Commerce, and (despite his guerrilla war with Regional Prefect Roussillon) editor of *Le Petit Courrier*, the official paper of the prefecture under the

Occupation. Brought to trial in September 1945, Manceau argued that he was 'a resister of the first hour', who had kept his newspaper going, instead of closing it, to 'limit German propaganda as much as possible'. He said that he had been prepared to take on Vichy over its vilification of parliamentarians, had refused to let collaborationist movements dictate to his paper, and had belonged to a group of 'resisting senators' that met weekly under the Occupation. Like the Marquis de La Ferronnays, he was supported by the local community and the professional institutions to which he belonged: the Cholet Chamber of Commerce, the Liberation Committee of Cholet, dominated as it was by good Catholics such as Bernard Pellaumail, Dom Sortais and Canon Douillard, together with the new mayor. What he did not have on his side, however, was the support of the new political class. Not only was he regarded as a dinosaur of the Third Republic, but what he called the 'despoilment' of the *Le Petit Courrier* by the Christian Democrats of Angers around Albert Blanchoin and Charles Poisson had to be legitimated. Manceau was therefore sacrificed and sentenced to five months in prison, which he had already served, to the confiscation of half his assets, and to 'national indignity' for life. He died a broken man in 1948.[43]

The Cours de Justice did, on occasions, act more swiftly and decisively. There was reportedly great satisfaction amongst the crowd that gathered outside the Palais de Justice of Tours where the court sat on 7 November 1944 when the news emerged that Antoine Devaud, a former police officer, and Nicole Pluveau had been sentenced to death as Gestapo agents. Though Pluveau had her sentence commuted by de Gaulle to perpetual forced labour, Devaud was shot on 19 December. It soon became clear to the public, however, that while the small fry were being dealt with severely, the big fish were not being brought to justice or were being let off very lightly. In December 1944 the communist *Voix du peuple* fired a broadside about 'the Moracchini scandal'. Moracchini was the Tours police chief who had presided over the arrest, beating and handover to the Gestapo of five young communist militants, who were shot on 16 May 1942, and had now been promoted to secretary-general of police at Angers. Meanwhile the head of Sûreté, Maurice, who had been specifically cited by the young communists before they were shot, and by the father of one of them before he committed suicide, as the man who delivered them to the Germans, was promoted to

Paris. Only the aptly named Boucherie, well known to be in cahoots with Gestapo chief Brückle, was arrested. Rather than blame the chiefs, the internal police inquiry took the easy route of blaming the subordinates, but the communist press would not lie down. 'Have they protectors who are so powerful that they cannot be called to account?' demanded *La Voix du peuple*. And when Moracchini was promoted again to be divisional commissaire at Bordeaux it proclaimed sarcastically, 'To the good servants of Pétain and the Gestapo the Fourth Republic expresses its gratitude.'[44]

There was also a good deal of public discontent at Tours about the immunity that seemed to be enjoyed by former members of the prefecture. Tracou and Secretary-General Molas-Quenescourt, who were said to have drawn up lists of communists and other dissidents for the Gestapo to arrest, were known to be enjoying their freedom in Paris. The stakes were raised by René Feld, a previous secretary-general, who had been suspended at the Liberation from his post as subprefect of Saint-Malo, and was trying to save his skin by blaming his colleagues. Tracou and Molas, both with naval backgrounds, he declared, were the villains, while he, with a Jewish grandmother, had spent his time at the prefecture protecting Jews and Freemasons from the ire of Vichy.[45] Despite these attacks, the only prefecture official of Indre-et-Loire to stand trial was the last Vichy prefect, Fernand Musso, and the spectacle was moved by Michel Debré from Tours to Angers for greater security. Musso suffered a blistering attack from Paul Cay, the subprefect of Chinon whom he had sacked and who re-emerged at the Liberation as secretary-general of the prefecture. Musso, Cay said, was 'always very docile in the face of German orders', had welcomed the collaborationist Marcel Bucard to Tours and was fanatical about suppressing the Maquis. Regional Prefect Donati tried to defend Musso, saying that of all the five prefects of the region he had been 'the most "poisoned" by the Germans and their insatiable demands'.[46] Donati was shortly to give evidence at Pétain's trial, arguing that Pétain had sacrificed himself to protect France and that his maxim, to make the right decision, was 'When there are two courses open to you, always take the most difficult. Then you know you are on the right path.'[47] It was always possible for a Vichy prefect to claim that, while remaining at his post, and even without indulging in any *double jeu*, he had defended French interests as far as was reasonably possible. Unfortunately Musso did not even pass muster on these criteria and was sentenced to four years in prison.

Given the unedifying nature of many trials, not least as far as the French administration was concerned, the government was keen that cases liable to produce a death penalty should be processed by the Cours de Justice before 1 May 1945, so that things could get back to normal. It was precisely at this time, however, that patriots who had been deported to camps in Germany began to return to France, many of whom, astounded that collaborators who had denounced them were still free, were burning for revenge. It also coincided with the return of workers who had gone voluntarily to Germany and, unlike STO conscripts, were considered to be collaborators. A certain Macret, who had returned to Loches but was being taken by the police to Tours, was dragged out of the police vehicle and lynched by a crowd of 300, including former deportees and their families. Even where individuals were convicted, an angry public might still want to get hold of them. A Vietnamese domestic servant who worked at the Château of Vaux near Tours where parachuted weapons were hidden, together with his friend the local grocer, had denounced the *châtelaine* Hélène Bruneau and about twenty resisters involved in the enterprise.[48] The resisters were duly arrested and many of them shot, and this as late as 4 August 1944. Although condemned to death by the Cour de Justice, the two were lynched by a crowd as they emerged from the courtroom, and the Vietnamese died of his injuries.[49]

These incidents were no doubt barbaric, but they betrayed a genuine popular dissatisfaction with the effectiveness of the purges as administered by the courts. The courts, it should be stressed, were not the only instrument of the purges. Many professions were allowed to manage their own purges through their own bodies. In the case of industry, interprofessional purge committees for businesses (CIEEs) were set up in each region, presided over by a magistrate and including two representatives of the CDLs, together with representatives of workers, white-collar employees, technicians, engineers and employers. Who they were supposed to purge and for what, however, was a matter of debate. Workers obviously took a tougher line than employers. On 21 December 1944 the tramway workers of Nantes went on strike, firstly to complain that they were being driven like galley slaves, and secondly to remove a trio of

Belgian directors whom they held responsible for sending workers to Germany and for drawing the attention of the Germans to a communist worker who had been arrested and shot. The CIEE divided between Péneau, president of the CDL, who took a hard line, and the employers' representative, who wanted to go slow. The prefect was squeezed between the employers and workers of the tramway company but eventually the three Belgian managers were dismissed.[50]

The key issue with 'economic collaboration' was not *whether* a firm had worked for the German war economy. The shipyards, railway workshops and aircraft factories of the Nantes–Saint-Nazaire area, for example, had worked full out for the Wehrmacht, Luftwaffe and above all the Kriegsmarine until they were gradually prevented from doing so by Allied bombing. The consensual view was that employers had no choice about working for the Germans and that jobs had to be preserved. What was not acceptable was doing the Germans' bidding with too much enthusiasm and above all putting pressure on workers to go to Germany under the *Relève* scheme, usually by threatening to report them to the German authorities, but the penalties were mild. Jacquet, a manager of the Batignolles locomotive works, 90 per cent of whose orders were German, got into trouble for producing for the Germans with an 'excess of zeal' and for socializing with German officers, although all the CIEE did was to move him to another job.[51] At the Chantiers de Bretagne at Nantes the deputy director was accused of threatening workers with deportation to Germany if they did not work harder, but was only suspended without pay for a year. The director, meanwhile, was said to have protected workers who resorted to go-slows and 'passive resistance' in the face of German demands and indeed was praised for his 'irreproachable and entirely French attitude'.[52] Elsewhere, at the Chantiers de la Loire and the Chantiers Dubigeon, the employers and managers who gained the upper hand on the CIEE practised the usual formula of passing the buck down to lower echelons and giving their fellow employers a clean bill of health.

When the Commissaire de la République called on Mgr Villepelet, bishop of Nantes, on 17 August 1944, a portrait of Marshal Pétain still hung on the wall. In order to anchor the Comité de Libération more firmly in the department the commissaire was keen to have a member of the clergy sit on it, but the bishop refused to allow them to become involved in what he called 'partisan politics'. 'I reminded him of the position of the Church in respect of political power,' said the bishop. 'It recognized only one authority as legitimate until further notice, but bowed to the *de facto* power with which it was now confronted.' The bishop feared that the provisional government was not strong enough to contain the communists and that France was on the verge of a Spanish Civil War situation. At the very least the Church no longer enjoyed the influence it had under Vichy. On Armistice Day 1944 Mgr Villepelet complained that the best seats in the official stand were reserved for members of the CDL and that 'had some influential people not protested I would have been relegated to the second rank'. When de Gaulle visited Nantes in January 1945 and asked the bishop to celebrate a Mass for him he deferred, but found the General as frosty as the snow on the ground, 'a man of will rather than of feeling'.[53]

There was no question that bishops should suffer any punishment simply for being Pétainists; the issue was rather how to win them over to the new regime. In Angers, however, Debré was under pressure from the left wing of the CDL to send Mgr Vincent, the rector of the Catholic University, and two of his staff before the Cour de Justice on charges of collaboration. They had, it was argued, attacked the Resistance, preached up the STO and recruited their students to collaborationist parties and the Milice. Debré feared that any such trial would ignite 'a little war of religion' and put pressure on the hierarchy to set its house in order. Reluctantly, the bishops who acted as a board of governors of the Catholic University agreed to dismiss Rector Vincent and his two colleagues, which was a triumph for secret diplomacy.[54]

The Catholic faithful were nevertheless mobilizing in anticipation of a new episode in the ongoing struggle of Church and state. The Fédération Nationale Catholique, set up to defend the Church against the Cartel des Gauches in the 1920s, was revived in 1945 as the Fédération Nationale d'Action Catholique under the presidency of Jean Le Cour Grandmaison, mayor of Guenroët, a former member of Vichy's Conseil National and the future biographer of the Marquis de La Ferronnays. The diocesan branch of the FNC, the Ligue des Catholiques de l'Anjou, was revived in April 1945 as the Union des Catholiques de l'Anjou (UCA) and found a cause célèbre in the defence of state subsidies to church schools that Vichy had reintroduced after sixty years of republicanism and which the provisional government was to abolish.[55] Catholics who had initially sat on liberation committees and given the Liberation their blessing now resigned to fight the good fight for Church schools. The Catholic group, as we have seen, resigned from the CDL of Maine-et-Loire in March 1945. One of them, Canon Douillard, then publicly accused the government of using 'the sinister methods of the camps of Buchenwald and Dachau' to starve the Church schools attended by two-thirds of the children in the Mauges. He was involved in a Catholic demonstration at Cholet, 30,000 strong and presided over by Mgr Costes, on 2 September 1945, which was itself a prelude to the 60,000-strong demonstration at Angers on 7 October. Jean Le Cour Grandmaison drew the parallel with the FNC demonstration at Angers in March 1925, but the polemic was modernized to overcome the traditional association of the Church with reaction. 'Catholics, like all French people,' declared the leader of the UCA, 'shed their blood for France in front of German tanks in 1940, endured deportation and concentration camps, resisted the enemy and took part in the glorious liberation of the soil of the fatherland. For these reasons we refuse to be treated like pariahs, outside the national community.'[56]

Over a year previously, on 4 August 1944, American forces liberated the village of Guémené-Penfao at the northern extremity of Loire-Inférieure. A retired schoolteacher and Freemason, Mlle Rolland, and the local curate, Abbé Bersihaud, took over at the *mairie*. Mlle Marie Rolland was in fact a resister of some experience in the region, code name Annick, but since the village was still surrounded on three sides by the Germans she asked another retired schoolteacher, André Laurens, to organize an FFI unit to defend it. Although this was formally part of the same liberation committee, however, a power struggle broke out between Annick Rolland and Laurens, whom she accused of undermining the Resistance. Laurens was initially confirmed as FFI leader in the locality by Colonel Félix's minions at Châteaubriant, then dropped, complaining that 'I have been defeated by a woman of seventy-one and a discharged corporal stretcher-bearer.' Annick then discovered that the CDL at Nantes had endorsed a second liberation committee at Guémené, under Laurens, and asked 'what this farce means'. Both Annick and Laurens were summoned to appear before the CDL on 5 January 1945 and Laurens was given the benefit of the doubt. Meanwhile, the mayor of Guémené had been interned and a new muncipal council was confirmed by the CDL, including fifteen old councillors and six new ones (not including Annick or the abbé) who had emerged from the Resistance.[57]

In the anarchic period of the Liberation such uncertainty and faction-fighting were extremely common, yet the new Republic had to ensure a rapid transition to stable local government. Resistance groups set up liberation committees which looked to purge discredited local councils to make room for people with Resistance credentials. On the other hand the authorities had to be satisfied that the administration was in the hands of those who had local influence and could demonstrate competence. There was a far-reaching reorganization of municipal councils and *conseils généraux* after the Liberation, but what took place fell far short of a revolution. Criteria based on political correctness were constantly balanced against those based on effectiveness and consensus. The principles of republican legitimacy laid down in an ordinance of 21 April 1944 banned from elective office the 569 deputies and senators who had voted full powers to Marshal Pétain on 10 July 1940 and all those appointed by 'the usurper' to the Conseil National, departmental councils or municipal councils. Only notable service to the Resistance would permit such a ban to be lifted. Mayors and councillors who had 'directly favoured or served the interests of the enemy or the usurper' would also be dismissed. Vacancies caused by the dismissal, resignation or death of councillors would be filled provisionally ahead of municipal or cantonal elections due in 1945, but Resistance activity would not be the sole or even main criteria for selection. Just as important, so that the local council would be approved by local citizens, was the political profile of the commune as evidenced by the last municipal elections held in 1935.

In Tours, there was no return as mayor for the socialist politician Ferdinand Morin, who had voted full powers to Pétain in 1940. He was said to have distrusted the Maquis as communist-inspired and 'shown a certain sympathy for the Vichy government, notably for Laval, whom he knew personally'. His record as protector of the city was not enough to outweigh these factors, and he did not become a municipal councillor again till 1953.[58] At Angers, the po-faced mayor Victor Bernier, not having been a deputy, was not compromised in July 1940. Instead, he was still able to play on his 'saving' of the city from destruction in June 1940, and by going into semi-retirement at the beginning of 1944 he claimed that he was 'seriously disobeying the Occupation authorities' and he was welcomed back as mayor almost as a hero. His authority was endorsed by General de Gaulle who visited the city on 22 August 1944, twelve days after its liberation, and again on 14 January 1945. Walking with the General down the Boulevard du Maréchal Foch, the Angevin equivalent of the Champs-Élysées, gave the eternal trimmer Bernier a new dose of legitimacy.[59]

Developments at Nantes and Saint-Nazaire also strongly contrasted. Their present mayors, Henri Orrion and Toscer, both appointed by Vichy, were declared ineligible, despite Orrion's valiant attempt to dig up some 'acts of resistance'. Socialist mayors and deputies Pageot and Blancho, who had both voted full powers to Pétain in 1940, appeared before the CDL of Loire-Inférieure on 19 October 1944 in the hope of having their ineligibility quashed. Each explained that he had voted for Pétain as the least of all evils in the dire circumstances. Pageot said that he had been arrested by the Germans, forced to resign and expelled to the Free Zone over the war memorial affair, but thereafter he had published a few articles in a collaborationist journal. Blancho was more successful in demonstrating his Resistance credentials, as one of the second batch of fifty hostages threatened with execution after the killing of the Feldkommandant of Nantes, for resigning as mayor after a row with Darlan, and finally for being an active member of the Liberation in the Nice area. Most important, however, he had the support of the SFIO both in the department and nationally as the natural leader of the working class in Saint-Nazaire and the only politician capable of keeping the communists at bay there.[60] Blancho duly returned to Saint-Nazaire as mayor after the Pocket was liberated. In Nantes, Clovis Constant, the post-office workers' leader and vice-president of the CDL, became mayor of a totally new muncipality at the end of August 1944, the old councillors being so faction-ridden that Debré insisted on starting with a clean slate.[61] He had to wait long months, however, for an endorsement from de Gaulle, who had not forgiven the city for refusing his award of the Croix de la Libération after the execution of the fifty hostages in 1941. It was not until 14 January 1945 that the General visited the city to make the award, and then offended Constant and the municipality by visiting the prefecture and the cathedral but not the Hôtel de Ville, leaving Nantes at two o' clock in the afternoon.[62] The precariousness of Constant's position was confirmed in 1947 when Henri Orrion, the Vichy mayor, swept back to power.

The 'Nantes model' of a completely new council was the dream of small liberation committees of resisters who found themselves pitted against municipalities stuffed with Pétainists who actually enjoyed the support of the majority of the population. The liberation committee of Ancenis was keen to purge the local council which took its cue from the Marquis de La Ferronnay's *Journal d'Ancenis*, and urged a new one composed of socialists, communists, radicals, Front National and trade unions. But Prefect Vincent argued that the clean slate at Nantes was undertaken for exceptional reasons and was not a model. He saw Ancenis as a 'right-wing town, where radicals look like the extreme left', and proposed a more balanced 'municipality of conciliation'.[63] In one or two similar towns existing mayors were toppled where charges of collaboration stuck, although they did not necessarily go quietly or forfeit local support. Alphonse Darmaillacq was confirmed as mayor of Cholet in September 1944, but then the communists, who wanted four seats on the municipal council but got two, accused the mayor of sending a young man to Germany on STO because he did not want him to marry his daughter. Try as he might to paint himself as 'the first resister of Cholet', as a mayor who had risked his life six or seven times to protect the townsfolk, Darmaillacq could not remove the smear and resigned as mayor and member of the *conseil général* at the beginning of 1945.[64] Prefect Fourré-Cormeray was reluctant to let him go, but was able to replace him by another rich Catholic industrialist, Bernard Pellaumail, who commanded just as much local support and had the advantage of sitting for a time on the CDL. Other small towns, however, were in effect the pocket boroughs of certain notables, and even if the administration wanted to break a habit the shortage of candidates to take on the challenge was manifest. The mayor of Vouvray, on the Loire just east of Tours, was Charles Vavasseur, president of Vichy's *conseil départemental*, who made huge profits selling sparkling wine to the Germans, frequent visitors to his cellars, thought Laval was a fine diplomat and de Gaulle soft on communism.[65] Prefect Vivier reported that he was 'moderate, traditionalist, 100 per cent Vichyssois', but an opportunist who had celebrated the Liberation and looked like rallying to the new order. It was difficult to find 'a citizen whose authority and republican and patriotic convictions make it possible to replace M. Vavasseur with any advantage'. From this case he extrapolated the general rule that 'it is very difficult to appoint a provisional municipal council that is at one and the same time republican, not polluted by Vichy, and commands the approval of the population'.[66]

The ability of mayors and municipal councillors to weather the Liberation as they weathered Vichy was thus considerable. Figures for Indre-et-Loire are incomplete but suggest that between 50 per cent and 60 per cent of mayors were confirmed in office at the Liberation. In Loire-Inférieure, where the Occupation had been more turbulent, 40 per cent of mayors were confirmed, although this proportion fell to 30 per cent in the *arrondissement* of Saint-Nazaire, which remained under Occupation until May 1945 and where purges were correspondingly greater. In Maine-et-Loire, however, which had remained cushioned from the worst of the Occupation, nearly three-quarters (73 per cent) of all mayors who had been in office under Vichy were confirmed at the Liberation.[67]

Such phenomenal tenacity requires an explanation. Often there were few resisters who could provide an alternative focus and even if there were they found it difficult to displace a notable who had controlled the *mairie* for years and whose networks of patronage were well established. Even the Liberation authorities were reluctant to remove them. The crusty radical–socialist Édouard Tardif, mayor of Longué in the Saumurois, felt compromised by his reign under Vichy and sent in his resignation, but he had the support of the whole municipal council and three-quarters of the population. The subprefect, who persuaded him to stay on, told him, 'I am surprised that an old fighter like you is thinking of abandoning a post that he has held so honourably for twenty years. More than ever the Republic needs men like you.'[68] In the Mauges, where the Vendée begins, the mayor of La Jumellière belonged to the Groupe Collaboration and the PPF, and his son had been killed fighting for the LVF on the Russian front. A member of the local liberation committee nevertheless argued, 'It would be difficult to find another mayor to set against him because he has the ear of those he administers and will be returned at the next elections. Besides, he is flexible enough to follow the new government.'[69]

Even when many formal changes did take place, as in Loire-Inférieure, the reality was often rather different. Derval near Châteaubriant was run virtually as a seigneurial regime and the CDL was persuaded by the communist Bernier to arrest the mayor, Comte Hay de Slade, a millionaire *châtelain*, as a collaborator. This was in the teeth of a warning from Olivier de Sesmaisons, who said he was a great 'notability' and veteran of 1914–18, whose arrest would provoke an explosive reaction in the department.[70] The CDL sent in two emissaries who arrived with the subprefect of Châteaubriant only to find that the mayor's deputy, described as a recruiting sergeant for the Francists, had whipped in the peasants, telling them, that 'Two communists from Nantes have come to expel the mayor. If you are good Catholics, come and defend him.' When the emissaries arrived on 23 September they were met at the town hall by 150 angry people, most of them the mayor's farmers and labourers, shouting 'Down with communists! Down with hooligans! Down with outsiders! Long live the mayor! Locals must keep the town hall!' The emissaries were beaten up as they tried to leave. Hay de Slade congratulated his tenants, delighted that the CDL had been taught a lesson. He was dismissed as mayor but continued to open the mail and to give orders in conjunction with the curé as if he were still in office. A local doctor, councillor and member of the humiliated local liberation committee reflected that 'Cagoulards and curés are dictators in this region [*pays*].'[71]

The grip of local notables was demonstrated also by the reform of departmental assemblies in the autumn and winter of 1944–5. Vichy's appointed *conseils départementaux* were abolished and the elected *conseils généraux*, suspended in 1940, were brought back. Under the original republican legitimacy rules those who had accepted nomination to Vichy's departmental councils were not allowed to return to the *conseil général*, but this was soon felt to be too draconian, and in November 1944 it was decided that members of the *conseils départmentaux* would be allowed to rejoin their *conseil général* if they had been elected to them before 1940. As a result, the membership of the *conseils généraux* restored in 1944–5 bore a striking resemblance to those which had been abolished in 1940: 50 per cent (18/36, not including 10 in the Saint-Nazaire Pocket) of the *conseil général* of 1945 was carried over from 1940 in

Loire-Inférieure, and 50 per cent (12/24) in Indre-et-Loire. Again, however, continuity was highest in Maine-et-Loire where the figure was 59 per cent (20/34).

In terms of personalities Indre-et-Loire saw the return of radical–socialist notables such as Gounin to Amboise and Dr Guillaume-Louis to Montbazon. Two more radical–socialists, Jollit, mayor of Azay, and Dr Labussière, of Chinon, were included even though they had been deported to Germany; Labussière was in fact already dead. Camille Aron, unceremoniously expelled from his Château-Renault seat as a Jew by Vichy, duly took it up again.[72] Conservative nobles were still a powerful force on the *conseil général* of Loire-Inférieure: the Marquis de Sesmaisons at La Chapelle-sur-Erdre, the Comte de Landemont at Ancenis, François Le Cour Grandmaison at Vertou, the Comte Ferdinand de Charette at Saint-Julien de Vouvantes.[73] Maine-et-Loire had its quota of long-serving conservatives such as François de Polignac at Chemillé, Jean de Geoffe at Doué-la-Fontaine, Jean de Jourdan at Segré, and Jacques de la Grandière, excused his membership of Vichy's Conseil National because his son was in de Gaulle's entourage, at Le Lion d'Angers. Henri de Champagny was kept on at Vihiers, although he was in a German concentration camp. Victor Bernier was brought back for Angers NW and recycled radical–socialists in the Saumurois included Édouard Tardif at Longué, Jean Herard at Noyant and the veteran Robert Amy at Saumur, where he had also recovered the town hall.[74]

One of the reasons given by the Liberation administration for only a limited remodelling of municipal councils and *conseils généraux* was the conservatism of local populations, indebted as they were to the local notables who (in most cases) had protected their interests during the Occupation. What the electorate actually felt was not tested until a wave of elections in 1945: municipal elections on 29 April and 13 May, cantonal for the *conseils généraux* in September, and general elections to the Constituent Assembly in October. Many new factors came into play in these elections. Women, who had been prevented from voting in the Third Republic not least because they were seen as electoral fodder for the Church and thus for the Right, were given the vote, if only as a counterweight to the communists. There was a general sense that some contribution to the Resistance should be a condition of seeking election, and many electoral lists were based on Resistance groupings rather than party affiliations.

On the other hand, political parties whether old or new – such as the Christian Democratic Mouvement Républicain Populaire (MRP) – were keen to restore the familiar rules of party politics and the primacy of party. Most important, there was a sense that change was needed and that the old political class, which had spent the last few years wheeling and dealing, trimming and second-guessing, was too tired and too compromised to lead the virginal Republic. This, more than anything else, explained the fact that despite (or even because of) the near anarchy of 1944, the change in political personnel was rather limited, whereas the return to orderly democratic politics in 1945 was more dramatic. This did not mean, however, that Right was displaced by the Left, for one of the most impressive features of this moment was the ability of the Right to rebrand itself in a world that, thanks to the Resistance, had created new rules.

In the municipal elections of April–May there were attempts in the large towns to construct joint socialist–communist lists under a Resistance banner. In Tours the great elector was Jean Meunier, leading light in Libération-Nord and president of the CDL as well as SFIO boss and outgoing mayor of Tours. He did a deal with Louis Salmon, briefly the communist mayor of Saint-Pierre-des-Corps at the Liberation, and secured the Hôtel de Ville for the socialists and communists, who acquired eleven seats.[75] In Angers, Victor Bernier was swept from power by a socialist–communist coalition and a bearded socialist, Alphonse Allonneau, finally replaced him as mayor. In Nantes the socialist old guard like Pageot and Prieur had been expelled from the party but new socialist Clovis Constant held on. The MRP made an excellent showing overall, less in anticlerical Indre-et-Loire than further west, where it took up the slack from Catholic conservatives compromised by Vichy and even conquered the radical fiefs of Saumur. The radical–socialist party, which had been the ruling party of the Third Republic and characterized the Ancien Régime that Vichy wanted to destroy, was now on the defensive.

There were, of course, exceptions to this pattern. Many voters still felt loyal to Vichy, feared the communists and trusted the local notables who had guided them through troubled times. There were a number of cases of politicians who had been declared ineligible under the rules of republican legitimacy who nevertheless put themselves forward for election and were elected, which obliged the authorities to invalidate the poll. Henri Mattraits, radical–socialist mayor of Chinon, who had been declared ineligible as a member of Vichy's departmental council, was massively re-elected by his townspeople, as we saw.[76] Dutertre de la Coudre, conservative mayor and deputy of Machecoul (Loire-Inférieure), rendered ineligible by virtue of his vote for Pétain in 1940, stepped into the elections in the second round and was re-elected mayor. He had not engaged in any active resistance, he told the prefect, which might have provided mitigating circumstances, 'because of the heavy occupation of the coast and hinterland, and because of the configuration of the landscape, flat, denuded of woods and forests and thus of any hiding place', but he had, as mayor, limited as far as possible German demands for Todt workers, STO conscripts, horses and potatoes. The municipal council backed him up, saying that he alone, mayor for thirty-eight years, had the necessary authority and 'spirit of reconciliation' and that 'the population of Machecoul would feel it cruelly if the plebiscite it has just declared in favour of M. Dutertre de la Coudre were set aside'.[77]

In these cases republican legitimacy overruled popular consent and the ineligibility of these tarnished politicians was upheld. Meanwhile, the popular vote continued to whittle away the old political class in the cantonal elections of September 1945. Only 26 per cent (12/46) of *conseillers généraux* of 1940 survived in Loire-Inférieure, 17 per cent (4/24) in Indre-et-Loire, and this time a mere 12 per cent (4/34) in Maine-et-Loire. The game was up for compromised local notables. This did not mean, however, a massive shift to the Left. The only communist councillor elected in the three departments was elected in Nantes, although another lost by only seventy-nine votes in Tours-Centre. The number of SFIO councillors rose from four in 1940 to six in Indre-et-Loire, from none to three in Maine-et-Loire, including Mayor Allonneau and one of his deputies, Germaine Canonne, the first woman to be elected to the *conseil général* in any of the three departments. The most significant decline was that of the radical–socialists, from six to two councillors in Maine-et-Loire and from fourteen to ten in their stronghold of Indre-et-Loire. Though Dr Guillaume-Louis, who had broadened his appeal by joining the Front National, was elected president of the new *conseil général*, he presided over a dying empire.

The most exciting party in the region was the MRP, which took two seats in Indre-et-Loire and five in Maine-et-Loire. In Angers NW the sempiternal Victor Bernier was defeated by Jean Sauvage, a thirty-five-year-old textile manufacturer who was diocesan president of the ACJF. Though Bernier 'knew everyone', he recalls, the MRP had a 'new dynamism' that was disseminated through the *Courrier de l'Ouest*, which he and his friends had founded.[78] The MRP took up the baton from the traditional Right, having the advantage of association with the Resistance, but the traditional Right itself was by no means done for. A solid phalanx of the old guard, still influential in the countryside, weathered the return to democracy. In Maine-et-Loire the likes of Jean de Jourdan and Jean de Geoffre still clung on, while at Beaupréau Pierre de Blacas succeeded his deceased father. In Loire-Inférieure Olivier de Sesmaisons, Ferdinand de Charette and Henri de Landemont were re-elected to the *conseil général*, while in the liberated Pocket Henri Le Cour Grandmaison was returned for Savenay. The success of the Right, just as much as that of the MRP, however, was due to a new generation of conservatives who had not been blatantly compromised by association with Vichy and had even won some credit from the Resistance. In Maine-et-Loire René Le Bault de la Morinière, who had built up the Catholic conservative group on the CDL and the liberation committee of Cholet, was elected for Champtoceaux in the Mauges; later he would become the Gaullist deputy of Cholet. In Loire-Inférieure Jacques Chombart de Lauwe, alias Colonel Félix, now mayor of Herbignac, achieved his dream of succeeding Count Hubert de Montaigu as *conseiller général* of Herbignac, and now set his eyes on the Constituent Assembly.[79]

These developments were confirmed in the elections to the Constituent Assembly on 21 October 1945. The elections were organized on a list system, under proportional representation, giving a good reflection of the share of the vote but making it difficult for politicians used to cultivating a local clientele. One communist was elected in Indre-et-Loire, another in Loire-Inférieure. There were two SFIO deputies in Indre-et-Loire including Jean Meunier, two in Loire-Inférieure including Clovis Constant, and one in Maine-et-Loire (Alphonse Allonneau). The radical–socialists, who had been prised out of the towns of Touraine in the municipal elections and clung on to the countryside in the cantonal elections, now had no deputy elected to the Assembly from Indre-et-Loire, none from Maine-et-Loire either, and only one in Loire-Inférieure. The MRP made a breakthrough in Indre-et-Loire, neck and neck with the SFIO, both winning two seats, and romped home with three of the six seats in Maine-et-Loire. 'Ardently social,' its leader Charles Barangé told the *Courrier de l'Ouest*, 'it wants to offer something new while at the same time keeping its spirituality.'[80] In Loire-Inférieure, however, the MRP secured only one of the eight seats, since the Right clung on under the guise of the National and Republican Union. This union was the brainchild of Jacques Chombart de Lauwe, a repackaged Right with a list headed by a Resistance hero, General Audibert. Audibert was nevertheless a Resistance leader in the mould of the conservative west, a large landowner, head of the Clisson section of La Rocque's Parti Social Français in the 1930s, leader of the Armée Secrète in Brittany and the Loire valley, deported to Buchenwald in 1943, repatriated to a hero's welcome in April 1945. He somewhat outrageously attacked the programme of the Conseil National de la Résistance (CNR) as 'neither national . . . nor resistant', drawn up, he said, by émigrés who had no mandate from anyone.[81] Meanwhile Chombart de Lauwe kept up a massive barrage in his *Avenir de l'Ouest* to clear the terrain for the Right, attacking the radical–socialists as 'responsible for the moral decomposition of the country between 1918 and 1939', the MRP as 'intended to divide Catholics and nationalists', and the communists as stooges of Moscow, which meant 'dictatorship, a dictatorship similar to Nazi dictatorship, slavery'.[82] Audibert, Chombart de Lauwe and the faithful Marquis Olivier de Sesmaisons were elected from the department to fight the good fight of the Right in the era of the Cold War.

It becomes clear that the heroic profile of the Liberation has in many instances to be revised. The Forces Françaises de l'Intérieur, commonly portrayed as freedom fighters, were often ill disciplined and as likely to prey on their fellow French as on embattled Germans. Much is doubtless explained by the warlike context of the summer of 1944, but there is no doubt that they proved a headache for local councils, prefects and even the regular military itself. These elements were desperate to ensure as peaceful a transition as possible from one order to the next. At the same time those who might have been compromised by association with Vichy or the Germans were keen to recycle themselves as good patriots. For these reasons the Liberation did not see the dramatic break in French politics and society that might be expected. Summary justice gave way to formal courts which were reluctant to try to convict more than a minority of those who might be accused of collaboration. The economy now produced for the Allied war effort rather than for the German, but above all the economy needed to turn over with as little disruption as possible so that business leaders suffered little from the purges. Government had to continue at the regional and local as well as at the national level. The continuity of the state at the centre was reflected in the continuity of the state locally, but a local approach also reveals the tremendous continuity of local notables who carried influence in their communities. Only the elections of 1945 saw a sea change in political personnel, and even then this was not accompanied in the Loire area by a marked shift from Right to Left. One of the extraordinary stories of this region was the ability of the Right to rebrand itself in order to prepare for the next political challenge: the defence against communism. However skilfully political continuity was managed, however, there were huge expectations of freedom and plenty among French people, and those expectations were all too often disappointed.

16. DISAPPOINTMENT

It is a truth universally acknowledged that French people danced in the streets at the Liberation. Along with French women embracing American soldiers who passed through their towns and villages, this gesture captured in numerous images encapsulates the sense of joy that swept the country as the yoke of German Occupation was lifted.[1] What is less appreciated was that dancing remained formally prohibited until the end of hostilities in May 1945. The liberation of France merely opened the way to France rejoining the Second World War and there was much serious fighting yet to be done. Moreover, while French territory had been liberated there were over 2 million French people in German POW, labour and concentration camps, and there was a widespread feeling that it was in very poor taste for some to make merry while so many more remained separated from and fearful for their loved ones. This induced an ambivalence and confusion which was nicely articulated by Albert Chevalier-Valin, a musician from a village just outside Saumur, where he had his instruments confiscated by three gendarmes at an illegal dance on 6 January 1945:

> I would like to protest strongly about the action taken against me given that people are dancing everywhere, I repeat EVERY-WHERE. Do you need proof? The same evening that we were caught there was a big dance in the cinema of Longué and posters had even been put up. Recently dances have taken place at Fontevrault, Montsoreau and Parnay, with the acquiescence of the gendarmerie of Fontevrault, and gendarmes even attended the dance at Turquant . . . I have played regularly for the the Maquis-ards and then the FFIs in the woods of Breille and Vernantes . . . Here, in Maine-et-Loire, which is not perhaps the same France as

360

Paris, all requests to hold dances are systematically turned down
... The Fourth Republic has brought back the motto 'Liberty,
Equality, Fraternity', but are we to believe that it is just to adorn
the pediments of public buildings?[2]

It is true that this was a thorny issue and that there was an
inconsistency about public policy. Dancing was not only for pleasure
but highly profitable, tied into the black market and an obvious way
for peasants and traders to sell their food and wine at high prices. A
sixty-year-old farmer, Henri Fefeu, who owned the barn in which
Chevalier-Valin was playing that night, was indicted not only for
organizing an illegal ball but for opening a bar without a licence, for
selling bread without exchanging it for ration tickets, and for clandestine pig-killing to make rillette sandwiches.[3] There was massive
pressure to dance not only from locals but from FFIs, regular soldiers
and passing Americans who were less ready to take no for an answer.
When the Saumur gendarmerie raided an illegal dance that had been
organized by the NCOs of the Cavalry School, a sergeant asked,
'Why are dances allowed at Château-du-Loir [Sarthe] and not here?'
and then answered his own question: 'Because the prefect is an idiot
(*con*) and the subprefect too. If there is a fine, just send the bill to de
Gaulle who is my boss. No one is going to stop us from dancing.'[4]
Whereas under the Occupation dancers tended to scatter when the
gendarmerie arrived, now they were reluctant to leave and, reinforced
by soldiers from the Division Leclerc, were in a position to win a
stand-off.[5] Mayors were squeezed between the requirement to
enforce the law and the need to keep the local community happy,
and even the gendarmerie who hailed from those communities were
reluctant to be tough. An anonymous burgher of Charcé complained
to the subprefect of Saumur that dancing that had gone on three
evenings in a row was 'an insult to France's suffering and the three
million prisoners and deportees who, alas, have no desire to dance.
What is the point of ministerial and prefectoral bans?' Even the
father of one of the Saumur gendarmes, he continued, had told
the mayor not to worry about letting the dances go ahead, because
the gendarmerie were in the picture.[6] The confiscation of Chevalier-
Valin's instruments was part of a new clampdown which recognized
that fines of 100 francs were not enough, and that 'the organization
of clandestine dances in the region seems to be on the increase'.[7] On

14 March 1945 the prefect of Maine-et-Loire renewed the ban, but the pressure on the floodgates was almost irresistible. Even the government came to permit exceptions to the ban in certain cases, such as charity balls where money was being raised for POWs and deportees, traditional balls celebrating national or local festivals, and dances organized by Resistance groups and army units, but global permission for dancing was not finally granted until 7 May 1945.

This approach by the government may seem to have been unduly mealy-mouthed, but it was perfectly true that for many people the war was not over. Only 200 kilometres from Saumur and, more to the point, only 20 kilometres from Nantes, the German Occupation still continued. Bouvron, whose curate, the Abbé Ploquin, had recruited a number of local youths for the Maquis of Saffré, and whose villagers hoisted the tricolour on the *mairie* on 9 August, found themselves reoccupied by the Germans on 12 August and on the front line of a pocket bounded by the Vilaine river in the north and then, switching south-east, by the Brest–Nantes canal. Many of the urban population of Saint-Nazaire had long since been evacuated to Touraine, but there remained 125,000 inhabitants of the town, its hinterland and the Guérande peninsula famous for its salt-marshes, who seemed not to have been invited to the Liberation party and for whom occupation by 25,000 German soldiers would last another nine months.[8]

No doubt it was not the same proud and good-looking army that had marched into the region four years previously. On the contrary, 'it was a pathetic army', noted Abbé Verger, curé of Guenrouet, another occupied village on the canal 20 kilometres from Bouvron. 'Drawn and haggard faces, limbs worn out by tiredness, boney horses, unbelievable vehicles, the remains of a routed army. Spectators nodded their heads as they watched them and said, "We know all about that: now it's their turn!"'[9] Now that the main theatre of operations had moved elsewhere, and the Germans could expect to be held responsible for any ill-treatment to French citizens under international law, Franco-German relations were tolerable and not without humour. At Guenrouet the ambition of the commander, Lieutenant Scharnhorst, was to be allowed to play the church harmonium. Since the curé would not give way, his adjutant, a Viennese called Theo Damm, requisitioned a piano for him on his birthday. Damm was no saint, and was even caught killing the curé's rabbits, but he was a popular figure with the locals and, with his green Luftwaffe trousers and stripy top made out of tent material, was nicknamed 'Peau de Grenouille'. Frustration was directed towards the FFIs and French troops who patrolled the frontier without launching any offensive, and the Americans, who turned their big guns on the church towers of the region because they made excellent lookout posts for the Germans. On 18 November 1944 they destroyed the church tower of Bouvron, and on 7 December that of Guenrouet. Lieutenant Scharnhorst and Theo Damm offered their sincere condolences to the mayor, and drank a glass of cognac with him, 'for good times and bad'.[10]

The pressing issue for both French and Germans was supply. Resources were limited and both sides wanted them. The farming communities near the canal were not badly off and suffered a good deal of plunder by the Germans but the *paludiers* of the salt marshes who did not grow crops or raise cattle were going hungry. Durables such as sugar, coffee, oil, soap, wood and matches were also scarce. Negotiations took place between the subprefect of Saint-Nazaire, Benedetti, and the German military authorities. It was agreed that the Germans would put an end to plunder and share out foodstuffs equitably so long as the French farmers handed goods over. The farmers, however, resumed their age-old ploy of hiding their produce, and the Germans now demanded the evacuation of many of the French population to allow more resources for them. This was not a direct Franco-German issue but one which divided the French military from the civil administration. The prefect and subprefect took the Germans' point about the welfare of the population, but the French military had no wish to make the lot of the Germans easier. Nor did the local population want to move, for fear of having their empty properties and farms pillaged. A compromise was worked out whereby 10,000 of the population would be evacuated if they so wished, and a supply train would go to the Pocket once a month. A first batch of evacuees from the hard-pressed Guérande peninsula arrived at Nantes on 23 October, and a first supply train went to the Pocket on 30 December, returning with a load of salt. Far from being sympathetic to the plight of their fellow citizens in the Pocket, the overwhelming view of the Nantais was that they should sort themselves out (*'qu'ils se débrouillent'*), and farmers were reluctant to provide dairy products that might still go to feed the Germans. It was even rumoured that the salt train was to supply black marketeers in the west of France.[11]

The management of the Pocket was a good episode in Franco-German cohabitation and a good example of negotiation in time of war. Liberation came eventually on 11 May 1945 when, in the middle of a poppy-field at Bouvron, General Junck handed over his pistol to the US General Kraemer, flanked by the French General Cholmel, and formally surrendered. Now the local inhabitants could experience the joy their fellows had savoured months before, although the liberation of the Pocket brought credit to neither French FFIs and soldiers nor the local population. FFIs forced German soldiers to drag them in carriages around Saint-Nazaire, while the local inhabitants threw stones at them as open goods trucks ferried them away to POW camps.[12] General Cholmel's Army of Liberation in fact behaved no differently from any other Army of Occupation, moving into the holiday villas on the coast at La Baule and loading furniture and kitchen equipment into military lorries for their own use. Even a herd of cows at La Baule airfield, requisitioned by the Germans, was seized by the French military as booty instead of being returned to farmers. The prefecture noted sadly that 'pillaging is even worse than when the Germans were here'.[13]

The partial evacuation of the Pocket of Saint-Nazaire in 1944–5 was only another episode in the drama of evacuation that had started with the bombings of Lorient, Nantes and Saint-Nazaire in 1942–3 and continued with the Normandy landings of June 1944. For the Allied landings and bombardment of Norman towns drove columns of refugees away from the coast, many of them crossing Anjou and Loire-Inférieure on their way south. The mayors of Baugé and Noyant complained at the beginning of August that 'a wave of 600 to 800 homeless per day is exhausting local resources, using about 40 per cent of the horses that are currently needed for the harvest, and leaving a local population that has plenty of goodwill completely overwrought'.[14] In November local communities were warned to expect a new wave of evacuees from the Pocket of Saint-Nazaire and appeals were made to their sense of 'solidarity'. Many towns and villages were willing to make another effort, but there were also clear signs of refugee fatigue. One mayor in the Mauges said that 'We have already made a huge effort for two months for the refugees from the Calvados. We had seventy refugees while many neighbouring communes had none at all.' Another mayor of a village near Baugé said that they had recently looked after fifty-six people fleeing from Normandy with no possessions at all. 'We had to give them so much that our capacity to give is now much diminished, not to say exhausted.'[15]

The displacement of populations as a result of the war was a problem that long outlasted the Liberation and was still there after the war ended. In July 1945 there were still 15,000 refugees in Indre-et-Loire and 16,000 in Maine-et-Loire, but there were 150,000 in Loire-Inférieure in May 1945, and 100,000 in October. About two-thirds of displaced persons received some kind of benefit, either as evacuees or victims of bomb damage (*sinistrés*), but there were generally delays in the payment of benefits. A spokesman for 7–8,000 refugees in Vertou, a suburb of Nantes, asked in September for the benefit due in July and August to be paid, especially as local traders were still charging high prices, even though German requisitions had ceased and the harvest was in.[16] Meanwhile the pressure on accommodation was extremely severe, and refugees found themselves competing for a roof with private landlords, businesses and the army. Working-class refugees from the Pocket who had been housed in a local château by the municipality of Rézé, another suburb of Nantes, were told that they had to vacate the premises by 1 April 1945 as it was needed by the army for barracks.[17] The liberation of the Pocket of Saint-Nazaire in May 1945 should have eased the problem, but ruined Saint-Nazaire looked like a moonscape and pressure for food and accommodation simply shifted to La Baule and other resorts. Homeless Nazairians living in La Baule marched on the subprefecture in August 1945 to demand better supplies of milk, potatoes and meat, and back rations of sugar and tobacco that they had not been able to enjoy while the Pocket was still occupied.[18] Refugees on the coast had to compete with the army, industries like SNCASO and the Chantiers de Penhouët that were starting up again and needed to house their workforces, and the owners of holiday villas who wanted to rent them out for the season.[19] Those still bearing the scars of the war were thus pitted against those who now wanted a return to pleasure and profit. The Saint-Nazaire evacuees based at Saint-Brévin-les-Pins, a resort on the other side of the Loire estuary from the port, responded to these pressures by forming an association which met 800 strong in a local cinema to defend their interests.

They were still there in the spring of 1946, representing 4,500 refugees, writing to their local deputy to protest at 'the offensive of landlords who are using all means to try to recover their properties in time for the summer season'.[20]

While the homecoming of evacuees and bomb victims was slow and difficult, the return of POWs, STO workers and deportees happened fairly quickly in the spring of 1945, as German territory was conquered and camps thrown open. The joy felt as they were reunited with family and friends soon gave way, however, to anger and resentment when the reality of their condition struck home.[21] On 24 June 1945 a meeting of recently returned POWs at the Apollo Theatre, Nantes, became a demonstration of about 1,000 people in front of the prefecture. Regretting that their first meeting had not been 'the great emotional ceremony we had dreamed about in the camps', they now expressed their 'bitterness and disappointment'. Their demands included an increase in the compensation payable for every year spent in captivity to 3,000 francs, an increase from 1,650 to 4,000 francs in the pay for the single month's leave they were allowed on their return, and clothes and shoes to help them to rejoin civilian life.[22] The association of POWs of Rézé turned down an invitation from the prefect of Loire-Inférieure to attend a Grande Kermesse de Retour in August 1945, with music, dancing, sport and fireworks on the grounds that 'after five years of harsh captivity which has not generally been understood by those who have not gone through it, the POWs have returned depressed, most of them without resources, to a France where the black market is the norm and they have had enormous problems recovering their housing, jobs and income'.[23] The predicament of POWs in Nantes was contrasted not only with the wealth of the black marketeers but with the ease of German POWs at Saint-Nazaire, described by the wife of a French POW as 'reclining on deck chairs on their old boats, sunbathing or fishing'.[24] Another comparison made by the POWs of Tours was with the new French army. A thousand of them marched on the prefecture on 4 August 1945 with placards saying 'We want clothes' and 'We want shoes', having met at the Chamber of Commerce to denounce the beautiful new uniforms of the French army, and reminding the government that they too had been proud soldiers once.[25]

Had all those who had somehow been displaced stuck together

they might have been able to defend their interests more effectively. The provisional government saw things that way and from the end of 1943 in Algiers set up a Commissariat (later Ministry) for Prisoners, Deportees and Refugees to manage the repatriation of prisoners of war, of STO workers, of deportees, of French evacuees from combat zones and of foreign nationals. It organized a week to remember and collect funds for all those absent for Christmas between 23 December 1944 and 1 January 1945, and proposed that 14 July 1945 be dedicated to all the dead of the war and the Resistance, celebrating 'the equality of prisoners, deportees and resisters'. The message, as passed on by the prefect of Maine-et-Loire, was to exalt 'the sense of union that exists between those who fell in the fighting and those who came back'.[26]

Unfortunately, the rapprochement between the different groups did not last long. To begin with, quarrels soon broke out over the benefits allotted to each category. Returning STO workers in Touraine were incensed to receive double rations for only three months, whereas POWs and political deportees received them for six months. The political deportees of Maine-et-Loire protested that POWs were getting an additional coal ration, while they were not. 'What happened to the fine promises made when we returned?' asked their spokesman. 'Everything was promised to these miserable survivors of the Nazi hell, but until now they have received nothing.'[27]

Competition for material benefits, important though they were, was one way of expressing a much more powerful competition for honour. Honour was accorded after the Liberation to those who were deemed to have contributed most to that Liberation through participation in the Resistance. Those with greater Resistance credentials tried to separate themselves from those whose claims were less obvious or less secure, creating a hierarchy with heroes at the top, villains at the bottom, and all sorts of gradations in between. Disappointment was therefore felt by those who, though they had suffered for France and behaved like 'good Frenchmen', were told that their contribution had not been enough.

At the top of the pyramid were the political deportees. In the municipal elections of April–May 1945 political deportees came top of the poll, even if they had not yet touched French soil, like Dr Leccia of Bléré, or, indeed, like Dr Labussière of Chinon who, unknown to the electorate, was already dead. Welcoming Dr Leccia and others, Jean Meunier, stalwart of Libération-Nord, president of the CDL of Indre-et-Loire and mayor of Tours, called them 'among the most heroic of our absentees'. He organized a meeting in the municipal theatre at which Dr Leccia talked about Dachau, General Chasles about Buchenwald and Mme Fournier about Auschwitz, an event that was said to have 'made a vivid impression on the Tours public'.[28]

Heroes and heroines they may have been, but they were keen to keep their kudos to themselves. Early in 1944 a National Movement of Prisoners of War and Deportees (MNPGD) was set up to bring together POWs, STO workers and political deportees sent to concentration camps, using the motto: 'They are united, do not divide them!'[29] Political deportees were organized into a National Federation of Patriotic Deportees and Internees, which was affiliated to the MNPGD, but those who had been deported for 'acts of Resistance' wanted to distinguish themselves from those who had been deported simply for being communists, and set up a separate National Federation of Deportees and Internees *of the Resistance* (FNDIR) to 'defend the ideal and the spirit of the Resistance'. This, it has to be admitted, was also basically a non-communist and even anti-communist organization, which demonstrated a deep rift that ran through the heart of the Resistance.[30]

The political deportees, communist or non-communist, could nevertheless agree on one thing, that they were superior to those who had been conscripted for work in Germany under the *Relève* or STO. The latter set up organizations of labour deportees, and founded reviews with titles like *Forced Labour*, but the political deportees fought hard to deny them the right to call themselves deportees. Because some workers had gone to work voluntarily, a question mark always hung over *Relève* or STO workers who were judged to have had a choice as to whether to go or not. The Vichy labour inspector of Indre-et-Loire, Dos, summoned before the purging commission of the CDL, argued that workers were 'perfectly free to go or not' under the *Relève*, and that the relatively high ratio of STO departures in the department was explained by 'the apathy of Tourangeaux'. This may have been true or it may have been to rebut charges that he had conscripted labour under German authority. At any rate the CDL seemed to appreciate his argument, and Dos got away with simply being transferred to another department.[31] Volunteer workers, of course, were considered to be collaborators, and ran the risk of being interned or lynched on their return. But the ability of *Relève* and STO conscripts to resist was constantly emphasized by political deportees who repeatedly frustrated the campaign of the former to be recognized as 'labour deportees'.

Prisoners of war returning after an absence of nearly five years, far from being acclaimed as heroes, were virtually ignored. They had enjoyed almost a cult status under the Vichy government, which had acclaimed them as pure patriots who had paid a heavy price for the military and psychological unpreparedness of the Third Republic and for whom the civilian population must now make sacrifices. Once Vichy had gone, however, their fortunes changed. 'It seems that people want to forget us, to obliterate us,' complained a spokesman for a group of POWs in Tours in September 1944, pointing out that they had not been invited to the great celebrations of the Liberation. One reason, he surmised, was that many of those who had returned during the Occupation had been dragooned into the Pétainist cause and identified with Vichy.[32] Another reason, however, was that the POWs were the incarnation of the worst defeat in French history, shamed by comparison with their fathers who had won the Great War, and a constant reminder of national inferiority.

At the bottom of the hierarchy, in 1945 at least, were the Jews. Administratively they were almost invisible, known at best as 'racial deportees'. The vast majority, of course, did not return from the camps. Some, like Émile Aron, who had been dismissed under the Statut des Juifs and fled to the Free Zone early in 1942 to escape being arrested as a hostage, returned to Tours and managed to recover both his job and, after a court case, his family property of La Chauvinière, near Château-Renault.[33] As a notable in Tours society, he wielded a certain influence and could make the new law nullifying 'acts of despoilment undertaken by the enemy or under his control' work for him. Others were less fortunate. Three Jews who had entrusted their furnished property to the Tours firm of Coutancin-Chatry were told that it had been sold, because the firm did not expect them to come back.[34] Businesses that had been liquidated, moreover, were almost impossible to recover. The agenda of surviving Jews was to rebuild their lives as individuals and families rather than to promote the cause of the Jewish people, which did not happen for another thirty years. Anti-Semitism had not evaporated just because of the suffering of the Jews. Only a month before the liberation of Nantes, in July 1944, *Le Phare* was holding forth about 'the invasion of the Yids' and concluded that 'there is no place on our soil for the wandering Jew'.[35]

Disappointment was felt not only by those who had been displaced and had returned to a home that did not regard them as heroes but also by communities which had doggedly lived out the Occupation and hoped for something better after the Germans had gone. The most fundamental issue was bread. Now that the Germans were no longer there to requisition foodstuffs for their own needs it was felt that there should be more than enough for the French. The Vichy system of strict price controls, requisitioning on behalf of both Germans and the urban population and distribution agencies, would cease. The free market would be restored, supplied automatically to the satisfaction of both producers and consumers, and the black market would simply wither away.

Unfortunately, all this remained a pipe dream. Within weeks of the Liberation a petition was addressed to the prefect of Maine-et-Loire by 873 blue- and white-collar workers from the iron mines, tannery, sawmill and railway works of Segré asking why prices were still rising. Bread had gone up from 3 francs 80 to 4 francs a kilo, they said, butchers were buying animals for 16 francs a kilo and selling the meat for 70–80 francs a kilo, while charcutiers were selling pork for 90–100 francs a kilo. 'Is it necessary for the recovery of our country', they enquired, 'that traders in general continue to accumulate fortunes?'[36] They demanded strict price controls, but strict price controls and delivery quotas made producers reluctant to supply the market. The peasantry had become used to being embattled in a closed economy, hiding their wares from prying Germans or Ravitaillement (Food Supply) officials, and selling it on their own terms to the highest bidder. At the end of August the new prefect in Maine-et-Loire issued an 'Appeal to the peasants', pointing out that quotas were now imposed for the benefit of French people only and calling for 'patriotism' and 'solidarity' with urban consumers. Milk was in particularly short supply, and urgently required for 'children, women and old people'.[37] The following month, as the Vichy administration had done in 1942, he wrote to the bishop of Angers, Mgr Costes, asking him to support the campaign in his next pastoral letter.[38] By October, when milk deliveries had still not improved, the subprefect of Cholet switched from blandishments to threats, using the language of French revolutionaries. 'The names of the guilty parties have already been noted,' he told the mayors of the Mauges who as usual were particularly recalcitrant. 'Those who starve the towns (*les affameurs des villes*) will be treated like collaborators and interned with them. Heavy fines will be imposed on bad Frenchmen who oppose a just distribution of the country's resources.'[39]

Politics, religion and class may all have set some landowners and peasants against the new regime, but the main reason for their lack of cooperation was the beckoning of the black market, with lorries coming from as far away as Paris to scour the countryside for supplies. As Christmas approached, traffickers came to Touraine to buy geese, turkeys and other poultry at inflated prices that only the rich could pay. *La Nouvelle République* argued that a gulf was opening up between workers and small employees who could afford very little and 'the privileged' who were now, in easier times, openly flaunting their wealth. The problem was one of distribution as well as price. Very few vehicles were available for the official collection and delivery of quotas but, observed a Tours police chief who thought the food supply situation worse than it had ever been since 1940, 'the lorries of the black market pound up and down, never stopped and never checked, even though most bridges are still down and all the traffic has to cross the few that remain'. Just to make sure, the big restaurants in Paris were using army lorries which the gendarmerie would not dare look into.[40]

Unless officials were simply incompetent, it is a fair assumption that corruption was still rife. The Ravitaillement administration set up by Vichy was carried over at the Liberation, and had the dual reputation of harshness and corruptibility. The common assumption was that small fry were dealt with mercilessly, but the bigger the crook, the easier it was for him to corrupt the administration. Intendant Rouleau, the head of Vichy's Ravitaillement administration in the region with a reputation for militaristic brutality, was brought before the Cour de Justice in Angers, but his patriotic conduct was vouched for by his colleagues and former Regional Prefect Donati, and he was acquitted in June 1945.[41] M. Le Bonhomme, head of Ravitaillement in Indre-et-Loire, was said to be protecting a number of large black-market operators.[42] Opinion in Touraine was reassured when he was suspended in December 1944 and left his job the following January, but aghast when in February he was brought back to run another branch of the Ravitaillement. His reputation was a factor in the troubles that broke out in Tours at the end of the year, which we shall look at shortly.

One instrument available to the administration to clamp down on those who had made corrupt fortunes during the Occupation and since were the aptly named Committees to Confiscate Illicit Profits set up in each department under a law of 18 October 1944. These might have done excellent work clawing back some of the fortunes made on the black market, but at the highest level it seems that the Ministry of Finance did not want them to be too tough. CDLs were allowed to nominate three individuals per department, and the committees were not allowed to include anyone from commercial and industrial milieux, including lawyers. But they were dominated by tax officials who, in the opinion of the CDL of Maine-et-Loire, did not have 'the necessary repressive mentality to carry out effectively the task entrusted to them'.[43] In addition they lacked teeth, unable to intern suspects to stop them concealing their gains, or to have access to bank accounts bursting with German payments. When Commissaire Debré wrote to the Finance Ministry about these shortcomings he was told sharply that no one else had complained.[44] As a result, while two millers, a grain merchant, three wine merchants, a butcher, a builder, a garagist, a painter and decorator, a shoemaker, a hotelier, a stallholder and a rag-and-bone man went before the Indre-et-Loire committee between March and October 1945, these were relatively small-time crooks. A Vouvray producer had 334,000 francs confiscated, and a certain Szabo had 9 million francs confiscated and a fine of 27 million francs imposed for 'important black-market activities', but his was the only case in that league.[45]

If those who wanted to purge corruption at the Liberation were disappointed, so also were those who wanted to break down the autarky of the farmers by abolishing Vichy's Peasant Corporation and set up something that would make agriculture more responsive to the needs of the towns. The Peasant Corporation was duly abolished, and the new minister of agriculture who took over in September 1944, Pierre Tanguy-Prigent, was a Breton socialist who wanted to replace it by another single union, the General Confederation of Agriculture (CGA), in which practising farmers rather than rentier landowners were represented. Collaborators and Pétainists were to be excluded as far as possible, and responsibility given to those who had stayed clear of partisan conflicts and had proved their professional competence.[46]

In each department a Departmental Committee of Agricultural Action (CDAA) was set up to prepare the new organization, but what was striking was the continuity of personnel. In Loire-Inférieure Raymond Lefeuvre, former president of the Peasant Corporation in the department and member of its national council, was arrested in February 1945 but then released, the administration admitting an 'error'.[47] The weight in the CDAA shifted from landowners to practising farmers, but Olivier de Sesmaisons was still there as secretary, and only three of the nineteen members, from the CDL or Front National, had any Resistance credentials.[48] The CDAA of Maine-et-Loire decided by eight votes to two, on the proposition of a token agricultural labourer on the committee, to ban Henri Dèze, Vichy's regional syndic, who had belonged to Dorgères' Parti Agraire and was suspected of collaboration, from any responsible post in agriculture for five years.[49] Eugène Forget, however, who regarded Dèze as innocent of all collaboration and himself survived a 3–7 vote on whether he should be banned, was singled out by Tanguy-Pringent as the obvious leader of what the CGA became in March 1946, at its Paris congress, namely the National Federation of Farmers' Unions (FNSEA). Forget insisted that all parties, including the communists, be represented on its governing bureau, and demanded that all representatives to the congress take an Oath of Unity, on the lines of the Tennis Court Oath taken by the deputies to the Estates-General in 1789, to the effect that they would not adjourn until they had passed a new constitution.[50]

Agricultural leaders with a distinctly Pétainist background were thus able to put the unity demanded by Tanguy-Prigent to their own use and renew their grip on power. All this gave no advantage to the urban working and lower-middle classes who went just as hungry as before. Indeed, during the winter of 1945–6 it is possible to argue that they were hungrier than they had been during the Occupation. Certainly they were determined to vent that anger as never before, not only through trade unions and consumer organizations, but spilling beyond them into popular violence in scenes reminiscent of the French Revolution.

Faced by the rising cost of living, referred to now as in revolutionary times as *la vie chère*, the labour force launched a succession of strikes in pursuit of higher wages, to resist unreasonable productivity increases, to demand measures against the black market, the confiscation of war profits and the nationalization of trusts, much of which was promised in the programme of the CNR. Strikes took place not only in the industrial heartland of Nantes, where 10,000 of the engineering workers went on strike on 29 January 1945 and marched on the prefecture to deliver their demands, but in the much less industrialized and militant Anjou. In Trélazé, the industrial suburb of Angers, the slate-cutters went on strike on 17 October 1944, and 330 female match-makers refusing to work two machines instead of one were locked out.[51] When the Trélazé workers headed the May Day procession in Angers in 1945, 6,000 strong, shouting 'Death to Pétain!', 'Death to Hitler!', 'Death to the trusts!', the prefect realized that the CGT had parted company with the government.[52] By the end of the year civil servants were striking in Maine-et-Loire with the support of the CGT and the Catholic CFTC, and teachers went on strike in Loire-Inférieure.

Alongside the traditional labour movement specially dedicated consumer organizations were now springing up. Consumer defence committees were set up in Tours in February 1945 and 7,000 demonstrated peacefully on 7 April, presenting their demands to the prefecture.[53] The police were not sanguine about the peacefulness persisting, however, especially with the price of bread going up. In October 1945 the government abolished bread rationing to promote optimism in time for the elections to the Constituent Assembly. This was a reckless gamble that depended on supply being adequate to meet demand. Unfortunately it was not, and in December, after the elections, bread rationing was reimposed and the daily ration cut from 350 to 300 grams.[54] This was like a spark to a gunpowder barrel. In Tours the CGT and Federation of Consumers called a demonstration for 29 December. Prefect Vivier met the organizers at 3 p.m. in an attempt to defuse the situation, but even they realized that they were losing their grip on the situation. Some wanted to burn the reissued bread-ration cards in public. Vivier had a poor opinion of the Consumers' leader, Martin, thinking him not very bright and putty in the hands of a communist named Marchais and women such as Mme Mauger who grabbed hold of a loudspeaker and shouted, '*Tous à la préfecture!*' The prefect described what happened next in terms worthy of Zola or Taine:

> The demonstration, which was disorganized, became a howling mob. It was made up of disorderly elements, the scum of Tours ... women, fishwives, youths foreign to the town and even to the region. The organizers were swept aside by determined agitators, prostitutes, young people seen in previous demonstrations [the Boucherie affair] ... former collaborators wanting to exploit popular discontent for political ends ... a few Trotskyists, even anarchists ... the pillage and vandalism was the result of a fermentation in consumers' milieux such as the housewives' committees of *quartiers* like the *quartier* Beaujardin which think that the Consumers' Federation itself is not militant enough.

Police, gendarmes and the recently formed CRS were in short supply because of the holiday period. The crowd of 6,000 invaded the prefecture, pillaging its archives and throwing them out of the window. It then went to the town hall and sacked the offices looking for ration cards. Finally it went to the Ravitaillement offices where it found more ration cards and burned them. Vivier was forced to bring in the army to guard grain and flour supplies and to issue a whole new edition of ration cards.[55]

The account of Vivier, normally a moderate and discreet man, is a reflection on the powerlessness he felt. He fell back on a conventional discourse to describe the mob in terms of outsiders, extremists, the rising flotsam and jetsam of the suburbs and above all bloodthirsty and immoral women, the heirs of the *tricoteuses* around the guillotine and the *pétroleuses* of the Paris Commune. The demonstration was frightening because it escaped the organizational channels of the trade unions and the Consumers' Federation. Whatever Vivier said about Martin, however, the Communist Party in fact disowned the violence and urged the public to be calm. Other evidence shows that the agitators, far from being scum, included a lieutenant in the air force and a number of soldiers; those arrested were all from Tours and included an apprentice baker aged sixteen, a pharmacy assistant aged nineteen, a young married woman (twenty-two), a thirty-nine-year-old labourer at the railway workshops, the manager of the La Paix café and his forty-nine-year-old waitress.[56] The importance of Vivier's outburst lies in his subjective perception that the Liberation had failed to meet popular expectations, so that the dancing in the streets that had welcomed the retreat of the Germans sixteen months before had become a witches' sabbath, a *danse macabre*, a world turned upside down and destroying any confidence that had been built between government and people.

The Liberation has frequently been been characterized as a moment of deliverance and hope, a time of reform and renewal,[57] but for many ordinary French people hopes were all too soon and to often disappointed. France did not suddenly become a land of freedom and plenty after the Germans left. War continued, and many restrictions that had been imposed by Vichy simply remained, as those who wished to dance, for example, discovered. Populations displaced by bombing raids and the Allied invasion were confronted by communities which had little more to give, materially or morally. Returning POWs, labour conscripts and deportees were welcomed with open arms but then found themselves competing for jobs, rations, benefits and not least recognition of what they had suffered. Even basic foodstuffs remained in short supply, the corruption and black marketeering of Occupied France continued after the Liberation, and bread riots of the winter of 1945–6 suggested a France more familiar to the revolutionary Jean-Paul Marat than to the architect of modernization, Jean Monnet.

17. MEMORIES

Paris! Paris violated! Paris broken! Paris martyrized! But Paris
liberated! Liberated by its own efforts, liberated by its people with
the help of the armies of France, with the help of the whole of
France, of fighting France, of the one and true France, of eternal
France![1]

Thus, at the Paris Hôtel de Ville on 25 August 1944, was announced
the gospel of the Resistance according to Charles de Gaulle. As the
General marched down the Champs-Élysées to cheering crowds, his
appeal of 18 June 1940 in which he had called upon the French
people not to accept defeat and armistice was somehow made flesh.
The fact that Paris crowds had turned out in force to cheer Marshal
Pétain only a few months before was studiously ignored; collaboration was brushed aside as the sin of 'a handful of wretches'. The
gospel declared that the Resistance had been pure and heroic and
the vast majority of French people had behaved under the Occupation
as 'bons Français'.They had been inspired by the eternal values of
France, of patriotism and the rights of man, and it was around these
values that union could now be reforged. Above all it was declared
that the French had liberated themselves by their own efforts. The
shame of defeat and the guilt of having obeyed the orders of a foreign
power were now redeemed by the act of self-liberation by which
dignity and honour were recovered. De Gaulle made virtually no
mention of the role played in the ongoing liberation of France by the
British and Americans, apart from a mildly patronizing reference to
the 'help of our dear and admirable Allies'. Liberation meant the
recovery of freedom, national unity and greatness under the leadership of Charles de Gaulle.

This gospel had a wonderful mythic power in the years after the Liberation. The French were only too pleased to accept their role as 'bons Français' and to present the smallest gestures as 'acts of resistance' which had contributed to the ultimate liberation of the country. And yet the gospel according to de Gaulle never achieved the consensus for which it was designed. Other versions, putting forward different heroes and different villains, vied for an audience. Rival interpretations of what had happened under the Occupation divided the French from each other and split communities. De Gaulle preached the primacy in the Resistance of the Free French who had been under his control in London or Algiers, over the internal Resistance – the Maquisards and the FFIs. Communists insisted that they had been the most dynamic force in the Resistance, the Party counting 75,000 martyrs to the cause. Others argued that the communists, by accepting the Nazi–Soviet Pact of 1939, had undermined the war effort in 1940 and subsequently made things worse in France by their strategy of violent resistance. These might be Gaullists, but they also might be Pétainists who argued that de Gaulle had taken an easy option by escaping to London, while Marshal Pétain, who had stayed in France to protect the French people, had embodied the real Resistance. Some local communities were desperate to promote their own heroes, however tenuous the connection, while others which had suffered collective reprisals as a result of Resistance activity in the vicinity had only victims to commemorate. Those who returned from deportation were also deeply divided. People who had been deported for 'acts of resistance' claimed to be more heroic than those who had been deported simply for political opinions, notably membership of the Communist Party. Both, meanwhile, were keen to reject the claims of labour conscripts to deportee status and to minimize the claim to special recognition of deported Jews. The fact that the persecution of the Jews and the French part in it took literally decades to come to light reflected the effectiveness with which groups speaking for the Resistance were able to impose their version of events. Once the Holocaust factor came into play, however, it swept all before it, forcing a full reconsideration of both Vichy and the Resistance.[2]

Attempts were made to fix interpretations of the Resistance by formal commemoration through the erection of monuments.[3] Such commemorations were also bids to achieve orthodox status for cults that might otherwise be considered marginal, even heretical. We have traced the shaping of collective memories by the commemoration of heroes and martyrs in the Loire region, but also listened to individuals whose private memories may or may not have coincided with the public memory. To a large extent, as we suggested in the introduction, private accounts are shaped by dominant narratives, but they also diverge either fully or at crucial points, and these privileged moments may allow the historian to glimpse alternative interpretations which have hitherto been marginalized or suppressed.

The tension between de Gaulle's gospel and that of the internal Resistance was in part a tension between a national perspective and local views. It also, however, expressed a conflict for the leadership of the Resistance between de Gaulle's Free French, whose main aim was to prevent the establishment of an Allied Military Government in France, and the internal Resistance, which often had political goals of its own. De Gaulle, both in and out of power, was a frequent guest of honour at the unveiling of local monuments to the Resistance, but his gloss on events was not necessarily the same as that of local protagonists. In 1965, for example, as President of the Republic, he visited Saumur on the twenty-fifth anniversary of the valiant attempt of the cadets of the Cavalry School between 19 and 21 June 1940 to hold up the German crossing of the Loire. He told a crowd of 10,000 that the heroic action of the school 'prefigured . . . the Liberation and victory'. This presentation of the fighting at Saumur as the first act of the drama of the Resistance was relatively recent. Not until the tenth anniversary in 1955 was a link made explicitly between the 'despairing heroism' of 19–21 June and 'the date of 18 June [1940], sublime in more ways than one', as if the Saumur combats had been a direct response de Gaulle's BBC appeal.[4] Under Vichy the bravery of the cadets had been likened to that of the forlorn heroes of 1870 or 1815. The subprefect of Saumur had compared the skirmish at the nearby farmhouse of Aunis to the fighting at the farm of La Haye Sainte on the battlefield of Waterloo 125 years before, 'almost day for day'.[5] The comparison with 1870 was also instructive, because although as in 1940 the war had been lost, pockets of heroism in the fight against overwhelming odds had allowed French honour to be saved. The difference was that after

1870 patriots spoke of revenge against Germany, whereas after 1940 the lesson drawn by Vichy was 'revenge against ourselves', an internal moral revolution.[6]

De Gaulle had been appearing at local commemorations of the Resistance since his departure from office in 1946, but always to stress French unity in the Resistance under his leadership. In 1950, for example, accompanied by General Audibert, commander of the Armée Secrète in Brittany and before a crowd of 50,000, he unveiled a huge monument at Saffré in honour of the Maquisards who fell when they were attacked by German forces on 28 June 1944. General Audibert duly proclaimed that the Maquisards had been replying to de Gaulle's appeal of 18 June and that although they had joined the battle at the end of the Occupation, they had played as important a role in the French victory as those who fought from the beginning. In particular he was keen to reject the idea that the thirteen Frenchmen who had died on the spot in Saffré and the twenty-seven who were shot later had made a 'useless sacrifice'. De Gaulle, for his part, insisted that 'the action of the Saffré combatants must not be separated from that undertaken against the occupier outside France by the Free French. Everything was part of a whole and made up our national defence.' He also underlined that the survivors of the battle who remembered their comrades must contribute to 'national solidarity and the unity of our people'.[7]

The nagging question that the Maquisards of Saffré had been victims rather than heroes was confronted again in 1967, on the twenty-fifth anniversary of the event, when General de Jussieu-Pontcarrel, national chief of staff of the FFIs, delighted his audience by citing Eisenhower's memoirs to the effect that the internal Resistance was worth five or six divisions to the Allies.[8] A glance at Eisenhower's memoirs, however, reveals that this reading was somewhat free. The only possible reference to such divisions refers to the Sixth Army Group under the US General Devers which drove up from the south of France. Eisenhower praised the Free French for their 'inestimable value in the campaign', but in fact criticized the Maquis as 'separate armed bands' which refused to be integrated into the regular army and were heavily subverted by communism.[9]

The group of survivors of the Maquis of Saffré whom I met in 1997 were certainly not subverted by communism. They exalted the fraternity of the Maquis and its ecumenical nature. 'You didn't ask your mates to which religion or political party they belonged,' said Pierre Hervé, president of the Comité du Souvenir. And yet further conversation revealed that the ecumenism of the Maquis was relative: most belonged to Catholic organizations of workers, peasants and students, and were informed by a discreet but well-founded anti-communism. 'You didn't take anyone,' clarified François Boudet, secretary of the Comité, 'but a dozen guys you had known from school.' They were reluctant to enrol communists, he confessed, because they were already known to the authorities and might talk under torture. It was also evident that there was no necessary con-nection between joining the Maquis in June 1944 and the appeal of 18 June. François Boudet admitted to saying '*Ouf*' (Phew!) when Pétain requested an armistice. Far from being a rootless outlaw, he had been a local officer or syndic of Vichy's Corporation Paysanne and on good terms with Lieutenant Laurens, the local German quarter-master; Laurens, he said, knew that he was in the Resistance, but did not betray him. The official cult of the Maquis of Saffré emphasized efficacy, unity and the response to de Gaulle, but private conversation even with the Maquisards themselves paints a more complex picture.[10]

The tension between the Gaullist version and the local version was also evident 25 kilometres west of Saffré in the village of Bouvron. Bouvron annually celebrates the end of the Second World War in Europe, which is uncontroversial, except that it claims that the war in Europe actually ended in their village on 11 May 1945 with the surrender there of the German general commanding the Pocket of Saint-Nazaire. The surrender was commemorated before a humble wooden cross of Lorraine until October 1949 when a magnificent stone monument was unveiled, announcing that the moment the Germans of the Pocket surrendered 'the whole of France was liber-ated'. In his speech General Larminat, commander of the FFIs on the Atlantic, paid homage to 'the agents of *réseaux*, saboteurs, Maquis-ards, FFI soldiers and regular soldiers who took over from our armies that had been torn to pieces'.[11] An official seal of approval for the myth was given in 1951 when General de Gaulle himself attended the event. As at Saffré, however, he was quick to deflate the preten-sions of the internal Resistance. While the mayor, Walsh de Serrant, repeated that the monument marked 'the day of the total Liberation of the whole French nation', de Gaulle replied that the surrender of the Germans of the Pocket 'had not only a local significance. Saint-Nazaire was only a historical episode in the war of liberation won at the cost of huge sacrifice . . . What was done here, what was done during the last great war is only a link in the chain on which the life and greatness of France depend.'[12] This cool contextualization, however, was not permitted to undermine the local cult. In 1970, for the twenty-fifth anniversary, a new mayor of Bouvron, Hervy, misquoted de Gaulle in order to replace the surrender at the centre of the stage. Neatly omitting one 'only', he quoted the General as having said that the event 'had not only local significance but was an episode in the History of France'.[13]

Such local cults generally served to unite communities and link them to the grand narrative of the official Resistance. There were cases, however, in which discordant voices were heard, undermining the local cult and at the same time demonstrating its artificiality. This is scarcely surprising, because open resistance had not been at the forefront of most people's minds under the Occupation. Andrée Trudeau, whose father had a farm close to the château overlooking Saumur, remembered sheltering in the limestone caves in the hillside during the three-day German bombardment in 1940. Employed in the ration-card service of Saumur town hall, she admitted sometimes slipping extra ration tickets into the hands of hungry-looking people, but never became involved in the issuing of false identity cards to those who had been forced to go underground. This was dangerous work, for which her section head was arrested, and men's work into the bargain. 'It was only men who did that,' she confesses, 'women didn't have the same [role] as today.' Her sole patriotic gesture was of a symbolic nature, to attend the funeral of British airmen whose plane had crashed near Saumur in February 1943. 'There was a huge procession to the cemetery,' she recalls, 'which was covered with flowers. Oh, I shall always remember that, I was there along with everyone else.' She never attended the commemoration of the battle of Saumur because she found the heroism fictitious. She insisted that 1940 was 'a complete débâcle' as officers retreated and left the young cadets to their fate. 'It is common knowledge', she asserted, 'that they were massacred to no purpose.' Her image of a real hero in the mould of local patriotism was the extraordinary nun of the Bon Pasteur who, built like a man and working with fallen women as she did, had an excellent grasp of bad language. She had access to POWs who were housed for several months in the Cavalry School, fetching and carrying laundry in a horse-drawn waggon, and used to smuggle them out with the dirty linen before sending them on their way to the demarcation line. Although Andrée can no longer remember her name, she says that the nun was 'legendary, she is still talked about today'.[14]

Michel Ancelin, son of the chief magistrate of Saumur who in 1940 at great personal risk negotiated a peaceful outcome for the town,[15] remained the spokesman of the burghers who resented the folly of a battle on their doorstep which would only lead to heavy civilian casualties. Even more explicitly than Andrée Trudeau, he dismissed the patriotic celebrations organized each June by the military and local officials of the Souvenir Français as 'ridiculous'. He handed me a report written by Dr von Senger of the 24th Panzer Division which, he asserted, 'completely destroys the beautiful legend' of the cadets because it says that when they arrived at Aunis they found 'some young men, unarmed and completely drunk', whom they didn't think were soldiers. In fact the German report simply states that on 21 June a group of forty officers and 200 men of the Cavalry School of Saumur were 'taken totally by surprise and made prisoner at Chinon'. Yet Michel Ancelin's irritation points to a fault line between those with a vested interest in the Resistance story and those attuned to other priorities in 1940 when the military were in full flight, leaving mayors and other notables to prevent the bombardment and massacre of their townsfolk.[16]

Michel Ancelin's father, of course, later went on to join a Resistance network, as a result of which he was arrested and tortured. This brought up another issue for Ancelin, the discrepancy between the heroic status conferred on some Resistance leaders, and the evidence of neglect, if not worse, which led to the deportation of their comrades. In November 1994 the grand old man of the Resistance in the Saumur area, Aristide Royer, died at the age of ninety-two. His obituary stated that as commander of the Saumur gendarmerie, he had been responsible for clandestine military operations in Anjou and had 1,500 resisters under his command. 'Aristide Royer . . . no longer counted his distinctions and medals. Commander of the Legion of Honour, he had notably been awarded the Military Cross with palm, the Resistance Medal with rosette, the Voluntary Resistance Combatant Cross, the Deportation Medal and many others.'[17]

The story of a Resistance force of 1,500 went back at least to 1948 when Commandant Royer declared that in June–September 1943 his networks had twenty-two officers, thirteen NCOs and 1,210 men. This was contradicted by one of his former colleagues, Commissaire Eprinchard, who turned down the offer in 1949 to write the history of the Saumur Resistance, pointing out that 'in 1941–3 the number of resisters could be counted on the fingers of two hands, while in 1945 the crowd of heroes was innumerable at Saumur as elsewhere'.[18] There had also been a major disaster during the night of 17–18 September 1943 when the Gestapo arrested eighteen individuals, including the former chief magistrate Ancelin, and on 8 October, when they arrested another twenty-five. Only ten of the forty-three, including Royer, returned alive from German concentration camps.

Questions began to be asked after the Liberation about how Royer's networks had been exposed. Another of his colleagues, René Marnot, said that Royer had been warned of his impending arrest three days earlier by a comrade in the Resistance, Daniel Durand, thanks to a tip-off from a German known to him, the translator at the Feldgendarmerie of Saumur, Corporal Hubert Sommer.[19] Royer did not go underground, nor did he warn any of the members in the networks for which he was responsible. This allegation was substantiated in 1998 by Michael Nerlich, professor of Romance literature at the Technical University of Berlin, who published Sommer's 1942 Marburg thesis on French literature and uncovered the records of the Gestapo interrogations of Royer and Durand at Angers on 21 September 1943. He established that Sommer, who had taught as an assistant at the Lycée of Roanne in 1937–8, knew Durand via a German family which had cared for Durand's son when the latter was working in Germany, and had dined with Durand three times before returning on 15 September to warn him of Royer's impending arrest. Durand sent these warnings to Royer, who nevertheless decided to say nothing and remained at his post. As a result, concluded Nerlich, Royer's network remained ignorant of the threat and was decimated. Meanwhile Sommer, whom Durand sought to protect under interrogation, was allegedly betrayed by Royer and arrested by the Gestapo on 29 September. He was sentenced to five years' imprisonment and, then, a year later, enrolled into a disciplinary battalion on the French front, where he was killed.[20]

This well-documented catastrophe is a good example of how the Resistance story has often been elaborated in defiance of tricky contradictions. It shows how the size of *réseaux* ballooned after the Liberation when to have resisted was what one needed to have done. It illustrates how idols of the Resistance like Royer who were fêted as local heroes for fifty years may in fact have concealed secrets about how their comrades were arrested and deported. Michel Ancelin, who saw his father tortured at the Feldgendarmerie of Saumur, went as far as to suggest that 'Royer was in cahoots with the Gestapo and an infamous traitor.'[21] It demonstrates, finally, that relations between French and Germans were sometimes more complicated than a crude division between oppressors and oppressed. The relationship of Hubert Sommer and Daniel Durand, based on a common appreciation of French culture and services rendered, led to Sommer's risking his life for his French friends and eventually to his own death. These subtleties are, however, very difficult to integrate into the Resistance story. So when in 1994 Nerlich wrote to the mayor of Saumur to propose that Sommer's name be added to the town's monument to the Resistance, he received no answer. 'Do people not want to know what happened in Saumur in 1943?' he asked. 'Or don't they want a German in the French Resistance?'[22]

Saumur, it seems, has been able to rebuff criticisms both of its heroism in 1940 and of its later contribution to the Resistance. The memories of other towns have been much more painful and divisive. Nantes, it is true, had a wonderful local hero in Christian de Mondragon who, on Armistice Day 1940, at the age of sixteen, climbed the cathedral tower under cover of darkness, while Germans patrolled the streets below, to attach a tricolour to the lightning conductor. He says that news of the exploit spread 'like a powder trail', not only through the city, as crowds gathered to marvel, but throughout Brittany. This purely symbolic gesture provoked no reprisals and simply confirmed the Gallic *esprit frondeur*. De Mondragon's identity was unknown until the Liberation but thereafter, he said with pride, his exploit became the toast of Nantes. 'There is not a book that comes out on the Occupation that does not mention it,' he asserted. To prove his point he showed me a collection beginning with Perraud-Charmantier's *War in Brittany* (1947) and concluding with Jocelyn Gille's strip cartoon, *Nantes in Upheaval* (1993).[23]

Unfortunately the Nantais are much more divided about how to commemorate the events that occurred less than a year later: the shooting of the Feldkommandant of Nantes by a communist commando on 20 October 1941 and the execution by the Germans of nearly fifty hostages at Nantes, Châteaubriant and Paris two days later. Immediately after the Liberation a struggle broke out between the Communist Party, which wanted to use the communist hostages shot at Châteaubriant to develop their myth of the party of the '75,000 *fusillés*', and the families of those (mainly war veterans and Catholics) executed at Nantes, who were opposed to any communist appropriation of the tragedy. The Pétainist bishop of Nantes portrayed the Nantes victims as Catholic martyrs, promised to light a candle every year if a second batch of hostages destined for the firing squad were spared, and at a ceremony on 22 October 1945 declared that 'the Church would not forget them, any more than a mother could forget her children'.[24] That same afternoon, communists swamped the commemoration at Châteaubriant, brandishing banners demanding 'Avenge our dead' and power for the party secretary Maurice Thorez, and singing the *Internationale*, to the annoyance of the French officials and American officers present. The seventy-six-year-old Marcel Cachin called the PCF '*le parti des fusillés*' and warned, 'Much ill has been said of the communists but in future it will be prohibited to say that communists are not loyal to France . . . many died for her, and their tragic fate will be mourned, but their death showed France the way.'[25] Nine months later, when the bodies of the twenty-one Nantes hostages were ceremonially reburied, veterans' organizations delivered a riposte to the communist claims. They argued that Jost, Fourny and the others who were shot at Nantes were veterans of 1914–18 who had been imprisoned for organizing the escape of 50,000 POWs in the region. Their colleague, Maître Ridel, who had escaped execution, declared of the veterans, 'Resisters you were, when everyone else was keeping their heads down, you were the precursors of the Liberation.'[26]

The gulf between the Nantes families and the communists deepened as the latter tightened their grip on the Châteaubriant ceremony. In 1946 Thorez himself addressed the gathering, exalting the patriotism of the communists and denouncing the pro-Munich Daladier government which had thrown communists into jail, the Vichy minister Pierre Pucheu (executed on communist insistence in 1944) who had tried to 'decapitate the labour movement' by mass executions, and even de Gaulle who had tried to stop communist attacks on German personnel.[27] For the ceremony in October 1950 the communists unveiled a heroic statue of five nude figures with proud heads and muscular torsos, embracing each other in front of a stake, plainly singing the *Marseillaise* or the *Internationale*.[28] For its part, the city of Nantes launched a fund for its own quota of martyrs in October 1944 but complained a few months later that although 'there are plenty of traders, market gardeners, managers of restaurants at 500 francs a time and people from the wealthy classes who could easily donate a thousand-franc note', little money had actually been forthcoming.[29] It was not until 22 October 1952 that the city's memorial was unveiled, and the mayor, Henri Orrion, who had also been the Vichy mayor in 1942–4, endeavoured to associate the town as a whole with the suffering. He spoke of those, including Mayor Rondeau, who had offered themselves to avert a second batch of executions, of the courage of the chaplains who had visited the condemned men, and the dignity of the population, and warned that the hostages themselves belonged 'neither to a class nor to a clan'. This infuriated the communist press, which attacked the mayor as a Pétainist, boycotted the official ceremony and held an alternative, popular vigil in the evening of 22 October, after the factories closed.[30]

Controversy extended not only to the victims but also to the killer. This opposed those who defended the action of a communist militant who arrived from Paris, pulled a gun on the local German military commander, and was credited with launching the Resistance in the west of France, and those who had nothing but contempt for the outsider who had come unbidden into their midst to inflict suffering and grief. The identity of the killer was soon known to the Germans but it was not until 1950 that Gilbert Brustlein, a communist who had since broken with the Party, announced that he had shot Colonel Hotz.[31] There were plenty of Nantais for whom Hotz was not the villain but a good and fair administrator whose death had been a catastrophe for the city. Edmond Duméril, who had served as interpreter at the prefecture during the Occupation, had been to the same German university as Hotz and admired his anti-Hitlerian humanity, argued in 1959 that Hotz had been killed not by communists but by the Gestapo, because he was too Francophile.[32] This view was supported at the time of the fiftieth anniversary of the shooting in 1991 by a local historian, Étienne Gasche, who argued that although Brustlein had pulled the trigger, he had in fact been arrested, gone over to the Germans, and allowed to escape by the Gestapo.[33] Brustlein subsequently brought a libel case against Gasche and won it. Meanwhile Louis Oury, a metallurgical worker turned local novelist and historian, invited Brustlein himself to return to Nantes for the fiftieth anniversary. Brustlein found it difficult to convince onlookers at the spot where he had pulled the trigger that he had performed not a murder but an 'act of war' and had 'unleashed armed resistance in the west of France'.[34] Michel Jost, son of the most illustrious hostage to be shot, declared at the monument to the fifty hostages on 22 October 1991, 'Gilbert Brustlein is using the blood of the dead for publicity. This anniversary has not been organized in memory of the attack on Hotz, but in honour of the forty-eight dead of Nantes, Châteaubriant and Paris.'[35] The visitors' book of the exhibition to mark the affair of the fifty hostages showed twenty-one entries critical of Brustlein and only three in favour. He was accused of shooting the German in the back, of failing to turn himself in order to spare the lives of the hostages, and then of daring shamelessly to return to the scene of the crime.[36]

Controversy in Nantes then centred on whether a plaque commemorating the killing of Colonel Hotz might be unveiled in the rue du Roi Albert, where he was shot, and how the inscription might read. The campaign for the plaque was undertaken almost alone by Louis Oury, and was opposed initially not only by the families of the hostages under Michel Jost but also by the Resistance organizations headed by André Chauvel of the Nantes branch of the Fédération des Déportés et Internés de la Résistance (FNDIR). Oury proposed a text which honoured the execution by Brustlein and his comrades Spartaco Guisco and Marcel Bourdarias of 'the Feldkommandant of the occupying forces' under orders from the communist Organization Spéciale as 'the first offensive action in the Occupied Zone' undertaken to 'launch the armed struggle in the west of France'. The Resistance organizations and families of hostages responded by proposing their own text which stated baldly that 'the Feldkommandant of Nantes was shot (*abattu*) by resisters' and then went on to list the number and place of execution of the victims shot in reprisal. For Oury this was 'a scandalous text worthy of Vichy', which would have simply used the word 'terrorist' instead of 'resister', and he managed to force a reconsideration of the wording. A provisional version of the plaque was unveiled in the rue du Roi-Albert, in the presence of the Minister of War Veterans and Deputy Mayor of Nantes, on the sixtieth anniversary of the events, 22 October 2001. This aligned the 'execution' of the Feldkommandant by a resistance commando Communist Youth with the execution of the forty-eight hostages at Nantes, Châteaubriant and Paris 'by the occupying German authorities on the orders of Hitler and with the collaboration of the Vichy authorities'. The ceremony was attended by Gilbert Brustlein, this time brought in an official car from Paris, but while the names of his comrades Spartaco and Bourdarias were mentioned on the plaque, his own name was not. The reason given was that 'republican tradition' ruled that only the names of the dead could be publicly commemorated in this way, even though Louis Oury pointed out that a lycée and college bore the name of the living resister Lucie Aubrac. This disappointment, however, was redeemed by the poign-ant act of reconciliation as Michel Jost agreed to shake Gilbert Brustlein's hand in public, saying that Brustlein had only been obeying orders and had no idea what the consequences of his actions might be. Consensus was still not complete. Many hostages' families and non-communist resistance organizations around André Chauvel were still horrified by the presence of Brustlein and a plaque com-memorating the execution of the Feldkommandant, and twelve of the fifteen local resistance organizations boycotted the commemor-ation. 'The wound remains deep in Nantes', reported L'Ouest-France, 'among the families of hostages who held the commandos responsible for the death of their loved ones'. Moreover the Resist-ance was never a bloc, and its internal rivalries were never more clearly expressed than when celebrating an act of resistance.[37]

The enduring conflict at Nantes over the fifty hostages is a powerful expression of a hostility to communist claims to have played a leading role in the Resistance which has been voiced not only by Gaullists but also by Pétainists. Sometimes the distinction between Gaullists and Pétainists was not all that clear because Pétainists too claimed to have been '*bons Français*' in the front line of the Resistance. Marquis Olivier and Marquise Yolande de Sesmai-sons were members of the conservative establishment in Loire-Inférieure who were also master and mistress of the *double jeu* under the Occupation. Olivier, who was not a parliamentarian and had not voted to give full powers to Marshal Pétain in July 1940, nevertheless used his place on the CDL to defend the very Pétainist Marquis de La Ferronnays and was elected a conservative deputy of the Constituent Assembly.[38] Yolande was a society lady who made the best use of her contacts with the Germans and was awarded the Légion d'Honneur. Their sons, Marquis Donatien and General Yves de Sesmaisons, whom I met in 1997, argued that the defeat and Occupation were explained entirely by the Nazi–Soviet Pact. After that, they said, communists sabotaged the armaments industry and Thorez deserted the army, leaving conservatives to fly the patriotic flag. The politicians Daladier and Reynaud 'led us into the shit', they said, and when Pétain sued for an armistice '80 per cent of French people said "Ouf", at last an honest chap.' 'The Vichy motto "Work, Family, Fatherland" impressed the traditional Right,' they agreed, but they claimed that enthusiasm for Pétain did not exclude hostility to the Germans. Indeed, they asserted, the French long believed in a 'tacit agreement between Pétain and de Gaulle'. The military nobility, including their older brother Jean, an officer in the Armistice Army and then, after its dissolution, in the Armée Secrète, were among the first resisters. To reinforce this point after the interview, General de Sesmaisons wrote to me to say, 'It is thus false to argue, as the "politically correct" version would now have it, that the Right were all collabos and only the communists were resistants ... French people could be in favour of Vichy while at the same time hating the Germans.'[39]

Similar anti-communist views were expressed by Vicomte Gilles de la Grandière, the son of Senator Palamède de la Grandière, who was invited to join the CDL of Maine-et-Loire in August 1944 but was no less a Pétainist for that. The senator, Gilles was clear, was an admirer of Pétain because he had been at Verdun and was president of the Union des Anciens Combattants in Anjou. He said that his father was very close to the Marquis de La Ferronnays, but that Palamède himself 'was not involved in politics' under Vichy and in particular that (unlike his cousin Jacques) he refused to become a member of Vichy's Conseil National. Gilles – presumably echoing his father – called de Gaulle a 'deserter' who 'might have unified the French' but had fallen under the influence of the communists. He denounced the 'string of murders committed by the so-called Resistance' and pointed out that his father joined the CDL to 'counterbalance the Left'. His wife the Vicomtesse asserted that 'it was not only the Left that was involved in the Resistance', and explained that Resistance was in the 'military tradition' of the French nobility. They lent me a *Memorial of the French Nobility in the Fighting against the Invader, 1939–45*, which cited two members of the de la Grandière family as resisters and calculated that although nobles formed only 0.2 per cent of the population they accounted for 4.4 per cent of the Compagnons de la Libération. The resistance of the young Gilles consisted of squirting German sentries with his water-pistol from the battlements of the château. Unfortunately, he says, the Resistance movement in Maine-et-Loire was taken over by anti-Catholic and anti-aristocratic elements who discovered pro-German articles he had written for an Angers paper during the Occupation and forced him off the CDL, after which he went back to his traditional Catholic and conservative politics.[40]

Two more apologists of the Resistance credentials of Marshal Pétain were Paule de Beaumont, the daughter of Vichy's second regional prefect in the Loire region, Charles Donati, and her husband Louis. Mme de Beaumont put her cards on the table straight away, attacking the 'present climate of historical disinformation that passes off Pétain as a criminal against humanity'; she was concerned that this would be reinforced by the forthcoming trial of former Vichy official Maurice Papon. Pétain, she said, was close to her father, and 'opened his heart to him'. In return, Donati 'entirely espoused the theory of Pétain that you had to stay in France to protect the French population', the only alternative being a German Gauleiter. On the other hand, she insisted, he did not get on with head of government Laval, whose enthusiasm for collaboration was difficult to disguise and with whom 'no discussion was possible'. She described her father as a 'man of duty' and absolute rectitude, who fought every moment against German demands. On one occasion, she remembered, in a meeting with a Feldkommandant who was making unreasonable demands, he banged loudly on the table with his one fist and demanded, 'Is *that* what you call collaboration?' and obliged the German to give ground. He took great risks, she insisted, and was 'on the list for the next deportations', following the deportation of the former prefect of Loire-Inférieure, Bonnefoy. As a veteran who had lost his left arm in the 1914–18 war, Donati enjoyed a certain prestige vis-à-vis the Germans, which he exploited, but he 'never gave even the smallest reception' for them, nor did he invite them to dine.

For Paule de Beaumont and her husband Louis, Donati was a Pétainist but also a genuine resister. Louis, who made religious broadcasts and discovered that at their château 300 counter-revolutionaries were massacred by republican troops in 1795, argued that there were in fact two Resistances, the first staffed by former army officers and engaged in military operations, the second 'monstrous', full of 'hooligans' (*voyous*) who 'took to the Maquis to pillage and steal'. Paule de Beaumont continued the analysis, saying that her father hated communists because they sabotaged the armaments factories during the war, were 'practically deserters' in 1940 and had a policy of 'better a civil war than a war against Germany'. Fortunately there was an orderly transfer of power between high civil servants at the Liberation, notably between her father and the new Commissaire de la République, Michel Debré, who shook hands at the prefecture of Angers on 10 August 1944. She regretted only that de Gaulle did not hold out his hand to Pétain in the same way. Later she sent me an extract from Pétain's trial of her father's statement before he was bundled from the courtroom, to the effect that 'millions and millions of French people think that this trial is an immense political mistake'.[41]

What emerges from such interviews is that there is still in some French circles a coherent and passionately held Pétainist position. According to this view, Marshal Pétain was the legitimate ruler of France, acclaimed by the National Assembly and a martyr to the protection of his people. De Gaulle is seen as a deserter, who had in any case fallen a prey to the communists. The communists proved by the Nazi–Soviet pact of 1939 that they had no sense of patriotism, undermined the war effort in 1940 and used the Resistance for their own power-political ends. The real Resistance was that of Vichy officials who stayed their ground and negotiated eyeball to eyeball with the Germans on a daily basis; Maquisards who called themselves resisters were often no better than bandits and terrorists.

When I repeated these stories to the Académie de Tours they told me that such Angevin *hobereaux* or petty nobles were in no way typical, and that in Touraine a genuine left-wing Resistance held sway. As an antidote, they introduced me to Georges Audebert, an official at the prefecture of Tours during the Occupation. Although in public he told gallant stories about his Resistance activities, in private, as we saw, he adopted a different line which was dictated by his responsibilities under Vichy. He argued that in 1940 there was no alternative to the Armistice 'as people were getting killed and buildings were on fire. France was abandoned by everyone except England of course, but people said that England was finished.' 'People argued,' he continued, 'that perhaps a man like Pétain, who had the glory of being a Marshal of France and was respected by the Germans, could limit the damage and save something.' Resistance, he insisted, was impossible, so keen was German repression, and the Liberation was marked by 'terrible abuses and mistakes'. He simply waited for his moment, carrying a German pass in his pocket and one issued by the Resistance in his shoe, and managed to make the transition to the prefecture of Mayenne with special responsibility for 'preventing excessive purges'.[42]

This sentiment of relief at the Armistice went all the way down the social order, and was probably plainest among the peasantry, such as the future Maquisards of Saffré. As André Treulier, the winegrower of Le Thoureil near Saumur, poured me a glass of wine in his cellar, he opened the conversation by announcing that by suing for an armistice and letting him out of the army, 'Pétain saved my life.'[43] Max Ménard, a candlestick-maker from Beaupréau, a pious and conservative town in the Mauges, was a former seminarist who knew all the priests in the area and had a captive market for his candles. He made no bones of his sympathy for Pétain, who he said acted as a buffer between the Germans and the French population, and argued that it was ill considered to put him on trial. His wife Jeanne recalled that the Germans were well behaved (*corrects*) and Max agreed that he was not unduly troubled by them under the Occupation. When the Germans started to requisition vehicles in the locality, Max asked a mechanic to remove a piece from his so that it would not start. 'We conned them as much as we could,' he said, 'it was passive resistance.' 'I resisted in my own way,' he continued, by not replying to letters calling on him to report for STO. There was no question, however, of joining a Maquis. 'I would have done more resistance,' he apologized, 'if we hadn't been going to get married.'[44]

In the more educated classes Pétainism was a choice dictated as much by fervour as by self-preservation or family priorities. Abbé

Henri Richer, chaplain of the Little Sisters of the Poor at Angers, was a seminarist who went to Germany on STO in 1943. Some seminarists, he conceded, went into hiding or joined the Resistance rather than go to Germany, but in his opinion it was 'better to accompany' the workers to provide religious services, and he explained how he received support in his mission from German parish priests. The conversation, however, revealed another reason for leaving. Richer's father was a career army officer until 1925, when he became a bookseller in Angers. His father followed Pétain, and Henri followed his father. 'We were always Pétainists,' he confided, 'we never listened to the English radio. We gave ourselves over to prayer to ask for the liberation of the prisoners of war [and] the reconstruction of the country.' The Occupation saw 'an intense religious life, at least in Christian milieux', and the restoration of state subsidies to Church schools for the first time since the 1880s was 'a burst of oxygen . . . a joy'. He said, 'We knew very little about what was going on in the Resistance,' and thought de Gaulle was a 'troublemaker . . . disruptive, irritating'. When he returned to France in April 1945 he was told at the frontier to acclaim de Gaulle, but he could not, arguing that he was 'still more or less illegal'. That summer he followed the trial of Pétain in the press and thought the condemnation to death 'unjust'. In the Pétainist world of Abbé Richer, still intact after more than fifty years, the Vichy regime was the city of God, STO the opportunity for missionary work, and the Resistance open defiance of loyalty and discipline.[45]

Another cleric who remained true to Pétainism and criticized the excesses of the Resistance was Abbé Jamonneau, who had been a POW in Germany and at the end of the Occupation was secretary to Mgr Villepelet, the very Pétainist bishop of Nantes. He recalled that Michel Debré, when he came to Nantes in August 1944 to rally opinion to General de Gaulle, 'expressed great surprise' to find a portrait of the Marshal still hanging in the bishop's office. He insisted that those who preferred Pétain to de Gaulle were not for that reason 'unpatriotic Frenchmen' and that the German Occupation was 'not a gulag, anyway'. He had nothing but scorn for the Resistance and the Americans. The Maquis of Saffré was in his eyes guilty of 'imprudence' and 'stupidity', as was his own brother, who killed two Germans only a few kilometres from the family farm and got his uncle, his uncle's daughter and himself arrested by the Gestapo. He criticized the Americans for their artillery bombardment of churches in the Pocket of Saint-Nazaire and showed me a photograph of the ruined church of Bouvron where he became curé after the war. Although he was a regular attender at the Bouvron ceremonies marking the end of the war, he denounced the FFIs, recalling that while helping a community of nuns at Saint-Étienne-de-Montluc to move away from the front, an FFI officer demanded the nuns' beds to put in his men's trenches. 'I was in the war,' Jamonneau roared at the officer, 'you don't put beds in trenches!' For him the FFIs were not the heroic soldiers of the Year II but the republican 'infernal columns' that put counter-revolutionary Brittany and the Vendée to fire and sword in 1793. Over his door there was an engraving of a secret forest Mass celebrated by Vendeans, and he pointed out that his ancestors were massacred by the self-same 'infernal columns'. His vision of the Second World War was coloured by the heritage of the French Revolution, the revolutionaries of 1944 like those of 1793 being the force for evil.[46]

Nobles and clerics, of course, are not a cross-section of the French population and Pétainist opinion, however strongly expressed, is a minority view. But one point often raised by such people – that attacks by armed resisters on German personnel inevitably provoked collective reprisals against local populations and were therefore foolhardy – merits attention. In the Loire area there does not seem to have been the same community support for Resistance fighters as in the Midi, and the feeling of many Nantais that armed attacks were counterproductive has been echoed in other villages which experienced or nearly experienced brutal collective punishments. The massacres of Tulle, Saint-Amand and Oradour-sur-Glane in the violent months surrounding the Liberation were the most famous but unfortunately not the only ones.[47]

Yves de Saint-Seine was appointed by the Vichy mayor of the small village of Toutlemonde near Cholet where, following the discovery by the Germans of a van full of weapons on 8 August 1944, a tragedy was only just averted. The Breton resister, Michel Créac'h, had confessed under torture that the weapons were destined for 'tout le monde', and the linguistic confusion led to himself as mayor, the curé and every sixth man in the village being lined up against the schoolhouse wall to be shot, unless they revealed where the weapons had been hidden. After fifteen tense minutes, when the misunderstanding was cleared up by a German-speaking Alsatian interpreter, they were fortunately released. A monument was raised outside the village to Michel Créac'h but following a good lunch Yves de Saint-Seine revealed his true feelings about this cult. 'I am against the Resistance, which was responsible for the deaths of many decent people,' he let slip. This hostility to the Resistance was of a piece with his loyalty to Pétain, who he said had prevented France from becoming totally occupied and should never have been sentenced to death. In his opinion de Gaulle was a deserter, and he argued that 'The British and Americans would have liberated France just as well without the Resistance.' The Liberation authorities kept him on as mayor in 1944 because of his exemplary conduct under the threat of massive reprisals, and he was duly elected in 1945 and for forty years subsequently. He might have become the father of his village but the fact that he was initially appointed by Vichy denied him the honours that would normally be bestowed. He said he did not care that he had not been awarded the Légion d'honneur or the Ordre du Mérite National, but he clearly did.[48]

The villagers of Maillé in Touraine were not so lucky. On 25 August 1944, after Maquisards ambushed some retreating Germans in the vicinity, a German unit covering the retreat put the village to fire and sword, massacring 126 of the 627 inhabitants. Those who survived the massacre were torn between anger and despair. The first plaque, unveiled on 25 August 1945 in the presence of the archbishop of Tours, read: 'To the 124 inhabitants massacred by Nazi barbarism. Let us never forget'. The monument unveiled by Raoul Dautry, Minister of Reconstruction, on the main road to Bordeaux in 1947 commanded: 'Passer-by, the Nazis have pillaged, killed, burned'. In 1948 Maillé, along with Tours and Saint-Pierre-des-Corps, was awarded the Croix de Guerre for 'the sacrifice, spirit of Resistance and heroism of the citizens of the village'.[49] What the survivors did not want, however, was for the tragedy to be hijacked for political purposes. This almost happened in 1953 during the trial of members of the Das Reich SS division held responsible for the Oradour massacre, when Resistance groups from Chinon used the commemoration to protest against the amnesty of collaborators voted by parliament at the same time.[50] From that time the commemoration was held in silence, without speeches, a time to remember the dead, not to make political capital.

The villagers do not want to criticize the Resistance, because of its status and legitimacy, although their deep feeling is that it contributed to destroying their loved ones. Gilbert Chedozeau, the mayor, who lost his father in the carnage, admitted that 'if there had been no Resistance in France that would have helped the Occupation'. On the other hand he revealed that on the fiftieth anniversary of the massacre he received a letter from one of the Maquisards, now living outside Angers, saying, 'I feel that I am responsible for the massacre of Maillé.' He made no comment. The massacre remains unspeakable. Mme Guitton, who lost her grandparents, aunt and cousins in it, confessed that she had not been able to tell the full story to her six children. She stood in the middle of the village cemetery, head bowed, in tears. An Association for the Remembrance of Maillé to establish a Maison du Souvenir in one of the few remaining original buildings has only recently been founded. And yet the inhabitants of Maillé are pained that they have been forgotten by others. The village is not a focus of national concern, like Oradour. Nothing is known of the German soldier who was responsible for the massacre, apart from the fact that he was condemned to death *in absentia* in 1952. Ministers are regularly invited to the annual commemoration but never come, because the date is the same as that of the Liberation of Paris, and might cast a shadow on it. In the words of the local paper in 1994, 'A little recognition would be enough for this commune of Indre-et-Loire which fifty years on still suffers from not understanding what happened.'[51]

Mayor Chedozeau and the surviving villagers of Maillé were ambivalent about the Resistance: it redeemed France, but it brought tragedy to them. Most communities in the region, of course, did not participate in the Resistance, but were simply liberated by Allied forces. A survey undertaken by the Comité d'Histoire de la Deuxième Guerre Mondiale in Maine-et-Loire in 1948 indicated that only a third of communes claimed that they produced so much as one deportee or member of the FFI. Two-thirds of mayors reported that there had been no resistance at all in their communes. That of Chaudefonds-sur-Layon, for example, said that 'the population in general was obliged to tolerate the Germans but had an unfavourable opinion of them'. At most it was claimed that reluctance to meet German requistions was 'passive resistance'.[52] And yet the pressure to display Resistance credentials was such that many communities cultivated a special relationship with a resister or liberator whose glory might be reflected on to the town or village. If a local hero like Christian de Mondragon could not be found, a national or even foreign hero would do, so long as a local association could be demonstrated.

After the Liberation the little village of Grugé l'Hôpital in northern Anjou claimed that it acted as a launch pad of the Liberation, sending the great General (later Marshal) Leclerc on his long military adventure. As Captain Philippe de Hautecloque, wounded in the fighting, he had sought refuge with his sister, Mme Yvonne de Bodard, in the local château on 26 June 1940. The Germans had set up a temporary Kommandantur at the *mairie*, and with the help of the mayor and the curé, Abbé Brossier, the captain was able to obtain a pass in the name of Leclerc, wine merchant, to cross to the Free Zone. In September 1946 he returned to the village for a thanksgiving Mass celebrated by Abbé Brossier and signed a document in the *mairie* which described how the pass had allowed him to escape 'providentially' from the Germans, to join General de Gaulle and begin the 'glorious epic which, from the Cameroons, Chad and Tunisia to Normandy, Paris and Strasbourg was to finish at Berchtesgaden, with the Liberation of occupied France'.[53] Leclerc was killed in an air crash in North Africa the following year, but a plaque was unveiled on the façade of the *mairie* in 1953 announcing that 'Grugé l'Hôpital wishes to preserve the pious memory of he whom it considers in some measure to be one of its children'. In 1980, on the fortieth anniversary of the occasion, a statue of Leclerc was unveiled on the main square of the village in a ceremony attended by the Marshal's widow, the bishop of Angers, cadets of the Cavalry School of Saumur, where Leclerc had been a student, and veterans of the Deuxième Division Blindée. The Secretary of State for Ex-Servicemen neatly rewrote history by declaring that 'people often commit sins of omission when they narrate the events of history, for what the mayor and curé of Grugé l'Hôpital did in 1940, permitting him who freely chose the name of Leclerc to take the first steps towards glory, was one of the first acts of the Resistance'.[54]

This invention of an 'act of resistance' and appropriation of General Leclerc as one of its children contrasted with a real local fear of Resistance under the Occupation itself, relayed by both the documents and the oral record. The subprefect of Segré said of Grugé in 1941, 'I witnessed a national spirit that was most comprehensive and most committed to the country's restoration. The municipal assembly has the most complete confidence in the Marshal's policies.'[55] The mayor, Édouard Delanoë, son of the mayor in 1940, told me in 1997 how his father managed to avert a nasty incident in 1940 when the Germans arrived by persuading French troops 'armed to the teeth' in the forest not to fight, in return for providing them with civilian clothing to allow them to escape.[56] Francis Bossé, one of those farmers, said at the beginning of his memoirs that 'from my childhood I have had a horror of war, so much had I heard about it from my father and his ex-servicemen friends'. Born in 1921, he escaped the initial call-up and confessed that 'for us young people the Armistice was a relief, as we thought we were rid of the war for good'.[57] The Germans left the village in September 1940 and the community settled into a peaceable Occupation. Its war memorial bears the names of twenty-four dead of the First World War and only two from the Second, including a student teacher shot by the Germans in the affair of the *normaliens* of Angers.[58]

On Sunday, 7 August 1994, a plaque was unveiled at the Pont des Pruniers, Bouchemaine, outside Angers, to the memory of a sea-scout leader, Louis Bordier, by his brother Yann, now a rear-admiral. This was in memory of the true scouting exploit fifty years before, when Louis had led the advancing American forces to a lightly defended railway bridge over the Maine downstream of Angers, which they were able to cross to attack the Germans in the rear and thus liberate the city.[59] The Angevins, who had weathered four years of occupation under the same mayor, had no other local heroes to cultivate. In the absence of French liberators, they decided to raise their profile by associating their liberation with the great General Patton, who was awarded the freedom of the city. It was a visit that almost never happened, for clearly Angers needed the general more than the general needed Angers. Patton was due to be fêted at Angers on 5 August 1945 but the visit had to be cancelled. He visited a number of towns liberated by the Third Army that October, but was again unable to visit Angers. He thanked Mayor Allonneau for awarding him the freedom of the city but asked whether the mayor could come to Rennes and present it there. Allonneau went to Rennes with his deputy mayor, Germaine Canonne, who in fact prevailed upon Patton to travel the 130 kilometres to Angers, where he made a triumphal entry on 27 October.[60]

The significance of this moment for Angers and indeed for Germaine Canonne would be difficult to underestimate. Although Mme Canonne was the first woman deputy mayor of Angers, the first woman member of the *conseil général* of Maine-et-Loire and the pioneer of many welfare reforms including the closure of the city's brothels, these achievements were nothing compared with her triumph in persuading General Patton to come to Angers. The essence of her tale, which she read aloud to me from her manuscript memoirs, was that the airfield at Angers was out of action and that Patton had been warned by a clairvoyant not to travel by car. The subtext was that she spoke good English and that Patton was persuaded by her charms. In fact Patton was killed in a car crash two months later at Mannheim, and Germaine Canonne expresses relief that no accident happened on the road to Angers. Fifty years after the Liberation she was able to meet Patton's granddaughter, Helen, who told her that she was happy to shake hands with someone who had met her grandfather, as she had never known him.[61] For the Angevins Patton achieved the status of a hero or modern saint whom, though associated with them only tangentially, they could somehow claim for their own in order to privilege the liberation of their city in the history of the Second World War.

To have resisted personally or even by proxy conferred great legitimacy, but simply to claim Resistance credentials was not enough. The gateway to Resistance accreditation was policed by powerful Resistance organizations which established a hierarchy of credentials – certificates and medals – differentiating between various levels of resistance and blocking the claims of rivals. The most powerful of the Resistance organizations was the FNDIR, which obtained a special status equivalent to having served in the army for those who had been deported or interned for *acts* of resistance under a law of 6 August 1948. They were awarded the title of Voluntary Combatant of the Resistance (CVR) and the Resistance Medal. The CVR was given only to those who could demonstrate that they had joined the Resistance at least ninety days before the landings of 6 June 1944; those who joined later, such as FFIs, qualified only as Combatants in a Resistance Capacity. The prime intention of the

FNDIR was to see off the claims of the communist FNDIRP, whose members in their opinion had been deported or interned simply for being in a political party. The FNDIR was also determined to reject the claims of the STO workers, who campaigned repeatedly for the title of 'labour deportees'. Working in a German factory, the FNDIR argued, was nothing compared with slaving in a German concentration camp. Those who had been conscripted but refused to go – and could subsequently prove that the police were looking for them – were entitled to a *réfractaire* card but those who went to Germany were allowed no more exalted a title than 'person constrained to work in enemy territory'. In defiance of this ruling many STO organizations continued to call themselves 'labour deportees' and in 1985, under pressure from the FNDIR, the Appeal Court of Bourges ruled that enough had been said about 'the heroism and martyrdom of the Resistance deportees that an incomparable title should correspond to their incomparable fate'. Their monopoly of honour was thereby confirmed.[62]

The struggle for honour, heavily bureaucratized, was not free of partiality and corruption. The patronage of a Resistance chief like Jean Meunier in Tours or a Resistance organization was indispensable. As the Cold War began to bite the authorities became less and less willing to recognize communists as resisters. While many of the non-communist *fusillés* of Nantes, for example, were posthumously awarded the Resistance Medal and Légion d'honneur in 1948, these were refused to the communist *fusillés* of Châteaubriant.[63] Conditions were set impossibly high for communists seeking recognition as resisters. For example, the brother-in-law, mother and grandparents of two communist brothers from Rézé hunted by the Gestapo were arrested in their place and deported to Orianburg. They claimed that they too were resisters, but the prefect of Loire-Inférieure ruled in 1951 that 'they could not adduce any provable fact (act of sabotage, participation in an attack against the installations or members of the Army of Occupation)' and were 'considered to be hostages rather than resisters'.[64]

The FNDIR increased its profile still further through the National Day of Remembrance of the Victims and Heroes of the Deportation, an annual gala of the deportees instituted under a law of 14 April 1954 to mark the liberation of the concentration camps in 1945 and held on the last Sunday of April. The constant refrain of these gatherings was unity and, to prevent quarrelling between movements and organizations of deportees, the official speech was handed down each year from the Ministry of War Veterans. The gospel to be passed on to future generations was that the barbarism of the concentration camps must never be allowed to recur and that the survivors' dream of a free and fraternal world must now be realized. The subtext was nevertheless to link deportation and Resistance, highlighting the primacy of the Resistance deportees and the contribution of the deportees to the Resistance. This became explicit in 1964 when associations of resisters and deportees, under the auspices of the Education Ministry, founded an essay competition linking the themes of Resistance and deportation 'to develop an understanding of the civic and moral values that were at stake in the combat'.[65] Each year a different topic was set, ranging from the Resistance and the principles of 1789 in 1989 to Nazi concentration camps in 1991 and Women and the Resistance in 1997. In Loire-Atlantique, one of the first departments to participate under the enthusiastic guidance of André Chauvel of the FNDIR, the annual prize-giving at the prefecture is a gala where the ageing representatives of associations of deportees, resisters and veterans bestow laurels on the gilded youth of the department. In 1997 the Marquis Donatien de Sesmaisons, speaking on behalf of the sponsoring *conseil général*, paid homage to the Resistance activities of his mother and declared that the Resistance 'united brothers-in-arms of all social and political conditions'.[66] The winning essay, by Kristell Retière of Le Loquidy School, Nantes (of which Christian de Mondragon was an old boy), entirely fulfilled the expectations of the organizers. She explained how French women turned away from Marshal Pétain after his attacks on women's employment, contraception and abortion and argued that 'in spite of their different social situations, their opposing political opinions and diverse beliefs and ideologies, they overcame their particularities in order to unite for what was essential, in a struggle without quarter: they became resisters, with exactly the same credentials as men'.[67]

The most striking thing about the French commemoration of the deportation, however, is that for nearly fifty years the Jewish dimension was scarcely mentioned. The text from the Ministry of War Veterans habitually referred to the '200,000 French people' who had been deported, or to the 'ten million victims of the most diverse nationalities'. Since most Jews deported from France were immigrants they were hidden behind the term 'diverse nationalities'. In Angers the twenty-fifth anniversary of the liberation of the camps in 1970 was commemorated by a meeting addressed by a Free French officer, a Jewish survivor of Auschwitz, and Mme Geneviève Anthonioz-de Gaulle, niece of the General and a Ravensbrück deportee. Only Mme Anthonioz-de Gaulle attracted any attention, and was presented with the visitors' book signed by Angevins on the day of her uncle's funeral.[68] For the fortieth anniversary, in 1985, young people were brought much more fully into the commemorations, and at Nantes one of them read the official message, this time penned by a survivor. Even so, reference was made only to 'the degradation, the torture and the extermination of millions of people' and the familiar summons was to 'build that free and fraternal world of which we dreamed on the exhilarating day of our liberation, forty years ago'.[69]

This extraordinary omission requires explanation. The Resistance gospel, as we saw, always prioritized the hero over the victim, accorded the highest honours to *Resistance* deportees or internees, followed by *political* deportees and internees. It refused to recognize that STO workers were deportees at all and nursed the prejudice that far from resisting, the Jews went like lambs to the slaughter. The communists who dominated the association of Auschwitz survivors ensured that Auschwitz was regarded above all as a camp for political deportees, and in June 1946 inhumed the ashes brought back from Auschwitz in the Père Lachaise cemetery in Paris next to the Mur des Fédérés dedicated to the Communards of 1871. The inscription, 'To the memory of the 180,000 men, women and children deported from France and exterminated at Auschwitz, victims of Nazi barbarism', made no specific mention of the Jews.[70] The Resistance cult also insisted that over and above social, political, religious or ethnic differences, all individuals and movements dedicated to the struggle against Nazism shared the same fundamental values of the Rights of Man, Liberty, Equality and Fraternity, and were committed to rebuilding a 'One and Indivisible' France. For that reason Deportees Day always presented a united front, a single message was proclaimed, and any attempt at separatism was vehemently discouraged. A final explanation brings in the French state. The extermination of the Jews called into question the responsibility first of the Vichy state, then of the French state in general. The fact that de Gaulle declared the Vichy state null and void and restored republican legitimacy made things easy for the Republic. When President Mitterrand attended the commemoration on 16 July 1992 of the fiftieth anniversary of the round-up of French Jews by French police in Paris, he refused to accept the responsibility of the French state on the grounds that Vichy was not the Republic and the Republic was not Vichy. Only with the declaration of Prime Minister Chirac, on 16 July 1995, that 'the criminal folly of the occupier was, as everyone knows, assisted by the French, assisted by the French state', and that 'on that day France accomplished something irreparable', was the responsibility of the French state for the first time acknowledged, and the door opened to place the Holocaust at the centre of the deportation debate.

The Holocaust salvo took the Resistance organizations amidships and breached their monopoly of honour. At a meeting of the Nantes FNDIR chaired by André Chauvel in 1997, twelve or fifteen whitehaired resisters agreed that 'too much importance' had been given to the Jews for the fiftieth anniversary of the liberation of the camps in 1995. Chauvel acknowledged that the Jews had caught the media spotlight and regretted that 'the deportees [*sic*] were put to one side, forgotten'. School students answering a recent questionnaire on who was deported, he said, cited Jews first and workers second. He was concerned that homosexuals would soon want to lay their own wreath on Deportees Day, even though, he affirmed, 'no one was deported from France for homosexuality'.[71]

This resentment was confirmed to me by Ernest Gluck, an Auschwitz survivor of Slovak origin and president of the Jewish community of Nantes. He was present at a ceremony on 16 July 1993 to unveil alongside the monument to the fifty hostages in Nantes a plaque recording the homage of the Republic to 'the victims of racist and anti-Semitic persecution and crimes against humanity committed under the *de facto* Government of the French State, 1940–1944'. Gluck revealed that the local organizations of deportees and resisters had been extremely reluctant to concede a separate ceremony for Jewish deportees to coincide with the *rafle du Vel d'Hiv* rather than Deportees Day, although it had been decreed nationally, arguing that unity had to be maintained at all costs and that if the Jews obtained their own ceremony, the next request would come from the homosexual community.[72] Once the unitary nature of the commemoration was broken by the concession of a Jewish ceremony on 16 July, the next best option was to relativize the Jews. Thus in 1993 the deputy-mayor of Nantes, Jean-Marc Ayrault, attacked the 'shameful, unacceptable laws and decrees' of Vichy against the Jews, but spent much time dilating on the persecution of the gypsies.[73]

At Angers public recognition of the deportation of the Jews took place a year earlier. On 20 July 1992 a ceremony was held in the courtyard of the Grand Séminaire into which, exactly fifty years before, 824 Jews had been crammed before being loaded on to convoy no. 8 and taken directly to Auschwitz. The initiative for the dedication of a plaque was taken by one of the three remaining survivors of the convoy, Désiré Hafner, now living in Tours. The wording that he chose, and the speech that he gave, made the gesture easier to make by the Angevins, since he blamed the whole episode on the Nazis. The recognition, moreover, was superficial. The bishop of Angers, Mgr Orchampt, who paid for the plaque, said he had been totally unaware of the drama until a few weeks previously, and stated that the seminary had been requisitioned at the time by the Nazis (which was only partially correct). The mayor of Angers, Jean Monnier, simply threw up his hands, wondering innocently 'how such goings on could have taken place in our good city of Angers, without leaving any memory, except in the departmental archives'.[74] The fears of Charles Toubon, then head of the Jewish community of Angers, meanwhile, were not fully assuaged. He said privately that he had not pardoned the Church and that it was 'written in the gospels that the Jews were wrong'. There was still a danger, as evidenced by Poland and the likes of Mgr Lefebvre in France, that 'Catholicism misunderstood' would be anti-Semitic.[75]

The difficulty experienced by the Jewish community promoting its own version of events alongside the received orthodoxy was most clearly illustrated in the commemoration of the Camp de la Lande, near the village of Monts, outside Tours. The camp, as we saw in Chapter 11, had been used in 1940–42 as a detention camp for foreign and displaced Jews, and thereafter as a camp for communist women. The first initiative in collective remembrance came in 1983 from two communist women of Monts, Huguette Robin, whose father had been shot by the Germans in 1942, and Lucie Lancezeux, who had worked at the Ripault factory. They had an article published in L'Humanité and attracted a number of communist women who had once been prisoners in the camp and were willing to talk. The visitors, seeing that all signs of the camp had vanished under a housing estate, suggested that a monument should mark the spot, and Mmes Robin and Lancezeux, with the help of a sympathetic communist councillor, persuaded the somewhat reluctant conservative municipal council to adopt the idea.[76]

At this point a former Jewish internee of the camp from Nancy, Jérôme Scorin, learned of the scheme and contacted the Jewish community in Tours. When they discovered that the projected inscription for the monument contained no specific reference to the Jews, only to the 'victims of racial and political hatred interned here from 1940 to 1944', they asked the permission of the mayor, Dr Prunier, to place their own plaque. The mayor, ever the local politician, amiably promised to meet their request, but found himself opposed by his council, and therefore did nothing. As a consequence, on 16 October 1988, the unveiling ceremony was boycotted by the Jewish community of Tours which declared itself, in the words of its leader, Marcel Messalati, 'wounded and scandalized', insulted and betrayed.[77] The prefect, fearing controversy, did not come. The ceremony was attended by Serge Klarsfeld on behalf of the Association of Sons and Daughters of Deported Jews of France and Jérôme Scorin, but only to protest. In a violent speech which the mayor later said 'brought me down in flames', Scorin asked whether the 'hatred' described on the plaque was that of the Nazis or the French and asserted that 'not only does the laconic wording of the monument fail to express the horror of the racist crime and the extent of the human catastrophe, but it seems to minimize the reality'. He himself, he said, had managed to escape from the camp, but his mother, father and brother had been among 489 Jews taken from there to Auschwitz. 'Does the municipality of Monts', he asked, 'want to disguise the fact that the internees of La Lande exterminated at Auschwitz were all Jews? Does it want to agree with the pseudo-revisionists, the falsifiers of history, or with a certain political party which claims that the crime committed against so many innocent people was only a detail?'[78]

After this collision of memories a reconciliation was gradually negotiated. A more left-wing municipality was elected, and a more diplomatic leader of the Jewish community, François Guggenheim, emerged. A municipal commission was appointed, including two members of the Jewish community, to discuss the wording of a second plaque.[79] At the same time André Bellegarde, a local teacher, persuaded the College of Monts to undertake research into the Camp de la Lande and put on an exhibition. This exhibition, which opened early in 1995, brought the Holocaust to the village and had a powerful influence on local opinion. It mediated between the Jewish community and the local community and paved the way to the unveiling of the second plaque in honour of the deported Jews in the presence among others of the prefect and Serge Klarsfeld on 3 December 1995.[80]

Unfortunately public recognition did not completely efface private resentment. Like the non-communist resistance of Nantes, the communists of Monts felt that they had been marginalized in the interests of political correctness. In his large office on the outskirts of Tours François Guggenheim expressed satisfaction with developments: the Jews now occupied centre stage in the deportation memory. However at Lucie Lancezeux's little house in Monts, where we sat in the garage for coolness, the tone was somewhat different. 'What annoyed me', confessed Lucie Lancezeux, 'is that never, ever did a Jew thank us. They took it over for themselves. No one ever said that it's thanks to the Communist Party cell that there is a monument. We cleared the land and then they ploughed it up.' Huguette Robin set the issue in the context of the Resistance teaching on the deportation. 'During the war,' she says, 'if you were against the Occupation, against repression and all that, people didn't ask who you were or where you came from.' The Jews, however, she says, 'always want to make distinctions, Jews on one side, communists on the other'. 'That sort of thing didn't exist during the war,' adds Lucie Lancezeux, 'people were striving towards a single goal.' 'Besides,' concludes Huguette Robin, 'in this area they don't remember any Jews who took part in the Resistance.'

The public recognition of the special claim of the Jews had the effect of unseating the Resistance establishment from its pedestal and of highlighting the actions of 'bad Frenchmen', some of whom were belatedly brought to trial. In addition the Holocaust factor reminded French people that it was no longer essential to present themselves as 'good French' with a Resistance record; the role of 'poor French', who had also suffered the oppression and hardships of the Occupation, was possibly even more powerful.

When I met the Amis du Vieux Chinon in the elegant Maison des États Généraux I was introduced to 'a person who took part in the Resistance', René Arnoult, a large and powerful man who clearly enjoyed some status. A young man at the time, he had been active in Resistance activities with his father, who had become a member of the CDL of Indre-et-Loire. The conversation that afternoon, however, was dominated by the slight and wizened Christian Beugnet, older than his years, who held forth on the day the Germans irrupted into his childhood.

> Today I can still see the arrival of the German forces. For three days and three nights came first of all the tanks, then the soldiers on foot with their officers on horseback, in the direction of the Atlantic. Then in the days that followed columns of French prisoners moved up in the opposite direction . . . Hotels were requisitioned for the Kommandantur and the Feldgendarmerie and a number of other services answerable to the German army, and of course the swastika flew from all these buildings . . . From the moment these organizations were set up the curfew was imposed, one could only move around outside the authorized times with a pass, and patrols came by regularly in the town . . . You had to take precautions: some people were arrested just for things they said . . . If you had a disagreement with your neighbour he just had to go and find someone at the Kommandantur and you could be arrested . . . and then there were round-ups (*rafles*) in town, the German came by with a lorry and if by misfortune you didn't have your identity card, well then. . . . It was four years of fascist dictatorship.

This classic statement of the suffering of the 'poor French' was listened to with great respect, but it did not, however, command full agreement. M. Beugnet's wife Léonie interrupted to say that there had only been a few arrests at Chinon, while the jovial president of the Amis, Claude Bougreau, claimed that 'the Occupation at Chinon was very mild, in fact. There were no reprisals. . . . The majority of the population adjusted fairly well to the occupation and some people actually did well out of it, with the black market.'[81]

As in Tours, memories of French people differed about the severity of the Occupation. It is perhaps significant that the 'Nazi dictatorship' view is often espoused by those who might have resisted but did not, while women or those who were boys at the time are more likely to remember the Occupation as fairly mild. Many, of course, expected the Germans to repeat the atrocities of which they had been guilty in northern France in 1914–18 or even in 1870, particularly those who had family connections with the frontier area, and were pleasantly surprised when things did not turn out that way. French and Germans lived cheek by jowl with each other for four or five years and came to see each other as real people, not just the stereotypes of propaganda and myth. It also became clear that the Germans were as much the victims as the perpetrators of the war, far from home, suffering fear and hardship, and in this sense they had much in common with the French population.

'I heard so much about the Germans from my mother', said Andrée Trudeau of Saumur, 'that I lived with the memory of the '14 war, even though of course I hadn't known it.' Her mother came from Le Chemin des Dames, in the Aisne, which became a battlefield in 1917, and told of how they were under the Germans one day, the English on another, the Scots on a third. Her grandmother had been treated by a German doctor who left instructions for her care before he was obliged to retreat. Andrée was quite clear that 'there were good and bad' among the Germans. Of the Occupation at Saumur, she says, 'for the first few years, here as everywhere else, they left us alone'. Later in the war people were not allowed to talk on the bridge in groups of more than three; if they were caught, the punishment 'wasn't nasty', usually to polish boots at the Kommandantur or watch the Loire for an hour without turning round. Her view of the Germans at Saumur was that they too suffered from the war. The Kommandant was 'not bad ... humane, there because he had to be there. People make war because they are obliged to. Those who declare war don't make it, they send others.'[82]

Having heard stories of atrocities committed by the Germans in 1914–18, the parents of Michel Leterme, who lived in Angers, were racked by anxiety about the grandparents, who lived at Armentières, near the Belgian border. Later it transpired that they had tried to flee with a wheelbarrow, but only got as far as Hazebrouck, 25 kilometres down the road. Michel, ten at the time, remembers seeing his first Germans in Angers, 'young and handsome, clean and polite'. They were, he said, keen to 'efface the image of terror that had become associated with them', and they practised a 'policy of fraternization'. The French eyed them curiously and asked them for news of towns the tanks had come through, where they had friends or relations. He argued that 'the presence of the German army was not disagreeable'. Michel's sister married in 1942 and two 'kind and peaceable' workers for the Todt Organization billeted on them for five or six months used her vacant room. Sometimes they shared coffee in the kitchen and mused about their common plight in broken French: 'war, very unfortunate'. The military band used to play in the Jardin du Mail on a Sunday afternoon and French and Germans rubbed up against each other in cafés, cinemas and the opera. He declares, 'It was what people now call cohabitation.'[83]

When I delivered my paper to the Académie de Tours in 1997 I quoted Violette Lemasson, who grew up during the Occupation in the small Angevin village of Saint-Ellier-sur-Aubance. 'We never lacked anything,' she had told me, 'we never went hungry.' This assertion provoked a wave of disagreement in the audience, many of whom would have spent the Occupation in Tours. In his letter to me the Academy's secretary, Marcel Girard, drove the point home. 'What is striking', he wrote, 'is the memory of food shortages. Here one must distinguish between the farmers, who had ample food and sometimes even made a good deal of money, and those who produced nothing, in the large towns and even in the small ones, who lost on average (according to the statistics) twenty kilos!'[84] Hunger was of course one of the main characteristics of the *années noires* but French people are in fact much more eloquent about the tricks they got up to in order to obtain food than about standing forlornly in bread queues.

Huguette Robin was precisely the kind of person who should have starved under the Occupation. Her parents ran a café in the place Velpeau, Tours, between the railway station and Saint-Pierre-des-Corps, the clientele of which was working class, mainly railwaymen. When they were arrested for communist activities in 1942 she was left, at the age of eighteen, to manage the café with her younger sister. She remembered being cold and hungry and in debt to the local baker. But there were ways of getting by. They had little wine to sell but collected the wine-ration tickets to which (even at that age) they were entitled and built up a stock to which they treated their clients on market day. More importantly they had relations in the Free Zone who were bakers, and once the demarcation line was abolished after the total Occupation of France in November 1942 these were able to come to their assistance.[85]

Another inhabitant of Tours, Lucienne Despouy, who was arrested along with her husband for communist activities in 1942, returned to her business making rubber stamps after three months in prison, while he was executed. Bereaved like Huguette Robin, whose father was shot, her memories of the food situation were rather more positive. She remembered people raising rabbits and chickens at home, pointed out that the villages of La Riche, Chambray and La Ville-aux-Dames, now part of the conurbation of Tours, were then full of market gardeners, and said that the black market flourished. She also had her own country uncle, who used to arrive from the Sarthe in his gas-fired car (petrol being almost impossible to find) with wood and potatoes. 'The inhabitants of Tours', she concluded, 'did not really go without.'[86]

Just as memories of hunger under the Occupation are challenged by recollections of imaginative ways of getting by, of the famous Système D, so memories of Nazi dictatorship and the moralizing prohibitions of the Vichy regime are contradicted by memories of flourishing religious, cultural and social life. Sometimes the contradiction between obeying rules and creating friendship networks informed the same account, as if internalized orders were still in conflict with the desire to make life tolerable.

Odette Goxe, whose husband ran a textile business in Angers, began by saying that associative and social life was 'dormant'. There was the cinema, of course, but 'no more cultural meetings. People stayed at home.' Religious life, she said, was the exception. She was with a group of ladies who met under the supervision of the curé of Saint-Serge at Angers, hearing him read messages from Marshal Pétain 'which did not enthuse anyone', she says, making cakes and knitting for the charity sale for the parish funds. This of course was perfectly legal, but her son's Catholic Boy Scout camp was not. Nevertheless he went on a clandestine camp in the Vendée, 'around a little lake, with the French flag flying', and she showed me photographs of the event. She was most enthusiastic when conversation turned to the procession of the statue of Our Lady of Boulogne which, having been taken to Lourdes in 1942, began a long and ceremonial odyssey across France in 1943–4. She remembered the 'huge production, the church flooded with light' in Angers where the statue rested after one of its stages. 'People turned out in great numbers,' she recalled, many walking in bare feet and throwing written prayers into the boat in which she was carried. For Mme Goxe and for the crowds Our Lady 'represented hope, [divine] intercession for the liberation of France'.[87]

Pierre Boudet, at the time president of a student association, then a young doctor in the Sarthe, initially declared that 'all meetings of students, of scouts or other demonstrations were absolutely forbidden'. There was 'absolutely no' social or associative life, he asserted. He then let slip that 'we did all sorts of prohibited things'. These included demonstrating on Joan of Arc Day on instructions from de Gaulle, walking at some distance from each other so as to evade the ban on processions, and dancing secretly in each other's houses and even in bistros. With pleasure and nostalgia he cited Roberte Marnor's charming song, 'Le Bal défendu'.[88]

Abel Avenet, a peasant of Dierre, 'the little Moscow' in the Cher valley, emphasized that what young people were interested in during the Occupation was not politics but music and dancing. 'When you are young,' he confided, 'you only think about having fun.' 'We made music during the war,' and his own instrument was the trombone. He remembers that in the spring of 1941, feeling 'on a rein', they organized a clandestine ball one Sunday night in a barn. The second Sunday some youths came by train from Tours to join in the fun, and the locals decided to allow the girls in but not the boys. As a result they were denounced and fined 15 or 20 francs by the JP. After that they restricted the balls to locals, with local musicians (including himself), and had no recollection of being bothered by the gendarmerie. Sometimes they danced in a mill at Bléré, where the thick walls muffled the sound, although they had to take care returning home after the curfew because of German patrols near the demarcation line. Asked whether to dance in defiance of the law constituted Resistance, Abel Avenet shrugged his shoulders. 'The young people didn't see it like that,' he assures me, 'boys and girls just wanted to have fun, to amuse themselves.'[89] These sentiments were confirmed by André Roussel, the grocer's son from Bléré, who showed me the old accordion that he used to play at clandestine balls and lovingly squeezed a few chords out of it. 'Many things were forbidden', he recalled, 'but lots of things happened anyway.' At the time, he said, he was only eighteen, and 'at that age it's the time to live. The only thing that interested me was going out with girls and playing the accordion ... Those were the good old days, weren't they?'[90]

The official memories and the stories people tell have been and continue to be shaped by the dominant narrative of the 'good French' who resisted or who supported the Resistance. There has always, however, been conflict as to who the 'good French' were and what might be good actions. The Free French considered their role more important than that of the internal Resistance. Gaullists vied with Communists and Pétainists for recognition as the most effective resisters. Some communities sought to associate themselves with Resistance heroes while others, who had suffered the fallout of Resistance activity, were torn between praising heroism and mourning the tragedy that had befallen them. Deportees who were deported for 'acts of Resistance' claimed superiority over political dissidents, labour conscripts and Jews and exercised a sort of surveillance police in order to defend their position.

Conflicts over memory have not remained static in the years since the Liberation. The claim of resisters to deserve most public recognition because they were bravest has been challenged by Jews, on the grounds that they suffered the most. Suggestions that resisters may not have been as pure and heroic as they once seemed have also undermined their status. Meanwhile, in private, the Pétainist account of the Occupation has been voiced and may at some time be accorded a wider audience. Finally, the concept of the 'poor French' enduring the hardships of *les années noires* has enjoyed much popularity with historians, but should not be allowed to silence those who have spoken of the imagination, creativity and resourcefulness of the inhabitants of Occupied France. The least that can be claimed for oral history is that sometimes the *vox populi* may be allowed to guide historical reflection.

18. CONCLUSION

The main purpose of this book has been to break out of the strait-jacket of interpretations based on the Resistance/collaboration version of events, while also refusing to reduce the French to passive victims of the Occupation, cold, hungry and fearful. The model of 'good French', 'bad French' and 'poor French' is very attractive, but too simple to make sense of the diverse and contradictory experiences of ordinary people. I have tried to concentrate on the strategies they adopted, the networks they created and the institutions they subverted in order to negotiate a tricky passage through the Occupation. As often as not this involved keeping one's options open, not committing oneself irretrievably either to Resistance or to collaboration, playing a number of roles at once, being ready to change direction as the occasion demanded. This interpretation does not seek to downgrade the serious ideological and political commitments that some people had, but suggests only that prudence played a significant part in determining what decisions were made and when. Such an approach has the advantage of moving beyond praise and blame, which for a historian born several years after the war ended would seem anyway to be inappropriate. It tries to understand actions and sentiments in terms of the options and values that obtained under the Occupation, the one extremely limited and the other extremely fluid.

The first conclusion is that Franco-German relations under the Occupation were not always as brutal or even as one-sided as they have often been portrayed. Recent German research points in the same direction and reinforces the call for a reassessment.[1] The Germans were content to allow the French administration a certain autonomy, to practise indirect rule, so long as that administration delivered public order and resources. Indeed it was felt that these were more likely to be delivered by means of good relations with the French, with their tacit consent, than by means of what was called 'Polonization'. The French administration, isolated from Vichy, had no alternative but to do business with the German military administration, and like indigenous chiefs under indirect colonial rule, might find their authority thereby reinforced. Despite the hereditary enmity between French and Germans, reinforced by the ideology of Nazism, there was a counter-current of mutual respect based on a common sense of military honour shared by veterans of 1914–18, a common European civilization, and sometimes a common religion too. These relationships made it possible to defuse crises that arose when public order was threatened by either side. Prefects and mayors instructed French citizens how unwise it was to persist in graffiti campaigns or to demonstrate too openly. The consequences of deaths on each side were minimized by negotiation, especially when they seemed like accidents. Even when the military commander of Nantes was shot in October 1941, frantic negotiations at all levels saved the lives of a second batch of fifty hostages.

Ordinary French and Germans also learned to live together. German atrocities feared by the French population in the summer of 1940 never took place: troops arriving in towns and cities declared 'open' by their municipalities were more likely to distribute cigarettes and sweets. The billeting of German troops on French families could be very trying, but as we have seen there were cases of disruptive lodgers being moved on after appeal to the Kommandantur, and relations between German guests and French families were not always as icy as those described in *Le Silence de la mer*. The Germans requisitioned everything that could be requisitioned at various times, but they also gave lucrative contracts to French firms, did plentiful business with French people on the black market, and employed a vast array of French domestics with whom relations sometime became more intimate.

This interaction suggests that the French were not just the passive victims of the Occupation. Nor, however, were they only cynical collaborators. Informal rules were devised by the French governing what was legitimate and what illegitimate in Franco-German relations. As a rule of thumb, actions that undermined the family, community or nation were illegitimate. On the economic front it was deemed acceptable for a firm to accept a contract to supply the Wehrmacht, provided the employer did not force his employees to work with undue zeal or put pressure on them to go and work in Germany. To rip off the Germans by small-scale black marketeering was just Gallic cunning, but large-scale dealing which deprived the community of scarce resources was not considered right. Socially, it was acceptable to drink with a German in a bar but not to invite him home. If a German was billeted on a family it was not thought proper that he should dine at the family table. Flirting with Germans was normal and to have sex with them for money was not a crime, particularly as the German military were so worried about their men catching VD. However, exaggerated merry-making by French women and German soldiers was frowned upon, while affairs between Germans and married women such as the wives of POWs were beyond the pale on every count.

This is not to deny the brutality of the Occupation or the imbalance of power between French and Germans; rather, these both intensified as the Occupation dragged on. The German invasion of the Soviet Union, nullifying the Nazi–Soviet Pact, tipped some communists in France into a campaign of assassination directed against members of the Wehrmacht. It caused the Germans to increase their demands for resources and labour to fight a Total War and to seek to eliminate 'enemies within' who were seen to be sabotaging their war effort, notably communists and Jews. The Germans gradually concluded that the French authorities were not able to guarantee public order or deliver supplies in the quantities they required. The French authorities were steadily swept aside as indirect rule gave way to direct rule, and the German military was displaced by the secret police. A style of collaboration based on negotiation was replaced by *Diktat* – the imposition of terms – or rather by collaboration with those elements of the French administration and police who alone were prepared to do the Germans' bidding. Most officials found themselves squeezed in a vice between the ruthlessness and insatiable demands of the Germans and the growing fear and anger of the population. They pretended to keep faith while doing what they could to protect the population. Some made contact with Resistance organizations or were fingered for the post-Liberation administration by Gaullist moles like Michel Debré. Such a double game was of course extremely dangerous: the German security police were highly sensitized to any evidence of disloyalty and increasingly either put pressure on Vichy to remove unreliable officials or simply arrested and deported them. A small minority deserted their posts and went into hiding. By the summer of 1944 the Germans had only limited cooperation from French officials in the regions, who were preparing to switch their allegiance either to the Allied forces when they appeared or to de Gaulle's provisional government. All this led the way to a smooth transfer of power at the Liberation and ensured the continuity of the state.

The second conclusion is that from the perspective of Occupied France the Vichy régime seems neither as authoritarian nor as reactionary as it perhaps looked in the Free Zone. Isolated from Vichy and without the transmission belt of the Légion that was banned in the Occupied Zone, the French administration there had to fall back on the notables to ensure that the local population cooperated. These notables, whose influence was based less on party than on their independent standing in the community, served as mayors, municipal councillors and members of prefects' vestigial administrative councils. Parliament had been abolished, but all national politicians had local power bases and these could not simply be uprooted. There might be something to be said for handing local government over to reactionaries in the interests of 'Travail, Famille, Patrie', but a conservative landowner who had influence in Brittany would have no purchase in Touraine. Similarly a large industrial town needed a socialist mayor, so long as he 'rallied' to the regime, not a representative of the employers who had no authority over the workforce. Under the Occupation trimming was thus developed into a fine art.

As the Occupation wore on, however, the Vichy regime became less and less able to maintain adequate communications with local communities. It therefore replaced the small administrative commissions invented to advise prefects by larger departmental councils which were like the *conseils généraux* of the Third Republic, abolished in 1940, but now appointed rather than elected. The need to rebuild bridges to the political class of the Third Republic was felt particularly keenly by Pierre Laval when he returned to government in April 1942. Although he favoured close collaboration with the Germans in the war against communists and Jews, he also realized that local politicians would gravitate *en masse* to the alternative government established by de Gaulle in Algiers unless they were given more reason to stay loyal by Vichy. The Napoleonic experiment which removed the check of elective assemblies on prefects thus gave way to Vichy's search for a republican base.

The key function of the notables was to mediate between the demands of the Germans and the interests of local communities. If anyone acted as a shield under the Occupation it was they rather than the Marshal. In 1940 they protected their towns by persuading the retreating military not to defend them and declaring them 'open' to the advancing Germans. They negotiated regularly with the Germans to limit the number of horses, vehicles or food they demanded to requisition or the quota of STO workers they wanted to draft. Whether they protected all their citizens equally, however, is open to question. The distinction between 'Vichy' and the 'state' breaks down when considering local notables, who essentially represented one to the other. An interesting light is nevertheless cast on the responsibility of the French for the deportation of Jews in France by the fact that notables who protested about the requisitioning of their farmers' grain and the conscription of their local youths for STO did not protest about the Aryanization of local Jewish businesses or the deportation of the Jews in their midst.

The pressure on notables in effect to turn against their own communities became intolerable. Like officials they also began to look to the future. Hence the departmental councils were dogged by absenteeism, while mayors resigned office in droves. Vichy was unable to consolidate a republican base, and after the Liberation these trimmers were generally happy to rally to the new republican regime. Meanwhile the Liberation authorities, who initially had even less power than Vichy, were happy to confirm them in office so long as they had not violated the minimum requirements of republican legitimacy. After all, they needed to bring over communities whose Pétainism had often been tenacious, and to guarantee order against the revolutionary challenge of communism. The continuity of local elites across the turbulent years from 1935 to 1945 was thus remarkable. It was not until elections were held in more peaceful circumstances in 1945 that these notables, who had sacrificed consistency to longevity, were unceremoniously dumped by a popular vote that was seeking something fresh and untarnished. Even this, however, did not mean that the country suddenly lurched from Right to Left. Provided that they could demonstrate some association with the Resistance, parties of the Centre and Right were able, in parts of the region at least, to ensure the continuity of conservatism.

The third conclusion is that however great the hardships suffered by ordinary people under the Occupation the monolithic concept of *les années noires* needs to be nuanced. The danger of this term, as we have seen, enshrines the image of the 'poor French', paralysed by cold, hunger and fear. In spite of the repressive policies of both the Germans and Vichy a civil society remained, old and new networks and associations were sustained and created, and different subcultures of workers, peasants and youth developed. This is not to deny that the French were often cold, hungry and fearful under the Occupation but to underline that they demonstrated imagination, resourcefulness and Gallic cunning in order to make the Occupation liveable.

When it came to getting daily bread, for example, the image of food queues should be replaced by the image of bicycles and trailers scouring the countryside. A whole series of parallel markets sprang up to counter the evils of requisitioning and price controls, both local and long distance, setting to work relations between family members, neighbours or profiteers. Again, there were winners and losers, exploiters and exploited, but everyone took part in Système D, which was far more flexible and responsive to people's needs than the official hunger market. Economic life was neither anarchic, nor was it regimented, with workers and peasants marching in step to the prescriptions of the Labour Charter and the Peasant Corporation. Trade unions did not disappear under Vichy, which for some labour leaders was supposed to reach an apotheosis as a syndicalist state. Other labour leaders, including Catholic ones, remained totally suspicious of the Labour Charter as the tool of trusts and the state and effectively scuppered it by insisting on their autonomy. Farmers, arguably, were more subtle. They went along with the Peasant Corporation but only to convert it into a vehicle for their own interests, to challenge the traditional domination of agricultural organization by landowners and to defend the resources of the agricultural sector from the claws of the requisitioning agencies. Lastly, a more important economic role was undertaken by women, running farms and small businesses in the absence of their husbands in POW camps, despite Vichy's sermonizing about '*la femme au foyer*'.

Associational life, as we have seen, was not confined to satisfying basic needs. The Occupation was a flourishing moment for sport, cinema, the theatre, music and dancing, sometimes in accordance with the policies of Vichy and the Germans, sometimes against them, and often exploiting the contradictions between the two. For as we have seen, while Vichy was obsessed by moral regeneration the Germans were interested only in the security of their armed forces. The craze for clandestine dancing in particular demonstrates that the gloom and despondency that was Vichy's official policy was far from successful. French people, however, did not just indulge their hedonism. There was an explosion of religious activity, which was tolerated by the Germans and encouraged by Vichy but which represented for many of the faithful the best hope of deliverance from their current ills. The Catholic hierarchy was overwhelmingly Pétainist, but institutionally it offered protection from Nazism and many of the lower clergy and Catholic laity were active resisters. Above all, however, there was a massive development of prayer, of saint cults, of processions and pilgrimages as people turned to heaven for salvation from the bombs of the Allies as well as the bullets of the Germans. This religious upsurge was something that the Church was able to play on after the Liberation, mobilizing Catholic opinion which had been trained in opposing anti-religious ideologies to defend Church schools against another wave of republican anticlericalism.

Of course there were limits to how far solidarity extended. The shock of defeat and Occupation caused horizons to contract: people resorted for material and emotional support to their family, neighbourhood, village, town or *pays*. This can be seen clearly when it came to charity. The Secours National was supposed to mobilize charitable giving on a national scale, under the benevolent eye of Marshal Pétain. But local communities were far readier to provide for their own needy or their own prisoners of war than for the needy and prisoners of war of France as a whole. Likewise, inland communities were often reluctant to take in evacuees from the bombed seaports of the Atlantic or refugees from the Normandy battles of 1944, and evacuees had to set up their own pressure groups to ensure that they were properly cared for by the local authorities whose charges they had become.

Communities, as we have seen, also divided against themselves. Old rivalries and new threatened to undermine much collective work, such as that of the prisoner-of-war committee of Saint-Brévin-les-Pins. The presence of the Germans both attracted people into their orbit and antagonized others who thought that they were violating the conventions of the local community. But the accusation of Boche levelled against a French woman or man could easily set in train a mechanism of denunciation of the offender to the Germans, his or her arrest, and an inevitable settling of accounts with the denouncer by the victim (if still alive) and community after the Germans had left. Communities also turned on those who were not fully integrated. This was the experience of many Jewish traders, artisans and even company directors under the Aryanization laws. The enthusiasm of the French to squeeze out Jewish partners from company boards, to present themselves as agents for the liquidation and sale of Jewish businesses and to apply to buy up such businesses seems as good a sign as any of the extent of popular anti-Semitism.

The narrowing of horizons and community conflicts did not exclude demonstrations of patriotism. In one sense the political antennae of the French people were never more finely attuned, but under occupation they had to be imaginative about how to reconstruct the French nation symbolically. Every 'V' sign scrawled on a wall, every wreath smuggled beneath a statue of Joan of Arc, every tricolour flag or buttonhole sported for an hour, every glance exchanged at the appointed hour in a procession that pretended to be a crowd served to reflect the continued existence of the French nation to the French. As demands from the Germans increased, so they took to a more concrete but passive resistance. Hiding farm stocks targeted for requisition or sending the oldest horse, striking against the *Relève*, going to ground rather than turn up for STO, singing the *Marseillaise* on the STO or failing to report back after a period of leave from work in Germany were all ways of undermining the German war machine which did not carry too many risks. Not all *réfractaires* or draft dodgers were Maquisards and not all armed bands contributed anything to the Resistance. The Loire area, which is flat and lacks forests except on the frontier with Brittany, was not a good habitat for Maquisards in the way that the Massif Central or the Alps were. Armed attacks on retreating German units in the summer of 1944 gave the region its fair share of collective reprisals and made local communities very ambivalent towards the armed struggle. Liberation, in the end, came less from French insurgents, who in any case had difficulty acquiring weapons, than from the industrial firepower of the Allies. In this context, as we have seen, the steady pounding of the German military–industrial base from the air, inflicting substantial collateral damage on the French population, was a vital prelude to the land assault of June 1944.

The last point to be made is that from the point of view of ordinary French people the Liberation was a mixture of joy and disappointment. The joy is evident on the smiling faces in myriad pictures of the French welcoming the liberating forces into their towns and villages and dancing in the streets. The disappointment, however, was also very real, not only because dancing remained formally banned until the end of the war in Europe, but because hundreds of thousands of people remained homeless, shortages and the black market did not disappear overnight, and POWs, conscripted workers and deportees did not return to a home fit for heroes. But the gospel of Resistance and Liberation was already overlaying the complexities of the Occupation and it would be a long time before all the truths were out.

Notes

ABBREVIATIONS

AD	Archives Départementales
A. Dio.	Archives Diocésaines
AM	Archives Municipales
AN	Archives Nationales
BAMA	Bundesarchiv-Militärarchiv
CDAA	Comité Départemental d'Action Agricole
CDL	Comité Départemental de la Libération
CFLN	Comité Français de Libération Nationale
CFTC	Confédération Générale des Travailleurs Chrétiens
CGA	Confédération Générale de l'Agriculture
CGMA	Commissariat Générale à la Main d'Œuvre
CGPF	Confédération Générale du Patronat Français
CGQJ	Commissariat Général aux Questions Juives
CGT	Confédération Générale du Travail
CHDGM	Comité d'Histoire de la Deuxième Guerre Mondiale
CHOLF	Comité d'Histoire de l'Occupation et de la Libération de la France
CIEE	Comité Interprofessional d'Épuration des Entreprises
CIMT	Compagnie Industrielle de Matériel de Transport
CNR	Conseil National de la Résistance
CO	Comité d'Organisation
COSI	Comité Ouvrier de Secours Immédiat
COSR	Comité des Œuvres Sociales de la Résistance
CVR	Combattant Volontaire de la Résistance
DGGFTO	Délégué Général du Gouvernement Français dans les Territoires Occupées
FFI	Forces Françaises de l'Intérieur
FNC	Fédération Nationale Catholique

423

NOTES

FNDIR	Fédération Nationale des Déportés et Internés de la Résistance
FNDIRP	Fédération Nationale des Déportés et Internés de la Résistance Patriotes
FNSEA	Fédération Nationale des Syndicats d'Exploitants Agricoles
FTPF	Francs-Tireurs et Partisans Français
IHTP	Institut d'Histoire du Temps Présent
I-et-L	Indre-et-Loire
I-et-V	Ille-et-Vilaine
JAC	Jeunesse Agricole Chrétienne
JEC	Jeunesse Étudiante Chrétienne
JOC	Jeunesse Ouvrière Chrétienne
L-A	Loire-Atlantique
L-I	Loire-Inférieure
LVF	Ligue des Volontaires Français contre le Bolchévisme
M-et-L	Maine-et-Loire
MNPD	Mouvement National des Prisonniers de Guerre et des Déportés
MRP	Mouvement Républicain Populaire
ORA	Organisation de la Résistance Armée
PPF	Parti Populaire Français
PSF	Parti Social Français
SFIO	Section Française de l'Internationale Ouvrière
SNCASO	Société Nationale de Construction Aéronautique du Sud-Ouest
STO	Service du Travail Obligatoire
UNC	Union Nationale des Combattants
UNMRAC	Union Nationale des Mutilés, Réformés et Anciens Combattants

INTRODUCTION

1 Letter from Marcel Girard to the author, 13 Jan. 1998.

2 Interview with Georges Audebert (b. 1913), Tours, 24 June 1998.

3 *La Nouvelle République*, 20 March 1998.

4 For a comparative view see Timothy Garton Ash, 'Trials, purges and history lessons', in his *History of the Present. Essays, Sketches and Despatches from Europe in the 1990s* (London, Penguin, 2000), 294–314.

5 See for example Henri Michel, *Histoire de la Résistance, 1940–1944* (Paris, PUF, 'Que sais-je?', 1950).

6 Robert O. Paxton, *Vichy France. Old Guard and New Order, 1940–1944* (London, Barrie & Jenkins, 1972). Sarah Farmer et al., eds, *France at War. Vichy and the Historians* (Oxford and New York, Berg, 2000) is a *Festschrift* for Robert Paxton.

7 The key text on this subject is Henri Rousso, *The Vichy Syndrome. History*

and Memory in France since 1944 (Cambridge, Mass., Harvard University Press, 1991). See also Eric Conan and Henri Rousso, *Vichy, un passé qui ne passe pas* (Paris, Fayard, 1994) and Henri Rousso, *La Hantise du passé* (Paris, Textuel, 1998).

8 On these debates see Thierry Wolton, *Le Grand recrutement* (Paris, Grasset, 1993); Gérard Chauvy, *Aubrac: Lyon 1943* (Paris, Albin Michel, 1997); Pierre Péan, *Vie et morts de Jean Moulin* (Paris, Fayard, 1998); Daniel Cordier, *Jean Moulin. La République des catacombes* (Paris, Gallimard, 1999).

9 Robert Paxton and Michael Marrus, *Vichy France and the Jews* (New York, Basic Books, 1981), Serge Klarsfeld, *Vichy–Auschwitz. Le rôle de Vichy dans la solution finale de la question juive en France* (2 vols, Paris, Fayard, 1983–5). See also Paul Webster, *Pétain's Crime. The full story of French collaboration in the Holocaust* (London, Macmillan, 1990).

10 *Le Monde*, 18 July 1995.

11 Ibid., 21 Oct. 1997. On the Papon trial see Richard Golsan, *The Papon Affair. Memory and justice on trial* (New York, Routledge, 2000); Gérard Boulanger, *Maurice Papon. Un technocrate français sous l'Occupation* (Paris, Seuil, 1994) and his *Papon. Un intrus dans la République* (Paris, Seuil, 1997); Jean-Jacques Gandini, *Le Procès Papon* (Paris, Librio, 1999); Arno Klarsfeld, *La Cour, les nains et le bouffon* (Paris, Laffont, 1998); Maurice Papon, *La Vérité n'intéressait personne* (Paris, Bergès, 1999).

12 Conan and Rousso, *Vichy, un passé qui ne passe pas*, 268–75.

13 *Le Monde*, 28 Oct. 1997.

14 See Jean-Pierre Azéma and François Bédarida, eds, *Vichy et les Français* (Paris, Fayard, 1992).

15 Dominique Veillon, *Vivre et survivre en France, 1939–1947* (Paris, Payot, 1995), 105.

16 Jean Guéhenno, *Journal des années noires* (Paris, Gallimard, 1947); Henri Rousso, *Les Années noires. Vivre sous l'Occupation* (Paris, Gallimard, 1992); Jean-Pierre Azéma and François Bédarida, *La France des années noires* (2 vols, Seuil, 1993); Julian Jackson, *France The Dark Years 1940–1944* (Oxford, Oxford University Press, 2001).

17 AD M-et-L 95W63, prefect of M-et-L to subprefect of Cholet, 18 Dec. 1946; police superintendent of Cholet to subprefecture, 26 Dec. 1946.

18 See especially the 72AJ series in AN.

19 Alistair Thomson, 'Unreliable memories? The use and abuse of oral history', in William Lamont, ed., *Historical Controversies and Historians* (London, UCL Press, 1998), 23–34. See also Peter Thompson, *Voice of Past* (Oxford, Oxford University Press, 1978 and 1988) and Elizabeth Tonkin, *Narrating Our Pasts* (Cambridge, Cambridge University Press, 1992).

20 *Le Courrier de l'Ouest*, 3 April 1997.

21 Interviews with Andrée Trudeau (b. 1923), Saumur, 22 June 1998, Lucienne Despouy, Saint-Avertin, Tours, 9 June 1997, and Thérèse Boucher, Angers, 12 Dec. 1996.

22 Interview with André Chardonnnet (b. 1917), Angers, 11 April 1997.

23 Michelle Mouton and Helena Pohlandt-McCormick, 'Boundary crossings: oral history of Nazi Germany and Apartheid South Africa – a comparative perspective', *History Workshop Journal* 48 (1999), 41–63.

24 Karl Figlio, 'Oral history and the unconscious', *History Workshop Journal* 26 (1988), 120–32.

25 See, for example, Marc Ferro, *Pétain* (Paris, Fayard, 1987); Nick Atkin, *Pétain* (London, Longman, 1998); Fred Kupferman, *Laval* (Paris, Balland, 1987); Hervé Coutau-Bégarie and Claude Huan, *Darlan* (Paris, Fayard, 1989); George E. Melton, *Darlan – Admiral and statesman of France* (London, Praeger, 1998); Jean-Paul Brunet, *Jacques Doriot* (Paris, Balland, 1986); Daniel Cordier, *Jean Moulin. L'Inconnu du Panthéon* (Paris, Lattès, 1989).

26 Philippe Burrin, *Living with Defeat. France under the German Occupation, 1940–1944* (London, Arnold, 1996).

27 Pierre Laborie, *L'Opinion française sous Vichy* (Paris, Seuil, 1990).

28 See Yves Durand, *Vivre au pays au XVIIIe siècle* (Paris, PUF, 1984) and, importing the concept, Charles Pythian-Adams, ed., *Societies, Culture and Kinship, 1580–1850* (Leicester, Leicester University Press, 1993).

29 C. J. Calhoun, 'Community: towards a variable conceptualization for comparative research', *Social History* 5 (1980), 105–29. See also David Garrioch, *Neighbourhood and Community in Paris, 1740–1790* (Cambridge, Cambridge University Press, 1986), 4–6.

30 Michèle Cointet, *Vichy capitale, 1940–1944* (Paris, Perrin, 1993).

31 On First World War atrocities see Ruth Harris, 'The Child of the Barbarian: rape, race and nationalism during the First World War', *Past and Present* 141 (Nov. 1993), 170–206, Stéphane Audoin-Rouzeau, *L'Enfant de l'ennemi* (Paris, Aubier, 1995) and John Horne and Alan Kramer, *German atrocities 1914: a history of denial* (New Haven and London, Yale University Press, 2001).

32 See the survey of the Institut d'Histoire du Temps Présent, *Les Élites locales dans la tourmente Du Front populaire aux années cinquante*, ed. Gilles de Bégnee and Denis Peschanski (Paris, CNRS, 2000). For a suggestive anthropological approach see Marc Abélès, *Quiet Days in Burgundy. A study of local politics* (Paris and Cambridge, Éditions de la Maison des Sciences de l'Homme/Cambridge University Press, 1991).

33 On denunciation see L.-J. Colanéri and G. Gérante, *La Dénonciation et les dénonciateurs* (Paris, PUF, 1948); André Halimi, *La Dénonciation sous l'Occupation* (Paris, Alain Moreau, 1983); Sheila Fitzpatrick and Robert

Gellately, eds, *Accusatory Practices* (Chicago and London, University of Chicago Press, 1997).

1. CHINON

1 Margaret Aulton, *Fair Touraine* (London, John Lane at the Bodley Head, 1925), 38–9.

2 René Boylesve, *La Jeune Fille bien élevée* (Paris, Calmann-Lévy, 1924), 1–2.

3 *La Touraine Républicaine*, 29–30 April 1929; *L'Écho de Chinon*, 2 May 1929.

4 E. H. Tourlet, *La Statue de Rabelais d'Émile Hébert. Relation des fêtes données à Chinon les 1er, 2 et 3 juillet 1882 à l'occasion de l'inauguration du monument* (Chinon, 1894).

5 See in particular Mikhail Bakhtin, *Rabelais and his World* (Bloomington, Indiana University Press, 1984).

6 François Rabelais, *Œuvres*, vol. I, *Gargantua*, ch. 13, ed. Abel Lefranc (Paris, Champion, 1913), 130–8.

7 AM Chinon, Registre des délibérations du conseil municipal, 4 Sept. and 12 Nov. 1940.

8 AD I-et-L 10W65, subprefect of Chinon to prefect, 22 Nov. 1940.

9 *Le Chinonais*, 15 May 1941 and 13 May 1943.

10 Ibid., 15 and 29 Jan. 1942, 4 June 1942; *Bulletin de la Société des Amis du Vieux Chinon*, IV (1936–45), 315–17.

11 AD I-et-L 52W20, prefect of I-et-L to regional prefect, Jan. 1942, 11 March and 24 June 1942.

12 AD I-et-L 52W21, Associations et syndicats. Recensement à la demande de la Feldkommandantur, Nov. 1940.

13 AM Chinon, Registre des délibérations du conseil municipal, 19 Oct. 1941, 19 Dec. 1942, 30 March 1943.

14 *Le Chinonais*, 28 May 1941.

15 Ibid., 8 July 1943.

16 AD I-et-L 10W8, report of subprefect of Chinon, 25 Aug. 1942.

17 AM Chinon, Registre des délibérations du conseil municipal, report of finance commission, 19 Sept. 1943.

18 AD I-et-L 121W2, subprefect of Chinon to prefect, 2 June 1943; 10W53, police commissioner, Tours, to prefect, 26 June 1943.

19 AD I-et-L 1119W25, depositions for Cour de Justice of I-et-L in the case of Mme Longuépée by Mehmed Kapandji, 8 Jan. 1945, E. Ponset, 16 Nov. 1944, and Leopold Florens, 16 Nov. 1944.

20 AD I-et-L 10W84, Inspecteur Postal Pouyol to Directeur Départemental des

NOTES

PTT, Barra, 20 June 1941; report of Barra to prefect, 25 June 1941; Pouyol to Barra, 8 Aug. 1941; Barra to prefect, 21 Aug. 1941.

21 AD I-et-L 10W84, Subprefect Cay to prefect, 20 Aug. 1941.

22 AD I-et-L 46W94, Captain Arlot of Tours gendarmerie to prefect, 2 Aug. 1944.

23 AD I-et-L 1119W25, trials of Simone Peltier, Madeleine Longuépée and Adalbert Chevalier.

24 AD I-et-L 10W69, subprefect of Chinon to prefect, 12 Feb. 1942; AD M-et-L 12W2, report of Prefect Tracou, 3 March 1942; AD M-et-L 18W27, report of director of Maison Centrale, Fontevraud, 21 Feb.1941.

25 Account of Lieutenant Blée of Forces Françaises Libres and Bréhémont, cited in Jacques Maurice, *Cinquante mois sous la botte* (Tours, 1992), 40–1.

26 AN AJ 40/542, German note on Paul Cay, n.d.

27 AD I-et-L 10W8, Subprefect Cay to prefect, 23 Dec. 1942.

28 Émile Aron, *La Médecine en Touraine des origines à nos jours* (Chambray-lès-Tours, CLD, 1992), 240–1. See also Jack Vivier, 'Le docteur Labussière: destin d'un homme révolté', *Amis du Vieux Chinon*, vol. X, no. 5 (2001).

29 AD M-et-L 18W107, Notes et renseignements sur les personnalités de la région, 1942.

30 AD I-et-L 52W57, Gestapo report to Feldkommandantur of Tours, 8 March 1944; Subprefect Cay to Prefect Musso, 16 and 19 May 1944; Prefect Musso to Regional Prefect Donati, 20 March 1944, and Donati's reply, 29 March 1944. See also declaration of Cay after the Liberation, n.d.

31 AD M-et-L 7U4/104, trial dossier of Fernand Musso. See also below, p. 344.

32 AM Chinon, Registre des délibérations du conseil municipal, 18 Sept. 1944.

33 Ibid., 27 Sept. 1944.

34 Auguste Correch, *L'Activité du Docteur Henri Mattraits avant la guerre et pendant l'Occupation* (Chinon, n.d. but end 1944).

35 AM Chinon, Registre des délibérations du conseil municipal, 12 July 1945.

36 *Le Courrier de l'Ouest*, 27 Oct. 1948; *La Nouvelle République*, 27 Oct. 1948.

37 Interview with Christian and Léonie Beugnet, Chinon, 23 June 1998.

38 For denunciation as a female crime see Hanna Diamond, *Women and the Second World War in France, 1939–1948. Choices and constraints* (Harlow, Pearson, 1999), 88–90; Richard Cobb, *French and Germans, Germans and French* (Hanover and London, University Press of New England, 1983), 105–6, Philippe Burrin, *Living with Defeat. France under the German occupation, 1940–1944*, (London, Arnold, 1996) 208–9.

2. ENCOUNTER

1 Charles de Gaulle, *Discours et messages I, juin 1940–janvier 1946* (Paris, Plon, 1970), 4.

2 AD L-A 75W560, prefect of L-I to DGGFTO, 23 July 1940.

3 Marinette Rameau, 'Journal de Guerre', entry for 17 June 1940.

4 Fonds Goxe, Angers, Ninette Bordereau to Camille Charpentier, president of the Angers Tribunal de Commerce, 19 July 1940.

5 See below, p. 379–80, 383.

6 Élie Chamard, *Les Combats de Saumur* (Paris, Berger-Levrault, 1948), 8, 27–8, 127–32. Note that the reference to 'little rabbits' was removed by the municipality in Michel Ancelin's account in *Saumur 1990*, 33–5.

7 Winston S. Churchill, *The Second World War*, vol. II, *Their Finest Hour* (London, Cassell, 1949), 158–62; Martin Gilbert, *Winston S. Churchill*, vol. VI, *1939–1941* (London, Heinemann, 1983), 526–38; Sir Edward Spears, *Assignment to Catastrophe*, vol. II (London, Heinemann, 1954), 208–31; Paul Baudouin, *Neuf mois au gouvernement, avril–décembre 1940* (Paris, Éditions de la Table Ronde, 1948), 152–166. Paul Reynaud, *Au cœur de la mêlée, 1930–1945* (Paris, Flammarion, 1951), 764–84, denies that he asked to be allowed to sue for an armistice.

8 Philippe Pétain, *Actes et écrits*, ed. Jacques Isorni (Paris, Fayard, 1974), 448; Marc Ferro, *Pétain* (Paris, Fayard, 1987), 75–8.

9 Louis Chollet, *Les Heures tragiques. Tours, juin 1940* (Tours, Arrault et Cie, 1946), 38.

10 Elizabeth Prat and Jeannine Labussière, *Tours, cité meurtrie, juin 1940* (Chambray-lès-Tours, CLD, 1991).

11 AN AJ40/571, M. Collon, chief librarian and archivist of Tours, to Minister of Public Instruction, 2 Oct. 1940.

12 Chollet, *Les Heures tragiques*, 88–9; Jérôme Guillard, 'Les Catholiques Tourangeaux pendant la Deuxième Guerre Mondiale' (*mémoire de maîtrise*, University of Tours, 1996), 33–5; Michèle Cointet, *L'Église sous Vichy, 1940–1945* (Paris, Perrin, 1998), 14–15.

13 AM Tours, Bulletin Municipal de la Ville de Tours, 8 July 1940.

14 AM Tours, Livre d'Or offert à Ferdinand Morin, maire de Tours, par ses concitoyens, 1941. Presented at council meeting, 2 July 1941.

15 Rameau, 'Journal de Guerre', entry for 18 June 1940.

16 AM Angers, Conseil Municipal, 18 June 1940.

17 AD M-et-L 116J9, CHDGM, 'Extrait du journal illustré bimensuel', *Die Wehrmacht*, no. 25 (4 Dec. 1940); Michel Lemesle, *Chronique d'Angers sous l'Occupation, 1939–1945* (Angers, Philippe Petit, 1972), 44–58.

18 *Le Petit Courrier*, 20 June 1940.

19 Fonds Goxe, Marcel Moncany, wholesale hatter, to M. Charpentier, president of the Tribunal de Commerce, Angers, 24 July 1940.

20 AM Angers, Conseil Municipal, 8 Aug. 1940.

21 Churchill, *Second World War*, vol. II, 123, 161, 169.

22 Edmond Duméril, *Journal d'un honnête homme pendant l'Occupation, juin 1940–août 1944* (Thonon-les-Bains, L'Albaron/Société Présence du Livre, 1990), 28.

23 ADio Nantes, Livre de Paroisse, Sainte-Croix, entry by Abbé Jean Luneau, 19 June 1940.

24 AD L-A 13W40, police reports, 21 and 22 June 1940.

25 AN 72AJ 144, report of meeting of Conseil Municipal, Nantes, 20 June 1940.

26 Livre de Paroisse, Sainte-Croix, 26–27 June 1940.

27 AD L-A 75W551, circular of Feldkommandant, 8 July 1940.

28 AD L-A 13W40, Jean Loutrel to mayor of Nantes, 23 Sept. 1941.

29 AM Nantes 38W5, note of Assistant Mayor Duchemin on meeting with Feldkommandant, 31 Aug. 1940; AD L-A 27J18, 'Carnets de M. Soil, secrétaire général de la mairie de Nantes', n.d., 31 Aug. and 1 Sept. 1940.

30 AN AJ40 544, Feldkommandant of Nantes to chief of Bezirk B, Angers, 12 and 16 Oct. 1940, Bezirk B to Militärbefehlshaber, Paris, 28 Nov. 1940; AD L-A 13W26, résumé of the 'affaire Pageot'; Duméril, *Journal d'un honnête homme*, 67–71.

31 Heinrich Bucheler, *Karl-Heinrich von Stülpnagel. Soldat, Philiosoph, Verschwörer* (Berlin, Ullstein, 1989).

32 AD M-et-L 116J9, CHDGM, H. Godivier, 'Occupation de Segré par les Allemands' (MS, 11 pp., n.d.).

33 See, in general, on the German military administration, Hans Umbreit, *Der Militärbefehlshaber in Frankreich, 1940–1944* (Boppard-am-Rhein, 1968) and Rita Thalmann, *La Mise au pas. Idéologie et stratégie sécuritaire dans la France occupée* (Paris, Fayard, 1991).

34 Louis Oury, *Le Cours des cinquante otages/Die Strasse der Fünfzig Geiseln* (Saarbrücken, Geschichts Werkstatt, 1989), 22–3; Louis Oury, *Rue du Roi Albert. Les Otages de Nantes, Châteaubriant et Bordeaux* (Paris, Le Temps des Cerises, 1996), 20–1.

35 Yves de Sesmaisons, *Marquise de Sesmaisons, 1898–1977. Souvenirs de l'Occupation* (Craon, 1978).

36 Interview with Marquis Donatien and General Yves de Sesmaisons, Nantes, 16 July 1998.

37 Duméril, *Journal d'un honnête homme*, 30–1, 101–2, 129.

38 See below, p. 213.

39 A. Dio., Nantes, Mgr Villepelet, 'Le Diocèse de Nantes. 1940–1945', entry for 18 Dec. 1941. See also Laurent Berger, 'L'Episcopat Nantais de

Mgr Villepelet, 1936–1966' (*mémoire de maitrise*, University of Nantes, 1991).

40 For a comparison with the 'British policy ... to rule subject races through their own chiefs' see Frederick Lugard, *The Dual Mandate in British Tropical Africa* (Edinburgh and London, William Blackwood & Sons, 1922), Ch. 10.

41 AD M-et-L 24W1, Roussillon to Interior Minister, 4 Dec. 1940.

42 AD M-et-L 24W4, reports of Roussillon to Interior Minister, 9 May, I July and 28 Sept. 1941.

43 Report of Jean Chaigneau, 3 Dec. 1941, cited in Claude Morin, *Les Allemands en Touraine, 1940–1944* (Chambray-lès-Tours, CLD, 1996), 30.

44 AD I-et-L XV Z 27, report of Feldkommandant Marloh to Chief of District B, Angers, 13 Nov. 1940.

45 Interview with Émile Aron, Tours, 24 June 1998.

46 AD L-A 75W551, posters signed by General Braemer, end June 1940; Kommandantur of Nantes to town hall of Nantes, 28 June 1940.

47 AD I-et-L 10W7, circulars of General de la Laurencie, 2 Sept. and 9 Oct. 1940. On international law and occupation, see Gerhard von Glahn, *The Occupation of Enemy Territory* (Minneapolis, University of Minnesota Press, 1957) and Karma Nabulsi, *Traditions of War. Occupation, Resistance and the Law* (Oxford, Oxford University Press, 1999).

48 Marc-Olivier Baruch, *Servir l'État français. L'administration en France de 1940 à 1944* (Paris, Fayard, 1997), 90–5.

49 AN F1a 3664, Armistice Commission, 2 Aug. and 23 Dec. 1941.

50 AD L-A 13W41, Meeting at Feldkommandantur of Nantes, 26 Feb. 1942, Feldkommandant to prefect, 27 Feb. 1941.

51 AM Nantes 9Z1, Guineaudeau to CHOLF, 9 Dec. 1948.

52 AD L-A 243W163, cases of André Lenglart, Oct.–Dec. 1940 and Arthur Martineau, Oct. 1940–July 1941; 13W21, case of Abbé Tourillon, March 1941.

53 AD M-et-L 80W40, Fernand de Brinon to prefect of M-L, 23 May 1941.

54 AD I-et-L 10W5, military court councillor of Tours to Procureur de la République, Chinon, 14 Oct. 1941.

55 AD M-et-L 24W2, report of prefect of M-L, 28 Sept. 1941; 7U4 1–2, Registre des arrêtés rendus par le Tribunal Spécial de la Cour d'Appel d'Angers, 2 Oct. 1941.

56 AD M-et-L 18W27, subprefect of Saumur to prefect, 30 Dec. 1940.

57 AD M-et-L 18W29, subprefect of Saumur to prefect, 1 March 1941; Kloss to Roussillon, 5 March; Roussillon to Kloss, 5 March; Kloss to Roussillon, 15 March 1941; AD I-et-L XV Z 21, Kreiskommandant of Saumur to Kloss, 4 March 1941.

58 AD M-et-L 18W29, subprefect of Cholet to prefect, 1 March 1941; prefect to Interior Minister. 4 March, 1941; AD I-et-L XV Z 21, von Trotha to

Kloss, 3 March and 14 March 1941; Kloss to Chief of District B, Angers, 4 March and 21 March 1941; A. Darmaillacq, *Cholet sous l'Occupation* (Cholet, 1946, reissued. 1991), 39–40.

3. COHABITATION

1 Vercors [Jean Bruller], *Le Silence de la mer* (Paris, Éditions de Minuit, 1942).

2 Marinette Rameau, 'Journal de Guerre', entry for 21 July 1940.

3 Interview with Marinette Rameau, Charcé (M-et-L), 28 Oct. 1996.

4 Rameau, 'Journal de Guerre', entries for 5 May, 12 June and 7 July 1944.

5 AD I-et-L 52W48, survey by prefect of I-et-L, Sept.–Oct. 1940.

6 AD M-et-L 148J, CHDGM, 'Enquête de 1948 sur l'histoire de l'Occupation et de la Libération dans le département de Maine-et-Loire'.

7 AD M-et-L 116J9, H. Granger [secretary of the town hall], 'Une Commune d'Anjou pendant la Guerre, l'Occupation, la Libération: Nyoiseau' (MS, n.d.).

8 AD L-A 13W20, Major Graf Spee to Kommandant of Nantes and Kommandant of Nantes to prefect of L-I, both 27 July 1940.

9 AD M-et-L 95W108, Duc de Blacas to subprefect of Cholet, 16 July and 14 Sept. 1940.

10 Collection Michel Lemesle, Helmut Voss, 'Truppenbelegung in Stadt und Arrondissement Angers', in documentation from the Kommandantur of Angers taken in Aug. 1944 by General de Coulange, military attaché to General Bradley.

11 Rameau, 'Journal de Guerre', 18 July 1940.

12 AD M-et-L 140W94, Colonel de Sauvebeuf to Feldkommandantur of Angers, 21 Aug. 1940.

13 Interview with Odette Goxe (b. 1907), Angers, 14 April 1997.

14 Ludwig Tewes, *Frankreich in der Besatzungszeit, 1940–1943. Die Sicht deutscher Augenzeugen* (Bonn, Bouvier, 1998), 107, 140, 144, 157, 387. See also Wolfgang Geiger, *L'Image de la France dans l'Allemagne nazie* (Rennes, Presses Universitaires de Rennes, 1999) and Bertram M. Gordon, 'Ist Gott Französich? Germans, tourism and occupied France, 1940–1944', *Modern and Contemporary France* 4/3 (1996), 288–98.

15 Collection Michel Lemesle, Helmut Radssat to Lemesle, 16 Feb. 1972; Helmut Voss to Lemesle, 19 July 1973.

16 Rameau, 'Journal de Guerre', entry for 17 Oct. 1942.

17 Interview with Michel Leterme, Angers, 13 May 1997.

18 Interview with Jacques Hervé, Tours, 12 June 1997.

19 Léon Mousseau, *Le Pont cassé. Souvenirs d'un Médecin des bords de Loire* (Angers, J. Palussière, 1981), 35.

20 Collection Michel Lemesle, *Sturmmarch zur Loire* [History of the 6th Infantry Division of the 38th Army Corps in 1940] (Verlag Die Wehrmacht KG, Berlin, 1941), 142.

21 See above, p. 45.

22 Collection Michel Lemesle, Helmut Voss, 'Angers' [A History of the Sixth Pioneer Battalion], MS. n.d.

23 See above, pp. 29–30.

24 Claude Morin, *Les Allemands en Touraine, 1940–1944* (Chambray-lès-Tours, CLD, 1996), 196.

25 Jean Texcier, *Conseils à l'occupé* (Paris, 1940), conseil 10. Richard Cobb, *French and Germans, Germans and French* (Hanover and London, University Press of New England, 1983), 65–7, and Hanna Diamond, *Women and the Second World War in France, 1939–1948. Choices and Constraints* (Harlow, Pearson, 1999), 82–6, also see the need to reassess the significance of sexual relations between French and Germans.

26 Interview with Marinette Rameau, 28 Oct. 1996.

27 AD I-et-L 1119W5, reports of gendarmerie of Ligueil, 31 Oct. and 7 Nov. 1944.

28 AD M-et-L 7U4/26, case of M.-L. Coisnault before Chambre Civique of Angers, 14 March 1945.

29 AD L-A 13W19, subprefect of Saint-Nazaire to prefect of L-I, 24 March 1941.

30 AD L-A 13W41, report of police commissioner, Nantes, 22 Sept. 1941.

31 AD M-et-L 80W37, Kommandantur of Angers to police superintendent, Angers, 8 July 1940; text of poster placed in brothels forwarded by superintendent to prefect of M-et-L, 27 Aug. 1940; weekly statistics on prostitution in Angers, 13 July 1940–1 Aug. 1941.

32 AD M-et-L 12W20, Ernst to regional prefect of Angers, 10 July 1943; commissaire Cholet to police superintendant, Angers, 18 July 1943; regional prefect to Ernst, 19 July 1943.

33 AD L-A 13W41, Lieutenant Pana of Ancenis gendarmerie to prefect of L-I, 3 and 17 April 1943; letters of mayor and Dr Chauveau also on file.

34 AD M-et-L 12W3, prefect of L-I, to Interior Minister, 1 April 1942.

35 AD I-et-V 217W217 Chambre Civique of L-I, La Baule police reports on Mme Deflandre, May 1945.

36 AD I-et-L 52W3, curé of Le Loroux (I-et-L) to Pétain, 4 Oct. 1940; Directeur des Services Agricoles to prefect, 9 Dec. 1940.

37 AD L-A 13W40, prefect of L-I to General de la Laurencie, 4 Nov. 1940.

38 AD L-A 13W20, Mme Bar of École Normale d'Institutrices of Nantes to

prefect of L-I, 19 Oct. 1940; report of Duméril on his interview with Hotz, 18 Oct. 1940.

39 AD M-et-L 7U4/95, gendarmerie report of 28 Feb. 1945. Odile Talon was sentenced to two years in prison at the Liberation for collaboration.

40 René Leprince, ed., *La Pommeraye dans la Guerre par ceux qui l'ont vécue* (La Pommeraye, Bibliothèque de La Pommeraye, 1995), 75.

41 BAMA Freiburg RH36/312, Feldkommandantur of Nantes, report on food supply and agriculture, 7 Aug. 1940.

42 Collection Michel Lemesle, Angers. Helmuth Voss, 'Weinachten 1940. Der Heimat einen Gruss aus Frankreich'.

43 AD I-et-L III Z 1, reports of Feldkommandant Kloss, Angers, 29 July and 19 Sept. 1940.

44 AD I-et-L 52W52, Feldkommandant Witter of Tours to prefect of I-et-L Chaigneau, 5 Dec. 1940 and reply of prefect, 17 Dec. 1940; AD M-et-L 95W76, Kreiskommandant of Cholet to Subprefect Hudson, 17 Nov. 1941, circular of Hudson to mayors 19 Nov. 1941, and their replies, Nov.–Dec. 1941.

45 AD I-et-L XV Z 27, Propagandastaffel of Bezirk B, Angers, to Feldkommandant of Tours, 25 Nov. and 11 Dec. 1941.

46 AD L-A 65W11, dossier on campaigns against Colorado beetle, June 1941–June 1944.

47 AD I-et-L 10W5, Dr Herbig to prefect of I-et-L, 14 Sept. 1940, 2 May 1941; Prefect Chaigneau to mayors, 17 June 1941.

48 BAMA Freiburg RH36/312, report of Feldkommandantur of Nantes, 23 June 1943.

49 AD I-et-L XIV Z 29, reports of Feldkommandant Marloh of Tours, 14 and 31 Oct. 1940.

50 AD M-et-L 54W11, Jaujard, Directeur des Musées Nationaux, to prefect of M-et-L, 3 Dec. 1940.

51 AD I-et-L XIV Z29, list of 31 Jan. 1942.

52 AD M-et-L 97W79, subprefect of Saumur to president of Délégation Spéciale of Saumur, 19 Feb. 1941.

53 AN F1a 3658, list of statues for conservation and melting down, 1 March 1942.

54 BAMA Freiburg RH36/312, report of Kriegsverwaltungsrat Dr Jung, 7 Aug. 1940.

55 AD M-et-L 95W109, report of Ingénieur en Chef des Ponts et Chaussées, 7 May 1941.

56 AN F1a 3669 and AD M-et-L 12W2, Feldkommandantur of Tours to prefect of I-et-L, 22 Feb. 1942, and reply, 3 March 1942.

57 BAMA Freiburg RW24/126, orders from German army, navy and air force, 24 Aug. 1940–20 Feb. 1941.

58 BAMA Freiburg RW24/122, war diary of Rüstungsinspektion B, SW France, 24 Feb.–2 March 1941, 21–27 April 1941.

59 BAMA Freiburg RH36/512, orders on notepaper of Veltrup-Werke K.G., Aachen, May 1942–May 1944.

60 BAMA Freiburg RH36/511, list of 29 Sept. 1941; RH24/174, war diary of Rüstungskommando of Le Mans, 7 Sept. 1942.

61 AD M-et-L 74W2, report on Entreprises Dodin by sub-commission of Comité Interprofessionnel d'Épuration dans les Entreprises, n.d but early 1945; AD L-A 132W161, report of Commissaire de Police des Renseignements Généraux, Nantes, 8 Jan. 1945.

62 AD L-A 13W8, anon. report to DGGFTO, May 1941.

63 AM Nantes 38W27, report of M. Helbert, Nov. 1944.

64 BAMA Freiburg RW24/176, war diary of Rüstungskommando of Le Mans, 24–30 Jan. and 21–31 March 1943.

65 A. Beltran, R. Frank and H. Rousso, *La Vie des entreprises sous l'Occupation. Une enquête à l'échelle locale* (Paris, Belin, 1994), 22–3, 386. See also Renaud de Rochebrune and Jean-Claude Hazera, *Les Patrons sous l'Occupation*, vol. I, *Face aux Allemands* (new edn, Paris, Odile Jacob, 1997), 573–6.

66 Jacques Delarue, *Trafics et crimes sous l'Occupation* (Paris, Fayard, 1968, reissued. 1993) concentrates on the Bureau Otto buying agency of the Abwehr and big-time crooks such as the Russian Jew Mendel Skolnikoff, but touches only the tip of the iceberg.

67 AD L-A 96W13, note of officer of civil affairs, district of La Baule, 15 April 1945.

68 AD I-et-V 217W218, Chambre Civique of L-I, report of gendarmerie of Pont-Rousseau, 29 Sept. 1944, and report of Inspecteur de Police détaché aux Renseignements Généraux, 6 April 1945. Couturier received twenty years' national degradation.

69 AD M-et-L 48W34, report of Renseignements Généraux, 27 Nov. 1944.

70 AD I-et-L 46W112, reports of Captain Arlot of Tours gendarmerie, 8 May and 21 Sept. 1944.

71 AD L-A 132W161, prefect of L-I to president of Comité de Confiscation des Profits Illicites, 12 Feb. 1945.

72 AD I-et-V 217W217, Chambre Civique of L-I, report of gendarmerie of Coueron, 28 Dec. 1944.

73 AD I-et-V Cour de Justice of L-I, report of gendarmerie of Le Pellerin, 8 Dec. 1944.

74 Philippe Burrin, *Living with Defeat, France under the German Occupation, 1940–1944*, 197.

75 Ibid., 207.

4. SEPARATION

1 Fonds Goxe. Ninette Bordereau [the mother] to M. et Mme Camille Charpentier, 19 July 1940; handwritten account of the events of 2 July in Angers by Odette Goxe, given to the author 3 May 1997.

2 AD I-et-L 10W33, Feldkommandant Marloh of Tours to prefect, 2 July 1940.

3 AD I-et-L 52W52, Feldkommandant of Tours to prefect, 20 July, and reply, 30 July 1940.

4 AD L-A 13W8, Elizabeth Walter to secretary general of the prefecture, 25 Nov. 1940. The prefect was told by Fernand de Brinon on 14 Dec. that the Germans had no intention of exerting pressure on Alsatians and Lorrainers.

5 AD L-A 13W15, undated report of prefecture [Oct. 1940]; AD I-et-L III Z 1, situation report of Feldkommandantur of Angers, 19 Oct. 1940.

6 A. V. De La Gillette, *Via Dolorosa. De Nantes à Châteaubriant (juin–juillet 1940)* (Fontenay-le-Comte, 1945), 25.

7 AN 72AJ145, departmental inspector of hygiene to doctor-general in charge of the Nantes region, 30 June 1940.

8 Mgr Villepelet, 'Le Diocèse de Nantes, 1940–1945', entry for 10 July 1940.

9 AD L-A 13W15, mayor of Sucé in reply to prefect's circular of 20 Feb. 1941. See also AN 72AJ147, 'L'Œuvre d'une Française sous l'Occupation. Mme de Sesmaisons' (anon. account of 21 Nov. 1944) and Yves de Sesmaisons, *Marquise de Sesmaisons (1898–1977). Souvenirs de l'Occupation*, 8.

10 AN 72AJ145, 'Mouvement Bouvron, Nantes-historique', from collection of CHOLF, Nantes. See also Fernand Ridel, *Témoignages 1939–1945. Une page d'histoire* (La Baule, Éditions des Paludiers, 1974).

11 AN F9 3064 Commissariat Général aux Prisonniers de Guerre Repatriés et aux Familles des Prisonniers de Guerre. Statistics 1 Nov. 1942. See Yves Durand, *La Vie quotidienne des prisonniers de guerre dans les Stalags, Oflags et Kommandos, 1939–1945* (Paris, Hachette, 1987, new edn, 1994).

12 Sarah Fishman, *We Will Wait. Wives of French prisoners of war, 1940–1945* (New Haven and London, Yale University Press, 1991).

13 See Miranda Pollard, *Reign of Virtue. Mobilizing gender in Vichy France* (Chicago and London, University of Chicago Press, 1998) and Francine Muel-Dreyfus, *Vichy et l'éternel féminin* (Paris, Seuil, 1996).

14 AD M-et-L 24W11, Mme Bonin of Trélazé to prefect of M-et-L, 14 Oct. 1941.

15 A. Dio. Tours 1D6, Mgr Gaillard to Feldkommandantur of Tours, 15 and 22 Aug. 1940, and to Red Cross in Paris, 18 Sept. 1940.

16 AD I-et-L 10W33, Oberleutnant Brucher to prefect of I-et-L, 13 Aug. 1940; AD M-et-L 24W11, circular of Prefect Roussillon, 18 Sept, 1940, on new regulations of Feldkommandant Kloss, 12 Sept. 1940.

17 AD I-et-L 10W82, gendarmerie reports from brigades of l'Ile Bouchard, 21 Oct., Montbazon, 28 Oct., Ligueil, 1 Nov., Richelieu, 3 Dec. 1940 and Beaumont-la-Ronce, 27 March 1941.

18 See above, p. 62.

19 AD M-et-L 97W38, subprefect of Saumur to prefect of M-et-L, 23 Feb. 1941.

20 AD M-et-L 24W11, subprefect of Saumur to prefect of M-et-L, 14 April 1941.

21 Ibid., Marquis de Saint-Pern, deputy of M-et-L, to prefect of M-et-L, 25 March 1941.

22 AD M-et-L 80W36, press communiqué of 26 March 1941.

23 Fonds Grenouilleau (Angers), Georges Mazeaud to Gaston Grenouilleau, 5 July 1941.

24 AD M-et-L 97W38, subprefect of Saumur to mayor of Montsoreau, Gustave Tessier, 21 July 1941, and reply of latter, 25 July 1941.

25 AD M-et-L 97W120, *kermesse* of Meigné-sous-Doué, 20 Sept. 1942.

26 AN F9 3037, report of director of the Maison du Prisonnier of Angers, Aug. 1943, concerning Beaufort-en-Vallée.

27 AD L-A 65W2, instructions of Education Minister Jérôme Carcopino, 13 Nov. 1941.

28 AD M-et-L 41W3, Rémy René-Bazin, assistant regional delegate for La Jeunesse, to regional prefect, 22 and 29 Nov. 1941.

29 AD M-et-L 80W41, SS Hauptsturmführer Busch to Comte Gaël de Coniac of Secrétariat d'Éducation Populaire, 30 Sept. 1942.

30 Mgr Villepelet, 'Le Diocèse de Nantes, 1940–1945', entry for 29 Nov. 1941.

31 *La Semaine religieuse du Diocèse de Nantes*, 28 Nov. 1941. 1,000 of the 2,546 Catholic priests in German POW camps were authorized to serve as chaplains.

32 *La Semaine religieuse du Diocèse d'Angers*, 1 Feb. 1942.

33 A. Dio. Angers 9E41, letters to Mgr Costes of René Sallé of la Chapelle-sur-Oudon, 10 Jan. 1942, and Sergeant Jean Renaud, curé of La Trinité, 18 Nov. 1941.

34 A. Dio. Nantes, Lettres et cartes envoyés à Mgr Villepelet par les séminaristes et prêtres prisonniers. Letter of Pierre Roberdel, 12 Dec. 1943.

35 *La Semaine religieuse du Diocèse de Tours*, 2 May 1941.

36 AD M-et-L 97W133, speech of Mayor Moreau forwarded to subprefect of Saumur, 2 June 1942.

37 On the working of this law, which was repealed in 1942 when labour

became scarce, see Hanna Diamond, *Women and the Second World War in France, 1939–1948. Choices and constraints*, (Harlow, Pearson, 1999) 32–6, and Pollard, *Reign of Virtue*, 153–65.

38 AD M-et-L 95W109, rector of Rennes to Mme Talbot, 31 Jan. 1941, copied to subprefect of Cholet, 26 Sept. 1941.

39 AD L-A 13W7, M. Huteau to prefect of L-I, 1 June 1942.

40 AD L-A 51W28, Prefect Dupard to prefect delegate of Ministry of the Interior, Paris, 29 June 1942.

41 See for example Diamond, *Women and the Second World War*, 109–10, and Dominique Veillon, *Vivre et survivre en France, 1939–1947*, (Paris, Payot, 1995), 223.

42 AD M-et-L 80W47, Mme Hubert to prefect of M-et-L, 1 May 1943.

43 AD M-et-L 24W11, mayor of Concourson-sur-Layon to prefect of M-et-L, 3 Feb. 1943; reply of prefect, 9 Feb. 1943; reply of mayor, 13 Feb. 1943. Letter of Paul Grenouilleau (b. Concourson 1930), to the author, 28 Sept. 1999.

44 AD L-A 51W28, Paul Urien to prefect of L-I, 15 Nov. 1942.

45 AD I-et-L 52W41, card of Albert Loiseau to prefect of I-et-L, 12 July 1942; report of social worker of Saint-Pierre-des-Corps, 11 Aug. 1942; prefect to Loiseau, 17 Aug. 1942.

46 AD M-et-L 8W93, Lucien Vétault to mayor of Jumelles, 8 Nov. 1943; mayor of Jumelles to Secours National, 9 Dec. 1943; subprefect of Saumur to prefect of M-et-L, 12 Jan. 1944; prefect to Maison du Prisonnier, 15 Jan. 1944, and their reply, 29 March 1944.

47 See below, pp. 286–7.

48 AD L-A 51W28, prefect of L-I to Laval, 11 and 17 May 1943.

49 AD M-et-L 140W39, subprefect of Saumur to prefect of M-et-L, 12 Aug. 1943.

50 AN F9 3064, census of POWs, 22 July 1942.

51 AD I-et-L 6W20, director of the Office du Travail, Tours, to prefect of I-et-L, 29 Sept. 1943.

52 AN F9 3055, A. Tijou to M. Lot, public works administrator at Tours, 25 March 1943; AN F9 3081, report of Maison du Prisonnier, Angers, Jan. 1944.

53 AN F9 3049, reports of Maison du Prisonnier, Nantes, 29 Nov. 1943 and 7 Aug. 1944.

54 AD L-A 51W28, record of meeting at prefecture of L-I to set up the Comité Départemental d'Aide aux Prisonniers de Guerre, 28 July 1940; Ridel, *Témoignages 1939–1945*, 43–69.

55 AD L-A 6W1and 6W2, files of Comité Nantais d'Aide aux Prisonniers de Guerre, 1941–6.

56 AD L-A 13W14, director of Forges de Basse-Indre, 28 Dec. 1940; mayor of Vertou, 3 Jan. 1941, and mayor of La Baule, 9 Jan. 1941.

57 AD M-et-L 140W38, secretary of Commission des Manifestations pour les Prisonniers de Guerre of M-et-L to M. Vanneyre of Angers, 17 July 1943; reply of M. Vanneyre, 23 July 1943.

58 AD L-A 51W28, summary of dossier by departmental information delegate for Prefect Bonnefoy of L-I, 11 Nov. 1943; Modena to Prefect Vincent of L-I, 15 Nov. 1944; 10W34, Hérault to Prefect Vincent, n.d., and to Modena, president of CDL, 5 and 11 May 1945.

59 AD M-et-L 24W2, report of Regional Prefect Roussillon to Interior Minister, 1 Dec. 1941.

60 AN F9 3037, reports from Angers of M. Georges, inspector of the Mouvement du Prisonnier, to André Masson, leader of the Mouvement, 19 April 1943 and June 1943; report of M. de Clauzade to M. Zaepffel, Direction Générale des Maisons du Prisonnier, 5 July 1943.

61 AN F9 3055, report of Lardy, 5 July 1943; Zaeppffel to Lardy, 15 July and 26 Aug. 1943; Philipon to secretary general of the Mouvement du Prisonnier, 1 Sept. 1943; Zaeppffel to Renault, 25 Oct. 1943.

62 AD I-et-L 52W23, General de Witowski, delegate of the Comité Central d'Assistance aux Prisonniers de Guerre, to prefect of I-et-L, 18 Feb. 1942; AD M-et-L 140W38, Laval circular to prefects, 27 Oct. 1942.

63 AN F9 3055, Lardy to director of Maisons du Prisonnier, Paris, 21 April 1943.

64 AD M-et-L 24W11, prefect delegate of M-et-L, Pierre Daguerre, to André Masson, Commissaire Général au Prisonniers de Guerre Repatriés, 6 May 1943.

65 AD M-et-L 7U4–1, Register of judgements of Special Tribunal of Appeal Court of Angers, 6 May and 29 July 1943, 13 Jan. 1944.

66 AD L-A 51W29, Laurent Ollivier of Stalag VIIIC to prefect of L-I, 14 Sept. 1943; Roger Jeffredo of Stalag IIIA to prefect of L-I, 13 Aug. 1943.

67 AM Nantes 38W21, Kommando 106 to mayor of Nantes, 9 Nov. 1943.

68 A. Dio. Nantes, Lettres et cartes envoyés à Mgr Villepelet . . . , Louis Nouais to Mgr Villepelet, 12 Dec. 1943.

5. BREAD

1 Fonds Paul Grenouilleau (Angers), Georges Mazeaud to Gaston Grenouilleau, 3 Jan. 1941.

2 Ibid., letters of 13, 16, 23 and 30 Jan. 1941.

3 Ibid., Georges Mazeaud to Gaston Grenouilleau, 22 April 1942; Lucienne

Mazeaud to Gaston, 28 May and 17 June 1941; Paul Mazeaud to Gaston, 22 Feb. and 2 March 1943.

4 Ibid., Georges Mazeaud to Gaston Grenouilleau, 6 Feb., 10 April and 18 Aug. 1941, 13 March 1943, 14 Jan. 1944, 24 Feb. 1945 and 22 June 1946.

5 Dominique Veillon, *Vivre et survivre en France, 1939–1947* (Paris, Payot, 1995), 112–26; Jennifer Davies, *The Wartime Kitchen and Garden* (London, BBC Books, 1993), 19–20.

6 AD L-A 75W561, prefect of L-I to delegate general, Paris, 22 Oct. 1940.

7 AD M-et-L 7U4/99, report of commissioner attached to Angers Cour de Justice, 4 May 1945.

8 Dominique Veillon and Jean-Marie Flonneau, eds, *Le Temps des restrictions en France, 1939–1949* (Paris, IHTP, 1995), contrast the 'départements ruraux nourriciers' of the west and the 'départements affamés' of the Mediterranean.

9 AD M-et-L 24W2, prefect of M-et-L to Interior Minister, 9 May 1941.

10 AD M-et-L 80W6, prefect of M-et-L to Interior Minister, 31 Jan. 1943.

11 AD M-et-L 12W2, prefect of L-I to Interior Minister, 4 March 1942 and 4 Jan. 1943.

12 AD M-et-L 54W11, 'Les Angevines' to prefect of M-et-L, 5 Nov. 1940.

13 AD M-et-L 103W34, Henri Foquereau to mayor of Angers's deputy responsible for the municipal police, 16 July 1941.

14 AD I-et-L 10W55, police superintendent, Tours, to police commissioner, Tours, 21 June 1943.

15 AD I-et-L 10W55, Andrée Simonneau to prefect of I-et-L, 26 March 1941.

16 AD M-et-L 95W109, Robert Steux, accountant with Pellaumail, to prefect of M-et-L, 14 June 1941.

17 See above, p. 28.

18 AD I-et-L 10W53, report of police commissioner, Tours, 14 Aug. 1943.

19 AD M-et-L 18W9, Mathurin Legras of Groupe Collaboration, Fresne-sur-Loire, to Prefect Bonnefoy of L-I, Oct. 1943.

20 Interview with Michel Leterme, Angers, 13 June 1997.

21 See above, p. 39.

22 AD M-et-L 116J9, Dr J. Barbary, 'Histoire de la Guerre 1939–44 dans le canton de Chemillé', MS, n.d.

23 Interview with Andrée Trudeau, Saumur, 22 June 1998.

24 Interview with André Treulier, Le Thoureil, 13 May 1997.

25 Léon Mousseau, *Le Pont cassé. Souvenirs d'un médecin des bords de la Loire* (Angers, J. Palussière, 1981), 98.

26 Interview with Lucienne Cohu (b. 1907) and Jacqueline and Louis Denis, Trélazé, 18 April 1997.

27 See for example Julian Jackson, *The Popular Front in France. Defending*

democracy, 1934–38 (Cambridge, Cambridge University Press, 1988), 85–112; Gérard Noiriel, *Workers in French Society in the Nineteenth and Twentieth Centuries* (Oxford, Berg, 1990), Ch. 5; Jacques Danos and Marcel Gibelin, *June '36. Class Struggle and the Popular Front in France* (London and Chicago, Bookmarks, 1986); Jacques Kergoat, *La France du Front Populaire* (Paris, Éditions La Découverte, 1986); Georges Lefranc, *Juin 36* (Paris, Julliard, 1965).

28 Guy Bourdé, *La Défaite du Front Populaire* (Paris, Maspéro, 1977); J.-P. Rioux, A. Prost and J.-P. Azéma, *Les Communistes français de Munich à Châteaubriant* (Paris, FNSP, 1987).

29 Étienne Dejonghe, 'Les aspects économiques et sociaux du Nord pendant la première année de l'Occupation', *Revue du Nord*, Oct. 1969.

30 AD L-A 13W8, reports of police superintendent, Saint-Nazaire, 30 March 1941, special commissioner, Saint-Nazaire, 24 May 1941, and prefect of L-I to de Brinon, 3 Sept. 1941.

31 AD L-A 13W6, reports of subprefect of Saint-Nazaire, 7, 10 and 20 Oct. 1941.

32 AD L-A 270W476, Police des Renseignements Généraux to prefect of L-I, 4 and 9 July 1942.

33 AD M-et-L 116W7, circular of Belin to prefects, 23 Dec. 1940; circular of Roussillon to mayors of M-et-L, 17 Feb. 1941.

34 AD M-et-L 12W3, report of Prefect Dupard of L-I to Interior Minister, 1 Dec. 1941.

35 The best study of this to date is Jean-Pierre Le Crom, *Syndicats Nous Voilà! Vichy et le Corporatisme* (Paris, Les Éditions de l'Atelier/Éditions Ouvrières, 1995).

36 AD L-A 13W9, message of Pucheu to prefects forwarded by Prefect Dupard to his subprefects, 24 Nov. 1941.

37 Centre d'Histoire du Travail, Nantes, Fonds Pennaneach 4, Bernard Neau of Syndicat Général des Employés d'Angers et Environs to Jean Pennaneach, 10 July 1941.

38 AD M-et-L 18W16, account of visit of Regional Prefect Roussillon to Saint-Nazaire, 26 Feb. 1941.

39 See below, pp. 246–50.

40 Centre d'Histoire du Travail, Nantes, CGT 1939–45, Jouvance to Engineers' Federation, Paris, 13 Feb. 1942.

41 See below, p. 334.

42 Centre d'Histoire du Travail, Nantes, Fonds Pennaneach 4, Déaud to directors of Chantiers de la Loire, Dubigeon, de Bretagne, Batignolles and SNCASO, 19 April 1944.

43 AD I-et-L 6W64, secretary general of the Bourse du Travail, Tours, to Inspector of Labour Terpault, 2 April 1943.

44 AD M-et-L 12W2, report of Prefect Tracou of I-et-L to Interior Minister, 3 Nov. 1943.

45 AD M-et-L 136W24, report of chief superintendent of Renseignements Généraux, Angers, 12 Jan. 1944.

46 AD M-et-L 21W52, regional inspector of police to chief superintendent of Renseignements Généraux, 8 Jan. 1944.

47 AD M-et-L 25W61, dossiers on 29 occupational families in Angers region, 1943–4.

48 AD L-A 132W64, M. Bourget to prefect of L-I, 20 April and 9 May 1944; prefect to Bourget, 27 April and 17 May 1944.

49 See for example Christian Faure, Le Projet culturel de Vichy (Paris–Lyon, CNRS, Presses Universitaires de Lyon, 1989), 105–26.

50 AD M-et-L 24W2, Regional Prefect Roussillon to Interior Minister, 1 July and 28 Sept. 1941; AD M-et-L 12W4, Roussillon to Interior Minister, 1 Jan. 1942.

51 AD M-et-L 12W2, prefect of I-et-L to Interior Minister, 3 Nov. and 3 Dec. 1941.

52 AD M-et-L 12W3, report of Dupard, prefect of L-I, to Interior Minister, 1 April 1942; AN F1a 3659, press cuttings on visit of M. Charbin to Nantes, 10–12 March 1942.

53 La Semaine religieuse du Diocèse de Nantes, 21 March 1942; La Semaine religieuse du Diocèse d'Angers, 22 March 1942.

54 AD L-A 13W9, prefect delegate of M-et-L to regional prefect, 22 May 1942; prefect of L-I to regional prefect, 28 May 1942.

55 AD I-et-L 10W55, 'un paysan vrai' to prefect of I-et-L, 14 Feb. 1941.

56 AD L-A 13W6, Marquis de Sesmaisons to prefect of L-I, 29 Aug. 1941.

57 AN F1a 3659, Ravitaillement Minister Max Bonnafous to Interior Minister, 3 Oct. 1942.

58 AD M-et-L 97W145, mayor of Courléon to subprefect of Saumur, 3 March 1943.

59 AD M-et-L 103W26, district Ravitaillement officer of Pouancé to director of Ravitaillement Général, Maine-et-Loire, 24 Oct. 1942.

60 AD M-et-L 24W30, Société Maggi to prefect of M-et-L, 7 July 1941.

61 AD M-et-L 97W33, Jules Diot, mayor of Gennes, to tax collector, 22 Dec. 1943; subprefect of Saumur to prefect of M-et-L, 28 Jan. and 20 March 1944.

62 AD M-et-L 80W4, chief superintendent of Renseignements Généraux to prefect of M-et-L, 27 March 1942.

63 AD M-et-L 95W111, mayor of Saint-Macaire to subprefect of Cholet, 12 Oct. 1943; AD M-et-L 8W93, departmental delegate of Central Committee of Potato Supply to Intendant Ganot, departmental director of Ravitaille-

ment Général, M-et-L, 4 Sept. 1943, and Prefect Delegate Saissier to Ganot, 28 Oct. 1943.

64 AD M-et-L 140W150, Intendant Ganot to prefect of M-et-L, 17 March 1944; report of gendarmerie of Montjean, 10 March 1944; subprefect of Cholet to prefect, 24 and 31 March 1944.

65 See the standard study of Isabel Boussard, *Vichy et la Corporation Paysanne* (Paris, FNSP, 1980).

66 AD M-et-L 18W16, cutting from *La Dépêche*, 11 Dec. 1943.

67 Eugène Forget, *Le Serment de l'unité paysanne* (Paris, Nouvelle Cité, 1982), 104; Robert Paxton, *French Peasant Fascism. Henri Dorgères's Greenshirts and the crises of French agriculture, 1929–1939* (New York and Oxford, Oxford University Press, 1997), 195 n. 122 and 127, 120–1.

68 AD M-et-L 18W112, Dèze to director of Ravitaillement Général, 18 July 1942.

69 AD M-et-L 80W40, syndic of Chanteloup-les-Bois in meeting with Prefect Delegate Saissier, 26 April 1944; Regional Syndic Dèze to Regional Prefect Donati, 6 and 22 May, 2 June 1944.

70 Bernard Potier, 'Aspects de la vie économique en Maine-et-Loire sous l'Occupation allemande' (*mémoire de maîtrise*, Angers, Université Catholique de l'Ouest, 1985), 189.

71 AD L-A 31W41, proceedings for irregular slaughter and sale of meat, Dec. 1942–July 1943.

72 AD M-et-L 12W2, report of prefect of I-et-L to Interior Minister, 3 Sept. 1943.

73 AD I-et-L 10W53, chief superintendent of Renseignements Généraux, Tours, 24 April 1943.

74 AD M-et-L 80W40, Prefect Saissier to district chiefs of Ravitaillement Général, M-et-L, 24 Sept. 1943.

75 AD M-et-L 140W150, reports of gendarmerie of Chalonnes-sur-Loire, 24 Feb. 1944.

76 AD M-et-L 12W20, report of Special Controller Renaud, n.d. but 1943.

77 AD M-et-L 18W9, Paul Leroux, secretary of Francist party of La 'Baule, to regional prefect, 2 April 1944; prefect of L-I to regional prefect, 16 May 1944.

6. CIRCUSES

1 Interview with André Roussel (b. 1926), Bléré (I-et-L), 25 June 1998.

2 AD I-et-L 46W88, Dr Foussereau to prefect of I-et-L, 26 March 1941; Robert Vivier, inspector of Academy of I-et-L, 28 March 1941.

NOTES

3 AD I-et-L 10W7, Prefect Chaigneau of I-et-L to prefect delegated by the Interior Minister to Paris, 7 Aug. 1941.

4 AD I-et-L 10W7, report on meeting of Comité des Jeunes by Marcel Bocquet, departmental delegate of La Jeunesse, 31 March 1941.

5 AD I-et-L 52W22, special inspector of police to police commissioner, Tours, 11 March 1942; prefect of I-et-L to mayor of Bléré, 7 Jan. 1943.

6 AD I-et-L 52W21, census of associations and unions for the Feldkommandantur of Tours, Nov. 1940, Amboise.

7 AD I-et-L 52W21, census of associations and unions for the Feldkommandantur of Tours, Nov. 1940, Saint-Pierre-des-Corps; AD M-et-L 97W121, associations declared Oct. 1940, Saumur; AD M-et-L 95W121, associations declared Oct. 1940, Cholet.

8 AD M-et-L 140W95, president of Club des Fêtes of École des Arts et Métiers, Angers, to prefect of M-et-L, 8 May 1942; Prefect Delegate Daguerre to Feldkommandantur, 19 May, SS Hauptsturmführer Busch to prefect, 8 Oct. 1942. On these schools see Charles R. Day, *Education for the Industrial World: the Écoles d'Arts et Métiers and the rise of French industrial engineering* (Cambridge, Mass., MIT Press, 1987).

9 AD I-et-L 10W43, Feldkommandantur of Tours to prefect of I-et-L, 24 May 1941, police superintendent, Tours, to prefect, 29 May 1941.

10 AD M-et-L 54W5, librarian of Bibliothèque Saint-Michel, Angers, to prefect of M-et-L, 17 Feb. 1942.

11 AD I-et-L 10W48, note of Délégation Spéciale of Saint-Pierre-des-Corps, 11 Sept. 1940; AD L-A 270W491, police commissioner, Nantes, to prefect of L-I, 23 Feb. and 1 Aug. 1942.

12 Jean-Paul Cointet, *La Légion Française des Combattants, 1940–1944. La tentation du Fascisme* (Paris, Albin Michel, 1995).

13 Bernard Briais, *Le Lochois pendant la Guerre 1939–1945* (Chambray-lès-Tours, CLD, 1988), 61–5.

14 AD I-et-L 10W43, Feldkommandantur of Tours to prefect of I-et-L, 29 Oct. 1940.

15 AD M-et-L 41W2, subprefect of Saumur to prefect of M-et-L, 6 Nov. 1940, and reply, 8 Nov. 1940.

16 AD M-et-L 18W13, Panaget to Regional Prefect Donati, 19 March 1943, Donati to secretariat of Marshal Pétain, 29 July 1943.

17 On Vichy youth movements, see the pioneering work of W. D. Halls, *The Youth of Vichy France* (Oxford, Clarendon Press, 1981).

18 AD M-et-L 140W28, Feldkommandantur of Angers to prefect of M-et-L, 29 April 1941; AD L-A 13W25, Feldkommandant of Nantes to prefect of L-I, 29 Aug. and 10 Sept. 1941.

19 AD M-et-L 140W28, Rémy René-Bazin, assistant regional delegate for La Jeunesse in M-et-L to prefect, 28 May 1941.

20 AD M-et-L 54W3, director of Agricultural Services of M-et-L to prefect of M-et-L, 6 Nov. 1940; AD L-A 13W25, departmental delegate of the Mission for Peasant Restoration to prefect of L-I, 6 Oct. 1941.

21 AD I-et-L 52W21, note of Émile Chauveau, head of section at prefecture of I-et-L, based on verbal instructions from Feldkommandantur of Tours.

22 Rozenn Corre, 'Le Scoutisme Catholique à Nantes des origines au Jamborée de la Paix, 1925–1947' (*mémoire de maîtrise*, University of Nantes, 1992), 206–11; Jérôme Gaillard, 'Les Catholiques Tourangeaux pendant la Deux-ième Guerre Mondiale' (*mémoire de maîtrise*, University of Tours, 1996), 85–6, 106–8; AD M-et-L Bibliothèque 7304, 'Ici 3ème Angers, 1934–1944'; AD M-et-L 60W5, extract from *Le Courrier de l'Ouest*, 8 Nov. 1944; interviews with Odette Goxe, Angers, 14 April 1997, Abbé Henri Richer, Angers, 6 June 1997, and Abbé Jacques Ménard, Tours, 2 June 1997.

23 AD I-et-L 218W14, report of Colonel de Busnel of Touraine Secours National, 5 Feb. 1941; AD M-et-L 18W109, report of Colonel de Sauvebeuf of Anjou Secours National, 4 Nov. 1942.

24 AD M-et-L 41W3, René Hersen of Niort to prefect of M-et-L, 19 Feb. 1941.

25 Camille de Montergon, *Le Colonel François de Sauvebeuf* (Niort, Imprimerie Saint-Denis, n.d.), and de Montergon, *Une Victime de Flossenburg. Le Colonel François de Sauvebeuf* (Niort, Imprimerie Saint-Denis, n.d.).

26 AD M-et-L 71W2, reports of Colonel O'Kelly of Cuisines d'Entr'aide, Angers, 18 Sept. 1941 and 25 June 1942, report of Colonel de Sauvebeuf, 12 June 1942.

27 AD M-et-L 18W109, report of Colonel de Sauvebeuf, 4 March 1942.

28 AD I-et-L 10W3, statement of Interior Minister, Feb. 1942; AD M-et-L 41W3, report of subprefect of Saumur, 2 April 1942.

29 *Le Petit Courrier*, 26 and 28 Nov. 1941; Regional Prefect Roussillon to Interior Minister, 8 Dec. 1941.

30 AD I-et-L 218W17, M. Schmitt of l'Ile-Bouchard to Secours National of Touraine, 20 April 1943; 'Étude sur les modalités de secours avec l'appréciation et les suggestions des services sociaux des délégations', 1 Jan. 1944.

31 AD M-et-L 8W91, minutes of meeting at prefecture of M-et-L, 25 Aug. 1943.

32 AD M-et-L 41W3, prefect of M-et-L to Mme Vve Poirier, 22 Jan. 1942.

33 AD L-A 16W38, Director of Maison du Prisonnier Roy to prefect of L-I, 5 Feb. 1943.

34 AD I-et-L, report of prefect of I-et-L, n.d. but April 1943; prefect of I-et-L to Victor Mangeant of Cangey, 11 Dec. 1943, and reply of Mangeant, 14 Jan. 1944.

35 AD I-et-L 31W1, circulars of Prefect Chaigneau to mayors of Occupied

Zone of I-et-L, 9 June and 16 Oct. 1941; mayor of Bléré to prefect, 17 Oct. 1941.

36 AD L-A 132W159, circulars of Prefect Dupard to mayors, 18 Oct. 1941 and 20 March 1942; note of Feldkommandantur of Nantes, 27 March 1942.

37 AD I-et-L 31W1, circular of Prefect Tracou to mayors, 27 Aug. 1942, reply of mayor of Montlouis-sur-Loire, 4 Sept. 1942.

38 See for example AD M-et-L 48W34, protests of Marc Bigeard, struck off the municipal council of Pellouailles for hunting with and selling wood and charcoal to the Germans, n.d. but Sept./Oct. 1944.

39 AD M-et-L 80W36, mayor of Chênehutte-les-Tuffeaux, forwarded to Feldkommandantur with stamp of prefecture of M-et-L, 25 March 1942.

40 AD I-et-L 10W5, Dr Herbig to Baron de Champchevrier, 13 Sept. 1940; AD I-et-L IIZ3, reports of Dr Herbig to Head of Military Administration of District B, 25 Sept. 1940 and 13 Jan. 1943; Claude Morin, *Les Allemands en Touraine, 1940–1944* (Chambray-lès-Tours, 1996), 182–3.

41 AD I-et-L 106W76, Louis Théret to prefect of I-et-L, 5 March 1942, and prefect to Procureurs de l'État Français at Tours and Chinon, 14 March 1942; AD I-et-L IIZ2, departmental director of Ravitaillement Général to Feldkommandantur of Tours, 10 June 1943, and Feldkommandantur to prefect of I-et-L, 19 July 1943.

42 Collection Michel Lemesle, letter of Mme Delépine, La Ferrière-de-Flée, 28 Nov. 1973.

43 René Le Prince, ed., *La Pommeraye dans la Guerre par ceux qui l'ont vécue* (La Pommeraye, Bibliothèque de La Pommeraye, 1995), accounts of Serge and Joseph Plumeseau. See above, p. 129.

44 AD M-et-L 117W33, *arrêté* of Roussillon, 8 May 1941, letter of Ministry of Agriculture, 13 May, second *arrêté* of Roussillon, 28 May 1941.

45 AD M-et-L 80W5, Feldkommandant of Angers to Prefect Roussillon, 12 and 27 Aug. 1942.

46 AD M-et-L 80W36, Clément Varambier to prefect of M-et-L, 19 Sept. 1941; prefect to Feldkommandant at Tours, 24 Oct. 1941.

47 AD M-et-L 97W120, prefect delegate of M-et-L to subprefect of Saumur, 6 Aug. 1943.

48 AD L-A 75W560, Marcel Braud to mayor of Nantes, 23 Dec. 1940.

49 AD L-A 132W64, invitations to prefect of L-I, 1 Dec. 1941 and July 1943.

50 AD M-et-L 140W28, chief superintendent of Renseignements Généraux in M-et-L to chief superintendent of Renseignements Généraux in Vichy, 28 June 1943.

51 On the flourishing of sport under Vichy, see Jean-Louis Gay-Lescot, *Sport et éducation sous Vichy, 1940–1944* (Lyon, Presses Universitaires de Lyon, 1991).

52 AD I-et-L 10W9, report of departmental delegate for La Jeunesse, H. Biessy, 1 May 1943. See also his reports of 3 March and 31 Dec. 1943.

53 AD I-et-L 46W88, Goupil de Bouillé to prefect of I-et-L, 27 Dec. 1941.

54 AD M-et-L 140W98, Casadeus to prefect of M-et-L, 26 Jan. and 11 Feb. 1943.

55 AD I-et-L 52W23, authorizations by Sicherheitspolizei, 1942–4.

56 AD I-et-L 10W37, file of Propagandastaffel Sud-West, Aussenstelle Tours, 1942–3. The song was 'C'était Basile', by Charles Colmache.

57 AD M-et-L 140W95, prefecture note, n.d. but Aug. 1942; Jérôme Gaillard, 'Les Catholiques Tourangeaux pendant la Deuxième Guerre Mondiale' (*mémoire de maîtrise*, University of Tours, 1996), 153. See also Gabriel Jacobs, 'The role of Joan of Arc on the stage of Occupied Paris', in Roderick Kedward and Roger Austin, *Vichy France and the Resistance. Culture and ideology* (London and Sydney, Croom Helm, 1985), 106–22, and in general Serge Added, *Le Théâtre dans les années Vichy* (Paris, 1992).

58 In general see Jean-Pierre Bertin-Maghit, *Le Cinéma français sous Vichy. Les films français de 1940 à 1944* (Paris, Albatros, 1980), and Evelyn Ehrlich, *Cinema of Paradox. French Film-making under the German Occupation* (New York, Columbia University Press, 1987).

59 AN F1a 3868, CFLN Zone Handbook no. 7, part III, Nov. 1943.

60 AD L-A 13W41, subprefect of Saint-Nazaire to prefect of L-I, 21 Oct. 1940; AD I-et-L 10W69, Roger Morel to prefect of I-et-L, 8 Dec. 1940. Morel was in prison in Tours and asked permission to marry his girlfriend.

61 AD I-et-L 10W36, Feldkommandant of Tours to prefects of I-et-L and M-et-L, 22 Aug. 1941; AD I-et-L 52W31, police superindentent to police commissioner, Tours, and chief of Sicherheitspolizei to prefect of I-et-L, 8 March 1943; AD M-et-L 12W54, police superintendant of Angers region to regional prefect, 8 March 1943.

62 Muriel Paquelet, 'Le Cinéma paroissial en Loire-Inférieure de 1919 à 1958' (*mémoire de maîtrise*, University of Nantes, 1994), 25–31.

63 AD L-A 132W160, Jean Briand of JOC to Clément, assistant regional delegate for La Jeunesse, 15 July 1941.

64 *La Famille catholique. Bulletin mensuel des Chefs de Famille Catholique*, March 1942.

65 AD M-et-L 12W4, report of Prefect Daguerre, 2 Sept. 1942.

66 Robert Gildea, '*Les Années noires?* Clandestine dancing in Occupied France', in Ceri Crossley and Martyn Cornick eds, *Problems in French History* (Basingstoke, Palgrave, 2000), 197–212.

67 AD M-et-L 95W75, subprefect of Cholet to Kreiskommandant of Cholet, 7 July 1941.

68 AD I-et-L 52W24, petitions of 4, 6 and 10 Nov. 1940.

NOTES

AD I-et-L 52W24, prefect of I-et-L to mayor of Sorigny, 16 April 1941, and to mayor of Reugny, 4 July 1941.

70 AD M-et-L 8W93, Mireille Gense to prefect of M-et-L, 22 Sept. 1941, and reply of prefecture, 24 Sept. 1941.

71 AD M-et-L 56W17, regional prefect's *arrêté* of 30 July 1942.

72 AD M-et-L 117W32, circular of Prefect Daguerre of M-et-L to mayors, 27 July 1943.

73 AD M-et-L 117W32 and 80W34, reports of gendarmerie of Vernantes, 5, 28 and 29 Dec. 1943, 2 Jan. 1944.

74 AD I-et-L 10W38, report of gendarmerie of Monnaie, 7 June 1943.

75 AD I-et-L 52W24, Pierre Renou and Maurice Rigoureau of Semblançay to prefect of I-et-L, 18 July 1941.

76 AD M-et-L 18W50, Gendarmerie Legion of Anjou, synthesis of Sept. 1943.

77 AD M-et-L 80W34, report of gendarmerie of Longué, 18 May 1944.

78 AD I-et-L 218W17, report of cantonal representative of Neuillé-Pont-Pierre, April 1943.

79 AD I-et-L 10W38, letter of Raymond Couella, curé of Nouzilly, 24 April 1944.

7. DEMONSTRATORS

1 Bernard Briais, *Le Lochois pendant la Guerre, 1939–1945* (Chambray-lès-Tours, 1988), 35–42; *Le Progrès de Loches*, 17 July 1940.

2 André Goupille, *Mon village sous la botte. La Haye Descartes, juin 1940-septembre 1944* (Tours, n.d.), 29.

3 Eric Alary, *La Ligne de Démarcation, 1940–1944* (Paris, PUF, 'Que sais-je?' 1995), 39–41.

4 AD I-et-L 10W7, prefect of I-et-L to Interior Minister, 10 Feb. 1941.

5 See above, p. 90.

6 AD I-et-L 52W40, prefect of I-et-L to prefect of Ille-et-Vilaine, 20 March 1941.

7 AN 72AJ136, MS account by André Goupille, p. 3.

8 AD I-et-L 42J1, Fonds Goupille, letter from family in Wingles (Pas-de-Calais), 13 Nov. 1940.

9 AD I-et-L 10W75, Trainee Inspector Chavenne of Loches to special superintendent, Loches, 13 Nov. 1941.

10 AD I-et-L 34W4, Cour de Justice of I-et-L, testimony of Aimé Brédif, a farmer (seventy-two) and his son Marius (forty-one), 15 Nov. 1943. Sidonie Bichet was interned by the prefect of I-et-L for intelligence with the enemy, 5 Jan. 1945.

11 AD M-et-L 12W48, subprefect of Saumur to prefect of M-et-L, 24 Oct. 1940; prefect of M-et-L to General Laure, DGGFTO, 26 Oct. 1940, and to Interior Minister, 30 Oct. 1940.

12 On commemoration and French identity, see Pierre Nora, ed., *Les Lieux de mémoire* (Paris, Gallimard), vol. I, *La République* (1984), vol. II (1–3), *La Nation* (1986) and vol. III (1–3), *La France* (1992). See also Rosamonde Sanson, *Les 14 juillet. Fête et conscience nationale, 1789–1975* (Paris, Flammarion, 1976); Danielle Tartakowsky, *Les Usages politiques des fêtes aux XIXe-XXe siècles* (Paris, Publications de la Sorbonne, 1994); Robert Gildea, *The Past in French History* (New Haven and London, Yale University Press, 1994); Olivier Ihl, *La Fête républicaine* (Paris, Gallimard, 1996); Danielle Tartakowsky, *Les Manifestations de la rue en France, 1918–1968* (Paris, Publications de la Sorbonne, 1997). On official Vichy commemorations from a regional perspective see François Cochet, 'Les Fêtes publiques de la période pétainiste (1940–1944)', in Sylvette Guibert. ed., *Fêtes et politique en Champagne à travers les siècles* (Nancy, Presses Universitaires de Nancy, 1992), 276–85.

13 *Le Progrès de Loches*, 17 July 1940.

14 AD L-A 75W551, prefecture of L-I to subprefects and mayors, 11 July 1940.

15 Edmond Duméril, *Journal d'un honnête homme pendant l'Occupation, juin 1940–août 1944*, 10 Nov. 1940.

16 W. D. Halls, *The Youth of Vichy France* (Oxford, Clarendon Press 1981), 404–6, has an interesting appendix on this incident.

17 AD L-A 13W25, police commissioner, Nantes, to prefect of L-I, 9 Nov. 1940; AD L-A 51W21, prefect of L-I to Interior Minister, 17 Nov. 1940; Duméril, *Journal d'un honnête homme*, 82, entry for 12 Nov. 1940.

18 Gérard Le Marec, *La Bretagne dans la Résistance* (Rennes, Ouest-France, 1983), 18; Sarah Choyeau, 'La Mémoire de la Résistance à Nantes' (*mémoire de maîtrise*, University of Nantes, 1994), 10; Interview with Christian de Mondragon (b. 1923), Nantes, 29 April 1997. In general on student behaviour, see André Gueslin, *Les Facs sous Vichy. Actes du Colloque des Universités de Clermont-Ferrand et de Strasbourg, Nov. 1993* (Clermont-Ferrand, Publications de l'Institut d'Études du Massif Central Université Blaise-Pascal, 1994).

19 AD L-A 132W54, prefect of L-I to Interior Minister, 11 Dec. 1940.

20 AD M-et-L 80W36, appeal of prefect of M-et-L, copied to Feldkommandantur of Angers, 4 Feb. 1941.

21 AD M-et-L 97W33, Feldkommandant Kloss, communiqué of 14 March 1941 and letter to Prefect Roussillon, 31 March 1941.

22 AD L-A 51W21, police commissioner, Nantes, to prefect of L-I, 31 March 1941.

23 AD L-A 13W8, Feldkommandant Hotz to Prefect Dupard, 30 March 1941;

Prefect Dupard, instructions of 31 March and circular to mayors, 4 April 1941.

24 Maurice Dommanget, *Histoire du Premier Mai* (Paris, Société Universitaire d'Éditions et de Librairie, 1953).

25 AD M-et-L 132W54, prefect of L-I to Interior Minister, 15 May 1941.

26 AD L-A 13W19, tract forwarded to prefect of L-I by 'un Français', 6 May 1941.

27 AD M-et-L 18W119, prefect of L-I to regional prefect, Angers, and Interior Minister, 3 May 1941.

28 *La Semaine religieuse du Diocèse d'Angers*, 11 May 1941.

29 AD M-et-L 41W2, police commissioner, Angers, to prefect of M-et-L, 2 May 1941.

30 AD M-et-L 18W119, prefect of L-I to regional prefect of Angers, and Interior Minister, 7 May 1941.

31 AD M-et-L 41W2, police commissioner, Angers, to prefect of M-et-L, 2 May 1941.

32 On the cult of Joan of Arc since the Revolution see Gerd Krumeich, 'Joan of Arc between right and left' in Robert Tombs, ed., *Nationhood and Nationalism in France. From Boulangism to the Great War, 1889–1918* (London, HarperCollins Academic, 1991), 63–73; Krumeich, *Jeanne d'Arc in der Geschichte. Historiographie-Politik-Kultur* (Sigmaringen, Thorbecke, 1989); Robert Gildea, *The Past in French History* (New Haven and London, Yale University Press, 1994), 154–165.

33 *La Semaine religieuse du Diocèse d'Angers*, 18 May 1941. In general on this ceremony see Michèle Cointet, *L'Église sous Vichy*, 51.

34 AD I-et-L XV Z 23, Feldkommandant of Tours to head of German military administration, Bezirk B, Angers, 13 May 1941; AD I-et-L 10W84, report of gendarmerie of Bléré, 11 May 1941.

35 AD M-et-L 41W2, police commissioner, Angers, to prefect of M-et-L, 12 May 1941.

36 AD L-A 27J17, account of Les Fils de France by Luc Belliard and A. Praud (two-page TS, n.d.).

37 AD L-A 13W21, note of Duméril for prefect of L-I, 13 May 1941; AD L-A 51W21, police commissioner, Nantes, to prefect of L-I, 15 May 1941.

38 AD M-et-L 136W12, prefect of M-et-L to Feldkommandant of Angers, 8 Sept. 1941.

39 AD M-et-L 12W48, report of gendarmerie of Gennes, 18 July 1941; 'an indignant French woman' to prefect of M-et-L, 3 June 1941.

40 AD I-et-L III Z 1, report of Feldkommandant of Tours, 18 March 1941.

41 AD M-et-L 24W2, police commissioner, Angers, to Prefect, 1 Nov. 1941; Prefect Roussillon to Interior Minister, 1 Dec. 1941.

42 *La Semaine religieuse du Diocèse d'Angers*, 10 May 1942.

43 AD I-et-L 10W40, Prefect Tracou of I-et-L to directors of Le Corozo-Darzouge, 7 May 1942, and Établissements Schmid, 16 May 1942.

44 AD M-et-L 41W2, report of gendarmerie of Trélazé, 14 July 1942; subprefect of Saumur to prefect of M-et-L, 15 July 1942.

45 AD M-et-L 18W119, report of prefect of M-et-L, 16 July 1942.

46 Gildea, *The Past in French History*, 149–50.

47 AD L-A 243W163, reports of police commissioner, Nantes, with tracts appended, 18 and 20 Sept. 1942.

48 AD M-et-L 80W5, chief superintendent of Renseignements Généraux to prefect of M-et-L, 23 Sept. 1942.

49 AD M-et-L 18W13, rector of Academy of Rennes to Regional Prefect Donati, 27 Feb. 1943, and reply of Donati, 17 March 1943.

50 AD L-A 132W159, prefect of L-I to police commisioner, Nantes, 13 April 1943; reports of Nantes police, 27 April and 8 May 1943.

51 AN 72AJ145, complaint by M. Decure to Nantes police, 2 May 1943; AD M-et-L 18W13, Regional Prefect Donati to Laval, 27 May 1943.

52 AD I-et-L 10W40, prefect of I-et-L to Pétain's private secretariat, 1 May 1943; regional prefect of Angers to prefect of I-et-L, 18 May 1943.

53 AD M-et-L 18W119, circular of Laval to regional prefects and police superintendents, 21 April 1944; Déat to regional and departmental prefects, 4 April 1944.

54 AD I-et-L 10W40, prefect of I-et-L to Laval, 2 May 1944.

55 AD M-et-L 80W7, prefect of M-et-L to Interior Minister Laval, 17 July 1943.

56 AD M-et-L 18W119, prefect of L-I to regional prefect, Angers, 17 July 1943.

57 AD I-et-L 10W40, telegram of Laval to all prefects and police superintendents, 14 July 1944; police superintendent, Tours, to police commissioner, Tours, 15 July 1944; chief superintendent of Renseignements Généraux, I-et-L, to director of Renseignements Généraux, Vichy, 15 July 1944.

58 AD M-et-L 90W1, police superintendent, Angers, to prefect of M-et-L, 14 July 1944.

59 Jacques Maurice, *Cinquante mois sous la botte*, (Tours, 1992), 30. See also Jacques Semelin, *Unarmed against Hitler. Civilian Resistance in Europe, 1939–1943* (Westport, Conn., and London, Praeger, 1993).

8. TRIMMERS

1 Fonds Émile Aron, Tours, petition of teachers at the École de Médecine, Tours, to prefect of I-et-L, 16 Feb. 1942.

2 See the tribute to his mentor by Émile Aron in *Figures Tourangelles* (Chambray-lès-Tours, CLD, 1986), 187–204.

3 For this distinction see Max Weber, 'Politics as a vocation', in H. H. Gerth and C. Wright Mills, *From Max Weber. Essays in Sociology* (London and Boston, Routledge & Kegan Paul, 1970), 84–6.

4 Ernest Gellner and John Waterbury, eds, *Patrons and Clients in Mediterranean Societies* (London, Duckworth, 1977), 4–5; Marc Abélès, *Quiet Days in Burgundy. A study of local politics*, 222–8, and Mattei Dogan, 'Les filières de la carrière politique en France', *Revue Française de Sociologie* 8 (1967), 468–92.

5 Raymond Lavigne, *Saint-Pierre-des-Corps ou la Clarté républicaine* (Paris, Éditions Messidor, 1988), 60–75.

6 Julien Papp, 'Les pouvoirs locaux en Indre-et-Loire', in Gilles Le Béguec and Denis Peschanski, *Les Elites locales dans la fourmente. Du Front populaire aux années cinquante* (Paris, CNRS, 2000); J. Feneant, *Histoire de la Franc-Maçonnerie en Touraine* (Chambray-lès-Tours, CLD, 1981).

7 Jean Le Cour Grandmaison, *Le Marquis de La Ferronnays, 1876–1946* (Paris, Éditions Siloë, 1952) and Annik Lassus Saint-Geniès, *Jean Le Cour Grandmaison* (Paris, Beauchesne, 1980); Christian Bougeard, 'Regards sur les réseaux de notables en Bretagne, des années 1930 aux années 1950', *Annales de Bretagne et des Pays de l'Ouest* 103 (1996), 31–51; René Bourrigaud, *Le Développement agricole au 19e siècle en Loire-Atlantique* (Nantes, Centre d'Histoire du Travail, 1994), 462–75; René Bourreau, *Une Utopie religieuse et sa modernisation lors des élections en pays nantais contemporain. La Logique restitutionniste de la noblesse nantaise* (thesis, Paris, EHESS, 1992), 272–317; Jean-Clément Martin, *La Vendée de la mémoire* (Paris, Seuil, 1989); AD L-A 1M473, file of Association des Chefs de Famille Catholiques du Diocèse de Nantes, 1927–30. I am grateful to Frank Liaigre for drawing my attention to this organization.

8 AD L-A 132W54, minutes of meetings at prefecture of 26 June, 2, 10, 12 and 16 July 1940; Mgr Villepelet, 'Le Diocèse de Nantes, 1940–1945', entry for 18 Aug. 1940.

9 AN F1a 3630, circular of Interior Minister Adrien Marquet to prefects, 7 Aug. 1940.

10 AD L-A 132W54, Prefect Dupard of L-I to Interior Minister, 12 Nov. 1940; AD M-et-L 12W20, Prefect Dupard to Interior Minister, 13 Dec. 1941.

11 AD M-et-L 12W4, Prefect Roussillon of M-et-L to DGGFTO, 30 Oct. 1940.

12 AD M-et-L 18W136, Prefect Roussillon to Interior Minister, 22 Jan. 1941.

13 AD M-et-L 18W135, subprefect of Saumur to prefect of M-et-L, 29 Dec. 1941; AD M-et-L 18W120, article in *Le Petit Parisien*, 29 Dec. 1941, annotated by Roussillon.

14 Philippe Gabillard, 'L'Extrême Droite en Maine-et-Loire, 1919–1934' (*mémoire de maîtrise*, Catholic University of Angers, 1980), 81–6.

15 AD M-et-L 60W4, Regional Prefect Roussillon to Interior Minister, 8 Dec.

1941; AD M-et-L 12W74, article in *Les Nouveaux Temps*, 6 Dec. 1940, Feldkommandant Kloss to Roussillon, 12 Dec. 1940.

16 AD M-et-L 136W12, Prefect Roussillon to Feldkommandant of Angers, 25 June 1941; AD M-et-L 24W2, Prefect Roussillon to Interior Minister, 1 July and 1 Aug. 1941; AD M-et-L 303W85, subprefect of Cholet Georges Husson to Roussillon, 4 Aug. 1941; the minutes of the municipal council in AM Cholet contain no reference to the wayward vote, but only an effusive vote of confidence in Darlan, Huntziger, Barthélémy, Bouthillier 'and all the other members of the government'.

17 AD M-et-L 12W74, Prefect Roussillon to Interior Minister and DGGFTO, 15 Sept. 1941.

18 See above, p. 143.

19 *Le Petit Courrier*, 5 Dec. 1941; AD M-et-L 12W74, Roussillon to Ministry of Industrial Production, 5 Dec., and to General Matthaei, 8 Dec. 1941; AD M-et-L 60W4, Prefect Roussillon to Interior Minister, 8 Dec. 1941; AD M-et-L 116W3, Chamber of Commerce of Cholet, 15 Dec. 1941.

20 Lavigne, *Saint-Pierre-des-Corps*, 75; AD I-et-L XV Z 23, Prefect Chaigneau of I-et-L to Feldkommandant of Tours, 27 June 1941.

21 AD L-A 132W157, 'Notices on influential figures', 1942.

22 AD M-et-L 12W48, subprefect of Saumur to Prefect Roussillon, 11 Feb. 1941.

23 AD I-et-L 10W25, circular to prefects of Interior Minister Peyrouton, 6 Jan. 1941.

24 *Tours Soir*, 7 June 1941. Cutting in AD I-et-L XIV Z 17.

25 AD I-et-L 10W25, Prefect Chaigneau of I-et-L to Interior Minister, 20 Jan. 1941; see also Robert Vivier, *Touraine 39–45. Histoire de l'Indre-et-Loire durant la 2e Guerre mondiale* (Chambray-lès-Tours, CLD, 1990), 135.

26 AD L-A 13W19, Lamaigre-Dubreuil, president of Fédération Départementale des Contribuables de la Loire-Inférieure, to Prefect Dupard for forwarding to Pétain, 15 March 1941.

27 AD L-A 132W157, notices on influential figures, 1942.

28 AD L-A 132W159, text read to CDL of L-I, 19 Oct. 1944.

29 AD L-A 10W11, Subprefect Douay of Saint-Nazaire to Prefect Dupard, 5 July 1941.

30 AD L-A 13W9, 'Advice to the prefectoral administration' given at a meeting of Interior Minister and regional prefects, forwarded by Prefect Dupard of L-I to subprefects of Châteaubriant and Saint-Nazaire, 24 Nov. 1941.

31 Ad L-A 132W85, subprefect of Châteaubriant to prefect of L-I, 10 April 1942.

32 AD M-et-L 18W107, Information on regional personalities, 1942.

33 Statistic from details on individual communes in AD I-et-L 3W9 and 10W25.

NOTES

34 AD M-et-L 140W8, Subprefect Milliat of Saumur to Prefect Roussillon, 10 and 15 Feb. 1941.

35 AD M-et-L 140W5, report of Prefect Delegate Daguerre, 3 Feb. 1942.

36 AD M-et-L 97W179, police superintendent of Saumur to subprefect, 5 Feb. 1943; Drouart to subprefect, 28 March; Captain Narcisse Clochard, second *adjoint*, to subprefect, 5 April; anonymous letter to subprefect, 24 April; subprefect to prefect of M-et-L, 21 July 1943.

37 Pierre Barral, 'Idéal et pratique du régionalisme dans le régime de Vichy', *Revue Française de Science Politique*, 24, no.5 (Oct. 1974), 911–3; Robert Gildea, *The Past in French History*, 166–85.

38 Michèle Cointet, *Le Conseil National de Vichy, 1940–1944* (Paris, Aux Amateurs du Livre, 1989).

39 Mgr Villepelet, 'Le Diocèse de Nantes, 1940–1945', entry for 6 Aug. 1940.

40 AD L-A 132W157, Société Archéologique et Historique de Nantes et de la Loire-Inférieure to Marshal Pétain via Prefect Dupard, 17 Dec. 1940.

41 AD L-A 243W163, police commissioner, Nantes, to prefect of L-I, 23 Jan., 21 and 28 Feb., 6 and 17 March, 8 April and 4 May 1941. See in general Alain Déniel, *Le Mouvement breton* (Paris, Maspéro, 1976); Michel Nicolas, *Le Séparatisme en Bretagne* (Brasparts, Éditions Beltan, 1986); Paul Serant, *La Bretagne et la France* (Paris, Fayard, 1971); Olier Mordrel, *Breiz Atao ou Histoire et actualité du nationalisme breton* (Paris, A. Moreau, 1973).

42 On these see Henri Hauser, *Le Problème du régionalisme* (Paris, PUF, 1924), 69–113.

43 AD L-A 132W157, Prefect Dupard of L-I to prefect delegate of Interior Minister, Paris, summing up a paper by Durand, 18 Dec. 1940; report of Chamber of Commerce, Nantes, 23 Dec. 1940, forwarded to prefect delegate by Dupard, 2 Jan. 1941; Dupard to Darlan, 14 April 1941; Abel Durand, *Nantes dans la France de l'Ouest* (Paris, Plon, 1941), with a preface by Gaëtan Rondeau.

44 AD M-et-L 18W136, Prefect Roussillon to Interior Minister, 22 Jan. 1941.

45 AD M-et-L 18W120, paper by Jacques de la Grandière and Joachim du Plessis de Grénadan, 20 May 1941.

46 AD M-et-L 116W4, Chambre de Commerce de Saumur, *Bulletin des Séances, 1940–1954*.

47 AD I-et-L 52W4, report by vice-president of Chamber of Commerce of Tours, F. Martin, endorsed 14 Jan. 1941 and forwarded to prefect of I-et-L, 17 Jan. 1941.

48 AD M-et-L 12W48, draft of Prefect Roussillon, n.d. but Nov.–Dec. 1941.

49 AD L-A 13W9, resolution of Chamber of Commerce of Nantes, 7 July 1941, forwarded by prefect Dupard to prefect delegate of Interior Minister, Paris, 18 July 1941; Hervé Le Boterf, *La Bretagne sous le Gouvernement de Vichy* (Paris, France-Empire, 1982), 109–13.

50 AD L-A 13W6, Rondeau, Brossier and employers' leader Bertin to Laval, 26 Aug. 1942. The prefect delegate of the Interior Minister, J.-P. Ingrand, told the regional prefect of Angers, 25 Aug. 1942, that the government had no plans to revise the regions. See also Yvonnig Gicquel, *Le Comité consultatif de Bretagne* (Rennes, Simon, 1961).

51 AD 18W135, Prefect Roussillon to Interior Minister, 25 Oct. and 20 Dec. 1940, *arrêté* of appointment of Interior Minister, 30 Jan. 1941; *Le Petit Courrier*, 9 Feb. 1941. See also Marc Bergère, 'Permanences et ruptures au sein du Conseil Général du Maine-et-Loire (1935–1953). Étude prosopographique des élus', *Annales de Bretagne et des Pays de l'Ouest* 103 (1996), 69–77.

52 AD L-A 13W10, minutes of Administrative Commission of L-I, 5 March 1941.

53 AD I-et-L 225W1 and 10W3, correspondence on the composition of the Administrative Commission of I-et-L, 1940–1; Vivier, *Touraine 39–45*, 127–8.

54 AD I-et-L 225W2/3, minutes of the Administrative Commission of I-et-L, 1 March 1941–14 Nov. 1942.

55 AD M-et-L 12W23, speech of Interior Minister Pucheu, 19 Feb. 1942.

56 AD M-et-L 12W4, Prefect Delegate Daguerre to Interior Minister, 1 Feb. 1942.

57 AD M-et-L 18W9, Prefect Tracou of I-et-L to Roussillon, 9 Feb. 1942.

58 AD M-et-L 18W16, speech of Roussillon in Tours, 29 Jan. 1942; report of Roussillon to Interior Minister Pucheu, n.d. but early 1942.

59 AD M-et-L 18W13, Prefect Tracou to Roussillon, 24 Aug. 1942.

60 AN F1a 3634 and AD L-A 13W10, circular of Interior Minister Pucheu, 9 Dec. 1941; Prefect Dupard to Interior Minister, 11 April 1942.

61 AD I-et-L 225W1, Prefect Tracou of I-et-L to Interior Minister, 23 June 1942.

62 See below, pp. 265–6.

63 AN F1a 3635, unsigned note of Interior Minister, 13 May 1942.

64 AD I-et-L 10W3, minutes of meeting of regional prefects of Occupied Zone, n.d. but May 1942. On Hilaire and Bousquet see M. O. Baruch, *Servir l'État français. L'Administration en France de 1940 à 1944*, (Paris, Fayard, 1997), 336–7.

65 AD I-et-L 225W6, Comité d'Organisation des Pelleteries et Fourrures to prefect of I-et-L, 28 Aug. 1942.

66 Ibid., Prefect Tracou to Laval, 16 Oct. 1942.

67 AD M-et-L 2W4, Prefect Delegate Daguerre to Interior Minister, 3 May 1943.

68 AD M-et-L 18W138, Prefect Delegate Daguerre to Laval, 13 Oct. 1942.

69 AD M-et-L 7U4/98, Prefect Delegate Daguerre to Interior Minister, 29 Aug.

1942; Daguerre's testimony to examining magistrate in proceedings against Moreau, 17 April 1945.

70 AD L-A 13W10, Conseil Départemental of L-I, 7–8 June 1943.

71 AD M-et-L 18W138, Conseil Départemental of M-et-L, April 1943.

72 *Demain*, 30 April 1943, cutting in AD M-et-L 140W9.

73 AD I-et-L 225W8/9, Conseil Départemental of I-et-L, 8 July 1944.

74 AD M-et-L 95W112, report of subprefect of Cholet, 26 July 1941.

75 AD M-et-L 8W87, report of subprefect of Cholet, 31 Aug. 1943.

76 AD M-et-L 90W6, circular of Laval to mayors, 4 Dec. 1942; AD I-et-L 10W25, circular of Laval to prefects, 22 June 1942. Changes to the law of 16 Nov. 1940 on municipal councils were brought in on 13 Nov. 1941 and 4 Oct. 1943.

77 AD M-et-L 80W5, circular of prefect of M-et-L to mayors, 3 June 1942; 80W6, report of prefect to Interior Minister, 2 March 1943.

78 AD I-et-L 52W4, Guillaume-Louis to prefect of I-et-L, 4 Oct. 1943, cutting from *La Dépêche du Centre*, n.d.; AD I-et-L 18W133, list of mayors from the Angers region, Oct. 1943; AD M-et-L 24W24, notes of prefect delegate of M-et-L for Regional Prefect Donati, 5 Oct. 1943.

79 AD I-et-L 18W134, Prefect Tracou to Regional Prefect Roussillon, 3 April 1943, and reply 19 April 1943. On Gounin, see AD M-et-L 18W107, notes on regional personalities, 1942.

80 AD L-A 132W157, subprefect of Châteaubriant to prefect of L-I, 9 Nov. 1942.

81 AD M-et-L 18W138, Jacques Hedouin, mayor of Vernoil, to Regional Prefect Donati, 26 July 1944.

82 AD I-et-L 10W25, prefect of I-et-L to Laval, 10 Jan. 1944.

9. SAINTS

1 *La Semaine religieuse du Diocèse de Nantes*, 9 June 1944, 185–6. See also Mgr Villepelet, *Au service de l'Église. Choix de discours, 1936–1966* (n.p., n.d.), 89.

2 In general on this period see Gérard Cholvy and Yves-Marie Hilaire, *Histoire religieuse de la France contemporaine*, vol. III, 1930–1988 (Toulouse, Privat, 1988).

3 *La Semaine religieuse du Diocèse de Nantes*, 25 May and 8 June 1940.

4 *Le Courrier de Saint-Nazaire*, 22 June 1940.

5 *La Semaine religieuse du Diocèse de Tours*, 4 Oct. and 1 Nov. 1940, 10 Jan. and 21 Feb. 1941; *La Semaine religieuse du Diocèse d'Angers*, 9 March 1941; Mgr Villepelet, 'Le Diocèse de Nantes, 1940–1945', entries for 4–11 Oct. 1940; Michèle Cointet, *L'Église sous Vichy*, 16–21; W. D. Halls,

Politics, Society and Christianity in Vichy France (Oxford and Providence, Berg, 1995), 45–53.

6 Nicholas Atkin, *Church and Schools in Vichy France, 1940–1944* (New York and London, Garland, 1991).

7 See below, p. 228.

8 Mgr Villepelet, 'Le Diocèse de Nantes, 1940–1945', entry for 8 June 1941; *La Révolution Nationale*, 6 Feb. 1943.

9 A. Dio. Tours, Mgr Gaillard, 'Tournée pastorale, 1942'.

10 A. Dio. Angers, Recteur Vincent to Mgr Bressolles of Institut Catholique, Paris, 24 Aug. 1941.

11 AN F1a 3868, CFLN Zone handbook no. 7, part III, Nov. 1943.

12 *Le Sou de la presse*, July-Aug. 1939; Cholvy and Hilaire, *Histoire religieuse de la France contemporaine*, 29–36, 85–9.

13 James McMillan, 'France', in Tom Buchanan and Martin Conway, eds, *Political Catholicism in Europe, 1918–1965* (Oxford, Clarendon Press, 1996), 41–3.

14 Philippe Gabillard, 'L'Extrême Droite en Maine-et-Loire 1919–1934 (*mémoire de maîtrise*, Angers, Catholic University, 1980), 125.

15 See above, p. 152.

16 Fernand Boulard, ed., *Matériaux pour l'histoire religieuse du peuple français, XIXe–XX siècles. Région de Paris, Haute-Normandie, Pays de Loire, Centre* (Paris, Éditions de l'École des Hautes Études en Sciences Sociales, 1982), 117, 389, 417; André Siegfried, *Tableau politique de la France de l'Ouest sous la Troisième République* (Paris, A. Colin, 1964), 4–7, 40–1; Laurence Wylie, ed., *Chanzeaux. A village in Anjou* (Cambridge, Mass., Harvard University Press, 1966), 3–4.

17 See John S. Conway, *The Nazi Persecution of the Churches* (London, Weidenfeld & Nicolson, 1968).

18 Mgr Villepelet, 'Le Diocèse de Nantes, 1940–1945', entry for 24 July 1940.

19 AD L-A 75W551, Kommandantur to bishop of Nantes, 19 July 1940; Mgr Villepelet, 'Le Diocèse de Nantes, 1940–1945', entry for 19 July, 25 and 28 Sept. 1940; Laurent Berger, 'L'Épiscopat nantais de Mgr Villepelet, 1936–1966' (*mémoire de maîtrise*, University of Nantes, 1991), 192.

20 AD I-et-L 10W42, Feldkommandant of Tours to prefect of I-et-L, 15 Aug. 1940; AD L-A 13W25, Feldkommandant of Nantes to Mgr Villepelet, 25 Oct. 1940; mayors of St Étienne-de-Corcoué and Mauves-sur-Loire to prefect of L-A, 28 Oct. and 5 Nov. 1940; AD M-et-L 5W17, Feldkommandant of Angers to prefecture of M-et-L, 23 Oct. 1940, curé of Nueil-sur-Layon to prefect of M-et-L, 6 Nov. 1940.

21 Mgr Villepelet, 'Le Diocèse de Nantes, 1940–1945', entry for 24 Nov. 1940; Berger, 'L'Épiscopat nantais', 193.

22 AD M-et-L 95W75, Feldkommandant Kloss to prefect of M-et-L, 10 Oct.

1940, and report of gendarmerie of Champtoceaux, M-et-L, 3 June 1941; BAMA Freiburg RW35/1261, report of Neumann-Neurode, 22 Feb. 1941; AD I-et-L 10W43, Feldkommandant of Tours to prefect of I-et-L, 3 May 1941, and prefect to Mgr Gaillard, 17 and 26 May 1941; AD M-et-L 97W34, prefect of M-et-L to subprefect of Saumur, 24 May 1941, and latter to archdeacon of Saumur, 24 May 1941.

23 *La Semaine religieuse du Diocèse d'Angers*, 11 Aug. 1940 and 8 June 1941; AD M-et-L 80W36, Feldkommandant Kloss to Mgr Costes, 29 May 1941, prefect of M-et-L to Kloss, 4 June 1941; A. Dio. Angers, funeral oration for Mgr Costes by Mgr Cesbron, bishop of Annecy, 28 March 1950.

24 Mgr Villepelet, 'Le Diocèse de Nantes, 1940–1945', entries for 28 June, 20 July, 24 Sept., 12, 13, 14 and 24 Dec. 1940.

25 *La Semaine religieuse du Diocèse de Nantes*, 7 and 21 June 1941.

26 See *La Famille Catholique. Bulletin mensuel des Chefs de Famille Catholique*, 1941–3.

27 *La Semaine religieuse du Diocèse de Tours*, 16 June 1978; Jérôme Guillard, 'Les Catholiques Tourangeaux pendant la Deuxième Guerre Mondiale' (*mémoire de maîtrise*, University of Tours, 1996), 147–8. On Catholics and STO see Cholvy and Hilaire, *Histoire religieuse de la France contemporaine*, 100–3, and Émile Poulat, *Naissance des prêtres ouvriers* (Paris, Casterman, 1965).

28 See, for example, Vera Drapac, *War and Religion. Catholics in the churches of Occupied Paris* (Washington, DC, Catholic University of America, 1998), 278–84.

29 AN 72AJ136 and AD I-et-L 81J1, report on Canon Robin by J. M. Demezil, archivist of Loir-et-Cher, 15 March 1949; Robert Vivier, *Touraine 39–45. Histoire de l'Indre-et-Loire durant la Deuxième Guerre Mondiale* (Chambray-lès-Tours, CLD, 1990), 158–60; Jack Vivier, *Prêtres de Touraine dans la Résistance* (Chambray-lès-Tours, CLD, 1993), 22–34; Canon Robert Fiot, *Un Prêtre de Touraine; L'Abbé Georges Lhermitte, 1887–1944* (Tours, Barbot et Gallon, 1945); Abbé Joseph Perret, *Le Curé de Draché, 'Un Pur de la Résistance'* (n.p. 1948). For an upbeat account of clerical resistance see Charles Molette, *Prêtres, religieux et religieuses dans la Résistance au Nazisme, 1940–1945* (Paris, Fayard, 1995).

30 See pp. 151 and 261–2.

31 BAMA Freiburg RH36/228, report of Cholet office to Feldkommandant of Tours, 7 May 1942.

32 Interview with Suzanne Le Chat, Ingrandes (M-et-L), 15 April 1997; Dom Guy Oury, *Dom Gabriel Sortais* (Solesmes, 1975).

33 Guillard, 'Les Catholiques Tourangeaux', 140.

34 Mgr Villepelet, 'Le Diocèse de Nantes, 1940–1945', entry for 14 Sept. 1942.

On the differences between the lower clergy and the hierarchy over the Resistance see Cointet, *L'Église sous Vichy*, 308–9, 320.

35 E. R. Vaucelle, *La Collégiale de Saint Martin de Tours des origines à l'avènement des Valois*, *397–1328* (Tours, 1907), 165–6. I am grateful to Professor David Ganz of King's College, London, for this reference.

36 *La Semaine religieuse du Diocèse de Tours*, 12 and 19 Dec. 1940, 19 June and 17 July 1941.

37 A. Dio. Angers 2K50, Notre-Dame de Béhuard and 2K52, Notre-Dame des Gardes; *La Semaine religieuse du Diocèse d'Angers*, 27 Sept. 1942.

38 *La Semaine religieuse du Diocèse d'Angers*, 15 Aug. 1943, 23 Jan., 26 March and 30 April 1944.

39 Mgr Villepelet, 'Le Diocèse de Nantes, 1940–1945', entries for 23 Sept. and 14 Nov. 1943; A. Dio. Nantes, Livre de Paroisse, Ste Croix, Nantes, 23 Sept. 1943; *La Semaine religieuse du Diocèse de Nantes*, 25 Sept. and 4 Dec. 1943.

40 *La Semaine religieuse du Diocèse de Nantes*, 2 Aug. 1941; AD L-A 13W22, Feldkommandant of Nantes to prefect of L-I, 26 July 1943, report of police superintendent, 12 Aug. 1943.

41 *La Semaine religieuse du Diocèse de Nantes*, 20 May 1944. In general see Louis Perouas, 'Le Grand Retour de Notre Dame de Boulogne à travers la France (1943–48). Essai de reconstitution', *Annales de Bretagne et des Pays de l'Ouest* 90 (1983), 171–83. Reprinted in *Archives des Sciences Sociales des Religions* 56/1 (1983), 37–59.

42 *La Semaine religieuse du Diocèse de Tours*, 2 June 1944.

43 Interview with Abbé Jacques Ménard (b. 1922), Tours, 2 June 1997.

44 *La Semaine religieuse du Diocèse d'Anjou*, 19 and 26 March 1944.

45 Ibid., 16 April 1944; Michel Lemesle, *1939–1945. A Travers l'Anjou* (Cholet, Les Éditions du Choletais, 1976), 164–6.

46 A. Dio. Nantes, Livre de Paroisse, Sainte Croix, Nantes, entry for 15 June 1944.

47 Mgr Villepelet, 'Le Diocèse de Nantes, 1940–1945', entries for 12, 15 and 25 June and 27 July 1944; Mgr Villepelet, *Au service de l'Église*, 94; *La Semaine religieuse du Diocèse de Nantes*, 24 June and 1 July 1944.

48 See below, pp. 333–4.

10. SINNERS

1 AD I-et-L 10W73, police commissioner, Tours, to prefect of I-et-L, 18 Jan. 1941.

2 AD M-et-L 116J9, 'Les Camps de Montreuil-Bellay' (MS, 30 pp., n.d.);

NOTES

Jacques Sigot, *Un Camp pour les Tsiganes ... et les autres. Montreuil-Bellay, 1940–1945* (Châteauneuf-les-Martignes, Éditions Wallada, 1983), 54–5; Sophie Paisot-Béal and Roger Prévost, *Histoire des camps d'internement en Indre-et-Loire, 1940–1944* (Private Press, 1993), 46–53.

3 Renée Poznanski, *Les Juifs en France pendant la Seconde Guerre Mondiale* (Paris, Hachette, 1997), 21–2.

4 AD M-et-L 97W39, Subprefect Milliat of Saumur to prefect of M-et-L, 31 May 1941.

5 Annie Lambert and Claude Toczé, *Être Juif à Nantes sous Vichy* (Nantes, Siloë, 1994), 19–23.

6 AD M-et-L 12W41, register of Jews of M-et-L, 2 Oct. 1940.

7 AD M-et-L 37W10, register of Jews of I-et-L, 1 Oct. 1940, and of L-I, 31 Oct. 1940.

8 AD I-et-L 120W7, Prefect Chaigneau to general inspector of internment camps at Interior Ministry, 22 Oct. 1941; Paisot-Béal and Prévost, *Histoire des Camps d'Internement en Indre-et-Loire, 1940–1944*, 46–53, 77–8.

9 AD L-A 51W21, police commissioner, Nantes, to prefect of L-I, 30 Oct. 1940.

10 AD L-A 51W21, prefect of L-I to Interior Minister, 30 Nov. and 16 Dec. 1940, 2 Jan. and 19 Feb. 1941; police commissioner, Nantes, to prefect, 30 Oct. 1940.

11 AD I-et-L 10W7, prefect Chaigneau of I-et-L to prefect delegate of Ministry of the Interior, 9 April and 4 Oct. 1941. See also Yves Durand and Robert Vivier, *Libération des Pays de Loire. Blésois, Orléanais, Touraine* (Paris, Hachette, 1974), 37–40.

12 AD I-et-L 10W7, police commissioner, Tours, to prefect of I-et-L, 1 Feb. 1941; AD M-et-L 12W20, Police Inspector Charpentier to police commissioner, Tours, 5 Nov. 1942.

13 AD I-et-L 10W75, General Mouton to prefect of I-et-L, 6 and 8 Nov. 1941.

14 *La Dépêche*, 16 Aug. 1941, and *Le Petit Courrier*, 16 Aug. 1941. Cuttings in AD M-et-L 12W72. Both articles have identical wording.

15 AD M-et-L 140W24, circular of Interior Minister Pucheu to prefects, 13 Sept. 1941.

16 Denis Peschanski, *Vichy 1940–1944: Contrôle et exclusion* (Paris, Complexe, 1997).

17 See above, p. 182.

18 Fonds Émile Aron, minutes of municipal council of Le Boulay, 10 Nov. 1940.

19 AD M-et-L 8W93, chef de cabinet of prefect of M-et-L to subprefect of Saumur, 25 Sept. 1941; AD M-et-L 97W37, subprefect of Saumur to prefect of M-et-L, 9 Oct. 1941.

20 AD M-et-L 97W37, Commissaire Eprinchard to subprefect of Saumur, 14

and 22 March 1941; Déré to subprefect, 22 March 1941; Clémence Veau to DFGOT, 16 Sept. 1941; subprefect to prefect, 9 Oct. 1941.

21 AD M-et-L 60W2, Bousquet to Regional Prefect Roussillon, 18 Nov. 1942.

22 AD M-et-L 12W20, Prefect Tracou to Regional Prefect Roussillon, 9 Dec. 1942.

23 AD I-et-L 10W75, chief superintendent, Renseignements Généraux, Loches, to prefect of Indre, 26 April 1943; internment order of 2 June 1942.

24 AD L-A 132W160, director of Contributions Indirectes, Nantes, to prefect Dupard, 26 Nov. 1940; Roussillon to Dupard, 9 Oct. 1941; commissioner of Police Nationale (Sûreté) to Prefect Dupard, 13 Oct. 1941; Dupard to de Brinon, 19 Jan. 1943.

25 AM Nantes 38W9, chef de bureau du personnel, Nantes, to Adjoint Prieur, 27 Nov. 1940.

26 Poznanski, *Les Juifs en France*, 71.

27 AD I-et-L 10W66, Feldkommandant of Tours to prefect of I-et-L, 25 Oct. 1940.

28 AD M-et-L 97W39, police superintendent of Saumur to Subprefect Milliat, 13 Aug. 1941; Milliat to Kreiskommandantur of Saumur, 2 Sept. 1941, and reply 4 Sept. 1941; Prefect Roussillon to Milliat, 26 Aug. 1941, and Milliat to Prefect Daguerre of M-et-L, 28 Jan. 1942.

29 AD L-A 13W46, Ross to Pétain, 21 Oct. 1940 and to Interior Minister, 14 Feb. 1941, supported by letter of Prefect Dupard, 18 March 1941; Ross to Dupard, 26 Dec. 1941. AN AJ38/150 contains most of this dossier.

30 André Kaspi, *Les Juifs pendant l'Occupation* (Seuil, 1991, new edn 1997), 116–17.

31 AD M-et-L 97W39, Feldkommandant of Angers to prefect of M-et-L, 8 Nov. 1940; AD L-A 13W44, Feldkommandant of Nantes to Prefect Dupard, 18 and 19 Nov. 1940; AD L-A 75W560, Prefect Dupard to mayors, 28 Oct. 1940.

32 AD L-A 13W20, Prefect Dupard to Dr Rheinfels, 17 Feb. and 6 June 1941.

33 AD M-et-L 12W42, Inspecteur Départemental du Travail Lehlmann to Prefect Roussillon, 10 Dec. 1940.

34 AD M-et-L 97W39, Laraia to Subprefect of Saumur Milliat, 5 Nov. 1940; minutes of interview of Laraia with Commissaire René Drouart and report of Drouart to Milliat, 6 Nov. 1940.

35 AD L–A 13W49, return of questionnaire to prefect of L-I by Société Parisienne de Confection, 9 Nov. 1940.

36 AD M-et-L 12W42, prefect Roussillon to presidents of Chambers of Commerce of Angers, Cholet and Saumur, 10 and 19 Dec. 1940, and replies of 13 Dec. 1940 and 6 Jan. 1941 (Angers), 18 Dec. 1940 (Cholet) and 19 Dec. 1940 (Saumur).

37 AD M-et-L 61W3, Palamède de la Grandière to Xavier Vallat, 6 July 1941;

NOTES

table of Aryanization and administration of Jewish businesses in Angers by Prefect Daguerre, 19 May 1942. See also details of provisional administrators in AN AJ 38/977.

38 AD L-A 13W50, correspondence addressed to Prefect Dupard, 12 Jan. 1941–15 Sept. 1942.

39 See for example Poznanski, *Les Juifs en France*, 569–71; Michèle Cointet, *L'Église sous Vichy, 1940–1945* (Paris, Perrin, 1998), 197–207; and W. D. Halls, *Politics, Society and Christianity in Vichy France* (Oxford and Providence, Berg, 1995), 95–103. Lambert and Toczé, *Être Juif à Nantes*, 152, are more scathing about French complicity in the spoliation of the Jews.

40 AD M-et-L 61W4, ruling by prefect on Sainte-Radégonde, June 1941; David Sternschuss to prefect of M-et-L, 15 July 1941, Feldkommandantur of Angers to prefect, 2 Aug. 1941.

41 AD M-et-L 12W42, Secretary General Foulquié to police commissioner, Angers, 20 Aug. 1941.

42 AD M-et-L 61W4, Chené to Prefect Roussillon, 14 Oct. 1941, and reply, 23 Oct. 1941; chief of the Police des Questions Juives to Roussillon, 7 May 1942.

43 AD L-A 270W491, Subprefect Lecornu of Châteaubriant to Prefect Dupard, 26 May 1941; police commissioner of Nantes to Dupard, 27 May 1941, and internment decision of Dupard, 8 July 1941.

44 Interview with Abbé François Jamnoneau, Nantes, 26 May 1997.

45 AD I-et-L 120W7, statistics on population of La Lande, 18 July 1941; AD I-et-L 10W6, Feldkommandantur of Tours to prefect of I-et-L, 28 Aug. 1941.

46 CDJC CCXIII – 100, Œuvres sociales du Centre d'Acceuil de Monts, près Tours, n.d.

47 AD I-et-L 120W7, Prefect Chaigneau to Inspector General of Internment Camps, Ministry of the Interior, 22 Oct. 1941; Jérôme Scorin, *L'Itinéraire d'un adolescent juif de 1939 à 1945* (Nancy, Christmann, 1994), 19–34.

48 AD I-et-L 120W7, prefect of I-et-L to director of La Lande, 24 Oct. 1941, to station master of Monts, 29 Oct. 1941 and to Inspector General of Internment Camps, Ministry of the Interior, 9 Dec. 1941; AD I-et-L 52W13, Dr Haueisen of Feldkommandantur of Tours to prefect of I-et-L, 5 Nov. 194; Sigot, *Un Camp pour les Tsiganes . . .*, 81.

49 AD I-et-L 10W75, General Mouton to prefect of I-et-L, 6 and 8 Nov. 1941.

50 AD I-et-L 10W7, prefect of I-et-L to Ministry of the Interior, 4 Oct. 1941.

51 AD M-et-L 7U4/1–2, register of judgements of the Special Tribunal of the Appeal Court of Angers, 14 Aug. 1941.

52 AD M-et-L 136W12, Prefect Roussillon to Feldkommandant of Angers, 25 July 1941; AD M-et-L 7U4/1–2, Special Tribunal, Angers, 18 Sept. 1941.

53 See above, p. 91.

54 AD L-A 270W494, reports of camp governor Captain Leclercq, May, June, July and Aug. 1941.

11. MURDER

1 The fullest account of this incident is in Louis Oury, *Rue du Roi Albert. Les otages de Nantes, Châteaubriant et Bordeaux* (Paris, Le Temps des Cerises, 1996), 13–14, 89–93.

2 *Ouest-France*, 21 Oct. 1991.

3 Edmond Duméril, *Journal d'un honnête homme pendant l'Occupation, juin 1940–aôut 1944*, 20 Oct. 1941, 181.

4 AN 72AJ145 and AM Nantes H4/116, F. Soil, secretary general of the prefectures, 'Meurtre du Lieutenant-Colonel Hotz, Feldkommandant de Nantes, le 20 octobre 1941'. The file in the AM also includes examples of the posters.

5 AM Nantes 1134W9, letters to mayor of Nantes, 21 Oct. 1941.

6 *Le Phare*, 22 Oct. 1941. See cuttings in AM Nantes 1134W12.

7 On 21 October the communist commandos sent to Bordeaux shot Commandant Reimers of the Wehrmacht general staff. See Dominique Lormier, *Bordeaux pendant l'Occupation* (Bordeaux, Éditions Sud-Ouest, 1992), 122–4.

8 BAMA Freiburg 35/543, circular of Keitel, 16 Sept. 1941, circulars of Stülpnagel, 19 and 28 Sept. 1941. Eberhard Jäckel, *Frankreich in Hitlers Europa* (Stuttgart, Verlags-Anstalt, 1966), 191–2; Richard Cavill Fattig, 'Reprisal: The German Army and the execution of hostages during the Second World War' (PhD, University of California at San Diego, 1980), 63–5.

9 BAMA Freiburg 35/542, 'Das Geiselverfahren im Bereich des Militärbefehlhabers in Frankreich von August 1941 bis Mai 1942'.

10 See above, pp. 90–1.

11 AD L-A 243W163, notes of procureur on 'l'Affaire Jost', n.d., and report of Duméril on execution of Poirier, n.d. The latter is also in AN F1a 3667.

12 AM Nantes H4/116, poster dated 21 Oct. 1941.

13 Bernard Lecornu, *Un Préfet sous l'Occupation allemande. Châteaubriant, Saint-Nazaire, Tulle* (Paris, France-Empire, 1984, re-ed. 1997), 47–51, 85–95. See also his account in AD L-A 270W480.

14 Oury, *Rue du Roi Albert*, 114–15.

15 Archives du Diocèse de Nantes, Mgr Villepelet, 'Le Diocèse de Nantes, 1940–1945', entry for 22 Oct. 1941.

16 As note 4.

17 AD L-A 132W54, report of Lecomte, commander of the Gendarmerie Company of L-I, 29 Oct. 1941.

18 Philippe Pétain, *Actes et écrits* (Flammarion, 1974), 603–4; Marc Ferro, *Pétain* (Paris, Fayard, 1987), 344–7.

19 AM Nantes 1134W10, Mlle Benoîte to mayor of Nantes, 6 Dec. 1941; Duméril, *Journal d'un honnête homme*, 194.

20 Mgr Villepelet, 'Le Diocèse de Nantes, 1940–1945', entry for 23 Oct. 1941.

21 AM Nantes 1134W10, Mayor Rondeau to *chef de cabinet* of de Brinon, 23 Oct. 1941.

22 Ibid., Mayor Rondeau to Alphonse de Châteaubriant, 23 Oct. 1941.

23 *Le Phare*, 25 Oct. 1941; *L'Ouest-Éclair*, 25 Oct. 1941. Cuttings in AM Nantes 1134W12.

24 AD L-A 270W480, report of police superintendent, Nantes, 24 Oct. 1941.

25 AD L-A 270W480, letter of M. Méroviac to prefect, 24 Oct. 1941.

26 Mgr Villepelet, 'Le Diocèse de Nantes, 1940–1945', entries for 24, 25 and 27 Oct. and 18 Nov. 1941.

27 Fernand Ridel, *Témoignages, 1939–1945* (La Bautle, Éditions des Paludiers, 1974), 162–5; Yves de Sesmaisons, *Marquise de Sesmaisons (1898–1977). Souvenirs de l'Occupation*, 70, 93–5.

28 AD L-A 270W480, petition of families 25 Oct. 1941 and note of Duméril for prefect, n.d.; Duméril, *Journal d'un honnête homme*, 195; AM Nantes 1134W11, Mayor Rondeau to M. Glou, 27 Oct., and reply of Glou, 29 Oct. 1941.

29 BAMA Freiburg RW 35/1, von Stülpnagel to Major General Wagner, 24 Oct. 1941. See also Jäckel, *Frankreich*, 192–4, and Bücheler, *Carl-Heinrich von Stülpnagel*, 246–7.

30 Ernst Jünger, *Premier Journal parisien. Journal II, 1941–1943* (Paris, Christian Bourgois, 1980), 108–9.

31 Fattig, 'Reprisal', 153; Anatoly Kuznetsov, *Babi Yar: A documentary novel* (London, MacGibbon & Kee, 1967); George St George, *The Road to Babyi Yar* (London, Neville Spearman, 1967).

32 AD L-A 270W480, report of Commissaire Divisionnaire, Chef de la 1ere Brigade de la Police Judiciaire, 4 Nov. 1941.

33 AN 72AJ 145, questioning of Mme Huau, Nantes, 20 Oct. 1944.

34 AM Nantes 1134W11, address of Mayor Rondeau, 29 Oct. 1941. This was authorized by the Feldkommandantur but prohibited by the Propagandastaffel at Nantes.

35 Charles de Gaulle, *Discours et messages I, 1940–1946* (Paris, Plon, 1970), 122–5. Broadcast of 25 Oct. 1941, repeated 30 Oct.

36 AD M-et-L 12W3, Prefect Dupard to Interior Minister, 2 Nov. 1941.

37 AD M-et-L 12W48, report of Prefect Dupard, 1 Nov. 1941.

38 AM Nantes 1134W14, decree of 11 Nov. 1941.

39 AD L-A 132W54, report of Prefect Dupard, 1 Dec. 1941.

40 AD L-A 270W480, *La Bretagne ouvrière, paysanne et maritime. Édition spéciale de la Loire-Inférieure*, n.d.

41 Duméril, *Journal d'un honnête homme*, 236.

12. TERROR

1 AD I-et-L 10W81, account by the young men, 15 May 1942; report of Bossy, police commissioner of I-et-L, to prefect, 18/20 Oct. 1944.

2 AD M-et-L 60W10, accounts of André Maurice, 24 Oct. 1944, Jean Moracchini, 1 Dec. 1944, and Commissaire Georges Gouchet, 2 Jan. 1945.

3 AD I-et-L 10W8, Commissaire Central Moracchini to Prefect Tracou, 26 May 1942; AD M-et-L 12W2, Tracou to regional prefect, Angers, 28 May 1942.

4 Robert Guérinau and Jean-Claude Guillon, *La Touraine sous le règne des Feldkommandants* (Tours, Centre-Loire, 1985), 47. See also Robert Guérineau, *Les Martys du 16 mai 1942. Les premiers fusillés de la Touraine* (Tours, La Voix du Peuple, 1963). Guérineau and Guillon were communist militants who had met on 30 April 1942 to organize the campaign of tracts and graffiti.

5 AD M-et-L 12W2, report of Prefect Tracou to Interior Minister, 3 Feb. 1942.

6 Interview with Émile Aron, Tours, 19 March 1997.

7 AD M-et-L 12W2, report of Prefect Tracou to Interior Minister, 3 March 1942.

8 BAMA Freiburg RW35/542, order of Militärbefehlshaber in Frankreich, 17 Feb. 1942.

9 AD M-et-L 12W3, report of Prefect Dupard to Interior Minister, 1 May 1942; Bernard Lecornu, *Un Préfet sous l'Occupation allemande*, 122–34; Mgr Villepelet, 'Le Diocèse de Nantes, 1940–1945', entry for 1 May 1942.

10 AD I-et-L 10W8, Bousquet to Oberg, 29 July 1942, text of Oberg address, 8 Aug. 1942, Bousquet to prefects, 13 Aug. 1942; Maurice Rajsfus, *La Police de Vichy. Forces de l'ordre français au service de la Gestapo* (Paris, Le Cherche-Midi, 1995), 75–97.

11 AD M-et-L 12W20, Ernst to regional prefect of Angers, 3 July 1942.

12 AD M-et-L 10W18, Ernst to regional prefect of Angers, 10 July 1942; regional prefect to prefects, 16 July 1942.

13 AD I-et-L 60W6, report on the Germans in I-et-L by Commissaire Spécial Laforge, May 1945, based on captured archives of the Tours Gestapo; AD I-et-L 34W4, report by Brückle on Boucherie, 15 Aug. 1942; Claude Morin, *Les Allemands en Touraine, 1940–1944* (Chambray-lès-Tours, CLD, 1996), 71–9.

14 AD M-et-L 140W95, prefect to Feldkommandant of Angers, 25 Aug. 1942.

15 AD L-A 51W29, Prefect Dupard to prefect delegate of the Ministry of the Interior, Paris, 31 Oct. 1942.

16 AD M-et-L 18W24, Ernst to Roussillon, 29 Oct. 1942, Roussillon to Mgr

Costes, 2 Nov. 1942, Costes to Roussillon, 7 Nov. 1942; AD M-et-L 18W25, Ernst to Mgr Costes, 16 Dec. 1942.

17 See above, p. 216.

18 AD M-et-L 12W54, report of regional police superintendent, Angers, 30 Sept. 1942; AN 72AJ147, Court of Feldkommandantur 518, Nantes, charges against forty-two communist terrorists sent for trial by examining magistrate Dr Gottlob, 6 Jan. 1943.

19 AD L-A 132W89, report of Prefect Dupard on Commissaire Fourcade, 1942; AD M-et-L 12W3, report of Yves Bayet, 1 Sept. 1942, and of Prefect Dupard, 4 Nov. 1942.

20 Edmond Duméril, *Journal d'un honnête homme pendant l'Occupation, juin 1940–août 1944*, 260–72.

21 *Le Phare de Nantes*, 16 Jan. 1943, cited in ibid., 264–5.

22 AD M-et-L 12W3, Prefect Dupard to regional prefect, Angers, 4 March 1943.

23 AD M-et-L 60W6, meeting of regional prefects and chiefs of Sicherheitspolizei, 16 April 1943.

24 AM Nantes 38W9, Mayor Rondeau to Prefect Dupard, 20 June 1942, prefect to mayor, 16 July 1942.

25 AD M-et-L 12W41, Prefect Delegate Daguerre to mayor of Seiches-sur-Loire, 5 June 1942.

26 AD M-et-L 61W3, Daguerre to CGQJ, 8 July 1942, and reply, 11 July 1942.

27 Michelle Audoin Le Marec, *Le Maine-et-Loire dans la Guerre, 1939–1945* (Le Coteau, Horvath, 1987), 136.

28 Among others, Asher Cohen, *Persécutions et Sauvetages. Juifs et Français sous l'Occupation et sous Vichy* (Paris, Éditions du Cerf, 1993), and Renée Poznanski, *Les Juifs en France pendant la Seconde Guerre Mondiale*, 313–46.

29 AD L-A 13W45, reports of Squadron Leader Lecomte and Subprefect Lecornu of Saint-Nazaire to prefect, 16 July 1942.

30 AD M-et-L 140W97, police commissioner, Angers, to prefect, 16 July 1942.

31 AD M-et-L 97W40, Adjutant Barreau of Gennes to captain of Saumur gendarmerie, 23 Oct. 1942.

32 Interview with Abbé Henri Richer (b. 1920), Angers, 6 June 1997.

33 As note 30 [16 July].

34 AD M-et-L 12W4, subprefect on behalf of prefect delegate of M-et-L to regional prefect, Angers, 24 July 1942.

35 AD M-et-L 140W97, subprefect of Cholet to prefect of M-et-L, 18 July 1942.

36 AD M-et-L 12W4, Prefect Delegate Daguerre to Interior Minister, 2 Sept. 1942.

37 AD M-et-L, 12W2, Prefect Tracou to regional prefect, Angers, 24 July 1942.

38 AD I-et-L 120W8, report of director of Camp de la Lande, July 1942.

39 AD M-et-L 140W97, subprefect of Saumur to prefect delegate, Angers, 16 July 1942.

40 AD M-et-L 7W1, list of children of Jews arrested in Angers since 15 July 1942.

41 AD L-A 13W44, decision of Ernst communicated to prefect of L-I, 24 Aug. 1941.

42 AD M-et-L 7W1, details of arrests of Jews, 1942–4.

43 AD M-et-L 18W25, Dr Barrault to mayor of les Ponts-de-Cé, 18 July 1942. SS Kommandeur Pfleider gave a favourable reply to the prefect of M-et-L, 19 Aug. 1942.

44 AD M-et-L 7W1, police commissioner, Angers, to prefect, 27 July and 10 Aug. 1942.

45 Michelle Audoin Le Marec, *Le Maine-et-Loire*, 137.

46 AD L-A 13W45, Lucien Bernheim to prefect of L-I, 7 Sept. 1942.

47 AD L-A 13W45, Subprefect Lecornu to prefect of L-I, 6 Oct. 1942.

48 AD I-et-L 10W84, Maître Siecklucki to prefect of I-et-L, 29 July 1942, and reply of prefect, 4 Aug. 1942.

49 AD I-et-L 52W20, Regional Prefect Roussillon to Prefect Tracou, 1 Sept. 1942, and reply of Tracou, 18 Sept. 1942.

50 AD M-et-L 97W40, president of UGIF, to prefect of M-et-L, 7 Aug. 1942, and reply of Prefect Daguerre, 10 Aug. 1942; Prefect Daguerre to Dr Ernst, 10 Aug. 1942, and reply of Ernst, 18 Aug.; AD M-et-L 140W97, Daguerre to Laval, 10 Aug. 1942, and reply of prefect delegate of the Ministry of the Interior, 20 Aug. 1942.

51 See below, Chapter 13.

52 AD I-et-L 120W8, reports of director of Camp de la Lande, 13 Sept. and 16 Nov. 1942.

53 AD M-et-L 18W83, Lieutenant Colonel Chambon, commander of gendarmerie of M-et-L, to colonel commanding 9th Gendarmerie Legion of Tours, 8 Oct. 1942.

54 AD M-et-L 140W97, Daguerre to Laval, 19 Oct. 1942.

55 AD M-et-L 97W40, lists of arrested Jews, Angers, Oct. 1942.

56 AD I-et-L 44W421, identity cards of deported Jews returned by prefecture of I-et-L to prefecture of M-et-L, 7 April 1943.

57 AD I-et-L 10W66, A. and D. Aron to Prefect Tracou, 28 Oct. 1942, and reply of Tracou, 14 Nov. 1942.

58 AD M-et-L 12W4, Daguerre to Interior Minister, 3 Nov. 1943.

59 AD M-et-L 18W83, Prefect Dupard to regional prefect, 9 Oct. 1942.

60 AD M-et-L 80W7, chief superintendent of Renseignements Généraux, Angers, 26 June 1943.

61 AD M-et-L 97W40, report of Baugé gendarmerie to prefect of M-et-L, 22 Nov. 1943.

62 AD M-et-L 18W85, report of Police des Questions Juives, Angers, 2 Nov. 1943.

63 AD L-A 13W50, regional delegate of CGQJ, Angers, to police commissioner, Nantes, May 1943; police superintendent, 5th *arrondissement*, Nantes, to police commissioner, 1 June 1943; Paris CGQJ to prefect of L-I, 11 Jan. 1944; prefect to CGQJ, Angers, 26 April 1944.

64 Sheila Fitzpatrick and Robert Gellately, eds, *Accusatory Practices* (Chicago and London, University of Chicago Press, 1997).

65 AD I-et-L 10W53, report of police commissioner, Tours, 12 Nov. and 24 Dec. 1943.

66 AN F1a 3874, weekly bulletin of Renseignements Généraux, 14 Jan. 1943.

67 AD M-et-L 12W82, Roussillon to Laval, 26 March 1943.

68 AD M-et-L 136W12, prefect to Feldkommandant of Angers, 7 Aug. 1942.

69 AN AJ40 544, military chief of Angers region to Dr Medicus, Paris, 7 Jan. and 18 Feb. 1943.

70 Camille de Montgeron, *Le Colonel François de Sauvebeuf* (Niort, Imprimerie Saint-Denis, n.d.), 249. See above, p. 143.

71 AD I-et-L 10W84, police commissioner, Tours, to prefect of I-et-L, 3 May 1943.

72 AD M-et-L 80W6, police commissioner, Angers, to prefect, 17 and 24 April 1943.

73 AD M-et-L 12W4, Prefect Daguerre of M-et-L to Interior Minister, 3 May 1943.

74 AD M-et-L 12W2, Prefect Tracou of I-et-L to Interior Minister, 4 May 1943.

75 AD M-et-L 12W2, Prefect Tracou to Interior Minister, 3 Sept. 1943; AN AJ40 542, German notes on Molas-Quenescourt, 14 Jan. 1944, and Aubert, n.d; AD I-et-L 52W57, file on Molas-Quenescourt, 1944–5.

76 AD M-et-L 60W12, police commissioner, Angers, to prefect, 1 Sept. 1943, Regional Prefect Donati to Bousquet, 24 Sept. 1943, Prefect Bonnefoy of L-I to regional prefect, 15 Sept. 1943; AD M-et-L 60W13, report by Inspector Vairé, 12 July 1945. On Wilkinson, see M. R. D. Foot, *SOE in France. An Account of the Work of the British Special Operations Executive in France, 1940–1944* (London, Her Majesty's Stationery Office, 1966), 196–7, 222, 258, 314.

77 AD M-et-L 80W7, report of Renseignements Généraux, 25 Sept. and 9 Oct. 1943.

13. CONSCRIPTION

1 AD L-A 132W157, Colonel Mauris, departmental delegate of the Ministry of Information, to general delegate of the Ministry of Information, 2 Oct. 1942; Robert Tillaut to Colonel Mauris, 2 Oct. 1942.

2 AD M-et-L 18W35, tract sent by Regional Prefect Roussillon to Laval, 9 Oct. 1942.

3 Jacques Evrard, *La Déportation des travailleurs français dans le Troisième Reich* (Paris, Fayard, 1972), 39–41.

4 AD M-et-L 12W3, Prefect Dupard to Interior Minister, 4 Nov. 1942.

5 AD M-et-L 18W35, copy of *Phare*, 11 Aug. 1942, forwarded by Dupard to Regional Prefect Roussillon.

6 Mgr Villepelet, 'Le Diocèse de Nantes, 1940–1945', entries for 10 and 21 Aug. 1942.

7 AD M-et-L 18W36, Rondeau to regional delegate of the Ministry of Information, Cambier, 31 Aug. 1942, and reply of Cambier, 8 Sept., forwarded by Prefect Dupard to Roussillon, 28 Sept. 1942.

8 AD L-A 13W8, Rondeau to Pétain, 19 Aug. 1942.

9 AD M-et-L 18W134, Prefect Dupard to Laval, 10 Oct. 1942.

10 AD L-A 27J18, 'Carnets de M. Soil, secrétaire général de la Mairie de Nantes', 10, 13 and 20 Oct. 1942.

11 AD L-A 132W157, Prefect Dupard to Laval, 20 Oct. 1942; BAMA Freiburg RW24/125, report of Wehrwirtschaftsinspektion, SW Frankreich, 29 Oct. 1942.

12 AD L-A 132157, Dupard to Laval, 21 Oct. 1942.

13 AD M-et-L 12W54, report of police superintendent, Angers, 2 Nov. 1942.

14 AD M-et-L 18W134, Dupard to Laval, 20 Oct. 1942; AD L-A 27J18, Carnets de M. Soil, 31 Oct. 1942: *Le Phare*, 30 Nov. 1942.

15 AD L-A 132W157, Prefect Dupard to prefect delegate of the Ministry of Information, 8 Nov. 1942.

16 AN F1a 3869, report for CFLN, Saint-Nazaire region, 15 Nov. 1942.

17 AD M-et-L 12W3, Prefect Dupard to Interior Minister, 4 Nov. 1942.

18 Evrard, *La Déportation des travailleurs*, 74–83.

19 AD I-et-L 121W1, Prefect Tracou to Secrétaire d'État au Travail, 17 Oct. 1942, and to Feldkommandant of Tours, 22 Oct. 1942.

20 AD I-et-L 121W1, Feldkommandant of Tours to Prefect Tracou, 12 Dec. 1942, Inspecteur du Travail Dos to Tracou, 14 Dec. 1942.

21 BAMA Frerburg RH36/312, report of Kriegsverwaltungsrat, FK 518 Nantes, 23 March 1943.

22 BAMA Frerburgh RW24/179, war diary of Rüstungskommando, Le Mans, 1–14 Nov. 1943; Alan S. Milward, *The New Order and the French*

Economy (Oxford, Oxford University Press, 1984; Gregg Revivals, 1993), 157–67.

23 AD I-et-L 10W9, Inspecteur du Travail to prefect of I-et-L, 1 March 1943. This form of words was taken up exactly by Prefect Tracou in his report to the Interior Minister, 6 March 1943, in AD M-et-L 12W2.

24 BAM Freiburg RH36/138, reports to Chief of Militärverwaltung Bezirk B from Kriegsverwaltungsrat Buchholtz, Angers, 8 Feb. 1943, Kriegsverwaltung Nantes, 13 Feb. 1943, and Feldkommandant von Trotha, Nantes, 21 Feb. 1943.

25 AD M-et-L 7U4/95, Cour de Justice file on Hupfer, who was sentenced to three years' imprisonment and confiscation of property, 22 March 1945.

26 AD M-et-L 12W3, Prefect Dupard of L-I to Interior Minister, 4 Jan. 1943.

27 AD M-et-L 12W4, Prefect Daguerre to Interior Minister, 5 Jan. 1943.

28 AD M-et-L 12W3, Prefect Dupard to regional prefect, Angers, 4 March 1943.

29 AD M-et-L 12W2, Prefect Tracou of I-et-L to Interior Minister, 6 July 1943.

30 As note 27.

31 AD I-et-L 10W9, subprefect of Chinon to prefect of I-et-L, 24 June 1943.

32 AD M-et-L 12W4, Prefect Daguerre to Interior Minister, 2 March 1943.

33 AD M-et-L 12W2, Prefect Tracou of I-et-L to Interior Minister, 3 Sept. 1943.

34 AD L-A 132W157, minute of meeting of 8 March 1943 at Feldkommandantur of Nantes.

35 A. Darmaillacq, *Cholet sous l'Occupation* (Cholet, 1946; reissue 1991), 42–3, 63–4.

36 AD I-et-L 121W5, replies to Inspecteur du Travail, Tours, of mayor of Saint-Roch, 3 Feb. 1943, and mayor of Saint-Laurent-en-Gâtines, 5 Feb. 1943.

37 AD I-et-L XIV Z 17, correspondence of Kriegsverwaltungsrat of Feldkommandantur of Tours and Befehlshaber SW Frankreich, Angers, 13 April–8 June 1943; Feldkommandantur to prefect of I-et-L, 8 June and 1 July 1943, and reply of prefect, 7 July 1943.

38 AD I-et-L 10W61, Brückle to prefect of I-et-L, 1 Nov. and 13 Dec. 1943, prefect to Laval, 15 Nov. 1943, prefect to Brückle, 14 Jan. 1944.

39 AD L-A 132W157, report of subprefect of Châteaubriant, 9 Nov. 1942.

40 AN AJ40/544, note on Prefect Roussillon, n.d.; Befehlshaber der SP und der SD to Militärbefehlshaber in Frankreich, 4 March 1943.

41 AN F1a 3869, report of CFLN, 29 Aug. 1943.

42 See for example Jean Estèbe, ed., *Les Juifs à Toulouse et en Midi toulousain au temps de Vichy* (Toulouse, Presses Universitaires Le Mirail, 1996), 154–6; W. D. Halls, *Politics, Society and Christianity in Vichy France*, 118–24.

43 Michèle Cointet, *L'Église sous Vichy* (Paris, Perrin, 1998), 290.

44 Mgr Villepelet, 'Le Diocèse de Nantes, 1940–1945', entry for 19 April 1943.

45 Ibid., entry for 29 April 1943.

46 AD M-et-L 18W35, Donati to Laval, 14 May 1943.

47 AD L-A 13W26, Obersturmführer Doescher of Nantes Sicherheitspolizei to Prefect Dupard, 17 April 1943.

48 AD M-et-L 12W54, report of police superintendent, Angers, 3 May 1943.

49 AD M-et-L 80W7, report of chief superintendent, Renseignements Généraux, 26 June 1943.

50 AD M-et-L 12W2, prefect Tracou to Interior Minister, 4 May 1943; François Tauzun, 'Le STO en Touraine occupé, 1942–1944' (*mémoire de maîtrise*, University of Tours, 1996), 56.

51 AD L-A 40W24, report of Secretary-General Yves Bayet for prefect of L-I, 26 June 1943; AD M-et-L 18W50, report of Lieut.-Col. Pentel, commander of 11th Legion of Gendarmerie, Nantes, June and July 1943.

52 René Leprince, ed., *La Pommeraye dans la Guerre par ceux qui l'ont vécue*, 87–102, 146.

53 Collection Michel Lemesle, letter of Mme Delépine, La Ferrière-de-Flée (M-et-L), 28 Nov. 1973.

54 BAMA Freiburg RH 36/588, captain commanding in Cholet to Feldkommandantur of Tours, 7 May 1942.

55 AD M-et-L 80W7, report of chief superintendent, Renseignements Généraux, Angers, 3 July 1943.

56 AD M-et-L 12W3, Prefect Gaudard of L-I to Intendant du Maintien de l'Ordre, Angers, 3 May 1944.

57 AD M-et-L 18W47, daily reports of police superintendent, 19 and 25 May 1944. This file is a rich Vichy source for the activities of 'terrorists' in the region in 1944.

58 See Alain Brossat, *Les Tondues. Un carnaval moche* (Paris, Hachette, 1994); Corran Laurens, 'La Femme au turban: les femmes tondues' in H. R. Kedward and Nancy Wood, *The Liberation of France. Image and event* (Oxford and Washington, Berg, 1995), 155–79; Hanna Diamond, *Women and the Second World War in France, 1939–1948. Choices and constraints* (Harlow, Pearson, 1999), 134–42.

59 AD L-A 40W14, Viennot, director of Commissariat Général à la Main d'Œuvre (CGMO), L-I, to prefect, 7 March 1944; deputy director of CGMO to prefect, 6 April 1944.

60 AD L-A 40W14, General Feldt to Regional Prefect Donati, 16 May 1944.

61 AD M-et-L 18W36, press cuttings from *Le Petit Courrier*, 28 Feb., *Tours Soir*, 29 Feb., and *Le Petit Parisien*, 1 March 1944; letter from Lübeck worker to Donati, 2 March 1944; Donati to Laval, 20 March 1944. This is also in AN F1a 3870.

62 AD I-et-L 10W53, police commissioner, Tours, 19 Feb. 1944.

63 AD M-et-L 136W3, G. Michelet, departmental delegate of the Ministry of Information, to prefect of M-et-L, 19 Jan. 1944.

64 Cointet, *L'Église sous Vichy*, 291. The statement was dated 17 Feb. 1944.

65 AD M-et-L 12W54, police superintendent, Angers, to regional prefect, 15 June, 28 Aug. and 14 Sept. 1943.

66 AD L-A 40W15, departmental director of CGMO, L-I, to regional director, Angers, 26 May 1944.

67 AD L-A 40W15, police commissioner, Nantes, to prefect, 13 and 20 June 1944.

14. DISINTEGRATION

1 *Le Courrier de Saint-Nazaire*, 20 Feb. 1942.

2 AD L-A 75W553, Kreiskommandant Major von Hasselbach to Prefect Dupard, 16 May 1942.

3 BAMA Freiburg RW24/125, war diary of Wehrwirtschaftsinspektion, SW Frankreich, 23 Nov. and 16 Dec. 1942; AN F1a 3871, report for CFLN, 11 March 1943.

4 AN 72AJ 146, statistics of bombings of Saint-Nazaire, 1939–1944.

5 AD M-et-L 12W3, Prefect Dupard of L-I to regional prefect, Angers, 4 March, and to Interior Minister, 1 May 1943.

6 See above, p. 123.

7 *La Semaine religieuse du diocèse de Nantes*, 28 Feb. 1942.

8 Anne Curet, 'Quelques souvenirs de 1941 à 1945', communicated to the author, 14 April 1997.

9 AD M-et-L 18W39, president of COSI at Angers to regional prefect, 5 May 1943.

10 AD M-et-L 18W38, report of regional head of Refugees Service, 29 March 1943.

11 AD M-et-L 95W91, replies to subprefect of Cholet from mayor of Tilliers, 15 May 1943, and mayor of Jallais, 17 May 1943.

12 AD M-et-L 140W108, reports of chief superintendent, Renseignements Généraux, Angers, 31 Aug. 1943, and of inspector of regional police, Angers, 20 Sept. 1943.

13 Edmond Duméril, *Journal d'un honnête homme pendant l'Occupation, juin 1940–août 1944*, 293. Entry for 27 March 1943.

14 AD L-A 54W14, Abel Durand of Secours National to Prefect Dupard, 8 and 24 July 1943; Pompes Funèbres Générales, Nantes, to Orrion, president of special delegation, Nantes, 12 Aug; hospices civiles, Nantes, to Dupard, 22 Oct. 1943.

NOTES

15 AN F1a 3871 and AD M-et-L 18W24, M. Gon of SNCASO to Prefect Dupard, 19 July 1943.

16 AM Nantes 38W17, Police Officer Morillon to commander of Nantes police, 14 Sept. 1943.

17 BAMA Freiburg RW24/155, war diary of Rüstungskommando of Nantes, July–Sept. 1943; AN F1a 3872, report of Prefect Bonnefoy of L-I, 8 Nov. 1943.

18 BAMA Freiburg RH36/525, report by Feldkommandantur of Nantes on effect of Nantes bombings of food sector, n.d. but Oct. 1943.

19 AD M-et-L 12W3, Prefect Bonnefoy of L-I to Interior Minster, 5 Nov. 1943.

20 BAMA Freiburg RH36/146, report of Arbeitseinsatzstab, Nantes, 22 Oct. 1943.

21 AD M-et-L 136W2, subprefect of Cholet to prefect of M-et-L, 20 Dec. 1943.

22 AD M-et-L 18W38, evacuee statistics for 1 Oct. 1943.

23 AD I-et-L 218W14, Secours National director of propaganda to I-et-L delegate, 18 May 1943.

24 AD I-et-L 218W17, reports from Ligueil and l'Ile Bouchard, April 1943.

25 AD I-et-L 18W50, report of commander of 9th Legion of Gendarmerie, Tours, 3 April 1943.

26 AD I-et-L 10W63, report of police inspector, Renseignements Généraux, Tours, 25 Mar 1943.

27 AD I-et-L 108W8, Prefect Tracou to prefect of Morbihan, 7 April 1943.

28 BAMA Freiburg RW24/179–180, war diaries of Rüstungskommando, Le Mans, 17–23 Oct. 1943, 31 Jan.–5 Feb. 1944; AN F1a 3874, interview with engineer of Le Ripault, 15 Nov. 1943; AN F1a 3869, report on Le Ripault, 20 Feb. 1944.

29 AN F1a 3874, eyewitness account of air raid on Saint-Pierre-des-Corps, 13 April 1944.

30 AN F1a 3874, record of Vichy radio broadcast, 25 May 1944; diverse information, 26 May 1944. Claude Morin, *La Touraine sous les bombes* (Chambray-lès-Tours, CLD, 2000), 112–13, 140–1, 158–61.

31 BAMA Freiburg RW24/141, war diary of Rüstungskommando, Angers, 9–15 April, 14–20 May, 28 May–3 June 1944.

32 AD M-et-L 18W25, prefect of I-et-L to regional prefect, 21 Feb. 1944, regional prefect to secretary of state for Industrial Production, 2 and 18 March 1944.

33 AD M-et-L 136W4, subprefect of Saumur to prefect of M-et-L, 20 April 1944.

34 AN F1a 3874, report from Tours, 5 April 1944.

35 But see Alain Beltran, 'Le cas des entreprises d'électricité', in A. Beltran, R. Frank and H. Rousso, *La Vie des entreprises sous l'Occupation. Une enquête à l'échelle locale* (Paris, Belin, 1994), 69–89; P. Perraud, 'Électricité et défense: rôle et importance de l'électricité dans l'exploitation des potentiels

NOTES

industriels durant l'Occupation par la Wehrmacht' (*mémoire de maîtrise*, Université de Paul-Valéry, Montpellier II, 1987).

36 BAMA Freiburg RW24/180, war diary of Rüstungskommando, Le Mans, 9–15, 16–22 Jan., 30 Jan.–5 Feb. and 12–18 March 1944.

37 BAMA Freiburg RW24/141, report of Oberst Keil, Rüstungskommando Angers, 1 April–30 June 1944; RW24/159, report of Rüstungskommando Nantes, 30 June 1944.

38 AD M-et-L 12W16, 'Réception des personnalités du département du Maine-et-Loire et de la Ville d'Angers à l'occasion de l'installation du nouveau préfet régional, M. Donati, lundi 9 août 1943'.

39 AD M-et-L 12W17, *Bulletin mensuel de la Chambre de Commerce d'Angers et de Maine-et-Loire*, no. 9 (Oct. 1943), 227–30. The meeting was on 7 Oct.

40 AN AJ40/542, German assessment of Charles Donati, n.d.

41 AD M-et-L 18W25, Donati to Feld, 5 Dec. 1943, and reply, 18 Dec. 1943.

42 BAMA Freiburg RH36/131, report of Feldkommandantur of Nantes, 4 Jan. 1944.

43 Duméril, *Journal d'un honnête homme*, 347. Entry for 23 Sept. 1943.

44 AD M-et-L 12W3, Prefect Bonnefoy to Interior Minister, 3 Sept. 1943.

45 AD L-A 13W22, Bonnefoy to Lieutenant Doescher, head of Sicherheitspolizei, Nantes, 2 Sept. 1943.

46 AD L-A 13W22, police commissioner to chief superintendent of Renseignements Généraux, Vichy, 29 Dec. 1943; AN 72AJ/144, information on General Reinhardt by E. Duméril, 25 Jan. 1950.

47 AN AJ40/542, report of Feldkommandantur of Tours on Prefect Musso, 12 May 1944.

48 AD I-et-L 52W59, Prefect Musso to Feldkommandant Boehmer, 23 June 1944; AD I-et-L 66W4, unsigned minutes of a conference in the Hôtel de Ville, Tours, 30 June 1944.

49 AM Tours, *Bulletin municipal de la Ville de Tours*, 28 Dec. 1943.

50 See above, p. 37.

51 AN AJ40/542, report of Feldkommandant of Angers on Saissier, n.d. but Feb. 1944; AD M-et-L 136W3, departmental delegate of Ministry of Information to Donati, 28 Feb. 1944; AD M-et-L 18W13, Donati to Laval, 17 March 1944.

52 AN AJ40/542, reports of Feldkommandantur and Propagandastaffel of Nantes, 7 Nov. 1943; AN AJ40/544, Befehlshaber SW Frankreich to Militärbefehlshaber in Frankreich, 1 Jan. 1944; Bernard Lecornu, *Un Préfet sous l'Occupation allemande. Châteaubriant, Saint-Nazaire, Tulle*, 164–5; Mgr Villepelet, 'Le Diocèse de Nantes, 1940–1945', entry for 14 Feb. 1944.

53 BAMA Freiburg RH36/142, report of Feldkommandantur of Nantes, 28 Feb. 1944.

54 AN F1a 3869, report of Mission Militaire de Liaison Administrative on Gaudard, n.d.

55 AD L-A 13W22, Prefect Gaudard to Dr Baessler, 13 May 1944.

56 Mgr Villepelet, 'Le Diocèse de Nantes, 1940–1945', entry for 14 May 1944.

57 See below, p. 331.

58 AD M-et-L 12W2, prefect Tracou to Interior Minister, 3 Sept. 1943; AD I-et-L XIV Z 17, internal circular of Feldkommandantur of Tours, 4 Sept. 1943, Feldkommandantur to Sicherheitspolizei, Tours, 14 Sept. 1943.

59 AD M-et-L 12W2, Prefect Musso of I-et-L to Interior Minister, 2 March 1944.

60 AD M-et-L 18W134, Donati to Laval, 8 Feb. 1944, Donati to Bernier, 4 March, and reply of Bernier, 6 March 1944.

61 See above, pp. 200–1.

62 AD L-A 13W18, report of Renseignements Généraux, Nantes, 22 and 28 Feb. 1944.

63 AD M-et-L 140W9, Subprefect Trémeaud to Prefect Daguerre, 21 May 1943.

64 AN AJ40/542, German information on Subprefect Trémeaud, 11 March 1944. See below, p. 330.

65 AD-et-L 10W25, figures for resignation of mayors, 1942–3.

66 As note 59.

67 AD I-et-L 10W9, report of Prefect Musso, 13 May 1944.

68 Collection Michel Lemesle, Angers, Renaud de Razilly, 'La Résistance dans le Maine-et-Loire', MS, n.d.

69 AD M-et-L 19W13, Prefect Fourré-Cormeray to Interior Minister, 3 Sept. 1944.

70 Michel Debré, Trois Républiques pour une France. Mémoires I (Paris, Albin Michel, 1984), 308.

71 Pierre Laborie, L'Opinion française sous Vichy (Paris, Seuil, 1990), 262–70.

72 AD M-et-L 80W4, chief superintendent, Renseignements Généraux, Angers, to prefect of M-et-L, 27 March 1942.

73 AD M-et-L 24W27, letters to Marshal Pétain from Angevins, Jan. 1943 to July 1944. These letters were generally referred back to departmental prefects for handling.

74 AD M-et-L 24W30, Mme Legouic of Saumur to Pétain, 8 Feb. 1944.

75 AN 72AJ145, report of police superintendent, Nantes, 9 May 1943.

76 AD M-et-L 18W50, report of commander of 9th Legion of Gendarmerie, Tours, 3 July 1943.

77 See above, p. 300.

78 AD M-et-L 12W2, prefect Tracou to Interior Minister, 3 Jan. 1944.

79 AD L-A 13W7, Prefect Gaudard of L-I to Interior Minister, 11 April 1944.

80 AD M-et-L 136W4, Renseignements Généraux, Angers, to Interior Minister, 11 March and 15 April 1944.

81 BAMA Freiburg RW35/1252, Final report of military administration of SW France region for July, Aug. and Sept. 1944, 17–18.

82 AD M-et-L 21W58, Feldkommandant of Angers to prefect of M-et-L, 26 July 1943; Michel Lemesle, *L'Anjou des Années 40. Chroniques* (Angers, les Éditions du Choletais, 1984), 123–6.

83 AN 72AJ136, account of Jean Meunier, 22 May 1947; AD I-et-L 66W1, proceedings of interrogation of resisters arrested by the Gestapo, Oct.–Nov. 1943; Yves Durand and Robert Vivier, *Libération des Pays de la Loire* (Paris, Hachette, 1974), 57–9.

84 Marcel Baudot, *Libération de la Bretagne* (Paris, Hachette, 1973), 99. See also AN 72AJ144, account of Bernier, 9 March 1950.

85 AN 72AJ146, account of Abbé Ploquin, 1965.

86 AD L-A 96W138, reports of Lieutenant Broustal of gendarmerie of Châteaubriant, 6 July, divisional commissioner, Renseignements Généraux of Nantes, 8 July, and subprefect of Châteaubriant, 22 July 1944; statement of Saint-Herblain farmer Joseph Lucas to gendarmerie of Indre, 24 Oct. 1944; Mgr Villepelet, 'Le Diocèse de Nantes, 1940–1945', entries for 3 and 25 July. Villepelet took credit for the reprieve of Abbé Ploquin.

87 BAMA Freiburg RW24/159, diary of Rüstungskommando, Nantes, by Captain Zimmermann, dated Dresden, 11 Oct. 1944.

88 AD M-et-L 18W46, information note, 7 Aug. 1944.

89 P-A Fouet [subprefect of Segré], *Angoisses et espoirs. Segré, août 1944* (Maine Libre, 1945), in AD M-et-L 116J9.

90 A. Darmaillacq, *Cholet sous l'Occupation*, 55–9; *Toutlemonde 1944–1994. 50ème anniversaire du 8 août 1944* (Toutlemonde, 1994).

91 AD M-et-L 30W219, report of Meunier to Commissaire de la République Debré, 28 Aug. 1944.

92 AD I-et-L 46W124 and AD M-et-L 30W219, account of massacre of Maillé, 25 Aug. 1944. BAMA Freiburg RW35/1253, 'Experience and final reports of a few Feldkommandants of Bezirk B, Aug. 1944–Jan. 1945'. See also the account by the local curé, Abbé André Payan, *Maillé martyr* (Tours, Arnault et Cie, 1945).

15. LIBERATION

1 Interview with Paule and Louis de Beaumont, Daumeray (M-et-L), 20 May 1997.

2 Michel Debré, *Trois Républiques pour une France. Mémoires I. Combattre* (Paris, Albin Michel, 1984), 295. See also AD M-et-L 30W193, Debré to Commissaire à l'Intérieur Astier de la Vigerie, n.d.

3 Gérard Boulanger, *Papon. Un intrus dans la République* (Paris, Seuil, 1997), 233, 235.

4 BAMA Freiburg RW35/1252, Final report of German military authority in SW France, July, Aug. and Sept. 1944, p. 18. Emphasis in original.

5 Jacqueline Sainclivier, 'Le pouvoir résistant (été 1944)', in Philippe Buton and Jean-Marie Guillon, *Les Pouvoirs en France à la Libération* (Paris, Belin, 1994), 28. In this category she cites 8 departments out of 33 studied: Côtes-du-Nord, Mayenne, Sarthe, Oise, Haute-Garonne, Basses-Pyrénées, Haute-Saône, Vaucluse.

6 AD I-et-L 46W94, file on administration of Indre-et-Loire, July–Aug. 1944; Robert Vivier, *Touraine 39–45. Histoire de l'Indre-et-Loire durant la 2e Guerre mondiale* (Chambray-lès-Tours, CLD, 1990), 274–89.

7 Jacques Feneant, *Francs-Maçons et sociétés secrètes en Val de Loire* (Chambray-lès-Tours, CLD, 1986), 321–2.

8 Interview with Jack Vivier, Tours, 16 June 1997. See also Jack Vivier, *Les Instituteurs de Touraine dans la République* (Chambray-lès-Tours, CLD, 1997), 97.

9 Debré, *Trois Républiques pour une France*, 298–303; AD L-A 10W2, proceedings of CDL, 23, 25, 26 Aug. 1944; Mgr Villepelet, 'Le Diocèse de Nantes, 1940–1945', entries for 17 Aug. and 22 Sept. 1944.

10 Jacqueline Sainclivier (see note 5) proposes five models of prefect/police superintendent–CDL relations: subjection of the CDL, close collaboration, the CDL as pressure group, conflict provoked by the CDL, and conflict provoked by the prefect.

11 AD I-et-L 66W7, meetings of CDL, 13 and 20 Feb. 1945, congress of CLLs at Tours, 24 March 1945; 66W7, CDL sub-commission for purging of firms, 6 and 13 April 1944.

12 Guy Haudebourg, 'Le Parti Communiste Français en Loire-Inférieure à la Libération, 1944–1947 (*mémoire de maîtrise*, University of Nantes, 1987), 46–52.

13 See above, pp. 123–4.

14 Christian Bougeard, 'Regards sur les réseaux de notables en Bretagne des années 1930 aux années 1950', *Annales de Bretagne et des Pays de l'Ouest* 103 (1996), 33; Yves de Sesmaisons, *Marquise de Sesmaisons (1898–1978). Souvenirs de l'Occupation* (Craon, 1980), 135–8, 207–9, 216.

15 Marcel Baudot, *La Libération de la Bretagne*, 191.

16 Membership of CDLs in AN F1a 4020 and AD M-et-L 30W193.

17 AD M-et-L 30W197, CDL meetings of 17 and 26 Aug. 1944.

18 Interview with René Le Bault de la Morinière, Landemont (M-et-L), 7 May 1997.

19 Dom Guy Oury, *Dom Gabriel Sortais* (Solesmes, 1975), 162. See also Élie Chamard, *Vingt siècles d'histoire à Cholet* (Cholet, Farré et Fils, 1981), 323–5, 340.

20 Marc Bergère, 'Tensions et rivalités entre les pouvoirs issus de la Résistance

en Maine-et-Loire', in Jacqueline Sainclivier, *La Résistance et les Français. Enjeux stratégiques et environnement social* (Rennes, Presses Universitaires de Rennes, 1995), 297–304.

21 AD M-et-L 30W197, CDL meetings 30 Nov. and 4 Dec. 1944, 25 Jan. 1945.

22 Bergère, 'Tensions et rivalités', 304–5.

23 Roderick Kedward, 'The Maquis and the Culture of the Outlaw' in Roderick Kedward and Roger Austin, eds, *Vichy France and the Resistance. Culture and ideology* (London and Sydney, Croom Helm, 1985), 232–51.

24 Luc Capdevila, *Les Bretons au lendemain de l'Occupation. Imaginaire et comportement d'une sortie de guerre, 1944–1945* (Rennes, Presses Universitaires de France, 1999), 128, 146–9; Jean-Marie Guillon, 'Parti du mouvement et parti de l'ordre', in Philippe Buton and Jean-Marie Guillon, *Les Pouvoirs en France à la Libération* (Paris, Belin, 1994), 39. See also Richard Cobb, *Les Armées révolutionnaires: instrument de la Terreur dans les départements, avril 1793 – floréal an II* (Paris, Mouton, 1961–3), translated by Marianne Elliott as *The People's Armies* (New Haven and London, Yale University Press, 1987).

25 AD M-et-L 30W197, CDL meetings 20 and 21 Sept., 6 Oct. 1944.

26 AD I-et-L 66W6, Prefect Vincent to Commissaire Debré, 27 Sept. 1944; 66W7, CDL meetings, 26 Sept., 3 and 7 Oct. 1944.

27 AN 72AJ136, account by Robert Vivier on 'Les lendemains de la Libération en Touraine'.

28 AD I-et-L 81J1, Vivier to Commissaire de la République, Angers, 16 and 22 Sept., 4 Oct. 1944.

29 On the Le Coz affair see also Yves Durand and Robert Vivier, *Libération des Pays de la Loire*, 227–9; Bernard Briais, *Le Lochois pendant la guerre, 1939–1945* (Chambray-lès-Tours, CLD, 1988), 124–65; Alfred Hangouët, *L'Affaire Le Coz* (CLD, Normand et Cie, 1978).

30 See for example AD L-A 270W510, complaints of mayor of Plessé, 7 Nov., and municipal council of Fégreac, 24 Dec. 1944; AD M-et-L 19W13, Prefect Vincent to Debré, 7 Oct. 1944; AD L-A 132W159, prefecture memos, 12 and 14 Dec. 1944.

31 Interview with Pierre and Yolande (née Fitzgerald) de Montalembert, Neuilly, 9 Jan. 1999.

32 AD L-A 10W2, meetings of CDL of L-I, 26 Aug. and 2 Sept. 1944.

33 AD L-A 132W167, Prefect Vincent to Colonel Félix, 8 and 19 Sept. 1944; AD L-A 270W510, mayor of Le Gâvre to prefect, 25 Sept., who forwarded it to Col. Félix, 5 Oct. 1944.

34 Mgr Villepelet, 'Le Diocèse de Nantes, 1940–1945', entries for 16 and 25 Aug. 1944.

NOTES

35 AD L-A 10W18 & 27J16, General Hary to colonel commanding military region of Rennes, 18 Oct. 1944.

36 AD M-et-L 22W67, General Hary to Commissaire de la République, Angers, 31 Dec. 1945.

37 For instance, Philippe Bourdrel, *L'Épuration sauvage, 1944–1945* (Paris, Perrin, 1988). Other good accounts include Marcel Baudot, 'La Résistance française face aux problèmes de répression et d'épuration', *RHDGM* 81 (Jan. 1971), 23–47; Peter Novick, *The Resistance versus Vichy. The purge of collaborators in liberated France* (London, Chatto & Windus, 1968); Herbert Lottman, *The People's Anger. Justice and Revenge in Post-Liberation France* (London, Hutchinson, 1986).

38 Debré, *Trois Républiques pour la France*, 332.

39 To compare, see Megan Koreman, *The Expectation of Justice. France, 1944–1946* (Durham and London, Duke University Press, 1999), 98–100.

40 The trial dossier is in AD I-et-V 217W109. See especially note of CDL, 13 Aug. 1944, Captain Saint-Roch to Procureur de la République, Nantes, 10 Oct. 1944, Amicale of 170th and 174th infantry regiment, 22 Dec. 1944, statements of Jean Lucas, retired teacher, of CLL of Ancenis, 25 Jan. 1945, former teacher Anne-Marie Turbau, 30 Jan. 1945, and insurance agent/ municipal councillor Prosper Baudoin, 31 Jan. 1945. See also AD L-A 10W2, CDL debate, 16 Sept. 1944, and 132W167, Prefect Vincent to Debré, 9 Oct. 1944.

41 AD L-A 10W7, CLL congress, 24–5 Feb. 1945; AD M-et-L 19W13, Prefect Vincent to Debré, 1 March 1945.

42 Cited by Jean La Cour Grandmaison, *Le Marquis de La Ferronnays, 1876–1946* (Paris, Editions Siloë, 1952), 121–2.

43 AD M-et-L 22W76, trial dossier, including letters of Cholet's CLL, 8 Jan., Chamber of Commerce, 22 Feb. and 29 June, and Jean Soulard, 7 July 1945. See also Manceau's own *La Spoliation du 'Petit Courrier'* (Cholet, 1948), 7–9, 33–4, 54–6, 70–4.

44 AD I-et-L 60W10, divisional superintendent, Angers, to secretary general of police, Angers, 16 Dec. and latter to Debré, 28 Dec. 1944. *La Voix du peuple*, 2 and 9 Dec. 1944, 6 and 13 Jan., 10 and 24 Feb., 7 April 1945.

45 AD I-et-L 34W6, Prefect Vivier to Interior Minister, 17 Feb. 1945; 52W57, Feld to president of CDL, Tours, 24 Aug. 1944, and to president of Palais de Justice, Tours, 10 Oct. 1944.

46 AD M-et-L 7U4/104, trial dossier of Musso. See especially submissions of Cay, 21 Feb. and 17 April 1945, and of Donati, 6 April 1945.

47 *Le Procès du Maréchal Pétain* (Paris, Albin Michel, 1945), 814.

48 See above, p. 267.

49 AN 72AJ160, report of police commissioner, Tours, 20 June 1945; AD I-et-L 34W7, report of police commissioner, Tours, 29 June 1945; Yves Durand and Robert Vivier, *Libération des Pays de Loire, Blésois, Orléanais, Touraine* (Paris, Hachette, 1974), 246.

50 AD L-A 132W90, dossier on tramways of Nantes, Dec. 1944–March 1945; AD M-et-L 74W4, meetings of Comité Interprofessionnel d'Épuration dans les Entreprises (CIEE), 22 Dec. 1944, 8 and 22 Jan. 1945.

51 AD L-A 132W90, dossier on Batignolles locomotive works, Nantes, Jan.-Feb. 1945; AD M-et-L 74W4, meeting of CIEE, 19 Feb. 1945.

52 AD L-A 132W90, dossier on Chantiers de Bretagne, Nantes, Dec. 1944–March 1945.

53 Mgr Villepelet, 'Le Diocèse de Nantes, 1940–1945', entries for 17 Aug. and 11 Nov. 1944; AD L-A 210W508, note of chief superintendent, Renseignements Généraux, Nantes, 7 Oct., forwarded by Prefect Vincent to Debré, 12 Oct. 1944.

54 AD M-et-L 30W146, Debré to archbishop of Rennes, 25 Aug., and reply 4 Sept. 1944; Mgr Villepelet, 'Le Diocèse de Nantes, 1940–1945', entries for 14–15 Nov. 1944; Debré, *Trois Républiques pour une France*, 313. On the very limited nature of the purge of the clergy see Michèle Cointet, *L'Église sous Vichy, 1940–1945* (Paris, Perrin, 1998), 352–7, and W. D. Halls, *Politics, Society and Christianity in Vichy France*, 361–79.

55 A. Dio. Angers 4K42, 'Fédération Nationale d'Action Catholique. L'Union des Catholiques de l'Anjou', brochure dated 8 May 1945; Annik de Lassus Saint-Geniès, *Jean Le Cour Grandmaison* (Paris, Beauchesne, 1980), 196–205.

56 AD M-et-L 140W27, subprefect of Cholet to prefect of M-et-L, 3 Sept. 1945; *L'Avenir de l'Ouest*, 8 Oct. 1945. In general see Étienne Fouilloux, 'Les Forces religieuses', in Buton and Guillon, *Les Pouvoirs en France à la Libération*, 116–39.

57 AD L-A 10W13, dossier on Guémené-Penfao, Aug.–Sept. 1944; L-A 27J23, report of André Laurens, n.d; L-A 10W6, Mlle Rolland to CDL, 19 Oct. 1944. I am also grateful to the *mairie* of Guéméné-Penfao for documentation communicated on 2 Jan. 2000.

58 AD I-et-L 46W116, report of police commissioner, Tours, 29 Jan. 1945; AM Tours, dossier Ferdinand Morin.

59 AM Angers, minutes of municipal council of Angers, 7 Sept. 1944; AM Angers 1I141, speech of Bernier, 14 Jan. 1945; AD M-et-L 19W13, prefect of M-et-L to Debré, 8 Feb. 1945; Michel Lemesle, *Chronique d'Angers sous l'Occupation, 1939–1945* (Angers, Philippe Petit, 1972), 241–3.

60 AD L-A 10W2, proceedings of CDL, Nantes, 19 Oct. 1944; AD M-et-L 30W222, dossier on rehabilitation of Blancho, 1944–5.

61 AD L-A 10W13, reorganization of municipality of Nantes, Aug. 1944.

62 AM Nantes 1134W14 and AD M-et-L 30W49, visit of de Gaulle to Nantes, 14 Jan. 1945.

63 AD L-A 10W12, report of CLL, Ancenis, n.d.; Prefect Vincent to president of CDL, 5 Sept. 1944; 132W167, prefect to Debré, 26 Sept. 1944.

64 AD M-et-L 303W85, Darmaillacq to prefect of M-et-L, 26 Jan., 13 and 25 Feb. 1945. Darmaillacq wrote his *Cholet sous l'Occupation* in 1946 essentially to clear his name. On 14 March 1946 he was acquitted by the Chambre Civique of Angers.

65 AD I-et-L 46W116, police commissioner, Tours, to prefect, 29 Jan. 1945.

66 AD I-et-L 52W54, Prefect Vivier to Debré, 31 Oct. 1944.

67 Statistics calculated from returns for individual communes in AD I-et-L 3W9 and 10W25, AD L-A 10W11–13 and 132W85, and AD M-et-L 140W8 and 11.

68 AD M-et-L 97W154, subprefect of Saumur to Tardif, 31 Oct. 1944.

69 AD M-et-L 95W41, note of G. Cohn, 28 Sept. 1944.

70 AD L-A 10W2, CDL meeting of 31 Aug. 1944.

71 AD L-A 10W6, report of CDL emissary Thévenon, n.d., report of Dr Capel, 28 and 29 Nov. 1944.

72 AD I-et-L 46W117, Prefect Vivier to Interior Minister, 28 Jan. 1945.

73 AD M-et-L 30W196.

74 AD M-et-L 30W196 (L-I), 140W10 (M-et-L), AD I-et-L 46W117, give full details of the remodelling of *conseils généraux*. See also AD I-et-L 46W116 for personal comments on candidates in Touraine.

75 AD I-et-L 66W4, report of cabinet du préfet, 23 Aug. 1945.

76 See above, pp. 38–9.

77 AD L-A 132W159, Durtertre de la Coudre and municipal council of Machecoul to prefect, 21 April and 19 May 1945.

78 Interview with Jean Sauvage, Angers, 25 April 1997.

79 Cantonal election results in Conseil Général of Loire-Inférieure, 1945; AD M-et-L 30W153, AD I-et-L 3W326. See also AD M-et-L 19W14, report of Prefect Vivier, 4 Oct. 1944.

80 *Le Courrier de l'Ouest*, 23 Oct. 1945.

81 *La Résistance de l'Ouest*, 19 Oct. 1945. On Audibert's PSF background, see Jacques Nobécourt, *Le Colonel de La Rocque 1885–1946: ou les pièges du nationalisme chrétien* (Paris, Fayard, 1996), 884.

82 *L'Avenir de l'Ouest*, 15, 17, 18, 20–21 Oct. 1945.

16. DISAPPOINTMENT

1 See for example Antony Beevor and Artemis Cooper, *Paris after the Liberation, 1944–1949* (London, Penguin, 1995).

NOTES

2 AD M-et-L 97W123, Albert Chevalier to subprefect of Saumur, 31 Jan. 1945.

3 AD M-et-L 117W2, report of gendarmerie of Saumur, 7 Jan. 1945.

4 AD M-et-L 117W32, report of gendarmerie of Saumur on dances at Chacé, 18 and 19 Feb. 1945.

5 AD I-et-L 46W83, report of gendarmerie of Preuilly-sur-Claise, 5 April 1945.

6 AD M-et-L 97W123, anon. letter from inhabitant of Chacé to subprefect of Saumur, 28 Dec. 1944.

7 AD M-et-L 97W123, subprefect of Saumur to Captain Viala of Saumur gendarmerie, 30 Dec. 1944.

8 Hervé Tremblay, À Quédillac dans la Poche. Neuf mois dans la vie quotidienne des Bouvronnais, août 1944–11 mai 1945 (Bouvron, 1995), 11–13.

9 AD L-A 27J18, 'Journal de Guerre de M. l'Abbé Verger, curé de Guenrouet' (MS, 1947), 2.

10 'Journal de Guerre de M. l'Abbé Verger', 4–6, 19–22; Jean-Anne Chalet, Peau-de-Grenouille. Histoire d'un petit village dans la 'Poche' de Saint-Nazaire, août 1944–mai 1945 (Paris, Serge Godin, 1980).

11 AD L-A 270W503, prefecture memo, 24 Oct. 1944; 270W504, report of Subprefect of Saint-Nazaire Benedetti, 2 Dec. 1944; 270W502, report of Charles Mabit of Red Cross, 5 Jan. 1945, and gendarmerie of Ancenis, 13 Jan. 1945.

12 AN 72AJ146, 'Après la reddition', n.d.

13 AD L-A 270W504, note of prefecture of L-I, 15 June 1945.

14 AD M-et-L 97W99, mayors of Baugé and Noyant to prefect of M-et-L, 1 Aug. 1944.

15 AD M-et-L 95W93, mayor of Sainte-Christine to subprefect of Cholet, 27 Nov. 1944; 97W99, mayor of Cheviré-le-Rouge to subprefect of Saumur, 24 Nov. 1944.

16 AD L-A 132W72, former municipal councillor Étienne Louerat to prefect of L-I, 5 Sept. 1944.

17 AD L-A 80W8, postman Legault on behalf of Rézé refugees to prefect of L-I, 28 March 1945.

18 AD L-A 270W502, subprefect of Saint-Nazaire to prefect of L-I, 7 Aug. 1945.

19 AD L-A 80W64, correspondence of SNCASO and Chantiers de Penhouët with local authorities at Saint-Nazaire, Sept. 1944–June 1945.

20 AD L-A 132W72, Association des Réfugiés et Sinistrés de Saint-Nazaire/Section de Saint-Brévin to Deputy Moisan, 14 March 1946.

21 In general, see Christophe Lewin, Le Retour des prisonniers de guerre français. Naissance et développement de la FNPG, 1944–1952 (Paris, Publications de la Sorbonne, 1986), and François Cochet, Les Exclus de la

Victoire. Histoire des prisonniers de guerre, déportés et STO, 1945–1985 (Paris, SPM, 1992).

22 AD L-A 51W29, police commissioner, Nantes, to prefect, 25 June 1945.

23 AD L-A 52W29, motion of Association Communale des Prisonniers de Guerre de Rézé, 20 Sept. 1945.

24 AD I-et-L 46W97, unsigned letter from wife of POW at Semblançay to prefect of I-et-L, 25 June 1945.

25 AD I-et-L 46W122, extraordinary general meeting of Association Départementale des Prisonniers de Guerre d'Indre-et-Loire, 2 Aug. 1945; memo of prefecture, 7 Aug. 1945.

26 AD M-et-L 90W1, telegram of Frenay, Minister of Prisoners and Deportees, to Commissaires de la République and prefects, n.d. Prefect of M-et-L to subprefects and mayors, 9 July 1945.

27 AD I-et-L 46W122, Note d'information, 8 June 1945; AD M-et-L 140W50, Albert Charleux, president of the Association Départementale des Déportés et Internés Politiques, to prefect, 12 Oct. 1945.

28 AD L-A 10W8, Jean Meunier to Comité de Libération of Loire-Inférieure, 27 April 1945; AD I-et-L 46W122, memo of 22 June 1945.

29 Annette Wieviorka, *Déportation ou génocide* (Paris, Plon, 1992), 121–3.

30 AD L-A 165J3, meeting of Fédération Nationale des Déportés et Internés de la Résistance, Oct. 1948; Olivier Lalieu, 'La Crétation des Associations d'Anciens Déportés', in Christiane Franck, *La France de 1945. Résistances, retours, renaissances. Actes du Colloque de Caen, 17–19 mai 1995* (Caen, Presses Universitaires de Caen, 1996), 193–203.

31 AD I-et-L 66W8, purge commission of CDL of I-et-L, 19 Oct. 1944.

32 AD I-et-L 46W122, Bernard Montigaud for 'a group of ex-POWs' to secretary general of the prefecture, 22 Sept. 1944.

33 Fonds Émile Aron, decision of Tribunal Civil, Tours, 10 Jan. 1945.

34 AD I-et-L 46W102, CDL to prefect of I-et-L, 30 May 1945.

35 *Le Phare*, 13–14 July 1944.

36 AD M-et-L 103W26, petition of Segré workers to prefect of M-et-L, 31 Aug. 1944.

37 AD M-et-L 140W92, 'Appel aux paysans' of Prefect Fourré-Cormeray, 25 Aug. 1944.

38 AD M-et-L 103W23, Fourré-Cormeray to Mgr Costes, 20 Sept. 1944.

39 AD M-et-L 97W100, Subprefect Coiffard to mayors of *arrondissements* of Cholet, 10 Oct. 1944.

40 AD I-et-L 52W54, cuttings from *La Nouvelle République*, 20 and 27 Dec. 1944, reports of police commissioner, Tours, 2 and 16 Jan. 1945.

41 AD M-et-L 7U4/99, dossier on Rouleau trial, Dec. 1944–June 1945.

42 *La Voix du peuple*, 8 Nov. 1944.

43 AD M-et-L 22W100, motion of CDL of M-et-L, 25 Nov. 1944.

44 AD M-et-L 22W99, Debré to Minister of Finance, 14 Dec. 1944, and reply 22 Jan. 1945; Debré to Minister of Finance, 2 Feb. 1945.

45 AD I-et-L 1305W54, Comité de Confiscation des Profits Illicites, I-et-L, March–Oct. 1945.

46 AD M-et-L 140W30, circular of Minister of Agriculture to prefects, 25 Oct. 1944; Isabel Boussard, 'Résistance et syndicalisme agricole. Unité paysanne et liberté syndicale', in Franck, ed., *Résistances, retours, renaissances*, 27–48.

47 AD L-A 132W167, Prefect Vincent to Interior Minister, 22 March 1945.

48 Hervé Camus, 'La FDSEA de Loire-Inférieure, 1945–1957' (*mémoire de maîtrise*, University of Nantes, 1988), 45–7.

49 AD M-et-L 140W30, meeting of CDAA of M-et-L, 27 Nov. 1944.

50 Eugène Forget, Le *Serment de l'unité paysanne* (Paris, Nouvelle Cité, 1982), 113–28.

51 AD M-et-L 21W55, report of commander of Trélazé gendarmerie brigade, 20 Oct. 1944.

52 AD M-et-L 30W215, prefect of L-I to Interior Minister, 1 May 1945.

53 AD I-et-L 52W54, reports of police commissioner, Tours, 20 Feb. and 10 April 1945.

54 Megan Koreman, *The Expectation of Justice: France 1944–1946*, 251–7.

55 AD M-et-L 30W218, Prefect Vivier to Commissaire de la République, 29 and 30 Dec. 1945; Vivier to Interior Minister, 7 Jan. 1946.

56 AD M-et-L 302W218, chief superintendent, Renseignements Généraux, Angers, to director of Renseignements Généraux, Paris, 1 Jan. 1946; *La Nouvelle République*, 3 Jan. 1946.

57 See for example Andrew Shennan, *Rethinking France. Plans for Renewal, 1940–1946* (Oxford, Clarendon Press, 1989).

17. MEMORIES

1 Charles de Gaulle, *Discours et messages I* (Paris, Plon, 1970), 439–40.

2 Michael Marrus and Robert Paxton, *Vichy France and the Jews* (New York, Basic Books, 1981); Serge Klarsfeld, *Vichy-Auschwitz. Le rôle de Vichy dans la solution finale de la question juive en France* (2 vols, Paris, Fayard, 1983–5); Paul Webster, *Pétain's crime. The full story of French collaboration in the Holocaust* (London, Macmillan, 1990).

3 Serge Barcellini and Annette Wieviorka, *Passant, souviens-toi. Les lieux de souvenir de la Seconde Guerre Mondiale* (Paris, Plon, 1995). The authors use the term 'lieux de souvenir' rather than Pierre Nora's 'lieux de mémoire'

because they take the view that many sites simply commemorate the dead rather than 'structure the political field'. This interpretation, in my view, is unduly modest. See also *La Mémoire des Français. Quarante ans de commémoration de la Seconde Guerre Mondiale* (Paris, CNRS, 1986).

4 *La Nouvelle République*, 20 June 1955, 21 May 1965.

5 Robert Milliat, *Le Dernier Carousel. Défense de Saumur 1940* (Grenoble–Paris: B. Arthaud, 1943), 97.

6 Antoine Redier, *Les Cadets de Saumur* (Lyon–Paris, Emmanuel Vitte, 1940), 210. Robert Gildea, *The Past in French History*, 119–20.

7 *Ouest-France*, 12 June 1950.

8 *Presse-Océan*, 30 June 1969.

9 Dwight D. Eisenhower, *Crusade in Europe* (London, Heinemann, 1948), 322, 325, 349–50.

10 Interview with Pierre Hervé, Félix Boudet, Xavier Garçon and Louis David at Saffré, 30 May 1997.

11 *La Résistance de l'Ouest*, 10 Oct. 1949.

12 Ibid., 21 May 1951.

13 *Presse-Océan*, 11 May 1970.

14 Interview with Andrée Trudeau, Saumur, 22 June 1998. See also above, pp. 116–17.

15 See above, p. 45.

16 Interview with Michel Ancelin (b. 1933), Saumur, 22 June 1998. His account is taken up in 'Mes souvenirs d'enfant' in *Saumur 1990*, 33–5.

17 *La Nouvelle République*, 8 Nov. 1994.

18 AD M-et-L 116J9, reports of Commandant Royer, 25 June 1948, and Commissaire Principal Eprinchard, 4 Nov. 1940.

19 René Marnot, *Ma ville sous la botte* (Saumur, Éditions Roland, 1947).

20 Hubert Sommer, *Génie. Zur Bedeutungsgeschichte des Wortes von der Renaissance zur Aufklärung*, ed. Michael Nerlich (Frankfurt am Main, Peter Lang, 1998), IX–XLVI.

21 Michel Ancelin, 'Miettes – 18 septembre 1943', 8 pp., dated 26.7.96; interview of 22 June 1998.

22 Hubert Sommer, *Génie*, XLI; letter of Nerlich to the author, 16 July 1998.

23 Interview with Christian de Mondragon, Nantes, 29 April 1997.

24 Mgr Villepelet, 'Le Diocèse de Nantes, 1940–1945', entry for 22 Oct. 1945.

25 AD M-et-L 90W4, Inspecteurs du Service des Renseignements Généraux, Angers, 23 Oct. 1945.

26 AM Nantes 1205W1, speech of Maître Ridel, 9 June 1945.

27 Maurice Thorez, *Œuvres*, book 5, vol. 22 (Paris, Éditions Sociales, 1964), 231–4.

28 Barcellini and Wieviorka, *Passant, souviens-toi*, 331–2.

29 AM Nantes 1205W2, report of secretary general of Nantes, 9 Feb. 1945.

30 AM Nantes 1205WI, speech of Mayor Orrion, 22 Oct. 1952; cutting of *Ouest-Matin*, n.d.

31 *Humanité Dimanche*, 20 Aug. 1950. See file in AM Nantes 1134W12.

32 Edmond Duméril, 'Un témoignage capital: les cinquante otages de Nantes', *Historia* 154 (Sept. 1959), 254–62.

33 Etienne Gasche, *50 Otages, mémoire sensible* (Nantes, Editions du Petit Véhicule, 1991), 102–31.

34 *Ouest-France*, 21 Oct. 1991.

35 *Presse-Océan*, 23 Oct. 1991.

36 Livre d'Or. Exposition des 50 Otages, Nantes, 16 Oct.–24 Nov. 1991. I am indebted to Frank Liaigre for lending me a photocopy of these entries.

37 *Quest-France* and *Presse-Océan*, 23 Oct. 2001; letter of Oury to the author, 18 Nov. 2001.

38 See above, pp. 53, 253.

39 Interview with Marquis Donatien and General Yves de Sesmaisons, Nantes, 16 July 1997; letter from General de Sesmaisons to the author, 21 July 1997.

40 Interview with Vicomte and Vicomtesse de la Grandière, la Jumellière (M-et-L), 5 May 1997.

41 Interview with Paule and Louis de Beaumont, Daumeray (M-et-L), 20 May 1997; letter of Paule de Beaumont to the author, 5 June 1997, enclosing extract from the *Procès du Maréchal Pétain. Compte-rendu sténographique* (Paris, Albin Michel, 1945), 245.

42 Interview with Georges Audebert, Tours, 24 June 1998.

43 Interview with André Treulier, Le Thoreil, 13 May 1997.

44 Interview with Max (b. 1916) and Jeanne (b.1921) Ménard, Jallais (M-et-L), 22 April 1997.

45 Interview with Abbé Henri Richer (b. 1920), Angers, 6 June 1997.

46 Interviews with Abbé François Jamonneau, Nantes, 26 May and 5 June 1997.

47 Sarah Farmer, *Martyred Village. Commemorating the 1944 massacre at Oradour-sur-Glane* (Berkeley, University of California Press, 1999); Tzvetan Todorov, *A French Tragedy. Scenes of a civil war, summer 1944* (Dartmouth College, 1996).

48 Interview with Yves de Saint-Seine, Toutlemonde (M-et-L), 22 April 1997; *Toutlemonde. 50e anniversaire du 8 août 1944* (Toutlemonde, 1994). See also above, p. 327.

49 AD I-et-L 33W13, prefect to mayor of Maillé, 18 Aug. 1948.

50 AD I-et-L 46W124, press cuttings of 13 and 18 May 1953.

51 *La Nouvelle République*, 23 Aug. 1994; interview with Gilbert Chedozeau, Mme Guitton and Serge Martin, 6 June 1997.

52 AD M-et-L 148J, Comité d'Histoire de la Seconde Guerre Mondiale, survey of 1948.

53 AD M-et-L 116J9, documents on visit of General Leclerc to Grugé l'Hôpital, 17 Sept. 1946.

54 *Le Courrier de l'Ouest*, 13 Oct. 1980.

55 AD M-et-L 140W6, subprefect of Segré to prefect, 9 May 1941.

56 Interview with Édouard Delanoë, Grugé l'Hôpital, 14 April 1997.

57 Francis Bossé, Memoirs (MS, 1997), 1, 10.

58 See above, p. 324.

59 *Le Courrier de l'Ouest*, 8 Aug. 1994.

60 AM Angers 1I227, visit of General Patton to Angers.

61 *Le Courrier de l'Ouest*, 24 Oct. 1995; interview with Germaine Canonne, Angers, 28 April 1997; Germaine Canonne, 'Souvenirs de la première femme élue en Maine-et-Loire' (MS, n.d.).

62 Ruling of Cour d'Appel, Bourges, 23 July 1985; Letter of FNDIR to president of the Republic, 25 June 1986. Documents kindly communicated by André Chauvel, president of the FNDIR, Nantes.

63 AM Nantes 1134W13, mayor of Nantes to Interior Minister Jules Moch, 4 Aug. 1948, and reply, 15 Sept. 1948; AD L-A 270W480, prefecture of L-I to parents of Frédéric Creusé, 30 April 1948; Comité National des Héros de Châteaubriant to prefect of L-I, 10 Aug.1949.

64 AD L-A 161W350, prefect to secretary of state for Armed Forces, 23 June 1951.

65 Sarah Choyeau, 'La Mémoire de la Résistance à Nantes' (*mémoire de maîtrise*, University of Nantes, 1994), 110.

66 Remise des Prix du Concours départemental de la Résistance et de la Libération, Nantes, 18 June 1997.

67 Essay kindly communicated by André Chauvel.

68 AM Angers 1I265, *Le Courrier de l'Ouest* and *La Nouvelle République*, 24 Nov. 1970.

69 *Presse Océan*, 29 April 1985.

70 Annette Wieviorka, *Déportation ou génocide* (Paris, Plon, 1992), 136–9. This figure, accepted until the 1960s, was calculated on the basis of 120,000 Jews and 60,000 non-Jews.

71 Meeting of FNDIR, Nantes, 6 May 1997.

72 Interview with Ernest Gluck, Nantes, 22 June 1997.

73 *Ouest-France*, 19 July 1993.

74 Ibid., 18 and 21 July 1992.

75 Interview with Charles Toubon, Angers, 22 June 1997.

76 Interview with Lucie Lancezeux and Huguette Robin, Monts (I-et-L), 23 June 1998.

77 *La Nouvelle République*, 15 Oct. 1988.

78 Collège de Monts, Jérôme Scorin, speech of 16 Oct. 1988.

79 Interview with François Guggenheim, Tours, 30 June 1997.

80 *La Nouvelle République*, 4 Dec. 1995. Interviews with André Bellegarde of the Lycée Jean-Monnet, Joué-lès-Tours, and Marie-Paule Fresneau of the Collège de Monts, 30 June 1997.

81 Interview with Christian and Léone Beugnet (both b. 1929), Claude Bougreau (b. 1936) and René Arnoult (b. 1921), Chinon, 23 June 1998.

82 Interview with Andrée Trudeau, Saumur, 22 June 1998.

83 Interview with Michel Leterme (b. 1930), Angers, 13 May 1997.

84 Interview with Violette Lemasson (Belle-Beille, Angers), 16 April 1997; letter of Marcel Girard to the author, 13 January 1998.

85 Interview with Huguette Robin, Monts (I-et-L), 23 June 1998.

86 Interview with Lucienne Despouy, Saint-Avertin, Tours, 9 June 1997.

87 Interview with Odette Goxe, Angers, 14 April 1997. See also above, p. 221.

88 Interview with Pierre Boudet (b. 1915), Angers, 11 Oct. 1997.

89 Interview with Abel and Claudine Avenet, Dierre (I-et-L), 25 June 1998.

90 Interview with André Roussel (b. 1926), Bléré (I-et-L), 25 June 1998.

18. CONCLUSION

1 Ludwig Tewes, *Frankreich in der Besatzungszeit, 1940–1943. Die Sicht deutcher Augenzeugen* (Bonn, Bouvier Verlag, 1998). However, Alrich Meyer, *Die deutsche Besatzung in Frankreich, 1940–1944. Widerstandbekampfung und Judenverfolgung* (Darmstadt, Wissenschaftliche Buchgesellschaft, 2000), argues for a progressively more repressive occupation regime, not least by the Wehrmach.

Bibliography

1. Manuscript Sources

BUNDESARCHIV-MILITÄRARCHIV, FREIBURG

Three series were used:

(i) those of the Militärbefehlshaber in Frankreich/Military Administration in France (RW35), notably on hostages (RW35/536, 542–3), and of the Military Administration of Bezirk B, based at Angers, notably reports from 1940–2 (RW35/1254, 1260–4) and reports relating to the end of the Occupation (RW35/1252–3);

(ii) those of the Kommandanturen within the Bezirk B, notably Nantes (RH36/131, 133, 142, 146, 148, 312, 511, 512, 525) and Tours (RH36/26, 228);

(iii) those of the Rüstungsdienstellen in France (RW24): the Rüstungsinspektion of SW France based at Angers (RW24/122–6, 129, 131, 132) and the Rüstungskommandos based at Angers, Le Mans (RW24/174–80) and Nantes (RW24/153–60).

NATIONAL ARCHIVES, PARIS

Five series were used:

(i) F1a: Ministry of the Interior: personnel of prefectures (3630), administrative commissions (3634) and departmental councils (3635), questions of production and supply (3658–9), detailed reports on the situation within France by the Free French Mission Militaire de Liaison Administrative, 1943–4 (3868–9), and reports of the Service Central des Commissariats de la République (4020);

BIBLIOGRAPHY

(ii) F9: General Commissariat for repatriated POWs and their families (3037, 3049, 3055, 3064);

(iii) AJ 38: General Commissariat for Jewish Questions, notably personal questions (150) and Aryanization (977);
AJ 40: German Archives of the Second World War, dealing notably with French officials (542–4) and the Liberation (571);

(iv) 72 AJ: Archives of the Comité d'Histoire de la Deuxième Guerre Mondiale, which includes numerous first-hand accounts collected in the years after the war (136, 144–7, 160).

DEPARTEMENTAL ARCHIVES

The Departmental Archives of Loire-Atlantique (L-A), Maine-et-Loire (M-et-L) and Indre-et-Loire (I-et-L) provided the greatest mass of documentation. Since Angers was a regional capital some material relating to the other two departments is found under Maine-et-Loire. Series W relates to the Second World War. There are also judicial files in series U. The following grid gives a guide to the main sub-series within Series W; references to individual files are found in the endnotes.

	LOIRE-ATLANTIQUE	MAINE-ET-LOIRE	INDRE-ET-LOIRE
prefecture	12, 13, 22, 43 (Châteaubriant), 51, 75, 132W	8, 12, 18, 24, 60, 80, 95 (Cholet), 97 (Saumur), 136, 140W	10, 46, 52, 121W
Franco-German relations	13, 18, 43, 51, 65, 75, 118, 132, 161, 243, 270W	5, 18, 60, 80, 95, 97, 80, 136, 140W	10, 52, 66, 108W
Vichy regime:			
departmental assemblies	13, 132, 157W	18, 140W	10, 52, 225W
municipalities	10, 13, 132W	2, 12, 24, 80, 90, 140W	3, 10, 18, 52W

courts	243W	7U4	
police	13, 51, 132, 243W	12, 18, 24, 41, 60, 75, 80, 90 136, 140W	10, 44, 52, 120W
propaganda/ public opinion	1, 13W	18, 56, 136, 140W	10W
Church		140W	10W
Secours National	13, 54, 132W	8, 18, 41, 71W	46, 218W
refugees/evacuees	8, 54, 80, 132W	18, 54, 93, 136, 140W	10, 18, 52, 108W
POWs	6, 16, 38, 43, 51, 52, 75W	8, 24, 90, 140W	10, 46, 218W
bombings	13, 43, 54, 75, 253W	18W	10W
food supply	31, 46, 56, 75, 80, 161, 253W	21, 24, 30, 32, 54, 103, 117, 140W	10, 46, 52, 63, 106, 135W
Peasant Corporation	13W	18, 69, 95. 140W	63, 106W
labour	13, 18, 42, 132W	12, 21, 25, 30, 33, 69W	6, 52W
Relève, STO	16, 18, 40, 75, 132, 161W	18, 140W	6, 10, 63, 121W
Jews	13, 65, 270W	7, 12, 18, 24, 37, 61, 97W	10, 44, 46, 52, 120W
associations	75, 82, 132, 270W	18, 41, 54, 80, 97, 116, 140W	10, 28, 30, 31, 46, 52, 106W
clandestine dancing		8, 18, 56, 80, 117W	10, 46, 52, 218W

Liberation	10, 96, 270W	18, 30, 60, 140W	33, 46, 60, 66, 121, 124W
purges	96, 132, 243, 270W	22, 30, 46, 48, 60, 74, 140, 303W	34, 46, 52, 1305W
courts	*Archives of Ille-et-Vilaine* 217W	7U4, 2, 22W	7, 34, 46, 217, 1119W
Commissaire de la République	132W	19, 30W	46W
liberation committees	10, 96, 132, 270W	30, 48, 140W	46, 66W
local councils	30W	19, 30, 56, 140W	3, 46, 66W
FFIs	270W	22W	52W
Pocket of Saint-Nazaire	26, 270W		

The AD I-et-L also have a useful collection of documents recovered from the German authorities at the end of the Occupation:
II Z 3 (hunting)

III Z 1, situation reports from Feldkommandantur of Angers, 1940–1
XIV Z 17 (mayors), 27, 29 (art conservation), 32 (French officials)
XV Z 21 (Maine-et-Loire), 23 (enemy propaganda), 27 (French officials, Indre-et-Loire)

The Departmental archives also contain private collections (Series J) such as:
AD L-A 27J16–18, various contemporary accounts
    165J, archives of the FNDIR
AD M-et-L 116J9 and 148J, archives of the Comité d'Histoire de la Deuxième Guerre Mondiale
AD I-et-L 42J1, archives of Dr Goupille, veterinary surgeon near the demarcation line
    81J1, archives of Robert Vivier, Liberation prefect

BIBLIOGRAPHY

MUNICIPAL ARCHIVES

(i) Nantes
H4 116, diary of F. Soil, secretary general of the municipality
38W5, 9, 17, 27 municipal administration
134W9–12 Hotz/hostages affair, W14 visit of de Gaulle
1205W1–2 commemoration of hostages

(ii) Angers
1 I commemoration of visits of de Gaulle, 1944–5 (141), of General Patton
       (227), of liberation of Angers (253–4), of deportees (265)
1 D register of proceedings of municipal council, 1938–45

(iii) Tours
Bulletin municipal 1940
Golden Book presented to Ferdinand Morin by the citizens of Tours, 1941

(iv) Chinon
Register of proceedings of municipal council, 1940–5

DIOCESAN ARCHIVES

Nantes: Mgr Villepelet, 'Le Diocèse de Nantes, 1940–1945'. This diary is an
       indispensable source
   Register of the parish of Sainte-Croix, Nantes, 1940–4
   Letters and cards sent by Mgr Villepelet to seminarists and priests in POW
       camps

Angers: 1D12, file on Mgr Costes
   9E41, letters of Mgr Costes to seminarists and priests in POW camps
   4K42, Union des Catholiques de l'Anjou
   6J4 Université Catholique d'Angers

Tours: 1D6, correspondence of Mgr Gaillard and Feldkommandantur of Tours,
       1940
   'Prêtres de 1939 à 1945'
   Pastoral visit, 1942

To these must be added the printed *Semaine religieuse* for each diocese, 1940–4

BIBLIOGRAPHY

LABOUR ARCHIVES

Centre d'Histoire du Travail, Nantes:
  CGT, 1939–45
  Pennaneach papers

Bourse du Travail, Angers:
  Papers of Raymond Déaud

PRIVATE MEMOIRS AND DIARIES

Collection Lemesle: private collection of Michel Lemesle, local historian at
    Angers
Marinette Rameau, 'Journal de Guerre'
Francis Bossé, 'Mémoires'
Suzanne Le Chat, 'En souvenir de l'époque tourmentée vécue dans les années
    1939 à 1945'
Papers of Émile Aron, Tours
Papers of Odette Goxe, Angers
Papers of Paul Grenouilleau, Angers

Printed Sources

Abélès, Marc, *Quiet Days in Burgundy. A study of local politics* (Paris and
    Cambridge, Éditions de la Maison des Sciences de l'Homme/Cambridge
    University Press, 1991).
Added, Serge, *Le Théâtre dans les Années Vichy* (Paris, 1992).
Alary, Eric, *La Ligne de Démarcation, 1940–1944* (Paris, PUF, 'Que-sais-je?',
    1995).
Amouroux, Henri, *Quarante millions de Pétainistes: juin 1940–juin 1941*
    (Paris, R. Laffont, 1977).
Aron, Émile, *La Médecine en Touraine des origines à nos jours* (Chambray-lès-
    Tours, CLD, 1992).
Aron, Émile, *Figures Tourangelles* (Chambray-lès-Tours, CLD, 1986).
Atkin, Nicholas, *Church and Schools in Vichy France, 1940–1944* (New York
    and London, Garland, 1991).

BIBLIOGRAPHY

Atkin, Nicholas, *Pétain* (London, Longman, 1998).

Audoin Le Marec, Michelle, *Le Maine-et-Loire dans la Guerre, 1939–1945* (Le Coteau, Horvath, 1987).

Audoin-Rouzeau, Stéphane, *L'Enfant de l'ennemi, 1914–1918* (Paris, Aubier, 1995).

Aulton, Margaret, *Fair Touraine* (London, John Lane at the Bodley Head, 1925).

Azéma, Jean-Pierre, Bédarida, François, and Frank, Robert (eds), *Jean Moulin et la Résistance en 1943* (Paris, IHTP, 1994).

Azéma, Jean-Pierre and Bédarida, François, *Vichy et les Français* (Paris, Fayard, 1992).

Bakhtin, Mikhail, *Rabelais and His World* (Bloomington, Indiana University Press, 1984).

Barcellini, Serge, and Wieviorka, Annette, *Passant, souviens-toi. Les lieux de souvenir de la Seconde Guerre Mondiale* (Paris, Plon, 1995).

Barral, Pierre, 'Idéal et pratique du régionalisme dans le régime de Vichy', *Revue Française de Science Politique*, 24, no. 5 (Oct. 1974).

Baruch, Marc-Olivier, *Servir l'état français. L'administration en France de 1940 à 1944* (Paris, Fayard, 1997).

Baudot, Marcel, 'La Résistance française face aux problèmes de répression et d'épuration', *RHDGM* 81 (Jan. 1971), pp. 23–47.

Baudot, Marcel, *Libération de la Bretagne* (Paris, Hachette, 1973).

Baudouin, Paul, *Neuf mois au gouvernement, avril–décembre 1940* (Paris, Éditions de la Table Ronde, 1948).

Beevor, Antony and Cooper, Artemis, *Paris after the Liberation, 1944–1949* (London, Penguin, 1995).

Beltran, A., Frank, R. and Rousso, H., *La Vie des entreprises sous l'Occupation. Une enquête à l'échelle locale* (Paris, Belin, 1994).

Berger, Laurent, 'L'Épiscopat nantais de Mgr Villepelet, 1936–1966' (*mémoire de maîtrise*, University of Nantes, 1991).

Bergère, Marc, 'Permanences et ruptures au sein du Conseil Général du Maine-et-Loire (1935–1953). Étude prosopographique des élus', *Annales de Bretagne et des Pays de l'Ouest* 103 (1996), pp. 69–77.

Bergère, Marc, 'Tensions et rivalités entre les pouvoirs issus de la Résistance en Maine-et-Loire', in Jacqueline Sainclivier, *La Résistance et les Français. Enjeux stratégiques et environnement social* (Rennes, Presses Universitaires de Rennes, 1995).

Bertin-Maghit, Jean-Pierre, *Le Cinéma français sous Vichy. Les films français de 1940 à 1944* (Paris, Albatros, 1980).

Bougeard, Christian, 'Regards sur les réseaux de notables en Bretagne, des années 1930 aux années 1950', *Annales de Bretagne et des Pays de l'Ouest* 103 (1996), pp. 31–51.

BIBLIOGRAPHY

Boulanger, Gérard, *Papon: Un intrus dans la République* (Paris, Seuil, 1997).

Boulard, Fernand (ed.), *Matériaux pour l'histoire religieuse du peuple français, XIXe–XXe siècles. Région de Paris, Haute-Normandie, Pays de Loire, Centre* (Paris, Éditions de l'École des Hautes Études en Sciences Sociales, 1982).

Bourdé, Guy, *La Défaite du Front Populaire* (Paris, Maspéro, 1977).

Bourdrel, Philippe, *L'Épuration sauvage, 1944–1945* (Paris, Perrin, 1988).

Bourreau, René, *Une Utopie religieuse et sa modernisation lors des élections en pays nantais contemporain. La logique restitutionniste de la noblesse nantaise* (thesis, Paris, EHESS, 1992).

Bourrigaud, René, *Le Développement agricole au dix-neuvième siècle en Loire-Atlantique* (Nantes, Centre d'Histoire du Travail, 1994).

Boussard, Isabel, 'Résistance et syndicalisme agricole. Unité paysanne et liberté syndicale', in Christiane Franck (ed.), *Résistances, retours, renaissances. Actes du Colloque de Caen, 17–19 mai 1995* (Caen, Presses Universitaires de Caen, 1996).

Boussard, Isabel, *Vichy et la Corporation Paysanne* (Paris, FNSP, 1980).

Boylesve, René, *La Jeune Fille bien élévée* (Paris, Calmann-Lévy, 1924).

Briais, Bernard, *Le Lochois pendant la Guerre, 1939–1945* (Chambray-lès-Tours, CLD, 1988).

Brossat, Alain, *Les Tondues. Un carnaval moche* (Paris, Hachette, 1994).

Brunet, Jean-Paul, *Jacques Doriot* (Paris, Balland, 1986).

Bücheler, Heinrich, *Carl-Heinrich von Stülpnagel. Soldat, Philosoph, Verschwörer* (Berlin, Ullstein, 1989).

Burrin, Philippe, *Living with Defeat. France under the German Occupation, 1940–1944* (London, Arnold, 1996).

Camus, Hervé, *La FDSEA de Loire-Inférieure, 1945–1957* (*mémoire de maîtrise*, University of Nantes, 1988).

Capdevila, Luc, *Les Bretons au lendemain de l'Occupation. Imaginaire et comportement d'une sortie de guerre, 1944–1945* (Rennes, Presses Universitaires de Rennes, 1999).

Chalet, Jean-Anne, *Peau-de-Grenouille. Histoire d'un petit village dans la 'Poche' de Saint-Nazaire, août 1944–mai 1945* (Paris, Serge Godin, 1980).

Chamard, Élie, *Les Combats de Saumur* (Paris, Berger-Levrault, 1948).

Chamard, Élie, *Vingt siècles d'histoire à Cholet* (Cholet, Farré et Fils, 1981).

Chauvy, Gérard, *Aubrac, Lyon 1943* (Paris, Albin Michel, 1997).

Chollet, Louis, *Les Heures tragiques. Tours, juin 1940* (Tours, Arrault et Cie, 1946).

Cholvy, Gérard, and Hilaire, Yves-Marie, *Histoire religieuse de la France contemporaine, vol. III, 1930–1988* (Toulouse, Privat, 1988).

Choyeau, Sarah, 'La Mémoire de la Résistance à Nantes' (*mémoire de maîtrise*, University of Nantes, 1994).

Churchill, Winston S., *The Second World War, vol. II, Their Finest Hour* (London, Cassell, 1949).

Cobb, Richard, *French and Germans, Germans and French* (Hanover and London, University Press of New England, 1983).

Cobb, Richard, *Les Armées révolutionnaires: instrument de la Terreur dans les départements, avril 1793 – floréal an II* (Paris, Mouton, 1961–3), translated by Marianne Elliott as *The People's Armies* (New Haven and London, Yale University Press, 1987).

Cochet, François, *Les Exclus de la victoire. Histoire des prisonniers de guerre, déportés et STO, 1945–1985* (Paris, SPM, 1992).

Cohen, Asher, *Persécutions et sauvetages. Juifs et Français sous l'Occupation et sous Vichy* (Paris, Éditions du Cerf, 1993).

Cointet, Jean-Paul, *La Légion Française des Combattants, 1940–1944. La tentation du Fascisme* (Paris, Albin Michel, 1995).

Cointet, Michèle, *Le Conseil National de Vichy, 1940–1944* (Paris, Aux Amateurs du Livre, 1989).

Cointet, Michèle, *L'Église sous Vichy 1940–1945* (Paris, Perrin, 1998).

Colanéri, L.-J. and Gérante, G., *La Dénonciation et les dénonciateurs* (Paris, PUF, 1948).

Conway, John S., *The Nazi Persecution of the Churches* (London, Weidenfeld & Nicolson, 1968).

Cordier, Daniel, *Jean Moulin: L'Inconnu du Panthéon* (Paris, Lattès, 1989).

Corre, Rozenn, 'Le Scoutisme Catholique à Nantes des origines au Jamborée de la Paix, 1925–1947', (*mémoire de maîtrise*, University of Nantes, 1992).

Correch, Auguste, *L'Activité du Docteur Henri Mattraits avant la Guerre et pendant l'Occupation* (Chinon, 1944).

Danos, Jacques and Gibelin, Marcel, *June '36. Class struggle and the Popular Front in France* (London and Chicago, Bookmarks, 1986).

Darmaillacq, A., *Cholet sous l'Occupation* (Cholet, 1946, re-ed. 1991).

Davies, Jennifer, *The Wartime Kitchen and Garden* (London, BBC Books, 1993).

Day, Charles R., *Education for the Industrial World. The Écoles d'Arts et Métiers and the rise of French industrial engineering* (Cambridge, Mass., MIT Press, 1987).

Debré, Michel, *Trois Républiques pour une France. Mémoires I. Combattre* (Paris, Albin Michel, 1984).

Dejonghe, Étienne, 'Les aspects économiques et sociaux du Nord pendant la première année de l'Occupation', *Revue du Nord*, October 1969.

BIBLIOGRAPHY

Delarue, Jacques, *Trafics et crimes sous L'Occupation* (Paris, Fayard, 1968, re-ed. 1993).

Delpla, François, *Aubrac, les faits et la calomnie* (Pantin, Le Temps des Cerises, 1997).

Déniel, Alain, *Le Mouvement breton* (Paris, Maspéro, 1976).

Diamond, Hanna, *Women and the Second World War in France, 1939–1948. Choices and constraints* (Harlow, Pearson, 1999).

Dogan, Mattei, 'Les filières de la carrière politique en France', *Revue Française de Sociologie* 8 (1967), pp. 468–92.

Dommanget, Maurice, *Histoire du Premier Mai* (Paris, Société Universitaire d'Éditions et de Librairie, 1953).

Duméril, Edmond, *Journal d'un honnête homme pendant l'Occupation, juin 1940–août 1944* (Thonon-les-Bains, L'Albaron/Société Présence du Livre, 1990).

Duméril, Edmond, 'Un Témoignage capital: les cinquante otages de Nantes', *Historia* 154 (Sept. 1959), pp. 254–62.

Durand, Abel, *Nantes de la France de l'Ouest* (Paris, Plon, 1941).

Durand, Yves, *La Vie quotidienne des prisonniers de guerre dans les stalags, oflags et kommandos, 1939–1945* (Paris, Hachette, 1987, new edn 1994).

Durand, Yves and Vivier, Robert, *Libération des Pays de Loire, Blésois, Orléanais, Touraine* (Paris, Hachette, 1974).

Ehrlich, Evelyn, *Cinema of a Paradox. French film-making under the German Occupation* (New York, Columbia University Press, 1987).

Eisenhower, Dwight D., *Crusade in Europe* (London, Heinemann, 1948).

Estèbe, Jean (ed.), *Les Juifs à Toulouse et en Midi toulousain au temps de Vichy* (Toulouse, Presses Universitaires Le Mirail, 1996).

Evrard, Jacques, *La Déportation des travailleurs français dans le Troisième Reich* (Paris, Fayard, 1972).

Farmer, Sarah, *Martyred Village. Commemorating the 1944 massacre at Oradour-sur-Glane* (Berkeley, University of California Press, 1999).

Faure, Christian, *Le Projet culturel de Vichy* (Paris–Lyon, CNRS, Presses Universitaires de Lyon, 1989).

Feneant, Jacques, *Francs-Maçons et sociétés secrètes en Val de Loire* (Chambray-lès-Tours, CLD, 1986).

Feneant, Jacques, *Histoire de la Franc-Maçonnerie en Touraine* (Chambray-lès-Tours, CLD, 1981).

Ferro, Marc, *Pétain* (Paris, Fayard, 1987).

Figlio, Karl, 'Oral History and the Unconscious', *History Workshop Journal* 26 (1988), pp. 120–32.

Fiot, Canon Robert, *Un Prêtre de Touraine. L'Abbé Georges Lhermitte, 1887–1944* (Tours, Barbot et Gallon, 1945).

BIBLIOGRAPHY

Fishman, Sarah, *We Will Wait. Wives of French prisoners of war, 1940–1945* (New Haven and London, Yale University Press, 1991).

Fitzpatrick, Sheila and Gellately, Robert, *Accusatory Practices* (Chicago and London, University of Chicago Press, 1997).

Forget, Eugène, *Le Serment de l'unité paysanne* (Paris, Nouvelle Cité, 1982).

Fouet, P. A., *Angoisses et espoirs. Segré, août 1944* (Maine Libre, 1945).

Fouilloux, Étienne, 'Les Forces religieuses', in Philippe Buton and Jean-Marie Guillon, *Les Pouvoirs en France à la Libération* (Paris, Belin, 1994).

Gabillard, Philippe, 'L'Extrême Droite en Maine-et-Loire, 1919–1934', (*mémoire de maîtrise*, Catholic University of Angers, 1980).

Gasche, Etienne, *Cinquante otages, mémoire sensible* (Nantes, Éditions du Petit Véhicule, 1991).

Gay-Lescot, Jean-Louis, *Sport et éducation sous Vichy, 1940–1944* (Lyon, Presses Universitaires de Lyon, 1991).

Gaulle, Charles de, *Discours et messages I, juin 1940–janvier 1946* (Paris, Plon, 1970).

Gellner, Ernest and Waterbury, John (eds), *Patrons and Clients in Mediterranean Societies* (London, Duckworth, 1977).

Gicquel, Yvonnig, *Le Comité consultatif de Bretagne* (Rennes, Simon, 1961).

Gilbert, Martin, *Winston Churchill, vol. VI, 1939–1941* (London, Heinemann, 1983).

Gildea, Robert, 'Les Années Noires? Clandestine dancing in Occupied France', in Ceri Crossley and Martyn Cornick (eds), *Echoes and Insights: Problems in French History* (Basingstoke, Palgrave, 2000), 197–212.

Gildea, Robert, *The Past in French History* (New Haven and London, Yale University Press, 1994).

Golsan, Richard, *The Papon Affair. Memory and justice on trial* (New York, Routledge, 2000).

Goupille, André, *Mon village sous la botte. La Haye Descartes, juin 1940–septembre 1944* (Tours, n.d.).

Guérinau, Robert, *Les Martyrs du 16 mai 1942. Les premiers fusillés de la Touraine* (Tours, La Voix du Peuple, 1963).

Guérinau, Robert and Guillon, Jean-Claude, *La Touraine sous le règne des Feldkommandants* (Tours, Centre-Loire, 1985).

Gueslin, André, *Les Facs sous Vichy. Actes du Colloque des Universités de Clermont-Ferrand et de Strasbourg, Novembre 1993* (Clermont-Ferrand, Publications de l'Institut d'Études du Massif Central Université Blaise-Pascal, 1994).

Guillard, Jérôme, 'Les Catholiques Tourangeaux pendant la Deuxième Guerre Mondiale' (*mémoire de maîtrise*, University of Tours, 1996).

Guillon, Jean-Marie, 'L'Affaire Aubrac ou la dérive d'une certaine façon de faire l'histoire', *Modern and Contemporary France* 7/1 (1999), pp. 89–108.

BIBLIOGRAPHY

Guillon, Jean-Marie, 'Parti du mouvement et parti de l'ordre', in Philippe Buton and Jean-Marie Guillon, *Les Pouvoirs en France à la Libération* (Paris, Belin, 1994).

Halimi, André, *La Dénonciation sous l'Occupation* (Paris, Alain Moreau, 1983).

Halls, W. D., *Politics, Society and Christianity in Vichy France* (Oxford and Providence, Berg, 1995).

Halls, W. D., *The Youth of Vichy France* (Oxford, Clarendon Press, 1981).

Hangouët, Alfred, *L'Affaire Le Coz* (CLD, Normand et Cie, 1978).

Harris, Ruth, 'The "Child of the Barbarian": rape, race and nationalism in France during the First World War', *Past and Present* 141 (Nov. 1993), pp. 170-206.

Haudebourg, Guy, *Le Parti Communiste Français en Loire-Inférieure à la Libération, 1944-1947* (*mémoire de maîtrise*, University of Nantes, 1987).

Hauser, Henri, *Le Problème du régionalisme* (Paris, PUF, 1924).

Jäckel, Eberhard, *Frankreich in Hitlers Europa* (Stuttgart, Deutsche Verlags-Anstalt, 1966).

Jackson, Julian, *France The Dark Years, 1940-1944* (Oxford, Oxford University Press, 2001).

Jackson, Julian, *The Popular Front in France. Defending democracy, 1934-1938* (Cambridge, Cambridge University Press, 1988).

Jacobs, Gabriel, 'The role of Joan of Arc on the stage of Occupied Paris', in Roderick Kedward and Roger Austin, *Vichy France and the Resistance. Culture and ideology* (London and Sydney, Croom Helm, 1985).

Jünger, Ernst, *Premier Journal parisien. Journal II, 1941-1943* (Paris, Christian Bourgois, 1980).

Kaspi, André, *Les Juifs pendant l'Occupation* (Paris, Seuil, 1991, new edn 1997).

Kedward, Roderick, 'The Maquis and the Culture of the Outlaw', in Roderick Kedward and Roger Austin, *Vichy France and the Resistance. Culture and ideology* (London and Sydney, Croom Helm, 1985).

Kergoat, Jacques, *La France du Front Populaire* (Paris, Éditions La Découverte, 1986).

Klarsfeld, Serge, *Vichy-Auschwitz. Le rôle de Vichy dans la solution finale de la question juive en France* (2 vols, Paris, Fayard, 1983-5).

Koreman, Megan, *The Expectations of Justice. France 1944-1946* (Durham and London, Duke University Press, 1999).

Krumeich, Gerd, 'Joan of Arc between right and left', in Robert Tombs (ed.), *Nationhood and Nationalism in France. From Boulangism to the Great War, 1889-1918* (London, HarperCollinsAcademic, 1991).

Krumeich, Gerd, *Jeanne d'Arc in der Geschichte. Historiographie-Politik-Kultur* (Sigmaringen, Thorbecke, 1989).

Kupferman, Fred, *Laval* (Paris, Balland, 1987).

Laborie, Pierre, *L'Opinion française sous Vichy* (Paris, Seuil, 1990).

Lalieu, Olivier, 'La création des associations d'anciens déportés', in Christiane Franck, *La France de 1945. Résistances, retours, renaissances. Actes du Colloque de Caen, 17–19 mai 1995* (Caen, Presses Universitaires de Caen, 1996).

Lambert, Annie and Toczé, Claude, *Être Juif à Nantes sous Vichy* (Nantes, Siloë, 1994).

Lassus Saint-Geniès, Annik de, *Jean Le Cour Grandmaison* (Paris, Beauchesne, 1980).

Laurens, Corran, 'La Femme au turban: les femmes tondues', in Roderick Kedward and Nancy Wood, *The Liberation of France. Image and Event* (Oxford and Washington, DC, Berg, 1995).

Lavigne, Raymond, *Saint-Pierre-des-Corps ou la clarté républicaine* (Paris, Éditions Messidor, 1998).

Le Béguec, Gilles and Peschanski, Denis, *Les Élites locales dans la fourmente. Du Front populaire aux années cinquante* (Paris, CNRS, 2000).

Le Boterf, Hervé, *La Bretagne sous le Gouvernement de Vichy* (Paris, France-Empire, 1982).

Lecornu, Bernard, *Un Préfet sous l'Occupation allemande. Châteaubriant, Saint-Nazaire, Tulle* (Paris, France-Empire, 1984, re-ed. 1997).

Le Cour Grandmaison, Jean, *Le Marquis de La Ferronays, 1876–1946* (Paris, Éditions Siloë, 1952).

Le Crom, Jean-Pierre, *Syndicats Nous Voilà! Vichy et le corporatisme* (Paris, Les Éditions de l'Atelier/Éditions Ouvrières, 1995).

Lefranc, Georges, *Juin '36* (Paris, Julliard, 1965).

Le Marec, Gérard, *La Bretagne dans la Résistance* (Rennes, Ouest-France, 1983).

Lemesle, Michel, *L'Anjou des Années 40. Chroniques* (Angers, Les Éditions du Choletais, 1984).

Lemesle, Michel, *1939–1945. À Travers l'Anjou* (Cholet, Les Éditions du Choletais, 1976).

Lemesle, Michel, *Chronique d'Angers sous l'Occupation, 1939–1945* (Angers, Philippe Petit, 1972).

Leprince, René (ed.), *La Pommeraye dans la Guerre par ceux qui l'ont vécue* (La Pommeray, Bibliothèque de La Pommeraye, 1995).

Lewin, Christophe, *Le Retour des prisonniers de guerre français. Naissance et développement de la FNPG, 1944–1952* (Paris, Publications de la Sorbonne, 1986).

BIBLIOGRAPHY

Lottmann, Herbert, *The People's Anger. Justice and revenge in Post-Liberation France* (London, Hutchinson, 1986).

Lugard, F. D., *The Dual Mandate in British Tropical Africa* (Edinburgh and London, William Blackwood & Sons, 1922).

Marnot, René, *Ma ville sous la botte* (Saumur, Éditions Roland, 1947).

Marrus, Michael and Paxton, Robert, *Vichy France and the Jews* (New York, Basic Books, 1981).

Martin, Jean-Clément, *La Vendée de la mémoire* (Paris, Seuil, 1989).

Maurice, Jacques, *Cinquante mois sous la botte* (Tours, 1992).

McMillan, James, 'France', in Tom Buchanan and Martin Conway (eds), *Political Catholicism in Europe* (Oxford, Clarendon Press, 1996).

Melton, George F., *Darlan: Admiral and Statesman of France* (London, Praeger, 1998).

Milliat, Robert, *Le Dernier carousel. Défense de Saumur 1940* (Grenoble–Paris, B. Arthaud, 1943).

Milward, Alan S., *The New Order and the French Economy* (Oxford, Oxford University Press, 1984; Gregg Revivals, 1993).

Molette, Charles, *Prêtres, religieux et religieuses dans la Résistance au Nazisme, 1940–1945* (Paris, Fayard, 1995).

Montergon, Camille de, *Le Colonel François de Sauvebeuf* (Niort, Imprimerie de Saint-Denis, n.d.).

Montergon, Camille de, *Une Victime de Flossenburg. Le Colonel François de Sauvebeuf* (Niort, Imprimerie de Saint-Denis, n.d.).

Mordrel, Olier, *Breiz Atao ou histoire et actualité du nationalisme Breton* (Paris, A. Moreau, 1973).

Morin, Claude, *Les Allemands en Touraine, 1940–1944* (Chambray-lès-Tours, CLD, 1996).

Morin, Claude, *La Touraine sous les bombes* (Chambray-lès-Tours, CLD, 2000).

Mousseau, Léon, *Le Pont cassé. Souvenirs d'un médecin des bords de Loire* (Angers, J. Palussière, 1981).

Muel-Dreyfus, Francine, *Vichy et l'éternel féminin* (Paris, Seuil, 1996).

Nabulsi, Karma, *Traditions of War. Occupation, resistance and the law* (Oxford, Oxford University Press, 1999).

Nicolas, Michel, *Le Séparatisme en Bretagne* (Brasparts, Éditions Beltan, 1986).

Nobécourt, Jacques, *Le Colonel de la Rocque 1885–1946. Ou les pièges du nationalisme chrétien* (Paris, Fayard, 1996).

Noiriel, Gérard, *Workers in French Society in the Nineteenth and Twentieth Centuries* (Oxford, Berg, 1990).

Novick, Peter, *The Resistance versus Vichy. The purge of collaborators in liberated France* (London, Chatto & Windus, 1968).

Oury, Dom Guy, *Dom Gabriel Sortais* (Solesmes, 1975).

Oury, Louis, *Au soleil de la victoire* (Pantin, Le Temps des Cerises, 1999).

BIBLIOGRAPHY

Oury, Louis, *Le Cours des cinquante otages/Die Strasse der Fünfzig Geiseln* (Saarbrücken, Geschichts Werkstatt, 1989).

Oury, Louis, *Rue du Roi Albert. Les Otages de Nantes, Châteaubriant et Bordeaux* (Paris, Le Temps des Cerises, 1996).

Pacquelet, Muriel, *Le Cinéma paroissial en Loire-Inférieure de 1919 à 1958* (*mémoire de maîtrise*, University of Nantes, 1994).

Paisot-Béal, Sophie and Prévost, Roger, *Histoire des camps d'internement en Indre-et-Loire 1940–1944* (Private Press, 1993).

Papp, Julien, 'Les pouvoirs locaux en Indre-et-Loire', unpublished IHTP conference on 'Les Élites locales en France, 1935–1953', 12–13 June 1996.

Paxton, Robert, *French Peasant Fascism. Henri Dorgères's Greenshirts and the crises of French agriculture, 1929–1939* (New York and Oxford, Oxford University Press, 1997).

Payan, Abbé André, *Maillé martyr* (Tours, Arnault et Cie, 1945).

Perouas, Louis, 'Le grand retour de Notre Dame de Boulogne à travers la France (1943–48). Essai de reconstitution', *Annales de Bretagne et des Pays de l'Ouest* 90 (1983), pp. 171–83. Reprinted in *Archives des Sciences Sociales des Religions* 56/1 (1983), pp. 37–59.

Perraud, P., *Électricité et défense. Rôle et importance de l'électricité dans l'exploitation des potentiels industriels durant l'Occupation par la Wehrmacht* (*mémoire de maîtrise*, Université de Paul-Valéry, Montpellier, 1987).

Perraud-Charmantier, André, *Le Drame du Maquis de Saffré* (Nantes, Éditions du Fleuve, 1946).

Peschanski, Denis, *Vichy 1940–1944. Contrôle et exclusion* (Paris, Complexe, 1997).

Pétain, Philippe, *Actes et écrits*, ed. Jacques Isorni (Paris, Fayard, 1974).

Pétain, Philippe, *Haute Cour de Justice, Le Procès du Maréchal Pétain* (Paris, Albin Michel, 1945).

Pollard, Miranda, *Reign of Virtue. Mobilizing gender in Vichy France* (Chicago and London, University of Chicago Press, 1998).

Potier, Bernard, Aspects de la vie économique en Maine-et-Loire sous l'Occupation allemande (*mémoire de maîtrise*, Angers, Université Catholique de l'Ouest, 1985).

Poulat, Émile, *Naissance des prêtres ouvriers* (Paris, Casterman, 1965).

Poznanski, Renée, *Les Juifs en France pendant la Seconde Guerre Mondiale* (Paris, Hachette, 1997).

Prat, Elizabeth and Labussière, Jeannine, *Tours, cité meurtrie, juin 1940* (Chambray-lès-Tours, 1991).

Rabelais, François, *Œuvres*, vol. I. *Gargantua*, ed. Abel Lefranc (Paris, Champion, 1913).

BIBLIOGRAPHY

Rajsfus, Maurice, *La Police de Vichy. Forces de l'ordre français au service de la Gestapo* (Paris, Le Cherche-Midi, 1995).

Redier, Antoine, *Les Cadets de Saumur* (Lyon–Paris, Emmanuel Vitte, 1940).

Reynaud, Paul, *Au cœur de la mêlée, 1930–1945* (Paris, Flammarion, 1951).

Ridel, Fernand, *Témoignages 1939–1945. Une page d'histoire* (La Baule, Éditions des Paludiers, 1974).

Rioux, J.-P., Prost, A. and Azéma, J.-P., *Les Communistes français de Munich à Châteaubriant* (Paris, FNSP, 1987).

Rochebrune, Renaud de, and Hazera, Jean-Claude, *Les Patrons sous l'Occupation, vol. I, Face aux Allemands* (new edn, Paris, Odile Jacob, 1997).

Roper, Lyndal, *Oedipus and the Devil. Witchcraft, Sexuality and Religion in Early Modern Europe* (London and New York, Routledge, 1994).

Sainclivier, Jacqueline, 'Le pouvoir résistant (été 1944)', in Philippe Buton and Jean-Marie Guillon, *Les Pouvoirs en France à la Libération* (Paris, Belin, 1994).

Scorin, Jérôme, *L'Itinéraire d'un adolescent juif de 1939 à 1945* (Nancy, Christmann, 1994).

Semelin, Jacques, *Unarmed against Hitler. Civilian resistance in Europe, 1939–1943* (Westport, Conn., and London, Praeger, 1993).

Serant, Paul, *La Bretagne et la France* (Paris, Fayard, 1971).

Sesmaisons, Yves de, *Marquise de Sesmaisons, 1898–1977. Souvenirs de l'Occupation* (Craon, 1978).

Shennan, Andrew, *Rethinking France. Plans for renewal, 1940–1946* (Oxford, Clarendon Press, 1989).

Siegfried, André, *Tableau politique de la France de l'Ouest sous la Troisième République* (Paris, Armand Colin, 1964).

Sigot, Jacques, *Un Camp pour les Tsiganes . . . et les autres. Montreuil-Bellay, 1940–1945* (Bordeaux, Éditions Wallada, 1983).

Sommer, Hubert, *Génie. Zur Bedeutungsgeschichte des Wortes von der Renaissance zur Aufklärung*, ed. Michael Nerlich (Frankfurt am Main, Peter Lang, 1998).

Spears, Sir Edward, *Assignment to Catastrophe, vol. II* (London, Heinemann, 1954).

Tauzan, François, *Le STO en Touraine occupé, 1942–1944* (*mémoire de maîtrise*, University of Tours, 1996).

Tewes, Ludwig, *Frankreich in der Besatzungszeit, 1940–1943. Die Sicht deutcher Augenzeugen* (Bonn, Bouvier Verlag, 1998).

Texcier, Jean, *Conseils à l'occupé* (Paris, 1940).

Thalmann, Rita, *La Mise au pas. Idéologie et stratégie sécuritaire dans la France occupée* (Paris, Fayard, 1991).

Thorez, Maurice, *Œuvres*, Book 5, Vol. 22 (Paris, Éditions Sociales, 1964).

Todorov, Tzvetan, *A French Tragedy. Scenes of a civil war, summer 1944* (Dartmouth College, 1996).

Tourlet, E. H., *La Statue de Rabelais d'Émile Hébert. Relation des fêtes données à Chinon les premier, 2 et 3 juillet 1882 à l'occasion de l'inauguration du monument* (Chinon, 1894).

Tremblay, Hervé, *À Quédillac dans la poche. Neuf mois dans la vie quotidienne des Bouvronnais, août 1944–11 mai 1945* (Bouvron, 1995).

Umbreit, Hans, *Der Militärbefehlshaber in Frankreich, 1940–1944* (Boppard-am-Rhein, 1968).

Veillon, Dominique, *Vivre et survivre en France, 1939–1947* (Paris, Payot, 1995).

Veillon, Dominique and Flonneau, Jean-Marie (eds), *Le Temps des restrictions en France, 1939–1949* (Paris, IHTP, 1995).

Vercors, Jean Bruller, *Le Silence de la mer* (Paris, Éditions de Minuit, 1942).

Vidal-Naquet, Pierre, *Le Trait empoisonné. Réflexions sur l'affaire Jean Moulin* (Paris, Éditions de la Decouverte, 1993).

Vivier, Jack, *Les Instituteurs de Touraine dans la République* (Chambray-lès-Tours, CLD, 1986).

Vivier, Jack, *Prêtres en Touraine dans la Résistance* (Chambray-lès-Tours, CLD, 1993).

Vivier, Robert, *Touraine 39–45. Histoire de l'Indre-et-Loire durant la Deuxième Guerre Mondiale* (Chambray-lès-Tours, CLD, 1990).

Von Glahn, Gerhard, *The Occupation of Enemy Territory* (Minneapolis, University of Minnesota Press, 1957).

Weber, Max, 'Politics as a vocation', in H. H. Werth and C. Wright Mills, *From Max Weber. Essays in Sociology* (London and Boston, Routledge & Kegan Paul, 1970).

Webster, Paul, *Pétain's Crime. The full story of French collaboration in the Holocaust* (London, Macmillan, 1990).

Wieviorka, Annette, *Déportation ou génocide* (Paris, Plon, 1992).

Wolton, Thierry, *Le Grand recrutement* (Paris, Grasset, 1993).

Wylie, Laurence (ed.), *Chanzeaux. A village in Anjou* (Cambridge, Mass., Harvard University Press, 1966).

Interviews

Ancelin, Michel (Saumur), 22 June 1998

Arnoult, René (Chinon), 23 June 1998

Aron, Émile (Tours), 19 March 1997, 24 June 1998

BIBLIOGRAPHY

Audebert, Georges (Tours), 24 June 1998

Avenet, Abel and Claudine (Dierre, I-et-L), 25 June 1998

Beaumont, Paule and Louis, (Daumeray, M-et-L), 20 May 1997

Bellier, Madeleine (Angers), 30 April 1997

Beugnet, Christian and Léonie (Chinon), 23 June 1998

Bossé, Francis (Grugé l'Hôpital, M-et-L), 14 April 1997

Bouche, Thérèse (Angers), 13 Dec. 1996

Boudet, Pierre (Angers), 11 Oct. 1996

Bougreau, Claude (Chinon), 23 June 1998

Canonne, Germaine (Angers), 28 April 1997

Cavigneaux, André (Avrillé, Angers), 30 April 1997

Chardonnet, André (Angers), 11 April 1997

Chauvel, André, and meeting of FNDIR (Nantes), 6 May 1997

Chedozeau, Gilbert, Mme Guitton and Serge Martin (Maillé, I-et-L),
     6 June 1997

Cohu, Lucienne (Trélazé, M-et-L), 18 April 1997

Delanoë, Édouard (Grugé l'Hôpital, M-et-L), 14 April 1997

Denis, Jacqueline and Louis (Trélazé), 18 April 1997

Despouy, Lucienne (Saint-Avertin, Tours), 9 June 1997

Geindreau, Jeanne (Saint-Pierre-Montlimart, M-et-L), 11 Nov. 1996

Gluck, Ernest (Nantes), 22 June 1997

Goxe, Odette (Angers), 14 April 1997

Grandière, de la, Vicomte Gilles et Vicomtesse (La Jumellière, M-et-L),
     5 May 1997

Grenouilleau, Paul (Angers), 17 April 1997

Gros, Colonel Pierre (Avrillé, Angers) 23 April 1997

Guggenheim, François (Tours), 30 June 1997

Hervé, Jacques (Joué-lès-Tours), 12 June 1997

Hervé, Pierre, Félix Boudet, Louis David and Xavier Garçon (Saffré, L-A),
     30 May 1997

Idier, Marguerite and Jeanne (Angers), 6 Nov. 1996

Jamonneau, Abbé François (Nantes), 26 May and 5 June 1997

Lallemand, Georgette (La Genevraie, M-et-L), 13 May 1997

Lancezeux, Lucie and Robin, Huguette (Monts, I-et-L), 23 June 1998

Le Bault de la Morinière, René (Landemont, M-et-L), 7 May 1997

Le Chat, Suzanne (Ingrandes, M-et-L), 15 April 1997

Lemasson, Violette and Rémi (Belle-Beille, Angers), 16 April 1997

Leterme, Michel (Angers), 13 May 1997

Ménard, Abbé Jacques (Tours), 2 June 1997

Ménard, Max and Jeanne (Jallais, M-et-L), 22 April 1997

Mondragon, Christian de (Nantes), 29 April 1997

Montalembert, Pierre and Yolande (Neuilly), 9 Jan. 1999

BIBLIOGRAPHY

Peltier, Robert (La Poissonnière, M-et-L), 16 April 1997

Perruchaud, Aline (Angers), 12 Sept. 1996

Prévost, Roger (Chambray-lès-Tours), 9 June 1997

Rameau, Marinette (Chacé, M-et-L), 28 Oct. 1996

Richer, Abbé Henri (Angers), 6 June 1997

Roussel, André (Bléré, I-et-L), 25 June 1998

Saint-Seine, Yves de (Toutlemonde, M-et-L), 22 April 1997

Sauvage, Jean (Angers), 25 April 1997

Sesmaisons, Marquis Donatien and General Yves de (Nantes), 16 July 1997

Toubon, Charles (Angers), 22 June 1997

Treulier, André (Le Thoureil, M-et-L), 13 May 1997

Trudeau, Andrée (Saumur), 22 June 1998

Vivier, Jack (Tours), 16 June 1997

INDEX

509

INDEX

INDEX

INDEX

INDEX

INDEX

Hary, General, commander of 4th military region 340

Hasselbach, Major, Kreiskommandant of Nantes 251, 259

Hautecloque, Captain Philippe de see Leclerc, General

Hay de Slade, Comte, Breton notable 353

Hedouin, Jacques, mayor of Vernoil-le-Fourier (M-et-L) 204

Hénaff, Eugène, communist leader 241

Henault, Robespierre, mayor of Saint-Pierre-des-Corps 177, 182, 229

Henriot, Philippe, Vichy Minister of Information 324

Henry II, King of England 21

Herard, Jean , Angevin notable 354

Herbig, Dr, vet and hunting officer at Tours 147

Herbignac (L-I) 339, 357

Herriot, Édouard, radical-socialist leader 178

Hervé, Jacques, mayor of Château-Renault 203

Hervé, Jacques, STO conscript 72

Hervé, Pierre, of Maquis de Saffré 381

Hervé, Raymond, communist militant 268

Hervy, mayor of Bouvron (L-A) 382

Heydrich, Reinhard 265, 266

Hilaire, Georges, of Vichy Minister of Interior 198

Hitler, Adolf
  and Pétain 203, 208
  and hostage crisis 246, 249, 251, 253, 255
  and Laval 265
  and Jews 278, 374

Holocaust
  French involvement in 271–4
  commemoration of 402–9

Honneur et Patrie, resistance network 325

horse-racing 27, 149

hostages of Nantes-Châteaubriant 240–2, 246–50
  commemoration of 386–7

Hotz, Lieutenant-Colonel Karl, Feldkommandant of Nantes
  as Feldkommandant 50–1, 54–5, 59, 80, 164, 213, 247, 315
  shot (20 Oct. 1941) 168, 243, 246
  funeral (24 Oct. 1941) 252–3
  remembered 387–8

Huau, Marie-Louise, of Nantes 256–7

Huismes (I-et-L) 34

Hugo, Victor 22

hunting
  ban on 26–7, 146–7
  clubs 26, 147
  see also poaching

Huntziger, General 69

Hupfer, Xavier, of Feldkommandantur of Angers 293

Ille-et-Vilaine 190

indirect rule 14, 18, 41, 57, 249, 259

Indre, river 238

Ingrand, Jean-Pierre, delegate of Ministry of Interior 59

Internationale, The 61, 240, 290, 300, 387

Jammoneau, Abbé François, of Nantes 238, 394

Je suis partout 174, 201, 315

Jeunesse Ouvrière Chrétienne (JOC) 136, 152

Jews
  immigration of 224–5
  census of 225, 232
  definitions of 232, 272
  expelled from coastal areas (Dec. 1940) 225–6
  Vichy statutes governing (3 Oct. 1940, 2 June 1941) 228, 231, 233, 276
  dismissal of 229, 231, 232–4
  Aryanization of businesses 234–8
  internment of 237–40
  as hostages 234, 263
  and Yellow Star 271–2
  round-up and deportation of 2, 6, 33, 234, 272–80
  organisation of 277
  non-Jewish population and 274–6, 279–81
  return of 369–70
  see also Holocaust

Joan of Arc 21–2
  statues of 82
  plays about 22, 151
  commemoration of 17, 22, 24–5, 41, 166–7, 318

Jollit, Edmond, mayor of Azay (I-et-L) 354

Jost
  Léon (ex. 1941) 91, 103, 247, 249, 386
  Michel 388

Joué-lès-Tours (I-et-L) 172

Jourdan, Jean de, Angevin notable 354, 357

Jouvance, Emmanuel, labour leader 123–4

Junck, General 364

Jünger, Ernst 255

justice
  German military courts 60–1, 261, 269–70, 271, 281, 315–16
  overruled by SS 269
  Vichy Sections spéciales 34, 61, 107, 240
  Liberation Cours de Justice and Chambres civiques 340, 343–5, 358–9, 371

Jussieu-Pontcarrel, General 380

Kapandji, Mehmed, of Chinon 29

Keil, Oberst, of Le Mans Rüstungskommando 313

516

INDEX

517

INDEX

INDEX

INDEX

INDEX

INDEX

Vavasseur, Charles, mayor of Vouvray (I-et-L)
197–201, 203, 351
Veillon, Dominique, historian
Vendée
department of 190, 193
revolt in 1793 180–1
memory of 177, 218, 394
autarky of 129, 371
religious practice in 210, 218
brand of resistance 64, 216
opposition to STO 299–300
suspicion of evacuees 307
opposition to STO
Vercors, writer 65, 87
Vern d'Anjou (M-et-L) 324
Vernantes (M-et-L) 155
Vernet, Camille prefect of I-et-L (1936–40)
208
Vernoil-le-Fourrier (M-et-L) 229
Vertou (L-I) 354, 365
veterans' organisations 139–40
Viaud, Marcel, communist militant (ex. 1943)
269
Vichy
capital 13
purge of administration 178
and Third Republic politicians 174–5,
176–187
'rallying' to 2, 15, 35, 186–7, 194, 198, 202
direct administration by 15, 178, 196
decentralisation by 188, 193
power of 132, 417
and solidarity 142
exclusion by 4, 224, 228–9, 262, 272
and regeneration 28, 121, 139, 141, 164
and corruption 28, 106–7, 132
and POWs 94–6, 101–4, 105–6, 134
and labour 120–5, 165, 169, 171, 172,
185–6
and peasantry 125–33
and women 97–8
and youth 140–1, 150–7
Vienne, river 21, 93
Vihiers (M-et-L) 354
Vilaine, river 362
Villefranche-de-Rouergue 317
Villepelet, Mgr, bishop of Nantes
diary of 10
as a hostage (1940) 50
and German authorities 55, 213–14
and Vichy 209, 333, 346
and POWs 91, 96, 97, 108
and Our Lady of Boulogne 206–7, 221

and hostage crisis 249, 253, 386
and Relève 288
and STO 297, 298
and air-raid victims 306
and resistance 216, 339
and de Gaulle 333, 347
Vincent, Mgr, rector of Catholic University of
Angers 347
Vivier
Jack, local historain 332
Robert, prefect of I-et-L (Sept. 1944) 135,
331, 332, 334, 338, 351–2, 374–6
Voix du peuple, La 343, 344
Voltaire 22
Voss, Lieutenant Helmut, at Angers 71, 73,
74, 81
Vouvray (I-et-L) 197, 351, 372
Vue (L-I) 29

Wahrenburg, Major, Kreiskòmmandant of
Saumur 45, 62
Walsh de Serrant, mayor of Bouvron 381
War of 1914–18 14
Waterloo, battle of 379
Wehrmacht
economic needs of 14, 346
honour of 62
security of 25
Wilkinson, Ted, SOE agent 284
women
praised by Vichy 97–8
wives of POWs 91, 92, 97–101, 155, 160
and Church 96
employment of married 98, 99
running family businesses 99, 171, 419
and food supply 99, 118–19
employed by Germans 78–9, 99
relationships with Germans 73–9
and demonstrations 167
and labour service 312, 354
see also denunciation, Mothers' Day,
prostitution

Yacco, alias Briac le Diouron, Breton FFI 325
youth
subculture 135–6, 152, 156–7
organisations 140–1, 150
as Gaullists 167, 171
as communists 227, 324

Zay, Jean, Education Minister under Popular
Front 174
Zola, Émile 375

524